Practical Rails Projects

Eldon Alameda

Practical Rails Projects

Copyright © 2007 by Eldon Alameda

ISBN-13 (pbk): 978-1-59059-781-1

ISBN-10 (pbk): 1-59059-781-8

Printed and bound in the United States of America 9 8 7 6 5 4 3 2 1

Lead Editors: Ben Renow-Clarke and Chris Mills
Technical Reviewer: Paul Bentley
Editorial Board: Steve Anglin, Ewan Buckingham, Tony Campbell, Gary Cornell, Jonathan Gennick, Jason Gilmore, Kevin Goff, Jonathan Hassell, Matthew Moodie, Joseph Ottinger, Jeffrey Pepper, Ben Renow-Clarke, Dominic Shakeshaft, Matt Wade, Tom Welsh
Senior Project Manager: Tracy Brown Collins
Copy Editor: Heather Lang
Assistant Production Director: Kari Brooks-Copony
Senior Production Editor: Laura Cheu
Compositor: Pat Christenson
Proofreader: Lori Bring, Christy Wagner, Elizabeth Berry
Indexer: Becky Hornyak
Artist: April Milne
Cover Designer: Kurt Krames
Manufacturing Director: Tom Debolski

Distributed to the book trade worldwide by Springer-Verlag New York, Inc., 233 Spring Street, 6th Floor, New York, NY 10013. Phone 1-800-SPRINGER, fax 201-348-4505, e-mail orders-ny@springer-sbm.com, or visit http://www.springeronline.com.

For information on translations, please contact Apress directly at 2855 Telegraph Avenue, Suite 600, Berkeley, CA 94705. Phone 510-549-5930, fax 510-549-5939, e-mail info@apress.com, or visit http://www.apress.com.

The source code for this book is available to readers at http://www.apress.com.

Contents at a Glance

PART 1 ▪▪▪ Making the Right Preparations (Don't Skip This Part)

PART 2 ▪▪▪ Monkey Tasks: Managing a Daily Task List

PART 3 ▪▪▪ Exercisr

PART 4 ▪▪▪ Simple Blogs

PART 5 ▪▪▪ Building a Web Comic Using Caching

PART 6 ▪▪▪ Church Community Site

PART 7 ▪▪▪ GamingTrend

PART 8 ▪▪▪ Integrating with a RESTful Application Using Edge Rails (Rails 2.0)

v

Contents

PART 1 ■■■ Making the Right Preparations (Don't Skip This Part)

PART 2 ■■■ **Monkey Tasks: Managing a Daily Task List**

■CHAPTER 5   **Enhancing Monkey Tasks** 85

PART 3 ■■■ Exercisr

■CHAPTER 6   **Developing a REST-Based Application** 93

PART 4 ■■■ Simple Blogs

PART 5 ■■■ Building a Web Comic Using Caching

PART 6 ■■■ Church Community Site

PART 8 ■■■ Integrating with a RESTful Application Using Edge Rails (Rails 2.0)

About the Author

■ELDON ALAMEDA is a web developer who currently resides in the harsh climates of Kansas. He develops Ruby on Rails applications for a small technology startup in downtown Kansas City; prior to this, he did development for a variety of companies including local advertising firms, Sprint PCS, and IBM. During the '90s, he also acquired a nice stack of worthless stock options working for dot-com companies. When he's not sitting in front of a computer or irritating his wife by describing a new technology as "sexy," Eldon spends most of his time at home playing games with his young daughter.

About the Technical Reviewer

■PAUL BENTLEY has been writing software professionally for over a decade. He has experience in many areas of computing, from embedded devices to 3-D graphics. He is especially proficient in the telephony world, experienced with both traditional computer telephony and SIP-based solutions. He is currently working with Rails, developing web applications for corporations who want stable solutions to a variety of problems.

As an avid Go player, he tries to play every day—though he admits he still has a lot to learn before he can even be considered an amateur. He lives with his girlfriend and daughter in Harrogate, UK. If you feel like challenging Paul to a game of Go, he can be tracked down via `paulbentley.net`.

Acknowledgments

Blah, blah, writing a book is hard, blah, blah.

That being said, this book could not be possible without the help, patience, and wisdom of a number of people.

Keir Thomas, Chris Mills, and Ben Renow-Clarke, the holy trinity of editors who have been involved with this project. Thank you for your guidance, advice, and assistance throughout the project.

Paul Bentley, the technical reviewer. Thank you for the long hours that you spent going through the code in the book, your insightful comments (even when we didn't agree), and your many words of encouragement that helped along the way.

Tracy Brown Collins, the project manager for this book. Thank you for your tireless work at keeping things (which typically meant me) on track. Thank you for also being flexible when times called for it.

Heather Lang, the copy editor. Thanks for all of your suggestions on the text and for the wonderful polish that you applied to the text of this book. You truly went above and beyond for me on numerous occasions, and I want to let you know how much I appreciated it.

Laura Cheu and her production team. Thanks for all of your hard work to help get the book out into the stores as fast as possible and for putting up with my requests for last, last minute changes. You came to my rescue on a number of occasions, and words cannot express my appreciation.

Thanks go to my wife Dori for your kindness, support, encouragement, and for essentially taking on the role of a single mother to support me over the last nine months. And for (almost) never complaining when I asked you to go pick me up an order of hot wings for dinner.

Finally, I'd like to thank my daughter Kaylee for being my sunshine and always bringing a smile to my face.

Introduction

Practical Rails Projects is for developers who have already read a beginning Rails book (or worked though a series of introductory tutorials online) and are now looking to expand that knowledge by gaining practical experience developing a variety of web applications in Rails. It's for developers who want to gain hands-on experience of building Rails applications that do interesting things such as caching, RESTful routing, using Active Resource and RJS, and connecting Rails to legacy databases. While I do make the assumption that readers have read some previous Rails material, I believe that I've also provided enough review information that a highly motivated reader with previous experience in a model-view-controller framework and familiarity with another object-oriented language should be able to work through the material.

The Problem with Most Training Books and Courses

Over the course of my career, I've had to sit through an inordinate amount of technical training sessions, and I would estimate that 98 percent of them all suffered from the same major flaw—they didn't actually teach anything. I sat in a classroom for a week and proved that I could follow step-by-step directions. Heck, for the majority of them, I could even daydream about other things all day and still pass the course. It wasn't until I got back to the office and was confronted with having to work with the technology myself (without a safety net) that I actually learned anything. It was only when I was removed from the ideal environment and had to use the technology in the real world that its benefits or weaknesses were revealed. I'm sure many of you have suffered through similar things.

Unfortunately, it seems that many current programming books fall into that same trap. The ones that provide instruction on how to build applications tend to fall into this same paint-by-numbers mentality so that at the end of the book, you've simply proven that you can follow step-by-step directions as well. I wanted to write something different.

You see, I love Ruby on Rails. I truly believe that it's the best web development framework available today. I know that Rails has brought a lot of the fun of web development back to my work and that it has made me a better developer as well. So when the opportunity to write this book came to me, I wanted to write something that would help others develop the same love for Rails. As I reviewed the existing books available on Rails, I noticed that they fell into just a few categories:

- *Introductory Rails books* provide the necessary introduction to the structure, conventions, and features of Rails. Examples include *Beginning Rails: From Novice to Professional* (Jeffrey Allan Hardy, Cloves Carneiro Jr., and Hampton Catlin. Apress, 2007), *Agile Web Development with Rails* (Dave Thomas, David Hansson, Leon Breedt, and Mike Clark. Pragmatic Bookshelf, 2006), or even *Ruby on Rails for Dummies* (Barry Burd. For Dummies, 2007).

- *Single-project books* are designed to spoon-feed the reader, moving step-by-step through the creation of a single application in Rails, such as building a social network site or an e-commerce site with Ruby on Rails.

- *Recipe books* are designed for intermediate to advanced Rails developers that include short snippets of code to demonstrate solutions for solving common problems such as adding authentication.

- *Reference books* are designed for intermediate to advanced Rails developers and take you deeper into a single feature or component related to Rails development, such as the excellent *Ruby for Rails: Ruby Techniques for Rails Developers* (David Black. Manning Publications, 2006), and books such as *Pro ActiveRecord: Databases with Ruby and Rails* (Kevin Marshall, Chad Pytel, and Jon Yurek. Apress, 2007), *Deploying Rails Applications A Step-by-Step Guide* (Ezra Zygmuntowicz and Bruce Tat. Pragmatic Programmer, 2007), and so on.

Typically, I recommend people interested in learning Rails to use books in exactly this order. Start with a beginning Rails book, then move into doing a variety of the project-based books to gain hands-on experience. Finally, move onto the recipe and reference books as a means of deepening your knowledge.

How This Book Is Different

Of those listed above, I believe that people gain the most knowledge of Rails from the project-based books. Unfortunately, even when dealing with a subject as fun as Rails, it's still possible to shut off your mind while reading those books and just end up following the instructions without learning from them. That's not meant as a knock on any of those books. I've bought and read pretty much all of them myself.

I wanted to give you something that was focused on helping you bridge that gap from being a beginning Rails developer to becoming an experienced Rails developer. I wanted to give you more value for your book-buying dollar by not just showing you how I might build an application but instead giving you the tools and knowledge necessary to build these applications for yourself.

So, rather than simply taking you through the process of how to build a single solution, we'll tackle several different types of projects. Each project was selected to allow you to develop hands-on experience either working with a core feature of Rails (such as caching or RESTful routing) or to wrangle an interesting problem domain in an effort to spark your interest. Each of these projects could have easily been extended out into the single-project book format.

Learning to Ride a Bike

In addition, rather than expand each project out into a full book of its own and spoon-feeding you the step-by-step instructions for how to build the exact project that I would build, I chose to scale back the applications a bit, giving you the results of an initial rollout version of each application. This way, each application is workable yet still at a point where you can easily modify and extend it to suit your own needs. When describing this book, I've often used the analogy of teaching someone to ride a bike. My goal is to help you get past that initial hurdle of getting up and going—and then let go once you've got some momentum and balance so that you can finish the ride yourself.

At the end of each project, I include a number of exercise ideas for you. As I believe that you often learn some concepts the best when having to fix something broken, I've created some areas in the projects that are less than optimal and then point them out in the exercise sections for you to fix. Other ideas I give you point you in new directions to take our project that would be fun and interesting. I strongly recommend that you go through all of the exercises, as I truly believe that you will learn more from them than in the other sections of the book (which isn't to imply that I haven't tried to share a lot of cool and interesting web development techniques with you in the rest of the book).

What's Not in This Book

Of course, writing a book like this also requires a substantial amount of sacrifice of subjects that the geek in me would have liked to cover as well. Unfortunately, if I covered everything that I wanted to, this book would have turned out to be around 2,000 pages (and I would probably still be writing it). That said, some of the core elements that I don't cover in the book but are important for you to understand are mentioned in the following sections.

Database Tuning and Indexing

Since database tuning and indexing are absent, you'll notice that we're not adding any additional indexes onto the databases in most of the applications. This is fine while our data storage is small and our queries remain fairly simple. However, as our applications grow over time, this lack could cause significant performance issues. Perhaps because I came into web development by way of database administration, this was an important feature that was hard for me to remove from the book, but this subject is complex and deserves more attention than I would have been able to give it in this book. Perhaps I'll write a second book that's focused entirely on this subject.

Testing

Test-driven development (TDD) has certainly taken a strong foothold within the Rails community, and while I haven't yet become a convert to writing tests first, I'm a firm believer in the value of developing a comprehensive test suite before the application is deployed. I've heard it said that all applications are going to be tested—the question is if you'll write the tests yourself or simply dump the application on your users to test it for you.

Refactoring

Going hand-in-hand with a solid set of test cases is the need to refactor the code. As each project is at an initial rollout stage, there's always going to be lots of room for refactoring the code to make it cleaner, simpler, or in some cases optimized for performance and scaling.

In the exercise section of each project, I try to point you in the right direction for some common-sense refactorings and optimizations.

Icons Used in This Book

As much as I would love to be able to claim responsibility for all of the artwork used in this book, the simple truth is that I'm a coder, not an artist. So to give credit where credit is due, here is a short list of the people responsible.

MonkeyTasks Project

Some icons used in this project were modified versions of ones I downloaded from the Creative Commons Licensed Mini-Icons v2 by Timothy Groves. You can obtain the whole set at http://www.brandspankingnew.net/archive/2006/12/hohoho.html.

Exercisr Project

Icons used in this project were from Paul Armstrong's Gallery 2 Icon set, which is licensed under the GNU General Public License (GPL). They are available for download at http://paularmstrongdesigns.com/portfolio/.

Typo Blog Project

Icons used in this project were created by Amanda Dinkel, a talented Kansas City graphic designer whose portfolio can be found at http://creativehotlist.com/index.asp?linkTarget=fullProfile.asp&indID=83102.

GamingTrend Project

Icons used in this project were created by Mike Dunn of http://www.foolishstudios.com. For the navigation links, he utilized and modified the Creative Commons licensed FamFam Silk Icons available at http://www.famfamfam.com/lab/icons/silk/.

PART 1

■■■

Making the Right Preparations (Don't Skip This Part)

Yes, I know that there is probably a strong temptation to skip straight ahead to some project that's piqued your interest or looks like a good start to solving a specific problem that you're dealing with, but doing so would be a big mistake, perhaps even one with fatal consequences.

OK, maybe not *fatal* consequences, but it is very important that you don't skip this part, because here, we're going to go over some basic information that will be very helpful in completing the projects in this book. Even if you already have a fairly significant amount of Rails experience, it will be useful for you to at least review the information presented, to make sure you've got everything you need to complete all the projects in this book.

I'll start by discussing how to establish a good development environment for yourself and what tools you should consider using. Once those basic requirements are established, we'll close out Part 1 with a step-by-step breakdown of the common tasks that will be used in building each of our projects so as to eliminate redundancy in this book.

■■■

## CHAPTER 1

Building a Development Environment

Miracle Max: You rush a miracle man, you get rotten miracles.

——William Goldman, *The Princess Bride*

In order to run the projects in this book, you need to ensure that you have installed the following technologies on your development machine:

- *Ruby and Rails*: As Rails is a framework for and written in Ruby, you need to have a working installation of Ruby. For this book, you'll need to have Ruby 1.8.4 at a minimum. I'll point you in the right direction for some painless ways to get both Ruby and Rails installed.

- *Database*: Rails is a framework that was designed specifically for creating database-driven web applications. Therefore, the framework won't even start without a connection to a database. We'll discuss some of the popular database options for development machines.

- *Code editor*: While you can use any program that can create and edit text files, developing in Rails means switching among a lot of files, so you'll benefit from checking out some of the more advanced code editing solutions that we'll discuss.

- *Web Server:* Any good development machine needs a way for you to run your application. Fortunately, we've got several great ruby based options to choose from that we'll discuss.

Installing Ruby and Rails

Since you've more than likely read through a beginning Rails book already, we won't spend a lot of time going over how to install Rails. However, just in case there are some people who still need this information, I do want to at least point you in the right direction for getting Rails installed on your development machine. So, in this section, I'll give some high-level information on how to install Rails on Linux, Windows, and Mac OS X.

If you're looking for a beginning-level book, the best one is still *Agile Web Development with Rails* (Thomas, Dave et al. Pragmatic Programmers, 2006).

Installing on Linux

Unfortunately, because of the large number of different Linux distributions, attempting to document a single installation method would be an exercise in futility.

The good news, however, is that if you've installed any of the development packages with your distribution, there's a good chance that Ruby may already be installed. If it's not, it's typically just a matter of using whichever package manager your Linux distribution requires to add it, and it's generally fairly painless. If you're a bit more daring, you could even build from source.

A great resource to find step-by-step instructions for your specific Linux distribution is the official Ruby on Rails wiki (`http://wiki.RubyonRails.org`).

Installing on Windows

If you choose to develop Rails applications on a Windows machine, you can bypass all the installation and configuration headaches that come with building a development environment on other operating systems by downloading Instant Rails.

Instant Rails is a full Ruby on Rails development environment that is installable through a single executable. You can download the latest version of Instant Rails from `http://Rubyforge.org/projects/instantRails`.

At the time of this writing, an Instant Rails installation includes the following files:

- Instant Rails Manager 1.7

- Ruby 1.8.6 (from the One-Click Ruby Installer 1.8.6-25)

- Ruby on Rails 1.2.3

- Apache 1.3.33

- MySQL 5.0.27

- MySQL/Ruby 2.7.3 (native driver)

- Mongrel 1.01

- phpMyAdmin 2.10.0.2

- Two preinstalled Rails applications for you to experiment with:

    - A cookbook application taken from an ONLamp.com tutorial

    - Version 2.6 of the popular Rails blogging engine Typo

To simplify things even further, the Instant Rails Manager (see Figure 1-1) is a GUI management tool from which you can start or stop any of the processes (Apache, MySQL, and so on) or your individual Rails applications that you've installed into Instant Rails.

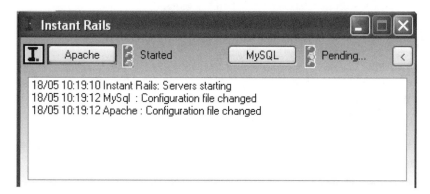

Figure 1-1. *Instant Rails management console*

Installing on Mac OS X

If you're running Mac OS X 10.5 (Leopard) or above, you'll be pleasantly surprised to find that Ruby on Rails is already included along with the OS in the development tools. Unfortunately, since Leopard's release has been postponed until after this book's publication date, you'll have to check back for updates to the book at http://www.RailsProjects.com or the Apress site for information on any gotchas associated with activating Rails.

If you're running Max OS X 10.4 (Tiger) or below, you have a few options to choose from to build your development environment. Regardless of which one you choose, it would be a good idea to first install the Xcode development tools. You can install these either from your Mac OSX CD/DVD or by downloading the latest version from http://developer.apple.com. Installing these tools will provide your Mac with the necessary compilers to build some of the packages that I recommend, such as Mongrel and SQLite.

Your first option for installing Rails is to install Locomotive, which is the Mac equivalent of Instant Rails. Within a single .dmg package, you'll find a complete development environment for Ruby and Rails along with a large number of commonly used Ruby gems. You can download Locomotive at http://locomotive.raaum.org. Locomotive also includes a management GUI similar to the Instant Rails Management tool (see Figure 1-2).

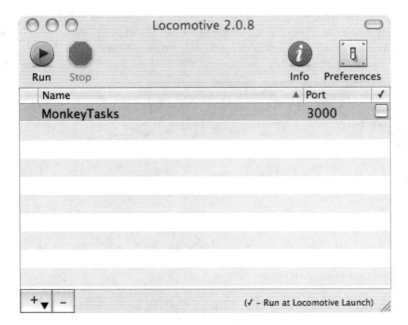

Figure 1-2. *Locomotive is the easiest way to set up Ruby on Rails for your Mac.*

Secondly, for those of you who (like me) would rather have full control over your development installation, you can do a full install manually by following the excellent step-by-step instructions found online at the Hivelogic blog (http://www.hivelogic.com/).

Installing a Database

As the ActiveRecord library in Rails does a fantastic job of abstracting your database connectivity from your code, switching databases underneath a Rails application is typically merely a matter of modifying the database.yml configuration file (found in /config) and rerunning your migrations to load the schema into your new database. As such, which database you choose to use for development will normally be more a matter of personal taste than a necessity of the eventual production environment. Gone are the days of having to use database-specific query commands such as PHP's mysql_query. In fact, it's also very easy to mix and match different databases for different environments, such as using SQLite for development and a PostgreSQL database for production.

Unless you need to connect to a legacy enterprise database, most Rails developers choose to use one of the popular open source database solutions such as MySQL, PostgreSQL, or SQLite. While I have a lot of respect for using PostgreSQL and MySQL as my database for production applications, I have found that SQLite is my preferred database for development for the following reasons, so I'll be using it in the projects in this book:

- SQLite is easy to manage. SQLite lives up to its description as "a self-contained, embeddable, zero-configuration SQL database engine." It provides support for most of SQL-92 and offers a simple command-line utility for interacting with its databases.

- Creating new databases is less of a hassle with SQLite. With SQLite, there is no need to run extra commands to create your database prior to running your migrations. Running your migrations will automatically create the database specified in your database.yml file.

- SQLite is easier to destroy. Since a SQLite database is merely a file sitting in the file system, I can easily blow it away using a simple rm or del command. During the early stages of development, if I find that I need to make a database schema change, I would prefer to modify the original migration file and re-create the database from scratch rather than build an additional migration to correct an oversight or mistake I may have made in my first attempt.

- SQLite is less resource intensive than MySQL yet provides excellent performance that is in most cases comparable to MySQL's. Also, unlike MySQL and PostgreSQL, which run as services and eat system resources even when you're not developing, SQLite has the advantage of running only when it's needed.

- SQLite is more portable. Since the database is merely a file in the file system, it can be distributed along with the application. This means that your development database can also be placed into your version control system so that it can be checked out along with the code.

Installing SQLite

Even if you choose to use another database for your development environment, it would behoove you to go through the process of installing SQLite and the SQLite Ruby gem so that you can utilize the sample databases that is included with most of the projects in this book (the sample databases are available in the Source Code/Download section of the Apress web site).

Installing SQLite on Windows

To install SQLite onto a Windows development box, you will need to download and install two files—the SQLite DLL and command line application—copying them into the bin directory of your Ruby installation (typically C:\Ruby\bin). You can download these from the SQLite home page at http://www.sqlite.org.

Installing SQLite on Linux/Unix

Most distributions offer a package manager that makes installing SQLite as simple as asking it to install. You could also install from source by checking out the latest build from the SQLite home page at http://www.sqlite.org.

Installing SQLite on Mac OS X

Starting with Tiger, Mac OS X began including SQLite along with the operating system, so there's no need to worry about installing SQLite. The necessary SQLite Ruby gem to interface to a SQLite database is a bit more complicated, however. Before you can install the Ruby gem, you will need to install an application named SWIG. Otherwise, the SQLite gem will not use the correct SQLite library but will default to a using a pure Ruby version of SQLite that doesn't work as well.

The easiest way to install SWIG is to first install the MacPorts tool. MacPorts is a free and open source application that simplifies installation of many open source tools that otherwise would require compiling from source manually. You can install the latest version of MacPorts from http://www.macports.org.

Once you have MacPorts installed, you can install the SWIG library from the command line with this simple command:

```
sudo port install swig
```

Install the SQLite Ruby Gem

Open a command prompt, and use RubyGems to install the SQLite Ruby gem:

```
sudo gem install sqlite3-Ruby
```

You'll see a list of possible install versions. You should choose the highest numbered version for your operating system (choose the Win32 version if you're on Windows or the Ruby version if you're on Unix/Linux or Mac OS).

■**Note** Even though I recommend using SQLite as your primary database during development, it certainly doesn't hurt to have MySQL installed on your development box as well. In fact, I often use SQLite during my initial development and switch over to a MySQL database as I get close to deploying the application into the wild. Installing MySQL is often a fairly painless procedure as well. Windows and Mac users have easy wizard-based setup tools can be downloaded from http://dev.mysql.com/downloads/mysql/5.0.html, whereas pretty much every Linux package manager has a way to easily add MySQL to your installation. For example, from a Debian-based Linux distribution (such as Ubuntu) you would merely run the following command: sudo apt-get install libmysql-Ruby1.8 mysql-server-5.0.

Code Editors

To create Rails application code, all you need is a basic editor that can create and modify text files. In fact, I built my very first Rails application on a Windows laptop using Notepad.

It worked, but the experience sure was a lot more painful than it needed to be, and I wouldn't recommend it. Since that time, I've developed Rails application on that same laptop running Windows and several different flavors of Linux, before switching to the Macbook that I use for development today. Having used the full gamut of operating systems, I've installed and experimented with different editors on each OS. Based on that experience, here are a few options for you to consider, as well as my recommendations for each OS.

Windows

If you're developing on Windows, you have a number of cross-platform and great Windows-only editors to consider.

Scite

This text editor, shown in Figure 1-3, should have been installed along with your Ruby one-click installation, and you should find it in your Ruby programs folder in your Start menu. Although a bit on the simple side, it does have a few nice features such as tabbed code editing, code block collapsing, and syntax highlighting. I tend to use this as my go-to editor if I just need to do something quick and small with an application that's running on a Windows server.

```
recipe_controller.rb - SciTE
File  Edit  Search  View  Tools  Options  Language  Buffers  Help
1 recipe_controller.rb
 6        @recipe = Recipe.new
 7        @categories = Category.find_all
 8      end
 9
10  -   def list
11        @category = @params['category']
12        @recipes = Recipe.find_all
13      end
14
15  -   def edit
16        @recipe = Recipe.find(@params["id"])
17        @categories = Category.find_all
18      end
19
20  -   def create
21        @recipe = Recipe.new(@params['recipe'])
22        @recipe.date = Date.today
23  -     if @recipe.save
24          redirect_to :action => 'list'
25        else
26          render_action 'new'
27        end
28      end
29
30  -   def delete
31        Recipe.find(@params['id']).destroy
32        redirect_to :action => 'list'
33      end
34    end
```

Figure 1-3. *Scite Text Editor, a cross-platform text editor*

jEdit

jEdit, another great programmer's text editor written in Java, has been around for a quite some time and supports a large number of languages (see Figure 1-4). Typically, the people who are using jEdit are people who have used it in the past. You can download the editor at `http://Rubyjedit.org` and the Ruby plug-in at `http://Rubyjedit.org`.

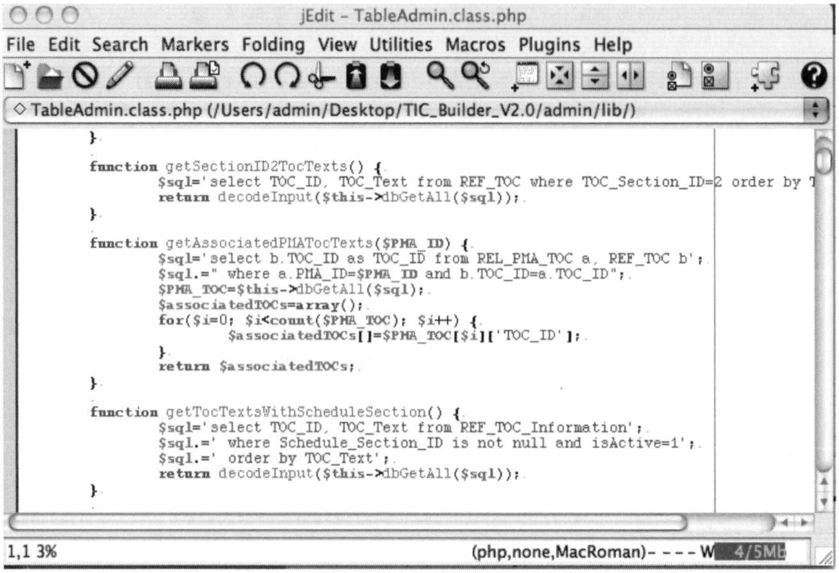

Figure 1-4. *jEdit is a popular cross-platform text editor for programmers.*

RIDE-ME

RIDE-ME, shown in Figure 1-5, is a great editor for those who are coming from a .NET background and have grown accustomed to the Visual Studio tools. It has a lot of nice features such as support for snippets, code folding, and an integrated Internet Explorer browser. You can check it out at `http://www.projectrideme.com`.

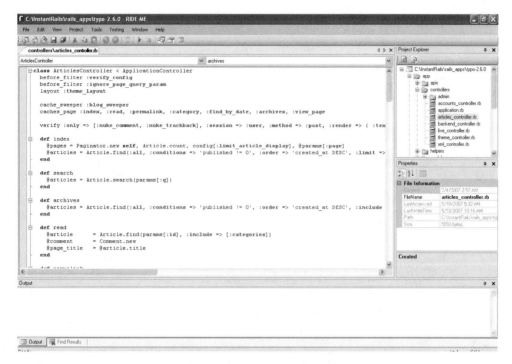

Figure 1-5. *RIDE-ME is a Rails IDE with a Visual Studio feel to it.*

RadRails

RadRails is an Eclipse-based integrated development environment (IDE) that's been custom-ized for Rails development (see Figure 1-6). It offers a number of nice features such as Subversion integration, generator and rake support, integrated testing, and snippet support. You can download it at http://www.radrails.org.

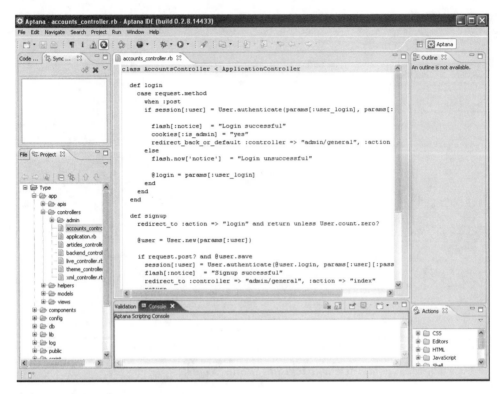

Figure 1-6. *RadRails is an Eclipse-based Rails IDE.*

E

E is a brand new entry into the realm of Windows editors that's hoping to prove that imitation truly is a sincere form of flattery. E strives to bring the power of TextMate over to the Windows world by not only supporting many of its features and functions but also providing full compatibility with TextMate's large library of bundles as well. You can download a copy of E from the official site at http://www.e-texteditor.com.

In addition, you may also want to check out a blog entry from Kansas City Rails developer Ben Kittrell on setting up a Mac-esque Rails development system in Windows using E at http://garbageburrito.com/blog/entry/391.

Figure 1-7 shows the E editor in action.

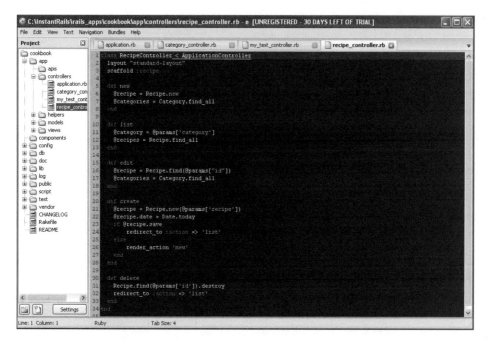

Figure 1-7. *The E text editor running the Vibrant Ink theme.*

Linux

Not only can Linux developers use familiar tools such as Gedit (included with the Gnome Desktop) or Kate (included with the KDE desktop) but they can also choose to use Linux versions of Scite, jEdit, or RadRails. Both Gedit and Kate should be easily installable from whichever package manager your specific flavor of Linux utilizes.

Figure 1-8. *Kate is an advanced text editor within the KDE desktop.*

Mac

While you could certainly use the Mac versions of cross-platform development tools such as RadRails, the simple truth is that TextMate truly rules the roost for Rails development on a Mac. TextMate is the editor that the entire Rails core team uses, and it is, by far, the most popular editor for Rails development.

TextMate, shown in Figure 1-9, provides excellent syntax highlighting support for Ruby, Rails, HTML, CSS, and anything else that you might need to use while developing Rails applications. It also features an incredible number of macros and Emacs-like shortcut commands that truly accelerate your development time.

It's so popular, in fact, that a large number of developers have switched to the Mac just so they can use TextMate. You can download a trial at http://macromates.com.

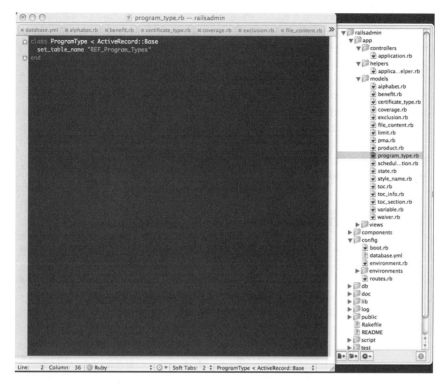

Figure 1-9. *TextMate by Macromates is considered by many to be the best Rails editor.*

Text Editor Recommendations

I started out developing with Rails in the Windows world; later, I switched to various Linux distributions so that I could match production servers and, finally, settled on Mac OS X as I started writing this book. My recommendations are based on personal experience with all of the editors I listed previously.

By far, my recommendation is to go with TextMate if you're on a Mac or can switch to a Mac.

If you're going to be developing on a Windows or Linux machine, I highly recommend using RadRails. RadRails provides excellent support for syntax highlighting. It also offers integrated tests, a database perspective that allows you to inspect and query your database, and Subversion integration. Also, its cross-platform compatibility means that this tool can grow with you no matter what type of system you develop on over the years.

Even though the editor you end up using is going to be a matter of your personal tastes, I do strongly recommend that you take the time to experiment with several and get a good feeling for what's out there. After you make your decision, dedicate some time to really getting to know the editor, and see what kind of additional shortcuts and features it may have that could help you out while you're developing. You're going to spend a lot of time in this editor, and investing the time to truly learn what it can do will pay you big dividends later on.

Installing a Web Server

Now that you have all of the tools in place to create a Rails application, you just need a way to run those applications on your development machine to see the fruits of your labors. While you're certainly free to go through the hassle of installing and configuring a full web server, like Apache, Lighttpd, or LiteSpeed, onto your development box, it strikes me as overkill for our needs—especially when we have a pair of excellent, lightweight, and fully functional solutions to use instead.

WEBBrick

The first solution we'll look at is WEBrick, which should already have been installed along with your Ruby installation. WEBrick is an HTTP server library written purely in Ruby that has been a part of Ruby's standard library since version 1.8.0. Ruby on Rails has always included bundled support for WEBrick. Running a Rails application in WEBrick is as simple as navigating to the root of your Rails application and running

```
ruby script/server
```

WEBrick also provides support for a large number of command-line configuration options as well such as:

```
    -p, --port=port
Runs Rails on the specified port. Default: 3000
    -b, --binding=ip
Binds Rails to the specified ip.  Default: 0.0.0.0
    -e, --environment=name
Specifies the environment to run this server under
I.E. test/development/production. Default: development
    -m, --mime-types=filename
Specifies an Apache style mime.types configuration file to
 be used for mime types  Default: none
    -d, --daemon
```

```
Make Rails run as a Daemon
(only works if fork is available -- meaning on *nix).
    -c, --charset=charset
Set default charset for output.  Default: UTF-8
    -h, --help
Show this help message.
```

While WEBrick provides a great, low-configuration option for running development code, it does suffer from a couple of minor problems. First, since WEBrick is a pure Ruby implementation, it will never run as fast as a web server written in a compiled language. This can be a pain, because you don't have a good scale for judging how fast your code will run when it's ported to production. Second, WEBrick has extremely limited scalability, which makes it impossible to use as a production web server for Rails applications (or at least, its use is highly discouraged).

Issues like these have caused a large number of developers to forgo using WEBrick to test their code. Instead, those developers installed a full-fledged web server, such as Lighttpd or FastCGI, on their development machines, but that all changed once Mongrel was released. Mongrel is a thing of beauty—it's what I use in both development and production, and I highly recommend that you do as well.

Mongrel

Frustrated with the complexity of Rails deployment using FastCGI, programmer Zed Shaw set out to develop a solution to simplify it. His first attempt to replace FastCGI was to develop a Simple CGI implementation, which looked very promising but unfortunately proved to be difficult to support within an existing web infrastructure. When he began working on a project for proxying HTTP requests into Simple CGI requests, he realized that he could just cut out Simple CGI completely, and thus Mongrel was born.

Today, Mongrel is a very fast web server written in Ruby and C and is an excellent alternative to WEBrick. It has quickly become the unofficial standard for development machines, and I recommend that you use Mongrel as your development web server. Mongrel is incredibly easy to install, much faster than WEBrick, and can also be used to power a production application.

To install Mongrel, open a command prompt and run the following line:

```
gem install mongrel
```

Once Mongrel is installed on your development box, you can start an application underneath it by navigating to the root directory of your application and running this command:

```
mongrel_rails start
```

Your application is now available on the local host at port 3000 with Mongrel running in the foreground. You can stop Mongrel by hitting Ctrl+C. Unfortunately, running your application in the foreground can get a tad annoying, as it means additional clutter on your desktop. But Mongrel supports a wide range configuration options including the capability to run as a daemon in the background (on Unix, Linux, and Mac OS). You can start a Mongrel process in the background by passing in the -d flag:

```
mongrel_rails start -d
```

You can pass Mongrel the following command line options:

```
-e, --environment ENV       Rails environment to run as
-d, --daemonize             Whether to run in the background or not
-p, --port PORT             Which port to bind to
-a, --address ADDR          Address to bind to
-l, --log FILE              Where to write log messages
-P, --pid FILE              Where to write the PID
-n, --num-procs INT         Number of processors active before client's
                              denied
-t, --timeout TIME          Timeout all requests after 100th seconds time
-m, --mime PATH             A YAML file that lists additional MIME types
-c, --chdir PATH            Change to dir before starting (will be
                              expanded)
-r, --root PATH             Set the document root (default 'public')
-B, --debug                 Enable debugging mode
-C, --config PATH           Use a config file
-S, --script PATH           Load the given file as an extra config script.
-G, --generate CONFIG       Generate a config file for -C
    --user USER

                            User to run as

    --group GROUP

                            Group to run as

    --prefix PATH

                            URL prefix for Rails app
-h, --help                  Show this message
    --version               Show version
```

Stopping a Mongrel process running in the background is similarly easy; use the following command:

```
mongrel_rails stop
```

Restarting a Running mongrel process can be done with the following command

```
mongrel_rails restart
```

Extra Tips that You'll Want to Adopt (Eventually)

At this point, you should have a pretty solid development environment that will enable you to complete all the projects in this book as well as your own development projects. Before we close this chapter, however, there are a few more items that I wanted to share with you. Even though we won't be explicitly using them in the projects in this book, I feel that these are critical elements for your development system, and I would be remiss if we didn't cover them in our discussion.

Use a Version Control System

Perhaps the most important tool to add to your development environment is a version control system. A solid version control system and discipline will undoubtedly save your tail end from the fire at some point. I remember with great clarity the first time that something went wrong with a large piece of code that I was working on and that wonderful feeling of joy I had when I realized that I didn't have to try and troubleshoot why it had gone wrong—since I could merely restore the previous (working) version of the code again.

One of the most popular version control systems today is Subversion, and if you're using TextMate or RadRails, you'll find that your code editor already has full support for integrating with a Subversion repository.

Going into the details of how to install or administer a Subversion repository is beyond the scope of this book. However, you can find a wonderful book online for free at `http://svnbook.red-bean.com`. I'm going to assume that you have already created your Subversion repository, and we'll discuss the process for importing your application into Subversion.

Let's assume a project named tickets, a Subversion repository at `svn://192.168.1.200/projects/` with a username of eldon and a password of password.

To start, open a command prompt, and navigate to the root of your application to perform your initial import:

```
svn import . svn://192.168.1.200/projects/tickets ➥
 --message "initial import" –username eldon
```

At this point, our application should be added to the repository. So now you'll want to check out a new copy of the application and make your modifications to the checked out version. You could simply delete the existing copy, but instead, it's a good idea to move your existing copy to a backup location just to be safe.

```
cd ..
mv tickets tickets_backup
svn checkout svn://192.168.1.200/projects/tickets tickets
cd tickets
```

Now that we have a copy from our Subversion repository, let's make some modifications to clean it up a bit. To start with, we obviously don't need to have our log files stored in version control, so let's get rid of those.

```
svn remove log/*
svn commit --message "removing all log files from subversion"
```

Though that command removed the existing log files from our existing copy and the copy in the repository, it won't prevent the addition of new log files to the repository. To do that, we'll need to tell Subversion to ignore any new log files added to the log directory:

```
svn propset svn:ignore "*.log" log/
svn update log/
svn commit –message "Ignore all log files in the log directory"
```

Let's also have Subversion ignore all the files in the /tmp directories (that is, cache, session, and socket files):

```
svn propset svn:ignore "*" tmp/sessions tmp/cache tmp/sockets
svn commit -message "Ignore all cache, sessions ,etc files in the tmp directory"
```

And that's it! Your project is now fully loaded into Subversion.

Automating Deployment with Capistrano

Assuming that you're not trying to deploy your applications to a Windows-based server for production, the final item that I strongly recommend is that you set up your applications to utilize Capistrano for deployment.

Capistrano is a tool that's designed to automate the normally painful task of moving your application from your development machine to your production servers. Capistrano is an incredibly powerful tool that can support virtually all of your deployment needs, from simple deployments on a single server to complex deployments in a server farm configured for share-nothing scalability. Capistrano is also fully extendable, so you can customize it to support any particular need that it doesn't support out of the box.

The first step to automating your deployments with Capistrano is to install the Capistrano gem:

```
gem install capistrano
```

Once you have that installed, you can configure an application to utilize Capistrano by opening a command prompt in the root of the application and running the following command to prepare the application for Capistrano deployment:

```
capify .
```

Running this command adds two files to your application: a new Capistrano capfile in the root of your application and a configuration file named deploy.rb in /config that you'll configure with your specific deployment options.

Using the same sample ticket application from the previous section, let's modify the deploy.rb file now. The first thing you need to do is to set the required variables—the application's name and the path to the Subversion repository:

```
set :application, "set your application name here"
set :repository, "set your repository location here"
```

For our example, we'll set these to

```
set :application, "tickets"
set :repository,  svn://192.168.1.200/projects/#{application}
```

Next, we need to define the servers that we want to deploy our application to in the Roles section:

```
role :app, "your app-server here"
role :web, "your web-server here"
role :db,  "your db-server here", :primary => true
```

Showing some marvelous forethought, Capistrano allows us to define many different server roles that we might want to deploy to: A web role would be where our actual files are served from. An application role would be useful if we wanted to farm out the actual processing of our application's code to application servers running Mongrel or FastCGI instances, and the database role provides a way to deploy elements to a separate database server. In addition, notice that Capistrano easily supports having multiple servers in each role, so even as your application grows and requires you to add more hardware, your deployment always remains just as easy.

For our example, we're just starting out with a single server for our application, so we'll define it like so:

```
role :web, "www.tickets.com"
role :app, "www.tickets.com"
role :db,  "www.tickets.com", :primary => true
```

Finally, we'll need to change some of the optional variables to more accurately match the way that our system administrators have set up things.

We have just a couple of minor changes to make to our deployment. First off, our system administrators have decided that all of our applications are to be deployed into the /home directory on our web servers, so we'll need to change the deploy setting from the default. Second, we'll need to set the login user name to use the eldon account instead of our system login name:

```
set :deploy_to, "\home\#(application)"
set :user, "eldon"
```

Go ahead and save your modified deploy.rb file, and Capistrano is now configured to deploy your application to your production servers.

Before we can deploy the application, though, we need to set up the production environments to receive our application code. We can do that through Capistrano using the setup task:

```
cap deploy:setup
```

During execution of the task, you'll be prompted to enter your password for the production server. That's normal, so go ahead and enter it to continue.

If you log on to the production server once the setup task has completed, you will find that Capistrano has created a new directory structure under /home/tickets on your server. You now have three new subdirectories that will be used to manage deployed revisions of your application.

The releases subdirectory is where Capistrano will deploy each revision of your application. The current subdirectory is a symbolic link to the active revision of your application under releases. The shared subdirectory is a single location where items that need to be shared among releases (such as logs) are stored.

Now that we have the server configured, let's go ahead and deploy our application:

```
cap deploy:cold
```

After entering your password again and waiting a few minutes for all the files to copy over, your application should be deployed to the production server. From now on, you can push out the latest version of your code that's stored in Subversion by running the cap deploy command.

If, for any reason, Capistrano encountered an error during deployment, it automatically rolls back any changes it has made. If you discover that your recently deployed revision isn't working and you need to revert to the previous version, you can do so by running the `rollback` task:

```
cap deploy:rollback
```

That's a decent enough introduction to using Capistrano, even though we barely touched on all the things you could do with it. For more information on Capistrano, check out the official site at `http://www.capify.org`.

Summary

In this chapter, we took a very high-level view of the steps necessary for installing Ruby and Rails onto your development machine. We touched on some of the bundled installation tools that make setting up a development environment even easier, such as Instant Rails and Locomotive.

We also looked a few options for tools that you can use to write your Rails code on different operating systems and discussed a few best practice ideas, such as using a version control system and using Capistrano to deploy your applications into production.

CHAPTER 2

■ ■ ■

Creating a Rails Application

Wiseman: When you removed the book from the cradle, did you speak the words?

Ash: Yeah, basically.

Wiseman: Did you speak the exact words?

Ash: Look, maybe I didn't say every tiny syllable, no. But basically I said them, yeah.

——Sam and Ivan Raimi, *Army of Darkness*

Now that you have a development environment put together, we're just about ready to begin creating some Rails applications. Before we dive into that though, we need to go over a few things to keep this book in line with the Don't Repeat Yourself (DRY) principle. Over the course of this book, we're going to be creating quite a number of Rails applications together, and we're going to do a lot of common things with each new application, such as creating the project structure and configuring the database connection.

I don't know about you, but for me, reading the same basic steps again and again can get pretty boring, so in an effort to save us both from some boredom, I'm going to document the basic setup process for all of our projects in this chapter. Since you're obviously one of the smart readers who chose not to skip the important set of chapters with the label "Don't Skip This," you'll know that, at the start of each project, when I say to create your Rails application, you should follow the steps in this chapter.

Kicking Things Off

At the start of each project, the first thing we'll need to do is to have Rails create our new application.

Step 1: Create the Project.

The first step to starting a new project is to use the `rails` command to generate the directory structure for our new project. From a command prompt, you'll run the following commands (for our example we'll assume we're creating an application named ticket):

```
rails ticket
    create
```

```
create  app/controllers
create  app/helpers
create  app/models
create  app/views/layouts
create  config/environments
create  components
create  db
create  doc
create  lib
create  lib/tasks
create  log
create  public/images
create  public/javascripts
create  public/stylesheets
create  script/performance
create  script/process
create  test/fixtures
create  test/functional
create  test/integration
create  test/mocks/development
create  test/mocks/test
create  test/unit
create  vendor
create  vendor/plugins
create  tmp/sessions
create  tmp/sockets
create  tmp/cache
create  tmp/pids
create  Rakefile
create  README
create  app/controllers/application.rb
create  app/helpers/application_helper.rb
create  test/test_helper.rb
create  config/database.yml
create  config/routes.rb
create  public/.htaccess
create  config/boot.rb
create  config/environment.rb
create  config/environments/production.rb
create  config/environments/development.rb
create  config/environments/test.rb
create  script/about
create  script/breakpointer
create  script/console
create  script/destroy
```

```
create  script/generate
create  script/performance/benchmarker
create  script/performance/profiler
create  script/process/reaper
create  script/process/spawner
create  script/process/inspector
create  script/runner
create  script/server
create  script/plugin
create  public/dispatch.rb
create  public/dispatch.cgi
create  public/dispatch.fcgi
create  public/404.html
create  public/500.html
create  public/index.html
create  public/favicon.ico
create  public/robots.txt
create  public/images/rails.png
create  public/javascripts/prototype.js
create  public/javascripts/effects.js
create  public/javascripts/dragdrop.js
create  public/javascripts/controls.js
create  public/javascripts/application.js
create  doc/README_FOR_APP
create  log/server.log
create  log/production.log
create  log/development.log
create  log/test.log
```

Creating the Rails Folder Structure

The `rails` command created the directory structure for your project. Let's take a quick look at the structure that's been created for us. A new Rails project contains the following directories:

app: The app directory contains the folders where the majority of your code will be stored. Subdirectories within this folder segregate your code into its specific functions.

app/controllers: Your controller classes will be stored here; these are the classes that serve as the general directors for responding to requests. Most of these should inherit from `ActionController::Base`.

app/models: Models are the classes that hold business logic and typically map to a database table. Subsequently, most model classes will inherit from `ActiveRecord::Base`.

app/views: All of your template files will be stored here. When you use the Rails generators to create your controllers, Rails will automatically create subfolders in this directory to match each of your controllers. Typically you'll store view files with extensions like `.rhtml`, `.rjs`, or `.rxml` here.

app/helpers: Helpers are small bits of code that you can call from your views. You'll want to push code out of your views and into these helpers to minimize the amount of Ruby code that's present in your view templates.

app/apis: You won't have this folder for a brand new project. It's created by the Action Web Service generator when you need to add a SOAP or XML-RPC interface to your application.

config/: Configuration files for your Rails application are stored here. Important ones that you'll typically modify are database.yml, routes.rb, and environment.rb.

components/: Components were an attempt at creating self-contained applets that could be dropped into any Rails application. They had a number of serious issues (primarily that they were *slow*), and they have pretty much been replaced by plug-ins.

db/: This folder stores database-specific files. Schema.rb is a helpful file that shows the current database schema and is auto-generated when you run your migrations. Its default behavior is to display this information in Ruby migration format, but you can change this to SQL format if you want. This folder also has a subdirectory named migrate where Rails stores your database migration files. Typically, I use this directory to store my SQLite databases as well.

doc/: Documentation for your application should be placed in this directory if you plan to share the application with others. You can even generate Rdoc documentation from your application within this directory by running the rake doc command.

lib/: Custom libraries that don't necessarily belong in one of the app folders are supposed to be stored here.

log/: Log files created by Rails are stored here.

public/: From the web server's perspective, this is the document root for your application. This directory also has several subdirectories for storing images, style sheets, and JavaScript files.

script/: This is where many of the important Rails scripts live, such as the generator script that you use to create controllers, models, migrations, and so forth.

test/: All the files you need to run unit, integration, and functional test are stored here.

tmp/: Temporary files such as cached files or session files are stored here.

vendor/: Third-party or external libraries that the application uses, such as plug-ins, are stored here.

Common Command-Line Options for the rails Command

The `rails` command also supports a number of command-line options that allow you to over-write the defaults or simplify your configuration. You can view all of the available options by running

```
rails --help
```

Three options that I use on a regular basis follow:

```
--version
```

This spits out information about the version of Rails that you have installed—very useful when you have applications deployed to a large number of servers or web hosts.

```
--freeze
```

This option extracts the currently installed version of Rails into the `vendor/rails` directory. Freezing your Rails applications to a specific version is strongly recommended, as it guarantees that your application will continue to work regardless of what some crazed system administrator decides to do to the installed version of Rails on the server. We won't be using this option in this book; instead, in the next few steps, we'll manually freeze to the version of Rails that was available while this book was being written.

```
--database=name
```

Rails generates a `database.yml` file with MySQL parameters by default. You can override this behavior by specifying your desired database with this parameter. Valid options are `mysql`, `oracle`, `postgresql`, `sqlite2`, and `sqlite3`. Obviously, I recommend using SQLite for your development environment, in which case, the correct way to create your new Rails application would be like this:

```
rails ticket --database=sqlite3
```

Step 2: Configure Database Settings.

Now that our application's structure is created, we need to configure the application with our specific database settings. That job is made considerably easier if you've used the correct database option when creating your application structure, as Rails uses that option when it generates `database.yml`:

```
# SQLite version 3.x
#   gem install sqlite3-ruby
development:
  adapter: sqlite3
  database: db/development.sqlite3
  timeout: 5000
```

```
# Warning: The database defined as 'test' will be erased and
# re-generated from your development database when you run 'rake'.
# Do not set this db to the same as development or production.
test:
  adapter: sqlite3
  database: db/test.sqlite3
  timeout: 5000

production:
  adapter: sqlite3
  database: db/production.sqlite3
  timeout: 5000
```

You could modify the names of the databases if you wanted, but there's really no need to.

If, on the other hand, you're using MySQL as your development database, you first need to create your database using either a tool such as PhpMyAdmin or the command-line mysqladmin tool:

```
mysqladmin -u root -p create ticket_development
```

Once your database is created, you should modify your database.yml file to match your newly created database:

```
development:
  adapter: mysql
  database: ticket_development
  username: root
  password:
  host: localhost
```

Testing Your Database Settings

After you've configured your database settings, you should do a quick test to verify that Rails can connect to your database with those settings by running the rake db:migrate task:

```
rake db:migrate
```

As long as you don't see any errors from that command, everything is working like it should, and Rails can connect to and create tables within your database.

Step 3: Test the Application.

Assuming that you're using Mongrel as your development web server, you can test that everything is working correctly at this point by starting up a Mongrel instance with this command:

```
mongrel_rails start
```

This command will start up a version of the application running on IP 0.0.0.0 and on port 3000. You can access it by opening a web browser and navigating to http://localhost:3000/. Once you do, you should see the Rails default test page that will confirm that your environment is configured correctly (see Figure 2-1).

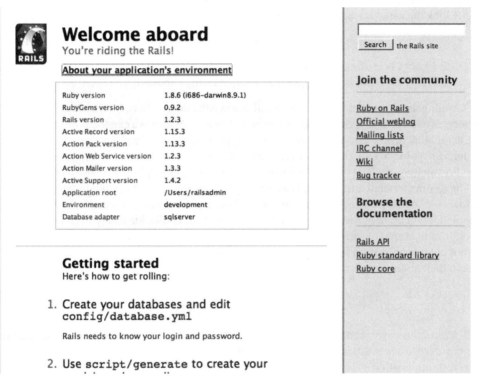

Figure 2-1. *The Rails "Welcome aboard" page*

Now that we know that the application is running, let's go ahead and get rid of this test page, so it won't be in our way later when we need our application to handle the default page for the application.

Navigate to the public folder, and delete index.rhtml to get rid of this page.

Step 4: Install Style Sheets.

Another element that I would like you to add to all of the projects in this book is a set of style sheet files from the Yahoo User Interface (YUI) library, an open source set of JavaScript controls designed to make it easy to build advanced web applications. The library includes three very powerful CSS stylesheets that we'll take advantage of in our projects to simplify the styling of our application front ends:

- `Reset.css` is a style sheet that removes all of a browser's default rendering by doing things like setting margins, padding, and borders to 0. Basically, this sets the style sheet rendering of all browsers back to a level playing field to help ensure that our applications look the same across different browsers.

- `Fonts.css` builds on `Reset.css` and provides normalization of text across browsers.

- `Grids.css` is the final piece of the puzzle and provides a flexible grid system for building CSS layouts. It provides over 200 preset layouts and allows for unlimited customizations.

Adding the three of these into our application will allow us to build the visual layout aspects of each project quickly and with minimal fuss. That way, we can focus our attention on the actual Rails applications that we're building instead of worrying about whether our applications are going to look the same in multiple browsers.

Fortunately, the YUI library also provides us with a lightweight way to use all three by providing a concatenated and minified (all whitespace removed) version called `reset-fonts-grids.css`. To further sweeten the deal and make using these files even easier, in April 2007, Yahoo opened up their own network to host the YUI library files for you (you can read more about this at `http://developer.yahoo.com/yui/articles/hosting/`). So within the application layout of any application from which we want to use the YUI style sheets, we can simply add a link to the Yahoo-hosted version of the `reset-fonts-grids.css` style sheet like this:

```
<link rel="stylesheet" type="text/css" href= ➥
"http://yui.yahooapis.com/2.2.2/build/reset-fonts-grids/reset-fonts-grids.css">
```

Alternatively, you can download the current version of the YUI library from the official site at `http://developer.yahoo.com/yui/` and manually copy the `reset-fonts-grids` style sheet into your application's `/public/stylesheets` directory (which may be useful if you tend to develop in a place where you don't always have an Internet connection). If you choose to do this, you'll need to link to the style sheet like this:

```
<%= stylesheet_link_tag 'reset-fonts-grids-min' %>
```

Step 5: Freeze Rails.

The final step you'll need to take with each application is to freeze the application to the 1.2 release of Rails. In essence, this means that we'll copy a specific version of the Rails gems (ActiveRecord, ActiveSupport, and so on) into `vendor/rails`, so our application will use those gems instead of whatever version may happen to be installed on the server.

Freezing the version of Rails into our applications means that you'll be building your applications with the same version of Rails that they were originally created and tested in, so you don't have to worry about future releases of Rails breaking things (especially considering the ever-increasing number of items planned to be deprecated in Rails 2.0).

You can freeze Rails by navigating to the root of your project and running this command:

```
rake rails:freeze:edge TAG=rel_1-2-3
```

Freezing Other Gems

Freezing the Rails gems is all well and good, but what if our application uses other Ruby gems? Unfortunately, there's no automated way to freeze those gems in a standard Ruby on Rails application, but we can add a custom task to our application to solve that problem and make it easier to deploy our applications to remote servers without worrying about whether or not all of the correct versions of the required gems are installed.

Geoffrey Grosenbach is the author of the rake task that we'll use, and you can download the task from his blog at `http://nubyonrails.com/articles/2005/12/22/freeze-other-gems-to-rails-lib-directory`. Once you have it downloaded, copy it into your `lib/tasks` directory, and edit the `libraries` line of the task to match the gems that you wish to freeze:

```
libraries = %w(shipping gruff)
```

Once you have saved it with your specific gems that you'll want to freeze, you can run this task like so:

```
rake freeze_other_gems
```

Summary

In this chapter, I explained some of the common tasks that we'll be performing in each of the projects in this book. We took a high level look at the directory structure of a new Rails application and discussed some of the useful options for defining a new application. From there, we discussed how to freeze the Rails version and gems into your Rails application to simplify deployment. With those final additions to our toolbox, we're now ready to start developing our projects.

## PART 2

Monkey Tasks: Managing a Daily Task List

If your life is anything like mine, you know how easy it is to get overwhelmed by the sheer number of things that we have to keep up with on a daily basis. It rarely seems to be the big items—like picking up the kids from school or finishing that report by noon—that get lost in the shuffle. It's the little ones—like picking up milk on the way home, updating that web page, sending that Netflix movie back, or remembering to return that coworker's call—that are so easily forgotten. I affectionately call all this little stuff "monkey work" (because it's so small and easy that you could train a monkey to do it).

Solving this problem requires some intelligent application of task management principles, an area where there are already endless theories, books, and software applications readily available. Unfortunately, the majority of them are designed for people who want to get much more organized than I care to. Even worse, these solutions make me feel increasingly guilty for not abdicating full control of my life and schedule to their collective wisdom on scheduling, prioritization, and task management.

What has worked for me is a much simpler method. At the very beginning of each day, I simply write out on a single sheet of paper all of the tasks that I plan to try to accomplish that day (trying very hard to be realistic about what I can actually accomplish in the few short hours of the day). It's a simple discipline but one that has worked wonders for my ability to keep on task and prevent items from slipping through the cracks.

So, for our first Rails programming project, we'll do a review of basic Rails development by building a simple task management application. As we build the application, we'll discuss some good practices for modeling our data, practice applying plug-ins to expedite some of our development, eliminate duplication by extracting portions of our code, and finish up by adding a bit of Ajax to our application using a powerful feature of Rails called Remote JavaScript, or RJS for short. By the time we're finished, we'll have a nice little application that can be used to manage tasks in a simple daily task list, but we certainly won't leave it there—throughout the course of this book, I'll refer to this application and discuss ways that you can enhance it.

CHAPTER 3

■■■

Implementing a User Registration and Authentication System

Let's kick things off by generating our project structure. Open a command line prompt, and create a new project named "monkey" using the instructions from Chapter 2.

For the sake of clarity, we're going to work from the outside in. That is, we're going to start by building our basic layout and view templates; next, we'll add in our user registration and authentication system, and then work backward from there to build the models, controllers, and methods that we'll need to bring our application to life.

With that in mind, I sketched out the basic design shown in Figure 3-1 (don't laugh; I never claimed I was a designer).

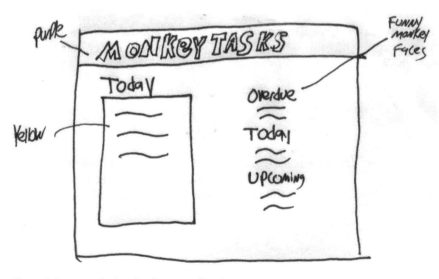

Figure 3-1. *A rough sketch of our application*

Once we have the application built, we'll have a fairly simple page layout. On the left-hand side of our application, we'll maintain our daily list of tasks that we want to accomplish. While over on the right-hand side of the page, we'll maintain a list of all of our uncompleted tasks placed into three groups (those that are now past their due dates, those due today, and those due in the future). We'll use these three task list groups to populate our daily task list.

Building Our Layout

Going from our design sketch, we're going to need a page that will serve as the primary interface for our daily task list. So let's go ahead and create a controller and define the first page. Since the primary purpose of this page will be to display today's tasks, let's name the controller "today."

Running the following command will create a new controller named today_controller.rb and build an empty index page:

```
ruby script/generate controller today index
```

```
exists  app/controllers/
exists  app/helpers/
create  app/views/today
exists  test/functional/
create  app/controllers/today_controller.rb
create  test/functional/today_controller_test.rb
create  app/helpers/today_helper.rb
create  app/views/today/index.rhtml
```

So our new controller was created in /app/controllers/ and our main view page (index.rthml) was created in /app/views/today. Opening our today_controller, we can see that Rails even built our index method for us as well:

```
class TodayController < ApplicationController
  def index
  end
end
```

Since we want to make this the default page for the application, let's go ahead and set that up as the default route now. Open routes.rb in /config, and add a route for request to '' (i.e., the root) to go to the today controller. So, minus the comments, your routes file should look like this:

```
ActionController::Routing::Routes.draw do |map|
  map.connect '', :controller => "today"
  map.connect ':controller/service.wsdl', :action => 'wsdl'
  map.connect ':controller/:action/:id.:format'
  map.connect ':controller/:action/:id'
end
```

Our Initial Layout

A web application should maintain a consistent look and feel, and Rails provides us with some wonderful tools to make it easy for us to maintain consistency as we build our application. One of the key ones, which we'll look at right now, is the ability to define layouts to wrap our templates. We can use layouts to separate common presentational items, such as headers and footers, into a file that can be used for every page request; we can simply populate the file with our specific, personalized content.

We're going to keep our design nice and simple so that we can get away with utilizing a single layout file for the entire application. However, before we do that, you'll need to download a few resources from the code archive for this application from the Apress web site's Source Code/Download section. First, you'll want to copy the file styles.css from the archive into your /public/stylesheets directory. Second, you'll need to copy all the images from the archive into /public/images.

With those resources added to your project, we can go ahead and create a standard layout that will wrap around all of our view templates. Create a new file named application.rhtml in /monkey/app/views/layouts, and edit that file to look like this:

```
<!DOCTYPE HTML PUBLIC "-//W3C//DTD HTML 4.01 Transitional//EN"
      "http://www.w3.org/TR/html4/loose.dtd">
<html>
    <head>
        <meta http-equiv="Content-type" content="text/html; charset=utf-8">
        <title>MonkeyTasks</title>
        <link rel="stylesheet" type="text/css" href= ➡
"http://yui.yahooapis.com/2.2.2/build/reset-fonts-grids/reset-fonts-grids.css">
        <%= stylesheet_link_tag 'styles' %>
        <%= javascript_include_tag :defaults %>
    </head>

    <body>
    <div id="content">
        <div id="header">
            <%= image_tag 'monkeyhead.gif' %>
            <%= image_tag 'monkeytasks.gif' %>
        </div>  <!-- End header  -->

        <ul id="topnav">
          <li>
            <%= link_to "Today", :controller => 'today', :action => 'index' %>
          </li>
          <li>
            <%= link_to "Logout", :controller => 'account', :action => 'logout' %>
          </li>
        </ul>

        <p style="color:green;"><%= flash[:notice] %></p>
```

```
        <%= yield %>
    </div>  <!-- End content  -->
    </body>
</html>
```

As you can see, it's really just standard HTML plus a few helper methods such as the following:

```
stylesheet_link_tag 'styles'
```

This is a helper method that will generate a standard link tag to the CSS style sheet passed as the parameter. It expects that your CSS style sheets are stored in the /public/stylesheets directory. In our layout, the method will generate the following HTML:

```
<link href="/stylesheets/styles.css?1179549309"
    media="screen" rel="Stylesheet" type="text/css" />
```

The image_tag helper method

```
image_tag 'monkeyhead.gif'
```

also generates common HTML elements; this time it will generate a link to the image name specified. It expects images to be stored in /public/images. This call will generate the following HTML:

```
<img alt="Monkeyhead" src="/images/monkeyhead.gif?1178180104" />
```

The following helper method

```
link_to "Today", :controller => 'today', :action => 'index'
```

will also generate the proper HTML links to controller methods. It is preferable to use these methods over building your links manually, as these helpers are able to more easily adapt to changes in your environment. This method generates the following HTML:

```
<a href="/">Today</a>
```

The magic yield method will pass control of rendering over to the template that is being rendered. In other words, it is at this location that our actual templates will be rendered within this layout.

```
javascript_include_tag :defaults
```

This is a convenience method that Rails provides to allow us to automatically pull in the standard prototype and script.aculo.us javascript libraries into our pages. In essence, it's the same as putting in the following commands, just with a lot less typing:

```
<%= javascript_include_tag 'prototype' %>
<%= javascript_include_tag 'effects' %>
<%= javascript_include_tag 'dragdrop' %>
<%= javascript_include_tag 'controls' %>
<%= javascript_include_tag 'application' %>
```

If you were to start up our application now (most likely using `mongrel_rails start`) and open a web browser to `http://localhost:3000/today`, you would see a result like in the one shown in Figure 3-2.

Today#index
Find me in app/views/today/index.rhtml

Figure 3-2. *Our application layout displaying the default template*

Our First View Template

Now, let's put together the main page of our application. Open `index.rhtml` in `/app/views/today` (this file was created when we generated our controller) and add the following content to it:

```
<div id="primary">
    <div id="add_task"> </div>

    <div id='main'>
        <h1>Today's Tasks</h1>
        <ul id="todo-list">
            <li>test</li>
            <li>test2</li>
        </ul>
    </div>
</div>

<div id='sidebar'>
    <div class="sidebar-tasks">
        <h1>Overdue Tasks</h1>
    </div>

    <div class="sidebar-tasks">
        <h1>Due Today </h1>
    </div>

    <div class="sidebar-tasks">
        <h1>Upcoming Tasks</h1>
    </div>
</div>
```

Fire up a web browser, and navigate to `http://localhost:3000/`, and you should see something similar to Figure 3-3:

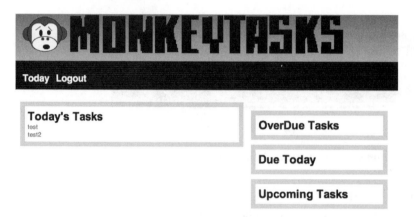

Figure 3-3. *Our page with content added to the view*

Within a few minutes, we've created a basic HTML mock-up of our site, which gives us a decent looking interface to use while we build our application (decent being a relative term, of course).

Adding User Registration and Authentication

Although I'm sure there's a wealth of people who would love to have the godlike ability to control my to-do list and force me to work on their pet projects today, I feel a lot more comfortable when I'm the only one who can control what goes into my daily task list. Since we want to be able to make our application open to other people to use, we're going to need to make sure that no one else is able to mess around with our daily schedules, which means adding user authentication.

Adding user authentication is an area where there has been a small amount of conflict within the Rails community. On one side is a large group of programmers who feel that user authentication is a common feature of most web applications and that Rails should provide an automated solution within the framework that can be added simply and easily. On the other side, many feel that adding basic authentication functionality is so easy within Rails that it is a bad idea to use over-the-counter solutions. In another project, we'll explore building our own simple authentication system, so you'll be able to make your own decision on what you want to use. I will say that in my most of my own development, I tend to roll my own authentication systems.

However, for the purpose of this project, we're going to use one of the most popular automatic authentication solutions, a plug-in developed by Rick Olsen called Acts as Authenticated.

Acts as Authenticated is a great plug-in that provides us with a rather large amount of functionality for supporting both automated user registration and user authentication with very little pain in configuration. Plus, since it's designed as a plug-in, we can easily integrate it into our application without being forced into any corners on how we use it.

So let's go ahead and install Acts as Authenticated. Go to the root of your application, and install the plug-in by running this command:

```
ruby script/plugin install ➥
http://svn.techno-weenie.net/projects/plugins/acts_as_authenticated/
```

```
./acts_as_authenticated/CHANGELOG
+ ./acts_as_authenticated/README
+ ./acts_as_authenticated/generators/authenticated/USAGE
+ ./acts_as_authenticated/generators/authenticated/authenticated_generator.rb
+ ./acts_as_authenticated/generators/authenticated/templates/authenticated_system.rb
+ ./acts_as_authenticated/generators/authenticated/templates/ ➥
authenticated_test_helper.rb
+ ./acts_as_authenticated/generators/authenticated/templates/controller.rb
+ ./acts_as_authenticated/generators/authenticated/templates/fixtures.yml
+ ./acts_as_authenticated/generators/authenticated/templates/functional_test.rb
+ ./acts_as_authenticated/generators/authenticated/templates/helper.rb
+ ./acts_as_authenticated/generators/authenticated/templates/index.rhtml
+ ./acts_as_authenticated/generators/authenticated/templates/login.rhtml
+ ./acts_as_authenticated/generators/authenticated/templates/migration.rb
+ ./acts_as_authenticated/generators/authenticated/templates/model.rb
+ ./acts_as_authenticated/generators/authenticated/templates/signup.rhtml
+ ./acts_as_authenticated/generators/authenticated/templates/unit_test.rb
+ ./acts_as_authenticated/generators/authenticated_mailer/USAGE
+ ./acts_as_authenticated/generators/authenticated_mailer/ ➥
authenticated_mailer_generator.rb
+ ./acts_as_authenticated/generators/authenticated_mailer/templates/activation.rhtml
+ ./acts_as_authenticated/generators/authenticated_mailer/templates/notifier.rb
+ ./acts_as_authenticated/generators/authenticated_mailer/templates/notifier_test.rb
+ ./acts_as_authenticated/generators/authenticated_mailer/templates/observer.rb
+ ./acts_as_authenticated/generators/authenticated_mailer/templates/ ➥
signup_notification.rhtml
+ ./acts_as_authenticated/install.rb
+ ./acts_as_authenticated generator
```

Now that we have the plug-in installed, we need to install it into our application by running the following generator to create the authentication models, views, and controllers that we'll be customizing for our needs:

```
ruby script/generate authenticated user account
```

```
exists  app/models/
exists  app/controllers/
exists  app/helpers/
create  app/views/account
exists  test/functional/
exists  test/unit/
create  app/models/user.rb
create  app/controllers/account_controller.rb
create  lib/authenticated_system.rb
create  lib/authenticated_test_helper.rb
create  test/functional/account_controller_test.rb
create  app/helpers/account_helper.rb
create  test/unit/user_test.rb
create  test/fixtures/users.yml
create  app/views/account/index.rhtml
create  app/views/account/login.rhtml
create  app/views/account/signup.rhtml
create  db/migrate
create  db/migrate/001_create_users.rb
```

Since we're going to want to make it easy for people to sign up for the application themselves (otherwise, we'd have to manually create accounts for all new users—and that just doesn't fit into my plans for doing less overtime work). To support this, we'll want to configure the mailer functionality of Acts as Authenticated as well. Generate the necessary mailer models and views by running this authenticated mailer generator:

```
ruby script/generate authenticated_mailer user
```

```
exists  app/models/
create  app/views/user_notifier
exists  test/unit/
create  app/models/user_notifier.rb
create  app/models/user_observer.rb
create  test/unit/user_notifier_test.rb
create  app/views/user_notifier/activation.rhtml
create  app/views/user_notifier/signup_notification.rhtml
```

As you may have noticed in the text that flew by while running those commands, Acts as Authenticated created a new controller (account_controller), several views, and, of particular note, a few models for us (User, User Notifier, and User Observer).

In order for that User model to be active, we're going to need to run a rake db:migrate command to load the database structure from the migration file it created. But before we can do that, we need to make a few minor modifications to support our application's needs.

We need to add in the necessary fields to support our automated user activation. Navigate to /monkey/db/migrate/, open the file 001_create_users.rb, and add the following two bold lines in the self.up block:

```
class CreateUsers < ActiveRecord::Migration
  def self.up
    create_table "users", :force => true do |t|
      t.column :login,                    :string
      t.column :email,                    :string
      t.column :crypted_password,         :string, :limit => 40
      t.column :salt,                     :string, :limit => 40
      t.column :created_at,               :datetime
      t.column :updated_at,               :datetime
      t.column :remember_token,           :string
      t.column :remember_token_expires_at, :datetime
      t.column :activation_code,          :string, :limit => 40
      t.column :activated_at,             :datetime
    end
  end

  def self.down
    drop_table "users"
  end
end
```

Those extra data elements will be used to store the activation code that we'll send along in the new users' activation e-mail. It will also provide us with a simple Boolean field to flag whether or not a user account is activated or yet. Go ahead and run rake db:migrate now to build the users table in our database:

```
rake db:migrate
```

```
== CreateUsers: migrating ===========================================================
-- create_table("users", {:force=>true})
   -> 0.1359s
== CreateUsers: migrated (0.1361s) =================================================
```

Configuring Acts as Authenticated

Now that we've installed Acts as Authenticated, we've gained a User model with some nice convenience methods for our use, an authentication system that uses SHA-1 to securely encrypt user passwords, and all the necessary login forms. But before we can make use of all of this, we still need to add the plug-in to our application and configure some of the additional functionality available, such as allowing the system to remember the user by storing a cookie on the user's system and the optional mailer functions we installed earlier.

Let's go back to /monkey/apps/controllers and tell our application to include the Authenticated System library when it starts up. We do that by reediting application.rb to look like this:

```
class ApplicationController < ActionController::Base
  session :session_key => '_monkeytasks_session_id'
  include AuthenticatedSystem
  before_filter :login_from_cookie
end
```

before_filter is a powerful command that we'll be using a lot. It allows us to define a method to call before any other methods are run in a controller. Here in application.rb, we're using it call the login_from_cookie method from Acts as Authenticated, which allows us to provide a remember-me feature to the Monkey Tasks application. In other controllers, we'll use that before_filter functionality to prevent unauthorized access to resources.

Limiting Access to Today

Now that we have Acts as Authenticated implemented in our application, we can start using it to limit access to our main page. Open today_controller in /app/controllers, and add the following bold line to it:

```
class TodayController < ApplicationController
  before_filter :login_required
  def index
  end
end
```

If we were to build other controllers in this application, we'd add that same before_filter :login_required method call to each of those as well to limit access to their methods to only those people who are logged in. Any requests from a nonlogged-in user will get redirected to the login screen, as shown in Figure 3-4.

Figure 3-4. *Our login page with a few display issues*

As you can see, we have a few minor issues with the login page view that we need to address. First off is the fact that our navigational elements are being displayed even though they serve no purpose to a nonlogged-in user. Second, we need to make a couple of small changes to the generated login page template to make it fit within our current styling.

To fix the navigation items from showing up when a user is not logged in, we'll need to make some additions to our layout template (/monkey/views/layouts/application.rhtml). To disable those elements, we'll take advantage of a helper method called logged_in? that was added by Acts as Authenticated. We'll utilize logged_in? to hide our navigation menu unless a user has signed in to the system. To do so, change the topnav unordered list to look like this instead:

```
<ul id="topnav">
  <% if logged_in? %>
    <li><%= link_to "Today", :controller => 'today', :action => 'index' %></li>
    <li><%= link_to "Logout", :controller => 'account', :action => 'logout' %></li>
  <% end %>
</ul>
```

Now that we've fixed that, let's add a div to the login template that Acts as Authenticated generated. Open login.rhtml in app/views/account, and add a surrounding div with an id of login-form around the form. For good measure, let's also add a link to a sign-up form:

```
<div id="login-form">
    <% form_tag do -%>
        <p><label for="login">Login</label>
        <%= text_field_tag 'login' %></p>

        <p><label for="password">Password</label>
        <%= password_field_tag 'password' %></p>

        <p><label for="remember_me">Remember me:</label>
        <%= check_box_tag 'remember_me' %></p>

        <p><%= submit_tag 'Log in' %></p>

        <p>Not a member yet?
            <%= link_to 'Click Here', :action => 'signup' %> to join today!</p>
    <% end -%>
</div>
```

While you're in app/views/account, go ahead and open the signup.rthml file as well, and enclose its contents in a login form div like we just did here in login.rhtml.

Last, delete the index.rhtml file out of /monkey/app/views/account, as this is just a sample file installed by Acts as Authenticated that provides us with no value.

Time to fire up the web browser again—you can see the fruits of our modifications in Figure 3-5.

Figure 3-5. *Our new (corrected) login screen*

While it would be tempting to go on over to the sign-up page and create a new user now, we still have a few modifications left to make to our user registration system before we'll be ready to do that.

Building User Registration

The goals of our user registration system should be fairly obvious—it needs to create a new user object within the system. If we were to document the intended flow of our user registration system, it should go something like this.

1. A visitor accesses site and is immediately directed to the login screen.

2. The visitor clicks the sign-up link, since he doesn't have an account yet.

3. The visitor submits the sign-up form, which consists of a login name, e-mail address, and password.

4. The application will run a number of validations on the data that was submitted and create a new user object.

5. The application redirects the user to a page that provides instructions on checking e-mail to activate the new account.

6. The application sends out an e-mail to the user with an activation code embedded into a link.

7. The visitor opens the e-mail and clicks the link to activate the account.

8. On all future visits, the user can simply log in via the login form to access the site.

We've already got our sign-up form built, but we need to make some modifications to support our sign-up process. When a new sign-up form is submitted, it goes to the sign-up method in account_controller, which attempts to use the submitted form parameters to create a new user. However, we also want the system to generate an activation code with every new user that's created, so we'll need to add some code to support that. To do so, we'll need to open the User model (/app/models/user.rb) and add a method that can generate that code.

We don't want anyone to be able to call this method directly, so we'll add it to the section of protected methods (near the bottom of the file):

```
def make_activation_code
  self.activation_code = ➥
Digest::SHA1.hexdigest(Time.now.to_s.split(//).sort_by{rand}.join)
end
```

If you're having any trouble following that line of code, a great tool for helping you see what each method is doing is script/console. Simply open a command prompt in the root of your application and run the following:

```
ruby script/console
```

```
Loading development environment.
```

```
>> require 'digest/sha1'
```

```
=> []
```

```
>> Time.now.to_s
```

```
=> "Mon May 14 00:44:08 CDT 2007"
```

```
>> Time.now.to_s.split(//)
```

```
=> ["M", "o", "n", " ", "M", "a", "y", " ", "1", "4", " ", "0", "0", ":", "4", "4",
   ":", "1", "2", " ", "C", "D", "T", " ", "2", "0", "0", "7"]
```

```
>> Time.now.to_s.split(//).sort_by {rand}.join
```

```
=> "0M40T4 C1:1 o2n0M4:7 0a Dy 2"
```

```
>> Digest::SHA1.hexdigest(Time.now.to_s.split(//).sort_by {rand}.join)
```

```
=> "95ca7cf4fbd94f7ce74e6f8063650b400f79233d"
```

In the end, our activation code is merely a hash of the randomized version of the current time stamp.

Now, we just need to make sure that our new `make_activation_code` method is called whenever we create a new user, so we'll add another filter for that. Scroll up to the top of the model, and add this line after the validation method calls:

```
before_create :make_activation_code
```

Even though we're not really set up to create a user using the sign-up form just yet, you can see the activation code being generated by creating a new user via `script/console` in sandbox mode:

```
ruby script/console -s
```

```
Loading development environment in sandbox.
Any modifications you make will be rolled back on exit.
```

```
>> u = User.new(:login => 'test', :email => 'test@test.com', ➥
:password => 'test', :password_confirmation => 'test')
```

```
=> #<User:0x2370160 @password_confirmation="test", @password="test", ➥
@new_record=true, @attributes={"salt"=>nil, "activated_at"=>nil, ➥
"updated_at"=>nil,"crypted_password"=>nil, "activation_code"=>nil, ➥
"remember_token_expires_at"=>nil, "remember_token"=>nil, "login"=>"test",➥
 "created_at"=>nil, "email"=>"test@test.com"}
```

```
>> u.save
```

```
=> true
```

```
>> u
```

```
=> #<User:0x2370160 @password_confirmation="test", @password="test", ➥
@errors=#<ActiveRecord::Errors:0x23328c4 @errors={}, @base=#<User:0x2370160 ...>, ➥
 new_recordfalse, attributes{"salt"=>"d56eb8eeff209aeaf397bbbba3a2315982866e69", ➥
"activated_at"=>nil, "updated_at"=>Mon May 14 23:18:20 CDT 2007, ➥
 "crypted_password"=>"dd086c2a04cf00200ec7ddf1d810fc6152a72a32", ➥
"activation_code"=>"2f0ca264b8839a37be7d00810de0e8d56ef4b822", ➥
"remember_token_expires_at"=>nil, "id"=>1, "remember_token"=>nil, "login"=>"test",➥
"created_at"=>Mon May 14 23:18:20 CDT 2007, "email"=>"test@test.com"}
```

Sending E-mail Notifications

Now that we've set up our model to create the activation code, our next step is to enable the process for sending it out to users in an e-mail when they sign up. In order to do that, we'll need to make a few small additions to our `environment.rb` in `/config` and then restart our web server to load those changes. After that, we'll configure the components that we set up with that authenticated mailer and finish up by making some modifications to our User model and controllers.

Configuring Outbound E-mails in Rails

Before we can send out e-mails from our Rails application, we need to configure Rails to let our application know how it should attempt to deliver e-mail. Rails supports two options for outbound e-mail: SMTP or SendMail. We select the option our application should use by adding one of the following lines to our `environment.rb` file.

```
config.action_mailer.delivery_method =  :sendmail
```

or

```
config.action_mailer.delivery_method = :smtp
```

In my experience, I've had better luck using the SMTP option; it seems to be a more portable solution as my applications have moved across servers. However, you should choose whatever you feel most comfortable with. If you do choose SMTP, you will also have to provide Rails with an SMTP configuration in your environment settings (replace these values with your own SMTP settings, of course):

```
config.action_mailer.server_settings = {
:address => "my.smtpserver.com",
:port => 25,
:domain => "my smtp domain ",
:authentication => :login,
:user_name => "username",
:password => "password"
}
```

Even though you might be tempted, you need to resist the urge to restart your web server to load these new configuration changes until we've made one more change to our environment file.

Earlier when we ran the `authenticated_mailer` generator, it added four new files to our application (not counting tests) that we'll be using to enable our outbound e-mails. The first one that we'll look at is an observer for our User model named `user_observer.rb`, which can be found in `/app/models`. Observers are very powerful tools for monitoring an ActiveRecord model and kicking off actions in response to events without having to add extra code to the model or force our model to take on responsibilities that it doesn't really need to have (such as sending out activation e-mails).

Our user_observer has two events that it's monitoring on the User model:

```
class UserObserver < ActiveRecord::Observer

  def after_create(user)
    UserNotifier.deliver_signup_notification(user)
  end

  def after_save(user)
    UserNotifier.deliver_activation(user) if user.recently_activated?
  end
end
```

After a new user is created in our system, this observer calls the User Notifier model to send out a signup_notification e-mail. And after a user has been updated, it will call the User Notifier model to send out an activation confirmation e-mail if that user was recently activated (we'll need to add the recently_activated method to our user model before we call this though).

In order to utilize this observer, we'll have to let Rails know that we want it to be enabled. We do that by uncommenting and editing a line in our environment.rb file to register our user_observer class:

```
# Activate observers that should always be running
config.active_record.observers = :user_observer
```

Once we restart our web server, all of our new configuration changes will be loaded into our Rails application. Now, whenever we create or update a user object, our user_observer will be notified and respond by calling UserNotifier to send out an e-mail.

User_Notifer.rb

The UserNotifier class is an Action Mailer class, where each method represents a different e-mail that can be sent from our application—the corresponding views for the methods are the actual e-mail text that is sent out. Each UserNotifier method sets up a set of instance variables that are used in the template, such as the subject line, recipients, and so on. As you can see, in UserNotifer, we have two methods available: a signup_notification method and an activation method. We can make a few minor modifications to these to reflect our applications name and settings:

```
class UserNotifier < ActionMailer::Base
  def signup_notification(user)
    setup_email(user)
    @subject    += 'Please activate your new account'
    @body[:url]  = "http://localhost:3000/account/activate/#{user.activation_code}"
  end

  def activation(user)
    setup_email(user)
    @subject    += 'Welcome to MonkeyTasks'
    @body[:url]  = "http://localhost:3000/"
  end
```

```
  protected
  def setup_email(user)
    @recipients   = "#{user.email}"
    @from         = "Monkeytasks"
    @subject      = "[MonkeyTasks] "
    @sent_on      = Time.now
    @body[:user]  = user
  end
end
```

We'll leave the actual e-mail templates as they are. However, if you want to modify the text of what's sent to the user in the e-mails, you can edit them. They're stored as `activation.rhtml` and `signup_notification.rhtml` in the `/app/views/user_notifier` directory.

Modifying the User Model

Before our observer will be able to work, though, we still need to make a few modifications to our User model—most notably, we need to fix the missing `recently_activated?` method that I mentioned was being called in the observer. Go to `/app/models`, and open our User model (`user.rb`) to fix our missing methods issue.

The first method we'll add is one that we'll use to activate a user. We'll call this from the controller when processing an activation request. In this method, we'll set an instance variable named `@activated` to true (which will come into play when we build our `recently_activated?` method) and update the current user to set `activated_at` to the current time stamp and erase the activation code from the record:

```
def activate
  @activated = true
  update_attributes(:activated_at => Time.now.utc, :activation_code => nil)
end
```

The second method we'll add is our missing `recently_activated?` method:

```
def recently_activated?
  @activated
end
```

If you were expecting this method to do some sort of date-time comparison between the time the user was activated and current time, you might be a little confused by the simplicity of this method. In essence, all we're doing is returning the `@activated` instance variable, which would be set to `true` only if the preceding request was a call to the `activate` method. Otherwise, our `@activated` variable would not be set, so it would be equal to nil. Therefore, when our `UserNotifier` calls `UserNotifier.deliver_activation(user) if user.recently_activated?`, the if statement will receive either a `true` if the update came from the activate method or nothing if it came from anywhere else (which evaluates to `false`).

Before we close out the User model, we need to make one last change. Currently, our login method in `account_controller.rb` calls the `authenticate` class method in the User model (`/app/models/user.rb`) to verify that the user is valid. Currently the `self.authenticate` method is only verifying that the username and password match. We need to modify the methods `find` parameters to also ensure that only a user who has an activated account will authenticate successfully. Modify the method like so:

```
def self.authenticate(login, password)
    u = find :first, ➡
     :conditions => ['login = ? and activated_at IS NOT NULL', login]
    u && u.authenticated?(password) ? u : nil
end
```

Modifying the Account Controller

We're almost finished now; all that's left is to make a few modifications to our account controller to handle our new activation process. Go ahead and open account_controller.rb in /app/controllers. The first thing we can do is remove the include AuthenticatedSystem and login_from_cookie filter calls from the controller, since we already added those to the Application controller (which means that they're included into every controller).

The next thing we want to change is our sign-up method. The current code will actually temporarily log in the user once she signs up even though she hasn't activated her account yet. We'll fix that by removing the line self.current_user = @user and changing the redirection method to take the user to a page that lets her know to check her e-mail. So you'll modify the signup method to look like this:

```
def signup
    @user = User.new(params[:user])
    return unless request.post?
    @user.save!
    redirect_back_or_default( :action => 'welcome')
  rescue ActiveRecord::RecordInvalid
    render :action => 'signup'
end
```

And create a new file named welcome.rhtml in /app/views/account that has the following content, which we'll display after a user has submitted a new sign-up:

```
<div id="welcome">
    <h1>Welcome to MonkeyTasks</h1>
    <p>You're just one step away from utilizing this simple daily task manager.</p>
    <p>An activation email has been sent to the e-mail address you provided.</p>
    <p>Follow the instructions in it to activate your account</p>
    <p>Thanks</p>
    <p>The MonkeyTasks Team</p>
</div>
```

We also need to redefine what our login and logout methods are going to display to a user by default. Currently, both make this call when choosing what to display:

```
redirect_back_or_default(:controller => '/account', :action => 'index')
```

redirect_back_or_default is a method that's added in acts_as_authenticated; you can find it in /lib/authenticated_system.rb, but here is the method, so you can see it firsthand:

```
def redirect_back_or_default(default)
  session[:return_to] ? redirect_to_url(session[:return_to]) : redirect_to(default)
  session[:return_to] = nil
end
```

All this method does is check for a return_to key in the current session. If one exists, the user is directed to that value; otherwise, the user is directed to whatever was passed in as an option to the method. This is useful for handling situations where you want to return the user to the requested page rather than a standard default page.

So barring the idea that the user went to an original page, the default for these method calls was to send the user back to the index method in the account_controller. However, the current index method merely redirects the user to the sign-up page. I think we should give some better defaults for our application.

Within the login method, it makes more sense to me that the default page should be the primary page our application, so change the redirect_back_default parameters in the login method to this:

```
redirect_back_or_default(:controller => '/today', :action => 'index')
```

After logging out, displaying the new user sign-up page could be confusing to an end user. A better choice would be to send users to the login screen, so change the redirect_back_default parameters in the login method to this:

```
redirect_back_or_default(:controller => '/account', :action => 'login')
```

Finally, let's add an activate method to this controller to support the e-mail activation functionality (and actually activate a user):

```
def activate
  @user = User.find_by_activation_code(params[:id])
  if @user and @user.activate
    self.current_user = @user
    flash[:notice] = "Your account has been activated."
  end
  redirect_back_or_default(:controller => '/account', :action => 'login')
end
```

With that, we're finally at the finish line and should be all set up to handle user registrations now. Since we don't have an account yet, let's go ahead and create one using the form shown in Figure 3-6.

Figure 3-6. *Our sign-up page*

After creating the account, you should find that you've been shown the welcome template that we created; meanwhile, the system has sent you an activation e-mail to the e-mail address that you specified. Go ahead and open that e-mail and paste the activation URL into your web browser to activate your account. Now, you should be able to log in and out of the application with no issues. If you can't find the e-mail or didn't have access to an SMTP server, you can also pull out the text of the e-mail that was sent from the logs. Open development.log in /log, scroll nearly to the bottom, and you will see something similar to this:

```
Sent mail:
 Date: Wed, 16 May 2007 13:51:00 -0500
From: ADMINEMAIL
To: test@test.com
Subject: [YOURSITE] Please activate your new account
Mime-Version: 1.0
Content-Type: text/plain; charset=utf-8

Your account has been created.

  Username: test
  Password: test

Visit this url to activate your account:

  http://localhost:3000/account/activate/58e11cd2d64a50abb8f8ff4a2062209e61dd2675
```

You can copy the URL from the log to activate your account as well. With that, we're now finished with our user registration and authentication system and can focus on building our daily to-do list manager.

Summary

We've covered a large amount of functionality in this chapter, including installing `acts_as_authenticated` and configuring it to meet our needs. Our end solution not only supports allowing users to sign up via the Web but requires them to prove that they gave us valid e-mail account information by requiring them to activate their accounts. We've also established a solid pattern for how we can provide security to our application by using the authentication system to limit access to our controllers to only those people who have logged in.

CHAPTER 4

■■■

Building a Daily To-Do Manager

We've made a pretty impressive amount of progress so far, even though we haven't done a lot of actual coding—but that's about to change. Now, we're going to start building our own models and controllers to support the application.

Creating Our First Model: task

Let's get this party started by defining our first model. We need to have a way to capture all of our tasks, so we can build a daily to-do list—our primary model for this application is going to be the task model. Let's think about the attributes of a task:

- A task should have a name or description.

- A task should know if it's been completed or not.

- A task should know when it's due, which also means that a task should know if it's overdue.

- A task should know which user it's associated with (so that no one else can view or edit another user's tasks).

Armed with that knowledge, let's go ahead and create our task model; from the root of your application, run this command:

```
ruby script/generate model task
```

```
exists  app/models/
exists  test/unit/
exists  test/fixtures/
create  app/models/task.rb
create  test/unit/task_test.rb
create  test/fixtures/tasks.yml
exists  db/migrate
create  db/migrate/002_create_tasks.rb
```

Looking back through the output, you'll notice that the generate model command is smart enough to know that it should also create a database migration file for us with the same name as the model that we just created.

Note What if you wanted to create a model that didn't need to create a database table? Are you going to be stuck leaving a bunch of empty migration files within your application or spending time going back and deleting them?

Nope, you can just run the command with the `-skip-migration` option to bypass the creation of a migration file, like this: `ruby script/generate model modelname --skip-migration`.

Now, let's edit our new database migration to build the fields that a task needs to be able to keep track of:

```ruby
class CreateTasks < ActiveRecord::Migration
  def self.up
    create_table :tasks do |t|
      t.column 'name', :string
      t.column 'complete', :datetime
      t.column 'due', :date
      t.column 'created_on', :datetime
      t.column 'updated_on', :datetime
      t.column 'user_id', :integer
    end
  end

  def self.down
    drop_table :tasks
  end
end
```

There's nothing too fancy here, but let's discuss a few of the field choices just to make sure that we're all on the same page as we move forward:

According to our database migration, a task field in the database has the following columns:

- name: This is set as a string in the migration file that will create a varchar (255-character) field in databases like MySQL, SQLite, and SQL Server. It will create a (note 1) field in PostgreSQL.

- complete: We will check this field to determine if a task has been completed. So why are we using a datetime field instead of a Boolean one? I've found that using a datetime stamp provides the same functionality as using a Boolean but also provides us with additional information—we know when the task was completed.

- due: This should be pretty straightforward. Some may ask, though, "Why not use a datetime field? After all, couldn't some tasks have a deadline that would require them to be completed by certain times?" Perhaps, but those tasks should be the exception rather than the norm; plus, adding that could change the scope of our application, making it more of a scheduling application. It also increases the level of complexity for us, as users, when adding tasks (e.g., what time should we mark a task due if it isn't due by a specific hour on the due date?). I'm a big believer in the idea that the simple application is actually more flexible in the long run. If a user needed to indicate that a task should be completed by a certain time, why couldn't that user simply put the time in the name (e.g., Pick up dry cleaning before 3 p.m.)?

- created_on and updated_on : These are just some extra sweetness for our application that Rails provides by convention. Simply because we include these two fields in our table, Rails will automatically populate them with the current time stamp whenever it creates or updates a task. We probably won't use them in our application, but I like adding them in my primary models, as they are sometimes of great assistance in troubleshooting issues.

- user_id: This is an integer field, as it stores a foreign key reference to the primary key of the task's associated user.

Now that we understand what we're building, let's run the migration:

```
rake db:migrate
```

```
== CreateTasks: migrating ========================================================
-- create_table(:tasks)
   -> 0.1320s
== CreateTasks: migrated (0.1321s) ===============================================
```

Modifying the task Model

Navigate to /app/models/, and edit our model files to create the associations between the user model and our brand new task model.

Modify task.rb to register that it is a child table to the User table with a belongs_to association:

```
class Task < ActiveRecord::Base
  belongs_to :user
end
```

Next, we'll modify the user model (user.rb in /app /models) to reflect that it has a one-to-many relationship with the task model by adding a has_many association underneath the validation calls:

```
has_many :tasks
```

And that's it—our models are now joined together so that a user object can now know about and reference the tasks associated with it, and a task object now knows to which user object it belongs.

Creating the Task Controller

Let's go ahead and create task_controller now; it will be the primary interface that we'll use to manage our task objects. Go back to the root of your application and run the following command:

```
ruby script/generate controller task
```

```
exists  app/controllers/
exists  app/helpers/
create  app/views/task
exists  test/functional/
create  app/controllers/task_controller.rb
create  test/functional/task_controller_test.rb
create  app/helpers/task_helper.rb
```

Open task_controller.rb from /app/controllers/, and edit it to match this:

```ruby
class TaskController < ApplicationController
  before_filter :login_required
  before_filter :find_task, :except => [:index, :new, :create]

def index
  @tasks = current_user.tasks
end

def show
end
def new
  @task = Task.new
end

def create
  @task = current_user.tasks.build(params[:task])
  if @task.save!
    redirect_to(:controller => 'today')
  else
    render :action => "new"
  end
end
```

```
def update
  @task.attributes = params[:task]
  @task.save!
  redirect_to(:action => "index")
end

def destroy
  @task.destroy
  redirect_to(:controller => "today", :action => "index")
end

protected
def find_task()
  @task = current_user.tasks.find(params[:id])
end

end
```

A few elements are important to point out about this controller. Obviously, you should notice right off the bat that we're using before_filter, which we discussed earlier to prevent unauthorized access to this controller:

```
before_filter :login_required
```

Second, we've added a new before filter that's calling a protected method from within the controller:

```
before_filter :find_task, :except => [:index, :new, :create]

protected
def find_task()
  @task = current_user.tasks.find(params[:id])
end
```

This is another shortcut that I use to avoid repetition in my code. Since many of the actions in this controller need to look up a task object, calling this filter allows me to build that lookup only once and prevent a lot of code duplication in this controller. Since some actions, such as new, would never need to look up a preexisting task object, I exclude them from the before_filter using the :except option.

Finally, one last important thing to note is that the default actions in this controller are built to follow along the standard CRUD (create, read, update, destroy) operations that a task would need. DHH, who, you'll recall, is the creator of Rails, gave a wonderful presentation at the 2006 Rails Conference challenging Rails developers to begin to think in terms of CRUD while designing their applications (the presentation is available online at http://media.rubyonrails.org/presentations/worldofresources.pdf).

CRUD is definitely a pattern that requires a bit of time to get used to. However, the benefits of implementing this design will pay off big in terms of cleaner controllers, more maintainable code, and easier implementation of web services (which you'll see when we start building REST-based interfaces into our applications).

The Add Task Form

Back when we were talking about the design of the application, we said that we needed to make it quick and easy to add new tasks to our application (so we can dump them out of our heads). The main page seems an ideal place to add tasks, so we don't have to navigate to another page just to add a task. So let's add a form that will allow us to do just that.

In the index page of our today controller, we included a placeholder div called add_task. We're going to place our add task form within that container. Go to /app/views/today/; open index.rhtml, and find this section:

```
<div id="add_task">
</div>
```

Rails provides an easy way to build a form for a given model using the form_for method. Create a form now by entering this form code inside of the add_task div:

```
<div id="add_task">
  <% form_for :task,
                    :url => {:controller => :task, :action => :create},
                    :html => {:id => 'addtaskform'} do |t| %>
    <p>
      <label for='task_name'>Task:</label>
      <%= t.text_field 'name' %>
    </p>
    <p>
      <label for='task_name'>Due Date:</label>
      <%= t.date_select 'due', :order => [:day, :month, :year] %>
    </p>
    <p>
      <%= submit_tag "Add Task" %>
    </p>
  <% end %>
</div>
```

Save your work, and open your web browser; you should see a page like the one shown in Figure 4-1.

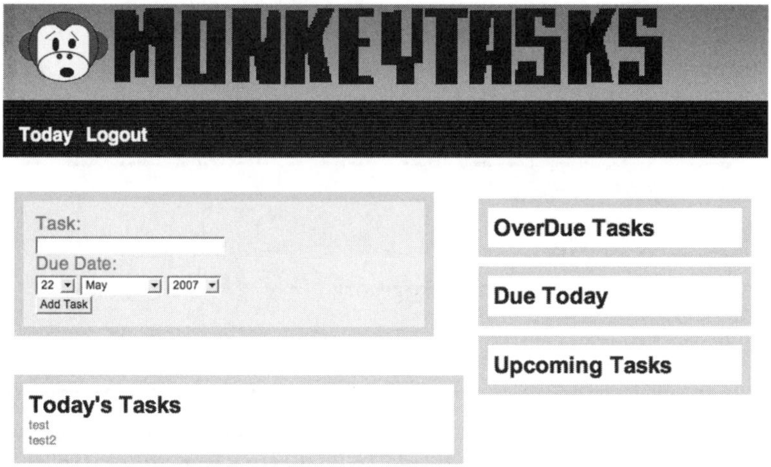

Figure 4-1. *Our add task form has been added.*

A Better Date Selector

While that form certainly doesn't look bad, I wouldn't exactly say it's very attractive either. Looking at the form, I think what bothers me the most are those date selection fields. Having those three selection boxes there on the page just looks so archaic—I know we can do better.

Even though there aren't many alternative options for the date selectors within Rails, there is a huge world of plug-ins and Ruby Gems available to us that we can use to enhance our rails applications. For our application, let's implement a Ruby gem by the name of Chronic (http://chronic.rubyforge.org) that will allow us to use natural language processing for the due date instead.

What does natural language processing mean? Quite simply, it means that we can enter dates in the same language that we would use to describe that date to a friend; it gives us the ability to enter our dates like this:

```
Tomorrow
3 weeks from tomorrow
this Monday
Friday
3rd Wednesday in November
7 days from now
yesterday
```

and Chronic will parse those into valid dates for our application. Cool stuff!

Installing Chronic

Open a command line, and run the following command to install the Chronic gem:

```
gem install chronic
```

```
Attempting local installation of 'chronic'
Local gem file not found: chronic*.gem
Attempting remote installation of 'chronic'
Updating Gem source index for: http://gems.rubyforge.org
Successfully installed chronic-0.1.2
Installing RDoc documentation for chronic-0.1.2...
```

Since Chronic isn't a part of the Rails framework, we'll have to tell Rails to load the Chronic gem into our applications environment when it starts up. To do that, navigate to /config, and edit the file named environment.rb. Scroll down to the very last line and add this command:

```
require 'chronic'
```

As always, any modifications to environment.rb will require you to restart your web server to have those changes loaded. Now that we have Chronic loaded into our Rails application, let's modify our application to use Chronic to allow users to enter dates in a much more friendly manner.

Our first step is to remove the date_select field from our add task form and replace it with a standard text field. So change that field to this:

```
<label for='task_due_date'>Due Date:</label>
<%= t.text_field 'due_date' %>
```

Now that we have our due date being captured in natural language, we need to set up our model to both accept this due_date field and use it to populate the due column in our database. We can do that by creating a pair of methods to handle due_date as a virtual attribute. In other words, we'll need to manually build getter and setter methods for due_date. So open task.rb, which is in /app/models, and let's start adding.

For our getter method, we'll simply return the due field converted back to a string.

```
def due_date
  due.to_s
end
```

Our setter method might require a bit more explanation:

```
def due_date=(str)
  self.due = Chronic.parse(str).to_date.to_s

  rescue
    @invalid_date = true
end
```

Chronic.parse is the main method that we use to convert our dates; parse will return a time object if it can parse the text. But we're not interested in times for our application—just dates—so we'll take that time object and immediately convert that to a date object with the to_date method. Finally, we'll pull back the string representation of that date object with to_s, and that's the value that will be pushed into the due column of our database for this record.

If, for some reason, Chronic cannot parse the text into a valid time, it will return nil. When we try to call the next method in the chain (to_date) on a nil object, we will generate an error. That's actually a good thing and puts us in a good position for validating our text. We merely need to rescue that error and set an @invalid date instance variable to true to indicate that we hit an error. We'll use that instance variable in our validations to set an error if that variable has been set to true. Add the following validate method to your task model:

```
def validate
  errors.add :due_date, 'is not a valid date' if @invalid_date
end
```

Now that we've added an error for the model, we just need to display that to the user. Since we already have a section on the page to display notification messages to the user, I like to reuse that so that informational messages are consistent. We'll modify our controller to send the errors back in the flash[:notice] hash. Open /app/controllers/task_controller.rb, and modify the create method to look like this:

```
def create
  @task = current_user.tasks.build(params[:task])
  if @task.save
    redirect_to(:controller => 'today')
  else
    flash[:notice] = @task.errors.full_messages.to_sentence
    redirect_to(:controller => 'today')
  end
end
```

If the task doesn't pass validations, we'll display the errors to the user, as shown in Figure 4-2.

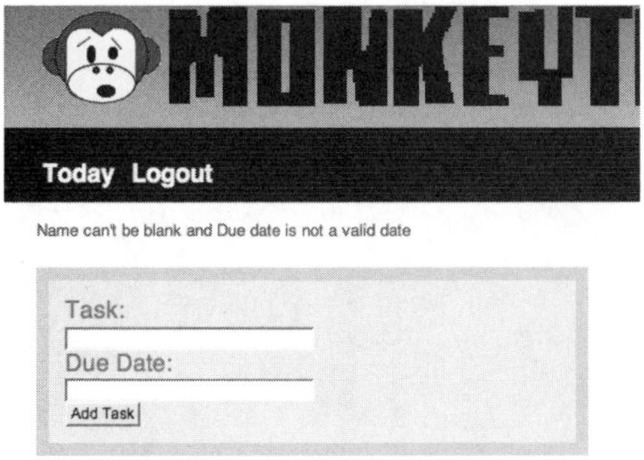

Figure 4-2. *Displaying errors above our add task form*

The schedule Model

The next object that we want to model is the ability to have a daily task list—not in the sense of the actual tasks that we have to do that day, more like the blank sheet of paper that we're going to place our daily list on. Coming up with a name for this was a bit of a challenge, but I finally decided on naming this object schedule.

So when we first log into the application each day, we're going to want the system to give us a brand new schedule object with no tasks added yet (simulating a blank sheet each morning) and give us that existing schedule as we go through our day; it should give us a new schedule only at the start of a new day.

Based on that description, a schedule object needs to know

- The day it's responsible for

- The user it's associated to

With that understanding, let's generate our schedule model:

```
ruby script/generate model schedule
```

```
      exists  app/models/
      exists  test/unit/
      exists  test/fixtures/
      create  app/models/schedule.rb
      create  test/unit/schedule_test.rb
      create  test/fixtures/schedules.yml
      exists  db/migrate
      create  db/migrate/003_create_schedules.rb
```

And now, let's build our migration file for this model. Navigate to the db/migrations folder, and edit migration file 003_create_schedules.rb to look like this:

```
class CreateSchedules < ActiveRecord::Migration
  def self.up
    create_table :schedules do |t|
      t.column :today, :date
      t.column :user_id, :integer
    end
  end

  def self.down
    drop_table :schedules
  end
end
```

The todo Model

Now, our users have a current schedule and many tasks that could be associated with that schedule, but we still need to find a way to associate a task with the current schedule. To do that, we're going to have to create another model to handle that association. We're going to name this model the todo model; the idea is that a scheduled task has now been upgraded to a todo object, that is, something to be done today.

At first glance, it might be tempting to build a many-to-many join table with a has_and_belongs_to_many association; after all, a schedule can have many tasks associated with it, and a task could be associated with multiple schedules (in the event that it didn't get completed the previous time it was added to a schedule). Doing that might prove too limiting, though, as we'll probably want to keep track of data beyond just the fact that the two are associated; one idea would be keeping track of a task's position within the current schedule to give a user the ability to change the order of the items in that schedule.

To accomplish this, our daily to-do items are going to require a full-fledged model of their own. We'll set it up to take advantage of the has_many :through associations that Rails added back in version 1.1.

Let's create our todo model:

```
ruby script/generate model todo
```

```
exists   app/models/
exists   test/unit/
exists   test/fixtures/
create   app/models/todo.rb
create   test/unit/todo_test.rb
create   test/fixtures/todos.yml
exists   db/migrate
create   db/migrate/004_create_todos.rb
```

Edit your migration to match this one:

```
class CreateTodos < ActiveRecord::Migration
  def self.up
    create_table :todos do |t|
      t.column :schedule_id, :integer
      t.column :task_id, :integer
      t.column :position, :integer
    end
  end

  def self.down
    drop_table :todos
  end
end
```

Run rake db:migrate to build the tables in the database, and then we'll set up all of our new models (/app/models) and their relationships to each other.

Ordering the todo Model

I really liked the idea of allowing users to be able to reorder their to-do items within their daily schedule. To support that, we added a position field within the database migration, so that, we can apply the Acts As List call on this model and use that functionality to support ordering and reordering our daily to-do lists. After adding the Acts as List call, a simple validation to prevent duplicates, and our associations to other models, our todo model (/app/models/todo.rb) should look like this:

```
class Todo < ActiveRecord::Base
  belongs_to :schedule
  belongs_to :task
  acts_as_list :scope => :schedule


validates_uniqueness_of :task_id, :on => :create,
            :message => "Cannot add the same task twice", :scope => "schedule_id"
end
```

Updating the schedule Model

Our schedule model (/app/models/schedule.rb) also needs to be set up with its associations to users, tasks, and to-do items. We also need to specify that our to-do items need to be pulled in the proper order by specifying an order clause on that association:

```
class Schedule < ActiveRecord::Base
  belongs_to :user
  has_many :todos, :order => :position
  has_many :tasks, :through => :todos
end
```

Updating the task Model

We'll also have to modify our task model (/app/models/task.rb) to let it know about its new association to the todo model:

```
class Task < ActiveRecord::Base
  belongs_to :user
  has_one :todo

  def validation
    errors.add :due, 'is not a valid date' if Chronic.parse(due.to_s).nil?
  end
end
```

Updating the user Model

Add the following association to the user model (/app/models/user.rb) just under the has_many :tasks call to grab the schedule for the current day for the user:

```
has_one :schedule, :conditions => ["today = ?", Date.today.to_s]
```

Making Our Task Lists Work

Now, it's time to start seeing some of the fruits of our labors. Let's start by building out the support for our task lists along the right-hand side of the page.

Looking back at the code we added in index.rhtml, we can see our div structures where we will be adding our code:

```
<div id='sidebar'>
  <div class="sidebar-tasks">
    <h1>OverDue Tasks</h1>
  </div>

  <div class="sidebar-tasks">
    <h1>Due Today </h1>
  </div>

  <div class="sidebar-tasks">
    <h1>Upcoming Tasks</h1>
  </div>
</div>
```

We can gather a list of tasks for a user by calling current_user.tasks, but that would give us one large list containing all tasks, instead of three separate lists based on due date. To get around this, we can modify the user model to enhance the has_many relationship with some block methods that will partition the data for us:

```
has_many :tasks do
  def overdue
    find(:all, :conditions => ["due < ? and complete is null", Date.today.to_s])
  end
  def today
    find(:all, :conditions => ["due = ? and complete is null", Date.today.to_s])
  end
  def upcoming
    find(:all, :conditions => ["due > ? and complete is null", Date.today.to_s])
  end
end
```

Now, we can call current_user.tasks.overdue to get a list of all tasks that should have been completed before today.

■**Tip** The `current_user.tasks.overdue` method does excel in being the most readable way for us to gather the relevant data, but it could cause problems at a later date because it requires three separate hits to the database to populate these lists. This shouldn't be an issue initially considering the small scale of our application. If the user base grows and performance becomes an issue, we could easily remove the block methods from the association and use an enumerable `select` method to partition the single, large dataset into the necessary collections. However, that's a lot of extra work that degrades the readability of the code to solve a problem that doesn't exist yet. We should always avoid premature optimization.

Now, armed with those methods, pulling in the relevant data is easy and looks pretty good too:

```
<div id='sidebar'>
  <div class="sidebar-tasks">
    <h1>OverDue Tasks</h1>
    <% for task in current_user.tasks.overdue %>
      <%= task.name %>
        <%= link_to " (Delete) ", :controller => "task",
                               :action => "destroy", :id => task.id %><br />
    <% end %>
  </div>

  <div class="sidebar-tasks">
    <h1>Due Today </h1>
    <% for task in current_user.tasks.today %>
      <%= task.name %>
        <%= link_to " (Delete) ", :controller => "task",
                               :action => "destroy", :id => task.id %><br />
    <% end %>
  </div>

  <div class="sidebar-tasks">
    <h1>Upcoming Tasks</h1>
    <% for task in current_user.tasks.upcoming %>
      <%= task.name %>
        <%= link_to " (Delete) ", :controller => "task",
                               :action => "destroy", :id => task.id %><br />
    <% end %>
  </div>
</div>
```

Open the page, and add some sample tasks (using the form shown in Figure 3-8) to check that the page is working correctly.

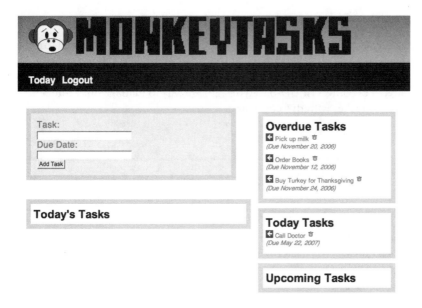

Figure 4-3. *Displaying our Task lists in the sidebar*

Making Our Daily Schedule Work

Let's get back to the primary focus of our application, making our actual daily task list. The first thing we need to do is make sure that we always have a schedule object for the current day. We'll do this through the use of a before_filter added to our today controller. We'll name this filter find_schedule:

```
before_filter :find_schedule
```

We'll add the method at the bottom of the today controller and make it a protected method, so a user would not be able to access this method directly. We'll either return the schedule that's already been created for today or we'll create a new one:

```
protected
  def find_schedule
    @today = current_user.schedule || ➥
current_user.create_schedule(:today => Date.today.to_s)
  end
```

You should recall that when we defined the association between a user and a schedule we included a condition on the association to match the current date (has_one :schedule, :conditions => ["today = ?", Date.today.to_s]). This means that if we were to access the page at 11:45 p.m., we would get one schedule object, and if we were to access the same page 15 minutes later (after midnight), we would get an entirely new object.

Moving Tasks to the Schedule

Now that we've ensured that we'll always have a schedule for the current day, we need to add some ways to move tasks to the current schedule. Let's look at our models. When we move a task to the current schedule, what we're really doing is creating a new todo object. Since we want to keep with our goal of using a CRUD-based design, the way to manage our to-do items is to create a new to-do controller with this command:

```
ruby script/generate controller todo
```

```
exists  app/controllers/
exists  app/helpers/
create  app/views/todo
exists  test/functional/
create  app/controllers/todo_controller.rb
create  test/functional/todo_controller_test.rb
create  app/helpers/todo_helper.rb
```

Within this controller, we'll want to restrict access to the to-do list unless a user is logged in, so we'll need to add our login_required filter again and create two methods: a create method will be responsible for the creation of a new to-do item based on the task that was sent to it, while delete will be responsible for removing a to-do item (which will effectively remove it from the user's current schedule). Our todo_controller should look like this:

```
class TodoController < ApplicationController
  before_filter :login_required

  def create
    task = current_user.tasks.find(params[:id])
    current_user.schedule.todos.create(:task_id => task.id)
    redirect_to(:controller => "today", :action => "index")
  end

  def destroy
    todo = current_user.todo.find(params[:id])
    current_user.schedule.todos.delete(todo)
    redirect_to(:controller => "today", :action => "index")
  end
end
```

Armed with a way to move tasks to and from our daily schedule, let's modify our main page to include links to these new methods. While we're at it, we'll also slap in a few icons for the actions associated with a task. Here's what our block to pull in the overdue tasks looks like:

```
<div class="sidebar-tasks">
  <h1>Overdue Tasks</h1>
  <% for task in current_user.tasks.overdue %>
    <%= link_to image_tag('arrow_left.gif', :title => "Do Today"),
          :controller => "todo", :action => "create", :id => task.id %>

    <%= task.name %>

    <%= link_to image_tag('trash.gif', :title => "Delete"),
            :controller => "task", :action => "destroy", :id => task.id %>

    <span class="duedate">(Due <%= task.due.to_s(:long) %>)</span>
  <% end %>
</div>
```

Implementing a Helper Method

Hopefully your spider sense is tingling at the very thought of putting multiple copies of that block of code onto our index page, because mine sure is. That's an awfully large amount of code to be in the template; it looks ugly; and worst of all, it's going to be duplicated several times. So let's move that out of the view, and create a helper method that we can use to build this block for us. Open today_helper.rb from /app/helpers, and let's create a method named sidebar_tasks that will build out that same block of code for us:

```
def sidebar_tasks(name)
    tasklist = content_tag(:h1, "#{name.capitalize} Tasks")
    for task in current_user.tasks.send(name)
      tasklist += link_to image_tag('arrow_left.gif', :title => 'Do Today'),
                    :controller => 'todo', :action => 'create', :id => task.id
      tasklist += " #{task.name} "
      tasklist += link_to image_tag('trash.gif', :title => 'Delete'),
                    :controller => 'task', :action => 'destroy', :id => task.id
      tasklist += content_tag(:span, "(Due #{task.due.to_s(:long)})",
                    :class => 'duedate')
    end

    content_tag :div, tasklist, :class => "sidebar-tasks"
  end
```

Now, within our index page, we can remove all those ugly blocks and use this instead:

```
<div id="sidebar">
  <%= sidebar_tasks "overdue" %>
  <%= sidebar_tasks "today" %>
  <%= sidebar_tasks "upcoming" %>
</div>
```

Displaying Our Schedule

We have a way to move tasks to the daily schedule, so now, we just need to add a way to display that schedule. Before we add the code to the main page, though, we need to set up an instance variable for our main page to display. Within the today_controller, add this line to the index method to gather a list of scheduled tasks for the current day:

```
def index
  @todos = @today.todos
end
```

We'll loop through the to-do items in the @todos instance variable in our main view to populate our daily task list. Open index.rhtml from /app/views/today/, and let's add the code to show our current tasks. For good measure, we'll also add two links in our list, one to mark the task as complete

```
<%= link_to image_tag("check.gif", :title => "Mark Complete"),
    :controller => "task", :action => "mark_complete", :id => todo.task.id %>
```

and a second to remove the task from our current schedule:

```
<%= link_to image_tag("arrow_right.gif", :class => 'unschedule',
    :title => 'Remove from Today'), :controller => "todo", :action => "destroy",
    :id => todo.id %>
```

So your index.rhtml will look like this with all of the code added:

```
<div id="primary">
  <div id="add_task">
    <% form_for :task, :url => {:controller => :task, :action => :create},
                                :html => {:id => 'addtaskform'} do |t| %>
    <p>
      <label for='task_name'>Task:</label>
      <%= t.text_field 'name' %>
    </p>
```

```erb
<p>
    <label for='task_due_date'>Due Date:</label>
    <%= t.text_field 'due_date' %>
  </p>
  <p>
    <%= submit_tag "Add Task" %>
  </p>
<% end %>
</div>

<div id="main">
  <h1>Today's Tasks</h1>
  <ul id="todo-list">
    <% for todo in @todos %>
      <li id="todo_<%= todo.id %>">
        <%= link_to image_tag("check.gif", :title => "Mark Complete"),
                                  :controller => "task",
                                  :action => "mark_complete",
                                  :id => todo.task.id %>
        <% if todo.task.complete %>
          <strike><em><%= todo.task.name %></em></strike>
        <% else %>
          <%= todo.task.name %>
        <% end %>

        <%= link_to image_tag("arrow_right.gif", :class => 'unschedule',
                                  :title => 'Remove from Today'),
                                  :controller => "todo",
                                  :action => "destroy",
                                  :id => todo.id %>
      </li>
    <% end %>
  </ul>
</div>
</div>

<div id="sidebar">
  <%= sidebar_tasks "overdue" %>
  <%= sidebar_tasks "today" %>
  <%= sidebar_tasks "upcoming" %>
</div>
```

Open a web browser again, and you should see that our application is well on its way, as shown in Figure 3-9.

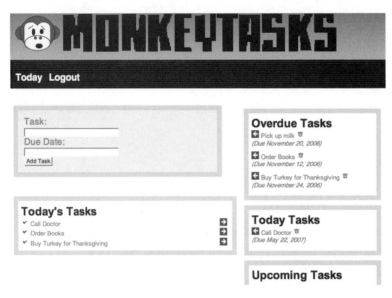

Figure 4-4. *The main page of our Application in its finished appearance*

Unfortunately, even a cursory glance at the sheer ugliness of the code in our index.rhtml is enough to churn my stomach. It was nice and clean to start out with, but now it's been made ugly by the inserted code. Let's fix that.

Utilizing Partials

Just as layouts give us a simple way to avoid repetition of the elements that surround our page content and helpers helped us to generate some dynamic code, partials are another powerful solution for eliminating duplication of code. Sound complicated? It won't be once you see them in action, so without further ado, let's convert some of these code elements to partials.

Converting Our Add Task Form to a Partial

Create a new file named _task.rhtml in the /monkey/app/views/today subdirectory, and copy the code for our add task form into it:

```
<% form_for :task, :url => {:controller => :task, :action => :create},
                            :html => {:id => 'addtaskform'} do |t| %>
  <p>
    <label for='task_name'>Task:</label>
    <%= t.text_field 'name' %>
  </p>
```

```
<p>
  <label for='task_due_date'>Due Date:</label>
  <%= t.text_field 'due_date' %>
</p>
<p>
  <%= submit_tag "Add Task" %>
</p>
<% end %>
```

Now, within the index.rthml file, let's remove the code we just moved to the partial and replace it with a call to render our partial here instead:

```
<div id="add_task">
  <%= render :partial => 'task' %>
</div>
```

We can repeat this process and move the schedule display code out of our page and into its own partial. Even better, since we can pass in the array of @todos to the partial as a collection, we can even eliminate the need to use a loop.

Copy the code that generates our to-do list into a partial named _todo.rhtml:

```
<li id="todo_<%= todo.id %>">
  <%= link_to image_tag("check.gif", :title => "Mark Complete"),
                        :controller => "task", :action => "mark_complete",
                        :id => todo.task.id %>
  <% if todo.task.complete %>
    <strike><em><%= todo.task.name %></em></strike>
  <% else %>
    <%= todo.task.name %>
  <% end %>

  <%= link_to image_tag("arrow_right.gif", :class => 'unschedule',
                        :title => 'Remove from Today'), :controller => "todo",
                        :action => "destroy", :id => todo.id %>
</li>
```

Then, we can reduce that section of the index page to merely this:

```
<ul id="todo-list">
  <%= render :partial => 'todo', :collection => @todos %>
</ul>
```

With those few changes, our main index.rthml page is now reduced to this:

```
<div id="primary">
  <div id="add_task">
    <%= render :partial => 'task' %>
  </div>
```

```
<div id="main">
  <h1>Today's Tasks</h1>
  <ul id="todo-list">
    <%= render :partial => 'todo', :collection => @todos %>
  </ul>
</div>
</div>

<div id="sidebar">
  <%= sidebar_tasks "overdue" %>
  <%= sidebar_tasks "today" %>
  <%= sidebar_tasks "upcoming" %>
</div>
```

Ah—so much nicer. Don't you agree?

Marking Tasks Complete

In our last iteration, we also added a link in our daily task list for marking a task as complete. Let's go ahead and finish that process up, so clicking that link doesn't generate a nasty error message. Open task_controller to add our mark_complete method, which will set the complete attribute to the current time and move the task to the bottom of the list in our daily schedule:

```
def mark_complete
  @task.complete = Time.now
  @task.todo.move_to_bottom
  @task.save!
  redirect_to(:controller => "today", :action => "index")
end
```

Marking a task complete will make the task list look like the one shown in Figure 4-5.

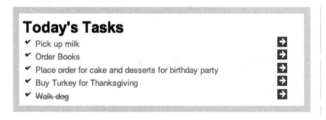

Today's Tasks
- ✔ Pick up milk
- ✔ Order Books
- ✔ Place order for cake and desserts for birthday party
- ✔ Buy Turkey for Thanksgiving
- ✔ ~~Walk dog~~

Figure 4-5. *Displaying our daily task list with an item crossed off*

But what happens if you click the mark-complete icon again? You would merely update the timestamp in the complete column of the database again, but it would appear to the user that nothing happened. That might be OK in some situations, but it would probably be more useful to our users if clicking that link would allow them to toggle whether a task is completed or not. We can do that by modifying the mark_complete method in the controller to first check to see if the complete attribute is `nil` or not. If it is, we'll continue as normal. If it's already populated with a timestamp (i.e., marked complete), we'll clear it out:

```
def mark_complete
  if @task.complete.nil?
    @task.complete = Time.now
    @task.todo.move_to_bottom
  else
    @task.complete = nil
  end
  @task.save!
  redirect_to(:controller => "today", :action => "index")
end
```

Ajaxification

The application looks good now, and we've cleaned up the code to make it both easier on the eyes and easier to maintain. But it's still lacking that certain something that makes it feel like a modern web application: Ajax.

Even if, like me, you absolutely hate that term, there's no denying that utilizing JavaScript to enhance our applications through the use of the `XMLHTTP` request (which technically is Ajax) and through the use of user interface enhancements (which technically is not Ajax). Unfortunately, the risk of using Ajax is that it becomes very tempting to start spreading it everywhere and soon your application is a horrible mess.

That being said, in my experience, a liberal amount of JavaScript can significantly improve your application, but you should be extremely critical when evaluating when and where to use it. In most of our projects, we'll be very conservative in our use of Ajax. However, let's add a few Ajax elements to our task application as an introduction to the basics.

Sortable Elements

You may remember that, when we built out our todo model, we added the `act_as_list` functionality to provide us with a mechanism for easily reordering our daily task list. Reordering elements in a list used to be handled by adding simple arrow icons next to each element and using methods in the controller called `move_up` and `move_down`, but that was always a bit painful if you needed to move an element multiple spaces, and it certainly added extra clutter to the interface. Using Ajax for this functionality is a much better solution, so let's make our daily task list sortable via a drag and drop mechanism.

Adding this functionality is amazingly easy thanks to the some of the JavaScript helpers that come standard with Rails. Simply open `index.rhtml`, and add the following block at the very bottom:

```
<%= sortable_element 'todo-list',
              :url => { :action => "sort" , :id => @today },
              :complete => visual_effect(:highlight, 'todo-list')
%>
```

That one command created a full drag and drop interface to our to-do list; with each change, it submits the reordered list to a sort method in the today controller. Unfortunately, since that method doesn't exist, our changes are not permanent, and the list goes back to the original order the next time we refresh the page. To make our changes permanent, let's add a sort method to today_controller.rb:

```
def sort
  @today.todos.each do |todo|
    todo.position = params['todo-list'].index(todo.id.to_s) + 1
    todo.save
  end
  render :nothing => true
end
```

This method simply loops over the list of the to-do items that were submitted and sets their current positions in the order they were submitted. Refresh our home page—we've now added true drag-and-drop sorting of our daily schedule in less than two minutes. Show it off to everyone you know, and they'll think you're a web programming god.

RJS

Another exciting feature added in Rails 1.1 was the ability to use RJS templates. RJS stands for Remote JavaScript, and it allows our applications to generate JavaScript code in response to XMLHTTP requests that will then be executed in the calling client, rather than an HTML page like our standard templates. RJS provides a unique and powerful solution for coding advanced JavaScript effects within our applications pages without having to resort to coding JavaScript.

Let's start with a practical example: don't you find it annoying that the simple action of marking one of our tasks complete forces us to refresh the entire page? That feels horribly inefficient for such a small change. Let's convert the mark-complete link to send that request to our controller via an Ajax call and use RJS to refresh only our daily task list, rather than force a full page reload.

Open the todo partial we created to manage our task list, and locate the line that marks the task as complete:

```
<%= link_to image_tag("check.gif", :title => "Mark Complete"),
        :controller => "task", :action => "mark_complete", :id => todo.task.id %>
```

To convert it to an Ajax call, we need to make a few minor modifications to that call; we need to convert the link_to method to a link_to_remote method and wrap our controller and action parameters within a :url block:

```
<%= link_to_remote image_tag("check.gif", :title => "Mark Complete"),
            :url => {:controller => "task", :action => "mark_complete",
            :id => todo.task.id} %>
```

And that's all there is to it. Clicking that link will now generate an Ajax callback to the server instead of submitting a GET request. However, we do need to make a few small changes to our controller method now. Currently, the mark_complete action in the task controller ends with the following command to redirect to the index page:

```
redirect_to(:controller => "today", :action => "index")
```

Since we now want to render an RJS template instead, we should delete that line and replace it with a call to create an updated list of our current to-do items, which we can use to refresh our list:

```
def mark_complete
  if @task.complete.nil?
    @task.complete = Time.now
    @task.todo.move_to_bottom
  else
    @task.complete = nil
  end
  @task.save!
  @todos = current_user.schedule.todos
end
```

Next, we need create a new RJS template in app/views/task, and name it mark_complete.rjs. Since we don't have an RHTML template for this method, our RJS template will be rendered when the mark_complete action is called. Within the mark_complete.rjs file, place the following code, which will replace the unordered to-do list with our partial, highlight the list to indicate to the user that it has indeed been updated, and reinstantiate our sortable list function on the new list:

```
page.replace_html 'todo-list', :partial => '/today/todo', :collection => @todos
page.visual_effect :highlight, 'todo-list'
page.sortable 'todo-list', :url => { :action => 'sort' }
```

Save your files; refresh the today page, and be amazed at how easily we've just added a pretty exciting effect.

Toggling the Add Task Form

Another one of the really cool things that we can do with RJS is to insert it directly into a page template, so we can add functionality within the page without having to make requests to the server or revert to creating JavaScript in our client-side code.

We create an inline RJS function through the use of the link_to_function helper method. Let's add a basic RJS inline function that we can use to hide or reveal the add task form by modifying index.rthml as follows:

```
<%= link_to_function "Add Task", update_page { |page|
                 page.visual_effect :toggle_blind, 'add_task' } %>
```

```
<div id="primary">
  <div id="add_task" style="display:none;">
    <%= render :partial => 'task' %>
  </div>
</div>

<div id="main">
  <h1>Today's Tasks</h1>
    <ul id="todo-list">
      <%= render :partial => 'todo', :collection => @todos %>
    </ul>
  </div>
</div>

<div id="sidebar">
  <%= sidebar_tasks "overdue" %>
  <%= sidebar_tasks "today" %>
  <%= sidebar_tasks "upcoming" %>
</div>

<%= sortable_element 'todo-list',
                        :url => { :action => "sort" , :id => @today },
                        :complete => visual_effect(:highlight, 'todo-list')
%>
```

The end result is definitely more appealing, as shown in Figure 3-11.

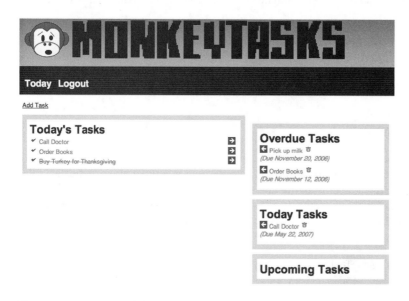

Figure 4-6. *Our add task form has been hidden.*

Summary

We've covered quite a lot of ground in this chapter, as we built our first basic Rails application. We used `acts_as_authenticated` to build out a full user registration and authentication system; we built our controllers and models around the idea of a CRUD-based design, and we finished things out by rolling in a bit of Ajax to enhance the application. The application that we built is simple but functional, and in the end, it should have served as a good primer for the traditional ways of building Rails applications. There's certainly a lot more that you can and should do to this application, and we will—in the next chapter there is a set of exercises that will help you begin to modify this application. Plus, at the end of most of the other projects in this book will be supplemental exercises that refer to the project.

But don't feel limited to just the exercises that I give you. Make this application your very own by modifying it in new and fun ways that I never thought of: Redesign it; add functionality that makes it better for your own personal needs. Open it to your friends, and get their feedback on how to make it better. Projects are never truly finished; they just get abandoned after time. In other words, don't ever stop coding and improving on this—keep applying new lessons you've learned to it and finding ways to enhance it; that is where your true learning will come from.

■ ■ ■

## CHAPTER 5

Enhancing Monkey Tasks

In this project, we took a high-level view of basic Rails development as we put together a daily task list manager. However, having me take you step by step through the development of an application will only get you so far; to truly enhance your learning what you need now is to solve some problems yourself. In this chapter, I've included a number of ideas to get you started. There are a few minor bugs you can fix, some basic refactoring to clean up the code, and some ideas for how you can take the application to a whole new level yourself.

Add Validations

I thought that one of the easiest ways to get you started on modifying the code that we just built was to leave some easy holes in our application for you to fix: namely one big hole in our model validations. For example, currently it's possible for a user to create a task without any text. That doesn't make any sense, does it? You can easily fix that by adding a `validates_presense_of` call to the task model. Are there any other validations you can think of that might be useful?

Edit a Task

Another area missing from our application is the ability to edit an existing task. Currently, the only way to modify a task is to delete it and create it anew. That works but is not exactly the most intuitive solution. You should be able to easily add the necessary edit and update methods to your task controller—but how are you going to work that process into the current interface?

Add a Calendar

While generating a list of the upcoming tasks on the sidebar is okay, sometimes we just need to see our tasks in the context of the bigger picture. In that situation, a calendar that shows the days that tasks are due would be a nice tool. You can easily build a calendar into the application with the Calendar Helper plug-in:

```
ruby script/plugin install http://topfunky.net/svn/plugins/calendar_helper/
```

To help you get started, here's some code I used in a similar project using this plug-in; it marks certain days on the calendar with different CSS styling based on whether or not a task is due on that day:

```
<%= calendar({:year => @year, :month => @month, :table_class => ➥
"calendar_helper"}) do |d|
  if @tasks.include?(d)
    [d.mday, {:class => "specialDay"}]
  else
    [d.mday, {:class => "day"}]
  end
end %>
```

Navigate Previous Days

One area that we didn't really develop in our application was the ability to navigate back over previous days to see our completed tasks by day. It's a minor point that won't be exceptionally useful, but every once in a while, it could be nice, so play around with the interface to add the ability to navigate backward and forward to see other daily task lists. Check out the Exercisr project for a simple approach to showing previous days.

Capture the Estimated Time for Each Task

Another area where we could add some distinction to our application would be to go beyond merely capturing our list of tasks to also include capturing an estimated amount of time that we expect each task to take. Then, as you're adding tasks to your daily to-do items, you could keep a running total of the estimated time to complete each day's tasks. This would be useful in ensuring that you don't commit yourself to eleven hours of work when you only have eight hours to complete it.

To make capturing estimated time easy, you should probably capture the time in a single format and convert it as needed. I would recommend adding an estimated time field to the task and storing the estimated times in minutes (so a 1-hour task would be entered as 60 minutes and converted into hours and minutes when you display it).

Display Percentage Completed

Going hand in hand with capturing an estimated amount of time that all of our tasks should take, it would be useful to be able to display the percentage of our total tasks completed as part of our daily list. Calculating the percentage from the sheer number of tasks doesn't really make sense, though. After all, if you have eleven tasks and six of them only took 10 minutes but the other five take an hour each, you're not necessarily close to 50 percent done with your daily work when you've marked five tasks completed. Instead, you should use the estimated time field from the previous exercise to calculate the total percentage completed. In this case, you'd only hit the 50 percent complete mark after you had completed three hours of your total tasks, irregardless of how many tasks that actually consisted of.

Develop an iPhone Interface

Being able to manage our daily task list is nice. However, for those of us who are mobile during the day, it will be a tad inconvenient to have to wait until we're at a computer to check the list again or to mark things as complete. For that reason, building a mobile interface to our application would be a huge boon. And what better mobile interface to develop for than the recently introduced iPhone?

To makes things easier, developer Joe Hewitt (creator of the insanely useful Firebug plug-in for Firefox) has created a set of JavaScript and style sheets for a solid and consistent iPhone user interface named iUI. You can read about iUI and download the latest version at http://www.joehewitt.com/iui/.

For this exercise, you'll probably find it easiest to simply create a new iPhone controller that provides the iPhone interface methods and views. This way, the iPhone interface could be accessed at www.monkeytasks.com/iphone for simplicity.

Optimize Database Queries

You should recall how we built those wonderful association proxies to show how we can make our code more expressive with calls, such as:

```
has_many :tasks do
    def overdue
      find(:all, :conditions => ["due < ? and complete is null", Date.today.to_s])
    end
    def today
      find(:all, :conditions => ["due = ? and complete is null", Date.today.to_s])
    end
    def upcoming
      find(:all, :conditions => ["due > ? and complete is null", Date.today.to_s])
    end
  end
```

Well, we talked about how that works, but three separate queries to the same model are also a bit of a hit on the database. You should rewrite this to be only a single call to the database and do your partitioning within your Ruby code.

Move Code into Models

We also have a few places where we're doing things in the controller that really scream to be made into methods in the models instead. For example, in our tasks controller, we have a method named mark_complete:

```
def mark_complete
  if @task.complete.nil?
    @task.complete = Time.now
    @task.todo.move_to_bottom
```

```
    else
      @task.complete = nil
    end
    @task.save!
    @todos = current_user.schedule.todos
end
```

This is just plain ugly, and this level of business logic should not be left in the controller. Why don't you fix this by creating a few methods in the task model, such as a `complete?` method that will let us know if a task is complete and `task.complete!` and `task.incomplete!` methods that will immediately mark a method as complete or incomplete? With those methods, you could rewrite this controller method to look like this:

```
def mark_complete
  if @task.complete?
    @task.complete!
  else
    @task.incomplete!
  end
  @task.save!
  @todos = current_user.schedule.todos
end
```

That's much nicer, but of course, even that could be simplified further with another model method named `toggle_complete`:

```
def mark_complete
  @task.toggle_complete!
  @task.save!
  @todos = current_user.schedule.todos
end
```

You see—the goal is to move as much of our logic as possible into our model methods, leaving our controllers nice and lean. For a great article on this process, check out the outstanding blog post "Skinny Controller, Fat Model" by Jamis Buck at `http://weblog.jamisbuck.org/2006/10/18/skinny-controller-fat-model`.

Freeze the Chronic Gem

Another point that you should consider is that if were to deploy this project to an external web server, you would first have to ensure that the Chronic gem was installed on the remote server (otherwise, the application wouldn't even start). Back in Chapter 2, we talked about a better solution involving freezing gems locally to the application. This is the perfect time to practice that procedure by freezing the Chronic gem into your application.

Summary

Congratulations are in order once you've finished these tasks. While these exercises may seem simple, now that you've done them, you've cleaned up the code, added new features, and almost certainly learned a substantial amount more about Rails development.

PART 3

■■■

Exercisr

Who would have thought that the stereotypical programmer lifestyle might not be the healthiest way to live? Once upon a time we could stay up all night hacking away at code, eating cold pizza, and drinking warm beer (or Dr. Pepper) without suffering any side effects or, worse, gaining weight. But those days are gone—now we're supposed to live healthy and that means making better choices for what goes into our bodies and investing time in regular exercise. While conventional wisdom has always thought that aerobic exercise was best for you, science over the last few years has given evidence that a regular resistance training program such as weight lifting is one of the best things you can do for your body. Because muscle requires more energy for your body to maintain, resistance training can significantly increase your metabolic rate (the rate at which your body burns calories).

So you've bitten the bullet and invested in a swanky new home gym so that you have no excuse for not working out. With that excuse removed, you only need to tackle the issue of how to keep yourself motivated once you start. A good way to do that is to maintain records of your progress as you begin a lifelong journey into fitness. In this project, we'll look at building a simple application that will help you do just that.

■■■

Developing a REST-Based Application

For this project, we're going to build a rails application that will provide a way for us to track our fitness goals and results. When we're finished, the final project should

- Allow us to maintain a list of our goals (such as weight loss or bicep size) and maintain records of our progress towards those goals over time.

- Allow us to maintain a record of when we worked out and what we did.

- Allow us to capture and track the progress of our workouts. We need to be able to capture data like how long it took us to jog three miles or how much we were able to lift using the bench press.

- Include an API for our application to open the door for us to make this data available elsewhere (such as on a personal blog).

- Provide a way to graph our progress over time. This will allow us to visually identify any problems in our workouts, such as a long period with no increase in our bench press weight. Seeing steady progress toward our goals is a great motivational asset as well.

REST-Based Development

As a means to accomplish these application goals, we're going to explore the new REST-based support that was added in Rails 1.2. It would be an understatement to say that RESTful development has been adopted by the Rails community big time, as evidenced by the overwhelming amount of discussions and posts that have been seen online since RESTful support was first announced during David Heinemeier Hansson's (DHH's) keynote address at the 2006 RailsConf entitled "A World of Resources" (available for download at http://media.rubyonrails.org/presentations/worldofresources.pdf). During that keynote, DHH introduced features of Rails designed to support the development of RESTful applications and challenged developers to embrace the constraints of RESTful development by viewing their controllers with a mindset of supporting CRUD operations (you should recall that we touched on these in Chapter 3).

So What Is REST?

From an academic standpoint, Representational State Transfer (REST) is a software architecture for distributed hypermedia systems. It refers to a collection of principles for how data is defined and accessed. It provides a simple way for external systems to access applications' data over HTTP without having to add an additional layer, such as SOAP. In web applications, REST is often used to describe a development style that provides a clean and unified interface that allows the same interface to serve multiple representations of the same data to various clients. In a REST-based system, we're often talking about interacting with resources. Examples of resources include such things as a Ruby object, a database result, and an image—essentially, a resource is anything that we might want to expose to our users to interact with.

Hopefully, that last paragraph didn't cause your eyes to glaze over too badly. If it did, don't worry, because from this point forward, we'll avoid the definitions and focus on what REST means for us. From a more practical view, when we're talking about building a RESTful application, we're talking about building a simple interface to our application where we're using the four core HTTP methods (GET, POST, PUT, and DELETE) to define the actions to perform on a resource rather than by placing method names within the URL as you can see in Table 6-1.

Table 6-1. *Comparison REST and Traditional URLs*

REST URL	Traditional URL
/exercises	/exercises/index
/exercises/1	/exercises/show/1
/exercises/new	/exercises/new
/exercises/1;edit	/exercises/edit/1
/exercises	/exercises/create
/exercises/1	/exercises/update/1
/exercises/1	/exercises/destroy/1

The goal of a REST design is to break things down into nouns and verbs. The verbs that we use in a RESTful application are the core HTTP methods GET, POST, PUT, and DELETE, while the nouns are the resources that we've made available. Those core HTTP methods have an obvious similarity to the CRUD database operations that you can see in Table 6-2.

Table 6-2. *Correlation of HTTP Methods to Database Operations*

Operation	Database	HTTP
Find	SELECT	GET
Create	INSERT	POST
Update	UPDATE	PUT
Destroy	DELETE	DELETE

The goal of REST is to get away from creating an endless series of method names that we might tack onto a URL to interact with an object such as `http://localhost/resource/add_resource` or `http://localhost/resource/list`. Instead, we want to move to using our verbs to interact with our nouns so that those same requests become a POST or GET request to `http://localhost/resources`.

The Value of REST

RESTful design provides a number of advantages; in his keynote, DHH brought up three main advantages for Rails developers:

Consistency: Designing a RESTful application provides us with a greater level of consistency—not just in our URLs but also in our controllers. Controllers built to the RESTful ideals will always have the same seven methods (`index`, `new`, `create`, `show`, `edit`, `update`, and `destroy`).

Simplicity: RESTful design takes away a lot of the questions about where things go; it lets every object focus primarily on its CRUD operations by implementing the seven methods discussed in the previous point. Simplifying these decisions effectively simplifies our design. There are already success stories out there, such as that of Scott Raymond who refactored IconBuffet.com to RESTful principles and discovered that he had reduced the number of actions in his application by 25 percent.

Discoverability: This goes hand in hand with consistency—as more and more developers embrace a common set of constraints, it eases integration between applications.

Our First Resource

Enough theory—let's kick off our project and see how Rails makes building a RESTful application a snap as we explore building our first resource. Open your development directory, and create a new project named exercisr using the instructions from Chapter 2. With our project created, let's take a brief look at some of the tools within Rails that we'll use to support building a RESTful application.

RESTful Tools

DHH, the creator of Ruby on Rails, has talked a number of times about how the core team tries to add syntactic sugar around certain programming styles or approaches to encourage their use, and that's highly apparent in the Rails support for building REST applications. Let's take a quick look at the three core features of Rails that support RESTful development.

map.resources

The first tool that we want to take a look at is a method that has been added for our routes. Traditionally we've had two methods that we could use within our routes. The oldest of these was `map.connect`, which is used to build our general `/:controller/:action/:id` style of routes in a manner like this:

```
map.connect '', :controller => 'home', :action => 'welcome'
map.connect '/post/:id', :controller => 'post', :action => 'show'
```

```
map.connect '/weather/:year/:month/:date, :controller => 'weather',
                                                :action => 'archive'
```

While the map.connect method was fine for awhile, it did cause Rails developers to be a bit too verbose a bit too often, when they wanted to refer to a specific route. If we wanted to create a link to the preceding routes, the correct way would have been

```
link_to 'Home', :controller => 'home', :action => 'welcome'
link_to 'Show Post', :controller => 'post', :action => 'show', :id => @post
link_to 'Weather Last Christmas', :controller => 'weather', :action => 'archive',
                                :year => '2006' :month => '12', :date => '25'
```

You can see how quickly it would become bothersome to constantly generate links by manually typing the controller, actions, and ID parameters each time, and you can imagine how quickly this was increasing the noise ratio within our view files. Named routes were added to our Rails arsenal to ease this pain for Rails developers. Building a named route is almost identical to building a regular route—except that we replace the connect method with a custom name of our own choosing for the route. So to convert the regular routes you saw previously, you might write them like this:

```
map.home '', :controller => 'home', :action => 'welcome'
map.post '/post/:id', :controller => 'post', :action => 'show'
map.weather_archive '/weather/:year/:month/:date, :controller => 'weather',
                                                :action => 'archive'
```

While this may seem like just a minor change, it makes a big difference for us. When we create a named route, Rails provides us with two new URL methods that make our lives much easier: {named_route}_path and {named_route}.url. So our previous map.home route would generate these URL methods as home_path and home_url, and they would generate the URLs for this route. The only difference between these two methods is that home_url will generate a fully qualified link including host and post (i.e., http://locahost:3000/) while home_path will only generate the relative path (i.e., /). So armed with our named routes, we could build links to those routes like this:

```
link_to 'Home', home_path
link_to 'Show Post', post_path(@post)
link_to 'Weather Last Christmas', weather_archive_path('2006', '12', '25')
```

While named routes are an incredibly powerful tool, they were still a bit underpowered for the needs of building RESTful routes, as we would be forced to build numerous named routes to support the seven CRUD style methods for each resource that we wanted to support. Fortunately, a new routing method by the name of map.resources was added to Rails; it's like scaffolding for RESTful routes. Let's take a look at a map.resources example by creating a resource named exercises. So imagine that we added a route such as this:

```
map.resources :exercises
```

Running map.resources :exercises generated a whole mess of dynamically generated routes that map to our RESTful actions, as well as a full plate of useful URL methods (the same as a named_route would), which you can see in Table 6-3.

Table 6-3. *map.resources Generated Routes*

Action	HTTP Method	URL	Generated URL Method
Index	GET	/exercises	exercises_path
Show	GET	/exercises/1	exercise_path(:id)
New	GET	/exercises/new	new_exercise_path
Edit	GET	/exercises/1;edit	edit_exercise_path(:id)
Create	POST	/exercises	exercises_path
Update	PUT	/exercises/1	exercise_path(:id)
Destroy	DELETE	/exercises/1	exercise_path(:id)

With one `map.resources` call, we've generated a full suite of RESTful routing actions for our application and saved ourselves a tremendous amount of typing. In fact, to do it by hand would have required us to create a routes configuration like this:

```
ActionController::Routing::Routes.draw do |map|
  # map.resources :exercises
  # gives us all this
  map.exercises 'exercises', :action => 'index', :conditions => {:method => :get}
  map.connect 'exercises', :action => 'create', :conditions => {:method => :post}
  map.formatted_exercise 'exercises.:format', :action => 'index',
                                              :conditions => {:method => :get}
  map.exercise 'exercises/:id', :action => 'edit', :conditions => {:method => :get}
  map.connect 'exercises/:id', :action => 'update', :conditions => {:method => :put}
  map.connect 'exercises/:id', :action => 'destroy',
                                              :conditions => {:method => :delete}
  map.formatted_exercise 'exercises/:id.:format', :action => 'edit',
                                              :conditions => {:method => :get}
  map.connect 'exercises/:id.:format', :action => 'update',
                                              :conditions => {:method => :put}
  map.connect 'exercises/:id.:format', :action => 'destroy',
                                              :conditions => {:method => :delete}
  map.new_exercise 'exercises/new', :action => 'new',
                                              :conditions => {:method => :get}
  map.formatted_new_exercise 'exercises/new.:format', :action => 'new',
                                              :conditions => {:method => :get}
  map.edit_exercise 'exercise/:id;edit', :action => 'edit',
                                              :conditions => {:method => :get}
  map.edit_exercise 'exercise/:id.:format;edit', :action => 'edit',
                                              :conditions => {:method => :get}
end
```

respond_to

The next tool within Rails that we'll use to support RESTful applications is the respond_to method within our controllers. Within a normal non-RESTful method, we might have an action that looks like this:

```
def index
    @exercises = Exercise.find(:all)
end
```

By default, this method will automatically render the first template file named index that it finds in its corresponding folder (in this example, index.rhtml). But one of our goals with REST is to be able to provide different variations of the same data from a single resource. For that, we'll modify the method to use the respond_to method:

```
def index
    @exercises = Exercise.find(:all)

    respond_to do |format|
        format.html
        format.xml { render :xml => @exercises.to_xml }
    end
end
```

In essence what this does is evaluate the desired response format that was sent with the request in the HTTP accept header and return the corresponding template. Therefore, a normal web request will be served back HTML, while an XML request would be served a list of exercises in XML format.

scaffold_resource

The last tool that we'll explore here is the new scaffolding generator for resource based routing named scaffold_resource. Over the last year or so, using the Rails scaffolding had fallen out of favor within the Rails community; and it was considered good for screencasts but not a tool that a professional Rails developer would use. Well, that changed with the release of the scaffold_resource generator, as scaffold_resource provides a wealth of functionality that truly speeds up your development in a clean and elegant manner. To get an understanding of how the new scaffold_resource works, you can run the command with no parameters to view some helpful information about how to use it:

```
ruby script/generate scaffold_resource
```

Usage: script/generate scaffold_resource ModelName [field:type, field:type]
. . .
Description:
    The scaffold resource generator creates a model, a controller, and a set of
templates that's ready to use as the starting point for your REST-like,
resource-oriented application. This basically means that it follows a set of
conventions to exploit the full set of HTTP verbs (GET/POST/PUT/DELETE) and is
prepared for multi-client access (like one view for HTML, one for an XML API, one
for ATOM, etc). Everything comes with sample unit and functional tests as well.

    The generator takes the name of the model as its first argument. This model
name is then pluralized to get the controller name. So "scaffold_resource post" will

generate a Post model and a PostsController and will be intended for URLs like
/posts and /posts/45.

    As additional parameters, the generator will take attribute pairs described
by name and type. These attributes will be used to prepopulate the migration to
create the table for the model and to give you a set of templates for the view. For
example, "scaffold_resource post title:string created_on:date body:text
published:boolean" will give you a model with those four attributes, forms to create
 and edit those models from, and an index that'll list them all.

    You don't have to think up all attributes up front, but it's a good idea of
adding just the baseline of what's needed to start really working with the resource.

    Once the generator has run, you'll need to add a declaration to your config/
routes.rb file to hook up the rules that'll point URLs to this new resource. If you
 create a resource like "scaffold_resource post", you'll need to add
"map.resources :posts" (notice the plural form) in the routes file. Then your new
resource is accessible from /posts.

Examples:
    ./script/generate scaffold_resource post # no attributes, view will be anemic
    ./script/generate scaffold_resource post title:string created_on:date ➡
body:text published:boolean
    ./script/generate scaffold_resource purchase order_id:integer ➡
created_at:datetime amount:decimal

Reading through that output should get you pretty excited about just how powerful the scaffold_resource generator is. From a single command, we can build out a full controller that's prebuilt to not only support the full line of CRUD operations but also HTTP verbs that we need for a REST application. The scaffolding will build our model and a complete set of generic view templates—yet it goes beyond the normal scaffolding for those items by also allowing us to pass in the database elements to be used in our migration to create the tables in the database. If it feels like we've just turbocharged our speed of development, it's because we have. Let's see it in action as we use scaffold_resource to build the first resource for our application.

Building the Exercise Resource

In our exercise project, whenever we record a workout, we'll be recording a series of exercises that we did. So, as we think about the attributes of an exercise, we recognize that what we really need here is just an object to identify each exercise that we could perform. Examples of exercises include things such as bench press, leg press, and biceps curl. We'll want to expose this list of possible exercises to an end user, so we'll build it as a resource using the new scaffold_resource generator.

At its core, an exercise resource should be a fairly simple thing—it will have to have a name, and a user that it's associated with. Knowing that, we can build our exercise resource by running this command:

```
ruby script/generate scaffold_resource Exercise name:string user_id:integer
```

```
exists   app/models/
exists   app/controllers/
exists   app/helpers/
create   app/views/exercises
exists   test/functional/
exists   test/unit/
create   app/views/exercises/index.rhtml
create   app/views/exercises/show.rhtml
create   app/views/exercises/new.rhtml
create   app/views/exercises/edit.rhtml
create   app/views/layouts/exercises.rhtml
create   public/stylesheets/scaffold.css
create   app/models/exercise.rb
create   app/controllers/exercises_controller.rb
create   test/functional/exercises_controller_test.rb
create   app/helpers/exercises_helper.rb
create   test/unit/exercise_test.rb
create   test/fixtures/exercises.yml
exists   db/migrate
create   db/migrate/001_create_exercises.rb
route    map.resources :exercises
```

Let's take a moment to examine a few important things that the scaffold_resource generator has added to our project.

First off, the new scaffold_resource generator added a map.resources line to our routes configuration (/config/routes.rb), which generated all the URL methods that we discussed previously in Table 6-3:

```
ActionController::Routing::Routes.draw do |map|
  map.resources :exercises
end
```

Second, the generator took the extra parameters that we passed it to prepopulate our database migration (/db/migrate/001_create_exercises.rb):

```
class CreateExercises < ActiveRecord::Migration
  def self.up
    create_table :exercises do |t|
      t.column :name, :string
      t.column :user_id, :integer
    end
  end

  def self.down
    drop_table :exercises
  end
end
```

When we created our exercise resource via the scaffold_resource generator, the generator also built a standard REST-based controller for us (we'll need to make some modifications to the generated controller code before it will work in our application). The generated controllers all have the same seven methods (index, show, new, edit, create, update, and destroy). Let's take a quick look at the index method in exercises_controller (/app/controllers/exercies_controller.rb):

```
# GET /exercises
# GET /exercises.xml
def index
  @exercises = Exercise.find(:all)

  respond_to do |format|
    format.html # index.rhtml
    format.xml  { render :xml => @exercises.to_xml }
  end
end
```

At the top of each of these generated methods, Rails added a comment to provide you with examples of what URLs could be used to access this method. After the comments, you'll see a standard find on the exercise model populating an instance variable named @exercises.

The respond_to block, though, is a pretty exciting thing, as it allows us to support multiple content requests from a single method. Rails has supported these respond_to blocks since Rails 1.1 came out in the spring of 2006, but it's within the context of the new RESTful routing that I think they really come alive.

One of the big problems with previous versions of the respond_to blocks was that they responded solely based on what was sent in the request header as the Accept content type. So a client that sent Accept: text/html was given an HTML template, and a client that sent Accept: text/xml was sent an XML template.

The trouble would come in, though, when a client sent an incorrect Accept request. RSS is a great example of that, as technically the client wants to pull down a specially formatted XML feed, yet many RSS requests come in as Accept: text/html.

Rails 1.2 fixed that by changing the way the routing works to also evaluate the file format requested—it evaluates the file extensions within the URL and gives those a higher priority over what's in the Accept header. In this way, a client that makes a GET request to /exercises.xml will be served the XML template even if the request came with Accept: text/html in the header. Nifty!

Let's take a quick glance at the full exercises controller that scaffold_resource generated for us:

```
class ExercisesController < ApplicationController
  # GET /exercises
  # GET /exercises.xml
  def index
    @exercises = Exercise.find(:all)

    respond_to do |format|
      format.html # index.rhtml
      format.xml  { render :xml => @exercises.to_xml }
    end
  end


  # GET /exercises/1
  # GET /exercises/1.xml
  def show
    @exercise = Exercise.find(params[:id])

    respond_to do |format|
      format.html # show.rhtml
      format.xml  { render :xml => @exercise.to_xml }
    end
  end

  # GET /exercises/new
  def new
    @exercise = Exercise.new
  end

  # GET /exercises/1;edit
  def edit
    @exercise = Exercise.find(params[:id])
  end
```

```ruby
    # POST /exercises
    # POST /exercises.xml
    def create
      @exercise = Exercise.new(params[:exercise])

      respond_to do |format|
        if @exercise.save
          flash[:notice] = 'Exercise was successfully created.'
          format.html { redirect_to exercise_url(@exercise) }
          format.xml  { head :created, :location => exercise_url(@exercise) }
        else
          format.html { render :action => "new" }
          format.xml  { render :xml => @exercise.errors.to_xml }
        end
      end
    end

    # PUT /exercises/1
    # PUT /exercises/1.xml
    def update
      @exercise = Exercise.find(params[:id])

      respond_to do |format|
        if @exercise.update_attributes(params[:exercise])
          flash[:notice] = 'Exercise was successfully updated.'
          format.html { redirect_to exercise_url(@exercise) }
          format.xml  { head :ok }
        else
          format.html { render :action => "edit" }
          format.xml  { render :xml => @exercise.errors.to_xml }
        end
      end
    end

    # DELETE /exercises/1
    # DELETE /exercises/1.xml
    def destroy
      @exercise = Exercise.find(params[:id])
      @exercise.destroy

      respond_to do |format|
        format.html { redirect_to exercises_url }
        format.xml  { head :ok }
      end
    end
end
```

Not only did the scaffolding generate a RESTful controller for us but it also built the full suite of associated templates for this controller. Extra nice is the fact that each of the templates also takes full advantage of the URL helpers, such as this one that was generated for the new method in /app/views/exercises/new.rhtml:

```
<h1>New exercise</h1>

<%= error_messages_for :exercise %>

<% form_for(:exercise, :url => exercises_path) do |f| %>
  <p>
    <b>Name</b><br />
    <%= f.text_field :name %>
  </p>

  <p>
    <b>User</b><br />
    <%= f.text_field :user_id %>
  </p>

  <p>
    <%= submit_tag "Create" %>
  </p>
<% end %>

<%= link_to 'Back', exercises_path %>
```

As you can see, the new scaffold_resource generator can be a huge timesaver for kick-starting a RESTful application. Now, let's continue our project development by adding in an authentication system.

■**Note** The only thing that I don't like about the scaffold_resource generator is that it also creates a corresponding layout file in /app/views/layouts. Since I prefer to create a global layout file named application.rthml, this scaffold generated layout causes unnecessary issues. Go ahead and remove the generated exercises.rhtml file.

Adding RESTful Authentication

If experience has taught us anything by now, it's that if we build anything remotely useful, some-one else is going to want to use it as well. We'll anticipate that our friends are also going to want to use the application by building in multiuser support from the get-go. Fortunately, Rick Olsen has made our job much easier, as he has already adapted his popular acts_as_authenticated plug-in to a REST-based implementation named restful_authentication. Using this plug-in will allow us to jump start our application with a full multiuser login and authentication system without sacrificing any of our RESTful ideals.

To install restful_authentication, open a command prompt and run the following command:

```
ruby script/plugin install http://svn.techno-weenie.net/projects/plugins/ ➥
restful_authentication
```

```
./restful_authentication/README
./restful_authentication/Rakefile
./restful_authentication/generators/authenticated/USAGE
./restful_authentication/generators/authenticated/authenticated_generator.rb
./restful_authentication/generators/authenticated/templates/activation.rhtml
./restful_authentication/generators/authenticated/templates/authenticated_system.rb
./restful_authentication/generators/authenticated/templates/ ➥
authenticated_test_helper.rb
./restful_authentication/generators/authenticated/templates/controller.rb
./restful_authentication/generators/authenticated/templates/fixtures.yml
./restful_authentication/generators/authenticated/templates/functional_test.rb
./restful_authentication/generators/authenticated/templates/helper.rb
./restful_authentication/generators/authenticated/templates/login.rhtml
./restful_authentication/generators/authenticated/templates/migration.rb
./restful_authentication/generators/authenticated/templates/model.rb
./restful_authentication/generators/authenticated/templates/model_controller.rb
./restful_authentication/generators/authenticated/templates/model_functional_test.rb
./restful_authentication/generators/authenticated/templates/model_helper.rb
./restful_authentication/generators/authenticated/templates/notifier.rb
./restful_authentication/generators/authenticated/templates/notifier_test.rb
./restful_authentication/generators/authenticated/templates/observer.rb
./restful_authentication/generators/authenticated/templates/signup.rhtml
./restful_authentication/generators/authenticated/templates/ ➥
signup_notification.rhtml
./restful_authentication/generators/authenticated/templates/unit_test.rb
./restful_authentication/install.rb
Restful Authentication Generator
====

This is a basic restful authentication generator for rails, taken from acts as
authenticated.  Currently it requires Rails 1.2 (or edge).

To use:

  ./script/generate authenticated user sessions --include-activation

The first parameter specifies the model that gets created in signup (typically a
user or account model).  A model with migration is created, as well as a basic
controller with the create method.
```

The second parameter specifies the sessions controller name. This is the controller
 that handles the actual login/logout function on the site.

The third parameter (--include-activation) generates the code for a ActionMailer and

its respective Activation Code through email.

You can pass --skip-migration to skip the user migration.

From here, you will need to add the resource routes in config/routes.rb.

```
map.resources :users, :sessions
```

Also, add an observer to config/environment.rb if you chose the --include-activation
 option
```
config.active_record.observers = :user_observer # or whatever you named your model
```

In the same manner that acts_as_authenticated did in our MonkeyTasks projects,
the Restful Authentication plug-in merely installs a generator that we use to create our
authentication system. Documentation for this generator should have been output during
the plug-in installation, but you can also find it in the plug-in's readme file (/vendor/plugins/
restful_authentication/README). We're not going to bother with adding the mailer and activation code functionality, since we already built that functionality in the MonkeyTasks project;
plus, we're designing this application for a smaller user base (i.e., just our friends and family).
With that said, let's use the generator to build our authentication system! Back at the command
prompt in the root our application, type the following command:

```
ruby script/generate authenticated user sessions
```

```
Don't forget to:

  - add restful routes in config/routes.rb
    map.resources :users, :sessions
    map.activate '/activate/:activation_code', :controller => 'users',
                                               :action => 'activate'

Try these for some familiar login URLs if you like:

  map.signup '/signup', :controller => 'users', :action => 'new'
  map.login  '/login', :controller => 'sessions', :action => 'new'
  map.logout '/logout', :controller => 'sessions', :action => 'destroy'

  --------------------------------------------------------------------------
```

```
exists  app/models/
exists  app/controllers/
exists  app/controllers/
exists  app/helpers/
create  app/views/sessions
create  app/views/user_notifier
exists  test/functional/
exists  app/controllers/
exists  app/helpers/
create  app/views/users
exists  test/functional/
exists  test/unit/
create  app/models/user.rb
create  app/controllers/sessions_controller.rb
create  app/controllers/users_controller.rb
create  lib/authenticated_system.rb
create  lib/authenticated_test_helper.rb
create  test/functional/sessions_controller_test.rb
create  test/functional/users_controller_test.rb
create  app/helpers/sessions_helper.rb
create  app/helpers/users_helper.rb
create  test/unit/user_test.rb
create  test/fixtures/users.yml
create  app/views/sessions/new.rhtml
create  app/views/users/new.rhtml
create  db/migrate
create  db/migrate/002_create_users.rb
```

The generator has added two new controllers to our application: a sessions controller and a users controller. It's also added a user model; associated views, helpers, and tests; and the authentication library to our project. The generator was even nice enough to remind us to add the necessary resource routes to our routes configuration. We'll take advantage of that reminder and go ahead and add those routes now. Edit your routes.rb file to look like this:

```
ActionController::Routing::Routes.draw do |map|
  map.resources :exercises
  map.home '', :controller => 'sessions', :action => 'new'
  map.resources :users, :sessions
  map.signup '/signup', :controller => 'users', :action => 'new'
  map.login '/login', :controller => 'sessions', :action => 'new'
  map.logout '/logout', :controller => 'sessions', :action => 'destroy'
end
```

We now need to set up our application to use the authentication system by default. When the generator ran, it added the necessary commands into the two controllers that it generated (sessions and users). But since we want all of the controllers in our application to use the authentication system, we need to move those commands out of those controllers and into the application controller (so that all controllers will inherit it). Open our three controllers (users_controller.rb, sessions_controller.rb, and application_controller.rb) in /app/controllers; remove the following lines out of the sessions and users controllers and add them into the application controller:

```
# Be sure to include AuthenticationSystem in Application Controller instead
include AuthenticatedSystem
# If you want "remember me" functionality, add this before_filter to ➥
   Application Controller
before_filter :login_from_cookie
```

Afterward, our application controller (/app/controllers/application.rb) should look like this:

```
class ApplicationController < ActionController::Base
  session :session_key => '_exercisr_session_id'
  include AuthenticatedSystem
end
```

Our application controller currently has two lines. The first line is automatically generated and is simply used to create the session keys that our application will use for any sessions it creates. The second line is the one that we just added, and it includes the authenticated system library from our /lib folder.

If we had wanted to enable a "remember me" level of functionality (i.e., setting a cookie in the user's browser that would enable them to be logged into the application without having to reenter their username and password each time), we could have also placed the before_filter :login_from_cookie line into this controller like we did for MonkeyTasks.

Meanwhile, our users controller (/app/controllers/users_controller.rb) should look like this:

```
class UsersController < ApplicationController
  # render new.rhtml
  def new
  end


  def create
    @user = User.new(params[:user])
    @user.save!
    self.current_user = @user
    redirect_back_or_default('/')
    flash[:notice] = "Thanks for signing up!"
  rescue ActiveRecord::RecordInvalid
    render :action => 'new'
  end
end
```

The users controller allows users to be added to our application and contains two methods. The new method is where our /signup route directs to and is used to display the form to create a new user account, which you can see in Figure 6-1.

Login

Email

Password

Confirm Password

Sign up

Figure 6-1. *The default signup form from Restful Authentication*

This signup form will POST to the create method in our users controller, which will create a new user from the form submission.

Finally, we have our sessions controller (/app/controllers/sessions_controller.rb), which handles the logging in and logging out functionality of our site:

```
class SessionsController < ApplicationController
  # render new.rhtml
  def new
  end

  def create
    self.current_user = User.authenticate(params[:login], params[:password])
    if logged_in?
      if params[:remember_me] == "1"
        self.current_user.remember_me
        cookies[:auth_token] = { :value => self.current_user.remember_token ,
                        :expires => self.current_user.remember_token_expires_at }
      end
      redirect_back_or_default('/')
      flash[:notice] = "Logged in successfully"
    else
      render :action => 'new'
    end
  end

  def destroy
    self.current_user.forget_me if logged_in?
    cookies.delete :auth_token
    reset_session
    flash[:notice] = "You have been logged out."
    redirect_back_or_default('/')
  end
end
```

The sessions controller contains three methods.

- new: This method is where our /login route is pointed. It displays the basic login form that a user would submit to log in to our application. That login form submits to the create method in this controller.

- create: This method is used to actually log in a user by creating a new session once the user has been authenticated.

- destroy: Finally, we have the destroy method, which removes our authenticated session, effectively logging out the user. This is where the /logout route is pointed.

Migrations

Finally, let's take a quick glance at the migration file that the generator created. Open 002_create_users.rb in /db/migrate:

```
class CreateUsers < ActiveRecord::Migration
  def self.up
    create_table "users", :force => true do |t|
      t.column :login,                    :string
      t.column :email,                    :string
      t.column :crypted_password,         :string, :limit => 40
      t.column :salt,                     :string, :limit => 40
      t.column :created_at,               :datetime
      t.column :updated_at,               :datetime
      t.column :remember_token,           :string
      t.column :remember_token_expires_at, :datetime
    end
  end

  def self.down
    drop_table "users"
  end
end
```

If we wanted to add any custom fields to our users model, such as capturing the first name, last name, or address, we could add them in here. However, for our application, we'll be just fine with the defaults. Go ahead and close this file, and let's run this migration to add the exercises and users tables to our database:

```
rake db:migrate
```

```
== CreateExercises: migrating ============================================
-- create_table(:exercises)
   -> 0.0780s
== CreateExercises: migrated (0.0780s) ===================================

== CreateUsers: migrating ================================================
-- create_table("users", {:force=>true})
   -> 0.0620s
== CreateUsers: migrated (0.0620s) =======================================
```

Fire up your web server (probably with the `mongrel rails_start` command) and load our application (it should be available at `http://localhost:3000`). You should be greeted by the login form shown in Figure 6-2.

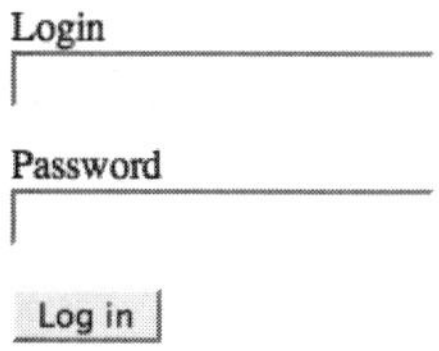

Login

Password

Log in

Figure 6-2. *The default login form created by Restful Authentication*

Refining the Look

Let's go ahead and create a layout template to get the visuals of our application more in line with the original goal as we build out our functionality. You can download the style sheets and images from the code archive. We need to create a new layout file named `application.rhtml` in `/app/views/layouts` and place the following content in it:

```
<!DOCTYPE html PUBLIC "-//W3C//DTD XHTML 1.0 Transitional//EN"
    "http://www.w3.org/TR/xhtml1/DTD/xhtml1-transitional.dtd">
<html>
   <head>
      <meta http-equiv="Content-type" content="text/html; charset=utf-8">
      <title><%= @title || "Exercisr" %></title>
      <link rel="stylesheet" type="text/css" href="http://yui.yahooapis.com ➥
/2.2.2/build/reset-fonts-grids/reset-fonts-grids.css">
      <%= stylesheet_link_tag 'styles' %>
      <%= javascript_include_tag :defaults %>
   </head>
```

```
<body>
    <div id="doc2" class="yui-t2">
        <div id="hd" class="box grad blue">
            <%= image_tag 'grad_black.png' %>
            <h1 id="masthead"><%= link_to "Exercisr", home_path %></h1>
        </div>

        <div id="bd">
            <div id="yui-main">
                <div class="yui-b">
                    <%= yield %>
                </div>
            </div>
            <% if logged_in? %>
            <div class="yui-b sidebar">
                <ul>
                    <li><%= link_to 'Exercises', exercises_path %></li>
                    <li><%# link_to 'Workouts', workouts_path %></li>
                    <li><%# link_to 'Goals', goals_path %></li>
                    <li><%= link_to 'Logout', logout_path %></li>
                </ul>
            </div>
            <% end %>
        </div>

        <div id="ft" class="box grad blue"><%= image_tag 'grad_white.png' %></div>
    </div>
</body>
</html>
```

Assuming that you still have a Mongrel instance running our application, reload the application in a web browser, and you should be treated with something like the login form shown in Figure 6-3, which is a little easier on the eyes (or at least good enough until we can afford to get a decent graphic artist to design something nicer).

Figure 6-3. *The login form with our layout and style sheet applied*

■**Note** You may have noticed that some of the links in our sidebar are placed within `<%#   %>` tags instead of the normal `<%=   %>` tags. These tags essentially comment out the code contained within them so that it isn't executed. I did this because, otherwise, the application would break if we tried to execute those lines, as we cheated a little by adding links to resources that we haven't built yet. But don't worry; we'll be building those resources soon.

Creating a New User

We're at a good point to go ahead and create our first user account within the system. Before we do that though, we'll need to make one minor change to the way that the Restful Authentication plug-in works. If you open the sessions controller (`/app/controllers/session_controller.rb`), you'll see that there are three methods in this controller (though only two with code). Currently, both the `create` and `destroy` methods utilize a method from the Authenticated System library (`/lib/authenticated_system.rb`) named `redirect_back_or_default`. This method is a great tool for user friendliness, as it will return users to the original page that they requested once they have logged in. So if a user bookmarked a page in our application and tried to access it while not logged in, that user would first be directed to the login page; however, after logging in, this method would send the user back to the originally requested page. That's a wonderful user experience, but to make it work, we need to change the parameter that's being passed in this method. Currently, the method is sending users back to the login form by default (even after they're logged in), so let's change that to a basic welcome page. To do that, we'll first need to build a good starting page.

Creating a Home Page

If this was an application that we wanted to push out professionally, we'd want to build a nice interactive welcome page that provided users with sample data, tutorials, and so on. However, since our application is really just for our own use and maybe a few friends, we can make do with a static page that gives the user a generic welcome to the site at login. To accomplish this, we'll simply create an additional method and template within our sessions template. This is a little bit of a kludge, as it's not really the session controller's responsibility to present a welcome template to the user, but considering the simple needs of our application, it's one that we can live with. If we were going to have more than a single informational page or wanted to add more functionality to these pages, we would want to create a new controller to mange them.

Let's add a new `welcome` method within our sessions controller (`/app/controllers/session_controller.rb`):

```
def welcome
end
```

And we'll also create the associated template (`/app/views/sessions/welcome.rhtml`) for this method to display the following welcome text:

```
<h1>Welcome to Exercisr</h1>
<h3>A RESTful place to keep track of your workouts</h3>
```

■**Note** Technically, we didn't have to create the `welcome` method within this controller, since there was no code that needed to be executed within that method. However, I feel that it's a good practice to always include a method for any template that you create in an application to avoid confusion when looking at the code at some point in the future.

With our welcome template defined now, let's add a named route to our routes configuration (`/config/routes.rb`) to access it (don't forget that the order of routes in this file is important):

```
ActionController::Routing::Routes.draw do |map|
  map.resources :exercises

  map.home '', :controller => 'sessions', :action => 'new'
  map.resources :users, :sessions
  map.welcome '/welcome', :controller => 'sessions', :action => 'welcome'
  map.signup '/signup', :controller => 'users', :action => 'new'
  map.login '/login', :controller => 'sessions', :action => 'new'
  map.logout '/logout', :controller => 'sessions', :action => 'destroy'
end
```

Finally, with our new named route to our welcome page, we can modify the default destinations of our methods in the session controller (`/app/controllers/session_controller.rb`) by changing the `create` method to go to our new welcome view and the `destroy` method to redirect back to the login page:

```
class SessionsController < ApplicationController

  def welcome
  end

  def new
  end

  def create
    self.current_user = User.authenticate(params[:login], params[:password])
    if logged_in?
      if params[:remember_me] == "1"
        self.current_user.remember_me
        cookies[:auth_token] = { :value => self.current_user.remember_token ,
                    :expires => self.current_user.remember_token_expires_at }
      end
      redirect_back_or_default(welcome_path)
      flash[:notice] = "Logged in successfully"
```

```
      else
        render :action => 'new'
      end
    end

    def destroy
      self.current_user.forget_me if logged_in?
      cookies.delete :auth_token
      reset_session
      flash[:notice] = "You have been logged out."
      redirect_back_or_default(login_path)
    end
end
```

The users controller (/app/controllers/user_controller.rb) also utilizes redirect_back_or_default in the create method when a user first signs up, so we'll need to also modify its default page:

```
def create
    @user = User.new(params[:user])
    @user.save!
    self.current_user = @user
    redirect_back_or_default(welcome_path)
    flash[:notice] = "Thanks for signing up!"
  rescue ActiveRecord::RecordInvalid
    render :action => 'new'
  end
```

With our code changes in place, you can go to localhost:3000/signup and create a new user account; afterward, you should be directed to our new welcome template, which you can see in Figure 6-4.

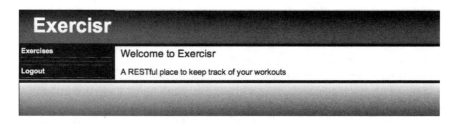

Figure 6-4. *Our welcome template*

Completing the Exercise Resource

If we're going to allow our friends and family to also have access to our Exercisr application, we'll need to provide some means to keep users' data separated. For our exercises resource, we only want each user to be able to view and edit his own list of exercises.

Building the Model Associations

The first step in maintaining separation among each users list of exercises is to build the associations between a user and an exercise. So within the user model (/app/models/user.rb) we'll add the following association:

```
has_many :exercises, :dependent => :destroy, :order => 'name asc'
```

Next, within our exercises model (/app/models/exercise.rb), we'll add the reciprocal association back to our user model:

```
belongs_to :user
```

With those associations added, we can now make a call to current_user.exercises within our controllers to pull back a list of the currently logged in user's exercises. However, before we start modifying our controllers to utilize that functionality—as long as we're already in our exercise model—let's go ahead and add some important validations to our model. Afterward, our exercise model will look like this:

```
class Exercise < ActiveRecord::Base
  belongs_to :user
  validates_presence_of :name
  validates_uniqueness_of :name, :scope => :user_id
end
```

For an exercise to be valid, we're going to require that it has a name. Secondly, we also want to ensure that a user doesn't submit the same exercise twice (for example, it would be confusing to allow a user to have bench press in her list twice). That uniqueness, though, has to be scoped to only a specific user, as we don't want to block two different users from adding the same exercise name.

Rescoping the Exercise Controller

While the generated code provided us with all the basic CRUD operations that we need to interact with each of our resources, it's doing it on a global level. What we need to do is reduce the scope, so that each of these actions is only capable of interacting with data that's associated to the current user. That way, little sister Susie can't accidentally (or maliciously) go in and delete all of our workout results for the last few months.

You should recall that when we created our scaffolded exercises controller (/app/controllers/exercise_controller.rb), it created a standard set of RESTful methods for us. If you look at them in your code editor, you'll notice that each of those methods starts by setting an @exercise instance variable (or @exercises in the case of the index method). The problem that we have is that the scaffolding had no idea that we wanted to limit the scope of our finds to only the exercises for a specific user, so it's currently set to retrieve any or all exercises regardless of the user, using code like @exercises = Exercise.find(:all) or @exercise = Exercise.new.

We'll modify this to always use the currently logged in user as the scope for these requests with the new associations that we built. To do that, we'll first need to ensure that no one could access this controller without first being logged in, so we'll add a before_filter :login_required call to the top of the controller.

Once we've added that filter, our next step will be to scope all of those finder methods based on the current user. We'll do that by changing our lookups to use our new association to find the exercises—so @exercises = Exercise.find(:all) will become @exercises = current_user.exercises.find(:all) and @exercise = Exercise.new will become @exercise = current_user.exercises.build. With those changes in place, our exercises controller should look like this:

```
class ExercisesController < ApplicationController
  before_filter :login_required

  # GET /exercises
  # GET /exercises.xml
  def index
    @exercises = current_user.exercises.find(:all)

    respond_to do |format|
      format.html # index.rhtml
      format.xml  { render :xml => @exercises.to_xml }
    end
  end

  # GET /exercises/1
  # GET /exercises/1.xml
  def show
    @exercise = current_user.exercises.find(params[:id])

    respond_to do |format|
      format.html # show.rhtml
      format.xml  { render :xml => @exercise.to_xml }
    end
  end

  # GET /exercises/new
  def new
    @exercise = current_user.exercises.build
  end

  # GET /exercises/1;edit
  def edit
    @exercise = current_user.exercises.find(params[:id])
  end
```

```ruby
# POST /exercises
# POST /exercises.xml
def create
  @exercise = current_user.exercises.build(params[:exercise])

  respond_to do |format|
    if @exercise.save
      flash[:notice] = 'Exercise was successfully created.'
      format.html { redirect_to exercises_url}
      format.xml  { head :created, :location => exercise_url(@exercise) }
    else
      format.html { render :action => "new" }
      format.xml  { render :xml => @exercise.errors.to_xml }
    end
  end
end

# PUT /exercises/1
# PUT /exercises/1.xml
def update
  @exercise = current_user.exercises.find(params[:id])

  respond_to do |format|
    if @exercise.update_attributes(params[:exercise])
      flash[:notice] = 'Exercise was successfully updated.'
      format.html { redirect_to exercises_url }
      format.xml  { head :ok }
    else
      format.html { render :action => "edit" }
      format.xml  { render :xml => @exercise.errors.to_xml }
    end
  end
end

# DELETE /exercises/1
# DELETE /exercises/1.xml
def destroy
  @exercise = current_user.exercises.find(params[:id])
  @exercise.destroy

  respond_to do |format|
    format.html { redirect_to exercises_url }
    format.xml  { head :ok }
  end
end

end
```

The Exercise Views

With our exercises controller finished, it's merely a matter of making a few modifications to the templates that were generated by the resource scaffolding to finish out our exercise resource.

One of the things that I like to do to keep my templates clean and DRY is to move the forms that are used to create and edit a resource into a single, separate partial, so let's create a new file in /app/views/exercises named _form.rhtml and place the following code into it:

```
<p>
    <label for="exercise_name">Name</label> <br />
    <%= f.text_field :name %>
</p>
<p>
    <%= submit_tag "Save" %>
</p>
```

With our form partial built, we can now rewrite several of our templates to utilize it; for example, the new template (/app/views/exercises/new.rhtml) can be used to create a new exercise or to display errors when creating a new exercise fails validation:

```
<h1>New exercise</h1>

<%= error_messages_for :exercise %>

<% form_for(:exercise, :url => exercises_path) do |f| %>
    <%= render :partial => 'form', :locals => {:f => f} %>
<% end %>

<%= link_to 'Back', exercises_path %>
```

For editing the name of an exercise once it's been added to the system, we'll modify the edit template found in /app/views/exercises/edit.rhtml to look like this:

```
<h1>Editing exercise</h1>

<%= error_messages_for :exercise %>

<% form_for(:exercise, :url => exercise_path(@exercise),
                          :html => { :method => :put }) do |f| %>
    <%= render :partial => 'form', :locals => {:f => f} %>
<% end %>

<%= link_to 'Show', exercise_path(@exercise) %> |
<%= link_to 'Back', exercises_path %>
```

We'll leave the show template (/app/views/exercises/show.rhtml) as it for now, but in the next chapter, we'll look at ways of adding additional value to that view when we add graphing capabilities to our application.

That just leaves us with the task of building our index template (/app/views/exercises/
index.rhtml), which will be the main page for our users to interact with the exercises. First,
we'll want to add some introductory text:

```
<h1>Exercises</h1>
<p>On this page you can create and manage the exercises that you use in your ➥
workouts.</p>
<p>You can also view reports on your progress for each exercises</p>
```

After our introductory text, we're going to want to iterate over the user's list of exercises
(stored in the @exercises instance variable). We could write that loop directly in our index template with something like this:

```
<% for exercise in @exercises %>
  <tr><td><%=h exercise.name %></td></tr>
<% end %>
```

But a cleaner way to do it is to move the row content into a partial and pass that partial the
collection. Let's create a new partial named _exercise.rhtml in /app/views/exercises, and
we'll place the content that we want to display for every exercise in it. We'll want to display the
exercise name and links to the view the exercise (show template), edit the exercise (edit template) and a link that will allow a user to delete the exercise from their list:

```
<tr>
    <td><%=h exercise.name %></td>
    <td><%=link_to image_tag("display.gif", {:title => "View Exercise Details"}),
                                        exercise_path(exercise) %></td>
    <td><%=link_to image_tag("edit_photo.gif", {:title => "Edit Exercise"}),
                                        edit_exercise_path(exercise) %></td>
    <td><%= link_to image_tag("delete_photo.gif", {:title => "Delete Exercise"}),
                                        :url => exercise_path(exercise),
                                        :confirm => 'Are you sure?',
                                        :method => :delete %></td>
</tr>
```

Within our index template, we can render this partial for every exercise in our @exercises
instance variable by calling it like this:

```
<%= render :partial => 'exercise', :collection => @exercises %>
```

Finally, to make things easier for the end user, we'll also include a form to create exercises on the index page, so users can instantly add a new exercise without having to go to yet
another page:

```
<div id="add_exercise">
  <% form_for(:exercise, :url => exercises_path,
                                :html => {:id => 'new_exercise'}) do |f| %>
    <%= render :partial => 'form', :locals => {:f => f} %>
  <% end %>
</div>
```

Once we put all of that together, we'll have an index template that looks like this:

```
<h1>Exercises</h1>
<p>On this page you can create and manage the exercises that you use in ➥
your workouts.</p>
<p>You can also view reports on your progress for each exercises</p>

<table id="exercise_details">
  <tr><th>Name</th></tr>
    <%= render :partial => 'exercise', :collection => @exercises %>
</table>

<br /><br />
<h1>Add a New Exercise</h1>

<div id="add_exercise">
  <% form_for(:exercise, :url => exercises_path,
                              :html => {:id => 'new_exercise'}) do |f| %>
    <%= render :partial => 'form', :locals => {:f => f} %>
  <% end %>
</div>
```

The template renders in a browser as shown in Figure 6-5.

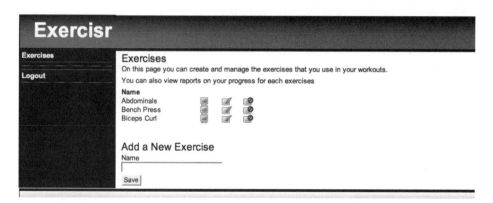

Figure 6-5. *The main index page for our exercises resource*

Now that we have an exercise resource, users need to build a way to record the fact that they worked out on a specific day and capture which exercises they did in each workout, so let's build those processes out now.

The Workout Resource

The next resource we'll build will handle capturing the fact that a user worked out on a specific day. To keep things simple, we'll call this new resource a workout resource. All we'll need to capture at this level is simply the date of the workout and an optional text description of what type of workout it was (e.g, upper body, abdominals, or arms). We'll create this resource like this:

```
ruby script/generate scaffold_resource Workout date:date label:string ➥
user_id:integer
```

```
output omitted for brevity
```

The first thing we need to do with our new scaffold is to remove the automatically generated layout (workout.rhtml) from /app/views/layouts so that it won't override our application layout. Once the layout is removed, we'll run our new migration to add the workouts table to the database:

```
rake db:migrate
```

```
== CreateWorkouts: migrating ======================================
-- create_table(:workouts)
   -> 0.0780s
== CreateWorkouts: migrated (0.0930s) ============================
```

The Workout Model and Associations

With the table added to the database, let's round out the models and associations. Since we built the workout model to capture the user_id, we'll add in a belongs_to :user and basic validation to ensure that we receive a date. Edit our workout model (/app/models/workout.rb) to look like this:

```
class Workout < ActiveRecord::Base
  belongs_to :user
  validates_presence_of :date
end
```

We'll also build out the reciprocal association from the user model (/app/models/user.rb) to add in a has_many :workouts relationship. We'll also pass that association a :dependent => :destroy option to ensure that Rails will delete all associated workout objects in the event that we ever delete a user (so we can avoid leaving orphaned data in the database):

```
has_many :workouts, :dependent => :destroy
```

The Workout Controller

The scaffolding added a new route to our routes file as map.resources :workouts, which we'll leave as is for now, so we can now turn our attention to modifying our workout controller. For the most part, we'll be able to keep the scaffold-generated code; we merely need to add in the before_filter :login_required call to limit access to the page, and by making the same types of modifications that we did in our exercises controller, we can scope the results based on the currently logged in user:

```ruby
class WorkoutsController < ApplicationController
  before_filter :login_required

  # GET /workouts
  # GET /workouts.xml
  def index
    @workouts = current_user.workouts.find(:all, :order => 'date desc',
                                           :limit => 10)

    respond_to do |format|
      format.html # index.rhtml
      format.xml  { render :xml => @workouts.to_xml }
    end
  end

  # GET /workouts/1
  # GET /workouts/1.xml
  def show
    @workout = current_user.workouts.find(params[:id])

    respond_to do |format|
      format.html # show.rhtml
      format.xml  { render :xml => @workout.to_xml }
    end
  end

  # GET /workouts/new
  def new
    @workout = current_user.workouts.build
  end
```

```ruby
# GET /workouts/1;edit
def edit
  @workout = current_user.workouts.find(params[:id])
end

# POST /workouts
# POST /workouts.xml
def create
  @workout = current_user.workouts.build(params[:workout])

  respond_to do |format|
    if @workout.save
      flash[:notice] = 'Workout was successfully created.'
      format.html { redirect_to workout_url(@workout) }
      format.xml  { head :created, :location => workout_url(@workout) }
    else
      format.html { render :action => "new" }
      format.xml  { render :xml => @workout.errors.to_xml }
    end
  end
end

# PUT /workouts/1
# PUT /workouts/1.xml
def update
  @workout = current_user.workouts.find(params[:id])

  respond_to do |format|
    if @workout.update_attributes(params[:workout])
      flash[:notice] = 'Workout was successfully updated.'
      format.html { redirect_to workout_url(@workout) }
      format.xml  { head :ok }
    else
      format.html { render :action => "edit" }
      format.xml  { render :xml => @workout.errors.to_xml }
    end
  end
end

# DELETE /workouts/1
# DELETE /workouts/1.xml
def destroy
  @workout = current_user.workouts.find(params[:id])
  @workout.destroy
```

```
    respond_to do |format|
      format.html { redirect_to workouts_url }
      format.xml  { head :ok }
    end
  end
end
```

Modifying the Views

Our modifications to the workout views will also be very similar to the modifications we did for exercises. We'll move the forms for creating and editing a workout into a partial, which we'll also include on the index page. For iterating over our list of workouts, we'll also use another partial.

So our index template (/app/views/workouts/index.rhtml) will look like this:

```
<h1>Listing workouts</h1>

<table>
  <tr><th>Date</th><th>Label</th></tr>
  <%= render :partial => 'workout', :collection => @workouts %>
</table>
<br />

<h1>Add a New Workout</h1>
<div id="add_workout">
  <% form_for(:workout, :url => workouts_path,
                                :html => {:id => 'new_workout'}) do |f| %>
    <%= render :partial => 'form', :locals => {:f => f} %>
  <% end %>
</div>
```

Of course, before this template will work, we'll need to build those workout and form partials, so let's build those now. The first one that we'll look at is the workout partial, which we'll use to iterate over each workout in the @workouts instance variable.

Create a new file in /app/views/workouts named _workout.rhtml and place the following content in it to display the basic information for the workout and provide links to the show, edit, and delete methods:

```
<tr>
  <td><%= workout.date.to_s(:long) %></td>
  <td><%= workout.label %></td>
  <td>
    <%=link_to image_tag("display.gif", {:title => "View Workout Details"}),
                                    workout_path(workout) %>
  </td>
```

```
<td>
  <%=link_to image_tag("edit_photo.gif", {:title => "Edit Workout Date/Label"}),
                                      edit_workout_path(workout) %>
</td>
<td>
  <%= link_to image_tag("delete_photo.gif", {:title => "Delete Workout"}),
                                  workout_path(workout),
                                  :confirm => 'Are you sure?',
                                  :method => :delete %>
</td>
</tr>
```

The second partial that we're including on the index page is the form that we use to create a new workout. Create a new file in /app/views/workouts/ named _form.rhtml and place the following form content in it:

```
<p>
    <b>Date</b><br />
    <%= f.date_select :date %>
</p>

<p>
    <b>Label</b><br />
    <%= f.text_field :label %>
</p>

<p>
    <%= submit_tag "Save" %>
</p>
```

Now that we have the workout form partial created, we can also utilize it in our edit and create templates in /app/views/workouts. So our show.rhtml template will look like this:

```
<h1>Editing workout</h1>
<%= error_messages_for :workout %>

<% form_for(:workout, :url => workout_path(@workout),
                                    :html => { :method => :put }) do |f| %>
    <%= render :partial => 'form', :locals => {:f => f} %>
<% end %>

<%= link_to 'Show', workout_path(@workout) %> |
<%= link_to 'Back', workouts_path %>
```

And our `new.rhtml` template will look like this:

```
<h1>New workout</h1>
<%= error_messages_for :workout %>

<% form_for(:workout, :url => workouts_path) do |f| %>
   <%= render :partial => 'form', :locals => {:f => f} %>
<% end %>

<%= link_to 'Back', workouts_path %>
```

Finally, now that we have our workout resource built, we can go back to our application layout (/app/views/layouts/application.rhtml) and uncomment the line from the sidebar area that will display the link to the workouts index page:

```
<% if logged_in? %>
  <div class="yui-b sidebar">
    <ul>
      <li><%= link_to 'Exercises', exercises_path %></li>
      <li><%= link_to 'Workouts', workouts_path %></li>
      <li><%# link_to 'Goals', goals_path %></li>
      <li><%= link_to 'Logout', logout_path %></li>
    </ul>
  </div>
<% end %>
```

Capturing Our Workouts

Now that we've built out the process for capturing when a user works out, we need to turn our attention to capturing what the user did at each workout. So after creating a workout, we will need to collect the following information:

- The exercises performed

- The number of sets of each exercise

- The weight or resistance used in each set

- The number of repetitions (i.e., how many times the user was able to perform the exercise) in each set

With those goals clearly in mind, determining our database structure should be fairly obvious. Each row of our table will represent one set of an exercise and capture the workout ID as a foreign key (so it can be associated back to the workout), the exercise ID as a foreign key (to associate it back to an exercise from our exercises resource), the amount of resistance used for the set, and the number of repetitions performed during that set.

So now all we need to do is determine a good name for this resource. It would be good to name this resource "exercises," but we've already used that name to maintain our master list of possible exercises. Another good name might be "sets," since each row in the database should match to a single set that we performed. Unfortunately, that would be a path fraught with pain as the word "set" is a reserved word within Ruby. That eliminates our two most obvious names for this resource. After much mental strain, I came up with the name of "activities," as in each workout we did many activities. With our name and our database structure ready, we'll create the resource like this:

```
ruby script/generate scaffold_resource Activity workout_id:integer ➥
exercise_id:integer resistance:integer repetitions:integer
```

```
output omitted for brevity
```

Once again, we'll need to delete the scaffold-generated layout (/app/views/layouts/activity.rhtml) and run our new migration to add the table to our database:

```
rake db:migrate
```

```
== CreateActivities: migrating =========================
-- create_table(:activities)
   -> 0.0780s
== CreateActivities: migrated (0.0780s) ===================
```

Building Our Activities Model and Associations

The activity model contains foreign keys to our exercise and workout models, so we'll need to include a pair of belongs_to methods in our model, and we'll want to have some basic validations. Our activity model (/app/models/activity.rb) should look like this:

```
class Activity < ActiveRecord::Base
  belongs_to :exercise
  belongs_to :workout
  validates_presence_of :resistance, :repetitions
end
```

We can also modify our workouts model (/app/models/workout.rb) to both recognize that a workout has many activities and to serve as a :through bridge to exercises:

```
class Workout < ActiveRecord::Base
  belongs_to :user
  has_many :activities, :dependent => :destroy
  has_many :exercises, :through => :activities
  validates_presence_of :date
end
```

With those associations we can now pull down the lists of associated activities or exercises for a given workout like this:

```
workout = Workout.find 5
```

```
=> #<Workout:0x14b709c @attributes={"date"=>"2007-01-17", "id"=>"5", ➡
"user_id"=>"2", "label"=>"Back / Biceps"}
```

```
workout.activities
```

```
=> [#<Activity:0x137db04 @attributes={"exercise_id"=>"9", "id"=>"10", ➡
"repetitions"=>"12", "workout_id"=>"5", "resistance"=>"150"}, ➡
#<Activity:0x137d758  @attributes={"exercise_id"=>"9", "id"=>"11", ➡
"repetitions"=>"12", "workout_id"=>"5", "resistance"=>"175"}, ➡
#<Activity:0x137d730 @attributes={"exercise_id"=>"9", "id"=>"12", ➡
"repetitions"=>"12", "workout_id"=>"5", "resistance"=>"180"}]
```

```
workout.exercises
```

```
=> [#<Exercise:0x27615a0 @attributes={"name"=>"Lat Pulldowns", ➡
"exercise_type"=>nil, "id"=>"9", "user_id"=>"2"}, #<Exercise:0x2761578 ➡
@attributes={"name"=>"Lat Pulldowns", "exercise_type"=>nil, "id"=>"9", ➡
"user_id"=>"2"}, #<Exercise:0x2761550 @attributes={"name"=>"Lat Pulldowns", ➡
 "exercise_type"=>nil, "id"=>"9", "user_id"=>"2"}]
```

We can also add an association back to our activities model from within the user model (/app/models/user.rb) by passing through the workouts model:

```
require 'digest/sha1'
class User < ActiveRecord::Base
  # Virtual attribute for the unencrypted password
  attr_accessor :password

  validates_presence_of     :login, :email
  validates_presence_of     :password,                   :if => :password_required?
  validates_presence_of     :password_confirmation,      :if => :password_required?
  validates_length_of       :password, :within => 4..40, :if => :password_required?
  validates_confirmation_of :password,                   :if => :password_required?
  validates_length_of       :login,    :within => 3..40
  validates_length_of       :email,    :within => 3..100
  validates_uniqueness_of   :login, :email, :case_sensitive => false
  before_save :encrypt_password
```

```
has_many :workouts, :dependent => :destroy
has_many :exercises, :dependent => :destroy, :order => 'name asc'
has_many :activities, :through => :workouts
(....remainder of User model ommitted for brevity)
```

Modifying the Activities Routes

Our activities resource is going to require some custom routing rules, though, so edit /config/
routes.rb to look like this:

```
ActionController::Routing::Routes.draw do |map|

  map.resources :workouts do |workout|
    workout.resources :activities
  end

  map.resources :exercises

  map.home '', :controller => 'sessions', :action => 'new'
  map.resources :users, :sessions
  map.welcome '/welcome', :controller => 'sessions', :action => 'welcome'
  map.signup '/signup', :controller => 'users', :action => 'new'
  map.login '/login', :controller => 'sessions', :action => 'new'
  map.logout '/logout', :controller => 'sessions', :action => 'destroy'
end
```

We've modified our workouts and exercises resources to place activities as a nested
resource underneath workouts. This is a way of declaring that a particular resource is only valid
within the subcontext of another resource. Let's use an analogy of parents and children to
hopefully make this clearer.

In a RESTful application, if I wanted to read a list of all parents I could simply issue a GET
request to /parents. While if I wanted to see the details on a specific parent, I might issue a
GET request to /parents/1.

Similarly, if I wanted to see a list of all children, I could use a GET /children request, and to
view the details of a specific child, I would use GET /children/1.

The problem comes in when it doesn't really make sense for me to access the list of children by themselves. What if I don't have any use for the children outside of their relation to
their parents? In that case, what I need is the ability to make my RESTful routing calls on a child
resource in relation to their parent, and that's exactly what nested routing provides us.

When we declare children as a nested resource underneath parents, we can avoid having
to pass additional parameters to our GET /children request to specify the specific parent to
whom we want to limit our request. We can now send a GET request to /parents/1/children to
see a list of all the children that belong to a particular parent or a GET request to /parents/1/
children/2 to see the details on a specific child.

Some other ideas of where a nested route might be used can be found in Table 6-4.

Table 6-4. *Nested Route Examples*

Parent	Child
Goal	Results
Forum	Posts
Article	Comments
Book	Chapters
State	Cities

Obviously, the resource routing capabilities of Rails are pretty exciting stuff, and the ability to easily nest resources like this is extra cool. In our application, we could make a GET request to /workout/1 to view the information on a specific workout and to pull in a list of all the exercises that in that workout would be a simple GET request to /workout/1/activities.

Modifying the Activities Controller

As usual, the first thing we'll need to add is a before_filter :login_required, so we can ensure that only a user who's logged in is able to access the methods in this controller. However, after that, those powerful nested resources changes do come with a small cost for us, as using them means we'll have to make a few more changes to the activities controller (/app/controllers/activities_controller.rb) than we have in previous controllers, primarily in terms of how we scope our finds. In previous controllers, we scoped all of our finds based on the currently logged in user, but in a nested resource, we'll also need to look up the parent resource.

In the case of an activity, we also will want to look up the associated workout to use in scoping our activities. We'll do this by adding a new before_filter and a new protected method to our activities controller. At the top of our controller, we'll add a before_filter like this:

```
before_filter :find_workout
```

And down at the bottom, we'll add a protected method named find_workout, which will look up the workout object and place it in an @workout instance variable:

```
protected
def find_workout
  @workout = current_user.workouts.find(params[:workout_id])
end
```

Now that we have the current user's workout available in the @workout instance variable, we can use it in all of our finds within our seven RESTful methods in the activities controller. So our activities controller will look like this:

```
class ActivitiesController < ApplicationController
  before_filter :login_required
  before_filter :find_workout
```

```ruby
# GET /activities
# GET /activities.xml
def index
  @activities = @workout.activities.find(:all)

  respond_to do |format|
    format.html # index.rhtml
    format.xml  { render :xml => @activities.to_xml }
  end
end

# GET /activities/1
# GET /activities/1.xml
def show
  @activity = @workout.activities.find(params[:id])

  respond_to do |format|
    format.html # show.rhtml
    format.xml  { render :xml => @activity.to_xml }
  end
end

# GET /activities/new
def new
  @activity = @workout.activities.build
end

# GET /activities/1;edit
def edit
  @activity = @workout.activities.find(params[:id])
end

# POST /activities
# POST /activities.xml
def create
  @activity = @workout.activities.build(params[:activity])

  respond_to do |format|
    if @activity.save
      flash[:notice] = 'Activity was successfully created.'
      format.html { redirect_to workout_url(@workout) }
      format.xml  { head :created, :location => activity_url(@workout, @activity)}
```

```ruby
      else
        format.html { render :action => "new" }
        format.xml  { render :xml => @activity.errors.to_xml }
      end
    end
  end

  # PUT /activities/1
  # PUT /activities/1.xml
  def update
    @activity = @workout.activities.find(params[:id])

    respond_to do |format|
      if @activity.update_attributes(params[:activity])
        flash[:notice] = 'Activity was successfully updated.'
        format.html { redirect_to workout_url(@workout) }
        format.xml  { head :ok }
      else
        format.html { render :action => "edit" }
        format.xml  { render :xml => @activity.errors.to_xml }
      end
    end
  end

  # DELETE /activities/1
  # DELETE /activities/1.xml
  def destroy
    @activity = @workout.activities.find(params[:id])
    @activity.destroy

    respond_to do |format|
      format.html { redirect_to activities_url }
      format.xml  { head :ok }
    end
  end

  protected
  def find_workout
    @workout = current_user.workouts.find(params[:workout_id])
  end
end
```

Modifying Activities View Templates

We will modify the view templates for our activities following the pattern we established with previous resources—with one important difference. Recall that because we've established activities as a nested resource, we've essentially said that activities are only valid in the context of their relationship to a workout. This means that whenever we link to an activity resource, we must always provide the workout_id as well. So we need to pass in the @workout instance variable as an additional parameter to all of our activities named route methods, such as

```
new_activity_path(@workout)
edit_activity_path(@workout, @activity)
```

With that knowledge, we can go ahead and modify our view templates for activities. We'll start out by building our two standard partials, the first being the activity partial that will be used to iterate over our list of activities. Create a new file named _activity.rhtml in /app/views/activities with the following links in it:

```
<tr>
  <td><%= activity.exercise.name %></td>
  <td><%= activity.repetitions %></td>
  <td><%= activity.resistance %></td>
  <td>
    <%=link_to image_tag("edit_photo.gif", {:title => "Edit Exercise"}),
                                  edit_activity_path(@workout, activity) %>
  </td>
  <td>
    <%= link_to image_tag("delete_photo.gif", {:title => "Delete Exercise"}),
                              activity_path(@workout, activity),
                              :confirm => 'Are you sure?',
                              :method => :delete %>
  </td>
</tr>
```

Next, we'll create the form partial that we'll use to create a new activity. Create a new file named _form.rhtml in /app/views/activities with the following content:

```
<p>
  <%= f.collection_select :exercise_id, current_user.exercises.find(:all), :id,
                                :name, :prompt => "Select an Exercise" %>
</p>
<p>One set of <%= f.text_field :repetitions %> with ➡
                    <%= f.text_field :resistance %> pounds of resistance</p>
<p>
  <%= submit_tag "Save" %>
</p>
```

We'll modify the edit template (/app/views/activities/edit.rhtml) to utilize our form partial like this:

```
<h1>Editing activity</h1>
<%= error_messages_for :activity %>

<% form_for(:activity, :url => activity_path(@workout, @activity),
                        :html => { :method => :put }) do |f| %>
    <%= render :partial => 'form', :locals => {:f => f} %>
<% end %>

<%= link_to 'Back', workout_path(@workout) %>
```

We'll also modify the index method for activities (/app/views/activities/index.rhtml) like this:

```
<h1>Listing activities</h1>

<table>
    <tr><th>Exercise</th><th>Reps</th><th>Resistance</th></tr>
    <%= render :partial => 'activity', :collection => @activities %>
</table>
<br />

<%= link_to 'New activity', new_activity_path(@workout) %>
```

We'll modify the new template (/app/views/activities/new.rhtml) like this:

```
<h1>New activity</h1>
<%= error_messages_for :activity %>

<% form_for(:activity, :url => activities_path(@workout)) do |f| %>
    <%= render :partial => 'form', :locals => {:f => f} %>
<% end %>

<%= link_to 'Back', workout_path(@workout) %>
```

Finally, we'll change the show template (/app/views/activities/show.rhtml) to look like this:

```
<p>
  <b>Exercise:</b>
  <%=h @activity.exercise.name %>
</p>
```

```
<p>
  <b>Resistance:</b>
  <%=h @activity.resistance %>
</p>

<p>
  <b>Repetitions:</b>
  <%=h @activity.repetitions %>
</p>

<%= link_to 'Edit', edit_activity_path(@workout, @activity) %> |
<%= link_to 'Back', activities_path(@workout) %>
```

Modifying the Show Method for a Workout

Even though we set up all the templates for the activities resource, in reality, we don't want a user to have to navigate to those pages—especially since we've nested activities underneath workouts. What we'll do instead is modify the show template in our workouts resource to serve as the primary interface for an end user to add activities to a workout.

Our first step in doing that is to modify the show method in our workouts controller (/app/controllers/workouts_controller.rb) to also generate an @activities instance variable containing a list of that workout's activities. To avoid doing N+1 queries to pull in the associated exercise name for each activity, we'll load the associated exercise object for each activity using :include => :exercise (you can see the result of this template in Figure 6-6):

```
def show
    @workout = current_user.workouts.find(params[:id])
    @activities = @workout.activities.find(:all, :include => :exercise)

    respond_to do |format|
      format.html # show.rhtml
      format.xml  { render :xml => @workout.to_xml }
    end
  end
```

With the @activities instance variable set, we modify the show template for our workouts (/app/views/workouts/show.rhtml) to render our activity partial to show the exercises that we performed in that workout and the activity form partial to be able to add a new exercise activity to the workout:

```
<h1><%= h @workout.label %> Workout on <%= h @workout.date.to_s(:long) %> </h1>
<table>
    <tr><th>Exercise</th><th>Reps</th><th>Resistance</th></tr>
    <%= render :partial => 'activities/activity', :collection => @activities %>
</table>
```

```
<h3>Add Exercise to this Workout</h3>
<% form_for(:activity, :url => activities_path(@workout)) do |f| %>
   <%= render :partial => 'activities/form', :locals => {:f => f} %>
<% end %>

<%= link_to 'Back', workouts_path %>
```

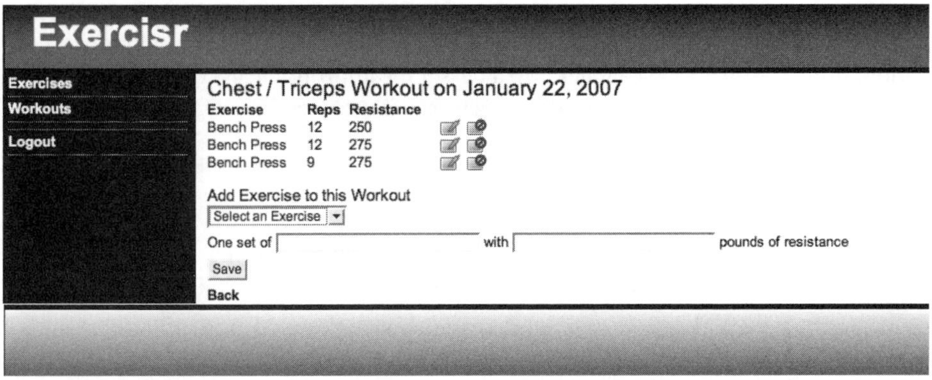

Figure 6-6. *Adding Exercises to a Workout*

Improving the Add Activity Form

The one thing that I really don't like about the current process is that if I realize that I'm missing an exercise in my drop-down list while I'm adding activities to a workout, my only option is to leave the workouts pages and go add my missing exercise back in the exercises section. Now, granted, the more I use the application, the less likely that situation will become, but it is still an irritation that I'd like to avoid if I can.

Fortunately, it is one we can solve with a fairly minor amount of additional code. To start with, let's add a new form field to our activity form partial (/app/views/activities/_form.rhtml) that can be used to capture a new exercise name:

```
<p>
  <%= f.collection_select :exercise_id, current_user.exercises.find(:all), :id,
                                    :name, :prompt => "Select an Exercise" %>
  or add a new exercise:
  <%= f.text_field :new_exercise_name %>
</p>
<p>One set of <%= f.text_field :repetitions %> with ➥
                        <%= f.text_field :resistance %> pounds of resistance</p>
<p>
  <%= submit_tag "Save" %>
</p>
```

Because the fields in this form are supposed to tie back to attributes in an activity model, this would currently generate an error if we tried to render it, since there is no corresponding field in the activities table named `new_exercise_name`. What we need to do is create `new_exercise_name` as a virtual attribute by modifying our activity model (`/app/models/activity.rb`) with the following line:

```
attr_accessor :new_exercise_name
```

Now that we have a way to capture the submitted value in memory, we can simply create a new method in our activity model named `create_exercise_if_submitted`. In this method, we'll call the `create_exercise` method (this method is added to our model by our `belongs_to` association) from a `before_save` callback. We'll pass it the appropriate `user.id` and the `new_exercise_name` virtual attribute to create a new exercise object directly from the activity model. So our activity model will look like this:

```
class Activity < ActiveRecord::Base
  belongs_to :exercise
  belongs_to :workout
  validates_presence_of :resistance, :repetitions

  attr_accessor :new_exercise_name
  before_save :create_exercise_if_submitted

  def create_exercise_if_submitted
    create_exercise(:user_id => workout.user_id, :name => new_exercise_name) ➥
unless new_exercise_name.blank?
  end
end
```

Our new workout view will look like the one shown in Figure 6-7 and will allow a user to either select an exercise from the drop-down list or create a new exercise directly.

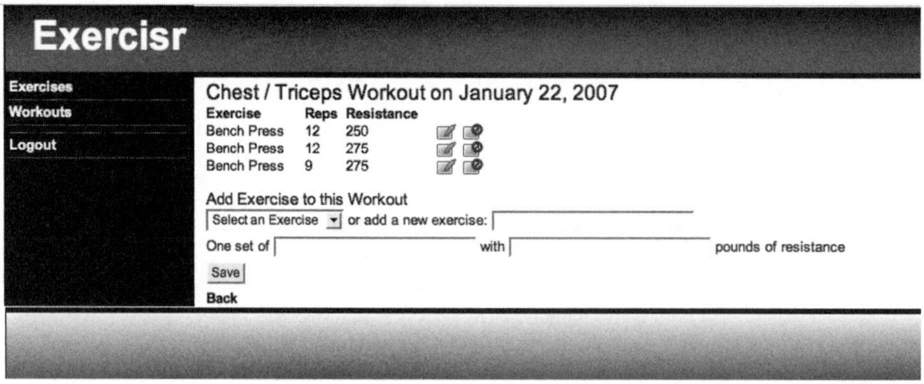

Figure 6-7. *Allowing users to create a new exercise while adding an activity*

Tracking Fitness Goals

The initial planning for this project also included supporting the ability to track general health goals such as weight, blood sugar, and so on. To accomplish this, we'll add yet another resource that we'll name "goals." Attributes for a goals resource would be the name of the goal that we're tracking and the target goal that we're trying to achieve, and we'll give ourselves a little cheat by storing the last result for this goal in the object as well (that way, we can very simply do things like calculate the difference between where we are currently and how much further until we reach our goal). We'll create our goal resource with this command:

```
ruby script/generate scaffold_resource Goal name:string value:decimal ➥
last:decimal user_id:integer
```

```
output omitted for brevity
```

Finally, we need a way to capture our individual results toward reaching our goals. For example, assuming that our goal is tracking our current weight, we'd want a place to capture weekly weigh-in results. We'll name this resource "results." The attributes for a results object would be to know which goal it's associated with, the date of this result, and the value that we're recording. We'll create this resource with this command:

```
ruby script/generate scaffold_resource Result goal_id:integer ➥
date:date value:decimal
```

```
output omitted for brevity
```

And with those few commands, we've just generated a significant portion of our application code to support tracking fitness goals. We can now go manipulate and massage the generated code into working the way that we want it to work. Before we do that though, let's run the migration files that our scaffolding generated to create our database tables.

```
rake db:migrate
```

```
== CreateGoals: migrating ====================================
-- create_table(:goals)
   -> 0.0780s
== CreateGoals: migrated (0.0780s) ===========================
== CreateResults: migrating ==================================
-- create_table(:results)
   -> 0.0780s
== CreateResults: migrated (0.0780s) =========================
```

With our database prepped for use, go ahead and remove the scaffold-generated `goals.rhtml` and `results.rhtml` layout files from `/app/views/layouts/`, and then we can direct our attention to configuring our models with our necessary associations and validations for our application.

Modifying Our Models

Our goals model (`/app/models/goal.rb`) should stay fairly simple for now; we'll associate it with our user model with a `belongs_to` association, add a `has_many` relationship to results, and add in some basic validations:

```
class Goal < ActiveRecord::Base
  belongs_to :user
  has_many :results, :dependent => :destroy
  validates_presence_of :name, :value
end
```

Next, we'll modify our results model (`/app/models/result.rb`) to include a `belongs_to` association with our goal, and we'll add in a basic `validates_presence_of` requirement for the date and value elements:

```
class Result < ActiveRecord::Base
  belongs_to :goal
  validates_presence_of :date, :value
end
```

Finally—we need to configure our user model (`/app/models/user.rb`) with an association back to the Goal mode:

```
has_many:goals
```

Setting Up a Nested Route

Open `/config/routes.rb`, and we'll modify our goals and results resources as a nested resource. Afterward, your `routes.rb` configuration file should look exactly like this:

```
ActionController::Routing::Routes.draw do |map|
  map.resources :goals do |goal|
    goal.resources :results
  end

  map.resources :workouts do |workout|
    workout.resources :activities
  end

  map.resources :exercises

  map.home '', :controller => 'sessions', :action => 'new'
  map.resources :users, :sessions
  map.welcome '/welcome', :controller => 'sessions', :action => 'welcome'
```

```
  map.signup '/signup', :controller => 'users', :action => 'new'
  map.login '/login', :controller => 'sessions', :action => 'new'
  map.logout '/logout', :controller => 'sessions', :action => 'destroy'
end
```

Configuring Our Controllers

The modifications that we need to make to the goals controller should be old hat to you by now. First, we'll need to add the login_required before filter, so we can control access to the methods. Second, we'll need to limit the scope all of our finds to only the currently logged in users goals. Finally, because we're going to display goal results on the show template, we need to generate a list of results in an @results instance variable within the show method.

Edit /app/controllers/goals_controllers.rb to look like this:

```
class GoalsController < ApplicationController
  before_filter :login_required

  # GET /goals
  # GET /goals.xml
  def index
    @goals = current_user.goals.find(:all)

    respond_to do |format|
      format.html # index.rhtml
      format.xml  { render :xml => @goals.to_xml }
    end
  end

  # GET /goals/1
  # GET /goals/1.xml
  def show
    @goal = current_user.goals.find(params[:id])
    @results = @goal.results.find(:all, :order => 'date desc')

    respond_to do |format|
      format.html # show.rhtml
      format.xml  { render :xml => @goal.to_xml }
    end
  end

  # GET /goals/new
  def new
    @goal = current_user.goals.build
  end

  # GET /goals/1;edit
  def edit
    @goal = current_user.goals.find(params[:id])
```

```ruby
end

# POST /goals
# POST /goals.xml
def create
  @goal = current_user.goals.build(params[:goal])

  respond_to do |format|
    if @goal.save
      flash[:notice] = 'Goal was successfully created.'
      format.html { redirect_to goal_url(@goal) }
      format.xml  { head :created, :location => goal_url(@goal) }
    else
      format.html { render :action => "new" }
      format.xml  { render :xml => @goal.errors.to_xml }
    end
  end
end

# PUT /goals/1
# PUT /goals/1.xml
def update
  @goal = current_user.goals.find(params[:id])

  respond_to do |format|
    if @goal.update_attributes(params[:goal])
      flash[:notice] = 'Goal was successfully updated.'
      format.html { redirect_to goal_url(@goal) }
      format.xml  { head :ok }
    else
      format.html { render :action => "edit" }
      format.xml  { render :xml => @goal.errors.to_xml }
    end
  end
end

# DELETE /goals/1
# DELETE /goals/1.xml
def destroy
  @goal = current_user.goals.find(params[:id])
  @goal.destroy

  respond_to do |format|
    format.html { redirect_to goals_url }
    format.xml  { head :ok }
  end
```

```
      end
end
```

Editing the Results Controller

Next, we'll need to modify the results controller (/app/controllers/results_controller.rb);
because it's a nested resource, it will require editing in a similar fashion to the activities
controller.

We'll start out by limiting access with the login_required before filter and then make
another before_filter call to populate the @goals instance variable with the parent goal for
these results. We'll then use that @goals variable to scope our finders within the standard
RESTful methods. Finally, we'll need to modify the redirect destinations for the create, update,
and destroy methods to send the user back to the goal detail page.

In the end, your results_controller.rb should look like this:

```
class ResultsController < ApplicationController
  before_filter :login_required
  before_filter :find_goal

  # GET /results
  # GET /results.xml
  def index
    @results = @goal.results.find(:all)

    respond_to do |format|
      format.html # index.rhtml
      format.xml  { render :xml => @results.to_xml }
    end
  end

  # GET /results/1
  # GET /results/1.xml
  def show
    @result = @goal.results.find(params[:id])

    respond_to do |format|
      format.html # show.rhtml
      format.xml  { render :xml => @result.to_xml }
    end
  end

  # GET /results/new
  def new
    @result = @goal.results.build
  end
```

```ruby
# GET /results/1;edit
def edit
  @result = @goal.results.find(params[:id])
end

# POST /results
# POST /results.xml
def create
  @result = @goal.results.build(params[:result])

  respond_to do |format|
    if @result.save
      flash[:notice] = 'Result was successfully created.'
      format.html { redirect_to goal_url(@goal) }
      format.xml  { head :created, :location => result_url(@result) }
    else
      format.html { render :action => "new" }
      format.xml  { render :xml => @result.errors.to_xml }
    end
  end
end

# PUT /results/1
# PUT /results/1.xml
def update
  @result = @goal.results.find(params[:id])

  respond_to do |format|
    if @result.update_attributes(params[:result])
      flash[:notice] = 'Result was successfully updated.'
      format.html { redirect_to goal_url(@goal) }
      format.xml  { head :ok }
    else
      format.html { render :action => "edit" }
      format.xml  { render :xml => @result.errors.to_xml }
    end
  end
end

# DELETE /results/1
# DELETE /results/1.xml
def destroy
  @result = @goal.results.find(params[:id])
  @result.destroy
```

```
    respond_to do |format|
      format.html { redirect_to goal_url(@goal) }
      format.xml  { head :ok }
    end
  end

  protected
  def find_goal
    @goal = current_user.goals.find(params[:goal_id])
  end
end
```

Configuring Our Views

The first thing we'll need to do is open our layout (/app/views/layouts/application.rhtml)
and uncomment the line in the sidebar div that provides a link to our goals index page:

```
<div class="yui-b sidebar">
  <ul>
    <li><%= link_to 'Exercises', exercises_path %></li>
    <li><%= link_to 'Workouts', workouts_path %></li>
    <li><%= link_to 'Goals', goals_path %></li>
    <li><%= link_to 'Logout', logout_path %></li>
  </ul>
</div>
```

The Goals Views

The modifications we made to our goals templates will be nearly identical to the ones that we made
to the workout templates. So let's jump right in by extracting out a partial named _form.rhtml for
the new and edit pages. Create _form.rhtml in /app/views/goals as follows:

```
<p><label for="goal_name">Name of the Goal:</label><br />
<%= f.text_field :name %></p>

<p><label for="goal_value">Goal to Reach:</label><br />
<%= f.text_field :value %></p>

<p><label for="goal_last">Current Result:</label><br />
<%= f.text_field :last %></p>

<p><%= submit_tag "Save" %></p>
```

Now, we'll modify the edit and new templates to use our new partial. We'll alter /app/
views/goals/edit.rhtml as follows:

```
<h1>Editing goal</h1>
```

```
<%= error_messages_for :goal %>

<% form_for(:goal, :url => goal_path(@goal), :html => { :method => :put }) do |f| %>
    <%= render :partial => 'form', :locals => {:f => f} %>
<% end %>

<%= link_to 'Show', goal_path(@goal) %> |
<%= link_to 'Back', goals_path %>
```

We'll alter /app/view/goals/new.rhtml in a similar fashion:

```
<h1>New goal</h1>

<%= error_messages_for :goal %>

<% form_for(:goal, :url => goals_path) do |f| %>
    <%= render :partial => 'form', :locals => {:f => f} %>
<% end %>

<%= link_to 'Back', goals_path %>
```

Once again, we'll extract out the iteration of our goals from the index page to a partial named _goal.rhtml that we'll use to render the collection. So create a file named _goal.rhtml in /app/views/goals with the following content in it:

```
<tr>
  <td><%=h goal.name %></td>
  <td> </td>
  <td>
    <%= link_to image_tag("display.gif", {:title => "View Report"}),
                                        goal_path(goal) %>
  </td>
  <td>
    <%=link_to image_tag("edit_photo.gif", {:title => "Edit Goal Details"}),
                                        edit_goal_path(goal) %>
  </td>
  <td>
    <%= link_to image_tag("delete_photo.gif", {:title => "Delete Goal"}),
                                        goal_path(goal),
                                        :confirm => 'Are you sure?',
                                        :method => :delete %>
  </td>
</tr>
```

Finally, we'll edit the index page (`/app/views/goals/index.rhtml`) to utilize our two new partials:

```
<h1>Listing goals</h1>
<table>
  <tr><th>Name</th></tr>
    <%= render :partial => 'goal', :collection => @goals %>
</table>

<br />

<h1>Add a New Goal</h1>

<div id="add_goal">
  <% form_for(:goal, :url => goals_path, :html => {:id => 'new_goal'}) do |f| %>
    <%= render :partial => 'form', :locals => {:f => f} %>
  <% end %>
</div>
```

The Results Views

Editing the templates for the results resource will also be old hat to you at this point, so we'll whip through these fairly quickly. First, we'll generate the same two partials that we have for previous resources and modify the standard templates to use them. Second, because this is a nested resource, we'll also modify any of our named routes to pass the @goals variable as well.

Create a new partial named `/app/views/results/_form.rhtml`:

```
<p><label for="">Date</label><br />
<%= f.date_select :date %></p>

<p><label for="">Value</label><br />
<%= f.text_field :value %></p>

<p><%= submit_tag "Save" %></p>
```

Next, we'll create the results partial to display our collection of results. Create `_result.rhtml` in `/app/views/results/`, and place the following content in it:

```
<tr>
    <td><%=h result.date.to_s(:long) %></td>
    <td><%=h result.value %></td>
    <td><%=link_to image_tag("edit_photo.gif", {:title => "Edit Result Details"}),
                            edit_result_path(@goal, result) %></td>
    <td><%= link_to image_tag("delete_photo.gif", {:title => "Delete Result"}),
                            result_path(@goal, result),
                            :confirm => 'Are you sure?',
                            :method => :delete %></td>
</tr>
```

Now, we'll modify our templates to utilize these partials. Edit /app/views/results/new.rhtml to look like this:

```
<h1>New result</h1>
<%= error_messages_for :result %>

<% form_for(:result, :url => results_path(@goal)) do |f| %>
    <%= render :partial => 'form', :locals => {:f => f} %>
<% end %>

<%= link_to 'Back', results_path(@goal) %>
```

And edit /app/views/results/edit.rhtml to look like this:

```
<h1>Editing result</h1>
<%= error_messages_for :result %>

<% form_for(:result, :url => result_path(@goal, @result),
                            :html => { :method => :put }) do |f| %>
    <%= render :partial => 'form', :locals => {:f => f} %>
<% end %>

<%= link_to 'Back to Goal', goal_path(@goal) %>
```

Meanwhile, the results index page (/app/views/results/index.rhtml) should look like this:

```
<h1>Listing results for <%= h @goal.name %></h1>

<table>
  <tr><th>Date</th><th>Value</th></tr>
      <%= render :partial => 'result', :collection => @results %>
</table>

<br />

<%= link_to 'Back to Goal', goal_path(@goal) %>
```

Finally, we can wrap up these templates by building the goals show template, which will utilize our two new results partials. Edit /app/views/goals/show.rhtml to look like this:

```
<h1>Results for <%= h @goal.name %> </h1>
<table>
    <tr><th>Date</th><th>Value</th></tr>
    <%= render :partial => 'results/result', :collection => @results %>
</table>
```

```
<h3>Record New Result for this Goal</h3>
<% form_for(:result, :url => results_path(@goal)) do |f| %>
   <%= render :partial => 'results/form', :locals => {:f => f} %>
<% end %>

<%= link_to 'Back', workouts_path %>
```

Capturing the Last Result

When we defined our goals resource, we included that we wanted it to break normalization by storing the duplicate data of the most recent result, but we haven't built a way to capture that data yet. Thanks to Rails's powerful callback support this is an easy problem to solve, as we can simply add an `after_create` callback in our results model to magically populate the last attribute for the associated goal. Open /app/models/results.rb, and add our functionality like this:

```
class Result < ActiveRecord::Base
  belongs_to :goal
  validates_presence_of :date, :value
  after_create :update_last_result

  def update_last_result
    goal.last = value
    goal.save
  end
end
```

Now, whenever we create a new result, its value will also be populated into the goals last field—incredibly powerful yet seriously easy.

Exploring the RESTful Interface

With that last change, our application is well on its way. We can easily use the HTML interface to create and manage our workouts and goals, but what if we wanted to play around with the XML interface that we gained for free with REST?

The easiest way to do that is to simply append a .xml to the end of any the URL strings in our browser, and Rails will serve us back the XML version of any of any of our resources. You can see the result of pulling back the list of activities in a specific workout at http://localhost:3000/workouts/7/activities.xml in Figure 6-8, but some other example URLs are

- http://localhost:3000/exercises.xml

- http://localhost:3000/exercises/6.xml

- http://localhost:3000/goals.xml

- http://localhost:3000/goals/3/results/1.xml

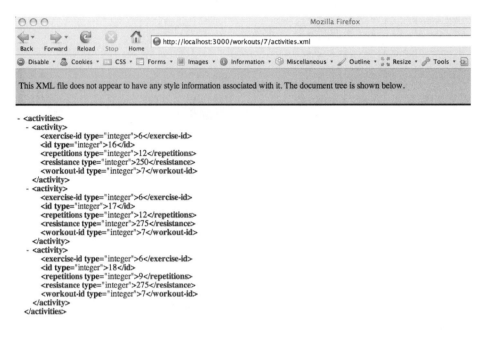

Figure 6-8. *Accessing the XML interface through a browser*

Using CURL to Interact with Our API

The limitation of using a web browser to experiment with your RESTful interface is that you're limited to mainly GET requests, so you can look but can't modify. Another alternative for interacting with your application that will allow you full access to read and modify your data is to use the command line utility curl.

Some common curl options that you should know are

- -X [ ]: Specifies the HTTP verb (i.e., GET, POST, PUT or DELETE)

- -d [ ]: Sets POST variables

- -H [ ]: Sets the content type

- -U [ ]: Sets the username:password for HTTP authentication

Using curl, you could access a list of all the exercises for a user ealameda (obviously, you'll need to use the username and password from the account that you created earlier) with the following command:

```
curl -X GET --Basic -u ealameda:test -H "Accept: text/xml" ➥
http://localhost:3000/exercises
```

```xml
<?xml version="1.0" encoding="UTF-8"?>
<exercises>
  <exercise>
    <exercise-type></exercise-type>
    <id type="integer">8</id>
    <name>Abdominals</name>
    <user-id type="integer">2</user-id>
  </exercise>
  <exercise>
    <exercise-type></exercise-type>
    <id type="integer">6</id>
    <name>Bench Press</name>
    <user-id type="integer">2</user-id>
  </exercise>
  <exercise>
    <exercise-type></exercise-type>
    <id type="integer">7</id>
    <name>Biceps Curl</name>
    <user-id type="integer">2</user-id>
  </exercise>
  <exercise>
    <exercise-type></exercise-type>
    <id type="integer">9</id>
    <name>Lat Pulldowns</name>
    <user-id type="integer">2</user-id>
  </exercise>
  <exercise>
    <exercise-type></exercise-type>
    <id type="integer">10</id>
    <name>Leg Press</name>
    <user-id type="integer">2</user-id>
  </exercise>
</exercises>
```

If you wanted to view the details of a specific exercise, you could simply specify it in the URL:

```
curl -X GET --Basic -u ealameda:test -H "Accept: text/xml" ➥
http://localhost:3000/exercises/6
```

```
<?xml version="1.0" encoding="UTF-8"?>
<exercise>
  <exercise-type></exercise-type>
  <id type="integer">6</id>
  <name>Bench Press</name>
  <user-id type="integer">2</user-id>
</exercise>
```

To create a new goal, however, we'll need to specify that we want to use the HTTP verb POST instead and use the -d parameter to set our post parameters:

```
curl -X POST --Basic -u ealameda:test -d "goal[name]=Daily Calories"
-d "goal[value]=1300" -H "Accept: text/xml" http://localhost:3000/goals
```

Once we've created the new goal, we can verify it's there by viewing the list of goals:

```
curl -X GET --Basic -u ealameda:test -H "Accept: text/xml" ➥
 http://localhost:3000/goals
```

```
<?xml version="1.0" encoding="UTF-8"?>
<goals>
  <goal>
    <id type="integer">3</id>
    <last type="decimal">250.0</last>
    <name>Weight Loss</name>
    <user-id type="integer">2</user-id>
    <value type="decimal">220.0</value>
  </goal>
  <goal>
    <id type="integer">4</id>
    <last type="decimal">110.0</last>
    <name>Blood Sugar (post lunch)</name>
    <user-id type="integer">2</user-id>
    <value type="decimal">100.0</value>
  </goal>
  <goal>
    <id type="integer">5</id>
    <last type="decimal"></last>
    <name>Daily Calories</name>
    <user-id type="integer">2</user-id>
    <value type="decimal">1300.0</value>
  </goal>
</goals>
```

AUTHENTICATION ERRORS?

At this time of this writing, a number of users were complaining of having issues authenticating through RESTful authentication and were proposing a workaround of making the following modifications to the login required method in `/lib/authenticated_system.rb`. Advocates of the modification suggest changing it from this:

```
def login_required
  username, passwd = get_auth_data
  self.current_user ||= User.authenticate(username, passwd) || :false ➥
if username && passwd
  logged_in? && authorized? ? true : access_denied
end
```

to this:

```
def login_required
  username, passwd = get_auth_data
  if self.current_user == :false && username && passwd
    self.current_user = User.authenticate(username, passwd) || :false
  end
  logged_in? && authorized? ? true : access_denied
end
```

You can read more about it at `http://www.railsweenie.com/forums/3/topics/1258` if you encounter similar issues.

Summary

In this chapter, we explored the basics of what RESTful applications are and why there's so much buzz about them within the Rails community. We even built our very first RESTful application in Rails using the `scaffold_resource` generator.

As a result, we now have a web application where we can enter all of our workout results. In the next chapter, we're going to develop another iteration of this application by further enhancing the interface design, integrating reporting capabilities using several popular Ruby graphing libraries, and adding some additional MIME types that can be called through the RESTful interface.

■ ■ ■

## CHAPTER 7

Adding Graphs to Our Application

In the previous chapter, you learned about RESTful development as we built a basic exercise tracking application in Ruby on Rails. Unfortunately, we left one glaring hole in the application—the inability to review our results in a meaningful way. We're going to solve that lack in this chapter, as I'll provide an overview of several graphing libraries that we can utilize from Ruby on Rails and then we'll implement several of them into our application.

Our Next Iteration

Being able to capture our exercise results is a powerful thing but not as powerful as being able to display those results in an attractive line or bar graph so we can visually track our progress over time. Fortunately, we have a number of great options available to us for the creation of attractive graphs and reports. Each solution has its own particular strengths and weaknesses that make each suitable for different needs. In your typical application, you would probably never need more than one of these solutions, but in this chapter, we're going to experiment with loading several of the most popular solutions into our application so that you'll have a bit of experience with each.

Of course, we first need to make sure that you have some data to graph. Since a few weeks have passed since I wrote the previous chapter, I've added several weeks' worth of data to the application. Unfortunately, this was during the holidays when sweets were plentiful and exercise wasn't. So to salvage a little dignity and not show off my holiday five, I've created a sample SQLite 3 database preloaded with data that we'll be using in this chapter that you can obtain from the Source Code/Download link on the Apress web site. Just copy this database in your /db directory over your existing development database, and your application will be loaded with enough data for our needs.

Graphing Options in Rails

Now that we have a database full of sample data to use, let's take a look at our options for creating graphs from our data. Many of these solutions will require that you have ImageMagick and its corresponding Ruby implementation library RMagick installed onto your development machine. See the "Installing RMagick" sidebar for tips on how to add it to your machine if you're missing it.

CSS Graphs

By far, the easiest option that we have available for adding graphs to our application is the CSS Graphs plug-in written by Geoffery Grosenbach (host of the *Ruby on Rails* podcast).

CSS Graphs provides several helper methods for generating pure CSS graphs directly in our view templates; it's based on a design from the Apples to Oranges blog (`http://applestooranges.com/blog/post/css-for-bar-graphs/?id=55`).

Using the CSS Graphs plug-in has the added benefit that it doesn't require the installation of any additional libraries such as RMagick. In addition, since the graphs are rendered on the client side, they have almost zero impact on our server load.

Unfortunately, the ease of the solution brings with it a number of severe limitations:

- It only supports three different types of graphs, all of which are bar graphs.

- You can't display more than one graph on a page.

- The graphs do not support numbers outside the 0–100 range.

- CSS graphs may not display correctly across all possible browser and OS combinations.

- CSS graphs don't print well.

Those limitations aside, if you're looking for a quick and simple way to add a basic bar graph to a page, it just doesn't get much easier than the CSS graphs plug-in.

The CSS graphs plug-in can generate three different types of graphs: bar graphs (see Figure 7-1), horizontal bar graphs (see Figure 7-2), and complex bar graphs (see Figure 7-3).

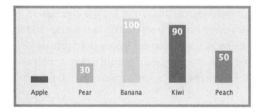

Figure 7-1. *A CSS bar graph*

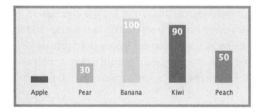

Figure 7-2. *A CSS horizontal bar graph*

Figure 7-3. *A CSS complex bar graph*

Installing CSS Graphs

To install CSS graphs, open a command-line prompt within the root directory of our Exercisr application and run the `plugin install` command:

```
ruby script/plugin install http://topfunky.net/svn/plugins/css_graphs
```

```
+ ./css_graphs/MIT-LICENSE
+ ./css_graphs/README
+ ./css_graphs/Rakefile
+ ./css_graphs/about.yml
+ ./css_graphs/generators/css_graphs/css_graphs_generator.rb
+ ./css_graphs/generators/css_graphs/templates/colorbar.jpg
+ ./css_graphs/generators/css_graphs/templates/g_colorbar.jpg
+ ./css_graphs/generators/css_graphs/templates/g_colorbar2.jpg
+ ./css_graphs/generators/css_graphs/templates/g_marker.gif
+ ./css_graphs/images/colorbar.jpg
+ ./css_graphs/init.rb
+ ./css_graphs/lib/css_graphs_helper.rb
```

That's all we need to do if all we desire are the basic and horizontal bar graphs. However, if we want to use the complex bar graph with its gradient images, we also need to copy the gradient images included with the plug-in into /public/images. Fortunately, the plug-in also includes a generator to handle that task for you. Simply run the following command to have the gradient images copied for you:

```
ruby script/generate css_graphs
```

```
create  public/images/css_graphs
create  public/images/css_graphs/colorbar.jpg
create  public/images/css_graphs/g_colorbar.jpg
create  public/images/css_graphs/g_colorbar2.jpg
create  public/images/css_graphs/g_marker.gif
```

INSTALLING RMAGICK

In order to utilize a number of these graphing libraries, you'll need to have RMagick installed onto your development machine. RMagick is a library that makes it easy to interface Ruby scripts with the ImageMagick suite of programs. ImageMagick is a software suite for the creation and editing of bitmap images such as GIF, JPG, PNG, and so on.

Windows

Windows developers actually have the easiest solution for installing and configuring ImageMagick and RMagick, as they can utilize a gem that includes a complete bundle of everything they need plus the most commonly used libraries. This bundled gem must be downloaded manually, as it's not available from your standard remote gems installation.

You can download the gem from the RMagick page on RubyForge at `http://rubyforge.org/projects/rmagick`. Once you have downloaded the gem, unzip it from its archive, and open a command shell in the directory where you unzipped the gem. From there, you'll install the gem from the command line with the `gem install` command:

```
gem install Rmagick-win32-1.13.0-mswin32.gem
```

After running the `gem install` command, you'll need to run an installation script to complete the installation.

```
ruby postinstall.rb
```

And you're done—easy as pie.

Linux

Most Linux distributions have the ability to install a functional ImageMagick suite via their package management solution. If for some reason your distro doesn't or you just don't like using those packaged solutions, you can download the installation files from the ImageMagick web site. There you'll find binary RPM versions (`http://www.imagemagick.org/script/binary-releases.php`), or if you're the adventurous type, you could choose to download and install from source (`http://www.imagemagick.org/script/install-source.php`).

You'll also want to install a number of development libraries such as `freetype` (for font support) and the support libraries for any graphics formats that you want to be able to support (libjpeg, libpng, libtiff, etc.

Once you have ImageMagick installed, you'll need to download and install the latest version of RMagick (`http://rubyforge.org/projects/rmagick/`) following the directions on that web site.

Mac OS X

If you chose to use Locomotive to build your Mac development system, adding the necessary RMagick support is a simple matter of downloading and installing the RMagick Rails bundle from `http://locomotive.raaum.org/bundles/index.html`; after that, you're good to go.

If you chose to do a manual install of Rails, your best bet is to follow the very detailed instructions written by Dan Benjamin available on his web blog at `http://hivelogic.com/narrative/articles/rmagick_os_x`.

With that simple installation, we now have three graph-generating helper methods available in our view templates:

```
<%= bar_graph [["Apple", 10], ["Pear", 30], ["Banana", 100], ["Kiwi", 90] , ➥
["Peach", 50]] %>
```

```
<%= horizontal_bar_graph [["Stout", 10], ["IPA", 80], ["Pale Ale", 50], ➥
["Milkshake", 30] ]%>
```

```
<%= complex_bar_graph [["Stout", 10], ["IPA", 80], ["Pale Ale", 50], ➥
["Milkshake", 30]] %>
```

Just plug those directly into any view and voilà—instant bar graph!

Sparklines

Another graphing solution that I want to highlight is the Ruby Sparklines library. The sparklines graph format was invented by Edward Tufte to create "data-intense, design-simple, word-sized graphics" that could be embedded inline with text or within small tables. They are designed to bring additional context to numbers within text, as they can show overall trends at a glance.

Figure 7-4. *An example of a sparkline*

The Ruby Sparklines library that we'll be using was originally coded by Dan Nugent as a port of the Python Sparklines web service script and later was converted into a module and modified for Rails integrations by Geoffrey Grosenbach.

Installing Sparklines

The first step in adding Sparklines to our application is to install the Sparklines gem:

```
gem install sparklines
```

```
Bulk updating Gem source index for: http://gems.rubyforge.org
Successfully installed sparklines-0.4.1
Installing ri documentation for sparklines-0.4.1...
Installing RDoc documentation for sparklines-0.4.1...
```

Since Sparklines is an external Ruby library, we need to let Rails know that it needs to load it along with your application by adding the following line to the very bottom of your environment.rb in /config:

```
require 'sparklines'
```

If your application was running, you'll need to restart it, as changes in `environment.rb` are only picked up during the initial startup of Rails.

Next, we need to install the Sparklines generator; the Sparklines generator will automate the process of adding controllers and helpers to our application to simplify using Sparklines from within Rails.

```
gem install sparklines_generator
```

```
Successfully installed sparklines_generator-0.2.2
```

With the generator added, let's go ahead and run it. The Sparklines generator will add a new controller and helper file to our application:

```
ruby script/generate sparklines
```

```
      create  app/controllers/sparklines_controller.rb
      create  app/helpers/sparklines_helper.rb
```

From here, we merely need to include the Sparklines helper within any controller from which we want to use Sparklines:

```
class SampleController < ApplicationController
  before_filter :login_required
  helper :sparklines
```

Implementing Sparklines into Exercisr

It seems that a good place to demonstrate a sparkline is the main page of our goals controller. Adding a simple sparkline at the end of each goal would provide a quick visual summary of our progress. So let's do a sample implementation of sparklines there.

We want to display a summary of our achievements toward our goals, so we'll first need to add the helper to the goals controller (/app/controllers/goals_controller.rb):

```
class GoalsController < ApplicationController
  before_filter :login_required
  helper :sparklines

    (... many lines ommitted...)
end
```

Since we want to graph our sparkline as a progression of our results over time, we need to ensure that we're pulling back those results in the proper order. We want our results to come back to us in a date-descending order rather than by ID (which would be the default). We can set this by adding an order-by conditional onto our association.

Open the Goal model (/app/models/goal.rb), and modify our has_many :results association like this:

```
class Goal < ActiveRecord::Base
  belongs_to :user
  has_many :results, :dependent => :destroy, :order => 'date'
  validates_presence_of :name, :value
end
```

With that, we're ready to actually add a sparkline to our goals, so open the goal partial
(/app/views/goals/_goal.rhtml). Here, we can create a sparkline graphic by adding a new
table cell with a call to the sparkline_tag helper method to our view:

```
<tr>
  <td><%=h goal.name %></td>
  <td> </td>
  <td><%= link_to image_tag("display.gif",
                            {:title => "View Report"}), goal_path(goal) %></td>
  <td><%=link_to image_tag("edit_photo.gif",
                    {:title => "Edit Goal Details"}), edit_goal_path(goal) %></td>
  <td><%= link_to image_tag("delete_photo.gif",
                        {:title => "Delete Goal"}), goal_path(goal),
                      :confirm => 'Are you sure?', :method => :delete %></td>
  <td><%= sparkline_tag (goal.results.collect {|g| g.value}),
                            :type => 'smooth', :height => '20',
                            :step => 4, :line_color => 'black'  %></td>
</tr>
```

When we open the web page at http://localhost:3000/goals, the preceding code should
produce a result similar to Figure 7-5.

ActionController::RoutingError in Goals#index

Showing *app/views/goals/_goal.rhtml* where line **#7** raised:

```
No route matches {:controller=>"sparklines", :line_color=>"black", :height=>"20", :type=>"smooth", :action=>"inde
```

Extracted source (around line **#7**):

```
4:    <td><%= link_to image_tag("display.gif", {:title => "View Report"}), goal_path(goal) %></td>
5:    <td><%=link_to image_tag("edit_photo.gif", {:title => "Edit Goal Details"}), edit_goal_path(goal) %></td>
6:    <td><%= link_to image_tag("delete_photo.gif", {:title => "Delete Goal"}), goal_path(goal), :confirm => 'Are
7:    <td><%= sparkline_tag (goal.results.collect {|g| g.value}), :type => 'smooth', :height => '20', :step => 4,
8:
9: </tr>
```

Figure 7-5. *The sparkline_tag helper blows up*

It blew up! What's up with that? Well, a quick glance at the error output on the page shows us
that it's failing because it can't find the route to the Sparklines controller (/app/controllers/
sparklines_controller.rb) that was added when we ran the Sparklines generator. A quick glance

at this controller reveals that it only has one method—an index method that will return a PNG sparkline graph based on the data it receives in the results parameter:

```
class SparklinesController < ApplicationController
  layout nil

  def index
    # Make array from comma-delimited list of data values
    ary = []
    params['results'].split(',').each do |s|
      ary << s.to_i
    end

    send_data( Sparklines.plot( ary, params ),
                  :disposition => 'inline',
                  :type => 'image/png',
                  :filename => "spark_#{params[:type]}.png" )
  end
end
```

All we need to do is add a route to this controller and action, so open routes.rb in /config, and let's add a route that will point to the index method of the Sparklines controller.

```
ActionController::Routing::Routes.draw do |map|
  map.resources :goals do |goal|
    goal.resources :results
  end

  map.resources :workouts do |workout|
    workout.resources :activities
  end

  map.resources :exercises

  map.home '', :controller => 'sessions', :action => 'new'
  map.resources :users, :sessions
  map.welcome '/welcome', :controller => 'sessions', :action => 'welcome'
  map.signup '/signup', :controller => 'users', :action => 'new'
  map.login '/login', :controller => 'sessions', :action => 'new'
  map.logout '/logout', :controller => 'sessions', :action => 'destroy'
  map.connect '/sparklines', :controller => 'sparklines', :action => 'index'
end
```

Alternatively, we could also have solved this issue by simply re-adding the map.connect ':controller/:action/:id' default route that we removed last chapter, but I prefer to avoid having that catch-all route when I'm striving to build a pure RESTful application. So with our new route added to our application, our sparklines should be working now. We can reload our goals again and see something similar to Figure 7-6.

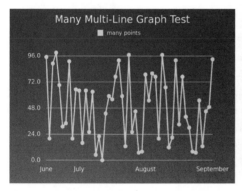

Figure 7-6. *Adding a sparkline to our goals*

Gruff Graphs

Another library written by Geoffrey Grosenbach is the Gruff graphing library for Ruby, which supports the creation of a wide variety of graphs including line, bar, pie, and area graphs. Each of the graphs is highly customizable, as you can specify colors, background images, and even fonts.

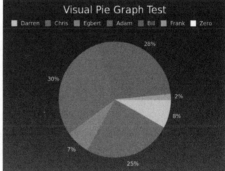

Figure 7-7. *Sample Gruff graphs*

Installing Gruff

Gruff uses RMagick to generate its graphs, so you'll need to ensure that it has been installed and configured correctly on your system.

Our first step towards creating graphs with Gruff is to install the Gruff gem:

```
gem install gruff
```

```
Bulk updating Gem source index for: http://gems.rubyforge.org
Successfully installed gruff-0.2.8
Installing ri documentation for gruff-0.2.8...
Installing RDoc documentation for gruff-0.2.8...
```

Next, we need to add the following line to the very bottom of our environment.rb in /config to let Rails know it needs to load Gruff when it starts up:

```
require 'gruff'
```

Once we restart our web server to load in our new environment.rb, we'll be all set to use Gruff graphs in our application.

Implementing a Gruff Graph

We've already added a summary view of our goal results, but let's take it a step further and add in a larger, detailed graph that a user could view or even save. The obvious place to add this graph would be in the goals show template, so we'll add it there. Open show.rhtml in /app/ views/goals/, and you'll see that currently the page looks like this:

```
<h1><%=h @goal.name %></h1>
<p>
  <b>Goal:</b>
  <%=h @goal.value %>
</p>

<p>
  <b>Current:</b>
  <%=h @goal.last %>
</p>

<%= link_to 'Back', goals_path %>
```

The easiest way to add a graph into this existing page would be to embed a request to generate the graph within an image tag on the page. Let's add that—while we're in there, we'll also remove the tag to display the last recorded value of the goal, since the graph will now be showing that. So your show.rhtml should now look like this:

```
<h1><%=h @goal.name %></h1>
<p>
  <b>Goal:</b>
  <%=h @goal.value %>
</p>

<p>
  <img src="<%= url_for(:action => "report",  :id => @goal.id) %>" />
</p>

<%= link_to 'Back', goals_path %>
```

Adding Member Routes to a REST Resource

Unfortunately, that report request will fail, since we have neither a report method in the goals controller nor any routing configured to direct a request to that method yet.

Remember that the map.resource command in our routes configuration created named routes for all of our standard methods (index, show, new, edit, create, update, and destroy). But what do we do when we need to break convention and introduce a new method on top of those standard ones? Fortunately, this is very easy to do by adding a member route onto our goals route. Open `routes.rb` in /config, and add a member route like this:

```
ActionController::Routing::Routes.draw do |map|
  map.resources :goals, :member => {:report => :get} do |goal|
    goal.resources :results
  end
(...lines omitted...)
```

That single command informs our routing that, within the goals controller, there is also a method named `report` that we want to be able to route to, and that requests to that method should use the HTTP verb of GET. It also introduces a new set of named routes to make it easy to link to that new resource method. So let's go ahead and modify /app/views/goals/show.rhtml to clean up our image tag to use the new named route:

```
<h1><%=h @goal.name %></h1>
<p>
  <b>Goal:</b>
  <%=h @goal.value %>
</p>

<p>
  <img src="<%= report_goal_url %>" />
</p>

<%= link_to 'Back', goals_path %>
```

Creating the Graph

Now that we have our view built, all that's left is the simple matter of adding a `report` method to the goals controller (/app/controllers/goals_controller.rb). Within that method, we can create a Gruff graph by instantiating a new object of the graph type that want to build such as this:

```
g = Gruff::Line.new
```

Once we have a new Gruff object, we can set attributes on it like this:

```
g.title = "Simpson Family Popularity"
```

and populate the graph with data like this:

```
g.data("Homer", [75, 85, 83, 90, 85, 94])
g.data("Marge", [40, 65, 57, 49, 28, 59])
g.data("Bart", [90, 87, 83, 80, 75, 70])
g.labels = {0 => '2003', 2 => '2004', 4 => '2005'}
```

Finally, we can convert the newly created graph object to an actual graph by choosing from a pair of methods. If we wanted to save the graph to the server's local file system, we could call the `write` method on the graph object to save it as a PNG image.

```
g.write('gruff.png')
```

For our needs, though, we don't need to store these graphs on the local file system, so instead, we can call the to_blob method, which will return the graph data back as a binary blob that we can then send directly back to the web browser using Rails send_data method. The send_data method supports a number of options:

- :filename: Specifies the file name that we should send to the browser

- :type: Specifies an HTTP content type; default is application/octet-stream

- :disposition: Specifies whether the file will be shown inline or downloaded as an attachment, which is the default

- :status: Specifies the status code used with the response; default is 200

We could send our graph back to the browser directly with a send_data call like this:

```
send_data(g.to_blob, :disposition => 'inline', :type => 'image/png', ➥
:filename => "gruff.png")
```

If we were to run this code within a controller, it would generate a graph like the one shown in Figure 7-8.

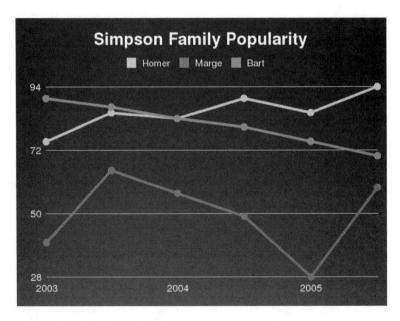

Figure 7-8. *A Gruff line graph*

But what if we wanted to render that graph into a different graph format? Well, that's just a simple matter of changing the object type of the graph that we instantiated.

By merely changing the object we instantiate to this:

```
g = Gruff::Pie.new
```

we get the pie chart result shown in Figure 7-9.

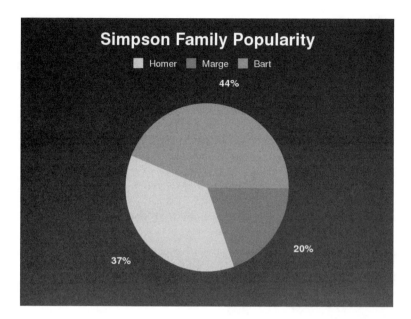

Figure 7-9. *A Gruff pie chart*

Or we'd get the graph in Figure 7-10 if we changed it to this:

```
g = Gruff::Area.new
```

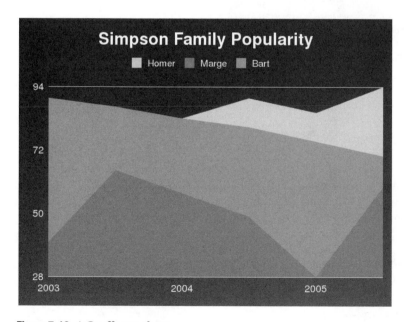

Figure 7-10. *A Gruff area chart*

Pretty easy, huh?

So let's go ahead build out the `report` method in our goals controller to respond to a request for a goals report:

```
def report
    g = Gruff::Line.new(400)
    goal = current_user.goals.find(params[:id])
    results = goal.results.collect {|r| r.value}
    g.title  = "#{goal.name} to date"
    g.data("#{goal.name}", results)
    send_data(g.to_blob, :disposition => 'inline', :type => 'image/png', ➥
:filename => "gruff.png")
  end
```

Load our new show page in the application, and you should see something like Figure 7-11.

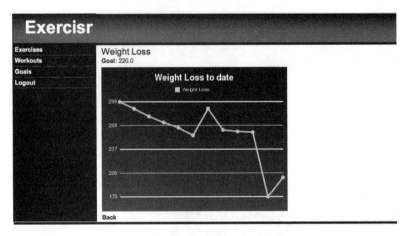

Figure 7-11. *A Gruff graph of weight loss*

A RESTful Change

Now, that's a perfectly workable solution, but the purist in me sure hates that it required us to muck up our routes with a new member route. While it's always acceptable to add a member route, we should always ask ourselves if it's really necessary. Is there a way we could provide the same response with our existing methods or by adding a new controller?

In this case, yes, we can. When you really think about it, our graph isn't really new data—it's just a different representation of a goals result data, an image representation. As we discussed in the last chapter, Rails supports sending different content for the same request through the `responds_to` method. So rather than defining a new method to gather this data in a visual format, it would be a much better solution to simply define this graph as a different format for a goal's results.

Defining a Custom MIME Type

The first step is to identify the format request that we need to respond to. Since we configured Gruff to send back the graph as a PNG, we'll add the PNG image format into the list of possible

MIME types that our Rails application will support. Open `environment.rb` in `/config`, and add the following line to the bottom:

```
(...lines omitted...)
# Add new mime types for use in respond_to blocks:
# Mime::Type.register "text/richtext", :rtf
# Mime::Type.register "application/x-mobile", :mobile
Mime::Type.register "image/png", :png


# Include your application configuration below
require 'sparklines'
require 'gruff'
```

Now that we've registered this MIME type with our application, we'll need to restart the application, since changes to `environment.rb` aren't picked up automatically.

Responding to PNG

Now that Rails has been informed that it should respond to requests for PNG files, we can configure our results controller to respond to a request for a PNG request by moving the report method code there. So let's go ahead and add PNG as a potential response in the show method of the goals controller and move our Gruff code out of the `report` method in the goals controller and into the index method of the results controller (`/app/controllers/results_controller.rb`).

```
def index
    @results = @goal.results.find(:all)

    respond_to do |format|
      format.html # index.rhtml
      format.xml  { render :xml => @results.to_xml }
      format.png  {
                    g = Gruff::Line.new(400, false)
                    results = @goal.results.collect {|r| r.value}
                    g.title  = "#{@goal.name} to date"
                    g.data("#{@goal.name}", results)
                    send_data(g.to_blob, :disposition => 'inline',
                                         :type => 'image/png',
                                         :filename => "gruff.png")
                  }
    end
  end
```

Since we've changed where the graph is being created, we also need to change the destination of our `image_tag` method in the goals show template (`/app/views/goals/show.rhtml`) so that it requests the PNG format from the results controller by calling `formatted_results_path` instead. With this change, we've now kept our application routes nice, clean, and restful.

```
<%= image_tag formatted_results_path(@goal, :png) %>
```

At this point, you can go ahead and remove the report member route from our routes configuration (/config/routes.rb) and the report method from our goals controller (/app/controllers/goals_controller.rb), which we originally added to build our graph.

Scruffy

A nice alternative to the Gruff library is a Ruby library developed by Brasten Sager by the name of Scruffy. Rather than utilizing RMagick to generate its graphs as Gruff does, Scruffy utilizes SVG. SVG stands for Scalable Vector Graphics and is an XML-based markup language for describing vector graphics. Vector graphics have a number of advantages over bitmap images, but the two most important ones for our application are these:

- They can be scaled to virtually any size with no degradation.

- They look wonderful in print.

Utilizing Scruffy within our projects is remarkably similar to using the Gruff graphs, as once again our first step is to install the Scruffy gem:

```
gem install scruffy
```

```
Successfully installed scruffy-0.2.2
Installing ri documentation for scruffy-0.2.2...
Installing RDoc documentation for scruffy-0.2.2...
```

Next, we include it in our Rails project by adding it to the bottom of config/environment.rb:

```
# Include your application configuration below
require 'sparklines'
require 'gruff'
require 'scruffy'
```

We start to see some really interesting differences between Scruffy and Gruff, though, in how we actually build a new graph. Rather than being limited to a single graph type, as we were in Gruff graphs, Scruffy takes a very different approach. In Scruffy, we instantiate a generic graph object, which can be thought of us as a blank canvas that we will be drawing our graphs on.

```
graph = Scruffy::Graph.new
```

With the graph object instantiated, we can then set attributes much like we did with Gruff graphs:

```
def graph.title = "#{goal.name} to date"
```

However, to draw our graphs, we'll add individual graphs to our graph within a block.

```
graph.add :stacked do |stacked|
    stacked.add :line, '', results
end
```

This is an extremely powerful approach, as we can now mix and match our graphs together into whatever formats make sense for our data. Once we've passed in the data that we want and set all of our attributes, we can create our graph with a simple render call:

```
graph.render
```

That will generate a 600 × 400 SVG graph for us. Unfortunately, because web browser support for SVG is still playing catch-up and is currently quite lacking, it's best to have the SVG rasterized into a bitmap image that won't give us any issues when displayed in a browser. That's easily accomplished by specifying the format for rendering the graph:

```
graph.render(:width => 400, :as => 'JPG')
```

Scruffy supports outputting our graphs into any format that RMagick supports.

Implementing a Scruffy Graph

With that understanding under our belts, we can convert the index method in our results controller to utilize Scruffy instead of Gruff graphs for serving up a PNG graph of our goals' results:

```
# GET /results
# GET /results.xml
def index
  @results = @goal.results.find(:all)

  respond_to do |format|
    format.html # index.rhtml
    format.xml  { render :xml => @results.to_xml }
    format.png {
              graph = Scruffy::Graph.new
              results = @goal.results.collect {|r| r.value}
              graph.add :stacked, 'Weight' do |stacked|
                stacked.add :line, '', results
              end
              send_data(graph.render(:width => 700, :as => 'PNG'))
            }
  end
end
```

And you can see the output in Figure 7-12.

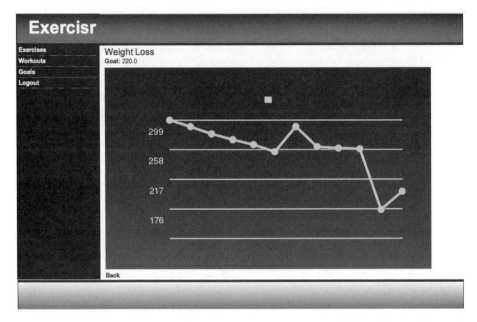

Figure 7-12. *A Scruffy graph of our weight*

Ziya

A relative newcomer to the Rails graphing solutions, Ziya is a solution that has gained a lot of acceptance in a short period of time. Ziya takes a completely different approach to graphs by utilizing the open source XML/SWF charts library (http://www.maani.us/xml_charts/) to build them. This allows us to move the rendering of our graphs to the client side while adding a significant number of "wow" features that we can't get in the previous solutions, such as animated graphs and making data elements on the graph clickable.

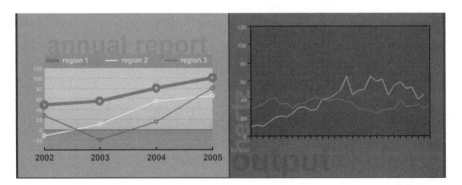

Figure 7-13. *Sample graphs from Ziya*

To begin the process of implementing Ziya graphs, install the plug-in:

```
ruby script/plugin install svn://rubyforge.org/var/svn/liquidrail/plugins/ziya/trunk
```

```
A    /Users/darkel/web/exercise/vendor/plugins/ziya
A    /Users/darkel/web/exercise/vendor/plugins/ziya/test
A    /Users/darkel/web/exercise/vendor/plugins/ziya/test/prefs
(............pages and pages of output deleted .................)
A    /Users/darkel/web/exercise/vendor/plugins/ziya/README
Exported revision 240.
>>> Copying Ziya charts to /Users/darkel/web/exercise/vendor/plugins/➥
ziya/../../../public directory...
>>> Copying Ziya styles to /Users/darkel/web/exercise/vendor/plugins/➥
ziya/../../../public/charts
```

With the plug-in installed, after we configure our controller, we'll be able to insert a Ziya graph into any of our views with the ziya_chart helper method:

```
<%= ziya_chart( url_for( :controller => 'blee', :action => 'refresh_my_graph' ),
                         :id => 'my_chart', :bgcolor => "transparent",
                         :width => 400, :height => 250 ) %>
```

The ziya_chart helper method requires that we pass a URL, along with a number of optional parameters:

- :id: The ID that will be set on the flash object; defaults to ziya_chart.

- :source_name: The controller and method that will generate the graph.

- :bgcolor: The background color of the Ziya graph; defaults to 00ff00.

- :align: Defaults to left. At the time of this writing, this option doesn't appear to have any effect.

- :class: At the time of this writing, this option doesn't appear to have any effect.

- :swf_path: Allows you to override where Ziya should look for the SWF files, in case you moved them to a new location. By default, they're installed in /public/charts.

- :wmode: Allows you to control the window mode of the Flash movie. Valid options are window, opaque, and transparent; defaults to transparent.

- :timeout: Allows you to override the amount of time the request should wait for a server request; defaults to nil.

- :cache: Added to help in some issues where Internet Explorer 6 displayed the charts in the middle of the canvas. If set to true, this option forces the browser to refresh the URL; defaults to false.

- :style: At the time of this writing, this option doesn't appear to have any effect.

- :width: The width of the Ziya graph on the page; defaults to 400. Alternatively, this could be set by passing it as :size => "400x300".

- :height: The height of the Ziya graph on the page; defaults to 300. Alternatively, this could be set by passing it as :size => "400x300".

Of course, to keep things RESTful, we'll first want to set up our application to recognize a request for a Flash file format (.swf). That way, we won't have to add any additional methods to our controller or our routes, and we'll be able to use a named route to request a Ziya graph. So open /config/environment.rb, and let's add the necessary MIME type extension for Flash movies near the bottom:

```
# Add new mime types for use in respond_to blocks:
# Mime::Type.register "text/richtext", :rtf
# Mime::Type.register "application/x-mobile", :mobile
Mime::Type.register "image/png", :png
Mime::Type.register "application/x-shockwave-flash", :swf


# Include your application configuration below
require 'sparklines'
require 'gruff'
require 'scruffy'
```

A quick restart of our web server to load the new environment.rb configuration file, and we're set to begin adding Ziya graphs to our controllers. Up to this point, we've been demonstrating all of our graphs from within the goals controller. However, for the Ziya graphs, let's try something different by graphing our exercise results instead.

Open our exercises controller (/app/controllers/exercises_controller.rb), and add Ziya to this controller. We do that by first requiring the Ziya library and then including it within our controller to keep its scope local:

```
require 'ziya'
class ExercisesController < ApplicationController
  include Ziya
  before_filter :login_required
  (...lines omitted...)
end
```

With Ziya added to our exercises controller, let's take a quick look at how we build a Ziya graph before we implement one. Within the controller, we instantiate a Ziya chart by creating a new object of the graph type that we wish to create:

```
graph = Ziya::Charts::Bar.new(nil, "My Cool Graph", 'bar_chart')
```

This object takes three optional parameters:

- License: XML/SWF is free to download and use, but the unlicensed version does have a few limitations; for example, clicking a chart will take the user to the XML/SWF charts homepage. You can purchase a license for your application from their page and place the license here to eliminate that.

- Chart Name: This is the name of your chart.

- Chart_id: This is a YAML-based configuration file stored in /public/charts that we can use to radically customize our graph. We'll look into this shortly.

Ziya supports a very large number of possible charts that you can create such as bar, line, pie, area, and stacked charts as well as 3-D graphs. The best place to learn about all the possible options is at the online Rdocs at http://ziya.liquidrail.com/rdoc/index.html.

With an instantiated chart object named graph, we can add our data and legends using the add method:

```
graph.add( :axis_category_text, [ "Dog", "Cat", "Rat"] )
graph.add( :series, "Series A", [10, -20, 30] )
```

There are a number of things that we can add to our graphs, such as

- :axis_category_text: This is an array of strings that will be used for the x and y axis ticks. You must set this parameter for every graph.

- :series: Use this to define the series name and chart's data points. The series name will be displayed in the chart legend. It is required that you have at least one of these defined per chart.

- :axis_value_text: This array of strings represents the ticks on the x and y axes that are used on the opposite side of the axis_category_text tags.

- :theme: This parameter allows you to specify a custom theme to use.

Next, we'll return the XML representation of our graph data back to the Flash movie with a render :xml call:

```
render :xml => graph.to_xml
```

In the next step, we need to add a format.swf call to the show method of our exercises_controller (/app/controllers/exercises_controller_rb):

```
# GET /exercises/1
# GET /exercises/1.xml
def show
  @exercise = current_user.exercises.find(params[:id])
  respond_to do |format|
    format.html # show.rhtml
    format.xml  { render :xml => @exercise.to_xml }
    format.swf  { }
  end
end
```

Now, within that `format.swf` block, we're going to want to generate the data necessary for our report, build the graph object, and render it as XML. Coming up with a good way to evenly show the results of each time we did an exercise, like the bench press, can be challenging when you take into account the variations that can occur between sets. In one set, you might lift 200 pounds 12 times, so you up the resistance for the next set to 250 and only lift it 8 times. What makes sense for me is to calculate the total weight lifted by multiplying the amount of resistance by the number of times it was lifted. In the examples I just listed, that would be 2,400 pounds and 2,000 pounds respectively. This gives us a nice even number that we can use to compare workouts.

Within our `show` method, we've already grabbed the exercise that we're interested in within the `@exercise` instance variable. So grabbing a collection of all of the times we performed that exercise is a simple matter of calling `@exercise.activities`. However, what we need is to extract the data that we care about for our report from that collection. We can do that through the use of Ruby's `collect` method, which, when called on a collection, will return a new array containing the results of running a block on each element within the collection. To create an array of the total weight lifted, we simply call this:

```
total_weight = @exercise.activities.collect {|e| e.repetitions * e.resistance}
```

Next, we'll want to gather an array of the dates of those workouts for populating our axes' ticks; we'll do that using the `collect` method again:

```
workout_dates = @exercise.activities.collect {|e| e.workout.date.to_s}
```

With the methods that we'll use to gather our exercise results, we can complete the `show` method like this:

```
# GET /exercises/1
# GET /exercises/1.xml
def show
  @exercise = current_user.exercises.find(params[:id])
  respond_to do |format|
    format.html # show.rhtml
    format.xml  { render :xml => @exercise.to_xml }
    format.swf  {
      total_weight =@exercise.activities.collect {|e| e.repetitions * e.resistance}
      workout_dates = @exercise.activities.collect {|e| e.workout.date.to_s}
      chart = Ziya::Charts::Bar.new
      chart.add( :series, "Total Weight Per Set", total_weight)
      chart.add( :axis_category_text, workout_dates)
      render :xml => chart.to_xml
    }
  end
end
```

At this point, all we need to do is modify the show template for our exercises (/app/views/exercises/show.rthml) to call our Ziya graph, and we'll be rewarded with a graph like the one shown in Figure 7-14:

```
<p>
  <b>Name:</b>
  <%=h @exercise.name %>
</p>
<p>
  <%= ziya_chart( formatted_exercise_path(@exercise, :swf),
                        :id => 'my_chart', :bgcolor => "transparent",
                        :width => 400, :height => 250, :align => 'center' ) %>
</p>
<%= link_to 'Back', exercises_path %>
```

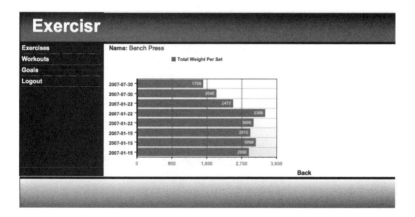

Figure 7-14. *Exercises graphed by Ziya*

That's nice and all, but it is a little bland for something as dynamic as a Flash-based graph. Fortunately, we don't have to settle for this. If you recall, there are a number of options that we can pass when we instantiate the chart object, including a YAML-based configuration file that we could use to customize our graph. So let's spice up our graph a little by building a custom YAML configuration for it.

The first step will be to change the chart instantiation in our show method to call a new YAML file that we'll name my_bar_chart.

```
chart = Ziya::Charts::Bar.new(nil, "", 'my_bar_chart')
```

That small change means that the method will now look for a YAML file named my_bar_chart.yml in /public/charts/themes/default/ when it instantiates the new Ziya graph. If you look in that directory, you'll see that there are already a set of YAML files in there, representing many of our basic chart types. Let's go ahead and open `bar_chart.yml`, as we'll use that as our base. Currently, it contains the following content:

```
<%= chart :bar %>
  <%=component :chart_border %>
    left_thickness:    3
```

Nothing too fancy—it just sets a chart type for this file and sets the thickness of the left border using a chart border component. Save this file in the `/public/charts/themes/default/` directory with the new name of `my_bar_chart`, and populate it with some more interesting configuration options to spice things up a bit:

```
<%= chart :bar %>

   # Set default chart border
  <%=component :chart_border%>
    left_thickness:    3
    bottom_thickness:  3
    top_thickness:     3
    right_thickness:   3

  <%=component :chart_transition %>
    type: zoom
    duration: 2

  <%=component :series_color%>
    colors:            333333,f8af68

   # Set y axis styles
  <%=component :axis_category%>
    color:             ff0000
    skip:              0
    font:              arial
    bold:              true
    size:              10
    alpha:             90
    orientation:       diagonal_up

   # Set x/y axis ticks color
  <%=component :axis_ticks%>
    value_ticks:       true
    category_ticks:    true
    major_thickness:   1
    major_color:       54544c
    minor_thickness:   1
    minor_color:       a19d91
    minor_count:       2
```

```
# Set chart background color
<%=component :chart_rect%>
   x:                 60
   y:                 35
   width:             300
   height:            195
   positive_color:    ff9900
   positive_alpha:    50
   negative_color:    f88868
   negative_alpha:    40

# Set horizontal grid color
<%=component :chart_grid_h%>
   thickness:         1
   color:             000000
   alpha:             7
   type:              solid

# Set vertical grid color
<%=component :chart_grid_v%>
   thickness:         1
   color:             000000
   alpha:             7
   type:              solid


# Set legend foreground color
<%=component :legend_label%>
   color:             000000
   size:              12
   layout:            horizontal
   bullet:            circle
   font:              arial
   bold:              true
   alpha:             75

# Set legend background color
<%=component :legend_rect%>
   x:                 60
   y:                 0
   margin:            10
   fill_color:        FF9900
   fill_alpha:        80
   line_color:        000000
   line_alpha:        50
   line_thickness:    1
```

Save the files and refresh our page; you should see the animated chart shown in Figure 7-15.

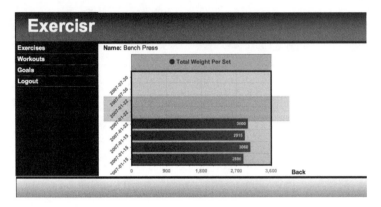

Figure 7-15. *Our animated, custom Ziya graph*

Summary

In this chapter, you learned about expanding our first RESTful application with new reporting features. Along the way, we explored a number of options that are available for producing graphs and implemented several of them within our application.

To integrate those graphs into our applications, we discussed how to add a custom MIME type to our application and set an existing method to respond to that new file type. You also learned how to expand generated route resources to include your own custom methods beyond the default CRUD operations.

■ ■ ■

## CHAPTER 8

Enhancing Exercisr

In this project we explored the exciting (and fun) world of building RESTful web applications in Rails as we put together a basic workout tracking application. To enhance the application we also added in a number of graphing libraries and discussed ways to keep our application RESTful even while supporting and displaying multimedia content. However, it's time again for you to enhance your own learning by continuing development on this application yourself. Below are a number of ideas of things that I would do as my next steps in development.

Add RJS to the Interface

One aspect of RESTful interfaces that we didn't cover in this project is using RJS actions to provide AJAX functionality. To be honest, in my first draft of the project, I actually put a fair amount of RJS into the Exercisr application; I decided to rip it all out, because after I was done, I realized that it was all too gimmicky and actually detracted from the simplicity of the application. So you do need to take caution if you choose to add AJAX functionality.

Calling an RJS template within a RESTful interface is a simple matter of adding a `format.js` call within the `respond_to` block of any controller like this:

```
def index
  @goals = current_user.goals.find(:all)

  respond_to do |format|
    format.html
    format.xml  { render :xml => @goals.to_xml }
    format.js
  end
end
```

Doing so will cause an AJAX request to look for an `index.rjs` template to render in response to this call, so as you can see, adding RJS to our application is a simple matter. Can you think of any places where AJAX might be useful (such as when adding exercises to a workout)?

Create a Calendar Showing When You Worked Out

Using the same calendar plug-in that we discussed in the Monkey Task exercises, you could add a useful calendar view that would mark each day of the month on which a user performed a workout.

Keeping track of your workouts builds a psychological motivation to keep working out, as after a few days, a user will build up a chain of days and will want to keep working out to avoid breaking the chain. For more information on this method of motivation (which is credited to Jerry Seinfeld), check out the blog post at `http://lifehacker.com/software/motivation/jerry-seinfelds-productivity-secret-281626.php`.

Cache Reports

While generating our report graphs on demand is nice, it's a task that is also a bit CPU intensive for each page view, especially when you consider how rarely the underlying data changes. There are a number of ways you could solve this. For one, you could explore caching, as we will do in Chapters 12 and 13. You could also create an external process to generate any necessary reports on a scheduled basis.

Make the Home Page RESTful

Currently, our application is fairly clean. However, we did cheat a little by generating our home page as a welcome method within the sessions controller. This is passable, but of course, not a very beautiful solution, as it undermines some of our ideals. Why don't you go ahead and create a new default controller and move this method over there as the `index` method so we can maintain our RESTful ideals?

Develop More Graphs

In Chapter 7, we explored some sample implementations of a number of different graphing libraries. Why not spend some time building some additional graphs with one or two of the graphing libraries? You could build additional views of our exercises, show the average weight lifted per workout, or provide a graph detailing a specific workout or exercise within a workout. The idea is to get a good feel for how each of the libraries work and what you can build with them, so that the next time you have a need to build graphs in an application, you're working from experience.

Fat Models / Skinny Controllers

We have a little bit of work to do if we want to get our code to the ideal of having our logic in our models and not in the controllers (like we discussed in Chapter 5). For example, to build a graph for our goal results, we built the index method in our results controller (/app/controllers/results_controller.rb) to look like this:

```
format.png {
  graph = Scruffy::Graph.new
  results = @goal.results.collect {|r| r.value}
    graph.add :stacked, 'Weight' do |stacked|
    stacked.add :line, '', results
  end
  send_data(graph.render(:width => 700, :as => 'PNG'))
}
```

While that works, a better solution would be to move all that code into the method in the goals model that will return this graph object. If we were to name this new method scruffy_graph, we could simplify our controller method to look like this:

```
def index
  respond_to do |format|
    format.png { send_data(@goal.scruffy_graph.render(:width => 700, :as => 'PNG'))}
  end
end
```

For more info on this process, check out the outstanding blog post "Skinny Controller, Fat Model" by Jamis Buck at http://weblog.jamisbuck.org/2006/10/18/skinny-controller-fat-model.

Develop Social Networking Features

If you want to take the application to a more advanced level, I suggest looking into adding some level of social networking into the application, such as the following:

- A community portal for sharing workout or goal results

- A "Find a workout partner" link or bulletin board

- A discussion forum

- Some sort of wiki where users could document things such as workout programs, exercise techniques, or even low-calorie recipes

Summary

That should be enough to get you started, but of course with an application like this – I'm sure you can come up with some creative idea that I haven't thought of. You could even take some of the ideas from other projects and apply them here as well (such as an iPhone interface, or caching the pages). If you come up with something realy cool, please share it with others at the RailsProjects.com forums.

Extending Monkey Tasks

The following exercises offer additional enhancements for Monkey Tasks.

Convert Monkey Tasks to a RESTful Design

As Monkey Tasks was already designed around CRUD-based methods, it's already got a decent head start toward a RESTful interface. Why not take it the rest of the way and rebuild it using the RESTful principles we used here? After you're done, compare the two applications. Is the code easier to read or follow when it's built to REST? Did you decrease controller methods or lines of code?

Experiment with Adding Reports to Monkey Tasks

Another way you can apply what you've learned in this project is to look at adding graphs to Monkey Tasks. Perhaps a graph that displays the number of tasks completed per day? Or if you followed the exercise to add an estimated time for each task, you could graph the estimated amount of time you've spent working on tasks per week.

PART 4

■ ■ ■

Simple Blogs

This project is actually going to be a bit different from the others. We'll start by exploring how quick and easy it is to get a blog up and running using an open source solution (we'll use Typo in this project). However, since that can be a little boring for programmer types like us, we'll take advantage of that project to expand our understanding about how Rails works and how to trace through someone else's code.

We'll wrap up the project by getting back into programming as we build a simple blog application that supports the MetaWeblog API, so that we can use a desktop blogging client to control our blog.

CHAPTER 9

■ ■ ■

Building a Blog Using Typo

In this chapter, we're going to explore how quick and easy it is to launch a web blog using an open source Rails application such as Typo (http://typosphere.org/) or Mephisto (http://mephistoblog.com/). For the purposes of this project, we'll build a simple blog using the Typo blog application.

Of course, in reality, this chapter's purpose isn't to document how to build a blog using Typo; rather it's our opportunity to explore the process of understanding a Rails application that someone else has built. So as we build the blog, we'll take a deeper look at the Rails startup process, how Rails delivers requests to the application, and take a journey into the Typo source as we trace a request all the way through the application. We'll start off our project by creating a fictional backdrop for why we're creating the blog so that we'll have a framework for the decisions we make in the application.

Our story starts out one Tuesday morning when Alanna, your company's new receptionist, pulls you aside to ask if you would consider building a web site for her.

It turns out that Alanna has dreams of one day becoming a recording artist and spends her nights and weekends performing at small venues around the state. She's even recorded her own CD that she sells when she performs. She's got all the normal venues covered, such as accounts on the major social networking sites, and of course, a page on MySpace. However, she's been advised by some friends that it's also a good idea to establish an official site of her own. As such, she'd like to have a basic web site where she could share thoughts and comments with her friends and fans, post her upcoming performance dates, and potentially allow people to sample some of the music from her CD.

You've had enough experience with previous receptionists to understand the power that they have to either be a deflector shield for you or to make your daily work life a living hell of constant interruptions. You wisely decide that it's in your best interest to do anything you can to be on her good side, so you agree to help her out. That's when she drops the bomb on you—she needs this web site up by this weekend, as she's heading out to a conference where she'll have the opportunity to meet record producers and would really like to be able to direct them to her web site for more information. That short time line pretty much rules out custom development, as you've already got a full week planned, so it's time to turn to an open source premade solution that you can customize.

Luckily, you've heard of just such a solution built in Ruby on Rails that you could take advantage of—the Typo blogging engine.

Introducing Typo

Typo was first developed back in January of 2005 (an eternity ago in Rails time) by Tobias Lütke. The story goes that Tobias had an appointment to meet with a client but had accidentally written the wrong time in his calendar (a typo). To pass the time while he was waiting, he found a local coffee shop and proceeded to bang out the first version of Typo in approximately six hours.

There wasn't a lot to that first version, as his goal was to create "the smallest possible weblog." It was built to run solely on the SQLite database, and since there was no administration interface, the only way to post to it was using XML-RPC via an application like MarsEdit. Interest and adoption in Typo built up like a tidal wave, and Typo soon became one of the most popular applications in the budding Ruby on Rails community.

Features of Typo

Two years later, Typo bears very little resemblance to that "smallest possible weblog" anymore, with approximately 10,000 lines of code and features such as:

- A gem-based installer

- A full backend administration system plus support for external clients

- Caching support

- Support for multiple text filters, including Textile, Markdown, and SmartyPants

- File uploads

- Theme support

- Feed support, including Atom 1.0 and RSS 2.0

- Support for comments and track backs

- E-mail notification of new comments and track backs

- Spam protection, including Askimet support

- Tags and categories

- Friendly URLs

- Migration scripts

- AJAX used for live previews, live search, commenting, sidebar management, and so on

And that's just the tip of the iceberg.

Installing Typo

Installing Typo couldn't be made any easier since the introduction of the gem-based installer in version 4. All you need to do to obtain the gem installer from RubyGems is to run the following command:

```
gem install typo -v 4.0.3
```

> ■**Note** During the time the book was being written, Typo went through another major release, which caused a significant amount of changes between the way the application will work as shown in this chapter and how it will work under the new release.
>
> However, since the purpose of this project wasn't to document the Typo blog engine, but to use it as a sample application to obtain a deeper understanding of how Rails works and to demonstrate how to trace through someone else's application code, I simply provided the instructions for installing the specific version of Typo that was used in this project.

Now that you've got the installer added to your system, you can create a new Typo instance by running the installer and telling it where you want to install your new Typo blog:

```
typo install alanna
```

Several pages of installation information later, you will see a message similar to this:

```
Running tests.  This may take a minute or two
 All tests pass.  Congratulations.
 Starting Typo on port 4533

Typo is now running on http://eldon-alamedas-computer.local:4533
Use 'typo start /Users/darkel/test/alanna' to restart after boot.
Look in installer/*.conf.example to see how to integrate with your web server.
```

How cool is that? With two simple commands, you've now got a fully functioning Typo instance using SQLite as its database and running Mongrel as its web server.

> ■**Note** We're going to go forward from this point using this default configuration, as this is fine for our example. However, if you're rolling this out for production use, go ahead and reconfigure your database settings to your production system and rerun your migration files manually, since all the upcoming configuration steps will be stored in whichever database Typo is configured to use.

Activating Our Typo Blog

Opening our web browser to the address that Typo started on (`http://eldon-alamedas-computer.local:4533` on my box) presents us with the initial configuration view shown in Figure 9-1, prompting us to create our primary administrative user.

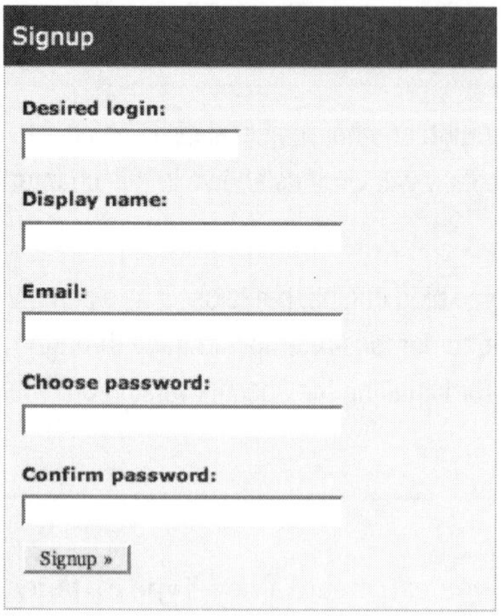

Figure 9-1. *Creating the administrative user in Typo*

Once you've set up the primary administrative user for your new blog, you'll be redirected to the settings configuration page (see Figure 9-2), where you can control how your blog functions. From here, you can set the name of your new Typo blog, enable or disable comments and track backs, control how many entries appear per page or in your RSS feed, configure spam protection, and control cache settings—among other things.

Go ahead and fill out the page with some basic settings, and click the Save Settings button on that page; your Typo blog is now live and serving a public blog. If you go ahead and click the "your blog" link in the upper right-hand corner, you can check it out; you should see something like Figure 9-3.

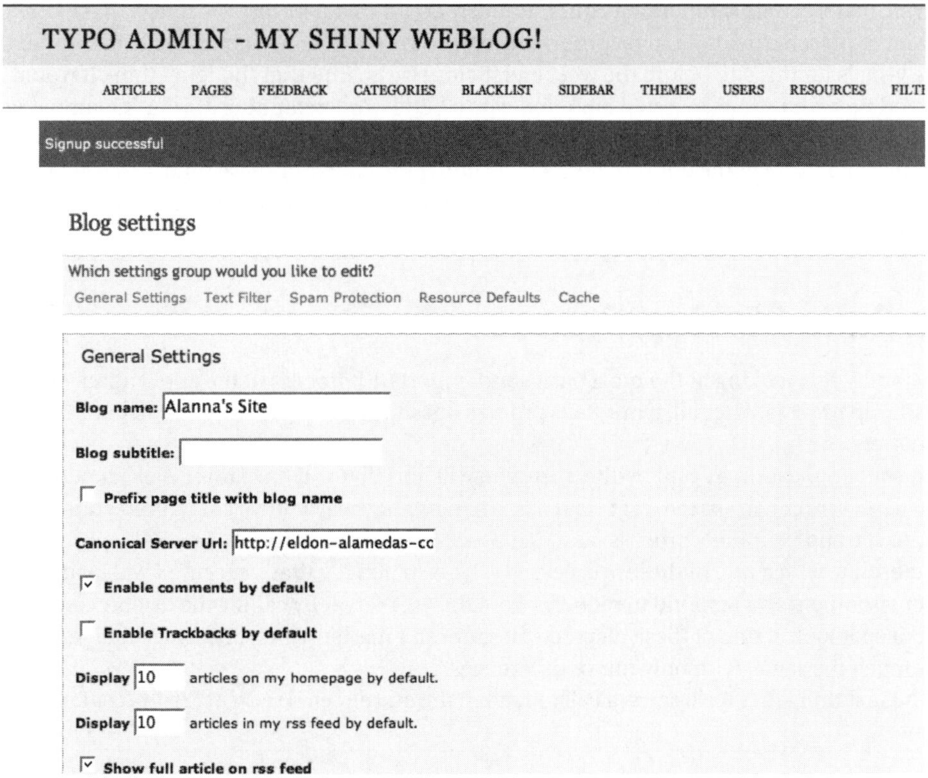

Figure 9-2. *Typo's general configuration settingsp*

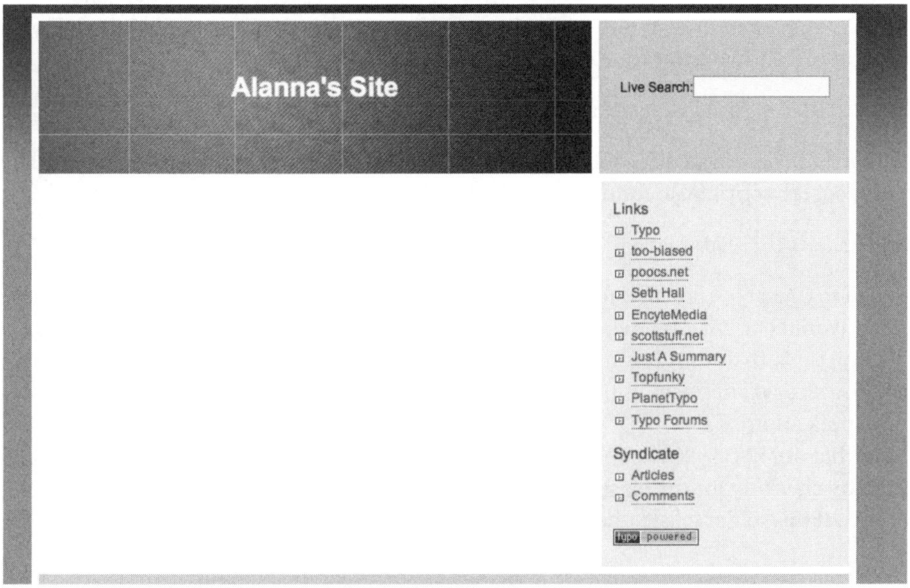

Figure 9-3. *A default Typo blog*

Well, that's certainly functional, but I seriously doubt that it's quite the image that Alanna will want to present to potential record producers. So we're definitely going to have to spruce up the visuals for this site before the weekend. Before we go into that though, I think it would be a good time for us to take a step back and gain a better understanding of what's happening in Rails and the Typo application to get us to this point. I'm always amazed at how many developers never go through the effort to take a peek under the covers of these things, as even the most basic understanding will certainly save you a lot of frustration if things ever go south in your application.

The Rails Startup Process

We'll start by first looking at the most basic (and important) process of the application—the Rails startup process. After all, if our Rails process doesn't start up, nothing else in our application matters one bit.

In your application's /public directory, you will find that you have three files named dispatch (dispatch.cgi, dispatch.fcgi, and dispatch.rb). The way you've configured your web server to start up your Rails process (as a CGI process, a FastCGI process, or a Ruby process) will determine which one of these is executed. The dispatch file that's executed will load our Rails environment and respond to requests from the web server by calling the dispatcher. Let's take a deeper look at one of these dispatch files (doesn't matter which one, since they're all pretty much the same, with only minor differences).

The first thing that we'll see is a call to read in the current environment.rb in /config with this line:

```
require File.dirname(__FILE__) + "/../config/environment" unless ➥
  defined?(RAILS_ROOT)
```

Let's go ahead and open environment.rb now. Typically present in a default Rails environment.rb yet absent from our Typo blogs configuration is the line that would define which version of Rails we want to use; it looks like this:

```
RAILS_GEM_VERSION = '1.2.3' unless defined? RAILS_GEM_VERSION
```

Since we don't have that element, the first thing we can see happen in this script is a call to load up the boot.rb script (also found in /config) with this line:

```
require File.join(File.dirname(__FILE__), 'boot')
```

We need to open boot.rb now to continue tracing our startup process. Now, boot.rb can look a bit convoluted at first, but what it's doing isn't really that difficult to understand. The very first thing boot.rb does is ensure that the RAILS_ROOT environment variable has been set. If it hasn't, boot.rb will define it as the directory one level beneath /config (i.e., the root directory of our application).

So now that our RAILS_ROOT constant has been set, boot.rb continues the process of loading up Rails by checking for the existence of a frozen Rails environment in #{RAILS_ROOT}/vendor/rails. If this folder exists, then boot.rb will require the Rails initializer from there.

If we don't have a local (frozen) copy of Rails, boot.rb will load the rubygems library and scan environment.rb to see if a RAILS_GEM_VERSION constant has been defined. If it has, boot.rb will load the intializer for that defined version of Rails (and raise an error if that version of Rails does not exist on the system). If RAILS_GEM_VERSION is not defined, boot.rb will attempt to initialize the most recent version of Rails installed on the system.

Now that we've determined the correct initializer, the final thing that boot.rb does is execute the run class method for the Initializer class in the Rails module:

```
Rails::Initializer.run(:set_load_path)
```

Since Typo includes a frozen version of Rails, let's load up the initializer.rb from /vendor/rails/railties/lib/; we can see that it has a module named Rails that contains two classes, Initializer and Configuration. The Intializer class is a bit boring but an important part of the startup process, as it's responsible for processing the settings from the configuration and setting the paths that Rails will search in when looking for files to load. The Configuration class, though, is much more interesting, as it maintains the parameters of our Rails environment.

Since boot.rb called the run class method, let's find it and see what it does:

```
def self.run(command = :process, configuration = Configuration.new)
  yield configuration if block_given?
  initializer = new configuration
  initializer.send(command)
  initializer
end
```

The run method accepts two parameters (that each have defaults): a command parameter that it will execute with the initializer.send(command) line and a configuration parameter that maps to the Configuration class. Since boot.rb didn't pass a configuration block, this configuration object will be loaded with the defaults of the Configuration class. So the next important thing that this method will do is call the set_load_path method in the Initializer class, which looks like this:

```
def set_load_path
  configuration.load_paths.reverse.each { |dir| $LOAD_PATH.unshift(dir) if ➥
File.directory?(dir) }
  $LOAD_PATH.uniq!
end
```

This method loads the $LOAD_PATH variable with the unique values that are in the configuration object's load_paths variable. So what was in that load_paths variable? Well, to answer that, we'll have to scroll down to the Configuration class and look at how it was initialized. We can see that, in the intialize method, load_paths was set to the value returned from a default_load_paths method:

```
def initialize
  self.frameworks  = default_frameworks
  self.load_paths = default_load_paths
  (…remainder of method omitted…)
```

Scrolling down a little bit further into the Configuration class, we can find the default_load_paths method, which sets us up with a number of directories that Rails should use when searching for files:

```
def default_load_paths
  paths = ["#{root_path}/test/mocks/#{environment}"]

  # Add the app's controller directory
  paths.concat(Dir["#{root_path}/app/controllers/"])

  # Then model subdirectories.
  # TODO: Don't include .rb models as load paths
  paths.concat(Dir["#{root_path}/app/models/[_a-z]*"])
  paths.concat(Dir["#{root_path}/components/[_a-z]*"])

  # Followed by the standard includes.
  paths.concat %w(
    app
    app/models
    app/controllers
    app/helpers
    app/services
    app/apis
    components
    config
    lib
    vendor
  ).map { |dir| "#{root_path}/#{dir}" }.select { |dir| File.directory?(dir) }

  # TODO: Don't include dirs for frameworks that are not used
  paths.concat %w(
    railties
    railties/lib
    actionpack/lib
    activesupport/lib
    activerecord/lib
    actionmailer/lib
    actionwebservice/lib
  ).map { |dir| "#{framework_root_path}/#{dir}" }.select { |dir| ➥
File.directory?(dir) }
end
```

With our $LOAD_PATH assembled, Rails will now be able to load any files in the directories listed in the preceding code. With that, this run through the intializer is complete, and we return to environment.rb (well, technically, we return to boot.rb, which ends and returns us to environment.rb).

Our next step within environment.rb, ironically enough, is to once again call the Intializers.run method—this time, the method passes in the custom configuration block from environtment.rb that starts with this line:

```
Rails::Initializer.run do |config|
```

We can see some of the custom configuration options that Typo loads, such as loading a large set of additional directories (where it has frozen a large set of Ruby gems) into the load path:

```
# Add additional load paths for your own custom dirs
# config.load_paths += %W( #{RAILS_ROOT}/app/services )
config.load_paths += %W(
  vendor/rubypants
  vendor/akismet
  vendor/redcloth/lib
  vendor/bluecloth/lib
  vendor/flickr
  vendor/syntax/lib
  vendor/sparklines/lib
  vendor/uuidtools/lib
  vendor/jabber4r/lib
  vendor/rails/railties
  vendor/rails/railties/lib
  vendor/rails/actionpack/lib
  vendor/rails/activesupport/lib
  vendor/rails/activerecord/lib
  vendor/rails/actionmailer/lib
  vendor/rails/actionwebservice/lib
).map {|dir| "#{RAILS_ROOT}/#{dir}"}.select { |dir| File.directory?(dir) }
```

We can also see a little lower where Typo selects that all session data should be stored in the database via ActiveRecord:

```
config.action_controller.session_store = :active_record_store
```

Going back to our run method, also note that, this time, no method was explicitly passed, so our command parameter will default to the process method:

```
def self.run(command = :process, configuration = Configuration.new)
```

The `process` method in the `Intializer` class sequentially steps through a series of initialization routines, such as:

- `set_load_path`: This sets the load path again—this time through it also uses the elements that were added to our load path from the `environment.rb`.

- `set_connection_adapters`: Determines which database adapters are loaded.

- `require_frameworks`: Determines which framework items are loaded (ActiveRecord, Action Web Service, etc.).

- `load_environment`: Loads the `development.rb`, `production.rb`, or `test.rb` environment configuration from `/config/environments` based on the environment that Rails is starting up with.

- `initialize_database`: Reads in `database.yml` and establishes the connection to the database.

- `initialize_logger`: Creates a new logger instance.

- `initialize_framework_logging`: Sets our logger instance as the logger for ActiveRecord, ActionController, and ActionMailer.

- `initialize_framework_views`: Configures `ActionController::Base` and `ActionMailer::Base` to look in `/app/views` for view templates.

- `initialize_dependency_mechanism`: Sets the dependency loading mechanism.

- `initialize_breakpoints`: If the breakpoint server setting is `true`, this will set the port to be used to listen for breakpoints (the `BREAKPOINT_SERVER_PORT`).

- `initialize_whiny_nils`: This configures Rails to complain if we attempt to call a method on a nil value.

- `initialize_framework_settings`: Initializes framework-specific settings for each of the loaded frameworks.

- `load_environment`: Loads the `development.rb`, `production.rb`, or `test.rb` environment configuration from `/config/environments` based on the environment that Rails is starting in (yes, this is called twice during processing—for supporting legacy configuration styles).

- `load_plugins`: Loads any plug-ins found in `/vendor/plugins`. Plug-ins are loaded in alphabetical order.

- `initialize_routing`: Loads the routing definitions and prepares to lazily load any requested controllers.

Finally, after the `process` method completes and our configuration is loaded, Rails loads any custom application configuration items from the bottom of our `environment.rb`:

```
# Include your application configuration below

# Load included libraries.
require 'redcloth'
require 'bluecloth'
require 'rubypants'
require 'flickr'
require 'uuidtools'
```

And with those final few calls, we're back to our dispatch file in `/public`, which finishes out with a call to the `Dispatcher` to respond to the incoming request—but we'll get into how that works in a few pages. Before we do that, let's take a deeper look at the Typo configuration.

Understanding Typo

Having a framework that dictates even something as simple as the directory structure makes it tremendously easy for us to understand code that was written by someone else, so our job of understanding the code behind Typo has become a hundred times easier.

Understanding the Database

Perhaps because of my background of starting out as a DBA before I moved into web development, I always like to start by checking out the database structure that the code base is built on.

If we were using something like Microsoft SQL Server as our primary database, we could just load up Enterprise Manager and have it build a new diagram to help us to see all the tables visually. Unfortunately, since Rails migrations abstract the database configuration down to the lowest common denominator, it doesn't define any of the referential constraints that would allow our generated diagram to show the relationships between tables.

Note So why doesn't Rails build those relationships in a database that supports referential integrity? That's a question that you'll see come up on mailing lists from time to time. The simple answer is that it would be repeating the same relationship information that we are creating in our model, so it would be redundant to create it in the database as well.

Since we're using SQLite in our application, we don't have any auto-generated diagram capabilities, so we could simply load the database in SQLite and explore the tables manually like this:

```
sqlite3 database.sqlite

SQLite version 3.3.7
Enter ".help" for instructions

sqlite> .tables
articles_categories  notifications      sessions
articles_tags        page_caches        sidebars
blacklist_patterns   pings              tags
blogs                redirects          text_filters
categories           resources          triggers
contents             schema_info        users

sqlite> .schema articles_categories
CREATE TABLE articles_categories (
  "article_id" integer,
  "category_id" integer,
  "is_primary" integer
);
```

But that would get old really fast, wouldn't it? Another option would be go through each of the migration files and follow the database as it's built, but—with 50 different files that add a column in one file and then remove it three migrations later—that's not exactly a fun-filled afternoon either.

Fortunately, Rails comes to our rescue again, as it automatically generates a full schema definition for us in Ruby migration format. You can find it in /db/schema.rb; here are a few highlights:

```
create_table "articles_categories", :id => false, :force => true do |t|
  t.column "article_id", :integer
  t.column "category_id", :integer
  t.column "is_primary", :integer
end

create_table "articles_tags", :id => false, :force => true do |t|
  t.column "article_id", :integer
  t.column "tag_id", :integer
end
```

Articles_categories and articles_tags are the join tables for a pair of has-and-belongs-to-many relationships.

```
create_table "blacklist_patterns", :force => true do |t|
  t.column "type", :string
  t.column "pattern", :string
end
```

Blacklist_patterns stores any user-created regular expression or string patterns that we want to scan new comments for.

```
create_table "blogs", :force => true do |t|
  t.column "settings", :text
end
```

The blogs table is the primary table about our blog. All of the values from the settings page are serialized into a hash and stored into the settings field.

```
create_table "categories", :force => true do |t|
  t.column "name", :string
  t.column "position", :integer
  t.column "permalink", :string
end
```

User-created categories are stored in the categories table. Categories are associated with articles via the articles_categories table.

```
create_table "contents", :force => true do |t|
  t.column "type", :string
  t.column "title", :string
  t.column "author", :string
  t.column "body", :text
  t.column "body_html", :text
  t.column "extended", :text
  t.column "excerpt", :text
  t.column "keywords", :string
  t.column "created_at", :datetime
  t.column "updated_at", :datetime
  t.column "extended_html", :text
  t.column "user_id", :integer
  t.column "permalink", :string
  t.column "guid", :string
  t.column "text_filter_id", :integer
  t.column "whiteboard", :text
  t.column "article_id", :integer
  t.column "email", :string
  t.column "url", :string
  t.column "ip", :string, :limit => 40
  t.column "blog_name", :string
  t.column "name", :string
  t.column "published", :boolean, :default => false
  t.column "allow_pings", :boolean
  t.column "allow_comments", :boolean
  t.column "blog_id", :integer, :null => false
  t.column "published_at", :datetime
  t.column "state", :text
  t.column "status_confirmed", :boolean
end
```

The contents table is another extremely important table, as this is the table that stores nearly all our user-created content. It utilizes single table inheritance (note the type field) to allow this field to be the storage mechanism for the Track Back, Pages, Feedback, Articles, Comment, and Content models.

```
create_table "redirects", :force => true do |t|
  t.column "from_path", :string
  t.column "to_path", :string
end
```

Redirects are used to handle upgrades where users might still need to access old blog posts from a different URL structure.

```
create_table "resources", :force => true do |t|
  t.column "size", :integer
  t.column "filename", :string
  t.column "mime", :string
  t.column "created_at", :datetime
  t.column "updated_at", :datetime
  t.column "article_id", :integer
  t.column "itunes_metadata", :boolean
  t.column "itunes_author", :string
  t.column "itunes_subtitle", :string
  t.column "itunes_duration", :integer
  t.column "itunes_summary", :text
  t.column "itunes_keywords", :string
  t.column "itunes_category", :string
  t.column "itunes_explicit", :boolean
end
```

Resources are used for storing information about uploaded files.

```
create_table "sidebars", :force => true do |t|
  t.column "controller", :string
  t.column "active_position", :integer
  t.column "config", :text
  t.column "staged_position", :integer
end
```

The sidebars table stores our current and activated sidebar components, and their respective configuration is stored as a serialized hash in the config field.

```
create_table "tags", :force => true do |t|
  t.column "name", :string
  t.column "created_at", :datetime
  t.column "updated_at", :datetime
  t.column "display_name", :string
end
```

User-created tags are stored in the tags table. Tags are associated to articles via the articles_tags table.

```
create_table "triggers", :force => true do |t|
  t.column "pending_item_id", :integer
  t.column "pending_item_type", :string
  t.column "due_at", :datetime
  t.column "trigger_method", :string
end
```

Triggers are created when an article is set to activate at a future date and time.

I still like things visual, so I usually draw out a quick little diagram like the one in Figure 9-4, so I can see the relationships.

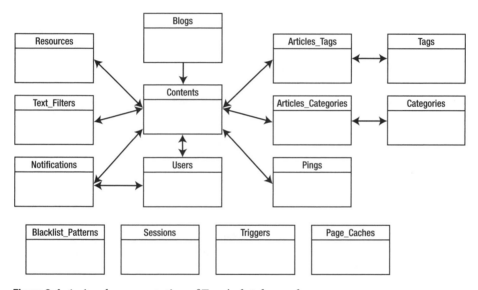

Figure 9-4. *A visual representation of Typo's database schema*

How Rails Routes Requests

After exploring the database schema and model files, I like to trace the full route path of a few of the key pages to get a good understanding of all that's going on behind the scenes to build those pages. The first step in doing that is taking a quick review of how Rails gets a request for a URL to the correct controller and action.

As I mentioned before, the web server will call the appropriate dispatch file in /public, which ensures that we have the Rails framework loaded before it calls Dispatcher.dispatch.

What does the dispatcher do? It takes the data passed to it from the web server, such as the request URL and any CGI parameters, and uses that data to determine the correct controller and action to respond to the request, instantiates an instance of that controller, sends that controller instance the request, and returns the response back to the web server. We can watch this happen within the interactive console by setting a few environment variables and calling `Dispatcher.dispatch` directly:

```
ruby script/console
```

```
Loading development environment.
```

```
>> ENV['REQUEST_URI'] = "/"
```

```
=> "/"
```

```
>> ENV['REQUEST_METHOD'] = "GET"
```

```
=> "GET"
```

```
>> Dispatcher.dispatch
```

```
Content-Type: text/html
Status: 200 OK
Cache-Control: no-cache

<!DOCTYPE html PUBLIC "-//W3C//DTD XHTML 1.0 Transitional//EN"
 "http://www.w3.org/TR/xhtml1/DTD/xhtml1-transitional.dtd">
<html xmlns="http://www.w3.org/1999/xhtml">
<head>
  <title>Alanna's Site</title>
  <meta http-equiv="content-type" content="text/html; charset=utf-8" />
  (…remainder of response omitted for brevity…)
```

We can see that a request to the root of our Typo application returned an HTML response. But let's go a step further and actually trace out that route request to the home page through our application controller.

Determining the Path

To start that trace, we need to find out where a default request to the root of the application is routed. If you open `routes.rb` in /config, you will find that this is routed to the index method of the articles controller:

```
map.index '', :controller => 'articles', :action => 'index'
```

However, you'd be wrong if you thought that our next step was to go straight to the articles controller. Since all of our controllers inherit from `ApplicationController` (`/app/controllers/application.rb`), we need to first look in `ApplicationController` for any filters that would be executed before, after, or around the articles controller execution.

The Application Controller

Here's the application controller:

```
class ApplicationController < ActionController::Base
  before_filter :get_the_blog_object
  before_filter :fire_triggers
  after_filter :flush_the_blog_object
  around_filter Blog
```

Sure enough, we've got several filters set to execute along with our request. You need to find out what these methods are doing if you want to be able understand the request when it reaches the articles controller, so let's break them down one by one.

before_filter :get_the_blog_object

Scrolling down into the protected methods of `ApplicationController`, you'll find our first filter method:

```
def get_the_blog_object
  @blog = Blog.default || Blog.create!
  true
end
```

The first thing our request does is create a `@blog` instance variable and populate it with either the result from the default method of the `Blog` class or with a new `Blog` object. I'm sure you can guess that the default method for the `Blog` class merely returns our `Blog` object, but to be safe, we can verify that by opening up the `blog.rb` in `/app/models/` and locating the default method.

```
def self.default
  find(:first, :order => 'id')
end
```

before_filter :fire_triggers

The second method that gets kicked off by our request is the `fire_triggers` method:

```
def fire_triggers
  Trigger.fire
end
```

Once again, we're calling a class method in one of the models. Opening `trigger.rb` in `/app/models` reveals that this method destroys any expired objects from the trigger model. You should remember from our earlier investigation that triggers are references to content that needs to activate at a future date. This method merely removes any references after the activation date has passed.

```
class Trigger < ActiveRecord::Base
class << self
    def fire
      destroy_all ['due_at <= ?', Time.now]
      true
    end
  end
```

after_filter :flush_the_blog_object

Finally, you have an `after_filter` to take a look at. This method is executed after all of our processing is done and the page has been rendered. In this case, it's just doing a little housecleaning by clearing out the `@blog` instance variable.

```
def flush_the_blog_object
  @blog = nil
  true
end
```

around_filter Blog

The final piece of code that we have to worry about from the `ApplicationController` is an `around_filter` from the Blog model that wraps our request. Opening the Blog model, we can find its relevant methods:

```
@@controller_stack = []
cattr_accessor :controller_stack

def self.before(controller)
  controller_stack << controller
end

def self.after(controller)
  unless controller_stack.last == controller
    raise "Controller stack got out of kilter!"
  end
  controller_stack.pop
end
```

In this case, Typo is doing some safety checks to ensure that the controller at the beginning of the request matches the controller at the end of the request. You can see this error pop up if you load some bad code in one of your sidebar components.

The Articles Controller

And with that, you can go ahead and open the articles controller (/app/controllers/articles_controller.rb). Unfortunately, a quick glance reveals that you still can't go straight to the index method just yet, as there are a few more obstacles in our way that we need to investigate.

```
class ArticlesController < ContentController
  before_filter :verify_config
```

ContentController

Our first obstacle is that ArticlesController doesn't inherit from the ApplicationController like you might have assumed. It's inheriting from another controller named ContentController, so we need to see what's going on there first.

Opening ContentController (/app/controllers/content_controller.rb), we find some methods to support Typo's caching, but it also has two important calls that I want to draw your attention to:

```
class ContentController < ApplicationController
  helper :theme
  before_filter :auto_discovery_defaults
```

The first method is a call to include the helper file from theme. This includes all the methods from the theme helper (/app/helpers/theme_helper.rb), which provides us with support for utilizing themes in the theme directory.

Second, it calls out another before_filter called auto_discovery_defaults. This method just sets up some instance variables that are used for auto-discovery of RSS and Atom feeds.

With that, we're finally ready to start running code in the articles controller, so let's go back to the articles controller and take a look at that last filter that stands between us and our index method.

before_filter :verify_config

The next method we see is before_filter calling the verify_config method:

```
def verify_config
  if User.count == 0
    redirect_to :controller => "accounts", :action => "signup"
  elsif ! this_blog.is_ok?
    redirect_to :controller => "admin/general", :action => "redirect"
  else
    return true
  end
end
```

Here's the method that redirected you to create your administrative user the first time you accessed the site. The first `if` condition checked whether we had any users created and saw that we had none, so it sent us to the `signup` method in the accounts controller to create one.

The second conditional makes sure that your blog is okay—but what does that mean? This is the first time we've seen a reference to a variable or method named `this_blog`, so your next step is determining what object `this_blog` is referring to. If you go back to the application controller, you'll find this method:

```
def this_blog
  @blog || Blog.default || Blog.new
End
```

So `this_blog` returns a reference to the `Blog` object, which by this point should always be returning the `@blog` variable that we populated earlier.

Now, how do we define if the blog is okay? `is_ok?` is a method from within the blog model (`/app/models/blog.rb`) that merely checks our settings hash to see if we have a key set for the blog_name. In essence, this is just verifying that you've made it past the initial settings screen and clicked the Save Settings button.

```
def is_ok?
  settings.has_key?('blog_name')
end
```

And with that, we're ready to tackle the index method.

index

It's taken some time to get here, but we're finally at the method that was called from our route request:

```
def index
  count = Article.count(:conditions => ['published = ? AND ➥
contents.published_at < ? AND blog_id = ?', true, Time.now, this_blog.id])
  @pages = Paginator.new self, count, this_blog.limit_article_display,➥
@params[:page]
  @articles = Article.find( :all,
    :offset => @pages.current.offset,
    :limit => @pages.items_per_page,
    :order => "contents.published_at DESC",
    :include => [:categories, :tags, :user, :blog],
    :conditions =>
      ['published = ? AND contents.published_at < ? AND blog_id = ?',
        true, Time.now, this_blog.id]
  )
end
```

Almost simple in comparison to everything that's come before, isn't it? Our `index` method sets up three variables: a count of the total active articles, a paginator object, and an `@articles` instance variable that contains the articles that we're going to display on the page view (but also includes the associated categories, tags, and user and blog objects to minimize database hits).

Displaying the Articles

It's actually standard fare from here out in the request. We pull in the layout from the currently selected theme and then open index.rthml in /app/views/articles, which loops through our @articles.

```
<% for article in @articles -%>
```

Within this loop, we can see that index.rhtml makes a call to display each of the articles in @articles using a partial named _article.rhtml.

```
<h2><%= article_link article.title, article %></h2>
<p class="auth">Posted by <%= author_link(article) %>
<%= js_distance_of_time_in_words_to_now article.published_at %></p>
<%= article.body_html %>
```

And, with that, we've just rendered our homepage.

■**Note** Observant readers may notice that we just bypassed exploring the code that renders the sidebar elements, and yes, that was on purpose. To render the sidebars, Typo still uses a feature of Rails called components that is strongly advised to avoid. Components were one of the few elements that added to the Rails core that weren't extracted from live production code. As such, there were a large number of issues with them—most noticeably, they were extremely slow. There is even talk that components will be officially deprecated by the 2.0 release of Rails. Don't worry, though—we will discuss the sidebars later on, and you'll even learn how to create your own sidebar component.

Working Out the Design

Now that you have Typo installed and have learned a bit about how Typo works, it's time to start putting Alanna's site together. To do that, though, we need to gain a better understanding of exactly what she wants. Being the smart one that you are, you're able to get her to take you out to lunch one afternoon to go over her requirements. So one free lunch later (at a place that wasn't too expensive but wasn't too cheap either), we've got a pretty good idea of what Alanna needs.

Over lunch, Alanna told you that she wants the main page to be the place for her blog posts to appear as well as any menu links to the extra content, and she'd like there to be some sort of music player built into the page to allow people to sample her music.

She gave you a few printouts of secondary content that she'd like. She was thinking we could have a set of secondary pages with names like:

- *The Girl*: A mini biography

- *The Music*: Lyrics to songs she's written

- *The Mission*: Concert dates

- *The Friends*: Photos and links to people she knows

- *The Extra Bits*: A few interviews she's done

From a visual standpoint, she asked if we could make the design use "earthy" colors and she gave us the picture in Figure 9-5 hoping that we could somehow incorporate it into the design.

Figure 9-5. *Our starting image for the blog*

After doodling page ideas for a few hours, we've come up with something that we think will work. The header bar will include a custom logo for Alanna and a row of icons linking to each of her secondary pages. Below that, we'll make a three-column layout: the left column will contain the Typo sidebar content; the middle column will hold her blog posts or secondary page data, and the right column will contain this photo that she provided us. Sketching this out, we expect that we'll build something that looks like Figure 9-6.

Figure 9-6. *A rough sketch of our final layout*

Armed with the information, we're ready to go ahead and build out the first version of Alanna's new site tonight.

Using Typo

Since most of our work for adding the initial content to Alanna's site is going to be using the administration system, let's take a 5,000-foot view of how that system works. The primary page that Alanna will be using to populate the home page with her blog posts is the Articles tab. The Articles overview page (see Figure 9-7) will allow her to navigate around all of her active blog posts.

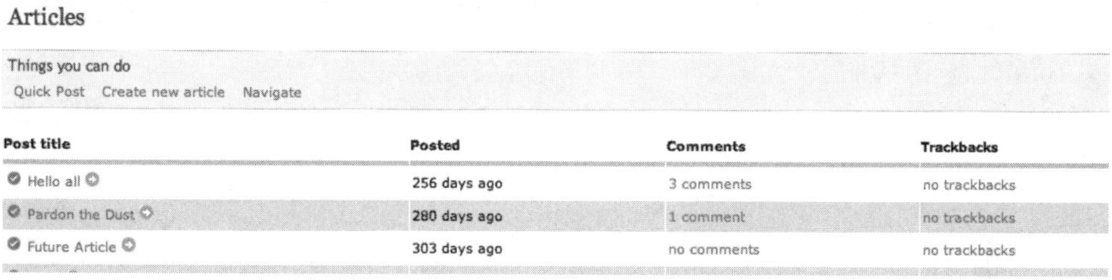

Figure 9-7. *The article management section*

Adding Articles Creating a new blog post (see Figure 9-8) uses a neat AJAX trick to provide a live preview of the post as it will be rendered on the page. While we're creating the article, we can also associate the articles with any categories that we created in the Categories tab or even assign custom tags.

___

■**Caution**   One limitation of the live preview is that, since the administration system uses a different style sheet than your selected theme, there can be significant differences on how the text will look on the main blog page versus the live preview, depending on the rules in your style sheet.

___

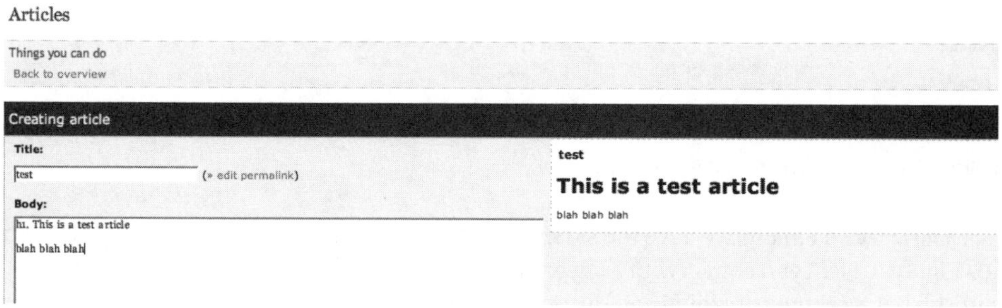

Figure 9-8. *Creating a new article*

Adding Pages Since we can expect that the supplementary content that Alanna would like to have on her page—such as concert dates, the about Alanna page, and the interview page—won't need to be updated very often, it makes sense for you to create them in the Pages menu.

You'll find that this interface is very similar to the Articles interface with an overview page and a live preview (see Figure 9-9). This should make sense, since they're both subclasses of the Content model. In addition, we can also set the URL location that an end user would use for navigating to this content page. So we can easily create URLs for Alanna like /pages/girl for her About the Girl page.

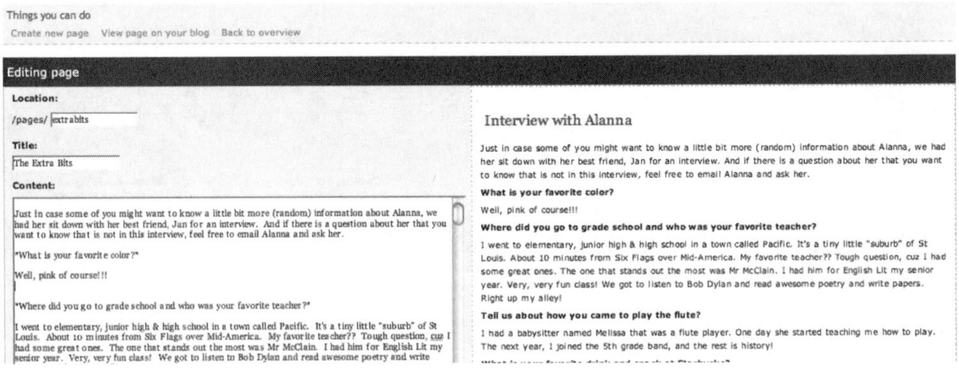

Figure 9-9. *Editing a page's content*

Uploading Content If Alanna would like to upload photos or some other type of file to use in any of her blog posts, she can do that herself using the Resources tab (see Figure 9-10). The resource page stores any uploaded files in the /public/files folder. An easy shortcut for using these files in a blog post is to simply right/Ctrl-click the file name, copy the link location, and paste that into your blog entry.

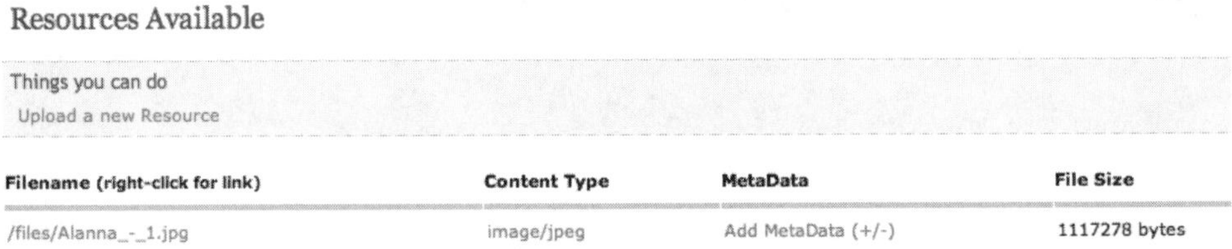

Figure 9-10. *Uploaded image management*

Managing Sidebars Finally, we have the sidebar modules that we can manage via the Sidebar tab (see Figure 9-11). Typo comes with a surprising number of useful items that you can add to your sidebar by simply dragging and dropping them to the active sidebar column on this page.

From pulling in content from your Flickr, Del.icio.us, or Tada list accounts to putting up static content, there's not a lot you can't do out of the box.

TYPO ADMIN - ALANNA'S SITE

ARTICLES   PAGES   FEEDBACK   CATEGORIES   BLACKLIST   SIDEBAR   THEMES   USERS   RESOURCES

Sidebar

Drag and drop to change the sidebar items displayed on this blog. To remove items from the sidebar just click remov

Publish changes

Available Items	Active Sidebar items
AIM Presence	**Archives**
Displays the Online presence of an AOL	Displays links to monthly archives
Instant Messenger screen name	☑ **Show article counts**
If you don't have a key, register here.	**Number of Months**
Amazon	10
Adds sidebar links to any amazon books	remove
linked in the body of the page	
Archives	**Categories**
Displays links to monthly archives	List of categories for this blog

Figure 9-11. *Options for sidebars*

Managing the Blog

Creating our blog structure is one thing—but we also need to have a number of tools to manage our blog. Typo provides several.

Spam Protection Alanna wants to allow her friends and fans to be able to post comments on her site. Considering the current situation of massive comment spam that plagues most blogs, that could be a recipe for a lot of aggravation. However, Typo provides us with a number of tools to assist in managing comments and blocking spam to help keep it from becoming a problem.

First off, you should configure the spam protection settings on the settings page of Alanna's blog. From here, you can enable the default spam protection, disable comments after a period of days, and set the maximum number of allowed links per comment post.

I also highly recommend that you utilize the Akismet integration by entering your Akismet key. Akismet is a spam protection service that will test any new comment on your site and provide either a thumbs-up or thumbs-down rating on the probability that the comment is spam. If you don't have an Akismet key yet, you can get a free one for personal use by applying at http://akismet.com/personal/.

Managing Comments Typo also provides a Feedback management page that will allow Alanna to view all of the comments on her blog in an overview fashion (see Figure 9-12). This makes it much easier to spot and deal with any comment spam or inappropriate comments that may have slipped in past the spam protection mechanisms.

Comments and Trackbacks for Alanna's Site

Things you can do
Limit to spam   Limit to unconfirmed   Limit to unconfirmed spam

Feedback Search:

| Delete Checked Items | Mark Checked Items as Ham | Mark Checked Items as Spam | Confirm Classification of Checked Items |

State Type	Article	Author	Body	IP	Po
		firmly1463@alannathornton.com			
Ham? Comment	Pardon the Dust	http://t Content-Transfer-...	firmly1463@alannathornton.com	67.43.156.69	21
		firmly1463@alannathornton.com			
		fighting8495@alannathornton.com			
Ham? Comment	Hello all	http://fighting8495@alannat...	fighting8495@alannathornton.com	61.18.170.111	21
		coma Content-Transfer-Encoding: 7bit C			

Figure 9-12. *Typo's interface for managing comments*

Banning Certain Content Finally, Typo also provides you with the ability to define your own blacklist patterns (see Figure 9-13) so that you block comments containing specific content from being posted to Alanna's site. You can create new blacklist patterns to match for explicit strings, or you can create a regular expression to match for more elaborate patterns.

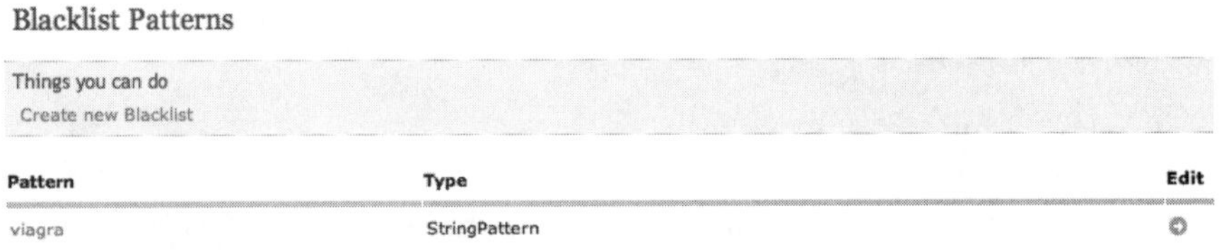

Blacklist Patterns

Things you can do
Create new Blacklist

Pattern	Type	Edit
viagra	StringPattern	⊕

Figure 9-13. *Blocking spam with blacklists*

Add the Content

Now, we have all the necessary tools needed to populate Alanna's new blog with all of the content that she gave us. After a few short hours of entering her content into the system and formatting it as text using Textile, her page is up and running with the default theme (see Figure 9-14).

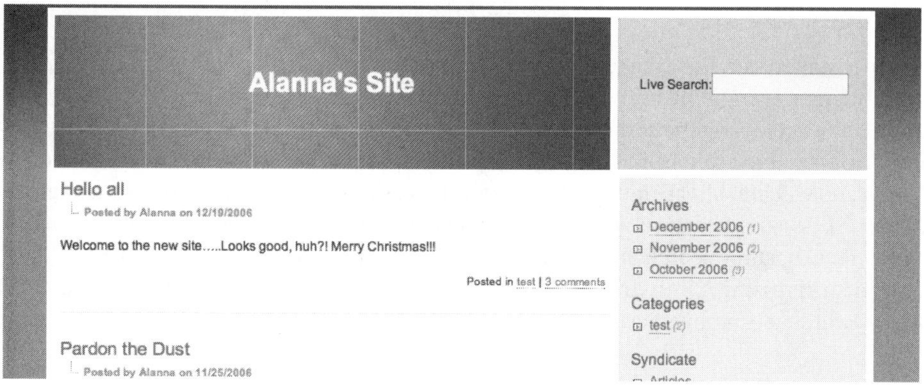

Figure 9-14. *The blog with additional content added*

Customizing Typo

So we've got Alanna's site up and running from a content perspective, but let's do the customization to truly make it her site now and give it a visual flair that fits with what she needs. Fortunately, Typo comes with a great theme system that makes customizing surprisingly easy.

Managing Themes

Within the administration system, you can view all of your installed themes within the Themes tab (see Figure 9-15). Typo comes with two preinstalled themes: Azure, which is the default theme that we just saw, and Scribbish, a stylish yet clean template that formats the blog posts using the microformat specification.

You can instantly switch between any installed themes by simply clicking the Activate link on the themes page.

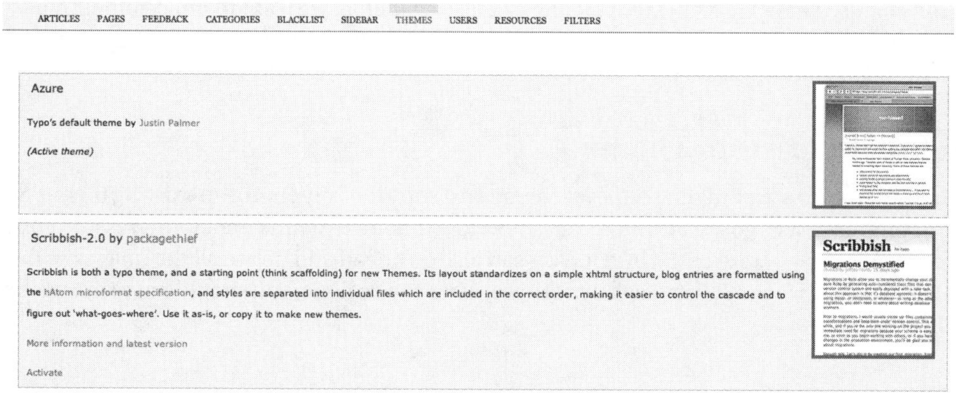

Figure 9-15. *Theme selection and management*

Exploring a Theme

Themes are installed into the /themes directory with each theme self-contained in its own subdirectory there. Navigating into each theme subdirectory, you can see that they follow a common pattern of using the same folder and file names within each. We have familiar-sounding folders named things like images, stylesheets, views, and layouts. The reason for this is that Typo will first check in these folders for the active theme when rendering a page to the end user. If Typo finds a file it needs here, it will use it; if not, it will search in the normal Rails paths. This dynamic search is extremely powerful, as it allows us to easily add a new theme by uncompressing it into this /themes directory without worrying about adding all the supporting style sheets, images, and so on into our public directories.

■Tip A good place to go to look for new themes for Typo is the Typo theme viewer at http:// www.dev411.com/typo/themes/, which provides thumbnails of all the themes that were submitted to the Typo theme contest (http://www.typogarden.org/). New themes are typically installed by simply uncompressing the file into the /themes directory.

One word of caution is that some older themes that were written for prior versions of Typo will break when you try to use them with the most recent version. A common issue in the older themes is a change in how the sidebars are rendered. If you see a call like this in the layout template:

```
<%= render_component(:controller => 'sidebars/sidebar',
  :action => 'display_plugins') %>
```

you may be able to fix the theme by changing that previous call to this instead:

```
<%= render_sidebars %>
```

Of course, we're not interested is using an existing theme, we want to build something unique for Alanna. Fortunately, building a custom theme within Typo is almost as easy as adding a premade one.

Building a Custom Theme

The easiest way to start building our own theme is to copy the contents of an existing theme. So for our purposes, let's go ahead and create a new folder named Alanna under /themes and copy the contents of the azure theme into it. You can also go ahead and delete all the images in the images folder, as we won't be using any of those. After you're done, you should have something similar to Figure 9-16.

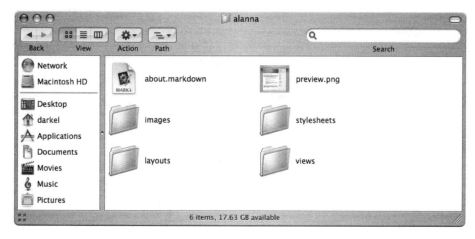

Figure 9-16. *Files for the custom theme for Alanna's blog*

The two files that will be used for the themes page in the administration system are the
`preview.png` and the `about.markdown`. We can capture a screenshot of the final design to replace
the `preview.png` after we're done, but for now, let's go ahead and edit `about.markdown`. This file
contains the description that is displayed about our theme on themes page of the administration system. We'll put something basic in there for now:

```
### Alanna
```

```
Custom theme for Alanna by Eldon Alameda
```

If we were going for the simplest way to create a custom theme, we could continue to use
the preexisting page layout and view files from our copied theme and merely replace the existing style sheet with the styles that we desire.

■**Tip** If you need some inspiration on what is possible by merely replacing the style sheet, I highly recommend checking out `www.csszengarden.com`. CSS Zen Garden is a site that demonstrates hundreds of
unique and highly artistic designs—all done using style sheets and without changing a single line of the
underlying HTML code.

As a starting point to help you in creating your own style sheet definitions, I documented
the overall page structure as it is laid out in the azure theme in Figure 9-17.

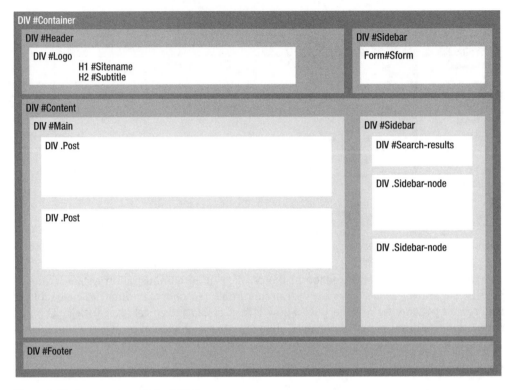

Figure 9-17. *An overview of the HTML structure*

I positioned the elements according to how they're laid out in the azure theme. Obviously, you're not limited to this layout, as you can use CSS positioning rules to change where elements appear on the page. So if you want to move the sidebar to the left side, you certainly can.

The post and the sidebar elements are actually repeated elements from partials that you may want to style a bit deeper. A breakdown of their structure can be found in Figure 9-18.

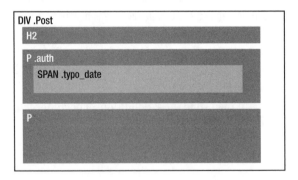
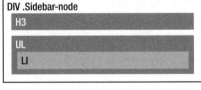

Figure 9-18. *Analysis of HTML structure for posts and sidebars*

Changing the style sheet gives us a lot of flexibility and power, but it's not going to easily allow us to create a three-column layout like we discussed earlier. So let's go ahead and create a new layout by changing default.rhtml in /themes/Alanna/layouts to this:

```
<!DOCTYPE HTML PUBLIC "-//W3C//DTD HTML 4.01//EN"
"http://www.w3.org/TR/html4/strict.dtd">
<head>
<title><%= h page_title </title>
  <%= page_header %>
  <link rel="stylesheet" type="text/css" href="http://yui.yahooapis.com/2.2.2/➥
build/reset-fonts-grids/reset-fonts-grids.css">
<%= stylesheet_link_tag "stylesheets/theme/alanna.css", :media => 'all' %>
  <%= javascript_include_tag 'niftycube' %>
  <script type="text/javascript">
    window.onload=function(){
    Nifty("div#sidebar,div#content");
    Nifty("div#hd","top");
    Nifty("div#ft", "bottom");
    }
  </script>
</head>

<body>
<div id="doc2" class="yui-t2">
  <div id="hd">
    <a href="/"><h1>Alanna Thornton</h1></a>
      <div id="navigation">
        <a href="/pages/girl"><%= image_tag 'girl_papyrus.png' %></a>
        <a href="/pages/guitar"><%= image_tag 'guitar_papyrus.png' %></a>
        <a href="/pages/music"><%= image_tag 'music_papyrus.png' %></a>
        <a href="/pages/mission"><%= image_tag 'mission_papyrus.png' %></a>
        <a href="/pages/friends"><%= image_tag 'friends_papyrus.png' %></a>
        <a href="/pages/extrabits"><%= image_tag 'extraBits_papyrus.png' %></a>
      </div>
  </div>
  <div id="bd">
    <div id="yui-main">
      <div class="yui-b">
        <div class="yui-gc">
          <div class="yui-u first">
            <div class="mod">
              <div class="wrapper">
                <div class="hd" id="content">
                  <%= @content_for_layout %>
                  <%= javascript_tag "show_dates_as_local_time()" %>
```

```
            </div>
          </div>
        </div>
      </div>

      <div class="yui-u">
      </div>
    </div>
  </div>
</div>

<div class="yui-b">
  <div id="sidebar">
    <% benchmark "BENCHMARK: layout/sidebars" do %>
      <%= render_sidebars %>
    <% end %>
  </div>
</div>
</div>

<div id="ft">
  <p>All music, images, and content copyright Alanna Thornton</p>
</div>
</div>
</body>
</html>
```

There are few things to highlight about this layout. Once again, we're utilizing the YUI library (http://developer.yahoo.com/yui/) to help us save time in developing a solid three-column layout that will work across all modern browsers:

```
<link rel="stylesheet" type="text/css" href="http://yui.yahooapis.com/2.2.2/➥
build/reset-fonts-grids/reset-fonts-grids.css">
```

Within our layout, we wanted to make the content boxes have rounded corners. We could do this through background images or by utilizing some complex CSS styling, but I've found a lot of success in taking advantage of a solution called Nifty Corners.

Nifty Corners is a JavaScript solution that dynamically modifies the DOM to create the illusion of rounded corners on block elements. To utilize the function, we first need to download the library from http://www.html.it/articoli/niftycube/index.html and copy all the .css and .js files from the archive into our /public/javascripts folder.

───

■**Note** We're putting the Niftycube style sheets in the JavaScript folder because the Niftycube JavaScript files dynamically load the style sheets—expecting them to be in the same directory. Normally when I deploy this, I edit the files so that I can maintain proper separation.

───

Once we have the files added to our application, our include call from the application layout will load Niftycube:

```
<%= javascript_include_tag 'niftycube' %>
```

And then we have our `onload` call to the `Nifty` function, which passes in the elements that we want rounded along with any options for how we want them rounded.

```
<script type="text/javascript">
  window.onload=function(){
  Nifty("div#sidebar,div#content");
  Nifty("div#hd","top");
  Nifty("div#ft", "bottom");
  }
</script>
```

All that's left to add are our own images and style sheets. Going into creating custom style sheets is really a topic for another book, so you can simply download the remaining style sheets and images from the code archive and add them to your application to see the final result, which should look like Figure 9-19.

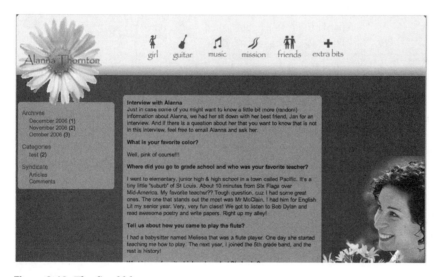

Figure 9-19. *The final blog*

■**Note** In the page that we built, we changed the layout template, but we didn't take advantage of Typo's ability to also override the view templates. We could have also created new templates within the view folder and changed the markup for how the blogs would be formatted to whatever format we desired. That means that, within any theme you create, you can have complete control over what the rendered output will be.

Creating a Sidebar Component

As a final customization to Alanna's new blog, let's explore how to create our own sidebar components. One of the issues that Alanna may encounter with this design is the fact that, because we'd like to try and keep the page from requiring the user to scroll, we limited the number of blog posts per page to only two. This means that posts can fall off the front page pretty quickly. It would be nice if we could provide a shortcut list of the most recent articles that have been added to the blog in the sidebar as well.

All of the sidebars are installed in the /components/plugins/sidebars directory. Within this directory, you'll find a controller for each sidebar element and a subdirectory with the same name that stores the view file for that sidebar component.

So go ahead and create a new file named recent_posts_controller.rb and a new subdirectory named recent_posts within this directory. Open your new controller, and put the following code into it:

```
class Plugins::Sidebars::RecentPostsController < Sidebars::ComponentPlugin
  display_name "Recent posts"
  description "Displays the most recent posts"

  def content
    @recent_articles = Article.find(:all, :limit => 7,
                          :conditions => ['published = ?', true],
                          :order => 'created_at DESC')
  end
end
```

Amazingly simple so far, isn't it? We merely made a couple of method calls and defined one new method named content. The display_name method sets the short name that will show up in the title block in the sidebar administration user interface, while the description method sets the description that will show there.

Our new content method is the method that will be called when this sidebar is rendered, so here we simply create a new instance variable named @recent_articles and populate it with an active record call for the last seven active articles based on the date that they were created.

Since Rails convention is to look for a display template with the same name as the method that was called, let's go ahead and create a content.rhtml in our new subdirectory /components/plugins/sidebars/recent_posts/:

```
<h3>Recent Posts</h3>
<div>
  <ul>
    <% for article in @recent_articles -%>
      <li>
        <%= article_link article.title, article %>
      </li>
    <% end %>
  </ul>
</div>
```

Now save our two new files, and load the administration system. Sure enough, our new sidebar plug-in is one of the available sidebar elements. We can activate it and reload our main blog page to now see a listing of the seven most recent articles added to our sidebar.

Customizing a Sidebar Component

Being able to add the recent blog posts is nice and all, but we chose seven as a rather arbitrary number of posts to show. What would we do if Alanna ever wanted to change that number to keep a recent post in the sidebar longer? Wouldn't it be much nicer if we could make that configurable within the sidebar administration interface?

Obviously, I wouldn't be asking these questions if it weren't possible. So reopen your recent_posts_controller, and modify it to look like this:

```
class Plugins::Sidebars::RecentPostsController < Sidebars::ComponentPlugin
  display_name "Recent posts"
  description "Displays the most recent posts"

  setting :count,   7, :label => "Number of Posts"

  def content
    @recent_articles = Article.find(:all, :limit => count,
                          :conditions => ['published = ?' , true],
                          :order => 'created_at DESC')
  end
end
```

Reloading the sidebar page in the administration system, you can see our new customizable settings (see Figure 9-20). By utilizing the setting method, you can create a wide variety of variables with custom controls in your sidebar component.

■Tip How does Typo store your customization settings? It stores it in the Sidebar model by creating and serializing the configuration settings and values as a hash into the config attribute of the Sidebar model.

These variables are accessible in your sidebar controller by name, or you can access them in your sidebar view by accessing them as hash elements of the @sb_config instance variable (e.g., @sb_config['count']).

One final note—you can also utilize other form controls besides a simple text box by passing an input_type option to the settings method. For example, if you want to create a text area element, you could do it like this:

```
setting :body, "Enter your text here", :input_type => :text_area
```

or if you wanted to capture a Boolean value, you can use a check box like so:

```
setting :show_user, true, :input_type => :checkbox
```

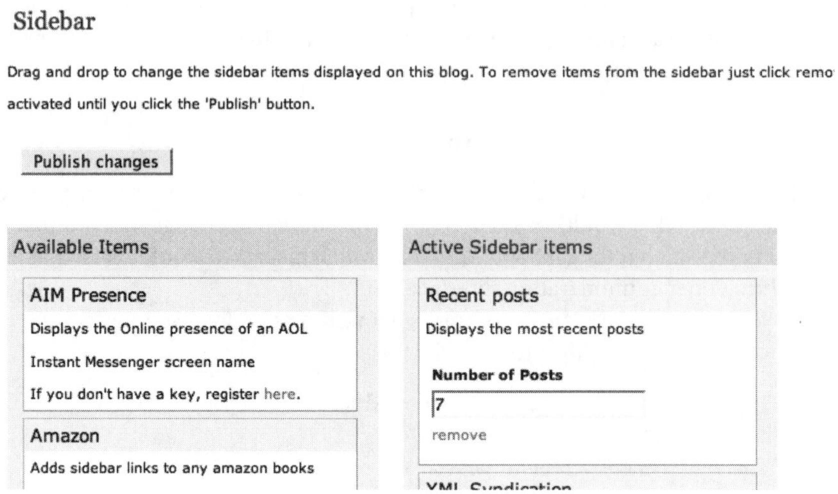

Figure 9-20. *Our custom sidebar*

Summary

You did it! You had to give up a few extra hours of free time, but Alanna now has her own blog page that provides her with all the tools that she needs to keep in touch with her fans.

Best of all, you were able to do it in just a few hours spread out over a few nights and meet her deadline. Thus she is able to confidently give out her new web address to anyone she meets at her conference this weekend. Alanna is thrilled, and you're going to be able to get at least a couple more free lunches out of this deal—plus, you made an office ally who can shield you from being interrupted every few minutes.

Along the way, you also gained a good understanding of Typo, one of the most popular Rails applications to date. The next time someone approaches you about building a blog, you should feel very confident in your ability to install and customize an instance of Typo for them in a short amount of time.

## CHAPTER 10

Building a Simple Blog Engine

While building a blog in an open source Rails application such as Typo is certainly easy enough, something about it just really bothers the programmer in me. Wouldn't it be more fun to build our own? That's the question that we're going to tackle together in this chapter as we build a basic blogging system tailored to our own specific needs.

To do that, we'll focus only on the features that we actually need (or care about) letting the others fall by the wayside to reduce bloat in our application and keep it streamlined. A blog, by definition, is a fairly simple thing. When you really break it down, all you need is a way to save some text to a database and a way to display that text on a web page. This is why we see so many web development frameworks building blogs for their introductory exvoamples and screencasts.

So What Are We Going to Build?

First off, our blog will need to be able to support the content that we want to post to it (that is, our posts), and since a blog is something that we could use for a number of years, it will need to be able to support a large number of posts. Whenever we start increasing the quantity of an item in a web application, it's always a good idea to find ways to classify our posts to make it easier for readers to find posts on specific subjects. To accomplish this, many blog engines provide support for tags. However, I think that's overkill for our blog. Tagging is a great tool for providing context to a site where many users are adding content or one that's a visual medium, such as a photo sharing site. But in every blog application I've used that had tagging support, I found that I ended up only using four or five tags to classify my posts. So we'll bypass tag support for our blog and go with the simpler solution of allowing each post to be simply joined to one or more categories.

Next, I've noticed that the blogs that I typically enjoy reading the most are those that embed a picture or some other graphic along with the posts. It's a small feature but one that really seems to add that extra oomph to the blog. So we'll definitely need to include the capability to upload images and include them in blog posts.

However, one key aspect of our simple blogging system is that we're not going to build a web-based admin for it. Instead, we'll be using a desktop blogging client to manage the posts on our new blog. My personal favorite is ecto, which features clients for both Mac and Windows. Figure 10-1 shows ecto in action.

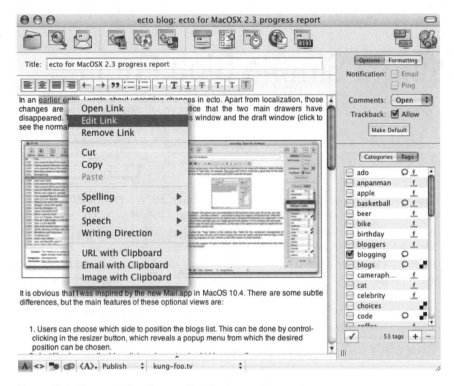

Figure 10-1. *The ecto blogging application*

ecto has all the standard features that we'll need to write and manage entries on our new blog, such as WYSIWYG editing and spell checking (see Figure 10-1). And ecto has one key feature that makes it my favorite—the ability to drag and drop images directly into a post from anywhere, including from a web browser. That feature alone saves me a huge amount of hassle when I come across a funny image that I want to share on my blog. In addition, ecto can handle most of the common image-related tasks that we might need, such as scaling, generating thumbnails, and converting to different formats. You can download a trial version of ecto from `http://ecto.kung-foo.tv/`.

Without further ado, let's kick things off by creating our new Rails project using the directions from Chapter 2 and naming it myblog. After that, we'll start our development by creating our basic blog and post models as our first models.

Building Our First Models

The first model we'll build is the blog model. This will be the core model of our blog and will be used to name the blog and potentially to store configuration settings specific to our blog. At this point in the project, our blog model doesn't need to hold a lot, just a name for our blog. Open a command prompt in the root of your application, and create our blog model with the following command:

```
ruby script/generate model Blog name:string
```

```
create  app/models/
create  test/unit/
exists  test/fixtures/
create  app/models/blog.rb
create  test/unit/blog_test.rb
create  test/fixtures/blogs.yml
exists  db/migrate
create  db/migrate/001_create_blogs.rb
```

Second, our blog will need to have posts (and lots of them). So what are the things that a post needs to have?

First off, it needs to know which blog it's associated with, so we'll need a blog_id reference.

Then, at a bare minimum, a post will need to have both a title and a body (to hold the actual content of the post), so we'll add those as well. For good measure, let's also add the created_at and updated_at fields.

```
ruby script/generate model Post blog_id:integer title:string body:text ➡
created_at:datetime updated_at:datetime
```

```
exists  app/models/
exists  test/unit/
exists  test/fixtures/
create  app/models/post.rb
create  test/unit/post_test.rb
create  test/fixtures/posts.yml
exists  db/migrate
create  db/migrate/002_create_posts.rb
```

From here, let's go ahead and edit our new blog and post models to add the necessary associations and validations. Our blog model (/app/models/blog.rb) should look like this:

```
class Blog < ActiveRecord::Base
  has_many :posts
  validates_presence_of :name
end
```

while our post model (/app/models/post.rb) should look like this:

```
class Post < ActiveRecord::Base
  belongs_to :blog
  validates_presence_of :blog_id, :title, :body
end
```

Before we run our database migrations, let's save ourselves a little hassle by creating our initial blog object and a sample post within our migration. So open our create blogs migration file (/db/migrate/001_create_blogs.rb), and add a Blog.create call for when we create the blog table:

```ruby
class CreateBlogs < ActiveRecord::Migration
  def self.up
    create_table :blogs do |t|
      t.column :name, :string
    end

    Blog.create(:name => 'My Simple Blog')
  end

  def self.down
    drop_table :blogs
  end
end
```

Next, let's also add a sample post to our newly created blog when we create our posts table, so edit /db/migrate/002_create_posts.rb to do that with these modifications:

```ruby
class CreatePosts < ActiveRecord::Migration
  def self.up
    create_table :posts do |t|
      t.column :blog_id, :integer
      t.column :title, :string
      t.column :body, :text
      t.column :created_at, :datetime
      t.column :updated_at, :datetime
    end

    blog = Blog.find :first
    blog.posts.create(:title => 'My Very First Blog Post',
                      :body => 'Nothing Interesting to see here yet')
  end

  def self.down
    drop_table :posts
  end
end
```

Now, we can go ahead and run our migrations to build the tables for these models in our database as well as create our blog and a sample post:

```
rake db:migrate
```

```
== CreateBlogs: migrating
-- create_table(:blogs)
   -> 0.0025s
== CreateBlogs: migrated (0.0027s)

== CreatePosts: migrating
-- create_table(:posts)
   -> 0.0028s
== CreatePosts: migrated (0.0030s)
```

If you want to make sure that your blog and post records got created, you can quickly do a double check from within the interactive console:

```
ruby script/console
```

```
Loading development environment.
```

```
>> blog = Blog.find :first
```

```
=> #<Blog:0x2769520 @attributes={"name"=>"My Simple Blog", "id"=>"1"}
```

```
>> blog.posts
```

```
=> [#<Post:0x2727bc0 @attributes={"updated_at"=>"2007-07-27 20:06:27",
"title"=>"My Very First Blog Post", "body"=>"Nothing Interesting to see here yet",
 "id"=>"1", "blog_id"=>"1", "created_at"=>"2007-07-27 20:06:27"}]
```

Building Our API

While we could continue to use migrations or the console to add content to our blog, that would get old really fast. So let's get cranking on building an API that ecto can use to control our blog; ecto can work with a variety of XML-RPC APIs including Blogger, MetaWeblog, and MovableType—unfortunately, though, there's no support for a REST-based API yet.

For this chapter, we'll focus on supporting the MetaWeblog API because of it's support for multimedia content. To do that, we'll take advantage of the Action Web Service library, which provides an easy way to build SOAP and XML-RPC web services in our Rails applications. Our first step in building a web service with Action Web Service is to use the built-in web service generator to give us a jump start. The web service generator will create a new API file and a new controller based on the name that we pass it to support our service. For our purposes, we'll name our service xmlrpc, and we'll create it from the command prompt like this:

```
ruby script/generate web_service xmlrpc
```

```
create  app/apis/
exists  app/controllers/
exists  test/functional/
create  app/apis/xmlrpc_api.rb
create  app/controllers/xmlrpc_controller.rb
create  test/functional/xmlrpc_api_test.rb
```

Let's take a quick glance at what our generator built. First, open the xmlrpc controller (/app/controllers/xmlrpc_controller.rb), and let's take a quick glance at it:

```
class XmlrpcController < ApplicationController
  wsdl_service_name 'Xmlrpc'
end
```

This controller will be used to serve any requests for our new web services. The wsle_service_name method is used to determine the name used in the SOAP bindings. We can see that by viewing the current WSDL file by starting up a Mongrel instance of the application and opening a web browser to http://localhost:3000/xmlrpc/service.wsdl:

```
<?xml version="1.0" encoding="UTF-8"?>
<definitions name="Xmlrpc" xmlns:typens="urn:ActionWebService" xmlns:wsdl=➡
"http://schemas.xmlsoap.org/wsdl/" xmlns:xsd=http://www.w3.org/2001/XMLSchema ➡
 xmlns:soap="http://schemas.xmlsoap.org/wsdl/soap/" targetNamespace= ➡
"urn:ActionWebService" xmlns:soapenc="http://schemas.xmlsoap.org/soap/encoding/" ➡
xmlns="http://schemas.xmlsoap.org/wsdl/">
  <portType name="XmlrpcXmlrpcPort">
  </portType>
  <binding name="XmlrpcXmlrpcBinding" type="typens:XmlrpcXmlrpcPort">
    <soap:binding transport="http://schemas.xmlsoap.org/soap/http" style="rpc"/>
  </binding>
  <service name="XmlrpcService">
    <port name="XmlrpcXmlrpcPort" binding="typens:XmlrpcXmlrpcBinding">
      <soap:address location="http://localhost:3000/xmlrpc/api"/>
```

```
      </port>
    </service>
</definitions>
```

Now, if we were to change that wsdl_service_name parameter to 'test' and reload the WSDL file, we would see the following:

```
<?xml version="1.0" encoding="UTF-8"?>
<definitions name="test" xmlns:typens="urn:ActionWebService" xmlns:wsdl= ➥
"http://schemas.xmlsoap.org/wsdl/" xmlns:xsd="http://www.w3.org/2001/XMLSchema" ➥
 xmlns:soap="http://schemas.xmlsoap.org/wsdl/soap/" targetNamespace= ➥
"urn:ActionWebService" xmlns:soapenc="http://schemas.xmlsoap.org/soap/encoding/" ➥
xmlns="http://schemas.xmlsoap.org/wsdl/">
  <portType name="testXmlrpcPort">
  </portType>
  <binding name="testXmlrpcBinding" type="typens:testXmlrpcPort">
    <soap:binding transport="http://schemas.xmlsoap.org/soap/http" style="rpc"/>
  </binding>
  <service name="testService">
    <port name="testXmlrpcPort" binding="typens:testXmlrpcBinding">
      <soap:address location="http://localhost:3000/xmlrpc/api"/>

    </port>
  </service>
</definitions>
```

■**Note** WSDL is short for Web Services Description Language; a WSDL file is an XML-based file that is used to describe how to access a web service and what operations the service supports. Typically, a client that wants to consume a web service will read in the WSDL file to create a proxy object for interfacing with the service.

The second file that the generator created that we'll look at is the API definition in /app/apis/xmlrpc_api.rb; after opening it, we can see that there's not much in there:

```
class XmlrpcApi < ActionWebService::API::Base
end
```

At this point, we need to make a decision about what sort of dispatching mode we'd like our web service to use. The dispatching mode in Action Web Service controls where we want client requests to go in our application and how those requests will be routed to the methods that will service them. Action Web Service suports three different dispatching modes:

- *Direct mode* is the default dispatching mode. It works by attaching the API definition directly to a controller. This means that all methods must be defined within a single controller. This mode is what you saw generated previously by the generator where the API file shared the same name as the controller. In this mode, our web service is only available at a single URL, and all API defintions must be in that single API file.

- *Delegated mode* is another option for dispatching. It allows your web service to have multiple API's that can then be attached to controllers. The downfall of this method, though, is that it requires each web service to maintain a separate URL.

- *Layered mode* is the final dispatching mode available for us to choose. It also allows for multiple APIs to be available to a single controller. However, it has an advantage over delegated mode in that all attached services are accessible via a single URL.

Even though we only plan to implement the MetaWeblog API for this project, it would be wise to build our configuration to be able to support other APIs in the future (especially since adding support for another API will be one of the exercises at the end of this project). Obviously, the best option for our needs is going to be to use the layered dispatching mode. We'll select layered dispaching by adding a web_service_dispatching_mode method to our Xmlrpc controller (/app/controllers/xmlrpc_controller.rb) and then mounting a MetaWeblog service—edit your Xmlrpc controller to look like this:

```
class XmlrpcController < ApplicationController
  web_service_dispatching_mode :layered
  web_service(:metaWeblog) { MetaWeblogService.new() }
end
```

You may have noticed that, in our web_service call, we instantiated a new MetaWebLogService object, but we haven't created it yet—let's rectify that now.

The MetaWeblog Service API

Before we create the new MetaWeblog service API definition, we first should go ahead and delete the Xmlrpc API file that was created (/app/apis/xmlrpc_api.rb), since we won't be using direct dispatching.

With that file gone, create a new file named meta_weblog_service.rb in that API folder. We'll use this file to store all of the necessary classes and modules that we need to support the MetaWeblog API for our blog. The first step to do that is to add a placeholder module to hold any structs that we'll use in our API:

```
module MetaWeblogStructs
end
```

Beneath that, we'll define the MetaWeblog API where Action Web Service requires us to define each of the methods for our API, including their expected input and output parameters. By default, ActionWeb Service will camel case the method names in its API definition and require that any requests use the camel cased version when making requests. We don't want that behavior, since it might cause conflicts with our blogging client, so we'll disable it with an `inflect_names false` call in this class:

```
class MetaWeblogApi < ActionWebService::API::Base
  inflect_names false
end
```

Finally, at the bottom of our file, we'll define the MetaWeblog service that we instantiated back in our Xmlrpc controller. Here is where we'll build the methods defined from our API class in the last step:

```
class MetaWeblogService < ActionWebService::Base
  web_service_api MetaWeblogApi
end
```

Putting that all together, your current `meta_weblog_service.rb` file should look like this:

```
module MetaWeblogStructs
end

class MetaWeblogApi < ActionWebService::API::Base
  inflect_names false
end

class MetaWeblogService < ActionWebService::Base
  web_service_api MetaWeblogApi
end
```

Why don't we go ahead and try to connect ecto to our new blog to see what sort of response we can get even with this most basic of configurations? Make sure that you have your Mongrel instance running the application and then open ecto and click the Accounts button in the toolbar. This will open the Account Manager dialog box where you can see a list of all of the blogs that ecto is configured to connect to.

Go ahead and click the Add button, so we can create a connection to our new blog. This opens the dialog shown in Figure 10-2, where we're asked for the web address of our new blog.

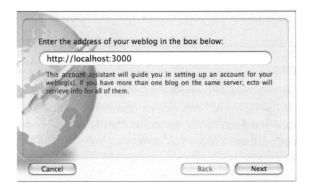

Figure 10-2. *Configuring our blog in ecto*

Assuming that you're running your blog locally for development, you can go ahead and enter `http://localhost:3000` in the dialog box.

Next, ecto is going to ask you to provide information on how and where it can access your blog (see Figure 10-3).

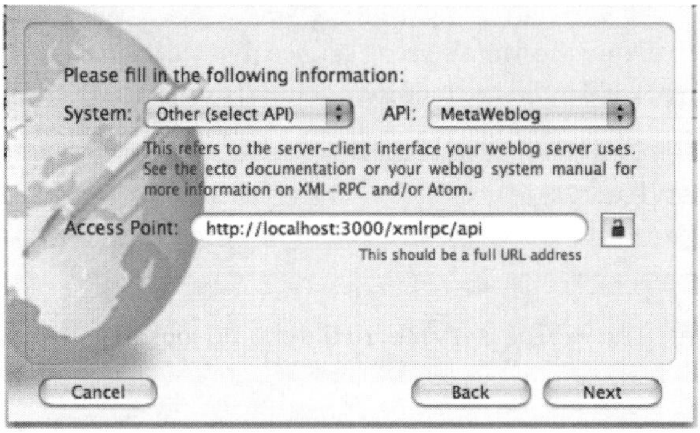

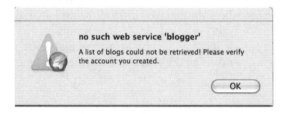

Figure 10-3. *Configuring our API*

Since this is our very own custom blog system, leave the system as Other. We've already decided that we'll use the MetaWeblog API, so select that from API the drop-down, and finally, we need to provide the URL for our API endpoint in our application. For our development purposes, go ahead and enter `http://localhost:3000/xmlrpc/api`.

From here, you'll just need to fill out the username and password that you'll want to use to access your API and a name for your blog to finish out our configuration and have ecto attempt to access our blog.

Unfortunately, once we do, ecto will greet us with the error message in Figure 10-4.

no such web service 'blogger'

A list of blogs could not be retrieved! Please verify the account you created.

OK

Figure 10-4. *Ecto is looking for a blogger API even though we specified MetaWeblog.*

Now, your first inclination will probably be to go back and check that you didn't accidentally select the wrong API when configuring your blog settings. But there's not really any need to, as this is expected behavior. Since the MetaWeblog API was originally designed to be an enhancement to some of the shortcomings in the Blogger API, a number of API methods were leveraged from the Blogger API and not created in MetaWeblog. It seems that one of our initial calls to the blog from ecto wants to use one of those, and it's failing because we have no Blogger API. So before we can go any further in implementing the MetaWeblog API, we'll need to add in support for a few Blogger API calls.

Adding Blogger Support

Our first step will be to add Blogger as an available web service by modifying our Xmlrpc controller in /app/controllers/xmlrpc_controller.rb to include a call to the Blogger web service:

```
class XmlrpcController < ApplicationController
  web_service_dispatching_mode :layered

  web_service(:metaWeblog) { MetaWeblogService.new() }
  web_service(:blogger)    { BloggerService.new }
end
```

Now, we'll need to create a new file in /app/apis named blogger_service.rb, which we'll populate with a similar structure as in our meta_weblog_service.rb:

```
module BloggerStructs
end

class BloggerApi < ActionWebService::API::Base
  inflect_names false
end

class BloggerService < ActionWebService::Base
  web_service_api BloggerApi
end
```

Fire up our configuration again in ecto, and let's try saving our account information now. We get another error message (shown in Figure 10-5), but at least this time it gives us a clearer picture of which Blogger method we need to build.

Figure 10-5. *ecto is looking for the Blogger getUsersBlogs method.*

Now ecto needs us to add the getUsersBlogs method from the Blogger API to move forward. After doing a little research on the Blogger API site, we can find the full documentation for this method at http://www.blogger.com/developers/api/1_docs/xmlrpc_getUsersBlogs.html. There, we discover that this method will pass three parameters to our API: an appkey (which is a unique identifier from the application sending the post), a username, and a password. The method should return a struct that features the blog ID, the name of the blog, and the URL where the blog can be found.

We'll start by adding an `ActionWebService` struct that we'll use to pass our blog data back to ecto. Open /app/apis/blogger_service.rb, and modify the `BloggerStructs` module at the top of the file to include this new struct:

```
module BloggerStructs
  class Blog < ActionWebService::Struct
    member :url,      :string
    member :blogid,   :string
    member :blogName, :string
  end
end
```

Now, we'll build our API definition for the `getUsersBlog` method by adding it to the `BloggerApi` section of our Blogger web service:

```
class BloggerApi < ActionWebService::API::Base
  inflect_names false

  api_method :getUsersBlogs,
    :expects => [ {:appkey => :string}, {:username => :string}, ➥
{:password => :string} ],
    :returns => [[BloggerStructs::Blog]]
end
```

All that's left is to add the actual controller logic that will respond to a `getUsersBlogs` request; we'll build that out as a method in the `BloggerService` section of our file:

```
class BloggerService < ActionWebService::Base
  web_service_api BloggerApi

  def getUsersBlogs(appkey, username, password)
    [BloggerStructs::Blog.new(
      :url      => 'http://localhost:3000',
      :blogid   => 1,
      :blogName => 'My Wonderful Blog'
    )]
  end
end
```

Retesting our configuration in ecto, we no longer see any errors—but we don't see our sample post pulled down either. Digging through the end of our development log (`tail log/development.log`) we discover this error:

```
ActionWebService::Dispatcher::DispatcherError (no such method 'getCategories'
on API MetaWeblogApi):
```

So the good news is that we're back on track toward using the MetaWeblog API after adding that one method from the Blogger API. The bad news is that it's now calling a getCategories method in the MetaWeblog API looking for a list of categories. Of course, that method doesn't exist, since we haven't even built any support for categories in our blog yet. Let's fix that by adding a Category model now:

```
ruby script/generate model Category name:string
```

```
exists  app/models/
exists  test/unit/
exists  test/fixtures/
create  app/models/category.rb
create  test/unit/category_test.rb
create  test/fixtures/categories.yml
exists  db/migrate
create  db/migrate/003_create_categories.rb
```

Before we run this migration to create categories, though, we also need to add another table to make it possible for us to associate a post to one or more of our categories. The simplest way to do that will be to use a join model that utilizes a has_and_belongs_to_many association. Let's edit our /db/migrate/003_create_categories.rb migration file to add that table as well:

```
class CreateCategories < ActiveRecord::Migration
  def self.up
    create_table :categories do |t|
      t.column :name, :string
    end

    create_table :categories_posts, :id => false do |t|
      t.column :category_id, :integer
      t.column :post_id, :integer
    end

  end

  def self.down
    drop_table :categories
    drop_table :categories_posts
  end
end
```

With that migration saved, we'll run our migration to create the new tables:

```
rake db:migrate
```

```
(in /Users/darkel/projects/myblog)
== CreateCategories: migrating =====================================================
-- create_table(:categories)
   -> 0.0027s
-- create_table(:categories_posts)
   -> 0.0028s
== CreateCategories: migrated (0.0059s) =======================================
```

Of course, we now need to modify our Post and Category models to know about each other by adding our has_and_belongs_to_many association method calls. So edit /app/models/post.rb to look like this:

```
class Post < ActiveRecord::Base
  belongs_to :blog
  has_and_belongs_to_many :categories
  validates_presence_of :blog_id, :title, :body
end
```

and /app/models/category.rb to look like this:

```
class Category < ActiveRecord::Base
  has_and_belongs_to_many :posts
end
```

After saving those models, let's go ahead and use the console to add a few categories to our blog from the console:

```
ruby script/console
```

```
Loading development environment.
```

```
>> Category.create(:name => 'Rails')
```

```
=> #<Category:0x2c87530 @new_record_before_save=true, @errors=#<ActiveRecord::Errors
:0x2d8aeb4 @errors={}, @base=#<Category:0x2c87530 ...>, new_recordfalse,
attributes{"name"=>"Rails", "id"=>1}
```

```
>> Category.create(:name => 'Personal')
```

```
=> #<Category:0x2d65808 @new_record_before_save=true, @errors=#<ActiveRecord::Errors
:0x2d60100 @errors={}, @base=#<Category:0x2d65808 ...>, new_recordfalse,
attributes{"name"=>"Personal", "id"=>2}
```

```
mypost = Post.find :first
```

```
=> #<Post:0x2c535f0 @attributes={"updated_at"=>"2007-03-25 13:11:05", "title"=>"My
Very First Blog Post", "body"=>"Nothing interesting to see here", "id"=>"1",
"blog_id"=>"1", "created_at"=>"2007-03-25 13:11:05"}
```

```
>> mypost.categories
```

```
=> []
```

```
>> personal = Category.find 2
```

```
=> #<Category:0x2c0ab70 @attributes={"name"=>"Personal", "id"=>"2"}
```

```
>> mypost.categories << personal
```

```
=> [#<Category:0x2c0ab70 @attributes={"name"=>"Personal", "id"=>"2"}]
```

```
>> mypost.save
```

```
=> true
```

```
>> mypost.categories
```

```
=> [#<Category:0x2c0ab70 @attributes={"name"=>"Personal", "id"=>"2"}]
```

Now that we have a bit of data to pull, let's build the getCategories method in our MetaWeblog API. Open /app/apis/meta_weblog_service.rb, and let's define the method in the API section:

```
class MetaWeblogApi < ActionWebService::API::Base
  inflect_names false
  api_method :getCategories,
      :expects => [{:blogid => :string},
                   {:username => :string},
                   {:password => :string}],
      :returns => [[:string]]
end
```

Now, we'll build the method within the `MetaWeblogService` class section. The `getCategories` method simply returns back a collection of of our category names:

```
class MetaWeblogService < ActionWebService::Base
  web_service_api MetaWeblogApi

  def getCategories(blogid, username, password)
    Category.find(:all).collect { |c| c.name }
  end
end
```

With that small addition, a quick check of attempting to save our blog configuration in ecto again reveals that we are now golden—there are no more errors in our logs, and Figure 10-6 shows that our categories are now available to select when creating a new post.

Figure 10-6. *A new blog post shows off our list of categories.*

Not bad—but a couple of things are still bothersome to me. First off, even though we created our blog configuration in ecto with a username and password and those were passed to the `getCategories` method that we just called, our actual API isn't doing anything with those parameters. That's about eight shades of bad, no matter how you look at it. Secondly, our sample post still hasn't been pulled down into the ecto application. We'll solve the mystery of the missing sample post when we create the methods for managing our posts, but let's fix that user authentication issue before we go any further.

Implementing Simple User Authentication

What we need is a simple way to verify that the username and password that were passed along in the request match with what we expect. If this was going to be a larger application with more than a single user, we would want to create a Users model that we would use to contain the logic to authenticate a user. However for our simple needs, we can get by with just a simple class method added to our Blog model (/app/models/blog.rb):

```ruby
class Blog < ActiveRecord::Base
  has_many :posts
  validates_presence_of :name

  def self.authenticate(username, password)
    if username == 'eldon' && password == 'test'
      true
    else
      false
    end
  end
end
```

We can now modify our getCategories method in /app/apis/meta_weblog_service.rb to utilize this Blog.authenticate method like this:

```ruby
module MetaWeblogStructs
end

class MetaWeblogApi < ActionWebService::API::Base
  inflect_names false
  api_method :getCategories,
      :expects => [{:blogid => :string},
                   {:username => :string},
                   {:password => :string}],
      :returns => [[:string]]
end

class MetaWeblogService < ActionWebService::Base
  web_service_api MetaWeblogApi

  def getCategories(blogid, username, password)
    if Blog.authenticate(username, password)
      Category.find(:all).collect { |c| c.name }
    end
  end
end
```

With that, we're now all set to begin building out the rest of our MetaWeblog API. Sticking to our CRUD methodology, we'll focus first on the basic create, read, update and delete methods for our blog posts.

Creating a New Post

We'll start off with the method that we'll be using the most with our new blog—the one that provides the ability to create a new post. A new blog post, according to the MetaWeblog API, will be submitted as a newPost request that passes the blogid, the username and password to use, a struct that contains the actual post, and a Boolean flag named publish that determines if the post should be activated or not. So outside of the struct that contains the post—the necessary values should be pretty straightforward.

That struct, however, is a fairly interesting thing. Rather than simply passing those values as strings, we instead pass them in as a struct that maintains all of the data fields we need for a post. In this way, the format of a new post can be modified easily without having to modify our API. For our purposes, the three basic elements of a post struct are the title, link, and description. This is a standard struct that we'll use throughout many of our methods for interacting with a post, so rather than retyping those same elements again and again, let's go ahead and create it as an Action Web Service struct in the MetaWeblogStructs module that we created in /app/apis/meta_weblog_service.rb:

```
module MetaWeblogStructs
  class Post < ActionWebService::Struct
    member :postid, :string
    member :title,  :string
    member :link, :string
    member :dateCreated, :time
    member :description, :string
    member :categories, [:string]
  end
end
```

Now, with our Post struct defined, we can build the newPost method definition and use that struct as one of the parameters in the API section of that same file:

```
class MetaWeblogApi < ActionWebService::API::Base
  inflect_names false
  api_method :getCategories,
      :expects => [{:blogid => :string},
                   {:username => :string},
                   {:password => :string}],
      :returns => [[:string]]
```

```
api_method :newPost,
  :expects => [
    {:blogid => :string},
    {:username => :string},
    {:password => :string},
    {:content => MetaWeblogStructs::Post},
    {:publish => :bool}
    ],
  :returns => [:string]
end
```

Our actual newPost method should be pretty straightforward—all we need to do is create a new Post object based on the data we received in the post struct, assigning any categories to the new post object as well:

```
class MetaWeblogService < ActionWebService::Base
  web_service_api MetaWeblogApi

  def getCategories(blogid, username, password)
    if Blog.authenticate(username, password)
      Category.find(:all).collect { |c| c.name }
    end
  end

  def newPost(blogid, username, password, content, publish)
    if Blog.authenticate(username, password)
      p = Post.new(:blog_id => blogid, :title => content['title'],
                        :body => content['description'])
      if content['categories']
        p.categories.clear
        Category.find(:all).each do |c|
          p.categories << c if content['categories'].include?(c.name)
        end
      end
      if p.save ? p.id.to_s : 'Error: Post cannot be created'
    end
  end
end
```

If we go ahead and create a new post in ecto and click Publish, our post is added to the page, but we also get back an error message complaining about a missing method (see Figure 10-7).

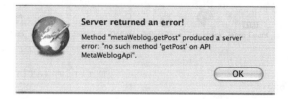

Figure 10-7. *ecto complaining about a missing method*

Getting Posts

We'll solve that problem by building out the getPost method to gather the details from a specific post. According to the specifications, it should be pretty easy. We'll issue a request with a postid (representing the ID of our post), a username, and a password, and in response, we'll receive back a Post struct. Still within /app/apis/meta_weblog_service.rb, we'll add the getPost definition to the API:

```ruby
class MetaWeblogApi < ActionWebService::API::Base
  inflect_names false
  api_method :getCategories,
    :expects => [{:blogid => :string}, {:username => :string},
                 {:password => :string}],
    :returns => [[:string]]

  api_method :newPost,
    :expects => [
      {:blogid => :string},
      {:username => :string},
      {:password => :string},
      {:content => MetaWeblogStructs::Post},
      {:publish => :bool}
      ],
    :returns => [:string]

  api_method :getPost,
    :expects => [{:postid => :string}, {:username => :string},
                 {:password => :string}],
    :returns => [MetaWeblogStructs::Post]

end
```

We can build the following getPost method by simply finding the post with the ID that was passed to us and building out a Post struct to return:

```ruby
class MetaWeblogService < ActionWebService::Base
  web_service_api MetaWeblogApi
```

```
def getCategories(blogid, username, password)
  if Blog.authenticate(username, password)
    Category.find(:all).collect { |c| c.name }
  end
end

def newPost(blogid, username, password, content, publish)
  if Blog.authenticate(username, password)
    p = Post.new(:blog_id => blogid, :title => content['title'],
                       :body => content['description'])
    if content['categories']
      p.categories.clear
      Category.find(:all).each do |c|
        p.categories << c if content['categories'].include?(c.name)
      end
    end
    p.save ? p.id.to_s : 'Error: Post cannot be created'
  end
end

def getPost(postid, username, password)
  if Blog.authenticate(username, password)
    post = Post.find(postid)

    MetaWeblogStructs::Post.new(
      :dateCreated => post.created_at || '',
      :postid => post.id.to_s,
      :description => post.body,
      :title => post.title,
      :categories => post.categories.collect { |c| c.name })
  end
end
end
```

If we resubmit our new post, everything works like a charm this time.

Getting Recent Posts

We'll go a step further by building a function that builds on our last post—the getRecentPosts method. Whereas getPost pulled back a single post, getRecentPosts will deliver back a collection of recent posts to our requesting client. According to the MetaWeblog API, this function submits four parameters to us: the blog identifier, the number of posts to return, a username, and a password. Our method should return an array of Post structs back.

So here's our API definition; note that we wrap our Post struct in the return within an extra set of array brackets to signify that we want to pass back an array of more than one Post struct:

```
class MetaWeblogApi < ActionWebService::API::Base
  inflect_names false
  api_method :getCategories,
    :expects => [{:blogid => :string}, {:username => :string},
                    {:password => :string}],
    :returns => [[:string]]

  api_method :newPost,
    :expects => [
      {:blogid => :string},
      {:username => :string},
      {:password => :string},
      {:content => MetaWeblogStructs::Post},
      {:publish => :bool}
      ],
    :returns => [:string]

  api_method :getPost,
    :expects => [{:postid => :string}, {:username => :string},
                    {:password => :string}],
    :returns => [MetaWeblogStructs::Post]

  api_method :getRecentPosts,
    :expects => [{:blogid => :string}, {:username => :string},
                    {:password => :string}, {:numberOfPosts => :int}],
    :returns => [[MetaWeblogStructs::Post]]

end
```

Building the actual method will be very similar to creating the getPost method, except this time, we'll be returning a collection of posts. But for good measure, let's abstract the process of building a Post struct into a separate method named buildPost:

```
def buildPost(post)
  MetaWeblogStructs::Post.new(
    :dateCreated => post.created_at || '',
    :postid => post.id.to_s,
    :description => post.body,
    :title => post.title,
    :categories => post.categories.collect { |c| c.name })
end
```

With this abstraction, we can now create the getRecentPosts method like this:

```
def getRecentPosts(blogid, username, password, numberOfPosts)
  if Blog.authenticate(username, password)
```

```
    Post.find(:all, :order => 'created_at desc',
                    :limit => numberOfPosts).collect do |p|
      buildPost(p)
    end
  end
end
```

We can also simplify the getPost method to use the new buildPost method as well to keep all of the logic in one place:

```
def getPost(postid, username, password)
  if Blog.authenticate(username, password)
    post = Post.find(postid)
    buildPost(post)
  end
end
```

Editing Posts

Even using a nice client like ecto providing built-in spell checking and preview capabilities, occasionally, we're going to post something to our blog that will need to be fixed or updated, so let's add the ability to edit a post. The MetaWeblog API defines an editPost method for doing so that requires us to accept a request with a username, password, the ID of the post that we want to edit, a Post struct containing the updated content, and a publish value (which we won't use but would be used to determine if this post should be a viewable on the site or not). In response, we'll return a Boolean value indicating that the edit was successful. Our editPost API definition should look like this:

```
api_method :editPost,
  :expects => [ {:postid => :string}, {:username => :string},
                {:password => :string}, {:struct => MetaWeblogStructs::Post},
                {:publish => :int} ],
  :returns => [:bool]
```

And the actual editPost method should be fairly straightforward: pull back the post based on the ID, update its content, and return a Boolean true if we didn't encounter any problems:

```
def editPost(postid, username, password, content, publish)
  if Blog.authenticate(username, password)
    post = Post.find(postid)
    post.attributes = {:body => content['description'].to_s,
                       :title => content['title'].to_s}

    if content['categories']
      post.categories.clear
      Category.find(:all).each do |c|
        post.categories << c if content['categories'].include?(c.name)
      end
    end
```

```
    post.save
    true
  end
end
```

Deleting Posts

We'll round out our CRUD methods of our posts' management with the ability to delete a post from the blog. Unfortunately, there doesn't seem to be a method within the MetaWeblog API that supports this. Instead the API depends on the Blogger deletePost method. We can confirm this by trying to delete a post from ecto and looking at the logs to determine what method it tried to use:

```
ActionWebService::Dispatcher::DispatcherError (no such method 'deletePost' ➥
on API BloggerApi):
```

Let's build this functionality in our Blogger API. Open the blogger.service.rb file in /app/apis/ that we created earlier, and add the deletePost definition in the BloggerApi class:

```
class BloggerApi < ActionWebService::API::Base
  inflect_names false

  api_method :getUsersBlogs,
    :expects => [ {:appkey => :string}, {:username => :string},
                        {:password => :string} ],
    :returns => [[BloggerStructs::Blog]]

  api_method :deletePost,
    :expects => [ {:appkey => :string}, {:postid => :string},
                        {:username => :string}, {:password => :string},
                        {:publish => :int} ],
    :returns => [:bool]
end
```

Next, add the deletePost method to the BloggerService class, which will simply pull back the post based on the ID, delete it, and return true if we don't have any errors:

```
def deletePost(appkey, postid, username, password, publish)
  if Blog.authenticate(username, password)
    post = Post.find(postid)
    post.destroy
    true
  end
end
```

Supporting Images

Now that our basic CRUD operations are built, we can get to the meat of our API and one of the key reasons we wanted to use the desktop blogging client—the ability to quickly and easily add images to our blog. For this support, we'll have to build in a new API method called newMediaObject. This method will require us to define two new structs to the MetaWeblog API.

Our first struct will be what the API will use to pass the image data to us. It contains three members:

- *Name*: A string that determines how the web log refers to the uploaded object

- *Type*: A string that includes the standard MIME type, such as image/jpeg

- *Bits*: A base-64-encoded binary value that contains the content of the uploaded object

Using that information, we'll create a new struct named MediaObject in /app/apis/ meta_weblog_service.rb and define it like this:

```
module MetaWeblogStructs
  class Post < ActionWebService::Struct
    member :postid, :string
    member :title,  :string
    member :link, :string
    member :dateCreated, :time
    member :description, :string
    member :categories, [:string]
  end

  class MediaObject < ActionWebService::Struct
    member :bits, :string
    member :name, :string
    member :type, :string
  end
end
```

The second new struct that we'll add to the MetaWeblog API will only have a single member that we'll use to pass back the URL for how to access the uploaded image:

```
class Url < ActionWebService::Struct
  member :url, :string
end
```

Now, with those two new structs added to our MetaWeblog API, we can define the newMediaObject method in our API definition using those structs like so:

```
api_method :newMediaObject,
  :expects => [ {:blogid => :string}, {:username => :string},
                {:password => :string},
                {:data => MetaWeblogStructs::MediaObject} ],
  :returns => [MetaWeblogStructs::Url]
```

Now, all that's left is to build the method to handle the uploads. The first step in this process is going to be to build out a place to store the files that we upload to the server. For that, let's create a new subdirectory named uploaded_images within the /public directory of our

Rails application. You'll also need to make sure that you've set the appropriate permissions on this new folder so that your Rails application can write to this directory.

Next, we'll need to create a new model that will handle the logic for our uploaded images as well as store a reference to any images that we upload:

```
ruby script/generate model Image
```

```
exists  app/models/
exists  test/unit/
exists  test/fixtures/
create  app/models/image.rb
create  test/unit/image_test.rb
create  test/fixtures/images.yml
exists  db/migrate
create  db/migrate/004_create_images.rb
```

We'll edit the new migration (/db/migrate/004_create_images.rb) to capture the name and extension of our uploaded image:

```
class CreateImages < ActiveRecord::Migration
  def self.up
    create_table :images do |t|
      t.column "name", :string
      t.column "extension", :string
      t.column 'created_at', :datetime
    end
  end

  def self.down
    drop_table :images
  end
end
```

Go ahead and run your migration to create the images table in our database, and then we'll edit our Image model. We'll have to build a few special features into our Image model in order to support our specific needs.

For one, we need to configure where our images are going to be stored. We could specify this in environment.rb, but for this project I think it will make more sense to keep that configuration within the model so that all of the logic is self-contained. Create a constant in the Image model (/app/models/image.rb) that references our newly created uploaded_images subdirectory:

```
DIRECTORY = 'public/uploaded_images'
```

Next, create a method in this model that will return the full file path reference to our image. We can create this by joining our DIRECTORY constant with the file name and extension:

```
def path
  File.join(DIRECTORY, "#{self.id}.#{extension}")
end
```

Of course, even more useful for our blog will be a URL reference to the image. We can generate this by simply modifying the result of our path method with a regular expression to remove the public reference:

```
def url
  path.sub(/^public/,'')
end
```

Finally—and probably most importantly of all—we need a method that will actually allow us to save uploaded image data to our application. We're going to keep this as simple as possible, merely accepting whatever is uploaded and saving it to the uploaded_images directory:

```
def save_file(data)
  File.open(path, 'wb') { |f| f.write(data) }
end
```

Putting it all together, we end up with an Image model like this:

```
class Image < ActiveRecord::Base
  validates_presence_of :name, :extension
  validates_uniqueness_of :name

  DIRECTORY = 'public/uploaded_images'

  def path
    File.join(DIRECTORY, "#{self.id}.#{extension}")
  end

  def url
    path.sub(/^public/,'')
  end

  def save_file(data)
    File.open(path, 'wb') { |f| f.write(data) }
  end
end
```

With our Image model built, let's finish out our image uploading support by building the newMediaObject method back in our /app/apis/meta_weblog_service.rb, where we'll create a new image object using the name of our uploaded file, and then saving its data to the file system using the save_file method we created in the Image model. Once we've created a new image, we'll return the URL to the image as the response:

```
def newMediaObject(blogid, username, password, data)
    image = Image.create(:name => data['name'],
                         :extension => data['name'].split('.').last.downcase)
    image.save_file(data['bits'])
    MetaWeblogStructs::Url.new("url" => image.url)
  end
```

With that, your final MetaWeblog API (/app/apis/meta_weblog_service.rb) should look like this:

```ruby
module MetaWeblogStructs
  class Post < ActionWebService::Struct
    member :postid, :string
    member :title,  :string
    member :link, :string
    member :dateCreated, :time
    member :description, :string
    member :categories, [:string]
  end

  class MediaObject < ActionWebService::Struct
    member :bits, :string
    member :name, :string
    member :type, :string
  end

  class Url < ActionWebService::Struct
    member :url, :string
  end
end

class MetaWeblogApi < ActionWebService::API::Base
  inflect_names false
  api_method :getCategories,
    :expects => [{:blogid => :string},
                 {:username => :string},
                 {:password => :string}],
    :returns => [[:string]]

  api_method :newPost,
    :expects => [
      {:blogid => :string},
      {:username => :string},
      {:password => :string},
      {:content => MetaWeblogStructs::Post},
      {:publish => :bool}
      ],
    :returns => [:string]

  api_method :getPost,
    :expects => [{:postid => :string},
                 {:username => :string},
                 {:password => :string}],
    :returns => [MetaWeblogStructs::Post]
```

```ruby
  api_method :getRecentPosts,
    :expects => [{:blogid => :string},
                 {:username => :string},
                 {:password => :string},
                 {:numberOfPosts => :int}],
    :returns => [[MetaWeblogStructs::Post]]

  api_method :editPost,
    :expects => [ {:postid => :string},
                  {:username => :string},
                  {:password => :string},
                  {:struct => MetaWeblogStructs::Post},
                  {:publish => :int} ],
    :returns => [:bool]

  api_method :newMediaObject,
    :expects => [ {:blogid => :string},
                  {:username => :string},
                  {:password => :string},
                  {:data => MetaWeblogStructs::MediaObject} ],
    :returns => [MetaWeblogStructs::Url]
end

class MetaWeblogService < ActionWebService::Base
  web_service_api MetaWeblogApi

  def getCategories(blogid, username, password)
    if Blog.authenticate(username, password)
      Category.find(:all).collect { |c| c.name }
    end
  end

  def newPost(blogid, username, password, content, publish)
    if Blog.authenticate(username, password)
      p = Post.new(:blog_id => blogid, :title => content['title'],
                       :body => content['description'])
      if content['categories']
        p.categories.clear
        Category.find(:all).each do |c|
          p.categories << c if content['categories'].include?(c.name)
        end
      end
      p.save ? p.id.to_s : 'Error: Post cannot be created'
    end
  end
```

```ruby
def getPost(postid, username, password)
  if Blog.authenticate(username, password)
    post = Post.find(postid)
    buildPost(post)
  end
end

def getRecentPosts(blogid, username, password, numberOfPosts)
  if Blog.authenticate(username, password)
    Post.find(:all, :order => 'created_at desc',
                    :limit => numberOfPosts).collect do |p|
      buildPost(p)
    end
  end
end

def editPost(postid, username, password, content, publish)
  if Blog.authenticate(username, password)
    post = Post.find(postid)
    post.attributes = {:body => content['description'].to_s,
                       :title => content['title'].to_s}

    if content['categories']
      post.categories.clear
      Category.find(:all).each do |c|
        post.categories << c if content['categories'].include?(c.name)
      end
    end
    post.save
    true
  end
end

def newMediaObject(blogid, username, password, data)
  image = Image.create(:name => data['name'],
                       :extension => data['name'].split('.').last.downcase)
  image.save_file(data['bits'])
  MetaWeblogStructs::Url.new("url" => image.url)
end
```

```
def buildPost(post)
  MetaWeblogStructs::Post.new(
    :dateCreated => post.created_at || '',
    :postid => post.id.to_s,
    :description => post.body,
    :title => post.title,
    :categories => post.categories.collect { |c| c.name })
  end
end
```

Creating a new blog post with an image gives us the successful result shown in Figure 10-8.

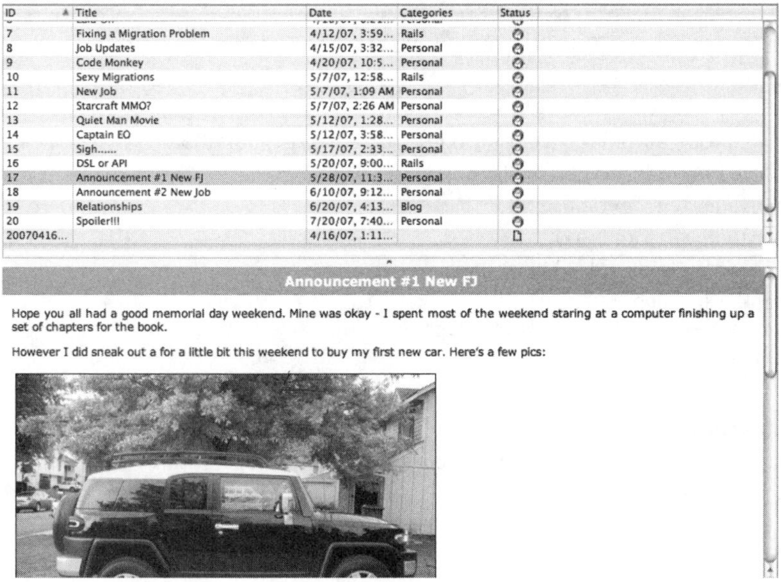

Figure 10-8. *A blog post with an image*

Building the Public-Facing Side of Our Blog

Now that we have our API built, let's round things out by putting together the external pages that will make up our new blog. After all, what good is a blog if no one can see it?

Creating a Basic Layout

The first thing that we need to do is put together a basic layout for our blog. We'll keep things really simple by putting together an uncomplicated layout consisting of a header, a main content area, and a navigation area on the right-hand side. To make things even easier in building this layout, we'll take advantage of the page layout capabilities of the Ext JavaScript library. I'll go into greater detail on how to use that library in Chapter 18 (including how to automate it's installation with a generator), but for now, you can get by with merely downloading the latest version from www.extjs.com. Once you have that file uncompressed, we'll need to copy over a few key files into our application:

- Copy ext-all.css from /resources/css into our /public/stylesheets directory.

- Copy ext-all.js from the root of the archive into our /public/javascripts directory.

- Copy ext-base.js from /adapter/base into our /public/javascripts directory.

Once you have those files copied over as well as the application.css style sheet and images downloaded from the code archive for this project, we can build our layout by creating a new file in /apps/views/layouts named application.rhtml and placing the following content into it:

```
<!DOCTYPE HTML PUBLIC "-//W3C//DTD HTML 4.01 Transitional//EN"
"http://www.w3.org/TR/html4/loose.dtd">
<head>
  <meta http-equiv="Content-type" content="text/html; charset=utf-8">
  <title>My Personal Blog</title>
  <%= javascript_include_tag 'ext-base' %>
  <%= javascript_include_tag 'ext-all' %>
  <%= stylesheet_link_tag 'ext-all' %>
  <%= stylesheet_link_tag 'application' %>
  <script type="text/javascript" charset="utf-8">
    Blog = function(){
      return {
        init : function(){
          var layout = new Ext.BorderLayout(document.body, {
            north: {
              split:false,
              initialSize: 105
            },
            east: {
              split:false,
              initialSize: 200
            },
            center: {
              autoScroll: true
            }
          });
          layout.beginUpdate();
          layout.add('north', new Ext.ContentPanel('header', {fitToFrame:true}));
          layout.add('east', new Ext.ContentPanel('navigation',
                        {title: 'Navigation', fitToFrame:true, closable:false}));
          layout.add('center', new Ext.ContentPanel('main'));
          layout.endUpdate();
        }
      }
```

```
    }();
    Ext.EventManager.onDocumentReady(Blog.init, Blog, true);
  </script>
</head>

<body>
  <div id="header" class="ylayout-inactive-content">
   <h1 id="welcome_to_my_blog">My Blog</h1>
  </div>

  <div id="main">
    <div id="content"  class="ylayout-inactive-content">
      <%= yield %>
    </div>
  </div>

  <div id="navigation" class="ylayout-inactive-content">
    <ul id="nav">
      <li><%= link_to 'Home', home_path %></li>
      <% for cat in Category.find(:all).collect { |c| c.name } do %>
        <li><%= link_to "#{cat}", "/category/#{cat}" %></li>
      <% end %>
    </ul>
  </div>
</body>
</html>
```

So our layout will have three main blocks: the header, which displays the name of our blog; the main block, which is where our content will be inserted via the `yield` method; and a navigation block, in which we simply iterate over our categories to build the navigation links. Now, if we were to view this layout (which won't work until we add some controllers), you would see that this layout produces an output like the page shown in Figure 10-9

Figure 10-9. *Our page layout*

Editing the Application Controller

Now that we have our layout built, we need to set up our application to utilize it and begin to display our blog posts in it. Open `application.rb` from `/app/controllers/`, and let's modify it to add a `before_filter` that will populate an `@blog` variable with a reference to our blog:

```
class ApplicationController < ActionController::Base
  session :session_key => '_myblog_session_id'
  before_filter :get_blog

  protected
  def get_blog
    @blog = Blog.find(:first)
  end
end
```

Creating the Home Page

With the layout built and a reference to our blog obtained, the next thing we should tackle is a way of presenting our blog posts onto the main page. We'll start out by first creating a new controller named `public` with a default method of index:

```
ruby script/generate controller public index
```

```
exists   app/controllers/
exists   app/helpers/
create   app/views/public
exists   test/functional/
create   app/controllers/public_controller.rb
create   test/functional/public_controller_test.rb
create   app/helpers/public_helper.rb
create   app/views/public/index.rhtml
```

Next, we'll modify our routes configuration to make the `index` method of our public controller the default root page by adding the following line to `/config/routes.rb`:

```
ActionController::Routing::Routes.draw do |map|

  map.home '', :controller => 'public'

  map.connect ':controller/service.wsdl', :action => 'wsdl'
  map.connect ':controller/:action/:id.:format'
  map.connect ':controller/:action/:id'
end
```

A request to the root of our application will now look for the index method in our public controller, so let's edit that method to retrieve a list of the posts now:

```
class PublicController < ApplicationController

  def index
    @posts = @blog.posts.find(:all, :order => "created_at desc")
  end
end
```

Afterward, we can edit the index.rhtml view in /app/views/public to add the following content, which will give us the results that are shown in Figure 10-10:

```
<% for post in @posts %>
  <h3><%= post.title %></h3>
  <p><%= post.body %></p>
  <hr />
<% end %>
```

Figure 10-10. *Our blog displaying our posts*

Adding in Pagination

Our blog page is going to fill up very fast if we're posting with any regularity, so to keep the content accessible, we should add in some basic pagination to split up our posts across multiple pages. If you've read a beginning Rails book, you're probably aware that Rails includes a few helpers for pagination—unfortunately, they have quickly fallen out of popularity with the Rails community because of the some scalability issues with the overall design. They will be moved out of the Rails core and into a separate plug-in named classic_pagination for Rails 2.0, so even though that pagination code would probably be sufficient for our simple blog, we might be better served with putting in a more scalable solution, so that we don't have problems down the road.

However, there's no need to be afraid that we're worrying about premature optimization too much, as it turns out we can add a better solution with not much more work than it would take to utilize the current Rails pagination helpers—thanks to the will_paginate plug-in released by Rails developer P.J. Hyett. But enough discussion, let's go ahead and install the plug-in to our blog, so you can see it in action:

```
ruby script/plugin install svn://errtheblog.com/svn/plugins/will_paginate
```

```
A    /Users/darkel/book/revision/myblog/vendor/plugins/will_paginate
A    /Users/darkel/book/revision/myblog/vendor/plugins/will_paginate/test
A    /Users/darkel/book/revision/myblog/vendor/plugins/will_paginate/test/helper.rb
A    /Users/darkel/book/revision/myblog/vendor/plugins/will_paginate/test/console
A    /Users/darkel/book/revision/myblog/vendor/plugins/will_paginate/test/boot.rb
A    /Users/darkel/book/revision/myblog/vendor/plugins/will_paginate/test/lib
A    /Users/darkel/book/revision/myblog/vendor/plugins/will_paginate/test/lib➡
/activerecord_test_connector.rb
A    /Users/darkel/book/revision/myblog/vendor/plugins/will_paginate/test/lib/➡
load_fixtures.rb
A    /Users/darkel/book/revision/myblog/vendor/plugins/will_paginate/test/➡
finder_test.rb
A    /Users/darkel/book/revision/myblog/vendor/plugins/will_paginate/test/fixtures
A    /Users/darkel/book/revision/myblog/vendor/plugins/will_paginate/test➡
/fixtures/topic.rb
A    /Users/darkel/book/revision/myblog/vendor/plugins/will_paginate/test/fixtures➡
/user.rb
A    /Users/darkel/book/revision/myblog/vendor/plugins/will_paginate/test/fixtures➡
/developers_projects.yml
A    /Users/darkel/book/revision/myblog/vendor/plugins/will_paginate/test/fixtures➡
/topics.yml
A    /Users/darkel/book/revision/myblog/vendor/plugins/will_paginate/test/fixtures➡
/users.yml
A    /Users/darkel/book/revision/myblog/vendor/plugins/will_paginate/test/fixtures➡
/replies.yml
A    /Users/darkel/book/revision/myblog/vendor/plugins/will_paginate/test/fixtures➡
/developer.rb
A    /Users/darkel/book/revision/myblog/vendor/plugins/will_paginate/test/fixtures➡
/company.rb
A    /Users/darkel/book/revision/myblog/vendor/plugins/will_paginate/test/fixtures➡
/project.rb
A    /Users/darkel/book/revision/myblog/vendor/plugins/will_paginate/test/fixtures➡
/projects.yml
A    /Users/darkel/book/revision/myblog/vendor/plugins/will_paginate/test/fixtures➡
/admin.rb
A    /Users/darkel/book/revision/myblog/vendor/plugins/will_paginate/test/fixtures➡
/reply.rb
A    /Users/darkel/book/revision/myblog/vendor/plugins/will_paginate/test/fixtures➡
/companies.yml
A    /Users/darkel/book/revision/myblog/vendor/plugins/will_paginate/test/fixtures➡
/schema.sql
```

```
A    /Users/darkel/book/revision/myblog/vendor/plugins/will_paginate/test➥
/pagination_test.rb
A    /Users/darkel/book/revision/myblog/vendor/plugins/will_paginate/Rakefile
A    /Users/darkel/book/revision/myblog/vendor/plugins/will_paginate/init.rb
A    /Users/darkel/book/revision/myblog/vendor/plugins/will_paginate/lib
A    /Users/darkel/book/revision/myblog/vendor/plugins/will_paginate/lib➥
/will_paginate
A    /Users/darkel/book/revision/myblog/vendor/plugins/will_paginate/lib/➥
will_paginate/finder.rb
A    /Users/darkel/book/revision/myblog/vendor/plugins/will_paginate/lib/➥
will_paginate/core_ext.rb
A    /Users/darkel/book/revision/myblog/vendor/plugins/will_paginate/lib➥
/will_paginate/collection.rb
A    /Users/darkel/book/revision/myblog/vendor/plugins/will_paginate/lib/➥
will_paginate/view_helpers.rb
A    /Users/darkel/book/revision/myblog/vendor/plugins/will_paginate/lib/core_ext
A    /Users/darkel/book/revision/myblog/vendor/plugins/will_paginate/README
Exported revision 313.
```

Once the plug-in is installed, we need to make a few minor modifications to our application to enable some exceptionally nice pagination functionality.

First, let's modify our finder from the index method in /app/controllers/public_controller.rb to use the new paginate method added by will_paginate. We'll have to pass the paginate method two new parameters: a :per_page option to configure the number of posts to show per page and a :page option to let will_paginate know which page in the collection we're wanting to display:

```
class PublicController < ApplicationController

  def index
    @posts = @blog.posts.paginate(:per_page => 7, :page => params[:page],
                                  :order => "created_at desc")
  end
end
```

Second, in the index view (/app/views/public/index.rhtml), we simply need to add a single line at the bottom to include our pagination links:

```
<% for post in @posts %>
  <h3><%= post.title %></h3>
  <p><%= post.body %></p>
  <hr />
<% end %>

<%= will_paginate @posts %>
```

Adding in a small amount of CSS styling (influenced heavily by the sample CSS included in the will_paginate plug-in), our pagination links end up looking like the ones shown in Figure 10-11.

Figure 10-11. *Styled pagination links for our blog*

Viewing a Single Post

We also need to create the ability to support viewing a single blog post, so that readers can easily bookmark or link to a specific post that we have written. We'll do that by adding a show method and template to the public controller of our blog—within /app/controllers/public_controller.rb, add the following method.

```ruby
class PublicController < ApplicationController

  def index
    @posts = @blog.posts.paginate(:per_page => 2,
                                   :page => params[:page],
                                   :order => "created_at desc")
  end

  def show
    @post = @blog.posts.find(params[:id])
  end
end
```

Next, create a new show.rhtml template under apps/views/public. In here, we'll simply display the content of our post within the existing layout:

```
<h3><%= @post.title %></h3>
<p> <%= @post.body %></p>
```

Now, we just need to provide a way to route to this page. Open /config/routes.rb, and add the following named route:

```ruby
ActionController::Routing::Routes.draw do |map|

  map.home '', :controller => 'public'
  map.post '/:id', :controller => 'public', :action => 'show'

  map.connect ':controller/service.wsdl', :action => 'wsdl'
  map.connect ':controller/:action/:id.:format'
  map.connect ':controller/:action/:id'
end
```

With those simple additions, we can go back and modify the index template (/app/views/public/index.rhtml) to now make the headline for each post also link to the individual post:

```
<% for post in @posts %>
  <h3><%= link_to post.title, post_path(post) %></h3>
  <p><%= post.body %></p>
  <hr />
<% end %>

<%= will_paginate @posts %>
```

Now, if people want to access a single post, they can access the page by simply navigating to http://localhost:3000/2. That's fine but not exactly the prettiest URL for a blog post. Typically, it's better if the links to our blog posts are a bit more descriptive and user friendly. We can do that fairly easily by overriding the to_param method in our Post model to return the ID plus a nice textual description of our post's title.

Add the following method to your Post model:

```
class Post < ActiveRecord::Base
  belongs_to :blog
  has_and_belongs_to_many :categories
  validates_presence_of :blog_id, :title, :body

  def to_param
    "#{id}-#{title.gsub(/[^a-z1-9]+/i, '-')}"
  end
end
```

Now, if we click one of the links from our main page, we'll see that our URL shows a much friendlier link like /posts/1-This-is-my-first-blog-post. That's certainly going to be a lot nicer for sharing links to our blog and for search engine optimization, but how does that work?

It's pretty simple actually; we're taking advantage of a couple of nice features within Rails. In the link to the show template, we're passing a Post object to our link_to method (link_to post.title, post_path(post) rather than explicitly passing the object's ID to the link_to method (link_to post.title, post_path(post.id)). By doing it this way, we cause Rails to call its to_param method on the object to obtain the ID, but we've overridden that method in the model to return the ID plus the post's title (which we've run through a regular expression to convert whitespaces to hyphens).

Then, when this URL is delivered to the controller to do its lookup, Rails will automatically convert what it receives as the ID to an integer, stripping off any text that it finds after the last digit. So what comes after the ID is irrelevant to the find methods.

■**Note** This solution is a bit on the simplistic side; for a slightly more thorough implementation, you might consider using another of Rick Olsen's plug-ins by the name of permalink_fu available at http://svn.techno-weenie.net/projects/plugins/permalink_fu/.

Adding a Category Filter

You might have noticed that we're using our category listings as our only navigational links within the sidebar of our layout (/app/views/layouts/application.rhtml):

```
<% for cat in Category.find(:all).collect { |c| c.name } do %>
    <li><%= link_to "#{cat}", "/category/#{cat}" %></li>
<% end %>
```

This code generates a set of links like /category/Rails and /category/Blog with the idea that we would use those links to provide a filtered view of our blog posts showing only the posts that were tagged with that specific category. Now, it's time to make those links work.

Our first step will be to add a route in our routes.rb in /config that will map these requests to a category method in our public controller and grab the category name from the URL placing it in a :name parameter:

```
ActionController::Routing::Routes.draw do |map|

  map.home '', :controller => 'public'
  map.category '/category/:name', :controller => 'public', :action => 'category'
  map.post '/:id', :controller => 'public', :action => 'show'

  map.connect ':controller/service.wsdl', :action => 'wsdl'
  map.connect ':controller/:action/:id.:format'
  map.connect ':controller/:action/:id'
end
```

Within our /app/controllers/public_controller.rb, we'll add the category method that we just targeted for these links to search for all the blog posts tagged with the category name that we received. To avoid duplication, we'll just render our existing index template to handle the displaying of blog posts:

```
class PublicController < ApplicationController

  def index
    @posts = @blog.posts.paginate(:per_page => 7,
                                  :page => params[:page],
                                  :order => "created_at desc")
  end

  def show
    @post = @blog.posts.find(params[:id])
  end

  def category
    @category = Category.find_by_name(params[:name])
    @posts = @category.posts.paginate(:per_page => 7, :page => params[:page],
                                      :conditions => ["blog_id == ?", @blog.id],
                                      :order => "created_at desc")
```

```
    render(:action => "index")
  end
end
```

Building an RSS Feed

Our simple blog has come together pretty nicely in a short time. We just have one last feature that every blog requires these days—an RSS feed. Just in case you aren't aware, RSS stands for Really Simple Syndication and is a way of representing our blog content into a specialized XML format that external applications can read. End users can configure these applications to subscribe to our site's content and be notified when a post is added to our site.

To start off, we'll create a new method in our public_controller.rb named rss, which will simply pull our most recent 25 posts. Since we want this method to display an XML template, we'll also need to disable the layout for this method:

```
def rss
  @posts = @blog.posts.find(:all, :limit => 25, :order => 'created_at desc')
  render(:layout => false)
end
```

To keep things a little cleaner, we'll create a route to our new RSS feed by adding a line to our routes.rb file (found in /config):

```
ActionController::Routing::Routes.draw do |map|

  map.home '', :controller => 'public'
  map.category '/category/:name', :controller => 'public', :action => 'category'
  map.feed '/rss', :controller => 'public', :action => 'rss'
  map.post '/:id', :controller => 'public', :action => 'show'

  map.connect ':controller/service.wsdl', :action => 'wsdl'
  map.connect ':controller/:action/:id.:format'
  map.connect ':controller/:action/:id'
end
```

This makes our RSS feed accessible at http://localhost:3000/rss. Now, all we need to do is build our RSS template to display. Create a new file in /apps/views/public named rss.rxml, and paste the following code into it:

```
xml.instruct!
xml.rss "version" => "2.0", "xmlns:dc" => "http://purl.org/dc/elements/1.1/" do
  xml.channel do
    xml.title           "My Simple Weblog"
    xml.link            posts_url
    xml.pubDate         CGI.rfc1123_date(@posts.first.updated_at) if @posts.any?
    xml.description     "My Personal weblog"
```

```
    @posts.each do |post|
      xml.item do
        xml.title          post.title
        xml.link          post_url(post)
        xml.description  post.body
        xml.pubDate      CGI.rfc1123_date(post.updated_at)
        xml.guid          post_url(post)
      end
    end
  end
end
```

With that, we've got our basic RSS feed built for our blog, which will serve our basic needs in a nice, no-frills way. Personally, I've found a lot of value in taking a basic feed like this and using the optimizing features and tracking capabilities of a third-party tool like FeedBurner (http://www.feedburner.com).

Summary

In this chapter, we put together a nice, simple blog that should serve most of our basic needs. We learned about building a common API like MetaWebLog, adding pagination, creating friendly URLs by overwriting the to_params method, and supporting a basic RSS feed.

Building our own blog provided us with a much greater sense of accomplishment than simply using a prebuilt solution—plus we gained a lot more flexibility to modify it however we see fit.

## CHAPTER 11

Enhancing Our Blogs

This project was a bit different as we completed two separate blogs. Our first blog was put together using the open-source blogging engine Typo, and we took some extra time as we went through that to gain a deeper understanding of how Rails works. Afterward, building our own blog engine sounded like fun, so we created a simple blogging engine with support for features like the MetaWeblog API and an RSS feed. This chapter contains a number of ideas that you can use to continue your own personal development and enhance the applications.

Develop the Blogger API

To build the MetaWeblog API, we were forced to build several methods in the Blogger API as well. Why not go back and finish the job and implement the remainder of the core functionality necessary to support posting via the Blogger API?

Build a Blog Using Mephisto

Another popular Rails-based open source blogging system is Mephisto, which was created by Rick Olsen. You can download a copy of the latest version and read the documentation at the official site at www.mephistoblog.com. Try to build out a blog using Mephisto; particularly, spend time getting your feet wet implementing a page layout using the Liquid templating language. Spend some time digging through the source code for Mephisto, too, and you'll be amazed at some of the nifty things you'll learn.

Customize Typo

In Chapter 7, we spent a bit of time learning how to customize Typo with our own themes and building out a simple sidebar component. Now, it's time for you to expand on our little forays into Typo by customizing your own version.

You can start off by designing and implementing your own theme within the system.

Second, you can build out your own sidebar component. One idea might be a component to pull in the RSS feed from a Netflix queue and display your most recently watched DVDs. Or build a component that will pull in your daily tasks into our Monkey Tasks application using the API that you'll build in this chapter's "Extending Monkey Tasks" exercises.

Move Authentication Out of Methods

In our simple blog application, one element that should bother you about our current API implementation is the amount of duplication in our code base for the simple task of authenticating
a user for each method in the API. Each method has to call if Blog.authenticate(username,
password), and this really needs to be abstracted out to keep our code *dry*.

For a good start on how to do this, check out the API definitions in either Typo or Mephisto,
and you'll see how they've both defined a master WebService API that other web services (such
as Blogger and MetaWeblog) inherit from. In this master API, they define an authenticate method
and then in the individual web services, they simply call before_invocation :authenticate.

Add in Caching

One of the big shortcomings of our simple blog application is that, unless we're somehow magically hosting our blog on a set of monster servers, it's doubtful that our little blog would be able
to survive being Slashdotted or the Digg effect of a popular blog post. The best solution is to
implement a caching system so that each request to our blog content doesn't have to require a
full hit to our system resources.

Go though the project in Part 5 to learn more about implementing a system with caching
and then come back here and implement a solid dose of caching throughout our simple blog.

Add Comments and Akismet Spam Filtering

We avoided adding a commenting system into our simple blog due to my strong annoyance with
having to deal with blog spam in other blog systems. However, for this exercise, go ahead and add
one to your blog. You could go the automated route and use a plug-in such as acts_as_commentable
(http://juixe.com/svn/acts_as_commentable), but I recommend building your own.

Here are a few things you could consider for your commenting system:

- You should consider disabling comments on blog posts a set number of days after the
  post was created.

- You should never trust content that was submitted by users and thus you should filter
  it vigorously. A good starting point is a plug-in by the name of white_list (http://
  svn.techno-weenie.net/projects/plugins/white_list/). The white listing plug-in does
  a number of helpful things, such as HTML encoding all tags and stripping href/src tags
  with invalid protocols.

- You could also help eliminate spam by adding a CAPTCHA service from a service like
  www.captchator.com.

- Finally, you should look into implementing a spam filter using the Akismet spam
  filtering service. Check out Ryan Bates's excellent screencast on the subject for more
  information (http://railscasts.com/episodes/65).

Add Web Administration

We built our simple blog with the idea that we'd forgo the usual web administration pages due to the richer interface and features of using a desktop blogging client. However, there can always be those odd times when we want to do a little blog administration when we might not have access to our desktop application. So go ahead and experiment with building a backend web administration that will allow you to do your basic CRUD operations on blog posts.

RSS Feed for Categories

Currently, we're providing a generic RSS feed for the site as a whole. However, it's possible that some people may only want to subscribe to a certain category of posts (after all, your mother may want to know about your personal posts, but her eyes would gloss over trying to read your posts in the Rails category). Solve this problem by building an RSS feed for each category.

Implement Tagging

Now personally, I think tagging on a blog site isn't a practical use of the technology; that's why we opted to use categories to classify our posts instead. However, for those of you who disagree, this exercise is for you.

Add tagging capabilities to your blog. You can easily find a wealth of articles and how-tos for implementing tagging using the `acts_as_taggable` plug-in or the `acts_as_taggable` gem. However, I'd like to point you in a different (and in my opinion better) direction. Evan Weaver has put together a very powerful plug-in named `acts_as_polymorph` that can be used to build a much more resilient tagging system. You can find detailed information at `http://blog.evanweaver.com/articles/2007/01/13/growing-up-your-acts_as_taggable`.

Summary

That should be enough to get you started on enhancing our blogs. Obviously, my preference for the blog application is to keep it small and simple. However, feel free to enhance it any way that suits your fancy and share your innovations with others on the `RailsProjects.com` forums.

Extending Monkey Tasks

The following exercises offer additional enhancements for Monkey Tasks.

Build an API for the CRUD Operations of Daily Tasks

See if you can add a WebService API to MonkeyTasks that will allow you to do all of your standard CRUD operations or tasks. You'll need methods such as `buildTask`, `addTask`, `getTask`, `editTask`, and `deleteTask`. In addition, you should have some methods like `getTodaysTasks` that will pull back a list of today's task and `AddToToday`, which will add a task to the current day's task list.

Of course, you should make sure that API is multiuser safe and is only pulling back the tasks for the authenticated user.

Add an RSS Feed

In addition to building out an API that could allow you to manage your tasks, it will also be good practice to add an RSS feed of your daily tasks that you could subscribe to.

PART 5

■ ■ ■

Building a Web Comic Using Caching

The question of Rails scalability still seems to surface each and every week in much the same way that people once questioned the scalability of PHP before Yahoo adopted it. However, with the recent advent of several high-profile Rails sites, such as Twitter (which handles spikes of 11,000 requests per second) or the popular gaming comic Penny-Arcade (serving over 2 million page views a day), the question of whether Rails applications can scale is no longer valid. The better question is, "How do we scale a Rails application?"

Unfortunately it would be far outside the scope of this book to go over the external things that we can do to handle those levels of traffic, such as implementing memcache, clustering our database access, optimizing our databases (tuning indexes and denormalizing for performance), utilizing content delivery networks, or simply distributing our processing out among multiple servers into a share-nothing architecture.

Fortunately, most of us won't ever have to endure the pain that is required to serve such high amounts of traffic through our Rails applications—even so, that doesn't prevent us from having to worry about scalability, as we've seen how quickly a front-page link from the likes of Slashdot, Digg, or Penny Arcade can cause an ill-prepared application to leave a server screaming for mercy.

Among the most powerful tools within our Rails arsenal for building applications that can handle a sudden increase in page views are the included caching features. A solid understanding of the Rails caching system and a thoughtful implementation of caching can remove expensive database queries and page generation processing out of each request and exponentially improve our applications' availability under load.

In this project, we'll take a look at building a basic web comic application. We'll start out by creating a system for image uploads, and then explore the different caching capabilities that we can add to the application to support the comic as it grows.

CHAPTER 12

■ ■ ■

Building Our Base System with Page Caching

In this first phase of the project, we're going to build a basic web comic site that will allow us to upload our comics. Let's start out by creating a new project named webcomic, using the instructions from Chapter 2. With our basic application structure ready, we need to start thinking about exactly what it is that we want to build. What are some of the key features of a web comic? Obviously, we'll need to make it easy to upload and display new comics, but taking a look around the web at some of the popular web comics, we can see several other key features that we'll want to support:

- The default (home) page should always provide the most current comic.

- In order to support the site, most web comics need to provide space for some level of advertising.

- We need to provide an easy way for visitors to navigate previous comics.

With that high-level understanding, I put together a basic sketch of what our application should look like; it's shown in Figure 12-1.

Figure 12-1. *Rough sketch of our web comic*

We can reasonably facilitate this layout with YUI grids in a standard layout, so go ahead and create an `application.rhtml` layout file in your /app/views/layouts folder with this content:

```
<!DOCTYPE HTML PUBLIC "-//W3C//DTD HTML 4.01//EN"
 "http://www.w3.org/TR/html4/strict.dtd">
<html>
<head>
  <title>Method Missing Web Comic</title>
  <link rel="stylesheet" href="http://yui.yahooapis.com/2.2.0/build/➥
reset-fonts-grids/reset-fonts-grids.css" type="text/css">
  <%= stylesheet_link_tag 'styles' %>
</head>
<body>
<div id="doc2" class="yui-t4">
  <div id="hd"><%= image_tag 'methodmissing.jpg' %></div>
  <div id="bd">
    <div id="yui-main">
      <div class="yui-b">
        <div class="yui-g"><%= image_tag 'topbanner.jpg' %></div>
        <div class="yui-g"><%= yield %> </div>
      </div>
    </div>
    <div class="yui-b"><%= image_tag 'sidebanner.jpg' %></div>
  </div>
  <div id="ft"> &copy; Method Missing</div>
</div>
</body>
</html>
```

It would be a good idea to go ahead and load the style sheets and images from the source archive now. With those loaded, once we add our first view to the applications (which we'll do shortly), this layout should produce a page like the one shown in Figure 12-2.

Figure 12-2. *The initial layout for the web comic application*

A Basic Administration System

With a basic layout defined, the first task that we'll tackle in building our web comic is handling the administration side of things. This will allow us to begin adding and managing comics on the site. We'll keep our administration side fairly simple (leaning on the scaffolding templates) so that we can spend more time on the meat and potatoes subjects of handling image uploads, building our own authentication system, and implementing the various types of caching for this project.

Uploading Comics

Obviously, one of the most important aspects that we'll need to address is the ability to easily upload new comics (images) to the site. To handle our image uploading needs, we'll take advantage of a plug-in by the name of `attachment_fu` written by Rick Olsen.

Attachment Fu is actually a significant rewrite of an earlier plug-in named Acts as Attachment, which extended Active Record models with a number of convenience methods for handling file uploads. Acts as Attachment had a number of extremely nice features, such as

- Allowing you to select whether to store your uploaded files on a file system or in a database

- Providing an interface to RMagick for easy image resizing and thumbnail creation

One of the most beautiful things about the rewrite is the way that key components of the plug-in, such as the storage engine and the image processing system, have been modularized. This allows us much more flexibility in how Attachment Fu will work in our specific environment, and it should make adding new options to Attachment Fu much easier in the future. To give you an idea, before the Attachment Fu rewrite, as you saw previously, there were only two options for storing images in Acts as Attachment. However, the modularization of the storage engine has now made it easy to add the Amazon Simple Storage Solution (or S3 for short) as a third option. Similarly, Attachment Fu has also added new image-processing options so that now we can choose from RMagick, ImageScience, or even MiniMagick to handle our image resizing or thumbnailing needs.

Attachment Fu is probably the easiest way to add file upload capabilities to your application (especially if you need to be able to handle different upload configurations in each model). For example, a console games store might use one model for box shots where the images would be stored in the database and another model for screenshots, which would allow for larger file sizes, that stores the images on the file system.

Installing Attachment Fu

We can install `attachment_fu` through the `plugin` install command like so:

```
ruby script/plugin install ➥
http://svn.techno-weenie.net/projects/plugins/attachment_fu/
```

```
+ ./attachment_fu/CHANGELOG
+ ./attachment_fu/README
+ ./attachment_fu/Rakefile
+ ./attachment_fu/amazon_s3.yml.tpl
+ ./attachment_fu/init.rb
+ ./attachment_fu/install.rb
+ ./attachment_fu/lib/geometry.rb
+ ./attachment_fu/lib/technoweenie/attachment_fu/backends/db_file_backend.rb
+ ./attachment_fu/lib/technoweenie/attachment_fu/backends/file_system_backend.rb
+ ./attachment_fu/lib/technoweenie/attachment_fu/backends/s3_backend.rb
+ ./attachment_fu/lib/technoweenie/attachment_fu/processors/➥
image_science_processor.rb
+ ./attachment_fu/lib/technoweenie/attachment_fu/processors/mini_magick_processor.rb
+ ./attachment_fu/lib/technoweenie/attachment_fu/processors/rmagick_processor.rb
+ ./attachment_fu/lib/technoweenie/attachment_fu.rb
+ ./attachment_fu/test/amazon_s3.yml
+ ./attachment_fu/test/backends/db_file_test.rb
+ ./attachment_fu/test/backends/file_system_test.rb
+ ./attachment_fu/test/backends/remote/s3_test.rb
+ ./attachment_fu/test/base_attachment_tests.rb
+ ./attachment_fu/test/basic_test.rb
+ ./attachment_fu/test/database.yml
+ ./attachment_fu/test/extra_attachment_test.rb
+ ./attachment_fu/test/fixtures/attachment.rb
+ ./attachment_fu/test/fixtures/files/fake/rails.png
+ ./attachment_fu/test/fixtures/files/foo.txt
+ ./attachment_fu/test/fixtures/files/rails.png
+ ./attachment_fu/test/geometry_test.rb
+ ./attachment_fu/test/processors/image_science_test.rb
+ ./attachment_fu/test/processors/mini_magick_test.rb
+ ./attachment_fu/test/processors/rmagick_test.rb
+ ./attachment_fu/test/schema.rb
+ ./attachment_fu/test/test_helper.rb
+ ./attachment_fu/test/validation_test.rb
attachment-fu
=====================
```

Now that we've added `attachment_fu` to our application, all we need to do is build out some models and configure them to utilize `attachment_fu`'s functionality.

So let's go ahead and build the most obvious model that we'll need—the comic model.

Our Comic Model

The comic model is going to be the core model of our entire application. It's the model that we'll use to track each of our individual comics. Each comic will be stored on the local file system for now, and each comic will have a title and basic text description. In addition to those fields, Attachment Fu requires that we also add the following columns to our database design for this model:

`Content_type`: Required for all attachments, this column stores the content type of the upload. For example, uploading a JPG image would result in `image/jpeg` being stored here.

`Filename`: This column is required for all attachments and stores the name of the file being uploaded.

`Size`: Required for all attachments, this column stores the size, in bytes, of the file being uploaded.

`Thumbnail`: Used for images only if we're creating thumbnail versions, this column stores the reference key to the thumbnail we've created. If we're storing the image on the file system, `attachment_fu` will append this key onto the file name when creating the name for the thumbnail version. If we uploaded an image named `avatar.jpg`, the thumbnail version might be called `avatar_thumb.jpg`.

`Parent_id`: This column is used only if we're creating thumbnail versions for images. It stores a foreign key reference to the ID of the full-sized version of the image.

`Width`: This column, required only if we're handling image uploads, stores the width, in pixels, of our uploaded image.

`Height`: This column, also required only if we're handling image uploads, stores the height, in pixels, of our uploaded image.

Armed with that knowledge, we can go ahead and use the `scaffold_resource` command to build out our comics controller and model:

```
ruby script/generate scaffold_resource Comic content_type:string filename:string➥
  size:integer width:integer height:integer title:string description:text
```

```
exists   app/models/
exists   app/controllers/
exists   app/helpers/
create   app/views/comics
exists   test/functional/
exists   test/unit/
create   app/views/comics/index.rhtml
create   app/views/comics/show.rhtml
create   app/views/comics/new.rhtml
create   app/views/comics/edit.rhtml
create   app/views/layouts/comics.rhtml
create   public/stylesheets/scaffold.css
create   app/models/comic.rb
create   app/controllers/comics_controller.rb
create   test/functional/comics_controller_test.rb
create   app/helpers/comics_helper.rb
create   test/unit/comic_test.rb
create   test/fixtures/comics.yml
create   db/migrate
create   db/migrate/001_create_comics.rb
 route   map.resources :comics
```

Unfortunately, the scaffolding also created a layout that we didn't want, so go ahead and remove comics.rhtml from /app/views/layouts/:

```
rm app/views/layouts/comics.rhtml
```

With that file out of our way, we can now modify our new Comic model to utilize attachment_fu. We start out by calling the method has_attachment from within our Comic model to add the attachment_fu functionality. This method takes a number of configurations options:

:content_type: By default, attachment_fu puts no restrictions on the types of files that can be uploaded. However, we can (and should) specify the specific file types that we want to allow through the content type configuration option. As a convenience, we can pass it :content_type => :image to account for most standard image types. We could also pass it a specific file type such as :content_type => 'image/jpeg' or :content_type => 'text/plain'. If we wanted to support a variety of content types, we could pass it an array like :content_type => ['image/jpeg', 'application/msword', 'application/pdf'].

:min_size: This sets the minimum size that we'll allow for an uploaded file. The Rails number helpers are a godsend for this, allowing us to specify parameters in convenient formats like :min_size => 1.byte or :min_size => 5.megabytes.

:max_size: Just as you'd expect, this sets the maximum size that we'll allow for an uploaded file. If nothing is provided, it will default to 1.megabyte.

:size: This is a more convenient way to specify the minimum and maximum file sizes allowed; we can pass this configuration option a range of sizes allowed such as :size => 1.kilobyte..4.megabytes. This configuration option will take precedence over the min_size and max_size options, so you should use one or the other.

:resize_to: If we're dealing with images, we can pass this configuration option in to use our image processing library to resize an image to specified dimensions. We can pass this configuration option an array containing the height and width to which we want the image resized (e.g., :resize_to => [640,480]) or, more usefully, we can pass it a geometry string such as :resize_to => "650x650>".

Note Geometry strings are a very powerful tool for providing better control over how our images will resize, especially in regards to ensuring that we maintain aspect ratios.

To resize to a specific width yet maintain the current aspect ratio, simply pass in a geometry string containing only the desired width (e.g., "x480").

To resize an image only if its dimensions are currently larger or smaller than our target resize ratio, simply append a greater-than or less-than symbol (< or >) to the number. For example, if we were to pass in "640x480>" and the image size was only 128 × 128, then no resizing would take place. However, if we uploaded an image that was 1024 × 1024, then it would be resized to 480 × 480.

:thumbnails: This configuration option allows us to specify additional thumbnails to generate. The extra nice feature of this option is that it accepts a hash of thumbnail keys and resize options so that we can generate multiple variants of thumbnails. For example, we could pass it something like :thumbnails => { :frontpage => '300>', :thumb => '125' }.

:thumbnail_class: By default, if we configure attachment_fu to generate thumbnails, it will create them as objects of the same class as the full image. This option allows us to specify a different class for the created thumbnails. This flexibility means that the data for the thumbnail would be stored, which allows us to specify different validations and so on.

:path_prefix: This option allows us to configure the specific path where we will store the uploaded images. By default, it will store images in public/[table_name]—so for our Comic model, it will store comics in /public/comics. We can configure the option like this: :path_prefix => 'public/uploaded_files'.

:storage: We can specify where we want to store the uploaded files with this option. Current options are on the local file system (:storage => :file_system), in the database (:storage => :db_file), and in the Amazon Simple Storage System (:storage => :s3). If nothing is chosen, attachment_fu will default to database storage.

:processor: This option allows us to configure the image processor to use. Current options are ImageScience, RMagick, and MiniMagick.

Once we have set up our configuration options in our model, we can quickly and easily add validations for our configuration by adding the validates_as_attachment method to our model.

Initially, we're going to choose to store our uploaded comics onto the local file system. If the web site grows substantially, we may consider moving the storage out to Amazon S3, so we can take advantage of their distributed content delivery network. We're also going to forgo the creation of thumbnails for this model, since we're only interested in displaying the standard comics. We do want to make sure that our comics are displaying at a standard aspect ratio, so we'll resize the comic if necessary as well. With that understanding, we can go ahead and configure our Comic model with the following options:

```
class Comic < ActiveRecord::Base
  has_attachment :content_type => :image,
                 :storage => :file_system,
                 :max_size => 500.kilobytes,
                 :resize_to => '650x650>'

  validates_as_attachment
  validates_presence_of :title
end
```

Let's go ahead and run our migrations now:

```
rake db:migrate
```

```
(in /Users/darkel/book/webcomic)
== CreateComics: migrating =========================================
-- create_table(:comics)
   -> 0.0028s
== CreateComics: migrated (0.0031s) ================================
```

Modifying Our Routes

Since we don't want this to be a public-facing controller, we need to add a path_prefix to its route in our /config/routes.rb file so that our comics controller will only be accessible from the path /admin/comics:

```
ActionController::Routing::Routes.draw do |map|
  map.resources :comics, :path_prefix => '/admin'
end
```

Modifying the Scaffolding

Now that we've configured our model and routes, we just need to make a few small changes to the scaffolding pages that were generated to round out our administration side.

comics/new

This first section we need to change is the template that is used to create a new comic. Scaffolding created it as merely a set of text fields, but those fields will be automatically populated by attachment_fu, so we need to modify the view to be a file-upload form instead. Open /app/views/comics/new.rhtml, and change its content to this:

```
<h1>New comic</h1>
<%= error_messages_for :comic %>
<% form_for(:comic, :url => comics_path, :html => { :multipart => true }) do |f| %>
   <p>
      <label for="comic_title">Comic Headline:</label>
      <%= f.text_field :title %>
   </p>
   <p>
      <label for="comic_uploaded_data">Upload a new Comic:</label>
      <%= f.file_field :uploaded_data %>
   </p>
   <p>
      <label for="comic_description">Description:</label>
      <%= f.text_area :description %>
   </p>
   <p>
      <%= submit_tag "Create" %>
   </p>
<% end %>
<%= link_to 'Back', comics_path %>
```

This should give us a simple form like the one shown in Figure 12-3.

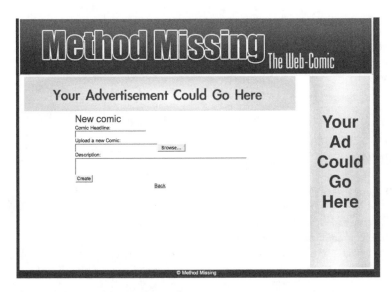

Figure 12-3. *Creating a new comic*

comics/show

Next, we want to modify the show view to provide us with a view of our uploaded comic and to remove some of the clutter. We can link to an attachment_fu image by calling the public_filename method within an image tag like so:

```
<%= image_tag @comic.public_filename %>
```

Our show.rhtml in /app/views/comics/ should look like this:

```
<p>
    <b>Title:</b>
    <%=h @comic.title %>
</p>
<p>
    <%= image_tag @comic.public_filename %>
</p>
<p>
    <b>Description:</b>
    <%=h @comic.description %>
</p>

<%= link_to 'Edit', edit_comic_path(@comic) %> |
<%= link_to 'Back', comics_path %>
```

comics/index

For our index.rhtml page in /app/views/comics/, we want to simplify our listing of comics by only displaying the information of interest to us:

```
<h1>Listing comics</h1>
<table>
   <tr>
      <th>Filename</th>
      <th>Title</th>
      <th>Description</th>
      <th> </th>
      <th> </th>
   </tr>

<% for comic in @comics %>
   <tr>
      <td><%=h comic.filename %></td>
      <td><%=h comic.title %></td>
      <td><%=h truncate( comic.description, 35) %></td>
      <td><%= link_to 'Edit', edit_comic_path(comic) %></td>
      <td><%= link_to 'Destroy', comic_path(comic), :confirm => 'Are you sure?',
                                              :method => :delete %></td>
```

```
</tr>
<% end %>
</table>

<br />

<%= link_to 'New comic', new_comic_path %>
```

You can see the results of our modified view in Figure 12-4.

Figure 12-4. *Displaying a list of our comics*

comics/edit

Finally, we also need to make a few minor modifications to our edit.rhtml template in /app/
views/comics/ to focus it solely on being able to update the headline and description fields
associated with the comic:

```
<h1>Editing comic</h1>
<%= error_messages_for :comic %>

<% form_for(:comic, :url => comic_path(@comic),
                              :html => { :method => :put }) do |f| %>
  <p>
    <%= image_tag @comic.public_filename %>
  </p>

  <p>
    <b>Title</b><br />
    <%= f.text_field :title %>
  </p>

  <p>
    <b>Description</b><br />
    <%= f.text_area :description %>
  </p>
```

```
<p>
  <%= submit_tag "Update" %>
</p>
<% end %>

<%= link_to 'Show', comic_path(@comic) %> |
<%= link_to 'Back', comics_path %>
```

Creating a Comic

Now that we have our comics controller built, let's use it to create our first comic. For the purpose of illustration in this book, I'm going to be using some of the comics from *Why's (Poignant) Guide to Ruby* (available online at http://poignantguide.net/ruby/), but you can use any that you want.

Note If you haven't read *Why's (Poignant) Guide to Ruby* yet, you have no idea how much you're missing. The book is not only the absolutely most unique programming book you will probably ever read, but it's an excellent guide to understanding some of the features that make Ruby so special.

Make sure that you have your Mongrel instance started. Open a web browser to http://localhost:3000/admin/comics/new, and you'll be greeted with the "New comic" page like the one shown in Figure 12-5.

Figure 12-5. *The "New comic" page of our administration system*

From here, we'll fill out the form and select a comic from our local file system. If our image passes all of our validations, when we click create, the Comic model saves our submission to the database and saves the modified image into /public/comics/0000/0001 (assuming that the

ID for our comic was 1). To see the information that is stored about our new comic, we can simply open a new console session at the command prompt and view our Comic object in it:

```
ruby script/console
```

```
Loading development environment.
```

```
>> comic = Comic.find 1
```

```
=> #<Comic:0x10b9a30 @attributes={"content_type"=>"image/png", "size"=>"7048",
 "title"=>"Chunky Bacon", "id"=>"1", "description"=>"CHUNKY BACON!!",
 "filename"=>"the.foxes-4c.png", "height"=>"242", "width"=>"286"}
```

After we have successfully saved our new comic, we should be redirected to the show page that is shown in Figure 12-6.

Figure 12-6. *The show template of the administration system and Chunky Bacon*

■**Note** At the time of this writing, some Windows users of the Attachment Fu plug-in were experiencing an occasional bug—the image upload would fail with an error message that said "Size is not included in the list". The common belief across many forums is that this error seems to be related to issues with Windows inconsistently reporting the populated temporary file size, and a number of users have reported that merely adding a small delay to the process eliminates the issue for them. You can read the most current details and workarounds for this issue at http://www.railsweenie.com/forums/3/topics/1257.

A Simple Authentication System

Now that we have our basic administration system working, we need to ensure that we keep the administration system secure so that no one else can access our backend and add unwanted content to our site. A comic declaring the wonders of Chunky Bacon on our site is certainly acceptable, but offensive images are not.

A full-blown user-registration and authentication system like Acts As Authenticated or RESTful authentication would be overkill for our simple needs. We don't need to be able to support multiple users, nor do we need an automated user registration system or the ability to scope objects back to the user who created them. Our simple application only needs to allow a single user to access the system and provide a way to block access to the site to anyone who doesn't know the password. That makes this a great opportunity to build our own simple security system.

The easiest way to limit access to a page is by setting a session variable with some data that we can use to determine if a user has authenticated successfully—so logging in and logging out are really just a matter of creating and destroying a session variable. Let's try to keep things clean by building that functionality into a sessions controller:

```
ruby script/generate controller sessions
```

```
   exists  app/controllers/
   exists  app/helpers/
   create  app/views/sessions
   exists  test/functional/
   create  app/controllers/sessions_controller.rb
   create  test/functional/sessions_controller_test.rb
   create  app/helpers/sessions_helper.rb
```

Now, within our new sessions controller, we'll need to add three methods:

- new: This method will display the login form when someone wants to log in.

- create: This is the destination method of the login form. It should process the submitted form parameters and create the necessary session variables.

- destroy: This resets all session variables—effectively logging out the user.

Now, let's edit our session controller and add those three methods:

```
class SessionsController < ApplicationController
  def new
  end

  def create
    session[:password] = params[:password]
    redirect_to comics_path
  end
```

```
    def destroy
      reset_session
      redirect_to home_path
    end
end
```

Our new method is the only method within our controller that will need to directly display a view template. Create new.rhtml in /app/views/session, and place the following login form within it:

```
<div id="login_form">
  <p style="color:red;"><%= flash[:notice] %></p>
  <h1>Please enter your access password: </h1>
  <% form_tag sessions_path do %>
    <%= password_field_tag :password %>
  <% end %>
</div>
```

Let's also add a pair of named routes to routes.rb in /config to make it easier to access our login and logout functionality:

```
ActionController::Routing::Routes.draw do |map|
  map.resources :comics, :path_prefix => '/admin'
  map.resources :sessions
  map.login '/login', :controller => 'sessions', :action => 'new'
  map.logout '/logout', :controller => 'sessions', :action => 'destroy'
end
```

With those changes, we can now access our login page at http://localhost:3000/login. When you do, you should see something similar to Figure 12-7.

Figure 12-7. *Our login page*

However, submitting our form doesn't currently do us a fat lot of good (security-wise), because our create method merely stores whatever we submitted into a password session variable and forwards us directly to the administration page. We still need to add some more logic if we want to actually secure our administration site from mischievous eyes.

Limiting Access

Now that we have a simple login form, our next task for limiting access is implementing a way to determine if the submitted password is the correct one. Since the needs of our application are pretty simple, we can do this by simply comparing what's in the session variable with the correct password in a method like this:

```
def admin?
  session[:password] == "my_ultra_secret_password"
end
```

Being merely a comparison check between two values, our admin? method will return either true or false, depending on whether or not the passwords match. Doing it this way means that anywhere we need to limit access, we can now simply ask the question, if admin?

Now, the question is, where do we put our new admin? method? If we were going to build a user model, I would probably recommend adding this method within that user model, so that we could query the administrative status of a specific user:

```
joe = User.find(params[:id])
if joe.admin?
  // allow joe to do adminy type stuff
else
  // stop it joe!!
end
```

But we don't need anything that granular—all we require is a simple way to see if the person requesting the page access knows the current password. Because of that, I recommend placing the method in your application_controller (/app/controllers/application.rb) so that our admin? method can be called from any controller:

```
class ApplicationController < ActionController::Base
  session :session_key => '_webcomic_session_id'

  protected
  def admin?
    session[:password] == "my_ultra_secret_password"
  end
end
```

■**Tip** If we needed to be able to call our new admin? method from within one our view templates, we could simply add a helper_method :admin? line command within our application controller; this would conveniently make our controller method accessible as a helper method as well.

Let's use our new `admin?` method to limit access to our administration section. We can do this easily by adding a before filter into our comics controller that verifies that only an administrator can access its methods:

```
class ComicsController < ApplicationController
  before_filter :verify_admin
  (ommitted code)
end
```

Now, down at the bottom of our comics controller, we'll add a protected block where we'll build our `verify_admin` method to redirect users to the login form if they're not administrators:

```
class ComicsController < ApplicationController
  before_filter :verify_admin
    (ommitted code)
protected
  def verify_admin
    unless admin?
      redirect_to login_path
      return false
    end
    true
  end
end
```

All that's left is to expand the `create` method in our sessions controller (`/app/controllers/sessions_controller.rb`) to check that the submitted password and display an error message if the password doesn't match:

```
def create
  session[:password] = params[:password]
  if admin?
    redirect_to comics_path
  else
    flash[:notice] = "That password was incorrect"
    redirect_to login_path
  end
end
```

The Public-Facing Side

Now that our administration system is working, we can focus on building the forward-facing (or public-facing) side of our web comic. We can start by defining a public controller:

```
ruby script/generate controller public webcomic
```

```
exists  app/controllers/
exists  app/helpers/
create  app/views/public
exists  test/functional/
create  app/controllers/public_controller.rb
create  test/functional/public_controller_test.rb
create  app/helpers/public_helper.rb
create  app/views/public/webcomic.rhtml
```

Our public controller needs only one method named webcomic, which will display a selected comic or the latest comic if it's called without a comic ID:

```
class PublicController < ApplicationController
  def webcomic
    @comic = Comic.find(params[:id])

    rescue
      @comic = Comic.find(:first, :order => 'id desc')
  end
end
```

Our webcomic method has an associated template in /app/views/public named webcomic.rhtml—place the following code within it to display the current comic and to build our next and previous comic links (albeit in a fairly brute force manner):

```
<h1 class="title"><%= @comic.title %></h1>
<%= image_tag @comic.public_filename %>
<br />
<hr />
<%= link_to image_tag('prev.jpg'), webcomic_path(@comic.id - 1) unless ➥
@comic.id == 1 %>
<%= link_to image_tag('next.jpg'), webcomic_path(@comic.id + 1) unless ➥
@comic.id >= Comic.count %>
<hr />
```

We'll need to add a few routes to our application to send requests to our new method, so open /config/routes.rb, and add the following bold lines to it:

```
ActionController::Routing::Routes.draw do |map|
  map.resources :comics, :path_prefix => '/admin'
  map.resources :sessions
  map.webcomic 'comic/:id', :controller => "public", :action => 'webcomic'
  map.home '', :controller => "public", :action => 'webcomic'
  map.login '/login', :controller => 'sessions', :action => 'new'
  map.logout '/logout', :controller => 'sessions', :action => 'destroy'
end
```

All of our hard work paid off with a basic web comic site, which is shown in Figure 12-8. Assuming that this comic is the most recent comic added to the site, it would be accessible at the root URL `http://localhost:3000/`. If we wanted to link to its permanent url, we would add `/comic/#{id}`, so this example would be at `http://locahost:3000/comic/2`.

Figure 12-8. *Our public-facing comic web site*

At this point, we've got a nice simple web comic site built that will serve our most basic needs. However, building our primary comic page with each request is going to be a little expensive because of the fact that we have at least two database hits occurring with each page view. In addition, the pages that are going to be viewed are fairly static, as the underlying data will not change very often.

In situations like that, a common pattern for increasing both scalability and response time is to implement some level of caching. Caching, in case you aren't aware, is the process of temporarily storing pre-rendered or precalculated data that is expensive to create in an easily accessible format so that future use can be made utilizing the cached version rather than re-rendering or recalculating the original data. Ruby on Rails provides three levels of caching out of the box: page, action, and fragment caching.

Page Caching

By far, the fastest caching system in Rails is page caching. Page caching works by saving the fully generated HTML page as a static file on the file system. On any future requests for that controller or method, the web server would find the static HTML version of the page and serve that saved copy instead of passing the request to the Rails dispatcher for processing. That means that Rails is completely removed from the request process, and the web server is just serving a static file.

The typical Rails request cycle can be seen in Figure 12-9: each request goes through the web server, which passes the request onto Rails to recognize the request, make queries to the database to collect data, and then renders a template view utilizing the data from the database.

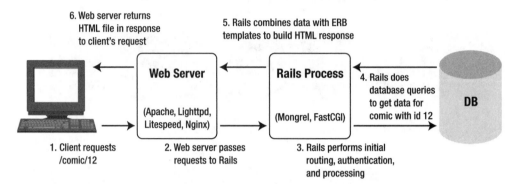

Figure 12-9. *The typical Rails request cycle*

Once we implement page caching, however, the request cycle changes, as both Rails and the database can be completely removed from the process to decrease the response time. Effectively, this means that we're going to rely on the speed of the web server to serve static content. You can see this cycle in Figure 12-10.

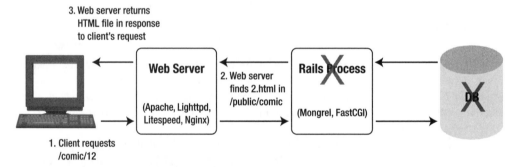

Figure 12-10. *The page caching request cycle*

Page caching sure sounds like a great idea on paper, doesn't it? Well, it is pretty good, but it does have some hard limitations that you need to be aware of.

First off, page caching saves the result of a request and then serves that same result to all subsequent requests. That means that everyone who makes this request will get exactly the same response, so we can't have any dynamic content displayed within the page. Since the subsequent requests are also bypassing Rails, that means that we have no opportunity to do any level of authentication either. And our final limitation is that page caching requires that the full page be rebuilt if we need to refresh the cache, so it's only going to be a good fit for situations where the content is going to remain static most of the time. Pages that are constantly being updated with new content would also be constantly expiring and re-creating their page caches and could effectively find themselves with lower performance than running Rails without caching.

Enabling Caching

If you're working in the development environment, you need to make a minor change to your configuration before we can start implementing caching within your project. You see, within the development environment, caching is turned off by default; you can modify that by editing development.rb in /config/environments and setting caching to true:

```
# Show full error reports and disable caching
config.action_controller.consider_all_requests_local = true
config.action_controller.perform_caching            = true
config.action_view.cache_template_extensions        = false
config.action_view.debug_rjs                         = true
```

Now that you have caching enabled within your environment, restart your web server, and let's turn on caching for our webcomic project by adding the caches_page method to our public controller (/app/controllers/public_controller.rb):

```
class PublicController < ApplicationController
  caches_page :webcomic

  def webcomic
    @comic = Comic.find(params[:id])
  rescue
    @comic = Comic.find(:first, :order => 'id desc')
  end
end
```

Believe it or not, that's all it takes. If you were to open a browser and hit the site now, that first page view would go through the Rails system normally, except that now Rails will also save a copy of the rendered HTML that it is going to send back to the browser in the /public directory. That means that each subsequent request would be served the cached version of the page, thereby eliminating the time required for our expensive database calls and template rendering. But how could we see that happen? After all, to the end user, there would be no difference between the two requests.

Probably the easiest way to see our page caching in action is to monitor the logs while we're accessing the site. So open a web browser, and view one of our comics by navigating to http://localhost:3000/comic/1.

Figure 12-11. *Viewing a comic on the site*

Afterward, we can review development.log (in /logs), and we can see that our page is being cached (the most recent log entries are at the bottom of the file). Here, we can see our initial view of the page with our multiple database queries—however, of special note is the line near the bottom that indicates that Rails has cached the page as /comic/1.html.

```
Processing PublicController#webcomic (for 127.0.0.1 at 2007-05-27 22:01:03) [GET]
  Session ID: fd2ac7920510a64fa9710dd30f1a1c65
  Parameters: {"action"=>"webcomic", "id"=>"1", "controller"=>"public"}
  Comic Load (0.000318)   SELECT * FROM comics WHERE (comics."id" = 1)
Rendering  within layouts/application
Rendering public/webcomic
  SQL (0.000225)   SELECT count(*) AS count_all FROM comics
Cached page: /comic/1.html (0.00051)
Completed in 0.02260 (44 reqs/sec) | Rendering: 0.00253 (11%) | DB: 0.00054 (2%)
 | 200 OK [http://localhost/comic/1]
```

From this point on, though, if you were to click refresh on your browser to view the page again, you might be surprised to see that there are no new log entries for any of your refreshes. That's because, once we've cached the page, all future hits to the page completely bypass Rails and are served directly by the web server.

Everything seems to be working splendidly now. Well, almost—because look what happens if we try to hit the root of our application at http://localhost:3000/:

```
Processing PublicController#webcomic (for 127.0.0.1 at 2007-05-27 22:04:33) [GET]
  Session ID: e7b4e99338a8bbb8aed9daedfb999567
  Parameters: {"action"=>"webcomic", "controller"=>"public"}
  Comic Load (0.000556)   SELECT * FROM comics ORDER BY id desc LIMIT 1
```

```
Rendering  within layouts/application
Rendering public/webcomic
  SQL (0.000255)   SELECT count(*) AS count_all FROM comics
Cached page: /comic.html (0.00193)
Completed in 0.02541 (39 reqs/sec) | Rendering: 0.00389 (15%) | DB: 0.00081
(3%) | 200 OK [http://localhost/]
```

And if we refresh again, we'll see another copy of this same entry get created in the log. Why's that? Well, it's because of the way that our routes are built: the page caching mechanism doesn't really understand that this is the root of our application (which would technically be http://localhost:3000/index), so it tries to save the file with the closest name it can determine—our named route.

Then when our next request comes in looking for the root (index), it doesn't find a match, since the cached page was saved as comic.html. That's just not going to work for our needs, because it means that the root page of our application will never be cached. Since that will also most likely be the most frequently visited page, it's the page that is the most important that we do cache.

I've heard of some people solving this problem by creating an after_save filter that copies the newly rendered comic.html cache file over index.html whenever the cache is created or updated. But that feels a bit hackish to me, especially when there's an easier way to solve this problem. The trade-off for the solution, though, is that we have to be willing to sacrifice a bit of our DRY methodology and introduce a bit of duplication.

To solve the problem, we can simply add an index method that will pull the most recent comic from the database (duplicating the same query from our webcomic method) and then use that result to render our existing webcomic template. So your public controller (/app/controllers/public_controller.rb) should be modified to look like this:

```ruby
class PublicController < ApplicationController
  caches_page :webcomic, :index

  def index
    @comic = Comic.find(:first, :order => 'id desc')
    render :template => 'public/webcomic'
  end

  def webcomic
    @comic = Comic.find(params[:id])
  rescue
    @comic = Comic.find(:first, :order => 'id desc')
  end
end
```

Now, to enable this new method, we also need to change the named route home to point to our new index method instead of to the webcomic method to which it currently routes. Edit /config/routes.rb like so:

```ruby
ActionController::Routing::Routes.draw do |map|
  map.resources :comics, :path_prefix => '/admin'
  map.resources :sessions
```

```
  map.webcomic 'comic/:id', :controller => "public", :action => 'webcomic'
  map.home '', :controller => "public", :action => 'index'
  map.login '/login', :controller => 'sessions', :action => 'new'
  map.logout '/logout', :controller => 'sessions', :action => 'destroy'
end
```

With those quick changes in place, let's try viewing http://localhost:3000 again; you should now see our caching working correctly, as the logs show that Rails is saving the cached page as index.html:

```
Processing PublicController#index (for 127.0.0.1 at 2007-05-27 22:10:38) [GET]
  Session ID: fd2ac7920510a64fa9710dd30f1a1c65
  Parameters: {"action"=>"index", "controller"=>"public"}
  Comic Load (0.000534)   SELECT * FROM comics ORDER BY id desc LIMIT 1
Rendering layoutfalsetemplatepublic/webcomic within layouts/application
Rendering public/webcomic
  SQL (0.000229)   SELECT count(*) AS count_all FROM comics
Cached page: /index.html (0.00227)
Completed in 0.02472 (40 reqs/sec) | Rendering: 0.00387 (15%) | DB: 0.00076
(3%) | 200 OK [http://localhost/]
```

Sure enough, we're back on track now. But caching the results of our pages is only half the battle. We also need to have a way of clearing out those cached versions of our pages so that changes to the underlying data will be reflected in what we display.

Cleaning Up the Cache

Since the page cache files are actually just static HTML files that are stored within the /public directory, we could clear out our page cache by simply deleting those files manually. But deleting those files every time we added a comic or updated a description would get old pretty quickly. Fortunately, we don't have to resort to this, as Rails provides us with several tools that we can utilize to remove caches.

At the most basic level is the expire_page method, which we can use to delete a specific cache file. We could be verbose and add this method to all of our controller methods that might trigger a need to update our cache, so after modifying the update method in our comics controller (/app/controllers/comics_controller.rb), it might look something like this:

```
def update
  @comic = Comic.find(params[:id])
  @comic.update_attributes(params[:comic])
  expire_page(:controller => 'public, :action => 'webcomic', :id => @comic.id)
  redirect_to comic_url(@comic)
end
```

But managing the sheer number of places where we would need to keep track of when to expire the cache would be both very error-prone (as we could easily miss calling the expire_page method in one of our methods) and a royal pain in the neck to manage. Fortunately, we have another tool that can make this process even easier for us—the sweeper.

Sweepers are part of a special class that is half observer and half filter—their whole purpose is to monitor the events on a model and allow us to override the standard filter methods with cache-expiring actions. That probably sounds a lot more complicated than it really is. Let's take a look at a real sweeper, and you'll see the true power of their simplicity.

Creating a Sweeper

Within your /app/models folder, create a new file named comic_sweeper.rb for our new sweeper, and let's put the following code in it:

```ruby
class ComicSweeper < ActionController::Caching::Sweeper
  observe Comic

  def after_save(comic)
    expire_cache_for(comic)
  end

  def after_destroy(comic)
    expire_cache_for(comic)
  end

  private
  def expire_cache_for(record)
    expire_page(:controller => 'public', :action => 'index')
    expire_page(:controller => 'public', :action => 'webcomic',
                                          :id => record.id)
    expire_page(:controller => 'public', :action => 'webcomic',
                                          :id => (record.id - 1))
  end
end
```

Within our sweeper, the first thing that we had to do was to specify what models it should be observing, which in our case is just the Comic model—one thing of note is that you do need to pass this method the name of the actual class that you want observed. That's why we're passing it Comic and not a string like "comics" or a symbol like :comic.

After specifying the models that we're observing, we override the event methods that we want to respond to. Typically, you'll want to create an after_save method that responds to both create and update calls and an after_destroy method, as these are going to be the core events that would cause you to need to update the cache. For our purposes here, we extract the duplicate code that would go into both the after_save and after_destroy methods into a private method named expire_cache_for, which is simply calling our expire_page methods.

For our application, anytime we change or update a comic, we're going to need to update three page caches:

- *The root of our application*: This cache needs updating in case our change introduces a new comic that needs to display as the most current.

- *The specific record that is created*: We update this cache in case our change alters some of the data on the page.

- *The comic directly preceding the one that triggers the event*: This is our safety net to make sure that our next and previous buttons are working correctly. For example, if the most recently added comic has an ID of 32, its display cache will not feature the Next Comic button since it is the last in the series. However, when we add a comic with an ID of 33, we need to expire the cache for comic 32 so that it will know it is no longer the last in the series and should now display a Next Comic button.

Before our sweeper will work, though, we also need to register this sweeper into any controllers that we'll be using to update our data—in our case, that's the comics controller. We do that by adding a cache_sweeper command to its related controller and specifying which methods it should be made aware of. So, open the comics controller (/app/controllers/comics_controller.rb), and add our cache_sweeper method call:

```
class ComicsController < ApplicationController
  cache_sweeper :comic_sweeper, :only => [:create, :update, :destroy]
  (lines omitted)
end
```

With our sweeper created and registered, let's do a quick test by opening up the administration site http://locahost/admin/comics/ and making a small modification to the description of one of the comics that you've added to the site. After that, you should be able to see that our existing page caches are expired in the logs:

```
Processing ComicsController#create (for 127.0.0.1 at 2007-05-27 22:26:30) [POST]
  Session ID: fd2ac7920510a64fa9710dd30f1a1c65
  Parameters: {"commit"=>"Create", "action"=>"create", "controller"=>"comics",
  "comic"=>{"title"=>"Screenshot", "uploaded_data"=>#<File:/tmp/CGI10356-1>,
  "description"=>"asdfajlksdfjladsf"}}
  SQL (0.000457)   INSERT INTO comics ("content_type", "size", "title",
"description", "filename", "height", "width") VALUES('image/png', 83788,
'Screenshot', 'asdfajlksdfjladsf', 'Picture_1.png', 349, 650)
Expired page: /index.html (0.00006)
Expired page: /comic/3.html (0.00004)
Expired page: /comic/2.html (0.00005)
Redirected to http://localhost:3000/admin/comics/3
Completed in 0.17315 (5 reqs/sec) | DB: 0.00046 (0%) |
302 Found [http://localhost/admin/comics]
```

Summary

In this chapter, we've put together the basics of our own little web comic site. We utilized Rick Olsen's fantastic Attachment Fu plug-in to quickly add a powerful and flexible image uploading solution to our application. We built our own simple authentication system, and we explored the process of caching the pages of our application to exponentially increase our scalability and performance.

In the next half of our project, we'll explore some of the limitations that our current caching solution has introduced and how we can overcome them using Rails's other two caching systems: action caching and fragment caching.

CHAPTER 13

■■■

Implementing Advanced Caching

Things have been going great for our little web comic. The site has been running like a champ, and our readership has continued to grow. Page caching has served the site extremely well, as it's been able to maintain consistent growth without having to add any additional processing.

However, a number of readers have voiced some complaints about the amount of advertising on the site and at the same time expressed desire to help support the site financially. So we're going to try an experiment by allowing readers to purchase a subscription to the site, whereby they'll be given a password that they can use to view an ad-free version of the site. If it's successful, we can look at adding additional features for subscribers later such as exclusive comics, desktop backgrounds, or even the ability to comment.

Unfortunately, since we want to introduce authentication into these pages, that pretty much eliminates page caching as an option. Fortunately, we do have a caching solution that can meet this need though—action caching. In action caching we'll still cache the full output of a rendered page so that we can serve that pre-rendered version to subsequent visits to the same page. If it sounds pretty similar to what we just did in the last chapter for page caching, that's because it is. Action caching, however, does provide us with two strong benefits that we couldn't get with page caching.

First, in page caching, Rails merely stores a static HTML file and leaves the web server in charge of finding and utilizing that stored page. This is great in that it eliminates any processing time from the request, but it completely blocks our ability to limit access to a page. In action caching, however, Rails maintains full control over the caching process by being the decision maker for finding and using cached pages.

Second, since the requests are now going through Rails to utilize the cache, we have the ability to add any number of before, after, or around filters in the processing of the request. This means that we can easily add a user authentication scheme and still utilize a cache of the page. Of course, we can't gain something for nothing—and thus while action caching does provide us more control over our pages, it comes at a cost of being slower than page caching. You can see a diagram showing the action caching process in Figure 13-1.

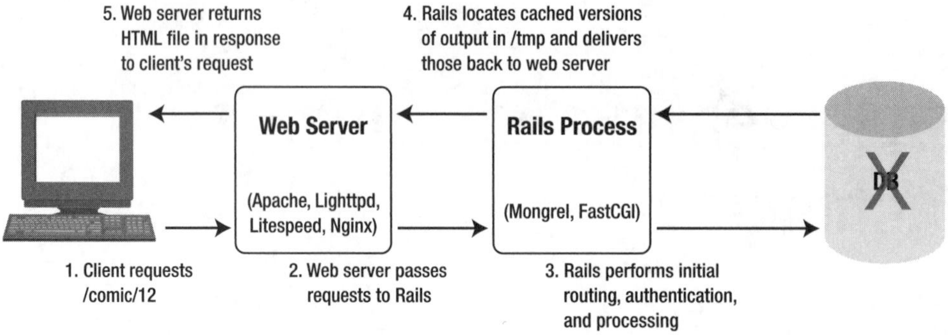

Figure 13-1. *Action Caching in Action*

For our needs, we'll be implementing a new section of the site that requires authentication, yet we still want to utilize caching in that section to maximize our performance and scalability—so action caching is definitely the way to go, so let's see how to implement action caching around a new paid members section.

The Members Controller

Our first step in implementing a subscriber's section of the site is to build a new controller that we will use to serve our paid members—we'll name this controller members:

```
ruby script/generate controller Members
```

```
    exists  app/controllers/
    exists  app/helpers/
    create  app/views/members
    exists  test/functional/
    create  app/controllers/members_controller.rb
    create  test/functional/members_controller_test.rb
    create  app/helpers/members_helper.rb
```

Next, since our goal is to provide paying members with an ad-free version of the site, we'll need to configure this members controller to utilize a different version of the layout with all ads removed. So create a new file in `/app/views/layouts` named `adfree.rhtml`, and place this layout content inside of it:

```
<!DOCTYPE HTML PUBLIC "-//W3C//DTD HTML 4.01//EN"➥
 "http://www.w3.org/TR/html4/strict.dtd">
<html>
<head>
  <title> Method Missing Web Comic</title>
  <link rel="stylesheet" href="http://yui.yahooapis.com/2.2.0/build/ ➥
reset-fonts-grids/reset-fonts-grids.css" type="text/css">
  <%= stylesheet_link_tag 'styles' %>
</head>
```

```
<body>
  <div id="doc2" class="yui-t7">
    <div id="hd"><%= image_tag 'methodmissing.jpg' %></div>
    <div id="bd">
      <div id="yui-main">
        <div class="yui-b">
          <div class="yui-g"> <%= yield %> </div>
        </div>
      </div>
    </div>
    <div id="ft"> &copy; Method Missing</div>
  </div>
</body>
</html>
```

We can make this new layout the default for our members by calling this layout from within our members controller (/app/controllers/members_controller.rb) with the simple addition of a layout method:

```
class MembersController < ApplicationController
  layout 'adfree'
end
```

While we're at it, let's also slip in this layout as the default in our comics controller (/app/controllers/comics_controller.rb). That way, we won't have to stare at advertising while we're administering the site:

```
class ComicsController < ApplicationController
  layout 'adfree'
  (...lines ommitted...)
end
```

Limiting Access to Subscribers

In order to secure access to the members-only pages, we'll first need to implement a way to determine if a user is a paying member or not. To do that, we should be able to reuse a large portion of the authentication design that we created to secure the administration side of our site with a few minor changes. We'll start by adding a member? method to our application controller (/app/controllers/application.rb) just as we did with the admin? method before:

```
class ApplicationController < ActionController::Base
  session :session_key => '_webcomic_session_id'

  protected

  def admin?
    session[:password] == "my_ultra_secret_password"
  end
```

```
  def member?
    session[:password] == "lambda-lambda-lambda"
  end
end
```

■**Note** Obviously, that's an awfully long password to type, so feel free to set it to anything that makes sense to you in your application. You do, however, get bonus points if you can name the movie that inspired that member password.

With a new member? function firmly in hand, we can now round out the members controller (/app/controllers/members_controller.rb) to mirror most of the same functionality of the public controller (/app/controllers/public_controller.rb) with the addition of a filter to a verify_member method that will keep unpaying eyes away from our ad-free pages:

```
class MembersController < ApplicationController
  layout 'adfree'

  before_filter :verify_member

  def index
    @comic = Comic.find(:first, :order => 'id desc')
    render :template => 'members/webcomic'
  end

  def webcomic
    @comic = Comic.find(params[:id])
  rescue
    @comic = Comic.find(:first, :order => 'id desc')
  end

  protected
  def verify_member
    unless member? || admin?
      redirect_to login_path
      return false
    end
    true
  end
end
```

The template that corresponds to the webcomic method in the members controller (/app/views/members/webcomic.rhtml) should be nearly identical to its sibling from the public controller with a few minor changes to where the next and previous buttons will redirect the user:

```
<h1 class="title"><%= @comic.title %></h1>
<%= image_tag @comic.public_filename %>
<br />
<hr />
<%= link_to image_tag('prev.jpg'), members_webcomic_path(@comic.id - 1) ➥
 unless @comic.id == 1 %>
<%= link_to image_tag('next.jpg'), members_webcomic_path(@comic.id + 1) ➥
unless @comic.id >= Comic.count %>
<hr />
```

I don't know about you, but the lack of DRYness in our implementation so far is really starting to annoy me. So let's add a little back by reusing our existing login form to handle subscriber logins in addition to our own administrator login. Open /app/controller/sessions_controller.rb, and modify the create method thusly:

```
def create
  session[:password] = params[:password]
  if admin?
    redirect_to comics_path
  elsif member?
    redirect_to members_path
  else
    flash[:notice] = "That password was incorrect"
    redirect_to login_path
  end
end
```

All that's left is to add a few routes to handle our member pages, and we'll have successfully finished our implementation of the subscribers' pages:

```
ActionController::Routing::Routes.draw do |map|
  map.resources :comics, :path_prefix => '/admin'
  map.resources :sessions
  map.webcomic 'comic/:id', :controller => "public", :action => 'webcomic'
  map.home '', :controller => "public", :action => 'index'
  map.login '/login', :controller => 'sessions', :action => 'new'
  map.logout '/logout', :controller => 'sessions', :action => 'destroy'
  map.members 'members', :controller => 'members', :action => 'index'
  map.members_webcomic '/members/comic/:id', :controller => 'members', ➥
:action => 'webcomic'
end
```

So now all we have to do is provide the current password and a link to the login form to any of our readers who choose to donate money to the web comic. It's a low-tech solution, but one that will work well for our current needs.

Caching Our Members Pages

As I said earlier, the problem with our members page is that we need to have Rails check the authentication prior to serving up the page, so that rules out page caching. Instead, we'll implement action caching, which should feel very similar—albeit a bit slower.

We can enable action caching on our controller's methods with the caches_action method:

```
class MembersController < ApplicationController
  layout 'adfree'
  before_filter :verify_member

  caches_action :index, :webcomic

  def index
    @comic = Comic.find(:first, :order => 'id desc')
    render :template => 'members/webcomic'
  end

  def webcomic
    @comic = Comic.find(params[:id])
  rescue
    @comic = Comic.find(:first, :order => 'id desc')
  end

protected
  def verify_member
    unless member? || admin?
      redirect_to login_path
      return false
    end
    true
  end
end
```

Just as we did with page caching, we can see our caching in action by monitoring what's going in the development.log in /logs while logging into the members-only page via the login form using the member's password:

```
Processing MembersController#index (for 127.0.0.1 at 2007-05-27 23:15:04) [GET]
  Session ID: 06304d6bb8a857c0084d7702ce11b6a8
  Parameters: {"action"=>"index", "controller"=>"members"}
```

```
Fragment read: localhost:3000/members (0.00013)
  Comic Load (0.000533)   SELECT * FROM comics ORDER BY id desc LIMIT 1
Rendering layoutfalsetemplatemembers/webcomic within layouts/adfree
Rendering members/webcomic
  SQL (0.000231)   SELECT count(*) AS count_all FROM comics
Cached fragment: localhost:3000/members (0.00081)
Completed in 0.01014 (98 reqs/sec) | Rendering: 0.00362 (35%) | DB: 0.00076 (7%)
| 200 OK [http://localhost/members]
```

We can see on our initial view of the members page that we did two database queries and saved the result as a cached fragment named localhost:3000/members. Let's click refresh and check the results in the logs:

```
Processing MembersController#index (for 127.0.0.1 at 2007-05-27 23:15:41) [GET]
  Session ID: 06304d6bb8a857c0084d7702ce11b6a8
  Parameters: {"action"=>"index", "controller"=>"members"}
Fragment read: localhost:3000/members (0.00012)
Completed in 0.00131 (763 reqs/sec) | 200 OK [http://localhost/members]
```

Nice! So with action caching enabled, when the page is requested, we're merely reading the fragment that was stored on the initial page view, and we've now removed all of the database hits as well. Another benefit is that Rails, rather than the web server, is now displaying our cached elements, so we can actually see the results of the cached actions being used within the Rails log.

Expiring Action Caching

Expiring action cache fragments is just as easy to do as it was with page caching—just a simple call to an expire_action command. In fact, since our sweeper is already monitoring the comics model, all we need to do is add a few expire_action calls to our existing sweeper (/app/models/comic_sweeper.rb):

```
private
  def expire_cache_for(record)
    prev_version = (record.id - 1)
    expire_page(:controller => 'public', :action => 'index')
    expire_page(:controller => 'public', :action => 'webcomic', :id => record.id)
    expire_page(:controller => 'public', :action => 'webcomic', ➥
:id => prev_version)
    expire_action(members_url)
    expire_action(members_webcomic_url(:id => record.id))
    expire_action(members_webcomic_url(:id => prev_version))
  end
```

You might have noticed that, while we were in there, I also cleaned up our calls to expire the previous record. I did that by first moving the calculation to determine the id of the previous record earlier in the process and to store that id in a variable named prev_version. With that id stored in the prev_version variable, I could then use it in the expire_page method to make it more readable (expire_page(:controller => 'public', :action => 'webcomic', :id => prev_version).

Once again, if we were to go back to the administration page and update one of the fields of an existing comic, we would see both our page and action caches being expired in the log:

```
Processing ComicsController#update (for 127.0.0.1 at 2007-05-27 23:50:44) [PUT]
  Session ID: 06304d6bb8a857c0084d7702ce11b6a8
  Parameters: {"commit"=>"Update", "_method"=>"put", "action"=>"update",
"id"=>"2", "controller"=>"comics", "comic"=>{"title"=>"Chunky Bacon 2",
"description"=>"Son of Chunky Bacon"}}
  Comic Load (0.000305)   SELECT * FROM comics WHERE (comics."id" = 2)
  Comic Update (0.000458)   UPDATE comics SET "content_type" = 'image/jpeg',
"size" = 325032, "height" = 650, "title" = 'Chunky Bacon 2',
"filename" = 'comic.jpg', "width" = 647, "description" = ' Son of Chunky Bacon '
WHERE "id" = 2
Expired page: /index.html (0.00005)
Expired page: /comic/2.html (0.00006)
Expired page: /comic/1.html (0.00023)
Expired fragment: localhost:3000/members (0.00016)
Expired fragment: localhost:3000/members/comic/2 (0.00014)
Expired fragment: localhost:3000/members/comic/1 (0.00014)
Redirected to http://localhost:3000/admin/comics/2
Completed in 0.15052 (6 reqs/sec) | DB: 0.00076 (0%) | 302 Found
[http://localhost/admin/comics/2]
```

Fragment Caching

While action caching did give us the ability to ensure that only authenticated readers were able to view the members-only version of the page, it also caused us to introduce a significant amount of duplication into our application by effectively recreating our public controller and views. To make matters even worse, the only benefit of all that duplication was merely to serve a different layout. Unfortunately, though, the inability to customize the pages content is inherent within the implementations of page and action caching. That's where fragment caching comes in.

While page and action caching were focused on caching results at the controller level, fragment caching is all about caching elements within a page. Using fragment caching, we can effectively cache selected portions of the page (such as a header or navigation menu), while allowing other sections of the page to have dynamic content. This is extremely useful in situations where certain elements in a page change frequently but others do not. Figure 13-2 shows a diagram of how fragment caching works.

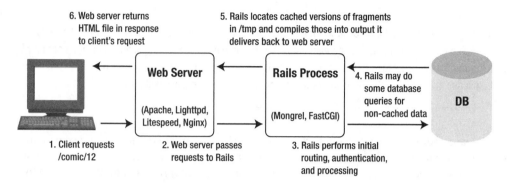

6. Web server returns
HTML file in response
to client's request

5. Rails locates cached versions of fragments
in /tmp and compiles those into output it
delivers back to web server

Web Server

(Apache, Lighttpd,
Litespeed, Nginx)

Rails Process

(Mongrel, FastCGI)

4. Rails may do
some database
queries for
non-cached data

DB

1. Client requests
/comic/12

2. Web server passes
requests to Rails

3. Rails performs initial
routing, authentication,
and processing

Figure 13-2. *Fragment Caching in action*

Additionally, unlike page caching, where our only option was to have the caches stored in the file system, fragment caching provides us with a number of options for where our cached fragments will be stored:

File store: This is the default behavior for fragment caching. Cached files will be stored within the /tmp/cache directory. This can be a bit slow and doesn't scale well, as cached elements are not shared among multiple web servers.

Memory store: Accessing fragments kept within server memory is much faster than accessing file-based storage but still suffers from the same scalability issues as storing on the local file system.

DRb store: A third option is to use a Distributed Ruby (DRb) store. DRb is a library that allows Ruby programs to communicate and share objects with each other across a network. For this option, we'd have to build and manage a distributed Ruby process that would store the caches in memory yet be accessible from any machine. This is a bit more complex to manage but scales very well, since all web servers would be utilizing a common storage system for cached elements.

Memcached store: Memcached is an open source application developed by Danga interactive (http://www.danga.com/memcached/) designed for sharing objects across multiple machines. Memcached is an extremely popular solution for large sites that need to be able to scale, and using it requires that you have both Memcached and the ruby-memcache library installed.

For our current needs, we'll keep the default and have our fragment caches stored on the local file system. If you ever needed to change that, all you need to do is simply add the appropriate line to your /config/environment.rb, such as:

```
ActionController::Base.fragment_cache_store = :memory_store
ActionController::Base.fragment_cache_store = :file_store, "/path/to/cache"
ActionController::Base.fragment_cache_store = :drb_store, "druby://localhost"
ActionController::Base.fragment_cache_store = :mem_cache_store, "localhost"
```

■Note You may have noticed, back when we were discussing action caching, that we never discussed where action caching stores its cached elements. The reason we didn't is because action caching actually uses fragment caching as the underlying solution, so it made more sense to wait until we got to this point and could discuss the various options for where our action and fragment caches will be stored.

Because additional processing such as database hits, template rendering, and so on can still occur when we're using fragment caching, fragment caching is going to be the slowest of all the caching mechanisms. However, it does provide the wonderful benefit of being able to pick and choose what sections of our page should be cached. This way we can easily leave portions of our page uncached where we want to display dynamic data such as the users name, flash messages, or other data that may need to update too frequently to cache—all the while, caching the sections of the page that are more expensive to render and/or are updated only on an infrequent basis.

So far in our project, we've implemented a little of both page caching and action caching—but let's convert those over to fragment caching before we end this project. By converting those to fragment caching, we'll be able to simplify our application to serve both members and nonmembers from a single controller rather than the being forced to use two, as we are now.

Let's start the conversion by first eliminating the page caching from our public controller, so either remove or comment out the caches_page :webcomic, :index line from /app/controllers/public_controller.rb.

With that commented out, we then need to remove any existing page caches from our /public directory. To do that, we need to delete the index.html file (if it exists) from the /public directory, as well as any HTML files in the /public/comic directory.

Customizing Our Layout

With those existing cached pages removed and page caching eliminated from our public controller, it's time to begin customizing our default layout to dynamically display advertising based on whether or not the reader is a member. Open application.rhtml from /app/views/layouts, and modify it like this:

```
<!DOCTYPE HTML PUBLIC "-//W3C//DTD HTML 4.01//EN"
 "http://www.w3.org/TR/html4/strict.dtd">
<html>
<head>
  <title>Method Missing Web Comic</title>
  <link rel="stylesheet" href="http://yui.yahooapis.com/2.2.0/build/ ➥
reset-fonts-grids/reset-fonts-grids.css" type="text/css">
  <%= stylesheet_link_tag 'styles' %>
</head>
```

```
<body>
  <% if admin? || member? %>
    <div id="doc2" class="yui-t7">
  <% else %>
    <div id="doc2" class="yui-t4">
  <% end %>

  <div id="hd"><%= image_tag 'methodmissing.jpg' %></div>
    <div id="bd">
      <div id="yui-main">
        <div class="yui-b">
          <% unless admin? || member? %>
            <div class="yui-g"><%= image_tag 'topbanner.jpg' %></div>
          <% end %>
          <div class="yui-g"><%= yield %> </div>
        </div>
      </div>
      <% unless admin? || member? %>
        <div class="yui-b"><%= image_tag 'sidebanner.jpg' %></div>
      <% end %>
    </div>
    <div id="ft"> &copy; Method Missing</div>
  </div>
</body>
</html>
```

So in our modified layout template, we'll call the `admin?` and `member?` methods to make the decision of whether or not to display the ads. However, since those are our controller methods currently, we can't use them in our view. So before we can attempt to view this page, we need to enable those methods as helper methods. We do that by adding a `helper_method` call to our application controller (`/app/controllers/application.rb`) like this:

```
class ApplicationController < ActionController::Base
  session :session_key => '_webcomic_session_id'
  helper_method :admin?, :member?

protected
  def admin?
    session[:password] == "my_ultra_secret_password"
  end

  def member?
    session[:password] == "lambda-lambda-lambda"
  end
end
```

Now that our page is configured to display or not display ads based on whether the user provided a valid password, our next step is to reconfigure our login method to send logged in members to the public controller, instead of to our members controller. To do that, we need to modify the create method in our sessions controller (/app/controllers/sessions_controller.rb), which processes logins:

```ruby
def create
  session[:password] = params[:password]
  if admin?
    redirect_to comics_path
  elsif member?
    redirect_to home_path
  else
    flash[:notice] = "That password was incorrect"
    redirect_to login_path
  end
end
```

So at this point, we're able to provide an ad-free version of the site to paying members and an ad-supported version to nonpaying members—all from a single controller—but we're not caching the pages. Let's fix that by adding fragment caching to our view; we'll do that by adding a cache block around the section of code in the layout that displays the current comic. Open webcomic.rhtml in app/views/public, and let's modify it to look like this:

```erb
<% cache do %>
  <h1 class="title"><%= @comic.title %></h1>
  <%= image_tag @comic.public_filename %>
  <br />
  <hr />
  <%= link_to image_tag('prev.jpg'), webcomic_path(@comic.id - 1) ➥
unless @comic.id == 1 %>
  <%= link_to image_tag('next.jpg'), webcomic_path(@comic.id + 1) ➥
unless @comic.id >= Comic.count %>
  <hr />
<% end %>
```

Let's open the main page of our application and look at the logs to see the results of our modifications. If we open a browser to http://localhost:3000 and view the development log, we can see that we're generating the fragment cache correctly:

```
Processing PublicController#index (for 127.0.0.1 at 2007-05-28 21:32:56) [GET]
  Session ID: 06304d6bb8a857c0084d7702ce11b6a8
  Parameters: {"action"=>"index", "controller"=>"public"}
  Comic Load (0.000521)   SELECT * FROM comics ORDER BY id desc LIMIT 1
Rendering layoutfalsetemplatepublic/webcomic within layouts/application
Rendering public/webcomic
Fragment read: localhost:3000/ (0.00015)
  SQL (0.000323)   SELECT count(*) AS count_all FROM comics
```

Cached fragment: localhost:3000/ (0.00050)
Completed in 0.01007 (99 reqs/sec) | Rendering: 0.00618 (61%) | DB: 0.00084 (8%)
| 200 OK [http://localhost/]

Now, if we refresh the page, our log shows that we're reading in the fragment and reducing our processing time:

```
Processing PublicController#index (for 127.0.0.1 at 2007-05-28 21:33:07) [GET]
  Session ID: 06304d6bb8a857c0084d7702ce11b6a8
  Parameters: {"action"=>"index", "controller"=>"public"}
  Comic Load (0.000533)   SELECT * FROM comics ORDER BY id desc LIMIT 1
Rendering layoutfalsetemplatepublic/webcomic within layouts/application
Rendering public/webcomic
```
Fragment read: localhost:3000/ (0.00012)
Completed in 0.00533 (187 reqs/sec) | Rendering: 0.00180 (33%) |
DB: 0.00053 (9%) | 200 OK [http://localhost/]

However, we have a problem—did you notice it in the preceding log?

The problem is that, even though we're caching the results of the fragment's rendering, we're still making a hit to the database to generate the data from our controller. You can see it in the line SELECT * FROM comics ORDER BY id desc LIMIT 1; that query correlates to the @comic = Comic.find(:first, :order => 'id desc') line in our index method. However, our usual database hit, which occurred within the fragment (SELECT count(*) AS count_all FROM comics, which came from our call for the Comic.count) was bypassed, because its result was cached.

That's an important distinction about page caching—it literally only caches the database queries and processing that occurs within the cached fragment. To solve this, you could consider moving your relevant database queries out of the controller and into the cache block in the view. The downfall with doing that, though, is that it really breaks our model-view-controller separation and has us putting logic that belongs in the model or controller into the view instead. Fortunately, there's another option. We can wrap our database calls in the controller with a method from ActionController by the name of read_fragment, like this:

```
unless read_fragment({})
  @comic = Comic.find(params[:id])
end
```

This method essentially says that if we have a matching fragment cache for the current request, we'll bypass the calls to the database. Adding these calls to our public controller (/app/controllers/public_controller.rb) will look like this:

```
class PublicController < ApplicationController

  def index
    unless read_fragment({})
      @comic = Comic.find(:first, :order => 'id desc')
    end
    render :template => 'public/webcomic'
  end
```

```
def webcomic
  unless read_fragment({})
    @comic = Comic.find(params[:id])
  end
  rescue
  @comic = Comic.find(:first, :order => 'id desc')
  end
end
```

Since we haven't yet modified our sweepers to clean up our fragment caches, we should clear out our existing cache by running rake tmp:cache:clear from the root of our application. Once any existing cached fragments are removed, we can retest our fragment caching by refreshing the home page again.

We can monitor the logs to see that our request to the page produced the same results but now it also caches the fragment:

```
Processing PublicController#index (for 127.0.0.1 at 2007-05-28 22:07:57) [GET]
  Session ID: 06304d6bb8a857c0084d7702ce11b6a8
  Parameters: {"action"=>"index", "controller"=>"public"}
Fragment read: localhost:3000/ (0.00013)
  Comic Load (0.000522)   SELECT * FROM comics ORDER BY id desc LIMIT 1
Rendering layoutfalsetemplatepublic/webcomic within layouts/application
Rendering public/webcomic
Fragment read: localhost:3000/ (0.00015)
  SQL (0.000250)   SELECT count(*) AS count_all FROM comics
Cached fragment: localhost:3000/ (0.00054)
Completed in 0.00971 (103 reqs/sec) | Rendering: 0.00505 (51%) | DB: 0.00077 (7%)
 | 200 OK [http://localhost/]
```

Now, if we refresh the page again, we should no longer see any requests to the database in our logs, as the read_fragment method detects the existing cache and prevents any unnecessary database hits:

```
Processing PublicController#index (for 127.0.0.1 at 2007-05-28 22:08:05) [GET]
  Session ID: 06304d6bb8a857c0084d7702ce11b6a8
  Parameters: {"action"=>"index", "controller"=>"public"}
Fragment read: localhost:3000/ (0.00012)
Rendering layoutfalsetemplatepublic/webcomic within layouts/application
Rendering public/webcomic
Fragment read: localhost:3000/ (0.00013)
Completed in 0.00290 (345 reqs/sec) | Rendering: 0.00128 (44%) | 200 OK
 [http://localhost/]
```

Clearing Our Fragment Cache

It should come as no surprise that modifying our fragment cache is just a simple matter of changing the expire_page commands in our comic sweeper to expire_fragment commands instead:

```
private
  def expire_cache_for(record)
    prev_version = (record.id - 1)
      expire_fragment(:controller => 'public', :action => 'index')
      expire_fragment(:controller => 'public', :action => 'webcomic', ➥
:id => record.id)
      expire_fragment(:controller => 'public', :action => 'webcomic', ➥
:id => prev_version)
  end
```

After those changes, if we make a modification to one of the comics (such as changing its name), we can see our fragments being expired:

```
Processing ComicsController#update (for 127.0.0.1 at 2007-05-28 22:24:23) [PUT]
  Session ID: 6d22fd6a722d8a707d6803ed16df0539
  Parameters: {"commit"=>"Update", "_method"=>"put", "action"=>"update",
"id"=>"2", "controller"=>"comics", "comic"=>{"title"=>"Chunky Bacon",
"description"=>"Chunky Bacon"}}
  Comic Load (0.000303)   SELECT * FROM comics WHERE (comics."id" = 2)
  Comic Update (0.000455)   UPDATE comics SET "content_type" = 'image/jpeg',
 "size" = 325742, "height" = 650, "title" = 'Chunky Bacon,
"filename" = 'comic.jpg', "width" = 647, "description" = 'Chunky Bacon'
WHERE "id" = 2
Expired fragment: localhost:3000/ (0.00148)
Expired fragment: localhost:3000/comic/2 (0.00023)
Expired fragment: localhost:3000/comic/1 (0.00016)
Redirected to http://localhost:3000/admin/comics/2
Completed in 0.14893 (6 reqs/sec) | DB: 0.00076 (0%) | 302 Found
[http://localhost/admin/comics/2]
```

With that, we've effectively implemented fragment caching and simplified our application by reducing duplication. Go ahead and delete the sessions controller and its related routes, templates, and so forth now, since they'll no longer be of any use to us.

Summary

Over the course of this project, we've explored quite a number of topics. We started out by implementing a file upload solution using the excellent plug-in attachment_fu. We next discussed and implemented a simple authentication solution that we could use to protect access to our application's pages and wrapped up our project by experimenting with the three different types of caching that are available within Rails.

You saw how page caching is a great solution in situations where the content never (or very rarely changes) and doesn't need any level of additional processing, such as inserting dynamic content or checking authentication.

We then explored action caching as a solution for still providing the benefits of caching while maintaining the ability to check authentication levels before serving the page. Action caching is a good solution where you need to be able to run before, after, or around filters for each request but don't need to be able to insert dynamic content into the page.

Finally, we explored fragment caching, which allows us to cache data within the page template, thereby allowing us to use dynamic data in the pages that we deliver to the end users while still gaining many of the benefits of caching.

■ ■ ■

## CHAPTER 14

Enhancing the Web Comic

In this project, we explored the powerful concepts of caching Rails applications as we put together a very simple web comic application. I pointed out some of the pros and cons of each of the different levels of caching that Rails supports and how they affected our application design. This chapter contains a number of ideas for you to use while enhancing the web comic application.

Add a Blog

Many web comics these days also communicate with users through blogs. Most often, these blog posts are located directly beneath the daily comic. However, some sites instead choose to push the blog to a separate page entirely. We build some basic blog-like functionality in a few of the projects in this book (such as the simple blog project in Chapter 10)—why not take that knowledge and add a basic blog to the web comic application? Be mindful of any necessary changes to your caching, though.

Integrate a Forum

Another key feature that many web comics add is a user forum for the community. While we could certainly build our own, it's often easier to simply install an open source one. In my opinion the best Rails-based forum is the Beast forum (which, unsurprisingly, is also written by Rick Olsen) that you can see in Figure 14-1. You can download the latest version of Beast from `http://svn.techno-weenie.net/projects/beast/`.

There's also a support forum available at `http://beast.caboo.se/forums/1`.

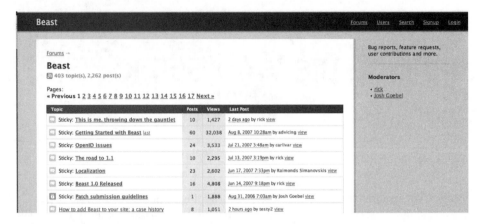

Figure 14-1. *The Beast forum*

Change Comics to Be Selectable by Date

Currently, our web comics are selectable by the IDs of the comics. However, another popular pattern is to make web comics accessible by date, so the URL might be something like http://localhost:3000/comic/2007/12/25. Doing so would require modifying your routes.rb file to something like this:

```
map.webcomic "comic/:year/:month/:day",
:controller => "public",
:action => "webcomic",
:requirements => { :year => /(19|20)\d\d/,
:month => /[01]?\d/,
:day => /[0-3]?\d/},
```

    After changing the routes file, you'll also need to change your controllers to search by date instead of ID. Why not go ahead and see if you can convert our web comic application to this pattern?

Enhance the Authentication System

For this project, we implemented an extremely simple authentication system. While this works for the simple needs of a single user who doesn't require any advanced functionality, there is definitely room for us to expand it. For one thing, it would be nice if we could store the passwords in the database instead of simply storing them in our code—that way, we could build a simple web form in the administration section so we could change it on a regular basis. Browse through the source of the restful_authentication plug-in for ideas on how to expand your authentication code.

Summary

At this point, you should have a fairly decent grasp on how caching works within Rails, and if you've used the ideas in this chapter, your web comic is starting to shape up nicely. Of course, there's always more you can do—look around other popular web comic sites and try to find features to add to this application (some of my favorite sites include xkcd.com, vgcats.com, penny-arcade.com, and pvponline.com).

To enhance your understanding of caching, go through all the other projects in the book and try to add caching to each. Often the best caching lessons are in the applications that you may have initially thought you wouldn't be able to cache.

Enhancing Monkey Tasks

The following exercise offers additional enhancements for Monkey Tasks.

Add Caching to Monkey Tasks

While the content of Monkey Tasks probably wouldn't be conducive to page caching, you could implement fragment caching to improve performance in some areas such as the sidebar containing your lists of upcoming tasks.

Summary

PART 6

■■■

Church Community Site

Take one glance at the job opportunities for web development lately and it's obvious that the success of social networking sites, such as MySpace and Facebook, have inspired quite the demand for copycat social networking sites—with good reason too. Social networking style sites are lots of fun and a great way to keep in touch with friends and family or to reconnect with old friends. There's no denying that social networks are a hot property right now. There are already a number of books published (or coming out shortly) that will take you step-by-step through putting together a large-scale social networking site. The problem with these sites is that, while they are excellent for large-scale networking, none of them have very solid tools for allowing a pre-established community of users to communicate.

For this project, we're going to put together a mini social network style site that will be suitable for use by a small community of users, such as a small church, a local Ruby users group, family members attending a reunion, and so forth. In keeping with our smaller community, we'll also provide a much smaller set of features and tools for our site than you would find on a large-scale social networking site. We'll primarily focus on the areas that will matter to a small, private community, such as providing a simple directory of members and allowing members to share what's going on in their lives through blog posts and photo galleries.

■■■

## CHAPTER 15

Managing Users and Profiles

For the purpose of this application, we'll pretend that we're building a site for a small church consisting of less than a hundred members. We'll start out by implementing support for users and user created content in this chapter. Once we have the ability to allow users to login and create content we'll move onto creating some simple community focused tools such as a community home page and a user directory in the next chapter.

So go ahead and create a new Rails application in your projects directory named church using the directions from Chapter 2.

Installing Restful Authentication

Once again, our first step for creating our new application will be to install the Restful Authentication plug-in to provide us with the user login and authentication system for our application.

We start by adding the plug-in to our application:

```
ruby script/plugin install http://svn.techno-weenie.net/projects/plugins/➥
restful_authentication/
```

```
+ ./restful_authentication/README
+ ./restful_authentication/Rakefile
+ ./restful_authentication/generators/authenticated/USAGE
+ ./restful_authentication/generators/authenticated/authenticated_generator.rb
+ ./restful_authentication/generators/authenticated/templates/activation.rhtml
+ ./restful_authentication/generators/authenticated/templates/➥
authenticated_system.rb
+ ./restful_authentication/generators/authenticated/templates/➥
authenticated_test_helper.rb
+ ./restful_authentication/generators/authenticated/templates/controller.rb
+ ./restful_authentication/generators/authenticated/templates/fixtures.yml
+ ./restful_authentication/generators/authenticated/templates/functional_test.rb
+ ./restful_authentication/generators/authenticated/templates/helper.rb
+ ./restful_authentication/generators/authenticated/templates/login.rhtml
+ ./restful_authentication/generators/authenticated/templates/migration.rb
+ ./restful_authentication/generators/authenticated/templates/model.rb
+ ./restful_authentication/generators/authenticated/templates/model_controller.rb
+ ./restful_authentication/generators/authenticated/templates/➥
```

```
model_functional_test.rb
+ ./restful_authentication/generators/authenticated/templates/model_helper.rb
+ ./restful_authentication/generators/authenticated/templates/notifier.rb
+ ./restful_authentication/generators/authenticated/templates/notifier_test.rb
+ ./restful_authentication/generators/authenticated/templates/observer.rb
+ ./restful_authentication/generators/authenticated/templates/signup.rhtml
+ ./restful_authentication/generators/authenticated/templates/➥
signup_notification.rhtml
+ ./restful_authentication/generators/authenticated/templates/unit_test.rb
+ ./restful_authentication/install.rb
```

With the plug-in installed, we run the included generator to create our user and session models:

```
ruby script/generate authenticated user sessions
```

```
    exists  app/models/
    exists  app/controllers/
    exists  app/controllers/
    exists  app/helpers/
    create  app/views/sessions
    create  app/views/user_notifier
    exists  test/functional/
    exists  app/controllers/
    exists  app/helpers/
    create  app/views/users
    exists  test/functional/
    exists  test/unit/
    create  app/models/user.rb
    create  app/controllers/sessions_controller.rb
    create  app/controllers/users_controller.rb
    create  lib/authenticated_system.rb
    create  lib/authenticated_test_helper.rb
    create  test/functional/sessions_controller_test.rb
    create  test/functional/users_controller_test.rb
    create  app/helpers/sessions_helper.rb
    create  app/helpers/users_helper.rb
    create  test/unit/user_test.rb
    create  test/fixtures/users.yml
    create  app/views/sessions/new.rhtml
    create  app/views/users/new.rhtml
    create  db/migrate
    create  db/migrate/001_create_users.rb
```

However, before we run the create_users migration that was generated by Acts as Authenticated, we'll want to modify our user model to include a number of other fields that we'd like to capture about a user such as the name, gender, and address. So we'll need to modify the `001_create_users.rb` migration in /db/migrate to add these fields:

```ruby
class CreateUsers < ActiveRecord::Migration
  def self.up
    create_table "users", :force => true do |t|
      t.column :login,                     :string
      t.column :email,                     :string
      t.column :crypted_password,          :string, :limit => 40
      t.column :salt,                      :string, :limit => 40
      t.column :created_at,                :datetime
      t.column :updated_at,                :datetime
      t.column :remember_token,            :string
      t.column :remember_token_expires_at, :datetime
      t.column :first_name,                :string
      t.column :last_name,                 :string
      t.column :gender,                    :string
      t.column :street,                    :string
      t.column :city,                      :string
      t.column :state,                     :string
      t.column :zip,                       :string
    end
  end

  def self.down
    drop_table "users"
  end
end
```

With these extra fields added to the user model, we can now run our migration to create the users table in the database:

```
rake db:migrate
```

```
(in /Users/darkel/book/church/church)
== CreateUsers: migrating =======================================================
-- create_table("users", {:force=>true})
   -> 0.0040s
== CreateUsers: migrated (0.0042s) ==============================================
```

Next, we'll want to remove the following lines out of our `sessions_controller.rb` and `users_controller.rb` in /app/controllers/:

```ruby
# Be sure to include AuthenticationSystem in Application Controller instead
  include AuthenticatedSystem
```

```
# If you want "remember me" functionality, add this before_filter to Application
 Controller
  before_filter :login_from_cookie
```

The appropriate place for those calls is really in our application controller, so edit /app/controllers/application.rb to look like this:

```
class ApplicationController < ActionController::Base
  session :session_key => '_church_session_id'
  include AuthenticatedSystem
end
```

With the Restful Authentication plugin library now added to our application, we'll want to wrap things up by creating a few custom routes in our /config/routes.rb file to provide easy access to our login/logout functionality, so edit your routes to look like this:

```
ActionController::Routing::Routes.draw do |map|
  map.resources :sessions
  map.login '/login', :controller => 'sessions', :action => 'new'
  map.logout '/logout', :controller => 'sessions', :action => 'destroy'
end
```

So What Are We Going to Build?

As we discussed in the opening of the chapter, we want to build a mini community site that allows users the ability to create blogs and galleries. In addition to this, we'll also need to add a few features, such as the ability for each user to create an informational profile about themselves and a directory of all users. To support those needs we also want to ensure that our URL scheme is a friendly one. But what should that look like? If we were to assume that our application was hosted under the domain name www.myhost.com, how would we want our URLs to look for that domain?

For starters, we'll take a lesson from MySpace in for how to navigate to a user's profile page by letting that be a single parameter after the domain name. So assuming a user profile name of Ash (yes, that's an *Army of Darkness* reference), we want to be able to view Ash's profiles at www.myhost.com/ash.

From there, we're going to want secondary pages of content for Ash to show up after his profile name, like so:

- www.myhost.com/ash/profile: Used to route a request to Ash's extended profile

- www.myhost.com/ash/profile/edit: Used by Ash to edit his own profile

- www.myhost.com/ash/posts: Provide a list of all of Ash's blog posts

- www.myhost.com/ash/posts/new: The place that Ash would go to create a new blog post

- www.myhost.com/ash/galleries: The place to view all of Ash's photo galleries

And so on and so forth—you get the general idea. In addition, we want to maintain a fairly standard layout throughout the application for consistency. So putting pencil to paper to sketch out a simple layout, I came up with the layout in Figure 15-1.

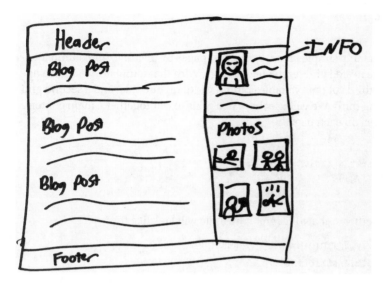

Figure 15-1. *Rough sketch of our layout*

Creating Our Shared Layout

Now that we have a general idea of what our application should look like, we can start putting together our default layout for the application. Create a new file named application.rhtml in /app/views/layouts. As we have in previous projects, we'll take advantage of the Yahoo CSS tools to speed up development of our layout and reduce our need to worry about cross-browser rendering differences. So within our new layout, we'll include the combined CSS tools directly from Yahoo with this call:

```
<link rel="stylesheet" href="http://yui.yahooapis.com/2.2.0/build/➥
reset-fonts-grids/reset-fonts-grids.css" type="text/css">
```

Next, we'll need to define our page structure in the containing div of the page. For our purposes, we'll choose a 950px centered layout (by specifying an id of 'doc2'), and we'll explicitly specify that we want to use the full column width by choosing the yui-t7 template:

```
<div id="doc2" class="yui-t7">
```

Within the main body (i.e., the 'bd' div) of our layout, we'll also add a navigation bar. We'll specify temporary values for now, just as a way to get to a few key pages and replace them with real navigational elements as we build out the backend code.

```
<div class="yui-g navigation">
    <a href="/">Home</a> |
    <a href="/ealameda">Eldon</a> |
    <a href="/directory">Directory</a> |
    <a href="/login">login</a>
</div>
```

Finally, we'll specify a fairly simple layout across our pages by dividing our column into two parts by specifying the nested grid template of yui-gc. With that template, we'll have one grid that will take up two-thirds of the available column width on one side, and a second grid that takes up the remaining third. We will use these two grids to put together a main content area and sidebar styled area on each page.

```
<div class="yui-gc">
    <div class="yui-u first"> </div>
    <div class="yui-u"> </div>
</div>
```

After putting it all together, our application.rhtml file will look like this:

```
<!DOCTYPE HTML PUBLIC "-//W3C//DTD HTML 4.01//EN"
 "http://www.w3.org/TR/html4/strict.dtd">
<html>
<head>
  <title>Church Family Pages</title>
  <link rel="stylesheet" href="http://yui.yahooapis.com/2.2.0/build/➥
reset-fonts-grids/reset-fonts-grids.css" type="text/css">
  <%= stylesheet_link_tag 'styles' %>
</head>
<body>
<div id="doc2" class="yui-t7">
  <div id="hd"> <h1>Church Family Pages<h1> </div>
  <div id="bd">
    <div class="yui-g navigation">
      <a href="/">Home</a> |
      <a href="/directory">Directory</a> |
      <a href="/logout">Logout</a>
    </div>
```

```
    <div class="yui-gc">
      <div class="yui-u first"> <%= yield %> </div>
      <div class="yui-u"> <div class ='sidebar'> <%= yield :sidebar %> </div> </div>
    </div>
  </div>
  <div id="ft"> </div>
</div>
</body>
</html>
```

The Avatar Model

With our layout built, we can now start creating some of the supplemental models for a user
that we'll need to build a users page. The first one that we'll tackle is the avatar model, which
we'll use to manage the profile picture that is displayed for a user. Open the command prompt,
and let's create our avatar model:

```
ruby script/generate model avatar user_id:integer parent_id:integer ➡
content_type:string filename:string  thumbnail:string size:integer width:integer ➡
height:integer created_at:datetime
```

```
      exists  app/models/
      exists  test/unit/
      exists  test/fixtures/
      create  app/models/avatar.rb
      create  test/unit/avatar_test.rb
      create  test/fixtures/avatars.yml
      exists  db/migrate
      create  db/migrate/002_create_avatars.rb
```

You may recognize those database fields from when we used them in Chapter 12 (for our
web comic project) as a way to simplify our image uploading process. Just like in that project,
we're going to take advantage of Rick Olsen's wonderful Attachment Fu plug-in.

To install attachment_fu, we'll run the following plugin install command from the root
of our application:

```
ruby script/plugin install http://svn.techno-weenie.net/projects/plugins/➡
attachment_fu/
```

```
+ ./attachment_fu/CHANGELOG
+ ./attachment_fu/README
+ ./attachment_fu/Rakefile
+ ./attachment_fu/amazon_s3.yml.tpl
+ ./attachment_fu/init.rb
+ ./attachment_fu/install.rb
+ ./attachment_fu/lib/geometry.rb
+ ./attachment_fu/lib/technoweenie/attachment_fu/backends/db_file_backend.rb
+ ./attachment_fu/lib/technoweenie/attachment_fu/backends/file_system_backend.rb
+ ./attachment_fu/lib/technoweenie/attachment_fu/backends/s3_backend.rb
+ ./attachment_fu/lib/technoweenie/attachment_fu/processors/➥
image_science_processor.rb
+ ./attachment_fu/lib/technoweenie/attachment_fu/processors/mini_magick_processor.rb
+ ./attachment_fu/lib/technoweenie/attachment_fu/processors/rmagick_processor.rb
+ ./attachment_fu/lib/technoweenie/attachment_fu.rb
+ ./attachment_fu/test/amazon_s3.yml
+ ./attachment_fu/test/backends/db_file_test.rb
+ ./attachment_fu/test/backends/file_system_test.rb
+ ./attachment_fu/test/backends/remote/s3_test.rb
+ ./attachment_fu/test/base_attachment_tests.rb
+ ./attachment_fu/test/basic_test.rb
+ ./attachment_fu/test/database.yml
+ ./attachment_fu/test/extra_attachment_test.rb
+ ./attachment_fu/test/fixtures/attachment.rb
+ ./attachment_fu/test/fixtures/files/fake/rails.png
+ ./attachment_fu/test/fixtures/files/foo.txt
+ ./attachment_fu/test/fixtures/files/rails.png
+ ./attachment_fu/test/geometry_test.rb
+ ./attachment_fu/test/processors/image_science_test.rb
+ ./attachment_fu/test/processors/mini_magick_test.rb
+ ./attachment_fu/test/processors/rmagick_test.rb
+ ./attachment_fu/test/schema.rb
+ ./attachment_fu/test/test_helper.rb
+ ./attachment_fu/test/validation_test.rb
attachment-fu

=====================
```

Now that we have the Attachment Fu plug-in loaded, we can add its functionality to our Avatar model with a small set of configuration options added to our model. Open /app/models/ avatar.rb, and add the following to it:

```
class Avatar < ActiveRecord::Base
  has_attachment :content_type => :image,
    :storage => :file_system,
    :max_size => 500.kilobytes,
    :resize_to => '110x110',
    :thumbnails => { :comment => '50x50>' }
  validates_as_attachment
end
```

With this configuration, we're letting the attachment_fu plug-in know that we're expecting an image (:content_type => :image) and that we want it to be stored to the local file system (:storage => :file_system).

The User Details Model

The second model that we need to add is the user details model. We'll use this model to allow users to provide supplementary information about themselves, their interests, and so on:

```
ruby script/generate model detail user_id:integer headline:string about_me:text➥
like_to_meet:text interests:text music:text movies:text television:text books:text
```

```
      exists   app/models/
      exists   test/unit/
      exists   test/fixtures/
      create   app/models/detail.rb
      create   test/unit/detail_test.rb
      create   test/fixtures/details.yml
      exists   db/migrate
      create   db/migrate/003_create_details.rb
```

Now that we have both models created, we need to run our migrations to add all of our new tables to the database:

```
rake db:migrate
```

```
(in /Users/darkel/book/church/church)
== CreateAvatars: migrating ======================================================
-- create_table(:avatars)
   -> 0.0141s
== CreateAvatars: migrated (0.0143s) =============================================

== CreateDetails: migrating ======================================================
-- create_table(:details)
   -> 0.0035s
== CreateDetails: migrated (0.0037s) =============================================
```

We'll wrap up adding these models by adding the necessary associations among them and our user model.

In /app/models/user.rb, we'll add a set of has_one method calls to build our associations back to the avatar and details models. We don't want to allow a user to be created without an associated detail, so we'll also add a new method named create_details that will be called by an after_create filter to ensure that we create an associated detail model for each new customer.

Finally, as long as we're in there, let's add a method to our user model named name that will combine user first and last name into a single result:

```ruby
require 'digest/sha1'
class User < ActiveRecord::Base
  # Virtual attribute for the unencrypted password
  attr_accessor :password
  validates_presence_of      :login, :email
  validates_presence_of      :password,                        :if => :password_required?
  validates_presence_of      :password_confirmation,           :if => :password_required?
  validates_length_of        :password, :within => 4..40, :if => :password_required?
  validates_confirmation_of  :password,                        :if => :password_required?
  validates_length_of        :login,    :within => 3..40
  validates_length_of        :email,    :within => 3..100
  validates_uniqueness_of    :login, :email, :case_sensitive => false
  before_save :encrypt_password
  after_create :create_details
  has_one :detail
  has_one :avatar

  def name
    "#{first_name} #{last_name}"
  end
  (...lots of  lines ommitted...)
```

```
  protected
    # before filter
    def encrypt_password
      return if password.blank?
      self.salt = Digest::SHA1.hexdigest("--#{Time.now.to_s}--#{login}--")➥
if new_record?
      self.crypted_password = encrypt(password)
    end

    def password_required?
      crypted_password.blank? || !password.blank?
    end

    def create_details
      self.create_detail
    end
end
```

Next, we'll need to add associations from our avatar and details models back to the user model as well. So edit your avatar model in /app/models/avatar.rb to look like this:

```
class Avatar < ActiveRecord::Base
  has_attachment :content_type => :image,
    :storage => :file_system,
    :max_size => 500.kilobytes,
    :resize_to => '110x110',
    :thumbnails => { :comment => '50x50>' }
  validates_as_attachment
  belongs_to :user
end
```

and your detail model in /app/models/detail.rb to look like this:

```
class Detail < ActiveRecord::Base
  belongs_to :user
end
```

Creating a Sample User

Due to the variety of methods that we could use for adding users to the application, we'll be saving that system as an exercise for the reader. However, even if we're not going to build the interface now, we still need to have at least one user in our database while we're building the application. So we'll use the console to allow us to easily add one or more users to the system interactively.

```
ruby script/console
```

```
Loading development environment.
```

```
>> user = User.new(:login => 'ealameda', :email => 'ealameda@email.com',
:first_name => 'Eldon', :last_name => 'Alameda', :gender => 'Male',
:street => '123 Test Lane', :city => 'Chico', :state => 'CA', :zip => '95926',
:password => 'test', :password_confirmation => 'test')
```

```
=> #<User:0x241408c @password="test", @new_record=true, @attributes={"city"=>"Chico"
, "salt"=>nil, "zip"=>"95926", "updated_at"=>nil, "crypted_password"=>nil,
"remember_token_expires_at"=>nil, "gender"=>"Male", "street"=>"123 Test Lane",
"remember_token"=>nil, "first_name"=>"Eldon", "last_name"=>"Alameda",
"login"=>"ealameda", "state"=>"CA", "created_at"=>nil,
"email"=>"ealameda@email.com"}, password_confirmation"test"
```

```
>> user.save
```

```
=> true
```

```
user.build_detail(:headline => 'A wild and crazy guy',
:about_me => 'This is my page - there are many like it but this one is mine')
```

```
=> #<Detail:0x2b35268 @new_record=true, @attributes={"headline"=>"A wild and crazy
 guy", "like_to_meet"=>nil, "about_me"=>"This is my page - there are many like it
but this one is mine", "music"=>nil, "television"=>nil, "movies"=>nil,
"user_id"=>1, "interests"=>nil, "books"=>nil}
```

```
>> user.save
```

```
=> true
```

Now that we have at least one user in our database, the necessary models, and an overall layout put together, we can shift our focus over to some controllers and views so that we can actually see some results from our application.

The Profile Controller

To display information about a user, we're going to create a new controller named profile that will contain three methods and associated template pages:

- index: To display users' pages

- show: To display extended information about users

- edit: To provide users with the ability to edit their profiles

Technically, there will be four methods when we're done, as we'll also need an update method that will be the destination for the form on the edit page, but we don't want a view template to be created, so we'll just add that method manually later.

```
ruby script/generate controller profile index show edit
```

```
exists  app/controllers/
exists  app/helpers/
create  app/views/profile
exists  test/functional/
create  app/controllers/profile_controller.rb
create  test/functional/profile_controller_test.rb
create  app/helpers/profile_helper.rb
create  app/views/profile/index.rhtml
create  app/views/profile/show.rhtml
create  app/views/profile/edit.rhtml
```

Now, we need to add a few named routes to our application in /config/routes.rb to facilitate our URL schemes and make it easy to create links:

```
ActionController::Routing::Routes.draw do |map|
  map.resources :sessions
  map.login  '/login', :controller => 'sessions', :action => 'new'
  map.logout '/logout', :controller => 'sessions', :action => 'destroy'

  map.showuser  ":user", :controller => 'profile', :action => 'index'
  map.showprofile  ":user/profile", :controller => 'profile', :action => 'show'
  map.editprofile  ":user/profile/edit", :controller => 'profile', :action => 'edit'
end
```

With those routes in place, we'll be able to pull up a user's page by going to http://localhost:3000/ealameda; we'll be able to view that user's profile at http://localhost:3000/ealameda/profile or allow that user to edit the profile by navigating to http://localhost:3000/ealameda/profile/edit. Well, we will once we finish our profile controller methods and views.

Because we want to use the username as the key for all of our routing to users' pages, we'll want to create some code that will pull in the User object for the requested user. To eliminate duplication, we can extract this into a single method that we'll call from a before_filter in our application controller so that we will always have the User object populated. Open application.rb in /app/controllers, and modify it with a find_user method:

```ruby
class ApplicationController < ActionController::Base
  session :session_key => '_church_session_id'
  include AuthenticatedSystem
  before_filter :get_user

  protected
    def get_user
      if !(@user = User.find_by_login(params[:user]))
        redirect_to :controller => 'welcome', :action => 'directory'
      end
    end
end
```

This method should be fairly straightforward: We'll create an @user instance variable with the user login name that was submitted in the URL. If none is found, we'll redirect the request to the user directory in a welcome controller (which we'll build in just a moment). So with this method in place, we'll now have an @user variable available that contains the requested user in all of the controllers that we build.

We'll build the full welcome controller in the next chapter as we build out a few community tools, but let's create a simple stub for now:

```
ruby script/generate controller welcome index directory
```

```
exists  app/controllers/
exists  app/helpers/
create  app/views/welcome
exists  test/functional/
create  app/controllers/welcome_controller.rb
create  test/functional/welcome_controller_test.rb
create  app/helpers/welcome_helper.rb
create  app/views/welcome/index.rhtml
create  app/views/welcome/directory.rhtml
```

One small problem with our new before_filter, though, is the fact that, because we're placing it in the application controller that means it will be executed in *all* controllers—even those where it doesn't make sense to look up a user such as when we display a login page. To fix this, we'll need to add a skip_before_filter :get_user method call to the top of our sessions and users controllers (/app/controllers/sessions_controller.rb and /app/controllers/user_controller.rb).

So now, let's turn our attention back to our profile controller and add in our index view. This page will be one of the most important pages in our application, as it will be the main page for each member of the community. On this page, we'll provide some basic information and some links to any recent blog posts or photos that the user has added. Since we don't have all the functionality built to support the data on this page just yet, we'll place some sample content in a few of the sections. Open /app/views/profile/index, and modify it with the following content:

```
<div class="blog">
  <h1 class="section_header">Blog<h1>
  <h3><a href="#">First Sample Blog Entry</a></h3>
  <p>This is a sample blog post.</p>
  <p>If it were a real blog post there would be more content here</p>
  <hr />

  <h3><a href="#">Second Sample Blog Entry</a></h3>
  <p>This is a sample blog post.</p>
  <p>If it were a real blog post there would be more content here</p>
  <hr />
</div>

<% content_for :sidebar do %>
  <div class='about'>
    <h1 class="section_header">About Me</h1>
    <p><%= @user.detail.headline %></p>
    <p><%= image_tag show_avatar %></p>
    <p><%= @user.detail.about_me %></p>
    <p><%= link_to '[Learn More About Me]',
                            showprofile_path(:user => @user.login) %></p>
  </div>

  <div class='gallery'>
    <h1 class="section_header">Photo Galleries</h1>
  </div>
<% end %>
```

The blog section is just placeholder content until we build out the blog post functionality. However, it's the sidebar section that we've added some real content to; mainly we're just displaying a few of the user details. However, we do have a little extra method in the `image_tag` section with the addition of a helper method named `show_avatar`.

We want to be able to display the user's avatar if it's been added, but if we attempt to display a nonexistent avatar, the whole page will break as we attempt to call a method on a `nil` object. We get around this by moving the necessary checks into a helper method. Open `/app/helpers/application_helper.rb`, and let's add the `show_avatar` method, which will return the user's avatar if it exists or a static image file if there's no avatar.

```
module ApplicationHelper
  def show_avatar
    if @user.avatar
      return @user.avatar.public_filename
    else
      return "no_avatar.gif"
    end
  end
end
```

Ensure that your web server is running and that you've copied the style sheets and images from the source archive for this project into your application, then load `http://localhost:3000/ealameda` (or whichever username you created) to see a result like the one shown in Figure 15-2.

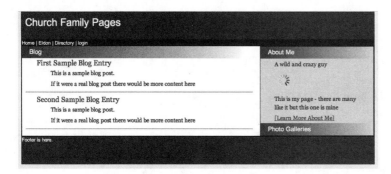

Figure 15-2. *Our initial user page*

Editing User Details and Avatars

Displaying our user page was fairly simple, albeit a bit boring, since we're using sample content. What we need now is the functionality to allow users to modify their avatars and user detail information, so that they can personalize the content on the page. We'll start by adding in an avatar controller that we can use to allow users to upload new avatar images:

```
ruby script/generate controller avatar
```

```
exists   app/controllers/
exists   app/helpers/
create   app/views/avatar
exists   test/functional/
create   app/controllers/avatar_controller.rb
create   test/functional/avatar_controller_test.rb
create   app/helpers/avatar_helper.rb
```

We'll modify our new controller to have just one method—the create method—which we'll use to save a new avatar image, associate it to the current user and finally redirect the request back to the user's profile page.

```
class AvatarController < ApplicationController
  before_filter :login_required
  def create
    @avatar = current_user.build_avatar(params[:avatar])
    @avatar.save
    redirect_to showprofile_path(:user => current_user.login)
  end
end
```

■**Note** You should notice that we used the current_user object that's provided by the Restful Authentication plug-in rather than the @user object that we might pick off from the URL parameters. The reason why is that we want to ensure that any uploaded images will only be modified for the current logged in user. That way, if someone tries to go around our forms and change the avatar for another user, he'll only end up changing his own.

Now that we have our create method in our avatar controller, we'll also add a named route for it in /config/routes.rb:

```
ActionController::Routing::Routes.draw do |map|
  map.resources :sessions
  map.login  '/login', :controller => 'sessions', :action => 'new'
  map.logout '/logout', :controller => 'sessions', :action => 'destroy'
  map.showuser   ":user", :controller => 'profile', :action => 'index'
  map.showprofile  ":user/profile", :controller => 'profile', :action => 'show'
  map.editprofile  ":user/profile/edit", :controller => 'profile', :action => 'edit'
  map.addavatar ":user/avatar/create", :controller => 'avatar', :action => 'create'
end
```

Editing a Profile

To allow users to update their profiles, we'll need to modify the edit method and add an update method to our profile controller in /app/controllers/profile_controller.rb to be able to support editing our profile. Also, since we don't want to allow any users to update a page that doesn't belong to them, this would be a good time to add our before_filter :login_required method call.

```
class ProfileController < ApplicationController
  before_filter :login_required
  def index
  end

  def show
  end

  def edit
    @detail = @user.detail
    @avatar = @user.avatar
  end

  def update
    @detail = current_user.detail
    @detail.update_attributes(params[:detail])
    redirect_to showprofile_path(:user => @user.login)
  end
end
```

With our controller methods ready and set to handle editing a user's profile, let's go ahead and modify the edit template for our profile controller in /app/views/profile/edit.rhtml to have two forms: one that will allow users to update their user details and another in the sidebar that will allow them to upload new avatar images.

```
<h1 class="section_header">Editing <%= @user.name.pluralize %> profile</h1>
<%= error_messages_for :detail %>

<% form_for(:detail,  :url => updateprofile_path,
                                   :html => { :method => :put }) do |f| %>
  <p><b>Profile Headline</b><br />
  <%= f.text_field :headline %></p>

  <p><b>About me</b><br />
  <%= f.text_area :about_me %></p>

  <p><b>Who I'd like to meet</b><br />
  <%= f.text_area :like_to_meet %></p>
```

```
<p><b>My Interests</b><br />
<%= f.text_area :interests %></p>

<p><b>Favorite Music</b><br />
<%= f.text_area :music %></p>

<p><b>Favorite Movies</b><br />
<%= f.text_area :movies %></p>

<p><b>Favorite Television</b><br />
<%= f.text_area :television %></p>

<p><b>Favorite Books</b><br />
<%= f.text_area :books %></p>

<p><%= submit_tag "Update" %></p>
<% end %>

<% content_for :sidebar do %>
  <p><%= image_tag show_avatar %></p>
  <% form_for(:avatar, :url => addavatar_path,
                      :html => { :multipart => true, :id => 'avatar' }) do |f| -%>
    <p><label for="mugshot">Upload A New Avatar:</label>
        <%= f.file_field :uploaded_data, "size" => 10 %></p>
    <p><%= submit_tag 'Create' %></p>
  <% end -%>
<% end %>
```

When rendered, the preceding code will give us a page like the one shown in Figure 15-3.

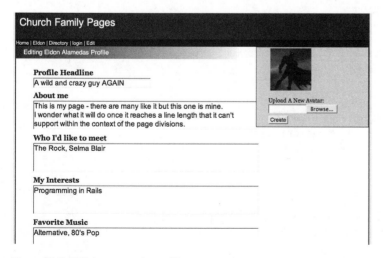

Figure 15-3. *Editing a user's profile*

All that's left is to add in one more named route in /configs/routes.rb for our details form to use to route to the update method in the profile controller.

```
ActionController::Routing::Routes.draw do |map|
  map.resources :sessions
  map.login  '/login', :controller => 'sessions', :action => 'new'
  map.logout '/logout', :controller => 'sessions', :action => 'destroy'

  map.showuser   ":user", :controller => 'profile', :action => 'index'
  map.showprofile  ":user/profile", :controller => 'profile', :action => 'show'
  map.editprofile  ":user/profile/edit", :controller => 'profile', :action => 'edit'
  map.updateprofile ":user/profile/update", :controller => 'profile', ➥
:action => 'update'
  map.addavatar ":user/avatar/create", :controller => 'avatar', :action => 'create'
end
```

Viewing a Profile

We'll wrap up our editing of profiles with the simple matter of building out the show template so that we can display a users profile. Open /app/views/profile/show.rhtml, and place the following content in it:

```
<% unless @user.detail.headline.blank? %>
  <h1 class="section_header">My Headline</h1>
  <p><%= h @user.detail.headline %></p>
<% end %>

<% unless @user.detail.about_me.blank? %>
  <h1 class="section_header">About Me</h1>
  <p><%= h @user.detail.about_me %></p>
<% end %>

<% unless @user.detail.like_to_meet.blank? %>
  <h1 class="section_header">Who I'd like to meet</h1>
  <p><%= h @user.detail.like_to_meet %></p>
<% end %>

<% unless @user.detail.interests.blank? %>
  <h1 class="section_header">My Interests</h1>
  <p><%= h @user.detail.interests %></p>
<% end %>

<% unless @user.detail.music.blank? %>
  <h1 class="section_header">Favorite Music</h1>
  <p><%= h @user.detail.music %></p>
<% end %>
```

```
<% unless @user.detail.movies.blank? %>
  <h1 class="section_header">Favorite Movies</h1>
  <p><%= h @user.detail.movies %></p>
<% end %>

<% unless @user.detail.television.blank? %>
  <h1 class="section_header">Favorite Television</h1>
  <p><%= h @user.detail.television %></p>
<% end %>

<% unless @user.detail.books.blank? %>
  <h1 class="section_header">Favorite Books</h1>
  <p><%= h @user.detail.books %></p>
<% end %>

<% content_for :sidebar do %>
  <div class='about'>
      <h1 class="section_header"><%= h @user.name %></h1>
      <p><%= h @user.street %></p>
      <p><%= h @user.city %>, <%= h @user.state %></p>
  </div>
<% end %>
```

For this page, we're going to wrap all of our user details within blocks that check if the value is set before we try to display it. That way, we'll only display the user detail fields for which a user has chosen to provide answers. So when viewing this page by opening http://localhost:3000/ealameda/profile, you should see a page like the one shown in Figure 15-4.

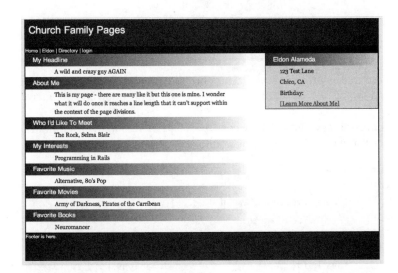

Figure 15-4. *Viewing a user's profile*

Adding Blogs

Now that we've allowed users to customize their pages with some basic profile information and add custom avatars, our next step will be to add some basic blogging support to their pages, so they can share their thoughts and life events with other members of the community. We'll do that by adding a new scaffold resource to our project named post:

```
ruby script/generate scaffold_resource post user_id:integer headline:string ➡
body:text created_at:datetime updated_at:datetime
```

```
    exists  app/models/
    exists  app/controllers/
    exists  app/helpers/
    create  app/views/posts
    exists  test/functional/
    exists  test/unit/
    create  app/views/posts/index.rhtml
    create  app/views/posts/show.rhtml
    create  app/views/posts/new.rhtml
    create  app/views/posts/edit.rhtml
    create  app/views/layouts/posts.rhtml
 identical  public/stylesheets/scaffold.css
    create  app/models/post.rb
    create  app/controllers/posts_controller.rb
    create  test/functional/posts_controller_test.rb
    create  app/helpers/posts_helper.rb
    create  test/unit/post_test.rb
    create  test/fixtures/posts.yml
    exists  db/migrate
    create  db/migrate/003_create_posts.rb
     route  map.resources :posts
```

The scaffold_resource command also created a new layout named posts.rhtml in /app/views/layouts that we don't want, as it will conflict with the default application layout that we built. So delete that file.

Next, we'll want to set up our associations between a post and user, so in the user model (/app/models/user.rb), we'll add the following association:

```
require 'digest/sha1'
class User < ActiveRecord::Base
  # Virtual attribute for the unencrypted password
  attr_accessor :password

  validates_presence_of     :login, :email
  validates_presence_of     :password,                 :if => :password_required?
  validates_presence_of     :password_confirmation,    :if => :password_required?
```

```
validates_length_of        :password, :within => 4..40, :if => :password_required?
validates_confirmation_of :password,                    :if => :password_required?
validates_length_of        :login,    :within => 3..40
validates_length_of        :email,    :within => 3..100
validates_uniqueness_of    :login, :email, :case_sensitive => false
before_save :encrypt_password
after_create :create_details
has_one :detail
has_one :avatar
has_many :posts

def name
  "#{first_name} #{last_name}"
end
(... Lines omitted...)
end
```

Meanwhile, in our posts model (/app/models/post.rb), we'll add the corresponding
belongs_to :user association:

```
class Post < ActiveRecord::Base
  belongs_to :user
end
```

With our associations defined, let's go ahead and add the posts table to the database by
running the database migrations:

```
rake db:migrate
```

```
== CreatePosts: migrating ==============================================
-- create_table(:posts)
   -> 0.0033s
== CreatePosts: migrated (0.0047s) =====================================
```

For adding the necessary routes for a post to our application, we'll utilize the map.resources
method so that all of our CRUD style of operations will be supported and to make it match our
routing scheme of #{username}/posts, we'll add in a path_prefix onto the route as well. So add
the following bold line to /config/routes.rb:

```
ActionController::Routing::Routes.draw do |map|
  map.resources :sessions
  map.login  '/login', :controller => 'sessions', :action => 'new'
  map.logout '/logout', :controller => 'sessions', :action => 'destroy'
  map.showuser   ":user", :controller => 'profile', :action => 'index'
  map.showprofile  ":user/profile", :controller => 'profile', :action => 'show'
  map.editprofile  ":user/profile/edit", :controller => 'profile', :action => 'edit'
  map.updateprofile ":user/profile/update", :controller => 'profile', ➥
```

```
    :action => 'update'
      map.addavatar ":user/avatar/create", :controller => 'avatar', :action => 'create'
      map.resources :posts, :path_prefix => ":user"
    end
```

Post Controller Methods and Templates

Obviously, the first thing we'll need to add to our posts controller (`/app/controllers/ posts_controller.rb`) is to add the `before_filter :login_required` method to limit access to the methods in this controller.

```
class PostsController < ApplicationController
  before_filter :login_required
  (...lines omitted...)
```

Now that we've limited access to this controller's methods, we can tackle the first piece of the CRUD pie that we'll build in our posts controller—the ability to create a new post.

New

We'll create our new method in the posts controller to build a new post associated to the current logged in user that will be used as the object for our data entry form.

```
def new
  @post = current_user.posts.build
end
```

And we'll build out the corresponding template (`/app/views/posts/new.rthml`) to look like this:

```
<div class="editblog">
  <%= javascript_include_tag 'tiny_mce/tiny_mce' %>
  <%= javascript_include_tag 'tinyconfig' %>
  <h1 class="section_header">New post</h1>
  <%= error_messages_for :post %>
  <% form_for(:post, :url => posts_path(:user => @user.login)) do |f| %>
    <p>
      <b>Headline</b><br />
      <%= f.text_field :headline %>
    </p>
    <p>
      <b>Body</b><br />
      <%= f.text_area :body %>
    </p>
    <p> <%= submit_tag "Create" %> </p>
  <% end %>
</div>
```

This is a fairly standard form; the only thing of note is that that we're adding in the TinyMCE JavaScript editor (included in the source archive or downloadable from `http://tinymce/moxiecode.com`) to provide a nicer HTML editor for users to format their blog posts. If we were to go to `http://localhost:3000/ealameda/posts/new`, we should see a page like the one shown in Figure 15-5.

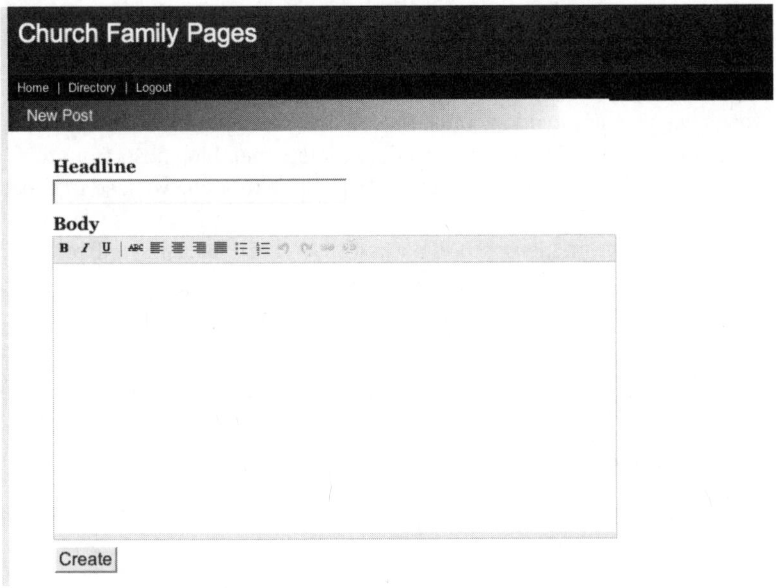

Figure 15-5. *Creating a new blog post*

Create

Our new form won't work without a method to actually save the new post to the database, so that's what our `create` method will do—edit the `create` method in the posts controller with this code, which will save the submitted form and redirect the user to their profile pages:

```
def create
  @post = current_user.posts.build(params[:post])
  if @post.save
    redirect_to showuser_path(:user => @user.login)
  else
    render :action => "new"
  end
end
```

Index

We're not going to be using the `index` method in our application, so go ahead and delete the auto-generated `index` method from the posts controller and the auto-generated `index.rthml` file from `/app/views/posts/`.

Show

Now that we have at least one blog post in our database, we can edit the show method and template that will be used to display it. Edit the show method in the posts controller to look like this:

```
def show
  @post = @user.posts.find(params[:id])
end
```

Now, in the show template (/app/views/posts/show.rhtml), we'll want to simply display the blog post in the page in much the same way that we'll display a summary of blog posts on the user's main page. However, we do want to add a touch more functionality though—it will be extra nice if we could also add in the ability for users to edit or delete their blog posts from this page, so we'll also add in a few links to make that possible. To do that, though, we need to make sure that we only provide those administration links if the person viewing the page is the owner of that blog post. So we'll create a new helper method named show_admin_menu that will return true or false based on whether or not the logged in user matches the user page.

Open /app/helpers/application_helper.rb, and add the show_admin_menu function to it:

```
module ApplicationHelper
  def show_avatar
    if @user.avatar
      return @user.avatar.public_filename
    else
      return "no_avatar.gif"
    end
  end

  def show_admin_menu
    current_user == @user
  end
end
```

With our helper method added, we're now ready to build the show template for a blog post. Add the following content to /app/views/posts/show.rthml:

```
<div class="blog">
  <h1 class="section_header"><%= @post.headline %><h1>
  <%= @post.body %>
  <p><span class="added">written on <%= @post.created_at.to_s(:long) %></span></p>
  <hr />

  <% if show_admin_menu %>
    <%= link_to 'Edit This Post',
              edit_post_path(:user => @user.login, :id => @post) %><br />
    <%= link_to 'Destroy This Post', post_path(:user => @user.login,
              :id => @post), :confirm => 'Are you sure?', :method => :delete %>
  <% end %>
</div>
```

```
<% content_for :sidebar do %>
  <div class='about'>
    <h1 class="section_header">About Me</h1>
    <p><%= @user.detail.headline %></p>
    <p><%= image_tag show_avatar %></p>
    <p><%= @user.detail.about_me %></p>
    <p><%= link_to '[Learn More About Me]',
                            showprofile_path(:user => @user.login) %></p>
  </div>
<% end %>
```

You can see the results of this template when viewing a page, such as `http://localhost:3000/posts/7`, shown in Figure 15-6.

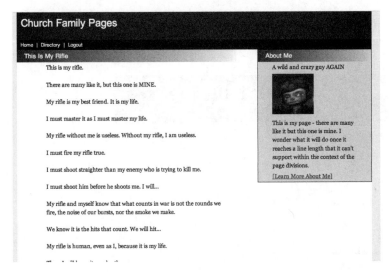

Figure 15-6. *Viewing a blog post ("Rifleman's Creed," by Major General William H. Rupertus)*

Edit

At the bottom of our blog post, we placed a pair of links; one of those was to edit the current blog post at `http://localhost:3000/ealameda/posts/7;edit`. Our `edit` method in the posts controller should look like this:

```
def edit
  @post = current_user.posts.find(params[:id])
end
```

The corresponding template in `/app/views/posts/edit.rhtml` will look very similar to the one that we created for the new template:

```
<div class="editblog">
  <%= javascript_include_tag 'tiny_mce/tiny_mce' %>
  <%= javascript_include_tag 'tinyconfig' %>
```

```
<h1 class="section_header">New post</h1>
<%= error_messages_for :post %>
<% form_for(:post, :url => posts_path(:user => @user.login)) do |f| %>
  <p>
    <b>Headline</b><br />
    <%= f.text_field :headline %>
  </p>
  <p>
    <b>Body</b><br />
    <%= f.text_area :body %>
  </p>
  <p><%= submit_tag "Create" %> </p>
<% end %>
</div>
```

When viewed on a page like `http://localhost:3000/ealameda/posts/7;edit`, the preceding code gives us the page appearance shown in Figure 15-7.

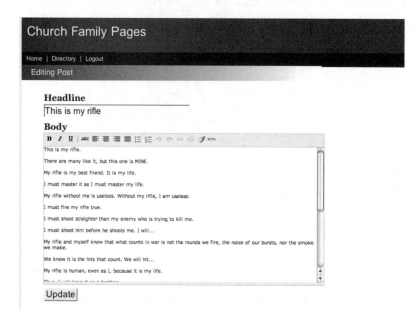

Figure 15-7. *Editing a blog post*

Update

The `update` method in the posts controller will simply be the destination of any posts from the edit template, so its job will be to simply save the updated post and then redirect the request to the user profile page.

```
def update
  @post = current_user.posts.find(params[:id])
  if @post.update_attributes(params[:post])
    redirect_to showuser_path(:user => @user.login)
  else
    render :action => "edit"
  end
end
```

Destroy

The final method that we'll modify in the posts controller is the destroy method, which will be called from the administration menu we created in the show template. It should look like this:

```
def destroy
  @post = current_user.posts.find(params[:id])
  @post.destroy
  redirect_to showuser_url(:user => @user.login)
end
```

The Full Posts Controller

When we combine all those methods, your final posts controller (/app/controllers/ posts_controller.rb) should look like this:

```
class PostsController < ApplicationController
  before_filter :login_required

  # GET /posts/1
  def show
    @post = @user.posts.find(params[:id])
  end

  # GET /posts/new
  def new
    @post = current_user.posts.build
  end

  # GET /posts/1;edit
  def edit
    @post = current_user.posts.find(params[:id])
  end
```

```
  # POST /posts
  def create
    @post = current_user.posts.build(params[:post])
    if @post.save
        redirect_to showuser_path(:user => @user.login)
    else
        render :action => "new"
    end
  end

  # PUT /posts/1
  def update
    @post = current_user.posts.find(params[:id])
    if @post.update_attributes(params[:post])
      redirect_to showuser_path(:user => @user.login)
    else
      render :action => "edit"
    end
  end

  # DELETE /posts/1
  def destroy
    @post = current_user.posts.find(params[:id])
    @post.destroy
    redirect_to showuser_url(:user => @user.login)
  end
end
```

Adding Blog Summaries to Our User Page

We're almost done with building our blog functionality; all that's left is to fill in the main user page with a list of the most recent blog posts. To do that, we'll need to come up with a good way of pulling back the list of recent blog posts. We could be verbose and create an instance variable in our controller that does something like this:

```
@recentPosts = @user.posts.find(:all, :order => 'created_at desc')
```

But that adds a bit too much ugliness to the code for my tastes; plus, it could force us into duplicating code if we needed to pull back that list somewhere else in our application. Instead, I'd rather build a method onto the association between users and posts. So open /app/models/user.rb, and let's modify the has_many posts method like so:

```
has_many :posts do
  def recent
    find(:all, :order => 'created_at desc', :limit => 6)
  end
end
```

Now we can simply call @user.posts.recent from anywhere in our application to retrieve the six most recent posts for the given user. Not only is this more concise but it improves the readability of our code. So let's go ahead and add the method call to the index method in our profiles controller, so we can utilize that list within the user page. Within /app/controllers/profile_controller.rb modify the index method, like so:

```
def index
  @posts = @user.posts.recent
end
```

Now, we can modify the related index template to replace our sample blog posts with some real code that will process our @posts instance variable and display those blog posts within the page. Open /app/views/profile/index.rhtml, and edit it to include the lines below

```
<div class="blog">
  <h1 class="section_header">Recent Blog Posts<h1>
  <% for post in @posts %>
    <h3>
      <%= link_to post.headline, post_path(:user => @user.login, :id => post) %>
    </h3>
    <span class="added">written on <%= post.created_at.to_s(:long) %></span>
    <p>
      <%= truncate(post.body.gsub!(%r{</?.*?>}, ""), 130) %>
      <%= link_to "[Read More]", post_path(:user => @user.login, :id => post) %>
    </p>
    <hr />
  <% end %>
</div>

<% content_for :sidebar do %>
  <div class='about'>
    <h1 class="section_header">About Me</h1>
    <p><%= @user.detail.headline %></p>
    <p><%= image_tag show_avatar %></p>
    <p><%= @user.detail.about_me %></p>
    <p><%= link_to '[Learn More About Me]',
                      showprofile_path(:user => @user.login) %></p>
  </div>

  <div class='gallery'>
    <h1 class="section_header">Photo Galleries</h1>
  </div>
<% end %>
```

One line in the preceding code that we should discuss is this line:

```
<%= truncate(post.body.gsub!(%r{</?.*?>}, ""), 130) %>
```

In this method, we want to display the `post.body` variable for the given post. However, in the event that a user was being particularly wordy, we want to limit how much data we display on the page—otherwise, our six most recent posts might extend the page through several full page lengths. To prevent that, we're going to pass the body of the post through the `truncate` method, which will evaluate the length of the body text, and if it's longer than 130 characters, it will truncate the text and append ellipsis on to the end to indicate that there is more text. However, that could still cause us some issues since we're allowing HTML tags into the body of a post, because if we were to truncate the text and cut off the closing of a `<b>` tag or truncate in the middle of an `<a href>` tag, we could screw up the formatting of the rest of our page. So to prevent us from having any issues like that, we want to strip out all HTML tags from our page and effectively convert our extracted blog post into pure text. To do that, we'll call the global substitution method on our body passing it the regular expression to convert anything contained within `<>` tags to an empty space.

Our user page at `http://localhost:3000/ealameda` will now look like Figure 15-8 with real blog posts added to the page.

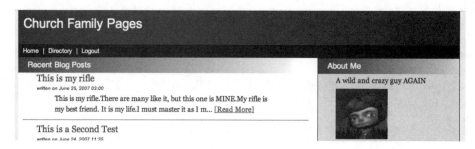

Figure 15-8. *Blog posts added to our user page*

Adding Galleries

The final piece of functionality that we'll add to our application in this chapter is the ability to create and view photos, organized into galleries. Since photos will be children of galleries, we'll start out by building the ability to create and manage galleries. Let's generate a scaffold resource for gallery:

```
ruby script/generate scaffold_resource gallery user_id:integer name:string ➡
description:text created_at:datetime photos_count:integer privacy:string
```

```
   exists  app/models/
   exists  app/controllers/
   exists  app/helpers/
   create  app/views/galleries
   exists  test/functional/
   exists  test/unit/
   create  app/views/galleries/index.rhtml
   create  app/views/galleries/show.rhtml
   create  app/views/galleries/new.rhtml
   create  app/views/galleries/edit.rhtml
   create  app/views/layouts/galleries.rhtml
identical  public/stylesheets/scaffold.css
   create  app/models/gallery.rb
   create  app/controllers/galleries_controller.rb
   create  test/functional/galleries_controller_test.rb
   create  app/helpers/galleries_helper.rb
   create  test/unit/gallery_test.rb
   create  test/fixtures/galleries.yml
   exists  db/migrate
   create  db/migrate/005_create_galleries.rb
    route  map.resources :galleries
```

Once again the scaffold_resource generator created a layout file that we don't need, so go ahead and delete the file galleries.rhtml from /app/views/layouts. Once that's deleted, let's run our migration and add the galleries table:

rake db:migrate

```
== CreateGalleries: migrating ==================================================
-- create_table(:galleries)
   -> 0.0033s
== CreateGalleries: migrated (0.0034s) =========================================
```

We'll need to add a route to our galleries as well, and we'll use a similar pattern as we did with posts, by adding a `path_prefix` onto our `map.resources` method:

```
ActionController::Routing::Routes.draw do |map|

  map.resources :sessions
  map.login  '/login', :controller => 'sessions', :action => 'new'
  map.logout '/logout', :controller => 'sessions', :action => 'destroy'
  map.showuser  ":user", :controller => 'profile', :action => 'index'
  map.showprofile  ":user/profile", :controller => 'profile', :action => 'show'
  map.editprofile  ":user/profile/edit", :controller => 'profile', :action => 'edit'
  map.updateprofile ":user/profile/update", :controller => 'profile', ➥
:action => 'update'
  map.addavatar ":user/avatar/create", :controller => 'avatar', :action => 'create'
  map.resources :posts, :path_prefix => ":user"
  map.resources :galleries, :path_prefix => ":user"
end
```

Finally, we'll wrap the base configuration of galleries by adding in the necessary associations between users and galleries. Within `user.rb` in `/app/models` add the following `has_many :galleries` association:

```
require 'digest/sha1'
class User < ActiveRecord::Base
  # Virtual attribute for the unencrypted password
  attr_accessor :password

  validates_presence_of     :login, :email
  validates_presence_of     :password,                       :if => :password_required?
  validates_presence_of     :password_confirmation,      :if => :password_required?
  validates_length_of       :password, :within => 4..40, :if => :password_required?
  validates_confirmation_of :password,                       :if => :password_required?
  validates_length_of       :login,    :within => 3..40
  validates_length_of       :email,    :within => 3..100
  validates_uniqueness_of   :login, :email, :case_sensitive => false
  before_save :encrypt_password
  after_create :create_details
  has_one :detail
  has_one :avatar
  has_many :posts do
    def recent
      find(:all, :order => 'created_at desc', :limit => 6)
    end
  end
  has_many :galleries
```

```
  def name
    "#{first_name} #{last_name}"
  end
  (...lines ommited...)
end
```

Then, within the gallery model (/app/models/gallery.rb), we'll add the complementary belongs_to :user association, as well as some basic validations:

```
class Gallery < ActiveRecord::Base
  belongs_to :user
  validates_presence_of :user_id, :name
end
```

Adding Photos

Now that we've added our model for galleries, our next step is to build support for a photos model. We'll build this by utilizing the attachment_fu plug-in once again to simplify our file upload process:

```
ruby script/generate scaffold_resource photo user_id:integer gallery_id:integer ➡
parent_id:integer content_type:string filename:string  thumbnail:string ➡
size:integer width:integer height:integer created_at:datetime
```

```
     exists   app/models/
     exists   app/controllers/
     exists   app/helpers/
     create   app/views/photos
     exists   test/functional/
     exists   test/unit/
     create   app/views/photos/index.rhtml
     create   app/views/photos/show.rhtml
     create   app/views/photos/new.rhtml
     create   app/views/photos/edit.rhtml
     create   app/views/layouts/photos.rhtml
  identical   public/stylesheets/scaffold.css
     create   app/models/photo.rb
     create   app/controllers/photos_controller.rb
     create   test/functional/photos_controller_test.rb
     create   app/helpers/photos_helper.rb
     create   test/unit/photo_test.rb
     create   test/fixtures/photos.yml
     exists   db/migrate
     create   db/migrate/006_create_photos.rb
      route   map.resources :photos
```

After deleting the `photos.rhtml` layout from /app/views/layouts, let's go ahead and run our migration:

```
rake db:migrate
```

```
== CreatePhotos: migrating ==============================
-- create_table(:photos)
   -> 0.0035s
== CreatePhotos: migrated (0.0041s) =========================================
```

Finally, we'll add in our associations in our user model in /app/models/user.rb; we'll define that a user can have many photos:

```
require 'digest/sha1'
class User < ActiveRecord::Base

 (...lines omitted...)

  has_many :posts do
    def recent
      find(:all, :order => 'created_at desc', :limit => 6)
    end
  end
  has_many :galleries
  has_many :photos

  def name
    "#{first_name} #{last_name}"
  end

  (...lines omitted...)
end
```

While in the gallery model (/app/models/gallery.rb), we'll define that a gallery can also have many photos:

```
class Gallery < ActiveRecord::Base
  belongs_to :user
  has_many :photos
  validates_presence_of :user_id, :name
end
```

A photo belongs to both users and galleries and should be configured for `attachment_fu` to store the photos to the file system, scale the image to a standard format, and create a thumbnail that maintains the correct aspect ratio while resizing the width to 140px:

```
class Photo < ActiveRecord::Base
  has_attachment :content_type => :image,
    :storage => :file_system,
    :max_size => 2.megabytes,
    :resize_to => '640x360>',
    :thumbnails => { :thumb => '140x105>' }
  validates_as_attachment
  belongs_to :gallery
  belongs_to :user
end
```

Finally, we'll add in a new route in `/config/routes.rb` for our photos using the same `path_prefix` as we used in galleries:

```
ActionController::Routing::Routes.draw do |map|
  map.resources :sessions
  map.login  '/login', :controller => 'sessions', :action => 'new'
  map.logout '/logout', :controller => 'sessions', :action => 'destroy'
  map.showuser  ":user", :controller => 'profile', :action => 'index'
  map.showprofile  ":user/profile", :controller => 'profile', :action => 'show'
  map.editprofile  ":user/profile/edit", :controller => 'profile', :action => 'edit'
  map.updateprofile ":user/profile/update", :controller => 'profile', ➥
:action => 'update'
  map.addavatar ":user/avatar/create", :controller => 'avatar', :action => 'create'
  map.resources :posts, :path_prefix => ":user"
  map.resources :galleries, :path_prefix => ":user"
  map.resources :photos, :path_prefix => ":user"
end
```

Galleries and Photo Controllers

Now that we've used the scaffold resource to build our photos and galleries models, and we've set them up with the necessary associations and routes, we're ready to configure their controller methods and view templates to implement photo-uploading functionality to our application. In addition to the modifications we'll make in the following sections, we'll also need to add a `before_filter :login_required` call to each controller to ensure that we're controlling access to these methods.

Creating a New Gallery

Since we'll have to create a gallery to hold our photos, our first process is to set up the functionality to create one. Open `galleries_controller` in /app/controllers, and let's edit the new method like so:

```
def new
  @gallery = current_user.galleries.build
end
```

Now, let's edit the new.rthml file in /app/views/galleries to contain the following form:

```
<h1 class="section_header">Create A New Gallery</h1>
<%= error_messages_for :gallery %>

<% form_for(:gallery, :url => galleries_path(:user => current_user.login)) do |f| %>
  <p><b>Name</b><br />
  <%= f.text_field :name %> </p>

  <p><b>Description</b><br />
  <%= f.text_area :description %> </p>

  <p><%= submit_tag "Create" %> </p>
<% end %>
```

You can see the result of our new create galleries form, as it would appear at http://localhost:3000/ealameda/galleries/new, in Figure 15-9.

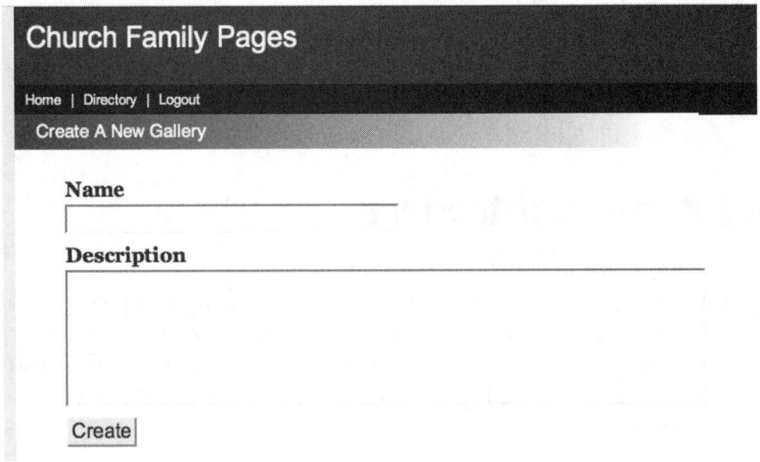

Figure 15-9. *Creating a new gallery*

Next, we'll need to update the `create` method of our galleries controller to save the submitted gallery, associate it to the current logged in user, and redirect the request to the gallery show method after successfully saving:

```
def create
  @gallery = current_user.galleries.build(params[:gallery])
  if @gallery.save
    redirect_to gallery_url(:user => current_user.login, :id => @gallery)
  else
    render :action => "new"
  end
end
```

Viewing a Specific Gallery

With the ability to create a new gallery completed, we now need the ability to show that gallery and provide an upload form to add photos to it. A gallery will be available at the URL http:// localhost:3000/ealameda/galleries/1—which will mean it will be routed to the show method in the galleries controller. Let's modify that method as so:

```
def show
  @gallery = @user.galleries.find(params[:id])
end
```

Now, we can modify the show.rhtml template in /app/views/galleries—this one will have a few new bits of code, so let's look at the template as a whole and then we'll break down a few of the more interesting parts afterward:

```
<h1 class="section_header"><%= @gallery.name %><h1>
<% @gallery.photos.in_groups_of(3, false) do |photos| %>
  <ul class="thumbnails">
    <% for photo in photos %>
      <li class="thumb">
        <%= link_to(image_tag(photo.public_filename(:thumb) ) + '<br />' + ➥
photo.description, photo_path(:user => @user.login, :id => photo) ) %>
      </li>
    <% end %>
  </ul>
<% end %>
```

```
<% content_for :sidebar do %>
  <h1 class="section_header">Gallery Description<h1>
    <p><%= @gallery.description %></p>
    <% if show_admin_menu %>
      <hr />
      <% form_for(:photo, :url => photos_path(:user => current_user.login),
                                :html => { :multipart => true }) do |f| -%>
        <label for="photo_uploaded_data">Upload New Photo:</label>
        <%= f.file_field :uploaded_data, "size" => 15 %>

        <label for="photo_uploaded_data">Describe Photo:</label><br />
        <%= f.text_field :description, "size" => 25 %>

        <%= f.hidden_field :gallery_id, :value => @gallery.id %>

        <%= submit_tag 'Upload Photo' %>
      <% end %>
    <% end %>
<% end %>
```

The interesting bit of code that we haven't discussed yet was the `in_groups_of` method that can be found in this line `@gallery.photos.in_groups_of (3, false) do |photos|`. This is a very useful method that we can use to iterate over an array dividing it into groups, which is extremely useful for building columns. To get a better understanding of it, let's take a look at the functioning of this method within `script/console`:

```
ruby script/console
```

```
Loading development environment.
```

Now, let's create an array of numbers 1 to 7 and pass it the `in_groups_of` method dividing the array into groups of three:

```
>> [1, 2, 3, 4, 5, 6, 7].in_groups_of(3)
```

```
=> [[1, 2, 3], [4, 5, 6], [7, nil, nil]]
```

You can see that the `in_groups_of` method divided our array up into a multidimensional array, where each of the subarrays holds three of the numbers from our array. Since our original array wasn't divisible equally by three, it padded the last subarray with `nil`s.

Since we want to prevent our arrays from being padded with `nil`s, we can simply pass the `in_groups_of` method a second parameter that it will use to pad any remaining slots, or we can pass it `false` to prevent it from placing any filler elements:

```
>> [1, 2, 3, 4, 5, 6, 7].in_groups_of(3, false)
```

```
=> [[1, 2, 3], [4, 5, 6], [7]]
```

Therefore, in our template, we're using the `in_groups_of` method to sort our photos into rows with three photos each, which gives us a result like you can see in Figure 15-10 when we view the page at `http://localhost/galleries/3` with a few photos added.

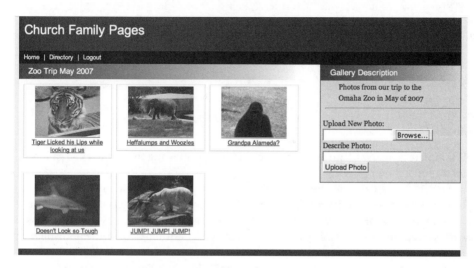

Figure 15-10. *Displaying the photos of a gallery*

Display All Users' Galleries

The code for displaying a list of all galleries (`http://localhost/ealameda/galleries`) will be very similar to the code that we just created to display all the photos in a gallery. First off, we'll modify the index method in the galleries controller (`/app/controllers/galleries_controller.rb`) like this:

```
def index
  @galleries = @user.galleries.find(:all)
end
```

And we'll modify the template file like this (`index.rhtml` in `/app/views/galleries`):

```
<h1 class="section_header">Galleries<h1>
<% @galleries.in_groups_of(3, false) do |galleries| %>
  <ul class="thumbnails">
    <% for gallery in galleries %>
      <% unless gallery.photos.count == 0 %>
        <li class="thumb">
          <%= link_to image_tag(gallery.photos.first.public_filename(:thumb)) + ➥
 '<br />' + gallery.name + '<br />' + pluralize(gallery.photos.count, 'Photo'), ➥
gallery_path(:user => 'ealameda', :id => gallery.id)  %>
        </li>
```

```
    <% else %>
      <li class="thumb">
        <%= link_to gallery.name + '<br />' + ➥
                          pluralize(gallery.photos.count, 'Photo'),
                          gallery_path(:user => 'ealameda', :id => gallery.id)  %>
      </li>
    <% end %>
  <% end %>
  </ul>
<% end %>


<br />


<% content_for :sidebar do %>
  <p><%= link_to 'Create New Gallery', new_gallery_path %></p>
<% end %>
```

This template is nearly identical to the one we used for showing the photos in a gallery except for a couple minor points.

First, by default, we'll display the thumbnail of the first photo in the gallery, but we want to check to ensure that there is at least one photo in the gallery first—otherwise, our page will crash when we try to call the filename of a nil object. We do a quick check by calling unless gallery.photos.count == 0 and using that response to pick between two different formats for displaying the gallery.

Second, we've added a count of the number of photos in that gallery by passing the photos.count response into the pluralize method: pluralize(gallery.photos.count, 'Photo').

In Figure 15-11, you can see the result of our gallery listing page as it would appear at http://localhost:3000/galleries.

Figure 15-11. *Displaying a list of galleries*

Summary

Well, this has certainly been quite a whirlwind chapter, as we've built a fairly significant amount of functionality in just a few short pages. We started this chapter with only a general idea of what we wanted to build and some HTML mock-ups, and now, we have a fairly functional site that allows users to manage their profiles, change their avatar images, create blog posts, and upload photos into galleries. Along the way, we picked up a few new tricks and set ourselves up to wrap up the project in the next chapter.

## CHAPTER 16

Rounding out the Community

In our last chapter, we built a fair amount of functionality to allow the users of our mini community to populate the site with their own content. However, there are few nagging items still missing from our application. In this chapter, we're going to finish up our application by adding a common navigation scheme throughout, building a community home page, and adding in some basic community tools such as a user directory.

Building the Community Home Page

The first task that we'll want to tackle is building a standardized home page for all users to go to after logging in. For the purposes of our initial application, we'll use this page to display a list of what's new within the community. However, this page could be expanded in the future to provide community calendars, community announcements, and so on. For now, though, we'll simply populate the page with a list of recently added blog posts and photo galleries. For good measure, we'll also provide the profile of a random user as a way of helping ensure that no one's profile is accidentally ignored by the community. The home for this page will be the index method of the welcome controller that we created in the last chapter.

Before we start editing the index method, however, there are a few things we need to add to our welcome controller. First off, we need to limit access to the pages controlled by the welcome controller to only members of our community, so we need to add a before_filter :login_required method call. Second, since the URLs within this controller are not going to be passing in a username like most of the controllers in the previous chapter, we'll need to also add the skip_before_filter :get_user method call to the controller to prevent an error from occurring. The welcome controller in /app/controllers/welcome_controller.rb should look like this as we start:

```
class WelcomeController < ApplicationController
  before_filter :login_required
  skip_before_filter :get_user

  def index
  end

  def directory
  end
end
```

Creating the Default Route

Since the index template in this controller will be the new home page for our application after someone has logged in, we'll build a route to map all requests for `http://locahost:3000/` to this index page. We'll accomplish this by creating a new named route named `home` within `/config/routes.rb`:

```
ActionController::Routing::Routes.draw do |map|
  map.home '', :controller => 'welcome', :action => 'index'
  map.resources :sessions
  map.login '/login', :controller => 'sessions', :action => 'new'
  map.logout '/logout', :controller => 'sessions', :action => 'destroy'
  map.showuser ":user", :controller => 'profile', :action => 'index'
  map.showprofile ":user/profile", :controller => 'profile', :action => 'show'
  map.editprofile ":user/profile/edit", :controller => 'profile', :action => 'edit'
  map.updateprofile ":user/profile/update", :controller => 'profile', ➥
:action => 'update'
  map.addavatar ":user/avatar/create", :controller => 'avatar', ➥
:action => 'create'
  map.resources :posts, :path_prefix => ":user"
  map.resources :galleries, :path_prefix => ":user"
  map.resources :photos, :path_prefix => ":user"
end
```

The Index Page

As we discussed earlier, we'll utilize the home page as the portal page to all the new content within the community. To keep things consistent, we'll keep the design of this home page similar to the design of the user profile pages. Make just a few minor modifications to the page to instead display the most recent blog posts from across all users, any galleries that have been updated with new photos recently, and a random user profile. To accomplish this, we'll set three instance variables in the `index` method of our welcome controller (`/app/controllers/welcome_controller.rb`):

```
def index
  @posts =
  @galleries =
  @user =
end
```

Now, we just need to build some methods in our models that we can use to populate those instance variables.

Grabbing the Most Recent Blog Posts

To grab the most recent blog posts, we'll add a new class method to our Post model named recent:

```
class Post < ActiveRecord::Base
  belongs_to :user

  def self.recent
    find(:all, :order => 'Posts.created_at desc', :group => 'user_id',
                                    :limit => 7, :include => :user)
  end
end
```

This method will pull back a list of seven (:limit => 7) of the most recent (:order => 'Posts.created_at desc') blog posts. However, if one user were to post seven short blog posts all at once, we wouldn't want to let that person dominate our front page, so we'll allow each user to only have one post on the main page by grouping the results by unique users (:group => 'user_id'). Finally, because we know that we're going to want to display the users' names along with their posts, we'll avoid doing a separate query for each of our results by eager loading the user record along with the post (:include => :user).

■**Tip** You may have noticed that, in our order_by clause, we specified the field with the full model name Posts.created_at instead of just created_at. This is because when we're eager loading an additional table (Users) and we need to reference a field name that exists in both tables (Posts and Users tables)—failing to fully specify which table and field we want would result in a database error for referencing an ambiguous column name.

We can now use the Post.recent class method within our controller to populate the @posts instance variable back in the index action of our welcome controller:

```
def index
  @posts = Post.recent
  @galleries =
  @user =
end
```

Within the associated template for this index method (/app/views/welcome/index.rhtml), we'll display the blog posts like this:

```
<div class="blog">
  <h1 class="section_header">Newest Blog Posts<h1>
  <% for post in @posts %>
```

```
    <h3>
      <%= link_to post.headline,
                              post_path(:user => post.user.login, :id => post) %>
    </h3>
    <span class="added">Written by <%= post.user.name %></span>
    <p>
      <%= truncate(post.body.gsub(%r{</?.*?>}, ""), 130) %>
      <%= link_to "[Read More]", post_path(:user => post.user.login, :id => post) %>
    </p>
    <hr />
  <% end %>
</div>
```

Grabbing the Most Recently Updated Galleries

Gathering our list of the most recently updated photo galleries will be very similar to the process that we just used to gather the most recent blog posts. In this case, we'll create a new recent class method within the Photo model:

```
class Photo < ActiveRecord::Base
  has_attachment :content_type => :image,
                        :storage => :file_system,
                        :max_size => 2.megabytes,
                        :resize_to => '640x360>',
                        :thumbnails => { :thumb => '140x105>' }
  validates_as_attachment
  belongs_to :gallery
  belongs_to :user

  def self.recent
    find(:all, :order => 'Photos.created_at desc', :limit => 4,
              :conditions => 'parent_id is null',
              :group => 'galleries.user_id', :include => :gallery)
  end
end
```

This recent method, much like the one we created for posts, will return the four most recently updated user galleries (:order => 'Photos.created_at desc', :limit => 4). Since we don't want to let any one user dominate the page, we will once again limit the query to display only one gallery per user (:group => 'galleries.user_id'). Also, since attachment_fu creates two records in the photos table for each picture (one for the picture and one for the thumbnail version), we need to remove the thumbnail images from our results by calling :conditions => 'parent_id is null'. Finally, we wrap up our method call by eager loading in the gallery name as well, so that we don't have a bunch of extra database calls to obtain the gallery name when displaying in our view.

Now that we have the recent method added to our Photo model, we can use it within our welcome controller to populate our @photos instance variable:

```
def index
  @posts = Post.recent
  @photos = Photo.recent
  @user =
end
```

The snippet that we'll use in the index template to display these photos will look like this:

```
<div class='gallery'>
  <h1 class="section_header">Photo Galleries</h1>
  <% for photo in @photos %>
    <p class="thumb">
      <%= link_to image_tag(photo.public_filename(:thumb)) + '<br />' +
            photo.gallery.name + '<br /> by ' + photo.gallery.user.name + '<br />',
          gallery_path(:user => photo.gallery.user.login, :id => photo.gallery) %>
    </p>
  <% end %>
</div>
```

Obtaining a Random User's Profile

The final instance variable left to set in our controller is the @user variable that we want to populate with a random user from our community. That way, we can ensure that everyone in the community is given a somewhat equal chance for exposure and hopefully help avoid hurt feelings.

Grabbing a random user, though, isn't as easy a task as you might think at first. There's no User.find(:random) type of functionality within Rails, so we'll have to look at how to build our own random user function.

Getting a Random User with Ruby

We could take advantage of the fact that there's a randomizing method within Ruby named rand to try and pull back a random customer using something like this:

```
class User < ActiveRecord::Base
  def self.random
    random = rand(User.count) + 1
    find(random)
  end
end
```

Unfortunately, there are a few negatives to this approach. For one, it's dependent on the idea that our user IDs are sequential, start with 1 (so they'll match the count), and have no missing numbers within their sequence.

We could bypass these problems by pulling back an array of all records and using the rand method to simply be used to specify a key within the array:

```
class User < ActiveRecord::Base
  def self.random
    users = User.find(:all)
    random = rand(User.count)
    users[random]
  end
end
```

This approach also has a number of problems with it—most specifically, the fact that it requires pulling back the complete dataset of our users just to get one record.

Getting a Random User with SQL

Another approach is to use database-specific functionality to pull back a random record. The function in most databases that provide this is named random() and could be invoked manually like this:

```
SELECT * FROM users ORDER BY random() LIMIT 1
```

We would invoke it using the ActiveRecord helpers like this:

```
user = User.find(:one, :order => 'random()')
```

One problem with this approach is that it can be a bit taxing on a database (less taxing than pulling back all records most likely). Since our goal is to have a solution for a small user base, that's an issue we could probably live with for now.

The other major problem with this approach is that it's not portable across all database solutions—for example, this function isn't available in a MySQL database, as MySQL uses a function named rand() instead. What we need is a solution that will extrapolate the correct randomize method across multiple database types. Fortunately, someone else already solved this problem with the Random Finder plug-in, which provides support for abstracting that database-specific functions into a common method for fetching random records across most common database types.

Using the Random Finder Plug-in

We can install the Random Finder plug-in like so:

```
ruby script/plugin install http://source.collectiveidea.com/public/rails/➡
plugins/random_finders/
```

```
+ ./random_finders/MIT-LICENSE
+ ./random_finders/README
+ ./random_finders/Rakefile
+ ./random_finders/init.rb
+ ./random_finders/lib/abstract_adapter.rb
+ ./random_finders/lib/base.rb
+ ./random_finders/lib/mysql_adapter.rb
+ ./random_finders/lib/postgresql_adapter.rb
+ ./random_finders/lib/sqlite_adapter.rb
+ ./random_finders/tasks/random_finders_tasks.rake
+ ./random_finders/test/random_finders_test.rb
```

Now that the plug-in is installed, we can pull back a random record by simply passing the :random symbol to the order clause in any finder method.

We can now use this plug-in to pull back a random user in our welcome controller like this:

```
def index
  @posts = Post.recent
  @photos = Photo.recent
  @user = User.find(:first, :order => :random)
end
```

As Borat would say, "*Nice!*"

Building the Home Page

With the index method in the welcome controller completed, we can modify the template we use to display a user's profile to instead be the community home page. Open /app/views/welcome/index.rhtml, and let's place all those snippets that we just discussed into that view:

```
<div class="blog">
  <h1 class="section_header">Newest Blog Posts<h1>
  <% for post in @posts %>
    <h3>
      <%= link_to post.headline, post_path(:user => post.user.login, :id => post) %>
    </h3>
    <span class="added">Written by <%= post.user.name %></span>
    <p>
      <%= truncate(post.body.gsub(%r{</?.*?>}, ""), 130) %>
      <%= link_to "[Read More]", post_path(:user => post.user.login, :id => post) %>
    </p>
    <hr />
  <% end %>
</div>
```

```
<% content_for :sidebar do %>
  <div class='about'>
    <h1 class="section_header">Have you met?</h1>
    <h3><%= link_to @user.name, showprofile_path(:user => @user.login) %></h3>
    <p><%= @user.detail.headline %></p>
    <p><%= image_tag show_avatar %></p>
    <p><%= @user.detail.about_me %></p>
    <p><%= link_to '[Learn More About Me]',
                            showprofile_path(:user => @user.login) %></p>
  </div>
  <div class='gallery'>
    <h1 class="section_header">Newest Photos</h1>
    <% for photo in @photos %>
      <p class="thumb">
        <%= link_to image_tag(photo.public_filename(:thumb)) +
                      '<br />' + photo.gallery.name + '<br /> by ' +
                      photo.gallery.user.name + '<br />',
                      gallery_path(:user => photo.gallery.user.login,
                                            :id => photo.gallery) %>
      </p>
    <% end %>
  </div>
<% end %>
```

The preceding code should give us a page similar to the one shown in Figure 16-1.

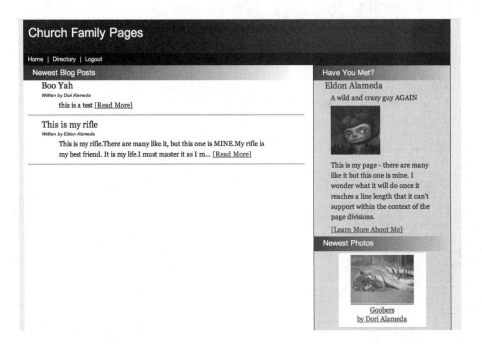

Figure 16-1. *Our community home page*

Adding a Directory of Users

The next important feature that we'll tackle is to provide our users with a way to find other users' pages within the site. To accomplish this, we'll build a basic user directory that can be used to navigate the list of users sorted by their last name. We expect that the directory will contain an alphabetical index that will look like Figure 16-2.

Figure 16-2. *The user directory navigation*

Generating an Alphabetical Index

The first challenge in solving this problem is in generating the list of alphabet characters for our directory index. Granted, we could build it by hand-typing all those links in HTML, but that would be a lot more pain than I'm willing to endure—especially when the problem can be solved with a simple array. What we need is an array containing all the letters of the alphabet which we can generate fairly simply by using Ruby's support for ranges to create a range of letters (`alphabet = 'A'..'Z'`) and then converting that range into an array with the `to_a` method. So we'll end up with something like this in our controller:

```
@alphabet = ('A'..'Z').to_a
```

Creating a Route

With the process of generating the alphabet index out of the way, let's add a route to our `/config/routes.rb` that will allow us to send requests to the directory method in our welcome controller.

What we want is a way for users to be able to go to `http://localhost/directory/B` to collect a list of users whose last name begins with the letter "B." However, we also want to support routing to the same method without an error if they omit the letter and simply request `http://localhost/directory`. We can accomplish this with a route that provides a default value:

```
map.directory '/directory/:char', :controller => 'welcome', ➥
:action => 'directory', :char => 'A'
```

The preceding route will support both of our needs: if a letter is provided, we'll pass that along to our controller method in the `:char` parameter; if a letter isn't provided, the route will pass "A" as the default value. Adding to this new route to our `/config/routes.rb` will look like this:

```
ActionController::Routing::Routes.draw do |map|
  map.home '', :controller => 'welcome', :action => 'index'
  map.resources :sessions
```

```
    map.login '/login', :controller => 'sessions', :action => 'new'
    map.logout '/logout', :controller => 'sessions', :action => 'destroy'
    map.directory '/directory/:char', :controller => 'welcome', ➡
:action => 'directory', :char => 'A'

    map.showuser  ":user", :controller => 'profile', :action => 'index'
    map.showprofile  ":user/profile", :controller => 'profile', :action => 'show'
    map.editprofile  ":user/profile/edit", :controller => 'profile', :action => 'edit'
    map.updateprofile  ":user/profile/update", :controller => 'profile', ➡
:action => 'update'
    map.addavatar    ":user/avatar/create", :controller => 'avatar', ➡
:action => 'create'
    map.resources :posts, :path_prefix => ":user"
    map.resources :galleries, :path_prefix => ":user"
    map.resources :photos, :path_prefix => ":user"
end
```

Adding the Directory Method

Finally, the directory method of our welcome controller (/app/controllers/welcome_
controller.rb) is completed and should be set up like this:

```
def directory
  @alphabet = ('A'..'Z').to_a
  @user = User.find(:first, :order => :random)
  @character = params[:char]
  @users = User.find(:all, :order => "last_name ASC",
                          :conditions => ["last_name like ?", params[:char] + "%"])
end
```

This directory method builds an @alphabet instance variable by converting a range of letters into an array. It creates an @user instance variable, which grabs a random user from the
database. It captures the current search character that was submitted into the @characters
instance variable, and finally, it performs a search against the users table for users whose last
names begin with our search character; if it finds any users that match, it places those results
into the @users instance variable.

Editing Our View Template

So with our variables set, we'll set up a simple display of the results in the /app/views/welcome/
directory.rhtml template file:

```
<h1 class="section_header">Alphabetical Index</h1>
<div class="directory">
  <% @alphabet.each do |letter| %>
    <% if letter == @character %>
      <span class="current"><%= letter %></span>
```

```
      <% else %>
        <%= link_to letter, directory_path(:char => letter), :class => "letter" %>
      <% end %>
   <% end %>
 </div>
 </div>
 <hr/>


 <% for user in @users %>
   <div class="result">
     <div class="userImage"><%= image_tag show_small_avatar(user) %></div>
     <div class="userInfo">
       <strong>Name: </strong><%= user.name %><br />
     </div>
     <div class="userActions">
       <%= link_to "View", showprofile_path(:user => user.login) %>
     </div>
   </div>
 <% end %>


 <% content_for :sidebar do %>
   <div class='about'>
     <h1 class="section_header">Have you met?</h1>
     <h3><%= link_to @user.name, showprofile_path(:user => @user.login) %></h3>
     <p><%= @user.detail.headline %></p>
     <p><%= image_tag show_avatar %></p>
     <p><%= @user.detail.about_me %></p>
     <p><%= link_to '[Learn More About Me]',
                                   showprofile_path(:user => @user.login) %></p>
   </div>
 <% end %>
```

For the most part, that template is pretty similar to everything that we've done so far. However, there is one small section that I want to discuss:

```
<% @alphabet.each do |letter| %>
  <% if letter == @character %>
    <span class="current"><%= letter %></span>
  <% else %>
    <%= link_to letter, directory_path(:char => letter), :class => "letter" %>
  <% end %>
<% end %>
```

In this block, we start out by looping over each letter in the alphabet instance variable. Within that loop, we check to see if the current letter matches the character that was received in the request with a `letter == @character` statement. If they match, we'll display the letter in a custom span; if not, we'll display the letter as a link to the `directory` method in the welcome controller.

Adding Navigation

The one major component of our site that is still missing is a common navigational structure. We'll add one now by building a split navigation scheme: we'll populate the upper navigation div that we created in our layout with the primary navigation, which will be the same for all users of the community, and we'll add a secondary navigation with user-specific links down in the footer.

The Upper Navigation

Our common navigation scheme should be fairly simple; we'll provide just three simple links: a link to the community home page, a link to the user directory page, and a link to log out of the application. Open /app/views/layout/application.rhtml, and edit the navigation div to look like this:

```
<div class="yui-g navigation">
  <a href="/">Home</a> |
  <a href="/directory">Directory</a> |
  <a href="/logout">Logout</a>
</div>
```

which should provide us with a common navigation scheme, as shown in Figure 16-3.

Figure 16-3. *The common navigation scheme*

The Footer Navigation

While the upper navigation provides some generic navigational items, we need to provide our users with links to perform common tasks that will be specific to their own content. To do that, we'll place those links in the footer, so that as the application and community continue to grow over the years, we'll have plenty of room to add new functionality.

Since we only want to display this user-centric menu if we actually know who the user is (i.e., if the user's logged in), we'll wrap the whole navigation section in a if logged_in? block.

Once inside that block, we'll provide the users with links to their user pages, the pages to edit their own profiles, the page for creating a new post, and the page to add galleries and photos.

```
<div id="ft">
  <% if logged_in? %>
    <div class="admin_menu">
      <%= link_to 'Your Page',
                      showuser_path(:user => current_user.login) %>
```

```
    <%= link_to 'Edit your Profile',
                            editprofile_path(:user => current_user.login) %>
    <%= link_to 'Create Blog Post',
                              new_post_path(:user => current_user.login) %>
    <%= link_to 'Manage Photo Galleries',
                            galleries_path(:user => current_user.login) %>
  </div>
 <% end %>
</div>
```

When our new footer is displayed to a user , it should look something like Figure 16-4 (assuming you have the style sheets from the code archive).

Figure 16-4. *User navigational links in the footer*

Adding Comments

The final thing that our site is missing is the ability for users to post comments about each other's content. For the purposes of this project, we only need to be able to place comments onto blog posts and photos, but we want to have a solution that can grow with us to support other types of contents as well. For that reason, we'll take advantage of a plug-in by the name of acts_as_commentable, which creates a single comment model that uses polymorphic associations, so that we can use it with any number of models.

Installing acts_as_commentable

To use the plug-in we'll first need to install it via the command line:

```
script/plugin install http://juixe.com/svn/acts_as_commentable
```

```
+ ./acts_as_commentable/CHANGELOG
+ ./acts_as_commentable/MIT-LICENSE
+ ./acts_as_commentable/README
+ ./acts_as_commentable/init.rb
+ ./acts_as_commentable/install.rb
+ ./acts_as_commentable/lib/acts_as_commentable.rb
+ ./acts_as_commentable/lib/comment.rb
+ ./acts_as_commentable/tasks/acts_as_commentable_tasks.rake
+ ./acts_as_commentable/test/acts_as_commentable_test.rb
```

Next, we need to generate a migration to create our comments table:

```
ruby script/generate migration add_comments
```

```
      exists  db/migrate
      create  db/migrate/007_add_comments.rb
```

We'll need to define the structure of our comments table by editing the new migration files that we just created (/db/migrate/007_add_comments.rb) to build the columns required by the plug-in:

```
class AddComments < ActiveRecord::Migration
  def self.up
    create_table :comments, :force => true do |t|
      t.column :title, :string, :limit => 50, :default => ""
      t.column :comment, :string, :default => ""
      t.column :created_at, :datetime, :null => false
      t.column :commentable_id, :integer, :default => 0, :null => false
      t.column :commentable_type, :string, :limit => 15, :default => "", ➡
:null => false
      t.column :user_id, :integer, :default => 0, :null => false
    end

    add_index :comments, ["user_id"], :name => "fk_comments_user"
  end

  def self.down
    drop_table :comments
  end
end
```

With our migration created, we just need to run the `migrate` command to add our comments table to our database:

```
rake db:migrate
```

```
== AddComments: migrating ======================================
-- create_table(:comments, {:force=>true})
   -> 0.0045s
-- add_index(:comments, ["user_id"], {:name=>"fk_comments_user"})
   -> 0.0029s
== AddComments: migrated (0.0078s) =============================
```

Now, to add comments to a model within our application, we merely need to add a single call to the `acts_as_commentable` method (added by the plug-in) to each model that we want to be able to support comments. Since we want to add comments to our Post model (/app/models/post.rb), we'll edit like so:

```
class Post < ActiveRecord::Base
  acts_as_commentable
  belongs_to :user

  def self.recent
    find(:all, :order => 'Posts.created_at desc', :group => 'user_id',
                                        :limit => 7, :include => :user)
  end
end
```

We are also going to want to allow comments on the Photo model (/app/models/photo.rb), so we'll need to add it there as well:

```
class Photo < ActiveRecord::Base
  acts_as_commentable
  has_attachment :content_type => :image,
                          :storage => :file_system,
                          :max_size => 2.megabytes,
                          :resize_to => '640x360>',
                          :thumbnails => { :thumb => '140x105>' }
  validates_as_attachment
  belongs_to :gallery
  belongs_to :user

  def self.recent
    find(:all, :order => 'Photos.created_at desc', :limit => 4,
            :conditions => 'parent_id is null',
            :group => 'galleries.user_id', :include => :gallery)
  end
end
```

Displaying Comments

Since the purpose of the commenting system was to be a way of communication, I really wanted to display the comments using speech bubbles.

There are a number of implementations out there that we can learn from, such as the open source CSS ones available on www.willmayo.com or the CSS-only versions at www.cssplay.co.uk/menu/bubbles.html, but in the end, I wanted something with a little more cartoonish look to it, so I built something that was heavily inspired by the code used to create the speech bubbles in an older version of a Rails-powered a forum application named Opinion. A pure HTML view of the source required to provide these speech bubbles looks like this:

```
<div id ="comments">
  <h1 class="section_header">Comments</h1>
  <ol id="comment-list">
```

```
    <li>
      <div class="comment-head">
        <div class="comment-author-details">
          <h3>
            <div class="user-img">
              <a href="/"><img alt="Underdog" ➥
src="/images/avatars/underdog.jpg" /></a>
            </div>
            <a href="#">Underdog</a> posted
          </h3>
        </div>
      </div>

      <div class="comment-body">
        <div class="comment-body-paragraph">
          <p>This is a great shot! </p>
          <p>You should print it out</p>
        </div>
      </div>
      <p class="comment-link small"><em> </em></p>
    </li>
  </ol>
</div>
```

When this HTML is rendered in a browser, you'll see it display a speech bubble like the one shown in Figure 16-5. To add some extra sizzle to the page, we'll also enhance the form to add a comment with a JavaScript-based rich text editor.

Figure 16-5. *Our commenting system with speech bubbles*

So now that we have the HTML structure for our comments defined, we just need to modify that structure to use Rails to populate it with content.

We'll first want to wrap the whole thing in an `@post.comments.any?` block so that we'll only try to display comments when there actually are some.

Next, if we have any comments, then we're going to want to create a loop to add each to the page, so we'll add `for comment in @post.comments` to our page.

Finally, we'll want to convert all of our hard-coded href and image tags to the Rails helper methods for generating those tags for the current comment:

```
<% if @post.comments.any? %>
<div id ="comments">
  <h1 class="section_header">Comments</h1>
  <ol id="comment-list">
    <% for comment in @post.comments %>
      <li>
        <div class="comment-head">
          <div class="comment-author-details">
            <h3>
              <div class="user-img">
                <%= link_to(image_tag(comment.user.small_avatar),
                                      showuser_path(:user => comment.user)) %>
              </div>
              <%= link_to comment.user.name,
                                showuser_path(:user => comment.user) %> posted
            </h3>
          </div>
        </div>

        <div class="comment-body">
          <div class="comment-body-paragraph">
            <p><%= comment.comment %></p>
          </div>
        </div>
        <p class="comment-link small"><em> </em></p>
      </li>
    <% end %>
  </ol>
</div>
<% end %>
```

The preceding code provides us a comment display like the one shown in Figure 16-6.

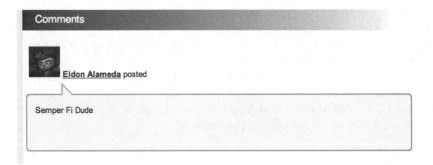

Figure 16-6. *Displaying a comment*

Adding Comments

So we've built a way to display comments, but we still need to add a way for users to create comments. The first step in that process is determining where we want our comment forms to post. We'll keep it simple and just add an addcomment method within our Post and Photo controllers.

However, to make those methods work, we'll also need to create routes to those methods. Since we defined both of those models as RESTful resources, we'll add them to those routes by defining a member action, such as :member => { :addcomment => :post }, onto each those routes. Afterward, your /config/routes.rb will look like this:

```
ActionController::Routing::Routes.draw do |map|
  map.home '', :controller => 'welcome', :action => 'index'
  map.resources :sessions
  map.login '/login', :controller => 'sessions', :action => 'new'
  map.logout '/logout', :controller => 'sessions', :action => 'destroy'
  map.directory '/directory/:char', :controller => 'welcome', ➥
:action => 'directory', :char => 'A'

  map.showuser  ":user", :controller => 'profile', :action => 'index'
  map.showprofile  ":user/profile", :controller => 'profile', :action => 'show'
  map.editprofile  ":user/profile/edit", :controller => 'profile', :action => 'edit'
  map.updateprofile  ":user/profile/update", :controller => 'profile', ➥
:action => 'update'
  map.addavatar  ":user/avatar/create", :controller => 'avatar', ➥
:action => 'create'
  map.resources :posts, :path_prefix => ":user", :member => { :addcomment => :post }
  map.resources :galleries, :path_prefix => ":user"
  map.resources :photos, :path_prefix => ":user", :member => ➥
{ :addcomment => :post }
end
```

Creating the Add Comment Form

With those new routes, we can access our controller methods through the `addcomment_post_path`
or an `addcomment_photo_path` named route helper method; let's use those named routes as we
create our comment forms now. Within the show template for the posts controller (`/app/views/
posts/show.rhtml`), we'll add this form:

```
<div id="comment_form">
  <h1 class="section_header">Post a Comment</h1>
  <% form_for :comment, :url => addcomment_post_path  do |c| %>
    <p>
      <label for "comment_body">Comment:</label><br />
      <%= c.text_area 'comment', "cols" => 70, "rows" => 5 %>
      <%= c.hidden_field 'user_id', :value => current_user.id %>
    </p>
    <p>
      <%= submit_tag 'Add Comment' %>
    </p>
  <% end %>
</div>
```

Enhancing the Form with a Rich Text Editor

You should recall that when we first discussed the add comment form we wanted to enhance
the form with a JavaScript-based rich text editor. In cases like these, I've had really good luck
with implementing an open source solution named TinyMCE. It's a highly configurable yet
lightweight solution, and in my experience, it produces HTML that is a lot cleaner than many
of the other solutions available. As an additional bonus, you can also configure TinyMCE with
an explicit list of allowed tags—so we can easily prevent users from submitting text with
embedded styles that might cause issues with the site's style sheets.

You can download TinyMCE from `http://tinymce.moxiecode.com/download.php`. Once
you uncompress the TinyMCE archive, copy the entire `tiny_mce` folder from the archive's
`/jscripts` subdirectory into our application's `/public/javascripts/` folder.

With TinyMCE installed, adding a TinyMCE editor to a page is simply a matter of including
the main file and adding in a few lines of configuration options for the editor. Because those
options are typically the same across any pages on which I use the editor, I usually push that
configuration into a separate JavaScript file that I include on any relevant pages. Go ahead and
create a new JavaScript file named `tinyconfig.js` in our `/public/javascripts` subdirectory
and place this configuration in it:

```
tinyMCE.init({
  mode : "textareas",
  theme : "advanced",
  theme_advanced_buttons1 : "bold,italic,underline,separator,strikethrough,➥
justifyleft,justifycenter,justifyright, justifyfull,bullist,numlist,undo,redo,➥
link,unlink,cleanup,code",
```

```
  theme_advanced_buttons2 : "",
  theme_advanced_buttons3 : "",
  theme_advanced_toolbar_location : "top",
  theme_advanced_toolbar_align : "left",
  extended_valid_elements : "a[name|href|target|title|onclick],➥
img[class|src|border=0|alt|title|hspace|vspace|width|height|align|➥
onmouseover|onmouseout|name],hr[class|width|size|noshade],➥
font[face|size|color|style],span[class|align|style]"
  });
```

Now, back in our show template (`/app/views/posts/show.rhtml`), we'll include the TinyMCE configuration at the top of the page like this:

```
<%= javascript_include_tag 'tiny_mce/tiny_mce' %>
<%= javascript_include_tag 'tinyconfig' %>
```

When we display our final page, the result of this comment form will look like the one shown in Figure 16-7.

Figure 16-7. *Our Post A Comment form*

The Final show Templates

Let's put all of our views together now. The show template for the posts controller (`/app/views/posts/show.rhtml`) will look like this:

```
<%= javascript_include_tag 'tiny_mce/tiny_mce' %>
<%= javascript_include_tag 'tinyconfig' %>

<div class="blog">
  <h1 class="section_header"><%= @post.headline %><h1>
  <%= @post.body %>
  <p><span class="added">written on <%= @post.created_at.to_s(:long) %></span></p>
  <hr />
  <% if show_admin_menu %>
    <%= link_to 'Edit This Post',
                    edit_post_path(:user => @user.login, :id => @post) %><br />
```

```
      <%= link_to 'Destroy This Post',
                         post_path(:user => @user.login, :id => @post),
                         :confirm => 'Are you sure?', :method => :delete %>
  <% end %>
</div>

<% if @post.comments.any? %>
  <div id ="comments">
    <h1 class="section_header">Comments</h1>
    <ol id="comment-list">
      <% for comment in @post.comments %>
        <% user = comment.user %>
        <li>
          <div class="comment-head">
            <div class="comment-author-details">
              <h3><div class="user-img"><%= link_to(image_tag(user.small_avatar),
                                        showuser_path(:user => user)) %></div>
              <%= link_to user.name, showuser_path(:user => user) %> posted</h3>
            </div>
          </div>

          <div class="comment-body">
            <div class="comment-body-paragraph"><p><%= comment.comment %></p></div>
          </div>
          <p class="comment-link small"><em> </em></p>
        </li>
      <% end %>
    </ol>
  </div>
<% end %>

<div id="comment_form">
  <h1 class="section_header">Post a Comment</h1>
  <% form_for :comment, :url => addcomment_post_path  do |c| %>
    <p>
      <label for "comment_body">Comment:</label><br />
      <%= c.text_area 'comment', "cols" => 70, "rows" => 5 %>
      <%= c.hidden_field 'user_id', :value => current_user.id %>
    </p>
    <p>
      <%= submit_tag 'Add Comment' %>
    </p>
  <% end %>
</div>
```

```
<% content_for :sidebar do %>
  <div class='about'>
    <h1 class="section_header">About Me</h1>
    <p><%= @user.detail.headline %></p>
    <p><%= image_tag show_avatar %></p>
    <p><%= @user.detail.about_me %></p>
    <p><%= link_to '[Learn More About Me]',
                                    showprofile_path(:user => @user.login) %></p>
  </div>
<% end %>
```

And the show template for our photos controller (/app/views/photos/show.rhtml) will
look like this:

```
<%= javascript_include_tag 'tiny_mce/tiny_mce' %>
<%= javascript_include_tag 'tinyconfig' %>

<h1 class="section_header">View Photo<h1>
<%= image_tag @photo.public_filename %>

<% if @post.comments.any? %>
  <div id ="comments">
    <h1 class="section_header">Comments</h1>
    <ol id="comment-list">
      <% for comment in @post.comments %>
        <% user = comment.user %>
        <li>
          <div class="comment-head">
            <div class="comment-author-details">
              <h3><div class="user-img"><%= link_to(image_tag(user.small_avatar),➥
showuser_path(:user => user)) %></div>
                <%= link_to user.name, showuser_path(:user => user) %> posted</h3>
            </div>
          </div>

          <div class="comment-body">
            <div class="comment-body-paragraph"><p><%= comment.comment %></p></div>
          </div>
          <p class="comment-link small"><em> </em></p>
        </li>
      <% end %>
    </ol>
  </div>
<% end %>
```

```
<div id="comment_form">
  <h1 class="section_header">Post a Comment</h1>
  <% form_for :comment, :url => addcomment_post_path  do |c| %>
    <p>
      <label for "comment_body">Comment:</label><br />
      <%= c.text_area 'comment', "cols" => 70, "rows" => 5 %>
      <%= c.hidden_field 'user_id', :value => current_user.id %>
    </p>
    <p>
      <%= submit_tag 'Add Comment' %>
    </p>
  <% end %>
</div>

<% content_for :sidebar do %>
  <%= @photo.description %>
  <% if show_admin_menu %>
    <h1 class="section_header">Photo Admin<h1>
    <%= link_to "Delete Photo", photo_path(:user => @user.login, :id => @photo),➡
  :confirm => 'Are you sure?', :method => :delete %>
  <% end %>
<% end %>
```

The Add Comment Methods

Now that we have everything configured to display a comment form for our posts and photos, we just need to build the addcomment methods in our controllers that will actually add the submitted comments to the database. This is made even easier, as our acts_as_commentable plug-in also added a method to each of our models named add_comment. So we can simply add the following methods.

Within our posts controller, we'll add this method:

```
def addcomment
  post = current_user.posts.find(params[:id])
  comment = Comment.new(params[:comment])
  post.add_comment comment
  redirect_to post_path(:user => params[:user], :id => post)
end
```

And within our photos controller, we'll add the addcomment method like this:

```
def addcomment
  photo = Photo.find(params[:id])
  comment = Comment.new(params[:comment])
  photo.add_comment comment
  redirect_to photo_path(:user => params[:user], :id => photo)
end
```

And with that, our comment functionality is complete.

Summary

In this chapter, we put together the few remaining elements of our application that will allow us to go live and let users start playing with it. While the elements that we added in this chapter, such as the user directory and commenting abilities, are going to be universal enough to go with most any community that might want to use an application like this, we're far from done. Individual communities' needs will drive the development directions of the application from here forward. A community that meets in lots of different places would probably benefit from a Google or Yahoo Maps integration, whereas a community that is technocentric might benefit from items such as tagging and instant message integration.

CHAPTER 17

■■■

Enhancing the Church Community Application

In this project, we put together a simple community application designed to foster community within a small group of users such as a local church, family, or users group. We provided a few basic tools for this community, including a user directory, photo galleries, blogging, and commenting. These are the generic things that would be useful for any mini community.

While I was building the application, you should have noticed that I had a fairly clear picture of my imaginary church group for which I was building the application, and thus I allowed the needs of that group to influence several key decisions while I was building the application.

For you to take the application further, I would strongly recommend you either find a group that could benefit from features like this or do your best to imagine a very specific group of people. An application like this really needs to be laser focused onto the users and their needs in order for it have any value at all. That being said, here are a number of additional ideas for you to consider while continuing to develop this application.

Create a User Import or Sign-Up Process

One key element that we touched on in the chapter was the need to build in a way to add users to our mini community site. I'm leaving this one up to you, as each community focus is going to have different needs for creating users. Some communities are going to want a traditional web sign-up process, which RESTful Authentication can provide for you. Other communities might want an administration page where only a single administrator is able to control who has access and who doesn't.

Yet others might want to bypass the administration portion completely and deal solely with creating users from a data import from a vendor application, such as Act or Outlook contacts. Some good libraries to look at for inputting from vCard or CSV are:

- http://rubyforge.org/projects/vpim/

- http://fastercsv.rubyforge.org/

Or you could go a completely different route and implement one of those hot new OpenID-based solutions. For a great tutorial on those, check out http://railscasts.com/episodes/68.

Batch Upload Photos Using SWFupload

One problem with the photo galleries that we're sure to hear about from our users is the fact that, currently, users can only upload a single photo at a time. There was a time not too many years back when we could have easily ignored that complaint and asserted that it's just the way things are, but too many sites allow batch uploads to overlook this complaint now. One interesting solution to this problem is an open source JavaScript and Flash solution named SWFupload that allows you to easily add batch file uploads. You can see a demonstration of the solution in Figure 17-1.

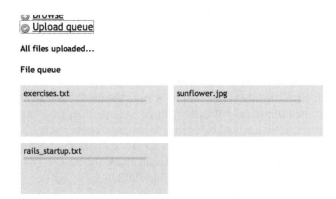

Figure 17-1. *An example of using SWFupload to upload multiple files*

For more information on using SWFupload, check out these sites:

- `http://swfupload.mammon.se/index.php`

- `http://blog.flornet.fr/2007/05/29/swfupload-using-ruby-on-rails-demo/`

- `http://code.google.com/p/activeupload/`

- `http://developer.assaydepot.com/?p=6`

- `http://blog.inquirylabs.com/2006/12/09/getting-the-_session_id-from-swfupload/`

Add an RSS Feed for Each User

Another area that we could easily expand on is the ability to create an RSS feed for each user that would contain the latest blog posts and photo uploads. This way, a user could simply subscribe to friends' RSS feeds to keep up on specific people. Check out our simple blog project (see Chapter 10) for an example of building an RSS feed using an `rxml` template.

Add Friends List Functionality

Of course, as long as we're talking about friends, we might also consider building in some basic friends list functionality. However, doing this in a small community is going to require a very delicate touch, as the potential for hurt feeling increases exponentially ("No one has asked to be my friend on the site!"). So you need to weigh the risks of adding a solution like this against your own desire to build something fun.

If I were to tackle this solution, I would probably hit it from the reverse angle and instead make it a permissions list of what you're willing to share with people. For example, with my close friends, I might be willing to share the fact that I'm looking for a new job or a funny (but unflattering) photo of myself. But I'd probably not want to share that information with *everyone* in the community.

For that scenario, I would create the ability for me to mark another user as my friend. Then, I would create a flag on all my content to specify whether it's available to the community at large or to my friends only. Of course, to keep jealousy and hurt feeling to a minimum, I would not give any indication to other users as to whether or not they are on my friends list. Users could simply see all of the content or only some of it.

Enhance the Home Page

Currently, our home page is informational but not very useful to the community. What it needs is some more content. Why don't you try to add some content and tools to populate that content? Some examples of content would be community announcements (which could probably be supported in the same manner as our blogs), a community calendar of upcoming events (perhaps reading in from a Google calendar feed), or even something as simple as a community bulletin board or classified ads. The goal here is to develop more enticement for users to visit the homepage (beyond the fact that we force them to when they log in).

Clean Up Some of Our Ruby Code

If you look back at the code in our galleries index template (`/app/views/galleries/index.rhtml`), you'll notice that we have a line in our code like this:

```
<% unless gallery.photos.count == 0 %>
```

While this is perfectly valid and acceptable code, it's not exactly the Ruby way of doing things. What we should be doing instead is taking advantage of enumerable methods such as `empty?` or `any?` that are available whenever we're dealing with hashes or arrays.

Doing so would allow us to change our code to something nicer such as:

```
<% if gallery.photos.any? %>
```

Sometimes those old C habits are hard to break. Look around the application—who knows what else you might find?

Move Code into Partials

As long as we're already in the galleries index template, did you happen to notice how noisy our template is? I mean, look at all this code we have in there to simply display our gallery thumbnails:

```
<h1 class="section_header">Galleries<h1>
<% @galleries.in_groups_of(3, false) do |galleries| %>
  <ul class="thumbnails">
    <% for gallery in galleries %>
      <% if gallery.photos.any? %>
        <li class="thumb">
          <%= link_to image_tag(gallery.photos.first.public_filename(:thumb)) +➡
'<br />' + gallery.name + '<br />' + pluralize(gallery.photos.count, 'Photo'),➡
gallery_path(:user => @user.login, :id => gallery.id)  %>
        </li>
      <% else %>
        <li class="thumb">
          <%= link_to gallery.name + '<br />' + pluralize(gallery.photos.count,➡
'Photo'), gallery_path(:user => @user.login, :id => gallery.id)  %>
        </li>
      <% end %>
    <% end %>
  </ul>
<% end %>
<br />
```

Considering that all we're doing here is looping over a collection of galleries, doesn't it make more sense that this should be moved into a partial? Do that, and this template could be made to look like this:

```
<h1 class="section_header">Galleries<h1>
<% @galleries.in_groups_of(3, false) do |galleries| %>
  <ul class="thumbnails">
    <% render :partial => 'gallery, :collection => galleries %>
  </ul>
<% end %>
<br />
```

Which is just a tad nicer on the old eyes, don't you think? I left a few other areas in the application that you can convert to partials. Why don't you go through and see how much you can clean up the code by converting to partials? As a hint, almost anytime you see that you're coding a `for foo in bars` type of loop, you're probably looking at a candidate for a partial.

For advanced credit, why not also see if you can convert some of the code so that different pages can share the same partial?

Implement Kropper for User Profile Images

Another potential problem for our users is going to come with the way that we're currently handling the profile pictures. Currently, we simply accept what they upload, which is a perfectly workable solution but can cause our less technically inclined users to have a nonoptimized profile picture. This would be the case especially for those users who may not have access to photo editing software.

A really interesting solution that came out as this book was getting close to completion is a tool named Kropper developed by Jonathon Wolfe of Kolossus Interactive (`www.kolossus.com`). Kropper provides a set of JavaScript, CSS, and Ruby functions to provide our Rails applications with an interactive photo cropping tool similar to what we would find in Apple's iChat application. Best of all, it was designed to work with the `attachment_fu` plug-in. You can see Kropper in action in Figure 17-2.

Figure 17-2. *Add Kropper to your application to optimize your profile's pictures.*

You can play with an online demonstration of Kropper at `kropper.captchr.com`, and you can download the latest version from `rubyforge.org/projects/kropper`. At the time of this writing, Kropper is only available as an open source application that you would have to manually integrate into your application. However, the creator has commented in his blog that he and Tim Lucas are working on converting it into a Rails plug-in.

Add Caching

Since we have a large amount of content in our community that won't be changing once it's been added, adding some intelligent caching into our application really makes a lot of sense. If our community isn't a group of comment-posting fiends, we should be able to get away with page caching the show methods of blog posts and photos. Other sections of the site, such as the community home page, would probably benefit best from a nice dose of fragment caching.

Summary

The ideas listed in this chapter should be more than enough to get you started and give you some tools to delight your user community. Visit the RailsProjects.com forums and share your enhancements with others. Every community is going to be different, but there are always things we can learn from each other.

PART 7

■■■

GamingTrend

In a perfect world, all Rails applications that we create would be greenfield applications with brand new databases that we could build from scratch according to the Rails conventions. Unfortunately, though, in the real world, we often either inherit or have previously written applications that we still need to maintain and support. In those situations, the temptation to rewrite those applications is hard to resist. Perhaps it's because somewhere deep down inside we believe that code slowly rusts over time, or perhaps we want to apply a new trick that we've learned about, or perhaps sometimes it's just because we want to have the opportunity to fix past mistakes.

In this project, we're going to succumb to that desire and take a look at one application that justifiably requires a rewrite. While the underlying data for the application is still good and must be maintained, the web application itself was written years ago in PHP/MySQL and is now too hard to maintain and unable to keep up with the needs of the client. As we build out a new version of this application, we'll explore some of the quirks that come into play when we develop to a nonstandard database structure.

Our application's story begins with an old college buddy named Ron who started his own web site a few years back. Originally, the site was created merely to track the release dates of upcoming video games, but as the readership grew, so did the site—today, it is a full-fledged gaming news and reviews web site.

A while ago, Ron decided that hand-editing every single page on the site was becoming far too painful as the quantity and frequency of the content grew, so he hired somebody to create a custom administration system for the site using PHP 4 and MySQL. That custom administration system was created to maintain data on all console games, as well as provide systems for adding reviews of those games and daily news. That little administration system has served the site pretty well for a number of years through the maintenance of a handful of developers. Unfortunately, the application is definitely showing its age. Staff members on the site have been complaining about the unwieldiness of the interface, and through the numerous developers (of varying quality), the applications code itself has degraded into a nightmare full of spaghetti code and one-off hacks.

That's where we come in—Ron is calling in some old favors (some might say it's blackmail—so much for that "what happens in Vegas stays in Vegas" line) to get our help in updating the backend administration of the site before he demonstrates the full site to some potential buyers.

Our mission, should we choose to accept it, is to build a new Rails application to replace the aging PHP administrative one. The legacy database must be used and maintained. Should we find ourselves buried deep in any legacy PHP code, the Secretary will disavow all knowledge of our actions. This book will self-destruct in five seconds.

■ ■ ■

## CHAPTER 18

Understanding the Problems of the Legacy PHP Site

As I stated, the current administrative system was written years ago in PHP4 with a MySQL backend and has served our buddy's site well, but the application's code has been maintained by a variety of pasta-loving amateur developers, which has led to a number of maintenance issues. For one, the site is an incredible hassle to maintain—even simple changes to the application often take days to complete and cause many other things to break. Second, the application's interface hasn't adapted and evolved with the needs of the site and has now become rather cumbersome for the staff to use. So Ron (the owner of the site) has opted that his best option before talking to any more buyers is to refresh the site, starting with the administrative tools that the staff uses on a daily basis.

While doing a complete rewrite of an existing application can sound very fun and exciting in the beginning, the reality is that rewrites can often degrade into a festering project from the very darkest bowels of hell itself. Fortunately for us, though, we're not going to have to spend our time digging through pages and pages of PHP code, as our emphasis is not on converting the actual PHP code that was originally used but on building a new Rails application that can speak effectively with the existing database. Rewriting the application into Rails won't be too terribly difficult, but the legacy database will almost certainly present some unique challenges that we'll have to deal with along the way.

Our goals for this rewrite are fairly straightforward:

- We want to make the code maintainable again, taking advantage of code reuse and cleaning up the database as necessary.

- A number of features that have been supported by the site no longer fit with the future direction of the web site, and Ron has decided that it's time to get rid of them during this rewrite.

- We want to update the user interface to make it modern as well as create an easier work-flow for the staff.

- We want to make changes to the database only where absolutely necessary so as to minimize any impacts to existing code on the primary (public-facing) site.

- The site originally launched under the name ConsoleGold but ran into some issues with using that name a few years back and was forced to rename. The administration site, however, was written before the naming issues and has remained a constant reminder of some painful times for the site. Ensuring that all references to ConsoleGold are removed from the new administration site is a feature that the staff has been longing for.

From its humble roots as a list of upcoming console games and expected release dates, the site has grown in leaps and bounds over the years. From originally having Ron as the sole contributor to the site, it now has over 20 volunteers on staff creating and adding content to the site daily. Today, the site maintains database records on approximately 4,000 PC and console games and generates a tremendous amount of daily content in the form of news, reviews, and previews.

There's a lot going on in this site and even a rewrite of the administration system alone would be a very large project that could easily fill up this whole book by itself. Some strategy will be necessary in what to convert in this project, as we won't be able to go over the complete application rewrite. Instead, I'll focus our efforts on covering several of the key features of the application, explore concepts for connecting Rails to a legacy database, and introduce you to some advanced tools that would be useful in a project like this. When we're done, you should have the tools that you need to feel confident addressing such a rewrite yourself one day. So, without further ado, let's take a look at what we're starting out with.

A Quick Tour of the Current System

At the core of the system are the game records—every game that the site covers has a record in the database. A game record includes information such as a description of the game, what genre a game belongs to (e.g., role playing, action, or sports), the publishers and developers for the game, and so on. You can see an example of a game record from the existing administration site in Figure 18-1.

Historically, the site has also tracked the release dates of each title as well as a list of advanced features that each title supports (such as which games run in HD, support 5.1 surround, or have online multiplayer components). However, as the site has evolved toward becoming a content-driven site rather than a reference-based site, those legacy features have become a burden on the staff to maintain. Ron has decided that maintaining that level of detail about each game has a decreasing value for the site's future and has asked us to eliminate support for release dates and features in our redesign. Only time will tell whether or not that was a good idea.

All content on the site (news, reviews, interviews, screenshots, etc.) is associated to at least one game record. In Figure 18-2, you can see the current administration page for editing a news story and see how it's been associated to several items in the database in the left side column.

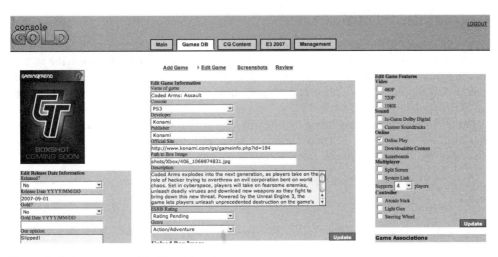

Figure 18-1. *A game record in the old system*

Currently, the staff is tasked with associating content such as news posts and game reviews to multiple items—games, consoles, publishers, and developers. However, only the association to the game record is actually being used on the public site, thus Ron has asked that we simplify the interface by removing the other associations.

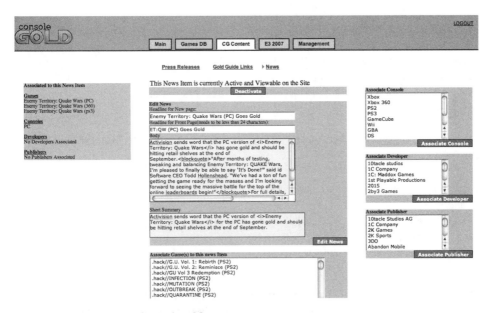

Figure 18-2. *A news story from the old system*

A Look at the Existing Code

To give you an idea of the mess that we're cleaning up, let's take a quick glance at a few lines of the code from the edit news post page. The first thing we notice is that each page in the administration application is actually its own self-contained mini application. Copy and paste seems to be the only method of code reuse in this application, and this is actually an above-average page in the application.

Forms on each page submit data to the same page for processing. At the very top of this page, there are seven blocks of SQL containing insert and update calls like the following ones—each one responding to a different form submission from this page:

```
if ((isset($HTTP_POST_VARS["MM_insert"])) && ($HTTP_POST_VARS["MM_insert"] == ➥
"adddev"))
  {
    $insertSQL = sprintf("INSERT INTO DevNews (NewsID,DevID)  VALUES(%s, %s)",
    GetSQLValueString($HTTP_POST_VARS['hiddenNewsID'], "int"),
    GetSQLValueString($HTTP_POST_VARS['Developer'], "int"));
    mysql_select_db($database_SQL, $SQL);
    $Result1 = mysql_query($insertSQL, $SQL) or die(mysql_error());
  }

if ((isset($HTTP_POST_VARS["MM_insert"])) && ($HTTP_POST_VARS["MM_insert"] == ➥
 "addpub"))
  {
    $insertSQL = sprintf("INSERT INTO PubNews (NewsID,PubID)  VALUES(%s, %s)",
    GetSQLValueString($HTTP_POST_VARS['hiddenNewsID'], "int"),
    GetSQLValueString($HTTP_POST_VARS['Publisher'], "int"));
    mysql_select_db($database_SQL, $SQL);
    $Result1 = mysql_query($insertSQL, $SQL) or die(mysql_error());
  }

if ((isset($HTTP_POST_VARS["MM_update"])) && ($HTTP_POST_VARS["MM_update"] ==➥
"activate"))
  {
    $updateSQL = sprintf("Update News Set Active=1, DateAdded = NOW() ➥
where NewsID = %s",
    GetSQLValueString($HTTP_POST_VARS['hiddenNewsID'], "text"));
    mysql_select_db($database_SQL, $SQL);
    $Result1 = mysql_query($updateSQL, $SQL) or die(mysql_error());
  }
```

After the page takes care of any form submissions, it runs though the following series of SQL select statements to populate content on the page; there are nine unique SQL select calls that all look like the following ones:

```
mysql_select_db($database_SQL, $SQL);
$query_PubPRList = sprintf("SELECT Publishers.Name, PubNews.PubID, PubNews.NewsID➥
FROM Publishers, PubNews where Publishers.PubID = PubNews.PubID ➥
and PubNews.NewsID = %s", $colname_PRList);
```

```
$PubPRList = mysql_query($query_PubPRList, $SQL) or die(mysql_error());
$row_PubPRList = mysql_fetch_assoc($PubPRList);
$totalRows_PubPRList = mysql_num_rows($PubPRList);

mysql_select_db($database_SQL, $SQL);
$query_ConsPRList = sprintf("SELECT Console, ConsNews.NewsID FROM ➥
ConsNews where ConsNews.NewsID = %s", $colname_PRList);
$ConsPRList = mysql_query($query_ConsPRList, $SQL) or die(mysql_error());
$row_ConsPRList = mysql_fetch_assoc($ConsPRList);
$totalRows_ConsPRList = mysql_num_rows($ConsPRList);

mysql_select_db($database_SQL, $SQL);
$query_GamesList = "SELECT GameID, Title, Console FROM Games ORDER BY Title ASC";
$GamesList = mysql_query($query_GamesList, $SQL) or die(mysql_error());
$row_GamesList = mysql_fetch_assoc($GamesList);
$totalRows_GamesList = mysql_num_rows($GamesList);
```

Finally, after all those SQL calls, we get into the HTML for the page, which has been made quite difficult to read thanks to a metric ton of embedded PHP intermixed with the HTML tags (though it could be worse; I have seen sites that have all the SQL queries mixed in with the HTML):

```
<form name="addgame" method="POST" action="<?php echo $editFormAction; ?>" id="add">
  <strong>Associate Game(s) to this news Item</strong>
  <input name="hiddenNewsID" type="hidden" value="➥
<?php echo $row_PRList['NewsID']; ?>"><br>
  <select name="GameID[]" size="10" multiple id="select" class="Xlongtext">
  <?php
    do {
  ?>
    <option value="<?php echo $row_GamesList['GameID']?>">
      <?php echo stripslashes($row_GamesList['Title']) . " (" . ➥
$row_GamesList['Console'] .")"?>
    </option>
    <?php
      }
    while ($row_GamesList = mysql_fetch_assoc($GamesList));
      $rows = mysql_num_rows($GamesList);
      if($rows > 0) {
        mysql_data_seek($GamesList, 0);
        $row_GamesList = mysql_fetch_assoc($GamesList);
      }
  ?>
  </select>
<div align="right">
  <input name="Submit" type="submit" value="Associate Game(s)" class="button">
</div>
  <input type="hidden" name="MM_insert" value="addgame">
</form>
```

Issues with the Old System

While it might seem funny and easy to poke fun at this code, it's always good to remember that sometime in all of our lives we've probably written code like this (or possibly even worse code). It's important to remember that this code has worked for the site for a number of years without many issues, so let's switch our focus instead to the issues that we need to solve:

- The first issue is that is that code is incredibly hard to maintain with its current design. A design like this might be okay for a small two- or three-page application but not when you're looking at trying to maintain several hundred pages like this. Suddenly, it's not a great mystery why the code hasn't been updated much over the years, is it?

- A minor but annoying issue is that the administration site still uses the old site name, which the site can no longer use. The administration page needs to be rebranded to use the site's new name GamingTrend.

- Currently, no code is reused at all. Each page is its own self-contained application with the same functions (apparently) copied and pasted from page to page.

- There are slow loading pages because the complete list of 4,000+ game titles is loaded into drop-down selection lists, which wasn't a problem when the site was first created and the complete list was only a few hundred records long.

- A number of times, staff members have copied and pasted in badly formed HTML from external sources that has caused issues with the layout of the main site. For example, they tried implementing a JavaScript-based WYSIWYG text area solution a few years back, but it only worked with Internet Explorer and produced horribly invalid HTML.

- There are a large number of historical features on the site that no longer make sense to support. While we're rewriting the backend application, we should also do a bit of housecleaning to remove those features.

- Staff members have complained that navigating around the content for a game can be pain. There's no easy way to get back to a game record after uploading screenshots for it without going back to a page that lists all games.

Setting Up Our Application

Throughout this book, I've preached the benefits of using smaller database solutions such as SQLite for our development purposes. However, when recoding to a legacy database, I've often found that it's best to match the database system of the source system, if possible. One reasons for this is that oftentimes a legacy system will utilize database-specific fields, features, and options that may not easily translate into another database solution. In addition, some legacy databases offer advanced features, such as views, that we can utilize to make our integration efforts easier that just aren't available in SQLite. For example, one of my first Rails applications was an interface to a legacy Microsoft SQL Server 2000 database. That database had an absolutely horrendous design with common data fields spread out among many tables (and in a few cases across multiple databases) and with each table using its own naming conventions. However, I was able to make my integration efforts tremendously easier by building a few views that could combine the data that I wanted into a cohesive whole (and using names that made my integration a thousand times easier).

For this project, I'll be utilizing a MySQL database on my development machine and will provide the sample data as a MySQL database export for your use as well. In the source archive for the application, you'll also find a MySQL import script that you can use to build a local copy of a smaller version of the legacy database. For maximum ease of use, I highly recommend using a MySQL management application by the name of Navicat (http://www.navicat.com). It's available for Windows, Mac, and Linux OS, and it offers a 30-day demonstration version for you to try it out. I use it on a daily basis for managing my production MySQL databases and truly believe it's worth the investment to purchase.

Let's go ahead and create our new Rails application according to the standard setup that we've used from Chapter 2 and call it "gaming". Once we have that new application configured, you'll want to ensure that you've loaded the sample database and downloaded the CSS and image elements that I've included in the archive. Within that archive, you'll find instructions on where all those elements will need to be placed, as well as some extra help detailing how to import the database for those who aren't familiar with the process.

Utilizing the Console

Now that we have an application created and the legacy database loaded, how do we ensure that the two can communicate? We'll do it using a tool that doesn't get nearly the attention that it deserves—the interactive console that comes with Rails. The console is a powerful tool that allows you to work directly with your Rails application from an interactive shell. Rather than wasting your time making changes and reloading your web pages to see if things are working correctly, you're able to work directly with your data using the same Rails method calls and see the explicit results that are returned from each method. It wouldn't be a stretch to say that I probably use the console on a daily basis. It's a great tool to learn from, an easy way to interact with my applications, and an especially powerful ally when building a configuration to a legacy database.

You initiate the console by opening a command prompt in the root of your project and entering the following command:

```
ruby script/console
```

```
Loading development environment.
>>
```

Once we're in the console, we'll be able to experiment with our model configuration by simply entering the same commands that we might enter into the code of our models and controllers. Let's start by defining a new Game model that we can use for the duration of this console session:

```
>> class Game < ActiveRecord::Base
>> end
```

```
=> nil
```

HAVING PROBLEMS?

When you're using a MySQL database you can run into minor issues of case sensitivity with regard to table names when using certain operating systems. This is due to the fact that, in MySQL, each table in the database will correspond to (at least) one file on the file system—if the file system is case sensitive, so are your queries.

This means that when running MySQL databases on most Unix-based distributions such as Ubuntu and Fedora, that your database and table names are case sensitive. Meanwhile, those same elements are case insensitive when running MySQL on Windows.

Mac-based systems can vary depending on the file system installed. Queries to the default file system (HFS+) are not case sensitive; however, if the file system is UFS, they will be.

Because the tables in this legacy database all begin with a capital letter and Rails expects that table names are all lowercase, we might run into some errors when attempting to query a table on a case-sensitive system.

In those situations, we'll need to explicitly tell Rails our table name using the set_table_name method, so we'd define our game model like this:

```
class Game < ActiveRecord::Base
  set_table_name 'Games'
end
```

Throughout this project, I'll include that set_table_name method in model definitions for those whose operating system may require it.

Now that we've built a simple Game model, let's see if it can read in a record from the legacy database:

```
>> @game = Game.find(:first)
```

```
=> #<Game:0x281ee68 @attributes={"updated_at"=>nil, "AddedBy"=>"0", "ESRB"=>"T",
 "SiteURL"=>nil, "BoximagePath"=>"shots/baldursgate_da.jpg", "Console"=>"Xbox",
 "PubID"=>"33", "Title"=>"Baldur's Gate: Dark Alliance", "GameID"=>"1",
 "GenreID"=>"4", "DevID"=>"15", "created_at"=>"0000-00-00", "Description"=>"It's
 the massively popular world of Baldur's Gate as you have never seen it before.
 Baldur's Gate: Dark Alliance is a revolutionary action adventure with an epic
 tale of intrigue, fierce alliances, explosive spell effects and highly detailed
 creatures and environments. Baldur's Gate: Dark Alliance is a benchmark of
 technology and gameplay. (...Lines Omitted...)"}
```

That's very promising—we're able to connect to the database and pull back a record, but what happens if we attempt to make a change to the record?

```
>> @game.Title
```

```
=> "Baldur's Gate: Dark Alliance"
```

```
>> @game.Title = "Kung Fu Phooey"
```

```
=> "Kung Fu Phooey"
```

```
>> @game.save
```

```
ActiveRecord::StatementInvalid: Mysql::Error: #42S22Unknown column 'id' in 'where
clause': UPDATE games SET `created_at` = NULL, `Title` = 'Kung Fu Phooey',
`GenreID` = 4, `SiteURL` = NULL, `AddedBy` = 0,
```

Boom! It blows up. Obviously, we're going to have to do a bit more work than normal to make our connection to Rails and this legacy database communicate correctly. We'll tackle those problems in the next chapter when we really build our Game model, but for now, I just wanted you to have a quick introduction to the console and see that we could connect to the legacy database even before we've written any code.

Utilizing Ext-JS to Create a Better Interface

Now that we know that we can connect to the legacy database (even though it's not working 100 percent perfectly), let's discuss how we're going to solve the problem of creating a new interface. Because we have full control over who's going to be utilizing this application, we can force some heftier requirements onto our users (modern, JavaScript-enabled browsers, etc.) so that we can take advantage of some new JavaScript libraries and add in some extra special features. We'll greatly enhance the look and feel of our application by utilizing a fairly new open source JavaScript framework by the name of Ext-JS.

Ext-JS began its life as the YUI-Ext (an extension to the Yahoo User Interface library) but has since developed into a full-fledged framework of its own that can be used to extend not only the Yahoo UI library but also jquery or Prototype/script.aculo.us. Ext is an incredible set of code that provides us not only with the standard JavaScript framework features such as Ajax, DOM utilities, and animations but also a wealth of impressive widgets such as grids, tabs, dialogs, and message boxes.

In our application, we'll be taking advantage of a basic implementation of several of those widgets to give our administration system a real cutting edge look and feel. In essence, many of our view templates for this application will be built almost entirely in JavaScript and will simply communicate with a Rails backend via XML or JSON (this is not entirely dissimilar to Flex/Rails applications in which there's been a recent surge of popularity). Before we start building our application's interface, let me whet your appetite for what we can do in Ext-JS by giving a quick overview of some of its key features.

Border Layout

Border layout is a widget for putting together advanced web interface layouts through some fairly simple JavaScript configuration. Using border layout, you build your application layout by defining a series of two to five panels (center, north, south, east, and west) and specifying what content you want to populate each panel. You can even include another border layout within a panel to build increasingly complex layouts.

To build a new layout, we create a new border layout and specify the container that the layout should be bound to and a configuration object, which defines the options particular to each of our panels.

```
var layout = new Ext.BorderLayout(document.body, {
  north: {
    split:false,
    initialSize: 35
  },
  west: {
    split:true,
    initialSize: 200,
    titlebar: true,
    collapsible: true,
    minSize: 100,
    maxSize: 400
  },
  center: {
    autoScroll: true
  }
});
```

With that layout object, we build our page by assigning what content we want in each of the panels we created:

```
layout.beginUpdate();
layout.add('north', new Ext.ContentPanel('header', {fitToFrame:true}));
layout.add('west', new Ext.ContentPanel('nav', {title: 'Navigation', ➥
fitToFrame:true}));
layout.add('center', new Ext.ContentPanel('content'));
layout.endUpdate();
```

And with that simple bit of code, we suddenly have the advanced web page layout shown in Figure 18-3, which provides a consistent look and feel across browsers.

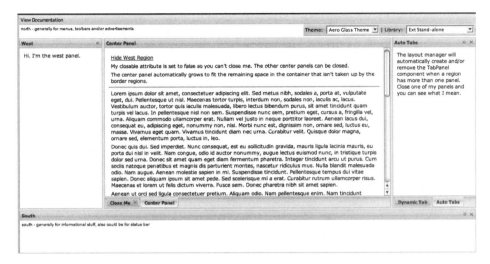

Figure 18-3. *An example of a border layout*

Grid

Another powerful tool that we'll be using is the Grid widget. Grids are a way of creating stylized tables that look similar to Excel spreadsheets. Grids can be configured to be sortable (on either the client or server side); have headers or footers that can house toolbars, buttons, or even paging controls; and are completely stylable via CSS.

To create a grid, the first thing we do is define the data store that will be used to populate the grid. A data store consists of a proxy object that fetches the data we'll use. Some of the available proxies include an in-memory proxy, an external proxy over HTTP, and an external proxy through a script (for pulling in data from another domain).

Second, we need to define a reader object for the data store. The reader is used to convert the data from the store into a format that the grid will understand. Available readers include array, JSON, and XML.

```
var ds = new Ext.data.Store({
  proxy: new Ext.data.MemoryProxy(myData),
  reader: new Ext.data.ArrayReader({id: 0}, [
    {name: 'company'},
    {name: 'price', type: 'float'},
    {name: 'change', type: 'float'},
    {name: 'pctChange', type: 'float'},
    {name: 'lastChange', type: 'date', dateFormat: 'n/j h:ia'}
    ])
  });
  ds.load();
```

The next element to configure for the grid is the column model. The column model can be thought of as simply defining what columns we want to display in our grid, how they should look, and what fields they map to from our data store.

```
var colModel = new Ext.grid.ColumnModel([
  {header: "Company", width: 200, sortable: true, locked:false, dataIndex: ➥
'company'},
  {header: "Price", width: 75, sortable: true, renderer: Ext.util.Format.usMoney,➥
 dataIndex: 'price'},
  {header: "Change", width: 75, sortable: true, renderer: change, dataIndex:➥
'change'},
  {header: "% Change", width: 75, sortable: true, renderer: pctChange, dataIndex:➥
'pctChange'},
  {header: "Last Updated", width: 85, sortable: true, ➥
renderer: Ext.util.Format.dateRenderer('m/d/Y'), dataIndex: 'lastChange'}]);
```

Once we have our data store and column model defined, we simply instantiate a new grid object and pass it the HTML container to use for our grid on the page, as well as our data store and column model objects.

```
var grid = new Ext.grid.Grid('grid-example', {
  ds: ds,
  cm: colModel
});
```

Finally, we merely give a call to the render method to display our grid, which is shown in Figure 18-4:

```
grid.render();
```

Company	Price	Change	% Change	Last Updated
3m Co	$71.72	0.02	0.03%	09/01/2007
Alcoa Inc	$29.01	0.42	1.47%	09/01/2007
Altria Group Inc	$83.81	0.28	0.34%	09/01/2007
American Express Company	$52.55	0.01	0.02%	09/01/2007
American International Group, Inc.	$64.13	0.31	0.49%	09/01/2007
AT&T Inc.	$31.61	-0.48	-1.54%	09/01/2007
Boeing Co.	$75.43	0.53	0.71%	09/01/2007
Caterpillar Inc.	$67.27	0.92	1.39%	09/01/2007
Citigroup, Inc.	$49.37	0.02	0.04%	09/01/2007
E.I. du Pont de Nemours and Company	$40.48	0.51	1.28%	09/01/2007
Exxon Mobil Corp	$68.10	-0.43	-0.64%	09/01/2007
General Electric Company	$34.14	-0.08	-0.23%	09/01/2007
General Motors Corporation	$30.27	1.09	3.74%	09/01/2007
Hewlett-Packard Co.	$36.53	0.03	0.08%	09/01/2007

Figure 18-4. *A grid widget from Ext-JS*

Dialogs

Ext-JS also has a powerful set of libraries for building interactive dialogs within our application. These dialogs can be draggable, resizable, and even configured with advanced layouts using border layout. Figure 18-5 shows an example.

```
dialog = new Ext.BasicDialog("hello-dlg", {
  autoTabs:true,
  width:500,
  height:300,
  shadow:true,
  minWidth:300,
  minHeight:250,
  proxyDrag: true
});
```

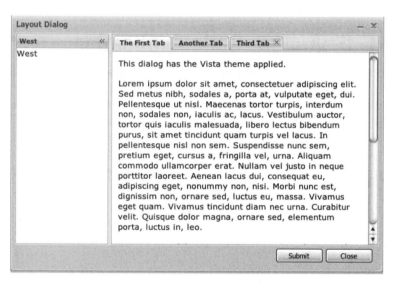

Figure 18-5. *An example of an Ext-JS modal dialog with a border layout applied*

Message Box

Similar to the dialog box functionality is the ability to simply create common modal message boxes such as alerts, confirmations (see Figure 18-6), and even progress bars (see Figure 18-7). These are much more attractive than your standard alert box, and adding one is as simple as typing a single line of code:

```
Ext.MessageBox.confirm('Confirm', 'Are you sure you want to do that?', showResult);
```

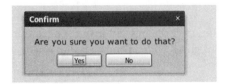

Figure 18-6. *A confirmation message box*

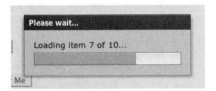

Figure 18-7. *A progress message box*

Installing Ext-JS into Our Rails Application

There's obviously a lot of power available within Ext-JS, so let's add it to our new application. You can download the current version of the library from the official site at http://www.extjs.com/download (I'm using version 1.1). Once you download and uncompress the archive, it creates the directory structure shown in Figure 18-8. I'll quickly explain what's where and discuss what we need to copy over into our Rails application.

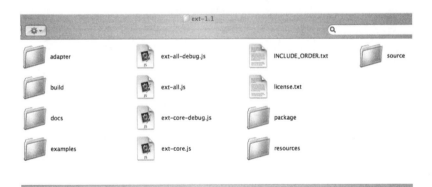

Figure 18-8. *The directory structure of Ext-JS*

There are obviously a number of folders within the archive but, fortunately, only a select few that we need to be concerned with:

- adapter/: Ext-JS works by extending a base library. In this folder, you'll find the necessary base libraries that you might want to use such as jQuery, Prototype/script.aculo.us, Yahoo UI, or the new Ext Base.

- docs/: This folder contains a fully functional copy of the online API docs and links to all of the examples.

- resources/: Here, you'll find any of the extra assets that you might need when using Ext-JS, such as CSS style sheets, images, and so on.

So let's go ahead and copy over the files that we'll need in our application:

1. In the root directory, there is the main Ext-JavaScript file named ext-all.js. Copy this file into the /public/javascripts folder of our application.

2. Next, we need to select one of the base libraries from the adapter folder. Since we'll probably be using a few of the Rails helper methods, it makes sense to use the prototype adapter. You'll need to copy all of the JavaScript files in here (effects.js, ext-prototype-adapter.js, prototype.js, and scriptaculous.js) into our application's /public/javascripts folder.

3. From the /resources/css folder, we'll need to copy the ext-all.css file and the three xtheme*.css files into our application's /public/stylesheets folder. The xtheme style sheets are custom color schemes for the standard Ext-JS widgets. We'll be using the xtheme-vista theme in our application, but I like to have them all installed in case I ever want to switch.

4. Finally, from /resources/images, you'll want to copy over all four folders (aero, default, gray, and vista) and all of the files within each into our application's /public/images directory. These are the associated background images, icons, and so on that are used by Ext-JS's widgets, based on the theme you specify.

Automating Ext-JS Installation

Copying those files over manually is well and good, but since this is a library that we're probably going to want to use again in future projects, it sure would be nice if we didn't have to do all that copying and pasting by hand, wouldn't it? Wouldn't it be great if we could simply run a generator like we do to create a new controller or model that would place all these files into the appropriate places in any application that we build? Well, let's stop dreaming about it, and go ahead and build one.

The first thing we need to decide is where we want to place our new generator. When you run the `script/generate` command, Rails will search in four places for a generator:

- The application's `vendor/plugins` directory

- Any installed Ruby gems

- The application's `/lib` directory

- The user's home directory on the system

Since we're not going to be building a new plug-in or a gem, those first two options are out. That just leaves the `/lib` directory or our home directory. If we place the generator in the `/lib` directory, it will only be available for use in this one application. If we place it in the user's home directory, we can use it across any of our applications. So placing it in the home directory seems to be the best option for this generator, unless of course you're using Windows, in which case there isn't a home directory defined by default.

Creating the Generator Files

Within our home directory, there should be a directory named `.rails`; you'll need to create it if it doesn't exist. Within this folder, we need to create a folder named `generators` and another subfolder named `extjs`, which will hold our new generator code.

Within our new `extjs` folder, we need to create three things:

- A file named USAGE that should contain information about how to use the generator

- A file named `extjs_generator.rb` that will hold all our generator code to copy over the Ext-JS resources

- A folder named `templates` where we'll place all of our Ext-JS files

The next step is to copy the files that we would have previously copied manually into our `templates` folder, as shown in Figure 18-9.

Figure 18-9. *Our Ext-JS files copied in the templates folder*

With our files copied into the `templates` directory, our next step is to add the necessary code into our new `extjs_generator.rb`. To start off, we'll need to create a new class that inherits from `Rails::Generator::Base`:

```
class ExtjsGenerator < Rails::Generator::Base
end
```

Within that class, we must have a method named `manifest`, which will be called automatically when the generator is executed:

```
class ExtjsGenerator < Rails::Generator::Base
  def manifest
    record do |m|
    end
  end
end
```

Within that `manifiest` block, we have a few core methods that we can call, but the two that we'll call most often are `file` and `directory`; `file` is used to copy a file from our `templates` folder into the Rails application:

```
m.file "shadow.png", "/public/images/shadow.png"
```

while `directory` is used to create a new folder within our application:

```
m.directory "/public/images/uploads"
```

So we could easily build out most of our generator by adding calls to copy files like this:

```
m.file "ext-all.js", "/public/javascripts/ext-all.js"
m.file "ext-all.css", "/public/stylesheets/ext-all.css"
m.file "prototype.js", "/public/javascripts/prototype.js"
m.file "scriptaculous.js", "/public/javascripts/scriptaculous.js"
m.file "effects.js", "/public/javascripts/effects.js"
m.file "ext-prototype-adapter.js", "/public/javascripts/ext-prototype-adapter.js"
```

But that's going to get really old once we start trying to copy the image folders, where each has multiple subfolders containing multiple images. But we can work around that with a simple loop. First, we can create an array of the subfolders from which we need to copy:

```
aero_images = %w(basic-dialog grid layout menu sizer tabs toolbar)
```

That array can then be looped over, so each array value is used to call a new method:

```
aero_images.each do |folder|
  copy_image_files( m, "aero/#{folder}")
end
```

Next, we need to create that `copy_image_files` method, which will create the subfolder (if it doesn't exist). Then it will open that folder in `templates` and loop over the files in the directory, copying each file into the local applications folders.

```
def copy_image_files( m, folder)
  m.directory "/public/images/#{folder}"
  Dir.open(File.join(File.dirname(__FILE__), "templates/#{folder}")).entries.each ➥
do |file|
    m.file "/#{folder}/#{file}", "/public/images/#{folder}/#{file}" unless ➥
File.directory?(file)
  end
end
```

With that, here's the final version of the new generator task:

```
class ExtjsGenerator < Rails::Generator::Base
  def manifest
    record do |m|
      m.file "ext-all.js", "/public/javascripts/ext-all.js"
      m.file "ext-all.css", "/public/stylesheets/ext-all.css"
      m.file "prototype.js", "/public/javascripts/prototype.js"
      m.file "scriptaculous.js", "/public/javascripts/scriptaculous.js"
      m.file "effects.js", "/public/javascripts/effects.js"
      m.file "ext-prototype-adapter.js", ➥
"/public/javascripts/ext-prototype-adapter.js"
      m.file "xtheme-aero.css", "/public/stylesheets/xtheme-aero.css"
      m.file "xtheme-gray.css", "/public/stylesheets/xtheme-gray.css"
      m.file "xtheme-vista.css", "/public/stylesheets/xtheme-vista.css"

      # CREATE IMAGE DIRECTORIES
      directories = %w(aero default gray vista)
      directories.each do |directory|
        m.directory "/public/images/#{directory}"
        m.file "/#{directory}/gradient-bg.gif", "/public/images/#{directory}/➥
gradient-bg.gif"
        m.file "/#{directory}/s.gif", "/public/images/#{directory}/s.gif"
      end

      # COPY AERO THEME IMAGES
      aero_images = %w(basic-dialog grid layout menu sizer tabs toolbar)
      aero_images.each do |folder|
        copy_image_files( m, "aero/#{folder}")
      end
```

```
      # COPY AERO THEME IMAGES
      default_images = %w(basic-dialog box dd editor form grid layout menu panel➥
  qtip shared sizer tabs toolbar tree)
      m.file "/default/shadow-c.png", "/public/images/default/shadow-c.png"
      m.file "/default/shadow-lr.png", "/public/images/default/shadow-lr.png"
      m.file "/default/shadow.png", "/public/images/default/shadow.png"
      default_images.each do |folder|
        copy_image_files( m, "default/#{folder}")
      end

      # COPY GRAY THEME IMAGES
      gray_images = %w(basic-dialog grid layout menu qtip sizer tabs toolbar)
      gray_images.each do |folder|
        copy_image_files( m, "gray/#{folder}")
      end

      # COPY VISTA THEME IMAGES
      vista_images = %w(basic-dialog grid layout qtip sizer tabs toolbar)
      vista_images.each do |folder|
        copy_image_files( m, "vista/#{folder}")
      end
    end
  end

  def copy_image_files( m, folder)
    m.directory "/public/images/#{folder}"
    Dir.open(File.join(File.dirname(__FILE__),"templates/#{folder}")).entries.each➥
  do |file|
      m.file "/#{folder}/#{file}", "/public/images/#{folder}/#{file}" unless ➥
File.directory?(file)
    end
  end
end
```

You can validate that the gem system is able to see your new generator by running the
ruby/script/generate task with no options to view a list of at the available gems:

```
ruby script/generate
Usage: script/generate generator [options] [args]
```

```
Rails Info:
    -v, --version                    Show the Rails version number and quit.
    -h, --help                       Show this help message and quit.

General Options:
    -p, --pretend                    Run but do not make any changes.
    -f, --force                      Overwrite files that already exist.
    -s, --skip                       Skip files that already exist.
    -q, --quiet                      Suppress normal output.
    -t, --backtrace                  Debugging: show backtrace on errors.
    -c, --svn                        Modify files with subversion. (Note: svn➡
  must be in path)



Installed Generators
  User: extjs
  Rubygems: sparklines
  Builtin: controller, integration_test, mailer, migration, model, observer, ➡
plugin, resource, scaffold, scaffold_resource, session_migration, web_service

(lines ommtted)
```

With the generator saved, we can now run it from any Rails application like this:

```
ruby script/generate extjs
```

```
     create  /public/javascripts/ext-all.js
     create  /public/stylesheets/ext-all.css
overwrite /public/javascripts/prototype.js? [Ynaqd] a
forcing extjs
      force  /public/javascripts/prototype.js
     create  /public/javascripts/scriptaculous.js
      force  /public/javascripts/effects.js
     create  /public/javascripts/ext-prototype-adapter.js
     create  /public/stylesheets/xtheme-aero.css
     create  /public/stylesheets/xtheme-gray.css
     create  /public/stylesheets/xtheme-vista.css
     create  /public/images/aero
     create  /public/images/aero/gradient-bg.gif
     create  /public/images/aero/s.gif
     create  /public/images/default
     create  /public/images/default/gradient-bg.gif
     create  /public/images/default/s.gif
     create  /public/images/gray
     create  /public/images/gray/gradient-bg.gif
     create  /public/images/gray/s.gif
     (...Lines Omitted...)
```

With that change, we'll call this chapter a wrap.

Summary

In this chapter, we began our journey into connecting our Rails application to a legacy database. We looked at some of the old PHP code that was being used and tested that we could connect to the legacy database from Rails. We then took a high-level overview of the powerful features available in Ext-JS and discussed how we were going to be using that library to power our new application. Finally, we closed out the chapter by creating a new generator that we can use to install the Ext-JS files and resources into our applications

■ ■ ■

## CHAPTER 19

Converting Game Records

As you saw in the last chapter, even with no configuration or code added, our basic Rails application was able to connect to and read in some simple data from the legacy database—at least, it could until we attempted to do anything more useful than pulling in the first record. In this chapter, we're going to solve that problem as we build the necessary models to allow our Rails application to communicate correctly with some of the core models of the gaming site. Once we have the models speaking correctly, we'll move onto building the first few pages of our administration application, which will be used to manage those records. We'll start in the most obviously useful place with building support for the games records, as they are the core resource of our application.

Converting Our Database to Migrations

Even though our database is already defined for us, I always think it's a good idea to convert it to a Rails migration format—that way, we can have a record not only of where the database structure is currently but also a baseline we can revert to as we make changes to the schema. The actual process for converting an existing database to a migration is a bit involved, but the end results are worth it.

Our first step is to gather a proper dump of the current schema by running the following command from the root of our application:

```
rake db:schema:dump
```

This rake task will create a fresh version of our schema.rb (found in /db) from the currently defined database. Once we have this, we can use it to set up our application to believe that this was our first migration. Let's start that process by creating an initial migration file to place our existing schema into:

```
ruby script/generate migration ExistingSchema
```

```
create  db/migrate
create  db/migrate/001_existing_schema.rb
```

Now, we merely need to copy all those create_table and add_index calls from /db/ schema.rb and paste them into the self.up block of our new migration (/db/migrate/ 001_existing_schema.rb):

```
class ExistingSchema < ActiveRecord::Migration
  def self.up
    create_table "ArtGame", :id => false, :force => true do |t|
      t.column "ArtID",  :integer, :default => 0, :null => false
      t.column "GameID", :integer, :default => 0, :null => false
    end

    add_index "ArtGame", ["ArtID"], :name => "ArtID"
    add_index "ArtGame", ["GameID"], :name => "GameID"

      (...Lines Omitted...)
  end

  def self.down
  end
end
```

We don't need to put anything into the self.down block, because we would never want to revert beyond this point. Don't try to run this migration just yet, unless you want to experience a complete loss of all the data in that database. That's because the schema dump added a bit of a bomb in the commands it created if they're used in a migration. That bomb goes by the name of the :force => true command appended at the top of each table creation. If you were to run your migration at this point, it would essentially drop all the existing tables (with their data) and create nice clean empty tables to replace them. So to save us from having to solve the mystery of the disappearing data, we'll simply need to remove that :force => true statement (and the comma in front of it) from each table creation in our migration (at times like this, a good code editor with a "search and replace all" feature can be your best friend). After all those :force => true commands are removed and you've saved the migration, we can go ahead and run our migration. The migration will fail but not before helping us out by creating the schema_info table in our database:

rake db:migrate

```
(in /Users/darkel/consolegold)
== ExistingSchema: migrating ====================================================
-- create_table("Announcements")
rake aborted!
Mysql::Error: #42S01Table 'announcements' already exists: CREATE TABLE ➡
Announcements (`id` int(11) DEFAULT NULL auto_increment PRIMARY KEY, ➡
`announcement` text DEFAULT '' NOT NULL, `date_added` datetime NOT NULL) ➡
ENGINE=InnoDB

(See full trace by running task with --trace)
```

It failed because the tables already existed, which is a good thing. Now that our schema_info table has been added, we can set it to 1 to reflect the current state of the database with our migration files. To do that, simply run the following command from the command line at the root of your application or edit the value manually using a tool such as Navicat:

```
ruby script/runner 'ActiveRecord::Base.connection.execute("UPDATE schema_info ➥
  SET version = 1")'
```

■**Note** In case you don't recall, the schema_info table is an automatically generated table added to all Rails databases that utilize migrations. It contains only a single field named version. The value of this field will match the current migration that has been executed. In our case, we're setting it to 1 to match the fact that the database currently matches the schema in 001_existing_schema.rb.

The Games Table

Now that we have our database migrations set to mirror the current configuration, we can start work on actually connecting our application to the games table. The first step is to take a look at what we have to work with. In our schema in /db/schema.rb, the current structure for the games record is like this:

```
create_table "Games", :id => false, :force => true do |t|
    t.column "GameID", :integer, :null => false
    t.column "Title", :string, :limit => 100, :default => "", :null => false
    t.column "Console", :string, :limit => 15, :default => "", :null => false
    t.column "DevID", :integer
    t.column "PubID", :integer
    t.column "SiteURL", :string
    t.column "BoximagePath", :string
    t.column "Description", :text
    t.column "ESRB", :string,  :limit => 2
    t.column "AvgReview", :integer, :limit => 4
    t.column "GenreID", :integer,  :default => 0,  :null => false
    t.column "AddedBy", :integer,  :default => 0,  :null => false
    t.column "DateAdded", :date, :null => false
    t.column "LastEditedBy", :integer, :default => 0,  :null => false
    t.column "DateEdited", :date, :null => false
    t.column "AssignedTo", :integer, :default => 0,  :null => false
    t.column "Verified", :date, :null => false
    t.column "E304", :integer, :limit => 4, :default => 0,  :null => false
  end
```

Also notice that the schema shows that there are a number of indexes that have been built on our Games table:

```
add_index "Games", ["Title", "Console"], :name => "NoDups", :unique => true
add_index "Games", ["Title"], :name => "Title"
add_index "Games", ["E304"], :name => "E304"
add_index "Games", ["Description"], :name => "descrip"
```

Doing a little research with Ron (the site owner) reveals the meaning behind each of these fields:

- *GameID*: This is the primary key used to identify the game record. It is an integer and auto-generated by the database.

- *Title*: The field stores the name of the game and is required.

- *Console*: The field indicates the console platform that this game runs on (e.g., Xbox 360, PlayStation 3). It is configured to store this information as a string, rather than as a foreign key to a separate consoles table (supposedly to avoid an extra join every time the game record is accessed).

- *DevID*: This is an integer foreign key reference to a Developers table to identify the developer of this game.

- *PubID*: This integer foreign key references the Publishers table to identify the publisher of this game.

- *SiteURL*: If there is an official web site for this game, this text field holds the URL to it.

- *BoximagePath*: Every game has a picture of the box uploaded along with it and stored on the file system. This text field holds the URL path to that file.

- *Description*: This field holds a synopsis of the game; it can hold paragraphs of text and HTML.

- *ESRB*: The Electronic Software Review Board rates all games with a recommendation of what age levels they are appropriate for. The rating for each game is stored here.

- *AvgReview*: Originally, there were plans to store the review scores of each game from other gaming sites and magazines. This field was supposed to store the computed average score of all reviews. A nice idea—sadly, it was never implemented, so this field is empty for all game records.

- *GenreID*: This field stores a foreign key reference to the Genres table, referencing the associated genre for this game.

- *AddedBy*: This stores the User ID of the staff member who initially created this record.

- *DateAdded*: The date that this game was added to the database is stored in this field.

- *LastEditedBy*: This stores the User ID of the staff member who last updated this game record.

- *DateEdited*: This is the date that this game record was last updated.

- *AssignedTo*: Before the database first launched on the site, Ron wanted to verify that there weren't any errors with data in the database. Every record was assigned to a staff member who was responsible for ensuring that the data was accurate. This field stored a foreign key reference to the Users table of the staff member responsible for validating the data in each. This field hasn't been used since that first push for complete verification and no longer serves any purpose.

- *Verified*: During the push for verification, staff members clicked a button that said "mark complete" whenever records were verified. That button stored the current date in this field to flag the record as verified and simultaneously record when it was checked. This field also hasn't been used since that first big push.

- *E304*: The Electronics Entertainment Expo (E3) used to be a huge annual gaming industry event at which a large number of new games were revealed or announced. This field was an experiment in marking that a game was first announced at the 2004 E3. Obviously, since there aren't any entries for the years since, this is another field that's just wasted space now.

Cleaning Up the Games Table

Overall, our games database isn't too bad; sure, it's not in line with the Rails conventions and it has a number of fields that need to be removed, but it's also got a few good points.

For one, it's got a nice integer primary key that's auto-generated (even if it is named differently than Rails would prefer). Second, whoever designed this schema recognized the need to prevent duplicate entries of a title/console combination, and fortunately, they solved that need by adding a unique index constraint on those fields, rather than going down the dark, dirty road of composite primary keys.

But that also leads us into one of the problems that we face: Because when the system was originally built, the majority of its validation logic was maintained in the database and not in the application itself, we have many rows that have restrictions on them, such as not allowing NULL values or forcing limits on the data entered (e.g., the 100-character limit on a game's title). Making matters worse is the fact that a good number of these fields aren't even being used—yet they're configured to not accept NULL.

As we build the new backend, we could choose to either continue to pump worthless data into those fields to satisfy the database constraints or do a little housekeeping on the database to eliminate these problems. Since I despise bad database designs, I chose housekeeping. Let's create a new migration that we can use to clean up those records from our games table:

```
ruby script/generate migration cleanup_games
```

```
exists  db/migrate
create  db/migrate/002_cleanup_games.rb
```

In keeping with the Rails way of doing things (and my own personal preference), I'd rather have the validation logic controlled by my models and not my database, so let's move all of those constraints out of the database and into the model.

Open our newly created `002_cleanup_games.rb` migration in /db/migrate/, and let's take care of the low hanging fruit by eliminating all of the unused fields from this table:

```
remove_column "Games", "AvgReview"
remove_column "Games", "LastEditedBy"
remove_column "Games", "AssignedTo"
remove_column "Games", "Verified"
remove_column "Games", "E304"
```

Next, we also have a pair of indexes that we can safely remove: the index on E304, since we're removing that field, and the index on the `descrip` field, since it makes no sense to have a standard index on a text field and a quick review of the current queries executed on this table reveals that it's not being used either.

```
remove_index "Games", :name => "E304"
remove_index "Games",  :name => "descrip"
```

The old backend administration system was capturing, for its own use, the date that a game was created or last edited with the `DateAdded` and `DateEdited` fields. While we could continue to support those, it would make things easier for us if we were to change those to the Rails conventions of `created_at` and `updated_at`, so that they would be auto-populated. Checking with Ron confirms that those fields aren't used on the main site at all, so we can safely modify those without fear of breaking anything on the primary site.

```
rename_column "Games", "DateAdded", "created_at"
rename_column "Games", "DateEdited", "updated_at"
```

Finally, we can modify the existing columns that have validation style rules on them and move them to our games model. We can start by first eliminating the no null values requirement and size limits from several of the columns.

```
change_column "Games", "Title",    :string,  :null => true
change_column "Games", "Console",  :string,  :null => true
change_column "Games", "ESRB",     :string
change_column "Games", "GenreID",  :integer, :null => true
change_column "Games", "AddedBy",  :integer, :null => true
```

Since this migration is really all about cleanup and we don't want to ever go back to the yucky state the database was in before, we can set Rails to throw an error if anyone ever tries to revert back by declaring that this migration is an irreversible migration, like this:

```
def self.down
  raise ActiveRecord::IrreversibleMigration
end
```

After putting all of that together, our 002_cleanup_games.rb migration should look like this (do take note that I reversed the order of the E304 migrations to first remove the index and then remove the column; otherwise, you may get an error when you try to run this migration):

```
class CleanupGames < ActiveRecord::Migration
  def self.up
    remove_column "Games", "AvgReview"
    remove_column "Games", "LastEditedBy"
    remove_column "Games", "AssignedTo"
    remove_column "Games", "Verified"
    remove_index  "Games", :name => "E304"
    remove_column "Games", "E304"
    remove_index  "Games", :name => "descrip"
    rename_column "Games", "DateAdded", "created_at"
    rename_column "Games", "DateEdited", "updated_at"
    change_column "Games", "Title",     :string,    :null => true
    change_column "Games", "Console",   :string,    :null => true
    change_column "Games", "ESRB",      :string
    change_column "Games", "GenreID",   :integer,   :null => true
    change_column "Games", "AddedBy",   :integer,   :null => true
  end

  def self.down
    raise ActiveRecord::IrreversibleMigration
  end
end
```

Let's go ahead and run our newly created migration:

```
rake db:migrate
```

```
== CleanupGames: migrating ============================
-- remove_column("Games", "AvgReview")
   -> 0.6623s
-- remove_column("Games", "LastEditedBy")
   -> 0.3534s
-- remove_column("Games", "AssignedTo")
   -> 0.3785s
-- remove_column("Games", "Verified")
   -> 0.3515s
-- remove_index("Games", {:name=>"E304"})
-> 0.3209s
-- remove_column("Games", "E304")
   -> 0.3704s
-- remove_index("Games", {:name=>"descrip"})
   -> 0.2168s
-- rename_column("Games", "DateAdded", "created_at")
   -> 0.3709s
-- rename_column("Games", "DateEdited", "updated_at")
   -> 0.3955s
-- change_column("Games", "Title", :string, {:null=>true})
   -> 0.3773s
-- change_column("Games", "Console", :string, {:null=>true})
   -> 0.3457s
-- change_column("Games", "ESRB", :string)
   -> 0.3917s
-- change_column("Games", "GenreID", :integer, {:null=>true})
   -> 0.3507s
-- change_column("Games", "AddedBy", :integer, {:null=>true})
   -> 0.3634s
== CleanupGames: migrated (2.8129s) ============================================
```

Creating the Games Model

Since we've now prepared the games table, let's create the Games model and add the validation rules that we just removed in our previous migration:

```
ruby script/generate model Game --skip-migration
```

```
      create  app/models/
      create  test/unit/
      create  test/fixtures/
      create  app/models/game.rb
      create  test/unit/game_test.rb
      create  test/fixtures/games.yml
```

Go ahead and open our new Game model, and set it up with our validation; also set the table name for MySQL variations that are case sensitive:

```ruby
class Game < ActiveRecord::Base
  set_table_name 'Games'
  validates_length_of :Title, :maximum => 100, :message => " must be less ➥
  than 100 characters"
  validates_presence_of :Title, :Console
end
```

Save the model, and let's fire up a console session to see if our new model is working:

```
ruby script/console
```

```
Loading development environment.
```

```
>> Game.new
```

```
=> #<Game:0x2038cc8 @attributes={"updated_at"=>nil, "AddedBy"=>0, "ESRB"=>nil,
 "SiteURL"=>nil, "BoximagePath"=>nil, "Console"=>"", "PubID"=>nil, "Title"=>"", "
GameID"=>nil, "GenreID"=>0, "DevID"=>nil, "created_at"=>nil, "Description"=>nil},
 new_recordtrue
```

```
>> g = Game.find :first
```

```
=> #<Game:0x27c820c @attributes={"updated_at"=>"2005-10-06", "AddedBy"=>"0",
"ESRB"=>"T", "SiteURL"=>nil, "BoximagePath"=>"shots/baldursgate_da.jpg",
"Console"=>"Xbox", "PubID"=>"33", "Title"=>"Baldur's Gate: Dark Alliance",
"GameID"=>"1", "GenreID"=>"4", "DevID"=>"15", "created_at"=>"0000-00-00",
"Description"=>"It's the massively popular world of Baldur's Gate as you have
 never seen it before. Baldur's Gate: Dark Alliance is a revolutionary action
adventure ..."}
(...lines ommited...)
```

```
>> Game.find 123
```

```
ActiveRecord::StatementInvalid: Mysql::Error: #42S22Unknown column 'Games.id' in
'where clause': SELECT * FROM games WHERE (games.id = 123)
        from /usr/local/lib/ruby/gems/1.8/gems/activerecord-
1.15.2/lib/active_record/connection_adapters/abstract_adapter.rb:128:in `log'
(...lines ommited...)
```

Look at the error that's generated by our last command; it indicates that Games.id is an unknown column. The obvious culprit is that nonstandard primary key named GameID instead of id. While it may be tempting to create a new migration to rename that column, the devastation of such a change to the front end would be on par with a plague of locusts. Plus, a new migration is unnecessary, as we can fix this issue fairly easily by telling our model which field to use as the primary key with the following method:

```
class Game < ActiveRecord::Base
  set_table_name 'Games'
  set_primary_key :GameID
  validates_length_of :Title, :maximum => 100, :message => " must be less ➥
than 100 characters"
  validates_presence_of :Title, :Console
end
```

Go back to our console session, and reload our configuration using the reload! command to test our model now:

```
reload!
```

```
Reloading...
=> {"ActiveRecord::Base"=>#<ActiveRecord::ConnectionAdapters::MysqlAdapter:0x281bc54
 (...Lines Ommited...)
```

```
>> Game.find 123
```

```
=> #<Game:0x26238d4 @attributes={"updated_at"=>"0000-00-00", "AddedBy"=>"0",
"ESRB"=>"E", "SiteURL"=>"http://www.sega.com/games/xbox/post_xboxgame.jhtml?
PRODID=10087", "BoximagePath"=>"shots/segasoccerslam.jpg", "Console"=>"Xbox",
"PubID"=>"8", "Title"=>"Soccer Slam", "GameID"=>"123", "GenreID"=>"6", "DevID"
=>"95", "created_at"=>"0000-00-00", "Description"=>"In Soccer Slam you'll unleash
 merciless kicks, tackles, and steals against excitable, colorful characters
from all over the world. Each character in this anything-but-ordinary soccer game
 wields special powers and moves that if executed properly earn the big score"}
```

Woohoo—success!

Creating the Developer and Publisher Models

Since, within the games table, there are several foreign key references to other tables in the database, let's also add those models. We'll start by building the models for the developers and publishers tables so that we can reference the names of each for a given game record.

The schema for the Developers and Publishers tables reveal that they are nearly identical to each outside of different primary key names.

```
create_table "Developers", :id => false, :force => true do |t|
    t.column "DevID", :integer, :limit => 10, :null => false
    t.column "Name",  :string,  :limit => 200, :default => "", :null => false
    t.column "URL",   :string,  :limit => 200
  end

create_table "Publishers", :id => false, :force => true do |t|
    t.column "PubID", :integer, :limit => 10,  :null => false
    t.column "Name",  :string,  :limit => 200, :default => "", :null => false
    t.column "URL",   :string,  :limit => 200
  end
```

Each table has a primary key field, which we'll have to explicitly set in our models since neither follows convention. Each has a name field, which stores the name of the company, and a URL field, which stores the URL to that company's home page.

We'll start off by once again removing the validation logic from these tables with a new migration:

```
ruby script/generate migration cleanup_devs_pubs
```

```
      exists  db/migrate
      create  db/migrate/003_cleanup_devs_pubs.rb
```

We'll edit that new migration (/db/migrate/003_cleanup_devs_pubs.rb) to remove the "no null" requirements from our name fields and the field length limits from the name and URL fields.

```
class CleanupDevsPubs < ActiveRecord::Migration
  def self.up
    change_column "Publishers", "Name", :string, :null => true
    change_column "Publishers", "URL",  :string
    change_column "Developers", "Name", :string, :null => true
    change_column "Developers", "URL",  :string
  end

  def self.down
    raise ActiveRecord::IrreversibleMigration
  end
end
```

We'll then run our new cleanup migration:

```
rake db:migrate
```

```
== CleanupDevsPubs: migrating ===========================
-- change_column("Publishers", "Name", :string, {:null=>true})
   -> 0.1365s
-- change_column("Publishers", "URL", :string)
   -> 0.0297s
-- change_column("Developers", "Name", :string, {:null=>true})
   -> 0.0402s
-- change_column("Developers", "URL", :string)
   -> 0.0567s
== CleanupDevsPubs: migrated (0.2637s) ===========================
```

With those validations removed, we can now create our models and add our validation logic to them:

```
ruby script/generate model Developer --skip-migration
```

```
exists   app/models/
exists   test/unit/
exists   test/fixtures/
create   app/models/developer.rb
create   test/unit/developer_test.rb
create   test/fixtures/developers.yml
```

```
ruby script/generate model Publisher --skip-migration
```

```
exists   app/models/
exists   test/unit/
exists   test/fixtures/
create   app/models/publisher.rb
create   test/unit/publisher_test.rb
create   test/fixtures/publishers.yml
```

As for the models, we'll apply the lessons we learned about the primary key from the Games table and set our primary keys correctly on the first pass this time. While we're at it, let's also create an association back to our game model (a developer would have many games and each game would belong to one developer) and add in the validations based on what was in the current schema.

Our developer model (/app/models/developer.rb) will look like this:

```
class Developer < ActiveRecord::Base
  set_table_name 'Developers'
  set_primary_key :DevID
  has_many :games, :foreign_key => 'DevID'

  validates_presence_of :Name
  validates_uniqueness_of :Name
  validates_length_of  :Name, :maximum => 200, :message => " must be less ➥
  than 200 characters"
  validates_length_of  :URL, :maximum => 200, :message => " must be less ➥
  than 200 characters"
  end
```

and our publisher model (/app/models/publisher.rb) will look like this:

```
class Publisher < ActiveRecord::Base
  set_table_name 'Publishers'
  set_primary_key :PubID
  has_many :games, :foreign_key => 'PubID'

  validates_presence_of :Name
  validates_uniqueness_of :Name
  validates_length_of  :Name, :maximum => 200, :message => " must be less ➥
  than 200 characters"
  validates_length_of  :URL, :maximum => 200, :message => " must be less ➥
  than 200 characters"
end
```

Let's also modify our game model to map to the publisher and developer models and add in some validations to require that we can't create a game without providing a Title and a Console that it's being released on:

```
class Game < ActiveRecord::Base
  set_table_name 'Games'
  set_primary_key :GameID
  belongs_to :publisher, :foreign_key => 'PubID'
  belongs_to :developer, :foreign_key => 'DevID'
  validates_length_of :Title, :maximum => 100, :message => " must be less ➥
  than 100 characters"
  validates_presence_of :Title, :Console
end
```

Saving all of our models and firing up a new console allows us to easily verify that our configuration is working correctly now:

```
ruby script/console
```

```
Loading development environment.
```

```
>> g = Game.find 123
```

```
=> #<Game:0x27f0e14 @attributes={"updated_at"=>"0000-00-00", "AddedBy"=>"0",
"ESRB"=>"E", "SiteURL"=>"http://www.sega.com/games/xbox/post_xboxgame.jhtml?
PRODID=10087", "BoximagePath"=>"shots/segasoccerslam.jpg", "Console"=>"Xbox",
"PubID"=>"8", "Title"=>"Soccer Slam", "GameID"=>"123", "GenreID"=>"6",
"DevID"=>"95", "created_at"=>"0000-00-00", "Description"=>"In Soccer Slam you'll
 unleash merciless kicks, tackles, and steals against excitable, colorful
characters from all over the world. Each character in this anything-but-ordinary
 soccer game wields special powers and moves that if executed properly earn
the big score"}
```

```
>> g.publisher.Name
```

```
=> "Sega"
```

```
>> g.developer.Name
```

```
=> "Visual Concepts"
```

```
>> g.publisher.id
```

```
=> 8
```

```
>> p = Publisher.find 8
```

```
=> #<Publisher:0x2728b30 @attributes={"Name"=>"Sega", "URL"=>
"http://www.sega.com/", "PubID"=>"8"}
```

```
>> p.games.count
```

```
=> 188
```

```
>> g.developer.id
```

```
=> 95
```

```
>> d = Developer.find 95
```

```
=> #<Developer:0x270a7fc @attributes={"Name"=>"Visual Concepts", "URL"=>
"http://www.segasports.com/", "DevID"=>"95"}
```

```
>> d.games.count
```

```
=> 83
```

Note The results that you get for the counts in the console session will differ from the results I listed in the examples, as I'm using the full 50MB database, and you'll be using a much smaller version from the source archive.

That takes care of our Developer and Publisher models; now we just have one foreign key relationship left to model—the genres table, which stores a list of genres (role playing, action, puzzle, etc.) that are used to categorize each game.

Creating Our Genres Model

The table schema for genres is once again very simple, merely a primary key and a genre name (as the TYPE field):

```
create_table "Genres", :id => false, :force => true do |t|
    t.column "GenreID", :integer, :null => false
    t.column "TYPE",    :string, :limit => 16, :default => "", :null => false
end
```

Once again, we'll want to clean up our database with a migration to remove the validation logic from the database:

```
ruby script/generate migration cleanup_genres
```

```
    exists  db/migrate
    create  db/migrate/004_cleanup_genres.rb
```

In this migration, we'll remove the null and field length requirements like this:

```
class CleanupGenres < ActiveRecord::Migration
  def self.up
    change_column "Genres", "TYPE", :string, :null => true
  end

  def self.down
    raise ActiveRecord::IrreversibleMigration
  end
end
```

Next, we'll run our cleanup_genres migration:

```
rake db:migrate
```

```
== CleanupGenres: migrating ==============================
change_column("Genres", "TYPE", :string, {:null=>true})
   -> 0.0494s
== CleanupGenres: migrated (0.0495s) =====================
```

At this point, we're ready to build our genre model:

```
ruby script/generate model Genre --skip-migration
```

```
    exists  app/models/
    exists  test/unit/
    exists  test/fixtures/
    create  app/models/genre.rb
    create  test/unit/genre_test.rb
    create  test/fixtures/genres.yml
```

We can edit the Genre model (/app/models/genre.rb) to define its table name and primary key, to recognize that one genre will have many games, and to place some validations onto the genres name. Your genre model should look like this:

```
class Genre < ActiveRecord::Base
  set_table_name 'Genres'
  set_primary_key :GenreID
  has_many :games, :foreign_key => "GenreID"
  validates_length_of :TYPE, :within => 1..16
  validates_uniqueness_of :TYPE
end
```

After creating the genre model, we'll also want to go back to our games model (/app/models/game.rb) and add our reciprocal belongs_to :genre method:

```
class Game < ActiveRecord::Base
  set_table_name 'Games'
  set_primary_key :GameID
  belongs_to :publisher, :foreign_key => 'PubID'
  belongs_to :developer, :foreign_key => 'DevID'
  belongs_to :genre, :foreign_key => 'GenreID'
  validates_length_of :Title, :maximum => 100, :message => " must be less than ➥
 100 characters"
  validates_presence_of :Title, :Console
end
```

By opening a new console window, or running reload! in an existing one to load in the new configuration, we should be able to easily view the associated genre for a game:

```
g = Game.find 123
```

```
=> #<Game:0xb7d1cb0 @attributes={"updated_at"=>"0000-00-00", "AddedBy"=>"0",
"ESRB"=>"E", "SiteURL"=>"http://www.sega.com/games/xbox/post_xboxgame.jhtml?
PRODID=10087", "BoximagePath"=>"shots/segasoccerslam.jpg", "Console"=>"Xbox",
"PubID"=>"8", "Title"=>"Soccer Slam", "GameID"=>"123", "GenreID"=>"6",
"DevID"=>"95", "created_at"=>"0000-00-00", "Description"=>"In Soccer Slam you'll
 unleash merciless kicks, tackles, and steals against excitable, colorful
characters from all over the world. Each character in this anything-but-ordinary
soccer game wields special powers and moves that if executed properly earn
the big score"}
```

```
>> g.genre.TYPE
```

```
=> "Sports"
```

```
>> genre = Genre.find 1
```

```
=> #<Genre:0xb7bdaf8 @attributes={"TYPE"=>"Action/Adventure", "GenreID"=>"1"}
```

```
>> genre.games.count
```

```
=> 2181
```

Setting Our Routes

Even though we're not building the new backend as a purely RESTful application, we can still benefit from some of the RESTful tools by using the map.resources method in our routes to generate the suite of friendly named routes. Open routes.rb in /config, and add the following lines.

```
ActionController::Routing::Routes.draw do |map|
  map.resources :games
  map.resources :publishers, :developers, :genres
  map.connect ':controller/:action/:id.:format'
  map.connect ':controller/:action/:id'
end
```

Creating Our Controllers

With our models built, our new administration system is now primed to connect to the legacy database and manage the existing records, so now it's time to build our controllers and views so we can start interacting with the data outside of simply using the interactive console.

By now, you've seen the value of building our controllers according to the philosophy of limiting ourselves to basic CRUD actions. We'll definitely want to take advantage of those benefits in this application as well—especially considering that our backend will need to respond to normal HTML requests as well as XML or JSON requests from the Ext front end. We'll start by generating our controllers with the following commands (output of each omitted):

```
ruby script/generate controller Publishers
ruby script/generate controller Developers
ruby script/generate controller Genres
ruby script/generate controller Games
```

At this point, we've got four new controllers that we need to populate with our standard RESTful actions, so we could do the usual boring thing and simply do a great big copy/paste and place slight variations of the following into each of them:

```
class GamesController < ApplicationController

  def index
    @games = Game.find(:all)

    respond_to do |format|
      format.html
      format.xml  { render :xml => @games.to_xml }
    end
  end
```

```ruby
def show
  @game = Game.find(params[:id])

  respond_to do |format|
    format.html
    format.xml  { render :xml => @game.to_xml }
  end
end

def new
  @game = Game.new
end

def edit
  @game = Game.find(params[:id])
end


def create
  @game = Game.new(params[:game])

  respond_to do |format|
    if @game.save
      flash[:notice] = 'Game was successfully created.'
      format.html { redirect_to game_url(@game) }
      format.xml  { head :created, :location => game_url(@game) }
    else
      format.html { render :action => "new" }
      format.xml  { render :xml => @game.errors.to_xml }
    end
  end
end


def update
  @game = Game.find(params[:id])

  respond_to do |format|
    if @game.update_attributes(params[:game])
      flash[:notice] = 'Game was successfully updated.'
      format.html { redirect_to game_url(@game) }
      format.xml  { head :ok }
```

```
      else
        format.html { render :action => "edit" }
        format.xml  { render :xml => @game.errors.to_xml }
      end
    end
  end

  def destroy
    @game = Game.find(params[:id])
    @game.destroy

    respond_to do |format|
      format.html { redirect_to games_url }
      format.xml  { head :ok }
    end
  end
end
```

That sure feels like a lot of duplication, doesn't it? It's not so bad when we use the scaffold_resource generator to build all those methods, but when faced with building them manually, the very idea of doing all that copying and pasting just makes me feel dirty inside. It sure seems like there should be a better way, doesn't it?

Well, there have been a number of attempts by different developers to come up with a solution for all that duplication; most of them have met with limited success at providing a DRY solution to RESTful controllers while maintaining the necessary flexibility to be useful in more than the most generic applications. One new solution seems to fill that need through the make_resourceful plug-in that was first announced at RailsConf 2007 by Hampton Caitlin (you can view the presentation slides of that announcement at http://www.hamptoncatlin.com/assets/2007/5/21/make_resourceful.pdf). With the make_resourceful plug-in installed, our games controller could be reduced to simply this:

```
class GamesController < ApplicationController
  make_resourceful do
    build :all
  end
end
```

That's much simpler, isn't it? Yet taking it even further is the fact that the make_resourceful plug-in also features a tremendous amount of additional flexibility, which you can see in the announcement presentation, to adapt to our applications needs. For now, though, let's see how we can use it within our application. Obviously, the first step to doing that will be to install the plug-in:

```
ruby script/plugin install http://svn.hamptoncatlin.com/make_resourceful/trunk
```

```
+ ./trunk/LICENSE
+ ./trunk/README
+ ./trunk/Rakefile
+ ./trunk/generators/resourceful_scaffold/resourceful_scaffold_generator.rb
+ ./trunk/generators/resourceful_scaffold/templates/controller.rb
+ ./trunk/generators/resourceful_scaffold/templates/functional_test.rb
+ ./trunk/generators/resourceful_scaffold/templates/helper.rb
+ ./trunk/generators/resourceful_scaffold/templates/layout.haml
+ ./trunk/generators/resourceful_scaffold/templates/partial.haml
+ ./trunk/generators/resourceful_scaffold/templates/view_edit.haml
+ ./trunk/generators/resourceful_scaffold/templates/view_form.haml
+ ./trunk/generators/resourceful_scaffold/templates/view_index.haml
+ ./trunk/generators/resourceful_scaffold/templates/view_new.haml
+ ./trunk/generators/resourceful_scaffold/templates/view_show.haml
+ ./trunk/init.rb
(...Lines Ommitted...)
```

After a quick restart of our web server, we can now build our four controllers the make_resourceful way. The games controller at /app/controllers/games_controller.rb will look like this initially:

```
class GamesController < ApplicationController
  make_resourceful do
    build :all
  end
end
```

The developers controller at /app/controllers/developers_controller.rb will look like this initially:

```
class DevelopersController < ApplicationController
  make_resourceful do
    build :all
  end
end
```

The publishers controller at /app/controllers/publishers_controller.rb will look like this:

```
class PublishersController < ApplicationController
  make_resourceful do
    build :all
  end
end
```

And finally, the genres controller at `/app/controllers/genres_controller.rb` will look like this:

```
class GenresController < ApplicationController
  make_resourceful do
    build :all
  end
end
```

Creating Our Views

We're in a really good position now. Our models are mapped to the database tables, and thanks to `make_resourceful`, our controllers are now configured to support all the common actions that we might need to perform on our models. So the sky is really the limit for what we want to do with the view templates. As I stated when we started this project, we're going to be using the Ext-JS framework to build our views and take them to a whole new dimension beyond the old administration system.

A Standard Layout

The first thing we should do is build a common layout that will be used by all of our site's pages. Create a new file named `application.rhtml` in `/app/views/layouts`. In this layout, we'll include all of our Ext JavaScript files and style sheets, a common header logo, and our standard navigation links for the application.

One important thing to keep in mind when using Ext is that it's very important to load the JavaScript files that you'll use in the correct order. To ensure that we do that correctly in this layout and any future layouts that we may add, I like to build a helper method that will add in the appropriate files. Open `application_helper.rb` in `/app/helpers/`, and add the following methods, which will add our Ext and Prototype JavaScript files in the correct order:

```
module ApplicationHelper

  def ext_javascript_tags
    sources = %w(prototype effects dragdrop controls ext-prototype-adapter ext-all)
    sources.collect do |source|
      source = javascript_path(source)
      content_tag("script", "", { "type" => "text/javascript", "src" => source })
    end.join("\n")
  end
end
```

When called from our layout, that helper method will essentially generate the following:

```
<script src="/javascripts/prototype.js?1178311282" type="text/javascript"></script>
<script src="/javascripts/effects.js?1178311282" type="text/javascript"></script>
<script src="/javascripts/dragdrop.js?1186705127" type="text/javascript"></script>
<script src="/javascripts/controls.js?1186705127" type="text/javascript"></script>
```

```
<script src="/javascripts/ext-prototype-adapter.js?1185915690" ➡
type="text/javascript"></script>
<script src="/javascripts/ext-all.js?1185915726" type="text/javascript"></script>
```

But why stop with just generating the necessary includes for our JavaScript files? In Ext, we also have a number of style sheets that we can use. So why not build a similar method for including our style sheets? In it, we'll include the ext-all.css style sheet, which provides all the standard formatting for the Ext widgets. Also, since we're going to be using the Vista theme that's included with Ext, we'll include the xtheme-vista.css style sheet, and for extra measure, we'll also include the blank style sheet for our own styles that we copied over in our generator. We'll name this helper method ext_stylesheet_tags:

```ruby
module ApplicationHelper

  def ext_javascript_tags
    sources = %w(prototype effects dragdrop controls ext-prototype-adapter ext-all)
    sources.collect do |source|
      source = javascript_path(source)
      content_tag("script", "", { "type" => "text/javascript", "src" => source })
    end.join("\n")
  end

  def ext_stylesheet_tags
    sources = %w(ext-all.css xtheme-vista.css application.css)
    sources.collect do |source|
      source = stylesheet_path(source)
      tag("link", { "rel" => "Stylesheet", "type" => "text/css",
                    "media" => "screen", "href" => source })
    end.join("\n")
  end
end
```

So with our helper methods ready, we can use them in our newly created application.rhtml layout that looks like this:

```html
<!DOCTYPE html PUBLIC "-//W3C//DTD XHTML 1.0 Transitional//EN"
  "http://www.w3.org/TR/xhtml1/DTD/xhtml1-transitional.dtd">
<html xmlns="http://www.w3.org/1999/xhtml" xml:lang="en" lang="en">
<head>
  <meta http-equiv="content-type" content="text/html;charset=UTF-8" />
  <%= ext_javascript_tags %>
  <%= ext_stylesheet_tags %>
</head>
<body>
  <div id='header' class="ylayout-inactive-content">
    <%= image_tag 'logo.gif' %>
  </div>
```

```
<%= yield  %>

<div id="sidebar" class="ylayout-inactive-content">
  <div id="sidebar-nav">
    <%= link_to image_tag('button_news.gif'), :controller => "news" %><br />
    <%= link_to image_tag('button_games.gif'), :controller => 'games' %><br />
    <%= link_to image_tag('button_publishers.gif'), :controller => "publishers" %>
    <br />
    <%= link_to image_tag('button_developers.gif'), :controller => "developers" %>
    <br />
    <%= link_to image_tag('button_genres.gif'), :controller => "genres" %><br />
  </div>
</div>
</body>
</html>
```

Enhancing Our Layout with Ext Border Layout

As we discussed in the previous chapter, Ext includes a very powerful widget named border layout that allows us to easily put together an advanced interface with some very simple
JavaScript. We'll want to use that to convert our simple block elements in our layout into something that will give us an impressive look and feel. So what is it that we want to build? Well, in
our layout that we just built, we defined a header div, a navigation div, and a block that we yield
to for each page's content. Putting together a rough sketch of our application, I came up with
Figure 19-1.

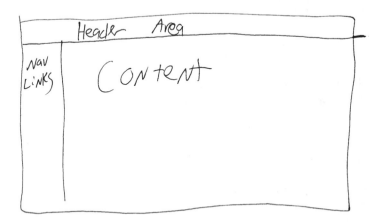

Figure 19-1. *A rough sketch of our general layout*

Building a page like this in Ext-JS is as easy as pie. We can even add interactivity to the navigation area by making it collapsible. We could build a page layout configuration using border layout like this:

```
var PageLayout = function() {
  var layout;
  return{
    init : function(){
      var layout = new Ext.BorderLayout(document.body, {
        north: {
          split:false,
          initialSize:65
        },
        center: {
          titlebar: true,
          autoScroll:true
        },
        west: {
          initialSize: 125,
          minSize: 125,
          maxSize:125,
          titlebar: true,
          split:true,
          collapsible:true,
          animate:true
        }
      });
      layout.beginUpdate();
      layout.add('north', new Ext.ContentPanel('header'));
      layout.add('center', new Ext.ContentPanel('content', {title:'Games'}));
      layout.add('west', new Ext.ContentPanel('sidebar', {title: 'Navigation'}));
      layout.endUpdate();
    }
  };
}();
Ext.EventManager.onDocumentReady(PageLayout.init, PageLayout, true);
```

To maintain a consistent look and feel throughout the application, all we have to do is add that border layout configuration to each page in our application. There's one important thing to note however: the line that adds a content div to the border layouts center area:

```
layout.add('center', new Ext.ContentPanel('content', {title:'Games'}));
```

also defines a title for that center block area, which we'll probably want to customize on each page to reflect the context of that specific page. We have a number of options for how we could add this border layout to our application:

- We could simply copy and paste the border layout configuration into every single page, modifying the header as necessary—*blech!*

- We could place the border layout into its own JavaScript file that we include in the page; however, that would make customizing the content header a pain in the rear.

- We could place the JavaScript into a partial that's included in each page. Doing that, we pass in the custom header using a local variable in the partial call. This solution's workable, but it's definitely been hit a couple of times with the ugly stick.

- We could place the JavaScript code in the application layout and pass in the custom header as an instance variable—not a bad idea but it does add some noise to our layout.

- We could generate a helper method that generates this JavaScript in each view template.

Of all those options, I like creating a new helper method the best, as it feels like the cleanest solution for this need. So open `application_helper.rb` in /app/helpers, and add the following method, which merely generates the same border layout configuration we created previously and accepts a single parameter that will be used to popualte the content header:

```
def ext_layout(titlebar)
    function = "var PageLayout = function() {"
    function << "var layout;"
    function << "return{"
    function << "init : function(){"
    function << "var layout = new Ext.BorderLayout(document.body, {"
    function << "north: {split:false,initialSize:65},"
    function << "center: {titlebar: true,autoScroll:true},"
    function << "west: {initialSize: 125,minSize: 125, maxSize:125,titlebar: ➥
true, split:true, collapsible:true, animate:true}"
    function << "});"
    function << "layout.beginUpdate();"
    function << "layout.add('north', new Ext.ContentPanel('header'));"
    function << "layout.add('center', new Ext.ContentPanel('content', ➥
{title:'#{titlebar}'}));"
    function << "layout.add('west', new Ext.ContentPanel('sidebar', ➥
{title: 'Navigation'}));"
    function << "layout.endUpdate();"
    function << "}};}();"
    function << "Ext.EventManager.onDocumentReady(PageLayout.init, ➥
PageLayout, true);"
    javascript_tag(function)
  end
```

Let's test our new helper method (and see our border layout) by creating a simple view template. Create a new file named index.rhtml in /app/views/games, and place this content inside it:

```
<%= ext_layout('Games') %>

<div id="content"> </div>
```

Save the files, and fire up your web server; you should then be able to go to http://localhost:3000/games and see the frame of our new administration system (see Figure 19-2).

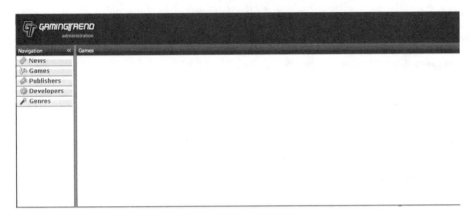

Figure 19-2. *Administration interface built with Ext border layout*

I'm always impressed by how simple it is to use border layout and how it feels more like I'm defining a configuration for a layout rather than writing JavaScript. You can also see in that screenshot that when we passed the string "Games" to the ext_layout helper method, this string shows up in the title bar directly over our content. Now that our application's layout is ready, let's take a momemt to further define how the new administration system should work and then get to work building some of the view templates so we can start using our application.

Defining the Workflow

With a standard layout defined for our application, we'll now turn our attention toward defining how we want the workflow of our application to go. Because each page in the previous administration system was its own mini application, there was a fair amount of inconsistency in how things worked from page to page. We're going to go exactly the opposite way in our application by creating a common system that will be used to manage all of the resources (games, publishers, genres, etc.) of the gaming site. As users go from page to page, they should always be presented with pages that are as similar in appearance and functionality as possible. Let's define how we're going to solve some of the common actions (such as listing a resource, editing a resource, etc.) in the following sections.

Listing the Current Resource

Obviously, we need to provide a way for staff members to view a list of all resources within the database, and the Ext grid components are the perfect solution to attractively and efficiently solve that problem. We'll be utilizing Ext grids on the index page of each resource (see Figure 19-3).

Title	Console
Final Fantasy Fables: Chocobo Tales	DS
Final Fantasy I & II: Dawn of Souls	GBA
Final Fantasy II	PSP
Final Fantasy III	DS
Final Fantasy IV	GBA
Final Fantasy Tactics Advance	GBA
Final Fantasy Tactics: The War of the Lions	PSP
Final Fantasy V Advance	GBA
Final Fantasy Versus XIII	ps3
Final Fantasy VI Advance	GBA
Final Fantasy VII: Dirge of Cerberus	PS2
Final Fantasy X	PS2
Final Fantasy X-2	PS2
Final Fantasy XI	360
Final Fantasy XI	PS2
Final Fantasy XI: Treasures of Art Urhgan	PC
Final Fantasy XI: Treasures of Art Urhgan	PS2
Final Fantasy XI: Chains of Promathia	PC
Final Fantasy XI: Chains of Promathia	PS2
Final Fantasy XI: The Vana'diel Collection	PC

Figure 19-3. *We'll use Ext grids to display a list of records.*

Creating a New Resource

We'll make the process of creating a new resource easily available by adding a button to the toolbar above each grid component (see Figure 19-4).

Figure 19-4. *A button to add a new record*

When that button is clicked, we'll pop open a dialog over the page that will provide the necessary fields to quickly and easily create a new record in the database.

Deleting a Specific Resource

Following the same logic as adding a new record, we'll make removing a record from the database easily accessible by adding a second button to the toolbar (see Figure 19-5).

Figure 19-5. *Adding a delete record button to the toolbar*

Clicking this button will first check that a row in the grid has been highlighted. If one hasn't, we'll open a message box alerting the user about the error.

If a row has been selected, we'll open a confirmation message box asking the user to confirm that this record should truly be deleted, and we'll only delete the record if the user clicks the yes button.

Editing a Specific Resource

Finally, for editing a record in the database, we'll attach an event handler onto the grid rows such that, if a user double-clicks any of the rows, we'll navigate the browser to the show template for the record that was double-clicked. That show template will need to be configured to support features such as in-place editing, so that the record can be both viewed and edited from the same place.

That show page will also have to be customized a bit, depending on the needs of each resource, but we'll try and keep things fairly consistent in our efforts here.

Building the Developer Pages

So with a basic understanding of how the system should work, we'll kick off the development of our view templates by first discussing how we can build the workflow in Ext for one of our resources. We'll then take that discussion and build some helper methods to simplify our deployment of that workflow to all the pages. We'll start by focusing on the needs of one of the reference tables—the developers model.

Listing Our Developers

The first problem that we'll address is the process of building an Ext grid to list all of our developers in the index page. Create a new file named `index.rhtml` in `/app/views/developers`, and place the following content into it to generate our surrounding layout:

```
<%= ext_layout('Developers') %>

<div id="content"> </div>
```

Adding a grid to the page is a fairly easy task; we'll start by defining a new empty JavaScript object named `pageGrid`, which will be used to build all of our functionality. Within this `pageGrid` object, we'll define a grid and a data store (`ds`) variable that will be used to reference the grid and data store objects from within all the various functions that we'll add. We'll also build a shell of this object's initialization with the `init` function. Finally, we'll close this block by calling an event handler to create our pageGrid object once the page is ready (i.e., when the page has fully loaded). Putting that all together will look like this:

```
<%= ext_layout('Developers') %>

<script type="text/javascript" charset="utf-8">
var pageGrid = function() {
  var grid;
  var ds;
  return{
    init : function(){
    }
  };
  Ext.onReady(pageGrid.init, pageGrid, true);
</script>

<div id="content"> </div>
```

You may recall, from our previous discussion on Ext grids, that the grid component displays a data store object, which can be configured to read its data from XML, JSON, a JavaScript array, and so on. So our next step is to establish a new Ext data store into which we'll pass two objects: We'll pass in a data proxy object specified as an HTTP proxy that will be used to pull back to the XML format of our developers list from Rails (proxy: new Ext.data.HttpProxy({url: 'developers.xml'})). Second, we'll pass in a reader object that is used to interpret the XML list of developers and map the fields that we're interested in into elements we can use in the grid (reader: new Ext.data.XmlReader({record: 'developer', id: 'DevID'}, ['DevID', 'Name', 'URL']). Putting that together will look like this:

```
ds = new Ext.data.Store({
  proxy: new Ext.data.HttpProxy({url: 'developers.xml'}),
  reader: new Ext.data.XmlReader({
    record: 'developer',
    id: 'DevID'
  }, [ 'DevID', 'Name', 'URL'])
});
```

Next, we'll establish the column model, which defines the fields that we'll display on the grid and how they'll look. You'll notice that it uses the data fields that we defined in the previous reader object. For good measure, we'll also set defaultSortable to true to enable client-side sorting of the records in the grid:

```
var cm = new Ext.grid.ColumnModel([
  {header: "Name", width: 300, dataIndex: 'Name'},
  {header: "URL", width: 250, dataIndex: 'URL'}
]);
cm.defaultSortable = true;
```

Now that all of our data is defined, we build the new grid on our page by creating a new Grid object and passing it its destination container, our data store, and the column model objects and then calling render on it.

```
grid = new Ext.grid.Grid('content', { ds: ds, cm: cm });
grid.render();
```

Finally, we call the ds.load method to make the request to the /developers.xml URL and pull in our list of developers, so the current developers index page (/app/views/developers/index.rhtml) should look like this:

```
<%= ext_layout('Developers') %>

<script type="text/javascript" charset="utf-8">
var pageGrid = function() {
  var grid;
  var ds;
  return{
    init : function(){
      ds = new Ext.data.Store({
        proxy: new Ext.data.HttpProxy({url: 'developers.xml'}),
        reader: new Ext.data.XmlReader({
          record: 'developer',
          id: 'DevID'
        }, [ 'DevID', 'Name', 'URL'])
      });

      var cm = new Ext.grid.ColumnModel([
        {header: "Name", width: 300, dataIndex: 'Name'},
        {header: "URL", width: 250, dataIndex: 'URL'}
      ]);
      cm.defaultSortable = true;

      grid = new Ext.grid.Grid('content', { ds: ds, cm: cm });
      grid.render();

      ds.load();
    }
  }
}();
  Ext.onReady(pageGrid.init, pageGrid, true);
</script>

<div id="content"> </div>
```

But the page won't work just yet, as we still have one more change to make—this time to our controller. You see, when we used the make_resourceful plug-in to build out RESTful controllers, it built the full suite of RESTful actions but only for standard HTML requests. We need to configure it to return an XML representation using the `response_for` method, so open /app/controllers/developers_controller.rb, and edit it to look like this:

```
class DevelopersController < ApplicationController

  make_resourceful do
    build :all

    response_for :index do |format|
      format.html {}
      format.xml { render :xml => @developers.to_xml }
    end
  end
end
```

If we open our web browser again and view `http://localhost:3000/developers`, our page now displays a basic grid of all of our developers (see Figure 19-6).

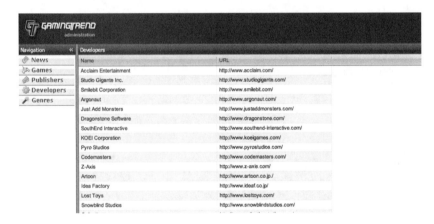

Figure 19-6. *Ext grid added to our Developers index page*

Unfortunately, we have a small problem with this page, as it's returning its results in order of DevID instead of by name. If we had built the `index` method, we could fix this by simply adding an order parameter to our finder like this:

```
@developers = Developer.find(:all, :order => 'Name ASC')
```

But what would be really cool is if we could define the default order that records should be returned in the model. While there are no methods within Rails that provide that functionality; fortunately, there is a plug-in that we can use by the name of the `default_order` plug-in. Unfortunately, at the time of this writing, the only way to install it is to check out the code from the Subversion repository, which you can do by opening a command prompt at the root of your application and running the subversion checkout command:

```
svn co http://svn.gwikzone.org/public/default_order/trunk vendor/plugins ➥
/default_order
```

```
A    vendor/plugins/default_order/trunk
A    vendor/plugins/default_order/trunk/test
A    vendor/plugins/default_order/trunk/test/default_order_test.rb
A    vendor/plugins/default_order/trunk/Rakefile
A    vendor/plugins/default_order/trunk/init.rb
A    vendor/plugins/default_order/trunk/lib
A    vendor/plugins/default_order/trunk/lib/default_order.rb
A    vendor/plugins/default_order/trunk/README
Checked out revision 2.
```

With the plug-in installed, we can now define the default order for any model by adding an order_by call to our models. So let's add that functionality to each of our models. We'll fix the developers model (/app/models/developer.rb) like this:

```
class Developer < ActiveRecord::Base
  set_table_name 'Developers'
  set_primary_key :DevID
  has_many :games, :foreign_key => 'DevID'
  order_by "Name"

  validates_presence_of :Name
  validates_uniqueness_of :Name
  validates_length_of  :Name, :maximum => 200, :message => " must be less ➥
than 200 characters"
  validates_length_of  :URL, :maximum => 200, :message => " must be less ➥
than 200 characters"
end
```

The publishers model (/app/models/publisher.rb) will be nearly identical and will also sort by name:

```
class Publisher < ActiveRecord::Base
  set_table_name 'Publishers'
  set_primary_key :PubID
  has_many :games, :foreign_key => 'PubID'
  order_by "Name"

  validates_presence_of :Name
  validates_uniqueness_of :Name
  validates_length_of  :Name, :maximum => 200, :message => " must be less ➥
than 200 characters"
  validates_length_of  :URL, :maximum => 200, :message => " must be less ➥
than 200 characters"
end
```

We'll sort the genres model (/app/models/genre.rb) by the genre type:

```
class Genre < ActiveRecord::Base
  set_table_name 'Genres'
  set_primary_key :GenreID
  order_by "TYPE"

  has_many :games, :foreign_key => "GenreID"
  validates_length_of :TYPE, :within => 1..16
  validates_uniqueness_of :TYPE
end
```

And finally, we'll sort the games model (/app/models/game.rb) by the game title:

```
class Game < ActiveRecord::Base
  set_table_name 'Games'
  set_primary_key :GameID
  belongs_to :publisher, :foreign_key => 'PubID'
  belongs_to :developer, :foreign_key => 'DevID'
  belongs_to :genre, :foreign_key => 'GenreID'
  order_by :title

  validates_length_of :Title, :maximum => 100, :message => " must be  ➡
less than 100 characters"
  validates_presence_of :Title, :Console
end
```

After restarting our web server and saving all those models, a quick refresh of our developers index page reveals that our page is now sorting the developers correctly.

Editing a Developer

As long as we have our grid loaded, let's add the functionality to it that will enable double-clicking a row in the grid to cause the browser to navigate to the show view for this selected record. We do this by first adding an event listener onto our grid for a double-click that will call the editResource method:

```
grid.on('rowdblclick', editResource);
```

Of course, we'll need to build an editResource method for this to work, which we'll add at the bottom of our pageGrid. The editResource method should be fairly simple; we'll simply grab the currently selected grid row and change the browser's destination with a window.location.href call:

```
function editResource(grid, rowIndex) {
  var id = grid.getSelectionModel().getSelected();
  if(id) {
    window.location.href = 'developers/' + id.get('DevID');
  }
}
```

So our current script in /app/view/developers/index.rhtml looks like this:

```
<script type="text/javascript" charset="utf-8">
var pageGrid = function() {
  var grid;
  var ds;
  return{
    init : function(){
      ds = new Ext.data.Store({
        proxy: new Ext.data.HttpProxy({url: 'developers.xml'}),
        reader: new Ext.data.XmlReader({
          record: 'developer',
          id: 'DevID'
        }, [ 'DevID', 'Name', 'URL'])
      });

      var cm = new Ext.grid.ColumnModel([
        {header: "Name", width: 300, dataIndex: 'Name'},
        {header: "URL", width: 250, dataIndex: 'URL'}
      ]);
      cm.defaultSortable = true;

      grid = new Ext.grid.Grid('content', { ds: ds, cm: cm });
      grid.render();

      ds.load();

      grid.on('rowdblclick', editResource);
    }
  }
  function editResource(grid, rowIndex) {
    var id = grid.getSelectionModel().getSelected();
    if(id) {
      window.location.href = 'developers/' + id.get('DevID');
    }
  }
}();
Ext.onReady(pageGrid.init, pageGrid, true);
</script>
```

Of course, we haven't built the show page yet, so double-clicking the grids won't do anything useful for us at the moment, but that functionality is ready for us once we do add that show template.

Enhancing the Grid

Before we go any further in our implementation, I'm really annoyed by the fact that the grid, in its current state, is pulling down an awfully big list of developers to display (over 1,000 in the full database). With that many records getting down to a developer whose name begins with the letter "S" currently involves a painful amount of scrolling. Not to mention that pulling down all those records is causing the load time for the grid to be increased to a near uncomfortable level. Enhancing our grid to support pagination can solve both of those problems, so let's go through that process now.

Adding Pagination

To support paging of our records, we're going to have to make a number of changes to our current implementation. Our first step is that to support pagination we need to convert our finder to support two new parameters that will be passed with each query from Ext's paginator: a limit parameter will be used to determine the number of records that should be returned, and a start parameter will be used to determine the starting point (or offset) for the first row to be returned. In our controller (/app/controllers/developers_controller.rb), we'll capture those parameters like this:

```
limit =  params[:limit] || 25
start = params[:start] || 0
```

Second, we'll have to modify the way that the finder in the index method works by writing it to utilize our limit and start parameters:

```
@developers = Developer.find(:all, :limit => limit, :offset => start )
```

Next, we'll need to provide an additional field in the response that we send from Rails that will contain the total number of records in the collection; Ext can use that count to determine the number of possible pages. We'll name this field totalCount, and it will need to be provided before the collection of developers in our response. While it's possible to add this totalCount field to our XML response by overriding the default to_xml method in Rails, I've found that it's a significantly easier task if we use JSON as the transport mechanism instead. Using JSON also provides us with extra benefits: since it is a much more compact transport, it will also help speed up our response times. Adding JSON support will be a simple matter of adding a format.json block to our responses. In this block, we'll create a new hash and populate it with the data from our Developers collection and the count of all developer records before sending it back to the client with the to_json method:

```
format.json {
  griddata = Hash.new
  griddata[:developers] = @developers.collect {|d|
    {:DevID => d.DevID, :Name => d.Name, :URL => d.URL}}
  griddata[:totalCount] = Developer.count
  render :text => griddata.to_json()
}
```

So we could put all of this together in our /app/controllers/developers_controller.rb to look like this:

```
class DevelopersController < ApplicationController
  make_resourceful do
    build :all
  end

  def index
    limit =  params[:limit] || 25
    start = params[:start] || 0
    @developers = Developer.find(:all, :limit => limit, :offset => start )

    respond_to do |format|
      format.html
      format.json {
        griddata = Hash.new
        griddata[:developers] = @developers.collect {|d|
          {:DevID => d.DevID, :Name => d.Name, :URL => d.URL}}
        griddata[:totalCount] =  Developer.count
        render :text => griddata.to_json()
      }
    end
  end
end
```

You should notice that, in the preceding changes, we removed the response_for block and instead redefined our index method manually; we did this because of our need to modify the default finder to utilize the limit and start parameters in its query. This highlights another of the great features of the make_resourceful plug-in—we're able to overwrite any of its implementations with our own. However, there is a subtle problem with this implementation. Have you noticed it?

The problem comes in the fact that, in our workflow, a request will be made to the index method, which will follow the HTML path and display the index view template. This view (once we modify it) will generate a request back to this same index method for the JSON representation of our developers list. The problem with all of this, though, is that we're making a database hit to generate the list of developers during both requests (even though we don't do anything with it for the HTML response). We can fix this by simply moving that query into the format.json request like this:

```
class DevelopersController < ApplicationController
  make_resourceful do
    build :all
  end
```

```
def index
  limit = params[:limit] || 25
  start = params[:start] || 0

  respond_to do |format|
    format.html
    format.json {
      @developers = Developer.find(:all, :limit => limit, :offset => start )
      griddata = Hash.new
      griddata[:developers] = @developers.collect {|d|
        {:DevID => d.DevID, :Name => d.Name, :URL => d.URL}}
      griddata[:totalCount] = Developer.count
      render :text => griddata.to_json()
    }
  end
end
end
```

With our controller set to deliver a JSON response, we can modify the pageGrid object back in our index template (/app/views/developers/index.rhtml) to process the JSON and display our results paginated. The first step in doing that will be to change our reader object from an Xmlreader to a JsonReader instead. Within that reader, we'll also define that it should recognize our totalCount variable:

```
reader: new Ext.data.JsonReader({
  root: 'developers',
  totalProperty: 'totalCount',
  id: 'DevID'
  }, [ 'DevID', 'Name', 'URL'])
});
```

Next, we'll need to add a paging toolbar to our grid in the footer using the prebuilt one included with Ext:

```
var gridFoot = grid.getView().getFooterPanel(true);
var paging = new Ext.PagingToolbar(gridFoot, ds, {
  pageSize: 20,
  displayInfo: true,
  displayMsg: 'Displaying topics {0} - {1} of {2}',
  emptyMsg: 'No topics to display'
});
```

Finally, we'll need to modify our ds.load method to now pass along the start and limit parameters when it makes its initial request for data:

```
ds.load({params:{start:0, limit:20}});
```

After putting all of that together, our current pageGrid script should look like this:

```
<script type="text/javascript" charset="utf-8">
var pageGrid = function() {
  var grid;
  var ds;
  return{
    init : function(){
      ds = new Ext.data.Store({
        proxy: new Ext.data.HttpProxy({url: 'developers.json'}),
        reader: new Ext.data.JsonReader({
          root: 'developers',
          totalProperty: 'totalCount',
          id: 'DevID'
        }, [ 'DevID', 'Name', 'URL'])
      });

      var cm = new Ext.grid.ColumnModel([
        {header: "Name", width: 300, dataIndex: 'Name'},
        {header: "URL", width: 250, dataIndex: 'URL'}
      ]);
      cm.defaultSortable = true;

      grid = new Ext.grid.Grid('content', { ds: ds, cm: cm });
      grid.render();


      var gridFoot = grid.getView().getFooterPanel(true);
      var paging = new Ext.PagingToolbar(gridFoot, ds, {
        pageSize: 20,
        displayInfo: true,
        displayMsg: 'Displaying topics {0} - {1} of {2}',
        emptyMsg: 'No topics to display'
      });
      ds.load({params:{start:0, limit:20}});
```

```
        grid.on('rowdblclick', editResource);
    }
  }
  function editResource(grid, rowIndex) {
    var id = grid.getSelectionModel().getSelected();
    if(id) {
      window.location.href = 'developers/' + id.get('DevID');
    }
  }
}();
Ext.onReady(pageGrid.init, pageGrid, true);
</script>
```

Save the scripts, fire up your web browser to view the developers index page again, and voilà—we get an empty grid (albeit one with a paginating footer). Troubleshooting this issue requires a bit more detective work than usual, because in all actuality, the code is working correctly. The easiest way to see the problem is to view the page in the Firefox web browser and use what I feel is one of the greatest gifts to the web developer—the Firebug extension (http://www.getfirebug.com/). Firebug provides a wealth of features such as the ability to tweak live CSS, debug and profile JavaScript, log JavaScript errors, and on and on. Seriously, I can't imagine how I used to do web development before Firebug, so if you don't have it installed yet, you need to go get it right now. Another of the features that makes Firebug essential is that it allows you to view AJAX requests as they occur. The result of our ds.load method in Firebug is shown in Figure 19-7.

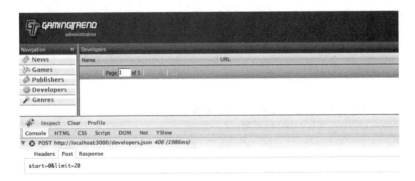

Figure 19-7. *Troubleshooting our error using Firebug*

If you recall our discussions of how RESTful routing works, you'll recall that in RESTful routing, it's not just the URLs that determine how the request is routed but the HTTP verb that's used as well. To access the index method of the developers controller, we need to use a GET request to /developers. However, the ds.load method is issuing the request as a POST (which would essentially cause the request to be routed to the create method). This happens because when we pass parameters to the ds.load method, Ext defaults to using the POST method (obviously, it wasn't designed around RESTful principles). Fortunately, this is a very easy fix, as all we need to do is make a small modification to our proxy object to use GET when it requests JSON representation of our developers.

```
proxy: new Ext.data.HttpProxy({method: 'GET', url: 'developers.json'}),
```

Make that change to our script, and reload the web page to see the fruits of our labors (as shown in Figure 19-8).

Developers	
Name	URL
#TBD	
10tacle studiosa	http://www.10tacle.com/
1C Company	http://int.games.1c.ru/
1C: Maddox Games	http://www.1c.ru/
1st Playable Productions	http://www.1stplayable.com/
2015	http://www.2015.com/
2by3 Games	http://www.2by3games.com
3000AD	http://www.3000ad.com/
369 Interactive	http://www.369interactive.com/
3D Ages	http://www.3d-ages.co.jp
3D Realms	http://www.3drealms.com/
3DO	http://www.3do.com
3G Studios	http://www.3gstudiosinc.com/
4 Kids Entertainment	www.4KidsEntertainment.com
49Games	http://www.49games-rz.com/index.php?id=147&L=
4A Games	http://www.4a-games.com/
4Head Studios	http://www.4head.de
4x Studio	http://www.4xstudio.com/
5000ft	http://www.5000ft.com/
7-Studios	http://www.sevenstudios.com/Welcome/welcomefr

Page 1 of 53 ▶ ▶| Displaying topics 1 - 20 of 1046

Figure 19-8. *Paginating our list of developers*

Adding a Filter

That pagination goes a long way toward making navigating our records easier, but getting to a specific record way back in the list can still be a bit of a pain. Let's fix that by enhancing the grid to support filtering the results. We'll start by first adding a text box to our grid that can be used by a user to enter a filter string.

```
var gridHead = grid.getView().getHeaderPanel(true);
var tb = new Ext.Toolbar(gridHead);
tb.add('-', 'Filter: ', "<input type='text' id='text_filter'>");
Ext.get('text_filter').on('keyup', filterResource);
```

In the preceding code, we first grabbed a reference to the header panel of grid, in which we then created a new Ext.Toolbar. Once we had that new toolbar, we added a text input to it and attached an event listener to call the filterResource method on it whenever the keyup event occurs (keyup is the event that is called whenever a keyboard key is pressed and released).

Now, let's build the filterResource method for handling our search.

```
function filterResource() {
  filtervalue = Ext.get('text_filter').dom.value;
  ds.proxy = new Ext.data.HttpProxy({method: 'GET', url: 'developers.json? ➥
search=' + filtervalue});
  ds.reload();
}
```

This method is pretty simple. We'll grab whatever text is currently in the filter box and then use this method as a search parameter as we redefine the proxy URL to pass our search text. Then, we reload the data store. At this point, the full script should look like this:

```
<script type="text/javascript" charset="utf-8">
var pageGrid = function() {
  var grid;
  var ds;
  return{
    init : function(){
      ds = new Ext.data.Store({
        proxy: new Ext.data.HttpProxy({url: 'developers.json'}),
        reader: new Ext.data.JsonReader({
          root: 'developers',
          totalProperty: 'totalCount',
          id: 'DevID'
        }, [ 'DevID', 'Name', 'URL'])
      });

      var cm = new Ext.grid.ColumnModel([
        {header: "Name", width: 300, dataIndex: 'Name'},
        {header: "URL", width: 250, dataIndex: 'URL'}
      ]);
      cm.defaultSortable = true;

      grid = new Ext.grid.Grid('content', { ds: ds, cm: cm });
      grid.render();


      var gridFoot = grid.getView().getFooterPanel(true);
      var paging = new Ext.PagingToolbar(gridFoot, ds, {
        pageSize: 20,
        displayInfo: true,
        displayMsg: 'Displaying topics {0} - {1} of {2}',
        emptyMsg: 'No topics to display'
      });
      ds.load({params:{start:0, limit:20}});

      grid.on('rowdblclick', editResource);
```

```
        var gridHead = grid.getView().getHeaderPanel(true);
        var tb = new Ext.Toolbar(gridHead);
        tb.add({ text: 'Create New Developer', handler: createResource }, '-', ➥
{ text: 'Delete Selected Developer', handler: deleteResource });
        tb.add('-', 'Filter: ', "<input type='text' id='text_filter'>");
        Ext.get('text_filter').on('keyup', filterResource);


    }
  }

  function filterResource() {
    filtervalue = Ext.get('text_filter').dom.value;
    ds.proxy = new Ext.data.HttpProxy({method: 'GET',
                        url: 'developers.json?search=' + filtervalue});
    ds.reload();
  }

  function editResource(grid, rowIndex) {
    var id = grid.getSelectionModel().getSelected();
    if(id) {
      window.location.href = 'developers/' + id.get('DevID');
    }
  }
}();
Ext.onReady(pageGrid.init, pageGrid, true);
</script>
```

Back in our developers controller, we need to modify our index method to also check for the presence of a search parameter:

```
def index
    limit =  params[:limit] || 25
    start = params[:start] || 0

    respond_to do |format|
      format.html
      format.json {
        if(params[:search])
          @developers = Developer.find(:all, :limit => limit, :offset => start,
            :conditions => ["Name like ?","%" + params[:search] + "%"])

          dev_count = Developer.count(:conditions => ["Name like ?","%" ➥
+ params[:search] + "%"])
        else
          @developers = Developer.find(:all, :limit => limit, :offset => start )
          dev_count = Developer.count
        end
```

```
        griddata = Hash.new
        griddata[:developers] = @developers.collect {|d|
          {:DevID => d.DevID, :Name => d.Name, :URL => d.URL}}
        griddata[:totalCount] = dev_count

        render :text => griddata.to_json()
      }
    end
  end
```

Our filtered results are shown in Figure 19-9.

Figure 19-9. *Filtering our results of developers*

Adding Buttons to Our Toolbar

With the enhancements to our grid navigation completed, we can get back to implementing our core functionality. All that we have left for this workflow is to add the ability to delete a record and the ability to create a new record. Since we already have a toolbar added to our grid, why don't we enhance it by placing buttons for those two functionalities onto the toolbar? We can do that easily by adding them with the add method within our existing toolbar definition:

```
var gridHead = grid.getView().getHeaderPanel(true);
var tb = new Ext.Toolbar(gridHead);

tb.add({ text: 'Create New Developer', handler: createResource }, '-', ➥
{ text: 'Delete Selected Developer', handler: deleteResource });

tb.add('-', 'Filter: ', "<input type='text' id='text_filter'>");
Ext.get('text_filter').on('keyup', filterResource);
```

Figure 19-10 shows what the buttons will look in our toolbar once we're done.

Figure 19-10. *Adding buttons to our toolbar*

■**Note** Of course, if you actually try to view the page without those functions defined, it will generate an error. So if you want to view the toolbar before we're done building the `createResource` and `deleteResource` functions, you'll need to define empty versions of the functions like this: `function createResource() {}` and `function deleteResource() {}` until we've populated them both.

Deleting a Developer

So what happens if a user clicks the delete button we just created? Nothing at the moment. Because, even though we set up the button to call a function named `deleteResource` when pressed, we haven't yet added the `deleteResource` function. So let's build it now:

```
function deleteResource() {
    var id = grid.getSelectionModel().getSelected();
    if(id){
      var news = id.get('DevID');
      Ext.MessageBox.confirm('Confirm', 'Are you sure you want to delete this ➥
Developer?', postDelete);
    } else {
      Ext.MessageBox.alert('DOH!', 'Maybe you want to try again after ACTUALLY ➥
selecting something?')
    }
  }
```

That function should be fairly easy to follow. Once the function is called, we grab the selected row from the grid. If a row has not been selected, we pop open a message box and let the user know (using what is hopefully perceived as a little bit of humor), as shown in Figure 19-11.

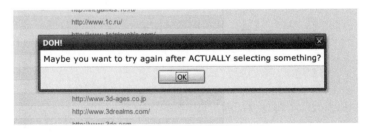

Figure 19-11. *Capturing a user error*

If a row has been selected, we simply prompt the user to confirm to the intention to delete this resource and then pass control to yet another function postDelete:

```
function postDelete(btn){
    if(btn == 'yes') {
      var id = grid.getSelectionModel().getSelected();
      var deleteme = id.get('DevID');
      window.location.href = '/developers/destroy/' + deleteme;
    }
  }
```

In postDelete, we check that the user did choose yes on the confirmation button, and if so, we redirect the page to our destroy method, which will destroy the specified resource and redirect the user to our current page.

Add those functions to our script, and it now looks like this:

```
<script type="text/javascript" charset="utf-8">
var pageGrid = function() {
  var grid;
  var ds;
  return{
    init : function(){
      ds = new Ext.data.Store({
        proxy: new Ext.data.HttpProxy({url: 'developers.json'}),
        reader: new Ext.data.JsonReader({
          root: 'developers',
          totalProperty: 'totalCount',
          id: 'DevID'
        }, [ 'DevID', 'Name', 'URL'])
      });

      var cm = new Ext.grid.ColumnModel([
        {header: "Name", width: 300, dataIndex: 'Name'},
        {header: "URL", width: 250, dataIndex: 'URL'}
      ]);
      cm.defaultSortable = true;

      grid = new Ext.grid.Grid('content', { ds: ds, cm: cm });
      grid.render();


      var gridFoot = grid.getView().getFooterPanel(true);
      var paging = new Ext.PagingToolbar(gridFoot, ds, {
        pageSize: 20,
        displayInfo: true,
        displayMsg: 'Displaying topics {0} - {1} of {2}',
        emptyMsg: 'No topics to display'
      });
```

```
        ds.load({params:{start:0, limit:20}});

        grid.on('rowdblclick', editResource);

        var gridHead = grid.getView().getHeaderPanel(true);
        var tb = new Ext.Toolbar(gridHead);
        tb.add({ text: 'Create New Developer', handler: createResource }, '-', ➥
{ text: 'Delete Selected Developer', handler: deleteResource });
        tb.add('-', 'Filter: ', "<input type='text' id='text_filter'>");
        Ext.get('text_filter').on('keyup', filterResource);

    }
  }

  function filterResource() {
    filtervalue = Ext.get('text_filter').dom.value;
    ds.proxy = new Ext.data.HttpProxy({method: 'GET',
                        url: 'developers.json?search=' + filtervalue});
    ds.reload();
  }

  function deleteResource() {
    var id = grid.getSelectionModel().getSelected();
    if(id){
      Ext.MessageBox.confirm('Confirm', 'Are you sure you want to delete this ➥
Developer?', postDelete);
    } else {
      Ext.MessageBox.alert('DOH!', 'Maybe you want to try again after ACTUALLY ➥
selecting something?')
    }
  }

  function postDelete(btn){
    if(btn == 'yes') {
      var id = grid.getSelectionModel().getSelected();
      var deleteme = id.get('DevID');
      window.location.href = '/developers/destroy/' + deleteme;
    }
  }

  function editResource(grid, rowIndex) {
    var id = grid.getSelectionModel().getSelected();
    if(id) {
      window.location.href = 'developers/' + id.get('DevID');
    }
  }
}();
```

```
Ext.onReady(pageGrid.init, pageGrid, true);
</script>
```

Creating a New Developer

The last feature we want to add to this page is the ability to open a dialog box to create a new developer. We'll build the content of the dialog for the form in the HTML structure of our page and merely use Ext to display it in a dialog when someone clicks the button, so in our index template (/app/developers/index.rhtml), add the following to the bottom:

```
<div id="newDialog">
  <div class="x-dlg-hd">Create New Developer</div>
  <div class="x-dlg-bd">
    <% form_for(:developer, Developer.new, :url => developers_path, :html =>
                {:id => 'create_resource', :name => 'create_resource'}) do |f| %>
    <p>
      <label for="developer_Name">Developer Name:</label>
      <%= f.text_field :Name %>
    </p>
    <p>
      <label for="develoer_URL">Developer Home Page</label>
      <%= f.text_field :URL %>
    </p>
  <% end %>
  </div>
</div>
```

We already added a button to our toolbar in our last step to launch the dialog. When the button is clicked, it calls the function createResource. Before we build that function, we need to add a variable to our pageGrid object—this one will store a reference to the dialog object that we can use to reference that value from anywhere in our code:

```
var pageGrid = function() {
  var grid;
  var dialog;
  var ds;
```

With that variable set, we can now build our createResource method like this:

```
function createResource() {
    if(!dialog) {
      dialog = new Ext.BasicDialog('newDialog', {
        width:300, height:170, shadow:true, minWidth:300, minHeight:170,
        proxyDrag:true, autoScroll:false, animEl:true
      });
```

```
    dialog.addKeyListener(27, dialog.hide, dialog);
    postBtn = dialog.addButton('Submit', submitResource, this);
    dialog.addButton('Close', dialog.hide, dialog);
    }

    dialog.show();
    dialog.on('hide', function(){
      document.create_resource.reset();
    })
  }
```

That function is a little bit bigger than our previous examples. Let's break down a few of the high points of this function. The first thing we do is check to see if we have a dialog created yet; if not, we'll create it from that form in our page:

```
if(!dialog) {
      dialog = new Ext.BasicDialog('newDialog', {
        width:300, height:170, shadow:true, minWidth:300, minHeight:170,
        proxyDrag:true, autoScroll:false, animEl:true
      });
```

Now that we have a dialog object created, we'll add a little functionality, including the ability to close the dialog box if the Esc key is pressed, and add a pair of buttons to our dialog. When a user clicks the submit button, it will call the submitResource function. If the user clicks the close button, we'll hide the dialog again.

```
dialog.addKeyListener(27, dialog.hide, dialog);
postBtn = dialog.addButton('Submit', submitResource, this);
dialog.addButton('Close', dialog.hide, dialog);
```

From here, we'll display the dialog and add in an event handler to reset the fields whenever the dialog is closed.

```
dialog.show();
    dialog.on('hide', function(){
      document.create_resource.reset();
    })
```

All that's left is to add in our submitResource function, and we'll have completed this functionality. Our submitResource function doesn't have to do anything fancy, merely submit the form.

```
function submitResource(){
  document.create_resource.submit();
}
```

The Create New Developer dialog box is shown in Figure 19-12.

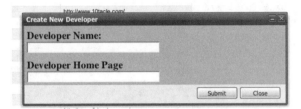

Figure 19-12. *Pop-up dialog box to create a new developer*

Abstracting Our Workflow into a Helper

We added quite a lot of functionality to support in the previous section. However, it required us to build a fairly substantial amount of code. That wouldn't be too much of an issue if it wasn't going to be duplicated, but we've already stated that we want to be able to use pretty much an identical set of code to also manage the index pages for other resources in our application such as the Publishers, Genres, and Games resources.

Let's take another look at the final version of our index page for developers (/app/views/developers/index.rhtml):

```
<%= ext_layout('Developers') %>

<script type="text/javascript" charset="utf-8">
var pageGrid = function() {
  var grid;
  var dialog;
  var ds;
  return{
    init : function(){
      ds = new Ext.data.Store({
        proxy: new Ext.data.HttpProxy({method: 'GET', url: 'developers.json'}),
        reader: new Ext.data.JsonReader({
          root: 'developers',
          totalProperty: 'totalCount',
          id: 'DevID'
        }, [ 'DevID', 'Name', 'URL'])
      });

      var cm = new Ext.grid.ColumnModel([
        {header: "Name", width: 300, dataIndex: 'Name'},
        {header: "URL", width: 250, dataIndex: 'URL'}
      ]);
      cm.defaultSortable = true;
```

```
      grid = new Ext.grid.Grid('content', { ds: ds, cm: cm });
      grid.render();


      var gridFoot = grid.getView().getFooterPanel(true);
      var paging = new Ext.PagingToolbar(gridFoot, ds, {
        pageSize: 20,
        displayInfo: true,
        displayMsg: 'Displaying topics {0} - {1} of {2}',
        emptyMsg: 'No topics to display'
      });
      ds.load({params:{start:0, limit:20}});

      grid.on('rowdblclick', editResource);

      var gridHead = grid.getView().getHeaderPanel(true);
      var tb = new Ext.Toolbar(gridHead);
      tb.add({ text: 'Create New Developer', handler: createResource }, '-', ➥
{ text: 'Delete Selected Developer', handler: deleteResource });
      tb.add('-', 'Filter: ', "<input type='text' id='text_filter'>");
      Ext.get('text_filter').on('keyup', filterResource);


    }
  }

  function filterResource() {
    filtervalue = Ext.get('text_filter').dom.value;
    ds.proxy = new Ext.data.HttpProxy({method: 'GET',
                       url: 'developers.json?search=' + filtervalue});
    ds.reload();
  }

  function submitResource(){
    document.create_resource.submit();
  }

  function createResource() {
    if(!dialog) {
      dialog = new Ext.BasicDialog('newDialog', {
        width:300, height:170, shadow:true, minWidth:300, minHeight:170,
        proxyDrag:true, autoScroll:false, animEl:true
      });
    dialog.addKeyListener(27, dialog.hide, dialog);
    postBtn = dialog.addButton('Submit', submitResource, this);
    dialog.addButton('Close', dialog.hide, dialog);
    }
```

```
      dialog.show();
      dialog.on('hide', function(){
        document.create_resource.reset();
      })
    }

  function deleteResource() {
    var id = grid.getSelectionModel().getSelected();
    if(id){
      Ext.MessageBox.confirm('Confirm', 'Are you sure you want to delete this ➥
Developer?', postDelete);
    } else {
      Ext.MessageBox.alert('DOH!', 'Maybe you want to try again after ACTUALLY ➥
selecting something?')
    }
  }

  function postDelete(btn){
    if(btn == 'yes') {
      var id = grid.getSelectionModel().getSelected();
      var deleteme = id.get('DevID');
      window.location.href = '/developers/destroy/' + deleteme;
    }
  }

  function editResource(grid, rowIndex) {
    var id = grid.getSelectionModel().getSelected();
    if(id) {
      window.location.href = 'developers/' + id.get('DevID');
    }
  }
}();
Ext.onReady(pageGrid.init, pageGrid, true);
</script>
<div id="content"> </div>

<div id="newDialog">
  <div class="x-dlg-hd">Create New Developer</div>
  <div class="x-dlg-bd">
    <% form_for(:developer, Developer.new, :url => developers_path,
        :html => {:id => 'create_resource', :name => 'create_resource'}) do |f| %>
      <p>
        <label for="developer_Name">Developer Name:</label>
        <%= f.text_field :Name %>
      </p>
```

```
  <p>
    <label for="developer_URL">Developer Home Page</label>
    <%= f.text_field :URL %>
  </p>
<% end %>
</div>
</div>
```

Sigh—that's an awful lot of code to copy and paste from index page to index page, and it sure adds a lot of visual noise to our template. Since I knew that was code that we were going to want to repeat, I did try and be a little more generic in the names of the function by naming them things like `deleteResource` rather than `deleteDeveloper`. By doing that, there's a lot less within these blocks of code that will need to be modified when we reuse them—mainly just things like URL paths and descriptive text.

So a good first step in abstracting out this code would be to determine exactly which items are going to be different if this same block of code were used in a Publishers index page versus a Games index page.

- The name of the resource will be different. We use this name in various places such as in our buttons like Create New Developer.

- The URL that it uses to pull down the JSON collection will need to change. However, this could also be derived by pluralizing the resource name.

- The primary key field will be different from resource to resource. If this was a standard Rails application that used `id` as the primary key for every resource, we wouldn't have that problem, but as it sits, we have primary keys like `DevID`, `PubID`, and `GameID`.

- The fields that will need to be mapped out of the JSON response in the column model will be unique from page to page.

- Our column model definitions in our grid are going to be unique from page to page as well.

- The height of our display dialog will need to be a variable based on the number of fields that may be passed to it.

That list isn't too long, as we could simply pass into a method the name of the resource and the majority of the unique elements could be derived from it. The primary key would have to also be passed to the method, as there would be no way to derive it from the resource name, since it doesn't follow conventions. As for the list of fields to map in our JSON response or our column model definitions, those could both be passed in as arrays or strings, which would be a little ugly but a vast improvement over where things are currently. So let's create a new helper method that will simply generate that same `pageGrid` JavaScript code based on the parameters we pass to it. Open /app/helpers/application_helper.rb, and create a new method named `ext_grid` like so:

```
def ext_grid(model, primary_key, fields, columns, height)
    xml_fields = fields
    xml_fields << primary_key
    xml_fields.collect! {|x| "'#{x}'"}
```

```
function = "var pageGrid = function() {"
function << " var grid; var dialog; var ds;"
function << " return{ init : function(){"
function << " ds = new Ext.data.Store({"
function << " proxy: new Ext.data.HttpProxy({method: 'GET', ➥
url: '#{model.pluralize}.json'})),"

function << "reader: new Ext.data.JsonReader({"
function << "root: '#{model.pluralize}',"
function << " totalProperty: 'totalCount',"
function << " id: '#{primary_key}'"
function << "}, [#{xml_fields.to_sentence(:connector => '')}])"
function << " });"

function << " var cm = new Ext.grid.ColumnModel([#{columns}]);"
function << " cm.defaultSortable = true;"
function << " grid = new Ext.grid.Grid('content', { ds: ds, cm: cm });"
function << " grid.render();"

function << "var gridFoot = grid.getView().getFooterPanel(true);"
function << "var paging = new Ext.PagingToolbar(gridFoot, ds, {"
function << "pageSize: 20,"
function << "displayInfo: true,"
function << "displayMsg: 'Displaying topics {0} - {1} of {2}',"
function << "emptyMsg: 'No topics to display'});"
function << "ds.load({params:{start:0, limit:20}});"


function << " grid.on('rowdblclick', editResource);"

function << " var gridHead = grid.getView().getHeaderPanel(true);"
function << " var tb = new Ext.Toolbar(gridHead);"
function << " tb.add({ text: 'Create New #{model.capitalize}', ➥
handler: createResource }, '-', { text: 'Delete Selected #{model.capitalize}', ➥
handler: deleteResource });"
function << " tb.add('-', 'Filter: ', \"<input type='text' ➥
id='text_filter'>\");"
function << " Ext.get('text_filter').on('keyup', filterResource);"
function << " }}"
function << "\n"
function << " function filterResource() {"
function << " filtervalue = Ext.get('text_filter').dom.value;"
function << " ds.proxy = new Ext.data.HttpProxy({method: 'GET', url:
```

```
#{model.pluralize}.json?search=' + filtervalue});"
    function << " ds.reload();}"
    function << "\n"
    function << " function deleteResource() {"
    function << " var id = grid.getSelectionModel().getSelected(); "
    function << " if(id){"
    function << " Ext.MessageBox.confirm('Confirm', 'Are you sure you want to ➥
delete this #{model}?', postDelete);"
    function << "  } else {"
    function << " Ext.MessageBox.alert('DOH!', 'Maybe you want to try ➥
again after ACTUALLY selecting something?')}}"
    function << "\n"
    function << " function submitResource(){"
    function << " document.create_resource.submit();}"
    function << "\n"
    function << " function postDelete(btn){"
    function << " if(btn == 'yes') {"
    function << " var id = grid.getSelectionModel().getSelected();"
    function << " var deleteme = id.get('#{primary_key}');"
    function << " window.location.href = '/#{model.pluralize}/destroy/' + ➥
 deleteme;}}  "
    function << "\n"
    function << " function editResource(grid, rowIndex) {"
    function << " var id = grid.getSelectionModel().getSelected();"
    function << " if(id) { "
    function << " window.location.href = '/#{model.pluralize}/' + ➥
id.get('#{primary_key}'); }}"
    function << "\n"
    function << " function createResource() {"
    function << " if(!dialog) {"
    function << " dialog = new Ext.BasicDialog('newDialog', {"
    function << " width:500, height:#{height}, shadow:true, minWidth:300, ➥
minHeight:#{height}, proxyDrag:true, autoScroll:false, animEl:true });"
    function << " dialog.addKeyListener(27, dialog.hide, dialog);"
    function << " postBtn = dialog.addButton('Submit', submitResource, this);"
    function << " dialog.addButton('Close', dialog.hide, dialog); }"
    function << "\n"
    function << " dialog.show();"
    function << " dialog.on('hide', function(){"
    function << " document.create_resource.reset();})"
    function << " } }();"
    function << " Ext.onReady(pageGrid.init, pageGrid, true);"
    javascript_tag(function)
  end
```

Using that helper method, we could easily reduce the index method for our developers down to just this:

```
<%= ext_layout('Developers') %>

<%= ext_grid("developer", "DevID", %w(Name URL),
  "{header: 'Name', width: 300, dataIndex: 'Name'},
  {header: 'URL', width: 250, dataIndex: 'URL'}") %>

<div id="content"> </div>

<div id="newDialog">
  <div class="x-dlg-hd">Create New Developer</div>
  <div class="x-dlg-bd">
    <% form_for(:developer, Developer.new, :url => developers_path,
        :html => {:id => 'create_resource', :name => 'create_resource'}) do |f| %>
    <p>
      <label for="developer_Name">Developer Name:</label>
      <%= f.text_field :Name %>
    </p>
    <p>
      <label for="developer_URL">Developer Home Page</label>
      <%= f.text_field :URL %>
    </p>
    <% end %>
  </div>
</div>
```

That's a lot nicer, and we if were to convert the create resource form at the bottom to a partial, we could reduce the code even further, but there's no reason to be greedy. In the meantime, though, let's use our new helper to finish the rest of the index methods for our resources.

Managing Games

Previously, we created an /app/views/games/index.rhtml template to demonstrate our layout; let's modify it now to use our new helper method and provide a fully functional page like this:

```
<%= ext_layout('Games') %>
<%= ext_grid("game", "GameID", %w(Title Console),
  "{header: 'Title', width: 300, dataIndex: 'Title'},
  {header: 'Console', width: 250, dataIndex: 'Console'}", 340) %>

<div id="content"> </div>
```

```
<div id="newDialog">
  <div class="x-dlg-hd">Create New Game</div>
  <div class="x-dlg-bd">
    <% form_for(:game, Game.new, :url => games_path,
         :html => {:id => 'create_resource', :name => 'create_resource'}) do |f| %>
      <p>
        <label for="game_Title">Title:</label>
        <%= f.text_field :Title %>
      </p>
      <p>
        <label for="game_Console">Console:</label>
        <%= f.select :Console,  %w(Xbox 360 PS2 ps3 PSP Cube GBA DS ➡
WII PC Nokia ) %>
      </p>
      <p>
        <label for="game_Description">Description:</label>
        <%= f.text_area :Description %>
      </p>
    <% end %>
  </div>
</div>
```

Also, we'll edit our games controller (/app/controllers/games_controller.rb) to look like this:

```
class GamesController < ApplicationController
  make_resourceful do
    build :all
  end

  def index
    limit =  params[:limit] || 25
    start = params[:start] || 0

    respond_to do |format|
      format.html
      format.json {
        if(params[:search])
          @games = Game.find(:all, :limit => limit, :offset => start,
            :conditions => ["Title like ?","%" + params[:search] + "%"])
          game_count = Game.count(:conditions => ["Title like ?","%" + ➡
params[:search] + "%"])
        else
          @games = Game.find(:all, :limit => limit, :offset => start )
          game_count = Game.count
        end
```

```
            griddata = Hash.new
            griddata[:games] = @games.collect {|g|
                    {:GameID => g.GameID, :Console => g.Console, :Title => g.Title}}
            griddata[:totalCount] =  game_count

            render :text => griddata.to_json()
        }
      end
    end
end
```

Managing Publishers

We can manage our Publishers by creating a new index.rhtml template in /app/views/
publishers and placing the following content in it:

```
<%= ext_layout('Publishers') %>
<%= ext_grid("publisher", "PubID", %w(Name URL),
  "{header: 'Name', width: 300, dataIndex: 'Name'},
   {header: 'URL', width: 250, dataIndex: 'URL'}", 170) %>

<div id="content"> </div>

<div id="newDialog">
  <div class="x-dlg-hd">Create New Publisher</div>
  <div class="x-dlg-bd">
    <% form_for(:publisher, Publisher.new, :url => publishers_path,
        :html => {:id => 'create_resource', :name => 'create_resource'}) do |f| %>
      <p>
        <label for="publisher_Name">Publisher Name:</label>
        <%= f.text_field :Name %>
      </p>
      <p>
        <label for="publisher_URL">Publisher Home Page</label>
        <%= f.text_field :URL %>
      </p>
    <% end %>
  </div>
</div>
```

We'll need to modify the Publishers controller to support our filter and paginating results
features as well, so edit /app/controllers/publishers_controller.rb to look like this:

```
class PublishersController < ApplicationController
  make_resourceful do
    build :all
  end
```

```
  def index
    limit =  params[:limit] || 25
    start = params[:start] || 0

    respond_to do |format|
      format.html {}
      format.json {
        if(params[:search])
          @publishers = Publisher.find(:all, :limit => limit, :offset => start,
            :conditions => ["Name like ?","%" + params[:search] + "%"])

          dev_count = Publisher.count(:conditions => ["Name like ?","%" + ➥
params[:search] + "%"])
        else
          @publishers = Publisher.find(:all, :limit => limit, :offset => start )
          dev_count = Publisher.count
        end

        griddata = Hash.new
        griddata[:publishers] = @publishers.collect {|p|
                  {:PubID => p.PubID, :Name => p.Name, :URL => p.URL}}
        griddata[:totalCount] =  dev_count

        render :text => griddata.to_json()
      }
    end
  end
end
```

Managing Genres

Finally, we'll pull our workflow into the index template for our genres resource as well, so create a new index.rhtml in /app/views/genres, and place the following content in it:

```
<%= ext_layout('Genres') %>
<%= ext_grid("genre", "GenreID", %w(TYPE GenreID),
  "{header: 'Genre', width: 300, dataIndex: 'TYPE'}", 120) %>

<div id="content"> </div>

<div id="newDialog">
  <div class="x-dlg-hd">Create New Genre</div>
  <div class="x-dlg-bd">
    <% form_for(:genre, Genre.new, :url => genres_path,
        :html => {:id => 'create_resource', :name => 'create_resource'}) do |f| %>
```

```
      <p>
        <label for="genre_TYPE">Genre Name:</label>
        <%= f.text_field :TYPE %>
      </p>
    <% end %>
  </div>
</div>
```

And modify the Genres controller (/app/controllers/genres_controller.rb) to look like this:

```
class GenresController < ApplicationController
  make_resourceful do
    build :all
  end

  def index
    limit =  params[:limit] || 25
    start = params[:start] || 0

    respond_to do |format|
      format.html
      format.json {
        if(params[:search])
          @genres = Genre.find(:all, :limit => limit, :offset => start,
            :conditions => ["Name like ?","%" + params[:search] + "%"])

          genre_count = Genre.count(:conditions => ["Name like ?","%" + ➥
params[:search] + "%"])
        else
          @genres = Genre.find(:all, :limit => limit, :offset => start )
          genre_count = Genre.count
        end

        griddata = Hash.new
        griddata[:genres] = @genres.collect {|g|
            {:GenreID => g.GenreID, :TYPE => g.TYPE}}
        griddata[:totalCount] =  genre_count

        render :text => griddata.to_json()
      }
    end
  end
end
```

Building the Show / Edit Template

Now that we have all of our index pages built to display lists of all of their records and provide functionality to create and delete as well, we need to build a way to interact with a single resource (e.g., the destination page when a row is double-clicked). Once again, let's start with building this page for the developer resource, and then we'll have a base set of code that we can migrate to other resources.

We'll need to create a new file named show.rhtml in /app/views/developers. After all that work building out our index page, you'll be happy to know that our next page will be much less involved. This will be the primary page from which a user will interact with an individual developer record. The page will display the information on a specific developer, but we'll add a little extra functionality to it by making all the fields editable in place.

In order to support in-place editing, we need to add the in_place_edit method for each field that we want to edit in place. So within the Developers controller (/app/controllers/developers_controller.rb), we'll add these methods for the Name and URL fields:

```ruby
class DevelopersController < ApplicationController
  in_place_edit_for :developer, :Name
  in_place_edit_for :developer, :URL

  make_resourceful do
    build :all
  end

  def index
    limit = params[:limit] || 25
    start = params[:start] || 0

    respond_to do |format|
      format.html
      format.json {
        if(params[:search])
          @developers = Developer.find(:all, :limit => limit, :offset => start,
            :conditions => ["Name like ?","%" + params[:search] + "%"])

          dev_count = Developer.count(:conditions => ["Name like ?","%" + ➥
params[:search] + "%"])
        else
          @developers = Developer.find(:all, :limit => limit, :offset => start )
          dev_count = Developer.count
        end

        griddata = Hash.new
        griddata[:developers] = @developers.collect {|d| {:DevID => d.DevID, ➥
:Name => d.Name, :URL => d.URL}}
        griddata[:totalCount] = dev_count
```

```
        render :text => griddata.to_json()
      }
    end
  end
end
```

Now, it's simply a matter of creating the show.rthml page in /apps/views/developers/:

```
<%= ext_layout('Edit Developer') %>

<div id='content' class="ylayout-inactive-content">
  <p>
    <label for="developer_Name">Company Name:</label>
    <%= in_place_editor_field :developer, :Name %>
  </p>
  <p>
    <label for="developer_URL">Developers Home Page:</label>
    <%= in_place_editor_field :developer, :URL %>
  </p>
  <%= button_to 'Back', developers_path, :method => :get %>
</div>
```

Firing up our new show page gives us a result like the one in Figure 19-13.

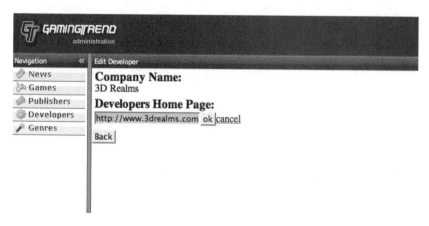

Figure 19-13. *In-place editing a developer's home page URL*

Nice and simple, huh? You should be able to take that example and extend it into creating the show.rthml pages for the Publishers and Genres sections by yourself at this point.

Capturing Failed Creations

Although "capturing failed creations" may sound like we're out hunting Frankenstein's monster, in reality, what I'm talking about is creating a new.rthml page for all of our resources. You see, even though we're using a dialog on the index page to create our new developers, our one big lack is determining how to respond to the user if the developer creation fails. While we could rewrite our index page to submit the new developer as a remote form via AJAX, doing that would introduce a significant amount of additional complexity without adding any additional value. It's much easier to just set up a standard new.rhtml page that will redisplay the creation form and any errors that occurred with the creation of the resource.

```
<%= ext_layout('Create New Developer') %>

<div id="content">
  <%= error_messages_for :developer %>
  <% form_for(:developer, Developer.new, :url => developers_path,
      :html => {:id => 'create_resource', :name => 'create_resource'}) do |f| %>
    <p>
      <label for="developer_Name">Developer Name:</label>
      <%= f.text_field :Name %>
    </p>

    <p>
      <label for="developer_URL">Developer Home Page</label>
      <%= f.text_field :URL %>
    </p>

    <p><%= submit_tag "Create" %></p>
  <% end %>
</div>
```

With that, we're done creating our tools to manage our developer resources. From here, you can either duplicate this process for the publisher and genre resources (modifying it to fit those resources obviously) or you can download the files straight from the source archive for this project. You'll need to create versions of this template for the Publishers and genres models as well.

Games

Now that we've built the pages necessary to mange our associated tables, it's finally time to tackle our page for displaying a specific game. While there will be some similarities among the games pages and our previous pages, the games detail pages will need to display a significant amount of additional data, as we'd like to make them the one-stop shop for any interactions with a game.

Building the Show Template

Sketching out a rough page layout, I came up with Figure 19-14, where the main content area is broken into a few new sections. We'll have a game information area, which will display information about the game and a picture of the game box. Below that, we'll have an area with multiple tabs. Within each tab, we'll display a different piece of data associated with this specific game, such as screenshots.

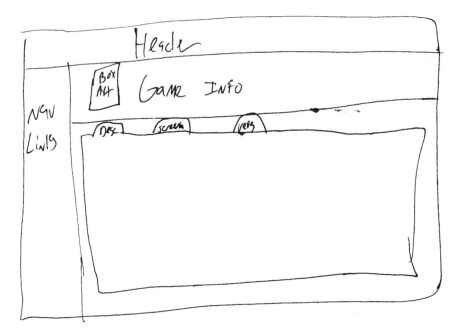

Figure 19-14. *A rough sketch of our game detail layout*

To accomplish this plan, we're going to have to make some modifications to our layout files and embed a nested layout into our center panel. To build this layout, we'll need to define the following new Ext border layout within the /app/views/games/show.rhtml template:

```
<script type="text/javascript" charset="utf-8">
  gameLayout = function() {
    var layout;
    return{

    init : function(){
      var layout = new Ext.BorderLayout(document.body, {
        north: {
          split:false,
          initialSize:65
        },
        center: {
          titlebar:false,
          tabPosition: 'top',
          alwaysShowTab: true,
          autoScroll:true
        },
```

```
      west: {
        initialSize: 125,
        minSize: 125,
        maxSize:125,
        titlebar: true,
        split:true,
        collapsible:true,
        animate:true
      }
    });
    layout.beginUpdate();
    layout.add('north', new Ext.ContentPanel('header'));

    var innerLayout = new Ext.BorderLayout('main', {
      north: {
        split:true,
        initialSize:155,
        titlebar:true,
        collapsible:true,
        animate:true
      },
      center: {
        autoScroll:true,
        tabPosition:'top'
      }
    });

    innerLayout.add('north', new Ext.ContentPanel('game_header', ➥
{title:"<%= h @game.Title %>"}));
      var tab1 = new Ext.ContentPanel('content', {title:'Description'});
      innerLayout.add('center', tab1);

      var tab2 = new Ext.ContentPanel('screenshots',{title:'ScreenShots'});
      innerLayout.add('center', tab2);

    layout.add('center', new Ext.NestedLayoutPanel(innerLayout));
    innerLayout.getRegion('center').showPanel('content');
    layout.add('west', new Ext.ContentPanel('sidebar', {title: 'Navigation'}));
    layout.endUpdate();}
  }
}();
Ext.EventManager.onDocumentReady(gameLayout.init, gameLayout, true);
</script>
```

Also, the HTML content of the page (directly beneath the script we just built) will need to have a structure like this:

```
<div id="container">
  <div id="game_header"> </div>

  <div id="main">
    <div id='content' class="ylayout-inactive-content"> </div>

    <div id="screenshots" class="ylayout-inactive-content">
      <h1>Screenshots will Go here</h1>
    </div>
  </div>
</div>
```

Putting these together produces the page layout shown in Figure 19-15.

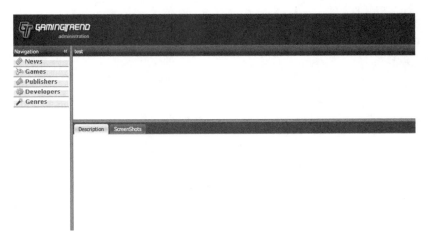

Figure 19-15. *Building our game display page*

Let's see about pulling in the appropriate data to each of those blocks now. We'll start by populating the game header:

```
<div id="game_header"> </div>
```

The first thing that we're going to want to display here is the box art for this game from the boximagepath attribute of the game record. When this field is populated, it will store the local file system path to the box art. However, if there is no box art uploaded, this attribute will be blank, and we'll need to display a "coming soon" image instead. Since we're dealing with the response of an object attribute, this sounds like the perfect place to add a new method to our

games model (/app/models/game.rb). Let's add a simple boxart method that will test if the
BoximagePath attribute is blank and return either the image path or our static empty image:

```ruby
class Game < ActiveRecord::Base
  set_table_name 'Games'
  set_primary_key :GameID
  belongs_to :publisher, :foreign_key => 'PubID'
  belongs_to :developer, :foreign_key => 'DevID'
  belongs_to :genre, :foreign_key => 'GenreID'
  order_by :title

  validates_length_of :Title, :maximum => 100, :message => " must be ➡
less than 100 characters"
  validates_presence_of :Title, :Console, :PubID, :DevID, :GenreID

  def boxart
    self.BoximagePath.blank? ? "/boxshots/empty.jpg" :  self.BoximagePath
  end
end
```

We can now use that method and our associations to populate our game header with general information about the game:

```erb
<div id="game_header">
    <table border="0" cellspacing="5" cellpadding="5">
      <tr>
        <td rowspan='6'> <%= image_tag "#{@game.boxart}" %> </td>
        <td> <label for="game_Console">Console</label> </td>
        <td> <%= @game.Console  %> </td>
        <td> <label for="game_PubID">Publisher</label> </td>
        <td><%= @game.publisher.Name %> </td>
      </tr>
      <tr>
        <td> <label for="game_Genre">Genre</label> </td>
        <td>  <%= @game.genre.TYPE %> </td>
        <td> <label for="game_DevID">Developer</label> </td>
        <td>  <%= @game.developer.Name %></td>
      </tr>
      <tr>
        <td> <label for="game_ESRB">ESRB Rating</label> </td>
        <td> <%= @game.ESRB %></td>
        <td><label for="game_SiteURL">Official Site</label></td>
        <td> <%= @game.SiteURL %></td>
      </tr>
    </table>
  </div>
```

which will give us a display like the one shown in Figure 19-16 when viewing a game record.

Figure 19-16. *The game header*

That's well and good, but what about making those fields editable? After all, we did intend to maximize the functionality of each page by making each of the fields editable in place. This will make it so that any changes are instantly saved. Our first step in accomplishing this is to add the in_place_edit method calls to our games controller:

```ruby
class GamesController < ApplicationController
  in_place_edit_for :game, :Console
  in_place_edit_for :game, :DevID
  in_place_edit_for :game, :PubID
  in_place_edit_for :game, :ESRB
  in_place_edit_for :game, :GenreID
  in_place_edit_for :game, :SiteURL


  make_resourceful do
    build :all
  end
  (...lines omitted...)
end
```

Unfortunately, we've also got a new challenge in making many of these fields editable in place. For many of the fields, using a text field won't make sense, because we don't actually store text but rather a foreign key to another table, and we need to control the available options. So, allowing a user to enter random text would be unacceptable and potentially disastrous. What we need to do instead is provide our users with a list of valid options in a select box.

Handling Select Boxes

Even though support for building in-place collection editors was added to the script.aculo.us library in the late spring of 2006, there are still no Rails helper methods built to use them. No worries though, as we have another option. A friend of mine and fellow Kansas City Ruby programmer named Sean Cribbs created a Rails plug-in that provides in-place editing with controls such as select boxes, check boxes, and radio buttons. We can install it by running the following command:

```
ruby script/plugin install svn://rubyforge.org/var/svn/inplacecontrols
```

```
A    /Users/darkel/consolegold/vendor/plugins/inplacecontrols
A    /Users/darkel/consolegold/vendor/plugins/inplacecontrols/test
A    /Users/darkel/consolegold/vendor/plugins/inplacecontrols/test/ ➥
in_place_controls_test.rb
A    /Users/darkel/consolegold/vendor/plugins/inplacecontrols/doc/classes/ ➥
InPlaceControls.html
...Many Lines Omitted...
A    /Users/darkel/consolegold/vendor/plugins/inplacecontrols/install.rb
A    /Users/darkel/consolegold/vendor/plugins/inplacecontrols/README
Exported revision 9.
```

Now that we have the plug-in installed, we can begin changing all the selection box areas in our games header with the new helper method in_place_select that our plug-in added to our application:

```
<div id="game_header">
  <table border="0" cellspacing="5" cellpadding="5">
    <tr>
    <td rowspan='6'>
      <%= image_tag "http://www.gamingtrend.com/#{@game.boxart}" %>
    </td>
    <td> <label for="game_Console">Console</label> </td>
    <td>
      <%= in_place_select :game, :Console, :choices => %w(Xbox 360 PS2 ps3 PSP ➥
  Cube GBA DS WII PC Nokia ) %>
    </td>
    <td> <label for="game_PubID">Publisher</label> </td>
    <td> <%= in_place_select :game, :PubID, :choices => ➥
Publisher.find(:all).collect {|p| [ p.Name, p.PubID ] }.sort %>
    </td>
  </tr>
  <tr>
    <td> <label for="game_Genre">Genre</label> </td>
    <td> <%= in_place_select :game, :GenreID, :choices => ➥
Genre.find(:all).collect {|p| [ p.TYPE, p.GenreID ] }.sort %>
    </td>
    <td> <label for="game_DevID">Developer</label> </td>
    <td> <%= in_place_select :game, :DevID, :choices => ➥
Developer.find(:all).collect {|d| [ d.Name, d.DevID ] }.sort %>
    </td>
  </tr>
  <tr>
    <td> <label for="game_ESRB">ESRB Rating</label> </td>
    <td>
      <%= in_place_select :game, :ESRB, :choices =>  %w(U T M EC E 10 AO RP) %>
    </td>
```

```
   <td> <label for="game_SiteURL">Official Site</label> </td>
   <td> <%= in_place_editor_field :game, :SiteURL %> </td>
  </tr>
 </table>
</div>
```

Now our header displays a list of selection boxes that will immediately make an AJAX call to the server whenever their values are changed. Figure 19-17 shows the result of the change.

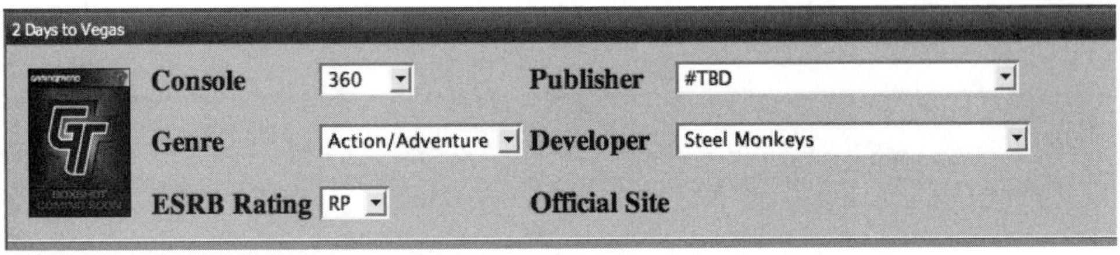

Figure 19-17. *Implementing in-place editors in our header*

We have introduced another minor problem, which you can see in Figure 19-17, when we made the SiteURL field editable. The problem lies in the fact that the SiteURL field is not required to be populated by any of our validation rules, so it's possible that it could be empty (as it is in the preceding record). Unfortunately, with an in_place_edit, if there's no text to display, there's also nothing that a user could click to add an entry. So what we need to do is find a way to return a default string that will still work with our in_place_edit control. We can fix this fairly easily by creating a virtual attribute in our Games model that has getter and setter methods and will populate the SiteURL attribute. Doing so is simply a matter of adding another pair of methods to our games model (/app/models/game.rb):

```
def homepage
  self.SiteURL || "Not Set"
end

def homepage=(value)
  self.SiteURL = value
end
```

Now, we can simply change our field on the page to reference homepage instead of SiteURL, and we'll always have some editable text displayed:

```
<%= in_place_editor_field :game, :homepage %>
```

The result of this change is shown in Figure 19-18.

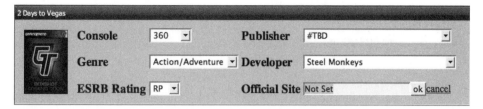

Figure 19-18. *Displaying a default value for the SiteURL attribute*

Providing WYSIWYG Functionality

Now that we have our game header completed, we need to turn our attention toward creating editing capabilities for the game title and game description in the content div. Assume that we've discussed with Ron how the new administration site was to provide a better solution for formatting large blocks of text like this. If this were a brand new application with no legacy data, we'd probably have been able to implement a text-based formatting language like Textile or Markdown. As it stands, though, the staff has grown quite accustomed to using a WYSIWYG text area replacement (even though the one they currently use has a significant number of problems) and would be resistant to learning a formatting language. So it looks like our hands are tied; we'll have to implement an HTML WYSIWYG editor and deal with storing HTML in the database. In cases like these, I've typically had good luck with implementing an open source JavaScript solution named TinyMCE (`http://tinymce.moxiecode.com/`). TinyMCE is a highly configurable, lightweight solution that, in my experience, produces pretty decent HTML. In fact, when I first wrote this chapter, I used that solution for this project. However, I was never very happy with the extra weight of adding yet another JavaScript library to the page.

Fortunately for us, though, just as the book was getting ready to go to print the new Ext 1.1 was released, which now includes its own HTML WYSIWYG editor, so I converted this section of the project to use it, so you could have the latest and greatest features.

Still working within our `/app/views/games/show.rhtml` page, we have a div named content that currently looks like this:

```
<div id='content' class="ylayout-inactive-content">
</div>
```

We're going to use Ext to build a new form within this content block and populate it with a text field to edit the game's title and an HTML editor to edit the game's description. Our first step in doing so will be to create a new `Ext.form` named game within an `Ext.onReady` block:

```
<div id='content' class="ylayout-inactive-content">
  <script type="text/javascript" charset="utf-8">
    Ext.onReady(function(){

    Ext.form.Field.prototype.msgTarget = 'side';
```

```
        var game = new Ext.form.Form({
          labelAlign: 'top',
          url:'<%= game_url(@game) %>'
        });

      });
    </script>
  </div>
```

The beautiful thing about this code is that even without knowing Ext, the code reads well and should be fairly self-explanatory. The only thing that might need a bit of explanation is the `Ext.form.Field.prototype.msgTarget = 'side';` line, which is merely used to indicate where we want to display any field validation errors (in this case, we'll display them next to the field). You'll also notice that in the `Ext.form` creation we specified the URL that the form should post to using one of our named helpers. With our new form created, we can add our title and game description fields to it with the `add` function:

```
game.add(
  new Ext.form.TextField({
    fieldLabel: 'Title',
    name: 'game[Title]',
    width:225,
    allowBlank:false,
    maxLength:100,
    value:'<%= @game.Title %>'
  }),

  new Ext.form.HtmlEditor({
    id:'description',
    fieldLabel:'Description',
    name: 'game[Description]',
    value: "<%= @game.Description %>",
    width:550,
    height:200
  })
);
```

Again, this should be fairly easy to read with only a few lines that we need to discuss. You may have noticed that we named both fields as elements of a game array (`name: 'game[Title]'` and `name: 'game[Description]'`). We do this to make our elements compatible with the default way that the Rails methods work. By passing all form elements in as elements of a game array, the controller can simply grab `params[:game]` to have access to the form data. The second bit to highlight is in our Title text field, where we've added a pair of validations to match our models validations: `allowBlank:false` will match our `validates_presence_of`, while `maxLength:100` maps back to our `validates_length_of` requirement.

With our form fields created, it's now time to create a button that will submit the data to the server. We'll do this with a simple addButton method, which will call the submit method if the form has passed its own validation checks:

```
game.addButton('Save', function(){
  if(game.isValid()){
    game.submit({
      params:{
        action: "update",
        _method: "put",
        commit:"Save",
        id: <%= @game.id %>
      }, waitMsg:'Saving Description Now...'
    });
  } else {
    Ext.MessageBox.alert('Errors', 'Please fix the errors noted.');
  }
}, game);
```

The key things to note in this block are the parameters that we pass along with the form submission—most notably the _method: "put" parameter, as that lets Rails know that we want to be routed to the update method. If we didn't have that parameter, this form would look like a request to create a new element rather than to edit an existing game record.

With our form built, all that's left is to render it out to the page—specifying the div element where we want form to display:

```
game.render('content');
```

After our modifications, our final function within the content div of /app/views/games/ show.rhtml looks like this:

```
<div id='content' class="ylayout-inactive-content">
  <script type="text/javascript" charset="utf-8">
    Ext.onReady(function(){

      var game = new Ext.form.Form({
        labelAlign: 'top',
        url:'<%= game_url(@game) %>'
      });

      game.add(
        new Ext.form.TextField({
          fieldLabel: 'Title',
          name: 'game[Title]',
          width:225,
          allowBlank:false,
          value:'<%= @game.Title %>'
        }),
```

```
        new Ext.form.HtmlEditor({
          id:'description',
          fieldLabel:'Description',
          name: 'game[Description]',
          value: "<%= @game.Description %>",
          width:550,
          height:200
        })
    );

    game.addButton('Save', function(){
      if(game.isValid()){
        game.submit({
          params:{
            action: "update",
            _method: "put",
            commit:"Save",
            id: <%= @game.id %>
          }, waitMsg:'Saving Description Now...'
        });
      } else {
        Ext.MessageBox.alert('Errors', 'Please fix the errors noted.');
      }
    }, game);

    game.render('content');
  });
</script>
</div>
```

The rendering of our new Ext form is shown in Figure 19-19.

If you were to click through numerous game records in the system, you would find that some of the records do not display our Ext form at all. If we pull up the Firebug console, on those pages, we see a JavaScript error being reported: `missing } after property list`. We see that error because many of the records existing in the database contain a bit of junk such as new line breaks and unescaped quotes, which are causing issues when it gets output in the `value: "<%= @game.Description %>"` line of our `HtmlEditor`. There are a number of approaches that we could take to solve this problem, but perhaps the easiest is to simply do a little chain of substitutions on our description when we display it. So we simply need to change that line to read as follows:

```
value: "<%= @game.Description.gsub("\n", "").gsub('"', '\"').gsub("'", "\'") ➥
.gsub("\r", "") %>",
```

In that chain, we remove all new lines (\n) and carriage returns (\r); meanwhile, we escape any double (") or single quotes(') found within the text as well

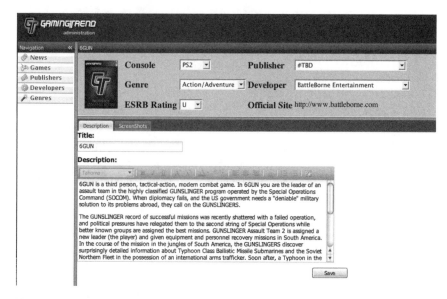

Figure 19-19. *An Ext form added to our game detail page to provide WYSIWYG functionality*

Viewing Screenshots

Before this chapter closes, let's throw one last piece of content onto our detail page—the thumbnails of any screenshots for a game. You should have noticed that we already added a tab to display the screenshots for a specific game into our initial layout. We've already done several projects that supported image uploads, so I'll leave adding images to the record as a good practice exercise for you, but we can have a little fun by building the screenshot model and adding a few functions to enable displaying them in our application.

The Screenshot Model

Our first step is, of course, to take a glance at the current schema for the screenshots:

```
t.column "shotID",    :integer, :limit => 20,                          :null => false
t.column "filepath",  :string,                   :default => "",       :null => false
t.column "filename",  :string,                   :default => "",       :null => false
t.column "caption",   :text,                     :default => "",       :null => false
t.column "GameID",    :integer,                  :default => 0,        :null => false
t.column "DateAdded", :date,                                           :null => false
t.column "E3year",    :integer, :limit => 4,     :default => 2006,     :null => false
```

Nothing too fancy—we have the path to the image on our file system stored in the `filepath` attribute and the name of the image on the file system stored in the `filename` attribute, and we've got a foreign key reference back to the Game model in the `GameID` attribute. We can add a basic model for accessing this table like so:

```
ruby script/generate model Screenshot --skip-migration
```

```
exists  app/models/
exists  test/unit/
exists  test/fixtures/
create  app/models/screenshot.rb
create  test/unit/screenshot_test.rb
create  test/fixtures/screenshots.yml
```

Let's think about the associations—a game can have many screenshots, but each screen-shot can only belong to a single game. We also have no need to call set_table_name for this model, as the table name (screenshots) is already lowercase. We can then build our screenshot model (/app/models/screenshot.rb) like this:

```
class Screenshot < ActiveRecord::Base
  set_primary_key :shotID
  belongs_to :game, :foreign_key => 'GameID'
end
```

And we'll have to add the following line to our Game model (/app/models/game.rb) so that we can call @game.screenshots:

```
has_many :screenshots, :foreign_key => 'GameID'
```

With our models configured, all we have left to do now is add the display logic to pull in our screenshots. We'll start by generating an empty screenshots controller.

```
ruby script/generate controller Screenshots
```

```
exists  app/controllers/
exists  app/helpers/
create  app/views/screenshots
exists  test/functional/
create  app/controllers/screenshots_controller.rb
create  test/functional/screenshots_controller_test.rb
create  app/helpers/screenshots_helper.rb
```

Creating this controller does two things for us: one, it sets up for the future when we'll build support for doing the full set of CRUD operations on our screenshots, and two (and more importantly to what we're doing right now), it created a screenshots folder under /app/views for us.

Within that screenshots folder, let's create a new partial that we'll use to display our screenshots. Create a new file named _screenshots.rhtml, and place the following line in it:

```
<img src="http://www.gamingtrend.com/<%= screenshots.filepath %>tb_<%= ➥
screenshots.filename %>">
```

In this line, all we're doing is building a link to the image by combining the `filepath` with the `filename` adding in a `tb_` in front of the filename to indicate that we want the thumbnail-sized version (as that was how they were saved by the old administration system).

Going back to our games detail page (`/app/views/games/show.rthml`), we'll change the content of our screenshots div to this:

```
<div id="screenshots" class="ylayout-inactive-content">
    <%= render :partial => '/screenshots/screenshots', :collection => ➥
@game.screenshots %>
</div>
```

Open a web browser, and view the ScreenShots tab from a game detail page; you should have something similar to Figure 19-20.

Figure 19-20. *Displaying associated screenshots*

Our final `/app/views/games/show.rhtml` template looks like this:

```
<script type="text/javascript" charset="utf-8">
  gameLayout = function() {
    var layout;
     return{

    init : function(){
       var layout = new Ext.BorderLayout(document.body, {
          north: {
             split:false,
             initialSize:65
          },
          center: {
             titlebar:false,
             tabPosition: 'top',
             alwaysShowTab: true,
             autoScroll:true
          },
```

```
          west: {
              initialSize: 125,
              minSize: 125,
              maxSize:125,
              titlebar: true,
              split:true,
              collapsible:true,
              animate:true
          }
      });
      layout.beginUpdate();
      layout.add('north', new Ext.ContentPanel('header'));

      var innerLayout = new Ext.BorderLayout('main', {
        north: {
            split:true,
            initialSize:155,
            titlebar:true,
            collapsible:true,
            animate:true
        },
        center: {
            autoScroll:true,
            tabPosition:'top'
        }
      });

      innerLayout.add('north', new Ext.ContentPanel('game_header', ➥
{title:"<%= h @game.Title %>"}));
      var tab1 = new Ext.ContentPanel('content', {title:'Description'});
      innerLayout.add('center', tab1);

      var tab2 = new Ext.ContentPanel('screenshots',{title:'ScreenShots'});
      innerLayout.add('center', tab2);

      layout.add('center', new Ext.NestedLayoutPanel(innerLayout));
      innerLayout.getRegion('center').showPanel('content');
      layout.add('west', new Ext.ContentPanel('sidebar', {title: 'Navigation'}));
      layout.endUpdate();}
      }
  }();
  Ext.EventManager.onDocumentReady(gameLayout.init, gameLayout, true);
</script>
```

```
<div id="container">
  <div id="game_header">
    <table border="0" cellspacing="5" cellpadding="5">
      <tr>
        <td rowspan='6'> <%= image_tag "#{@game.boxart}" %> </td>
        <td> <label for="game_Console">Console</label> </td>
        <td> <%= in_place_select :game, :Console, :choices => ➡
["Xbox", "360", "PS2", "ps3", "PSP", "Cube", "GBA", "DS", "WII", "PC", ➡
"Nokia"] %> </td>

        <td> <label for="game_PubID">Publisher</label> </td>
        <td><%= in_place_select :game, :PubID, :choices => ➡
Publisher.find(:all).collect {|p| [ p.Name, p.PubID ] }.sort %> </td>
      </tr>
      <tr>
        <td> <label for="game_Genre">Genre</label> </td>
        <td>  <%= in_place_select :game, :GenreID, :choices => ➡
Genre.find(:all).collect {|p| [ p.TYPE, p.GenreID ] }.sort %> </td>
        <td> <label for="game_DevID">Developer</label> </td>
        <td>  <%= in_place_select :game, :DevID, :choices => ➡
Developer.find(:all).collect {|d| [ d.Name, d.DevID ] }.sort %></td>
      </tr>
      <tr>
        <td> <label for="game_ESRB">ESRB Rating</label> </td>
        <td> <%= in_place_select :game, :ESRB, :choices => ➡
%w(U T M EC E 10 AO RP) %></td>
        <td><label for="game_SiteURL">Official Site</label></td>
        <td> <%= in_place_editor_field :game, :homepage %></td>
      </tr>
    </table>
  </div>

  <div id="main">
    <div id='content' class="ylayout-inactive-content">
<script type="text/javascript" charset="utf-8">
Ext.onReady(function(){

  Ext.form.Field.prototype.msgTarget = 'side';
```

```
var game = new Ext.form.Form({
  labelAlign: 'top',
  url:'<%= game_url(@game) %>'
});
game.add(
  new Ext.form.TextField({
      fieldLabel: 'Title',
      name: 'game[Title]',
      width:225,
      allowBlank:false,
      maxLength:100,
      value:"<%= @game.Title.gsub("\n", "").gsub('"', '\"').gsub("'", ➡
"\'").gsub("\r", "") %>"
      }),

  new Ext.form.HtmlEditor({
    id:'description',
    fieldLabel:'Description',
    name: 'game[Description]',
    value: "<%= @game.Description.gsub("\n", "").gsub('"', '\"').gsub("'", ➡
"\'").gsub("\r", "") %>",
    width:550,
    height:200
  })
);

game.addButton('Save', function(){
  if(game.isValid()){
    game.submit({
      params:{
        action: "update",
        _method: "put",
        commit:"Save",
        id: <%= @game.id %>
      }, waitMsg:'Saving Description Now...'
    });
  } else {
    Ext.MessageBox.alert('Errors', 'Please fix the errors noted.');
  }
}, game);
```

```
  game.render('content');
  });

</script>

    </div>

    <div id="screenshots" class="ylayout-inactive-content">
        <%= render :partial => '/screenshots/screenshots', :collection => ➥
@game.screenshots %>
    </div>
  </div>
</div>
```

Summary

We've configured our new Rails application to effectively communicate with our legacy database as we've built the beginning of our administration system. In building our administration system, you've learned about creating an advanced interface using the Ext JavaScript library using features such as border layout, grids, and dialog boxes. We came across a number of errors along the way, and we talked about how to troubleshoot and solve them. We've covered a lot of ground in this chapter, and at the end, we've put together a basic system for managing games, developers, publishers, and genres. All that we have left to do now is implement a solution for managing user-created content as well—which we'll do in the next chapter.

## CHAPTER 20

Supporting News

In the previous chapter, we built the capacity for our new administration system to manage the game records for our friend's gaming web site. While maintaining a database of all the games is important, since this is primarily a content site, it's critically important that new content is pumped through the site in order to keep visitors coming back on a regular basis. Ron keeps the site fresh through a variety of content such as daily news, press releases, reviews and previews of games, interviews with developers, and so forth. While each of those is important for the success of the site, the one that keeps readers coming back every day is the news—Ron and his staff provide daily content on the latest gaming news and information as it's occurring. Whether it's reporting about a newly revealed feature in an upcoming PlayStation 3 game or rumors of a potential price drop on the Nintendo Wii, daily news is a huge draw of the site; it's one of the most visited pages. It's also the page that cycles through the most content daily. On any given day, the staff can add two to twenty news stories.

So we're going to finish our project by building support for that core piece of the site in our new administration system. The nice thing about doing this, though, is that the other content pieces such as press releases, reviews, and so on are extremely similar to the news system, and you should have no problems building out the rest yourself.

Modifying the Database

Currently, the news is stored in a database table named news (oddly appropriate). Viewing the schema for this table in our /db/schema.rb gives us a good overview of the current structure for this news table:

```
create_table "News", :id => false, :force => true do |t|
    t.column "NewsID", :integer, :null => false
    t.column "Headline", :string, :default => "", :null => false
    t.column "FrontPage", :string, :limit => 26, :default => "", :null => false
    t.column "Body", :text, :default => "", :null => false
    t.column "Summary", :string, :default => "", :null => false
    t.column "DateAdded", :datetime, :null => false
    t.column "UserID", :integer, :limit => 8, :default => 0, :null => false
    t.column "E3year", :integer, :limit => 4, :default => 0, :null => false
    t.column "Active", :integer, :limit => 4, :default => 0, :null => false
  end
```

Doing a little research on the history of these fields with Ron revealed this information:

- *NewsID*: This is the primary key used to identify the news post.

- *Headline*: This is the headline for the news post. It is displayed at the top of each news post.

- *FrontPage*: This is an abbreviated version of the headline used on the front page of the site, where it must fit within a very narrow column—hence the 26-character limitation.

- *Body*: This is the content of the news post.

- *Summary*: This was originally intended to be a short version of the news post. However, it ended up not being used. Adding to the annoyance factor, though, is the fact that the current system requires that staff members enter something into this field every time they create a news post.

- *DateAdded*: The time stamp field that records when the news post was added to the system. It's updated again when the post is activated.

- *UserID*: This foreign key references the users table to record which staff member created the news post.

- *E3year*: This is another historical field for tracking if a news article was associated with a particular year's E3 exposition; it's not used anymore.

- *Active*: This is used to determine whether or not the article is active on the primary site. If the field's value is 0, then the article won't be showed; if the field's set to 1, the article will appear.

We obviously have a few cleanup needs here. Let's start by creating a new migration:

```
ruby script/generate migration cleanup_news
```

```
    exists  db/migrate
    create  db/migrate/003_cleanup_news.rb
```

We'll use this new migration to remove those unused fields, remove the database managed validations, and rename the DateAdded field to created_at so that Rails can manage keeping it populated for us. As long as we're in here, we'll also make one final change: we'll convert our active field from an integer to a Boolean—within the database. Doing so won't break the front end, as the data will still be stored as a 1 or a 0, but within our application, it will allow us to reference the field as true or false. In the end, our 003_cleanup_news.rb in /db/ migrate will look like this:

```
class CleanupNews < ActiveRecord::Migration
  def self.up
    remove_index "News", :name => "E3year"
    change_column "News", "Headline", :string, :null => true
    change_column "News", "FrontPage", :string, :null => true
```

```
      change_column "News", "Body",        :text,  :null => true
      add_column    "News", "Extended", :text
      remove_column "News", "Summary"
      rename_column "News", "DateAdded", "created_at"
      add_column    "News", "updated_at", :datetime
      change_column "News", "UserID",     :integer,  :null => true
      remove_column "News", "E3year"
      change_column "News", "Active", :boolean
      add_index  "News", "created_at"
   end

   def self.down
      raise ActiveRecord::IrreversibleMigration
   end
end
```

Now, we can run our migration to clean up our table:

```
rake db:migrate
```

```
== CleanupNews: migrating ==============================
-- remove_index("News", {:name=>"E3year"})
   -> 1.3279s
-- change_column("News", "Headline", :string, {:null=>true})
   -> 0.1115s
-- change_column("News", "FrontPage", :string, {:null=>true})
   -> 0.0137s
-- change_column("News", "Body", :text, {:null=>true})
   -> 0.0151s
-- add_column("News", "Extended", :text)
   -> 0.0096s
-- remove_column("News", "Summary")
   -> 0.0081s
-- rename_column("News", "DateAdded", "created_at")
   -> 0.1677s
-- add_column("News", "updated_at", :datetime)
   -> 0.0654s
-- change_column("News", "UserID", :integer, {:null=>true})
   -> 0.0224s
-- remove_column("News", "E3year")
   -> 0.0094s
-- change_column("News", "Active", :boolean)
   -> 0.0233s
-- add_index("News", "created_at")
   -> 0.0109s
== CleanupNews: migrated (1.7877s) ==========================
```

Creating a Model for News

In creating a model for the daily news, the first problem that we'll have to address is the name of the object itself. While it might feel tempting to build our model and try to name it News, in the end, that would be a path fraught with frustration. "Why?" you might ask. It has to do with Rails conventions of using singular and pluralized versions of names, and surely you can imagine what's going to happen when it tries to singularize "news"? Besides, we can't easily declare a New.new, can we?

Instead, we'll have to name our model something that won't cause us issues in our application. To keep it relevant, I decided to name the model Post:

```
ruby script/generate model Post --skip-migration
```

```
      exists  app/models/
      exists  test/unit/
      exists  test/fixtures/
      create  app/models/post.rb
      create  test/unit/post_test.rb
      create  test/fixtures/posts.yml
```

In our model configuration, we need to configure our model to know that it should look for its data in the News table by using the set_table_name method and by defining that its primary key should be NewsID. We'll also move our validations that we removed from the database into the model while we're in here. Our Post model (/app/models/post.rb) should look like this:

```
class Post < ActiveRecord::Base
  set_table_name 'News'
  set_primary_key :NewsID

  validates_presence_of :Headline, :Body
  validates_length_of :FrontPage, :within => 1..26, :on => :create, :message => ➡
 "must be present"
end
```

Firing up our console validates that we're able to connect to the data without any issues:

```
ruby script/console -s
```

```
Loading development environment in sandbox.
Any modifications you make will be rolled back on exit.
```

```
>> Post.find 9805
```

```
=> #<Post:0x24b19a4 @attributes={"updated_at"=>nil, "Body"=>"With <a href=
"http://www.e3expo.com">E3</a> out of the way, it's time for awards.  Today, <a
href="http://www.activision.com">Activision</a> has announced that Call of Duty
4: Modern Combat has been awarded <a href="http://www.gamingtrend.com/PressReleases
/index.php?PRID=6108">Best Action Game</a> from Game Critics Awards: Best of E3
2007.<blockquote>\223It\222s a tremendous honor to have Call of Duty 4: Modern
Warfare recognized as a best in class title by such experienced and knowledgeable
 individuals in the gaming community,\224 said Robin Kaminsky, executive vice
president of publishing, Activision, Inc.  \223Infinity Ward is committed to
setting the benchmark for action and these awards and honors are a testament to
their hard work and talent.\224</blockquote>Call of Duty 4: Modern Combat will be
out later this year.", "FrontPage"=>"CoD4 Best Action Game @ E3", "Extended"=>nil,
"NewsID"=>"9805", "Active"=>"1", "UserID"=>"27", "Headline"=>"Call of Duty 4 Named
Best Action Game At E3", "created_at"=>"2007-08-03 02:21:33"}
```

```
>> p = Post.new
```

```
=> #<Post:0x2458d04 @new_record=true, @attributes={"updated_at"=>nil, "Body"=>nil,
"FrontPage"=>"", "Extended"=>nil, "Active"=>false, "UserID"=>0, "Headline"=>"",
"created_at"=>nil}
```

```
>> p.Body = 'test'
```

```
=> "test"
```

```
>> p.save
```

```
=> false
```

```
>> p.Headline = 'test'
```

```
=> "test"
```

```
>> p.save
```

```
=> false
```

```
>> p.FrontPage = 'test'
```

```
=> "test"
```

```
>> p.save
```

```
=> true
```

```
>> p.id
```

```
=> 9861
```

Looks like we're off to a good start. We'll come back to this model a little later on when we're ready to map its associations back to the games records, but we're good for now.

Creating Our Controller

With the Post model ready and working, we're ready to create a Posts controller that we can use for all of our standard CRUD actions to the Post model. We'll create our controller like this:

```
ruby script/generate controller Posts
```

```
    exists  app/controllers/
    exists  app/helpers/
    create  app/views/posts
    exists  test/functional/
    create  app/controllers/posts_controller.rb
    create  test/functional/posts_controller_test.rb
    create  app/helpers/posts_helper.rb
```

Once again, we'll take advantage of our Make Resourceful plug-in to provide our controller with the standard REST actions (and keep us out of copy/paste hell). So our /app/controllers/posts_controller.rb will look like this:

```
class PostsController < ApplicationController
  make_resourceful do
    build :all
  end
end
```

Creating Our Resource

With our controller built, we just need to add our new posts resource to our routes.rb in /config so that we can take advantage of all the automatically generated named paths:

```
ActionController::Routing::Routes.draw do |map|
  map.resources :games
  map.resources :publishers, :developers, :genres, :posts
  map.connect ':controller/:action/:id.:format'
  map.connect ':controller/:action/:id'
end
```

Building Our List View

Once again, we'll be leveraging the layout and grid code that we've used on previous pages for many of the features of managing our news posts. Doing so not only helps speed up our development but also helps maintain a common and consistent interface throughout the application. However, the needs of a news post are going to require us to address a few key differences between a news post and previous resource pages by modifying our code and enhancing the view.

Redefining the Index Method

Since we want to reuse the grid code that we built in the previous chapter, we'll need to modify our Posts controller to redefine the index method to return our results into the JSON format again. So modify /app/controllers/posts_controller.rb to look like this:

```
class PostsController < ApplicationController
  make_resourceful do
    build :all
  end
```

```
  def index
    limit =  params[:limit] || 25
    start = params[:start] || 0

    respond_to do |format|
      format.html
      format.json {
        @posts = Post.find(:all, :limit => limit, :offset => start )
        griddata = Hash.new
        griddata[:posts] = @posts.collect {|p|
            {:NewsID => p.NewsID, :Headline => p.Headline, :Body => p.Body, ➥
:created_at => p.created_at.to_s, :Active => p.Active}}
        griddata[:totalCount] = Post.count
        render :text => griddata.to_json()
      }
    end
  end
end
```

A First Pass at the Index Page

Create a new page in /apps/views/posts named index.rhtml as the main view. In this file, we'll
start out by including our common layout code again:

```
<%= ext_layout('News') %>
<%=ext_grid("post", "NewsID", %w(Headline Body created_at Active),
  "{header: 'Headline', width: 300, dataIndex: 'Headline'},
  {header: 'Body', width: 650, dataIndex: 'Body'},
  {header: 'Created At', width: 200, dataIndex: 'created_at'},
  {header: 'Active?', width: 60, dataIndex: 'Active'}", 340) %>

<div id="content"> </div>

<div id="newDialog">
  <div class="x-dlg-hd">Create New Game</div>
  <div class="x-dlg-bd">
    <% form_for(:post, Post.new, :url => posts_path,
        :html => {:id => 'create_resource', :name => 'create_resource'}) do |f| %>
      <p>
        <label for="post_Headline">Story Headline:</label>
        <%= f.text_field :Headline %>
      </p>
      <p>
        <label for="post_FrontPage">Frontpage Headline:</label>
        <%= f.text_field :Headline %>
      </p>
```

```
    <p>
      <label for="post_Body">News Story:</label>
      <%= f.text_field :Body %>
    </p>
  <% end %>
 </div>
</div>
```

The preceding code, of course, will generate a view like the one shown in Figure 20-1 when accessed at `http://localhost:3000/posts`.

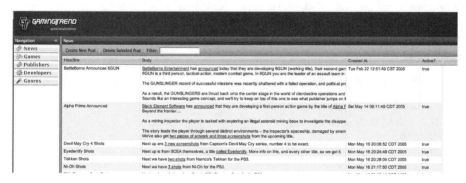

Figure 20-1. *Reusing our existing code to build the news post index page*

That was quick and easy, wasn't it? Too bad we're not done; we need to make a number of changes before this will be ready for use.

Changing the Default Order

The first thing we notice is that the news posts are being returned in a default order. To be useful for managing the posts, though, the news posts really should be delivered in newest to oldest. So we'll need to modify our Posts model (`/app/models/post.rb`) to include an `order_by` clause:

```
class Post < ActiveRecord::Base
  set_table_name 'News'
  set_primary_key :NewsID
  order_by "created_at DESC"

  validates_presence_of :Headline, :Body
  validates_length_of :FrontPage, :within => 1..26, :on => :create, ➥
:message => "must be present"
end
```

A quick refresh of the page, and we'll see that our news posts are now being returned in the correct order.

Modifying the Grid

Reordering the results in the grid was a small victory, but now, it's time to go onto some bigger things. We need to enhance the grid for the specific features that will be more in line with the type of content that we'll be displaying here. That means we're going to have to make modifications to the JavaScript grid code that we moved into a helper in the last chapter.

Perhaps the easiest place to begin our modifications is to take another look at the JavaScript code that our ext_grid helper method is generating for us and then make our modifications to that JavaScript. When we called

```
<%=ext_grid("post", "NewsID", %w(Headline Body created_at Active),
  "{header: 'Headline', width: 300, dataIndex: 'Headline'},
  {header: 'Body', width: 650, dataIndex: 'Body'},
  {header: 'Created At', width: 200, dataIndex: 'created_at'},
  {header: 'Active?', width: 60, dataIndex: 'Active'}", 340) %>
```

this is the JavaScript that was generated:

```
<script type="text/javascript" charset="utf-8">
  var pageGrid = function() {
    var grid;
    var dialog;
    var ds; return{
      init : function(){
        ds = new Ext.data.Store({
          proxy: new Ext.data.HttpProxy({method: 'GET',
          url: 'posts.json'}),
          reader: new Ext.data.JsonReader({root: 'posts',
          totalProperty: 'totalCount',
          id: 'NewsID'},
          ['Headline', 'Body', 'Active',  'NewsID'])
        });
        var cm = new Ext.grid.ColumnModel([
          {header: 'Headline', width: 300, dataIndex: 'Headline'},
          {header: 'Body', width: 650, dataIndex: 'Body'},
          {header: 'Active?', width: 60, dataIndex: 'Active'}
        ]);

        cm.defaultSortable = true;
        grid = new Ext.grid.Grid('content', { ds: ds, cm: cm });
        grid.render();

        var gridFoot = grid.getView().getFooterPanel(true);
        var paging = new Ext.PagingToolbar(gridFoot, ds,
```

```
      {
        pageSize: 20,
        displayInfo: true,
        displayMsg: 'Displaying topics {0} - {1} of {2}',
        emptyMsg: 'No topics to display'
      }
    );
    ds.load({params:{start:0, limit:20}});
    grid.on('rowdblclick', editResource);
    var gridHead = grid.getView().getHeaderPanel(true);
    var tb = new Ext.Toolbar(gridHead);
    tb.add(
      { text: 'Create New Post', handler: createResource },
      '-',
      { text: 'Delete Selected Post', handler: deleteResource }
    );
    tb.add('-', 'Filter: ', \"<input type='text' id='text_filter'>\");
    Ext.get('text_filter').on('keyup', filterResource);
    }}

    function filterResource() {
        filtervalue = Ext.get('text_filter').dom.value;
        ds.proxy = new Ext.data.HttpProxy({method: 'GET', ➥
url: '#{model.pluralize}.json?search=' + filtervalue});
        ds.reload();
    }

    function deleteResource() {
        var id = grid.getSelectionModel().getSelected();
        if(id){
            Ext.MessageBox.confirm('Confirm', 'Are you sure you want to delete ➥
 this post?', postDelete);
        } else {
            Ext.MessageBox.alert('DOH!', 'Maybe you want to try again after ➥
ACTUALLY selecting something?')
        }
    }

    function submitResource(){
      document.create_resource.submit();
    }
```

```
        function postDelete(btn){
          if(btn == 'yes') {
            var id = grid.getSelectionModel().getSelected();
            var deleteme = id.get('NewsID');
            window.location.href = '/posts/destroy/' + deleteme;
          }
        }

        function editResource(grid, rowIndex) {
          var id = grid.getSelectionModel().getSelected();
          if(id) {
            window.location.href = '/posts/' + id.get('NewsID');
          }
        }

        function createResource() {
          if(!dialog) {
            dialog = new Ext.BasicDialog('newDialog', {
              width:500,
              height:340,
              shadow:true,
              minWidth:300,
              minHeight:340,
              proxyDrag:true,
              autoScroll:false,
              animEl:true
            });
            dialog.addKeyListener(27, dialog.hide, dialog);
            postBtn = dialog.addButton('Submit', submitResource, this);
            dialog.addButton('Close', dialog.hide, dialog);
          }
          dialog.show();
          dialog.on('hide', function(){
            document.create_resource.reset();
          })
        }
      }();
    Ext.onReady(pageGrid.init, pageGrid, true);
</script>
```

Removing the Filter

One of the first things we'll do is remove the text filtering option from our grid (we removed it from the controllers index method when we created it). While there might be some moderate value in being able to search through the news posts, there are a couple of factors that make it unwieldy for our purposes. First off, the only field that really makes sense to do a search on would be the Body field, which is defined as a text field in the database. Second, the sheer number of news posts added to the system daily means that, before long, our searches would have to sort through too many records to be able to respond in a useful amount of time. If this was a feature that would be more useful for our application, we could solve this problem by implementing a full text search engine such as Sphinx using the Sphincter gem (http://seattlerb.rubyforge.org/Sphincter/).

Since we don't have a need to implement a full text search engine, we'll need to change our grid code by removing the lines that create the filter bar:

```
tb.add('-', 'Filter: ', \"<input type='text' id='text_filter'>\");
Ext.get('text_filter').on('keyup', filterResource);
```

We'll also need to remove the `filterResource` function, since it serves no purpose in this case:

```
function filterResource() {
  filtervalue = Ext.get('text_filter').dom.value;
  ds.proxy = new Ext.data.HttpProxy({method: 'GET', ➥
url: '#{model.pluralize}.json?search=' + filtervalue});
  ds.reload();
}
```

Formatting the Active Field

The next thing that we're going to want to do is format the Active field in our grid. Currently, it's converting the flag to display either "true" or "false". That's okay, but it would be a little bit nicer if we could make that display a "yes" or "no" instead. We'll do this by adding a new `formatBoolean` function that will simply test the value and return "yes" or "no."

```
function formatBoolean(value) {
  return (value == 1) ? 'Yes' : 'No';
}
```

Now that we have that function, we simply need to make our grid use it. Back in the column model definition, we need to define a renderer for the `Active?` column, which will cause Ext to call our `formatBoolean` function when it attempts to display each of these values:

```
{header: "Active?", width: 60, dataIndex: 'Active', renderer: formatBoolean}
```

Formatting News

The next enhancement to make to our news display is to reformat the way that a news article displays in the grid. Currently, we're displaying the headline of each news post in one column and the body text in a separate column. It would be much nicer if we could, instead, combine the two into a single column. We'll do that by again defining a new function that we'll call as a renderer within the column definition. This function will be named `renderNews` and will look like this:

```
function renderNews(value, p, record) {
  return String.format('<b>{0}</b><br />{1}', value, record.data['Body']);
}
```

So with that function available, we'll redefine our Headline column to use the renderNews function as its renderer, so our column model definition will look like this:

```
var cm = new Ext.grid.ColumnModel([
  {header: 'News Story', width: 610, dataIndex: 'Headline', id: 'Headline', ➥
renderer: renderNews},
  {header: 'Created At', width: 200, dataIndex: 'created_at', id: 'created_at'},
  {header: "Active?", width: 60, dataIndex: 'Active', renderer: formatBoolean}
]);
```

That's all well and good, but we have another issue we need to fix—we're still displaying the *full* news post, but that seems like a bit of overkill for the index page. It also causes issues with the display of the page when you consider that some news posts can be quite long. Let's fix that by reducing the amount of the news story that we display down to a preview. We'll do this by first stripping the body text of any HTML tags like this:

```
Ext.util.Format.stripTags(record.data['Body'])
```

Next, we'll truncate the text that's displayed using an Ext substring function to limit the results down to only the first 100 characters:

```
Ext.util.Format.stripTags(record.data['Body']).substr(0,100) + "...."
```

Putting that all together, our renderNews function should look like this and give us a display like Figure 20-2:

```
function renderNews(value, p, record) {
  return String.format('<b>{0}</b><br />{1}', value, ➥
Ext.util.Format.stripTags(record.data['Body']).substr(0,100) + "....");
}
```

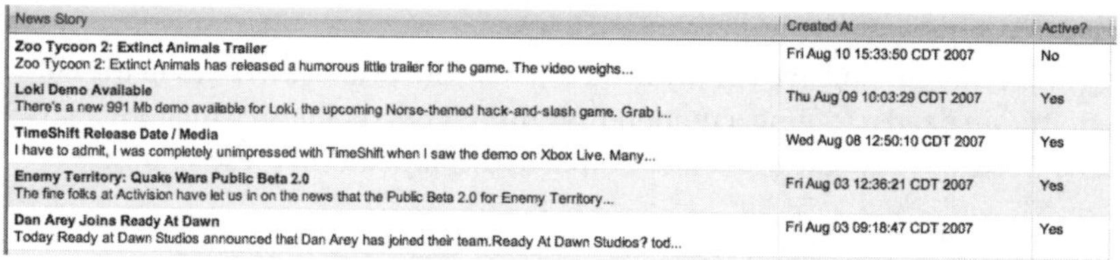

News Story	Created At	Active?
Zoo Tycoon 2: Extinct Animals Trailer Zoo Tycoon 2: Extinct Animals has released a humorous little trailer for the game. The video weighs...	Fri Aug 10 15:33:50 CDT 2007	No
Loki Demo Available There's a new 991 Mb demo available for Loki, the upcoming Norse-themed hack-and-slash game. Grab i...	Thu Aug 09 10:03:29 CDT 2007	Yes
TimeShift Release Date / Media I have to admit, I was completely unimpressed with TimeShift when I saw the demo on Xbox Live. Many...	Wed Aug 08 12:50:10 CDT 2007	Yes
Enemy Territory: Quake Wars Public Beta 2.0 The fine folks at Activision have let us in on the news that the Public Beta 2.0 for Enemy Territory...	Fri Aug 03 12:36:21 CDT 2007	Yes
Dan Arey Joins Ready At Dawn Today Ready at Dawn Studios announced that Dan Arey has joined their team.Ready At Dawn Studios? tod...	Fri Aug 03 09:18:47 CDT 2007	Yes

Figure 20-2. *Improving the display of our news posts*

Adding a Toggle

Another item that's not really a necessity but would be kind of nice to add is a toggle for the display of our news posts that turns on and off the display of the news post preview.

Our first step toward doing that will be to define a new renderer function that will display the news headline sans the news body preview:

```
function renderNewsPlain(value) {
  return String.format('<b><i>{0}</i></b>', value);
}
```

With two different renderers available, we need a way to rotate between them. We can do this fairly easily by adding a button to our toolbar that toggles between the two. Clicking the button will call a function named toggleNews:

```
tb.add('-',{ pressed: false,
  enableToggle: true, text: 'Detailed View',
  toggleHandler: toggleNews
});
```

Our new toggleNews function will simply call an if statement on the button-press state and use that to pick which renderer to apply:

```
function toggleNews(btn, pressed) {
  cm.getColumnById('Headline').renderer = pressed ? renderNews : renderNewsPlain;
  grid.getView().refresh();
}
```

So adding in a few minor size modifications, our page should look like this (building it all manually):

```
<%= ext_layout('News') %>
<script type="text/javascript" charset="utf-8">
  var pageGrid = function() {
    var grid;
    var dialog;
    var ds; return{
      init : function(){
        ds = new Ext.data.Store({
          proxy: new Ext.data.HttpProxy({method: 'GET', url: 'posts.json'}),
          reader: new Ext.data.JsonReader(
            {root: 'posts', totalProperty: 'totalCount', id: 'NewsID'},
            ['Headline', 'Body', 'Active', 'created_at', 'NewsID'])
        });

        function renderNews(value, p, record) {
          return String.format('<b>{0}</b><br />{1}', value, ➥
Ext.util.Format.stripTags(record.data['Body']).substr(0,100) + "....");
        }

        function renderNewsPlain(value) {
          return String.format('<b><i>{0}</i></b>', value);
        }

        var cm = new Ext.grid.ColumnModel([
          {header: 'News Story', width: 610, dataIndex: 'Headline', id: ➥
'Headline', renderer: renderNews},
          {header: 'Created At', width: 200, dataIndex: 'created_at', id: ➥
 'created_at'},
```

```
            {header: "Active?", width: 60, dataIndex: 'Active', renderer: ➥
    formatBoolean}
          ]);

        cm.defaultSortable = true;
        grid = new Ext.grid.Grid('content', { ds: ds, cm: cm });
        grid.render();

        var gridFoot = grid.getView().getFooterPanel(true);
        var paging = new Ext.PagingToolbar(gridFoot, ds,
          {
            pageSize: 13,
            displayInfo: true,
            displayMsg: 'Displaying topics {0} - {1} of {2}',
            emptyMsg: 'No topics to display'
          }
        );
        ds.load({params:{start:0, limit:13}});


        function toggleNews(btn, pressed) {
            cm.getColumnById('Headline').renderer = pressed ? renderNews : ➥
    renderNewsPlain;
            grid.getView().refresh();
        }

        grid.on('rowdblclick', editResource);
        var gridHead = grid.getView().getHeaderPanel(true);
        var tb = new Ext.Toolbar(gridHead);
        tb.add(
          { text: 'Create New Post', handler: createResource },
          '-',
          { text: 'Delete Selected Post', handler: deleteResource }
        );
        tb.add('-',{ pressed: true,
          enableToggle: true, text: 'Detailed View',
          toggleHandler: toggleNews
        });

      }}


        function formatBoolean(value) {
          return (value == 1) ? 'Yes' : 'No';
        }
```

```
function deleteResource() {
  var id = grid.getSelectionModel().getSelected();
  if(id){
    Ext.MessageBox.confirm('Confirm', 'Are you sure you want to delete ➥
this post?', postDelete);
  } else {
    Ext.MessageBox.alert('DOH!', 'Maybe you want to try again after ➥
ACTUALLY selecting something?')
  }
}

function submitResource(){
  document.create_resource.submit();
}

function postDelete(btn){
  if(btn == 'yes') {
    var id = grid.getSelectionModel().getSelected();
    var deleteme = id.get('NewsID');
    window.location.href = '/posts/destroy/' + deleteme;
  }
}

function editResource(grid, rowIndex) {
  var id = grid.getSelectionModel().getSelected();
  if(id) {
    window.location.href = '/posts/' + id.get('NewsID');
  }
}

function createResource() {
  if(!dialog) {
    dialog = new Ext.BasicDialog('newDialog', {
      width:630,
      height:420,
      shadow:true,
      minWidth:300,
      minHeight:340,
      proxyDrag:true,
      autoScroll:false,
      animEl:true
    });
    dialog.addKeyListener(27, dialog.hide, dialog);
    postBtn = dialog.addButton('Submit', submitResource, this);
    dialog.addButton('Close', dialog.hide, dialog);
```

```
          }
          dialog.show();
          dialog.on('hide', function(){
            document.create_resource.reset();
          })
        }
      }();
  Ext.onReady(pageGrid.init, pageGrid, true);
</script>


<div id="content"> </div>

<div id="newDialog">
  <div class="x-dlg-hd">Create New Game</div>
  <div class="x-dlg-bd">
    <% form_for(:post, Post.new, :url => posts_path, :html => {:id => ➥
'create_resource', :name => 'create_resource'}) do |f| %>
      <p>
        <label for="post_Headline">Story Headline:</label>
        <%= f.text_field :Headline %>
      </p>
      <p>
        <label for="post_FrontPage">Frontpage Headline:</label>
        <%= f.text_field :Headline %>
      </p>
      <p>
        <label for="post_Body">News Story:</label>
        <%= f.text_area :Body %>
      </p>
    <% end %>
  </div>
</div>
```

The preceding code gives us a nice clean page, like the one shown in Figure 20-3.

Since there's a good chance we'll reuse this interface to manage other content, let's go ahead and convert our JavaScript grid into a helper method again. This one will be nearly identical to the previous one, except for the changes we made in this chapter.

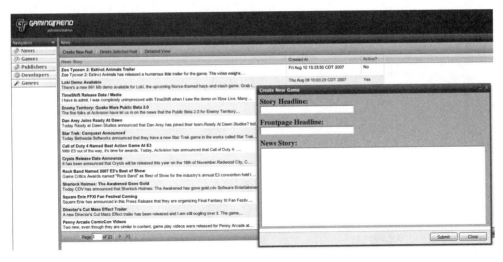

Figure 20-3. *The new index interface*

Back in /app/helpers/application_helper.rb, we'll create a new function named ext_news_grid, which will simply output our new JavaScript:

```
def ext_news_grid(model, primary_key, fields, columns, height)
    xml_fields = fields
    xml_fields << primary_key
    xml_fields.collect! {|x| "'#{x}'"}

    function = "var pageGrid = function() {"
    function << " var grid; var dialog; var ds;"
    function << " return{ init : function(){"
    function << " ds = new Ext.data.Store({"
    function << " proxy: new Ext.data.HttpProxy({method: 'GET', url: ➥
'#{model.pluralize}.json'}),"

    function << "reader: new Ext.data.JsonReader({"
    function << "root: '#{model.pluralize}',"
    function << " totalProperty: 'totalCount',"
    function << " id: '#{primary_key}'"
    function << "}, [#{xml_fields.to_sentence(:connector => '')}])"
    function << " });"
```

```
    function << "function renderNews(value, p, record) {"
    function << "return String.format('<b>{0}</b><br />{1}', value, Ext.util. ➥
Format.stripTags(record.data['Body']).substr(0,100) + \"....\");}"

    function << "function renderNewsPlain(value) {"
    function << "return String.format('<b><i>{0}</i></b>', value); }"

    function << " var cm = new Ext.grid.ColumnModel([#{columns}]);"
    function << " cm.defaultSortable = true;"
    function << " grid = new Ext.grid.Grid('content', { ds: ds, cm: cm });"
    function << " grid.render();"

    function << "var gridFoot = grid.getView().getFooterPanel(true);"
    function << "var paging = new Ext.PagingToolbar(gridFoot, ds, {"
    function << "pageSize: 13,"
    function << "displayInfo: true,"
    function << "displayMsg: 'Displaying topics {0} - {1} of {2}',"
    function << "emptyMsg: 'No topics to display'});"
    function << "ds.load({params:{start:0, limit:13}});"

    function << "function toggleNews(btn, pressed) {"
    function << "cm.getColumnById('Headline').renderer = pressed ? renderNews : ➥
renderNewsPlain;"
    function << "grid.getView().refresh(); }"

    function << " grid.on('rowdblclick', editResource);"

    function << " var gridHead = grid.getView().getHeaderPanel(true);"
    function << " var tb = new Ext.Toolbar(gridHead);"
    function << " tb.add({ text: 'Create New #{model.capitalize}', handler: ➥
 createResource }, '-', { text: 'Delete Selected #{model.capitalize}', handler: ➥
 deleteResource });"
    function << " tb.add('-',{ pressed: true,"
    function << " enableToggle: true, text: 'Detailed View',"
    function << " toggleHandler: toggleNews });"
    function << " }}\n"

    function << "function formatBoolean(value) {"
    function << "return (value == 1) ? 'Yes' : 'No';}"

    function << " function deleteResource() {"
    function << " var id = grid.getSelectionModel().getSelected(); "
    function << " if(id){"
    function << " Ext.MessageBox.confirm('Confirm', 'Are you sure you want to ➥
delete this #{model}?', postDelete);"
    function << "  } else {"
```

```
    function << " Ext.MessageBox.alert('DOH!', 'Maybe you want to try again ➥
after ACTUALLY selecting something?')}}\n"

    function << " function submitResource(){"
    function << " document.create_resource.submit();}\n"

    function << " function postDelete(btn){"
    function << " if(btn == 'yes') {"
    function << " var id = grid.getSelectionModel().getSelected();"
    function << " var deleteme = id.get('#{primary_key}');"
    function << " window.location.href = '/#{model.pluralize}/destroy/' + ➥
 deleteme;}}\n"

    function << " function editResource(grid, rowIndex) {"
    function << " var id = grid.getSelectionModel().getSelected();"
    function << " if(id) { "
    function << " window.location.href = '/#{model.pluralize}/' + ➥
id.get('#{primary_key}'); }}\n"

    function << " function createResource() {"
    function << " if(!dialog) {"
    function << " dialog = new Ext.BasicDialog('newDialog', {"
    function << " width:630, height:#{height}, shadow:true, minWidth:300, ➥
minHeight:#{height}, proxyDrag:true, autoScroll:false, animEl:true });"
    function << " dialog.addKeyListener(27, dialog.hide, dialog);"
    function << " postBtn = dialog.addButton('Submit', submitResource, this);"
    function << " dialog.addButton('Close', dialog.hide, dialog); }\n"

    function << " dialog.show();"
    function << " dialog.on('hide', function(){"
    function << " document.create_resource.reset();})"
    function << " } }();"
    function << " Ext.onReady(pageGrid.init, pageGrid, true);"
    javascript_tag(function)
  end
```

We'll utilize the ext_news_grid function in our index page (/app/views/posts/index.rhtml) like this:

```
<%= ext_layout('News') %>
<%= ext_news_grid("post", "NewsID", %w(Headline Body created_at Active),
"{header: 'News Story', width: 610, dataIndex: 'Headline', id: 'Headline', ➥
renderer: renderNews},
{header: 'Created At', width: 200, dataIndex: 'created_at', id: 'created_at'},
{header: 'Active?', width: 60, dataIndex: 'Active', renderer: formatBoolean}", ➥
 420) %>
```

```
<div id="content"> </div>

<div id="newDialog">
  <div class="x-dlg-hd">Create New Game</div>
  <div class="x-dlg-bd">
    <% form_for(:post, Post.new, :url => posts_path,
         :html => {:id => 'create_resource', :name => 'create_resource'}) do |f| %>
      <p>
        <label for="post_Headline">Story Headline:</label>
        <%= f.text_field :Headline %>
      </p>
      <p>
        <label for="post_FrontPage">Frontpage Headline:</label>
        <%= f.text_field :Headline %>
      </p>
      <p>
        <label for="post_Body">News Story:</label>
        <%= f.text_area :Body %>
      </p>
    <% end %>
  </div>
</div>
```

Capturing Creation Errors

Once again, if a new post can't be created, we'll direct the user to a default page to correct any mistakes and resubmit. Create a new file named new.rthml in /app/views/posts directory, and place the following content in it:

```
<%= ext_layout('Create News Post') %>

<div id='content'>
  <%= error_messages_for :post %>
  <% form_for(:post, :url => posts_path,
        :html => {:id => 'create_resource', :name => 'create_resource'}) do |f| %>
  <p>
    <label for="post_Headline">Story Headline:</label>
    <%= f.text_field :Headline %>
  </p>
  <p>
    <label for="post_FrontPage">Frontpage Headline:</label>
    <%= f.text_field :Headline %>
  </p>
```

```
  <p>
    <label for="post_Body">News Story:</label>
    <%= f.text_area :Body %>
  </p>
  <% end %>
</div>
```

The Edit News Page

The final page that we'll add is the edit news page. This is the page that users will see if they double-click a news story on the index page, and it will be the page that they will be redirected to after successfully creating a new post. On this page, we'll obviously need to provide users with the ability to reedit the news post if necessary, but we also want to provide staff members with the ability to control with which resources this news post should be associated.

Let's create a new template named show.rhtml in /app/views/posts, and in this new page, we'll add our layout helper and build our forms to edit the news post in a combination of Ext forms and Rails helpers. We'll also take advantage of the In-Place Controls plug-in again by creating an in_place_checkbox to allow toggling of the news post from active to deactivated.

We'll start with the most basic things that we need for our page to work by placing this into our new page:

```
<%= ext_layout('Edit News Post') %>

<div id="content">
</div>
```

Editing the News Post

We'll add to this page by adding in an Ext form to edit our news post headline, front page headline, and post text. To keep things nice and neat, we'll place this form in an edit_form div. This will be very similar to the form that we built in the previous chapter, so we'll focus solely on the implementation here.

```
<%= ext_layout('Edit News Post') %>

<div id="content">
  <div id="edit_form">
    <script type="text/javascript" charset="utf-8">
      Ext.onReady(function(){
        Ext.form.Field.prototype.msgTarget = 'side';
          var post = new Ext.form.Form({
          labelAlign: 'top',
          url:'<%= post_url(@post) %>'
        });
```

```
            post.add(
              post.fieldset(
                  {legend:'Edit News Post'},
                    new Ext.form.TextField({
                        fieldLabel: 'Headline',
                        name: 'post[Headline]',
                        growMin:225,
                        allowBlank:false,
                        grow: true,
                        value:"<%= @post.Headline.gsub("\n", "").gsub('"', '\"'). ➥
gsub("'", "\'").gsub("\r", "") %>"
                      }),

                    new Ext.form.TextField({
                        fieldLabel: 'FrontPage',
                        name: 'post[FrontPage]',
                        width:225,
                        allowBlank:false,
                        maxLength:26,
                        value:"<%= @post.FrontPage.gsub("\n", "").gsub('"', '\"'). ➥
gsub("'", "\'").gsub("\r", "") %>"
                      }),

                    new Ext.form.HtmlEditor({
                        id:'Body',
                        fieldLabel:'Body',
                        name: 'post[Body]',
                        enableFont: false,
                        value: "<%= @post.Body.gsub("\n", "").gsub('"', '\"'). ➥
gsub("'", "\'").gsub("\r", "") %>",
                        width:750,
                        height:200
                      })
                )
            );

        post.addButton('Save', function(){
          if(post.isValid()){
            post.submit({
              params:{
                action: "update",
                _method: "put",
                commit:"Save",
                id: <%= @post.id %>
              }, waitMsg:'Saving News Post Now...'
            });
```

```
      } else {
        Ext.MessageBox.alert('Errors', 'Please fix the errors noted.');
      }
    }, post);

    post.render('edit_form');
    });
  </script>
  </div>
</div>
```

You can see the results of our new form element in Figure 20-4.

Figure 20-4. *Editing a news post*

Activating the Post

We have a process for editing the content of a news post now—but that won't do us any good unless we also have the ability to activate the post so that it will show up on the main site. You should remember that we control the activated status through a simple Boolean flag set to either 0 or 1. An easy way to solve this is to take advantage of the in_place_checkbox method that was added by our In-Place Controls plug-in again.

We'll first need to configure our posts controller (/app/controller/posts_controller.rb) to accept in-place edits of the Active field:

```
class PostsController < ApplicationController
  in_place_edit_for :post, :Active

  make_resourceful do
    build :all
  end
```

```
  def index
    limit =  params[:limit] || 25
    start = params[:start] || 0

    respond_to do |format|
      format.html
      format.json {
        @posts = Post.find(:all, :limit => limit, :offset => start )
        posts_count = Post.count
        griddata = Hash.new
        griddata[:posts] = @posts.collect {|p| {:NewsID => p.NewsID, ➥
:Headline => p.Headline, :created_at => p.created_at.to_s, :Body => p.Body, ➥
:Active => p.Active}}
        griddata[:totalCount] =  posts_count
        render :text => griddata.to_json()
      }
    end
  end
end
```

Next, we can go back to our show.rhtml in /app/views/posts, add a new activated div in our content div, and place our in_place_checkbox method there:

```
<%= ext_layout('Edit News Post') %>

<div id="content">
  <div id="activated">
     <label for="post_Active" style="display: inline; margin-right: 5px;">Active ➥
 on Site?</label>
     <%= in_place_checkbox :post, :Active, :checked => true, :unchecked => false %>
  </div>
  <div id="edit_form">
    <script type="text/javascript" charset="utf-8">
      Ext.onReady(function(){
    (...Remaining Output Omitted...)
```

This enhances our edit news post page, as shown in Figure 20-5.

Figure 20-5. *Adding an activation control to our news post*

Building Associations to the Post

We're not done with our edit news page just yet though. As you may recall from our earlier discussions about how the current news system works, once a news post has been created, staff members are expected to associate that story with one or many game records as well. The table for storing these associations is merely a join table named GameNews; looking in db/schema.rb, we can see that it does have a traditional many-to-many relationship:

```
create_table "GameNews", :id => false, :force => true do |t|
    t.column "GameID", :integer, :default => 0, :null => false
    t.column "NewsID", :integer, :default => 0, :null => false
end
```

So this should just be a simple matter of establishing a has_and_belongs_to_many association between the Game model and the Post model. Of course, I say "should be" because building that association is going to be a little bit more work because of the unconventional ID fields.

In our Games model, we can create an association to our Posts model by adding the following line:

```
has_and_belongs_to_many :posts
```

However, because the legacy databases join table GameNews doesn't follow conventions (otherwise, it would be named game_news), we'll need to define the name of the join table like this:

```
:join_table => "GameNews"
```

Now that the model knows which table to look in for its associations, we still have the issue of mapping to our nonstandard ID fields. A has-and-belongs-to-many (HABTM) association expects that it will find fields named post_id and game_id in the GameNews table. We'll have to override these assumptions by manually specifying the foreign keys to look for.

The first value that we'll override is the :foreign_key, which is used to specify the key that maps back to this model. Its default assumption is that it will be the name of this class lowercased and with and _id appended. So within the Games model, it would expect that the foreign key in GamesNews would be game_id. We'll override this by setting :foreign_key => "GameID".

Second, we need to define the value that is used to map to the other table we're joining to. Rails assumes that this will be the lowercase version of the name of the associated class with an _id appended. So Rails expects this to be news_id, and we'll override it to NewsID by setting :association_foreign_key => 'NewsID'.

So putting that all together and our HABTM association in the Games model (/app/models/game.rb) should look like this:

```
class Game < ActiveRecord::Base
  set_table_name 'Games'
  set_primary_key :GameID
  belongs_to :publisher, :foreign_key => 'PubID'
  belongs_to :developer, :foreign_key => 'DevID'
  belongs_to :genre, :foreign_key => 'GenreID'
```

```ruby
  has_many :screenshots, :foreign_key => 'GameID'
  has_and_belongs_to_many :posts, :join_table => "GameNews",
              :foreign_key => "GameID", :association_foreign_key => 'NewsID'

  order_by :title
  validates_length_of :Title, :maximum => 100, :message => " must be less than ➥
100 characters"
  validates_presence_of :Title, :Console

  def boxart
    self.BoximagePath.blank? ? "/boxshots/empty.jpg" :  self.BoximagePath
  end

  def homepage
    self.SiteURL || "Not Set"
  end

  def homepage=(value)
    self.SiteURL = value
  end
end
```

Meanwhile, in our Posts model (/app/models/post.rb), we can map back to the Games model by adding the reciprocal version:

```ruby
class Post < ActiveRecord::Base
  set_table_name 'News'
  set_primary_key :NewsID

  has_and_belongs_to_many :games, :join_table => "GameNews",
              :foreign_key => "NewsID", :association_foreign_key => 'GameID'
  order_by "created_at DESC"

  validates_presence_of :Headline, :Body
  validates_length_of :FrontPage, :within => 1..26, :on => :create, :message => ➥
"must be present"
end
```

Now that we have our HABTM association mapped correctly, what we need to have is a simple way of maintaining the associations among game records and news posts in our edit news page. However, we'd like to be able to do it without having to resort to pulling in a full list of games again. We'll make this happen by adding a pair of new forms to our page and a little AJAX magic. The first form we'll add to the show.rhtml in /app/views/posts is a form that provides a list of any currently associated games to this news post as a check box.

```erb
<%= ext_layout('Edit News Post') %>
<div id="content">
  <div id="activated">
```

```
  <label for="post_Active" style="display: inline; margin-right: 5px;">Active ➥
on Site?</label>
    <%= in_place_checkbox :post, :Active, :checked => true, :unchecked => false %>
  </div>
  <div id="edit_form">
    (…code omitted for brevity…)
  </div>

  <div id="add_game_associations">
    <label>Associated Games</label>
    <% form_for :post, :url => { :action => "associate", :id => @post } do |f| %>
      <ul>
        <% @post.games.each do |g| %>
          <li><%= check_box_tag 'post[game_ids][]', g.id, 1 %>
                <%= "#{g.Title} (#{g.Console})" %>
          </li>
        <% end %>
        <div id="results"></div>
      </ul>
      <%= submit_tag 'Associate' %>
    <% end %>
  </div>
</div>
```

which will give us a list of associated games to each news post like, as shown in Figure 20-6.

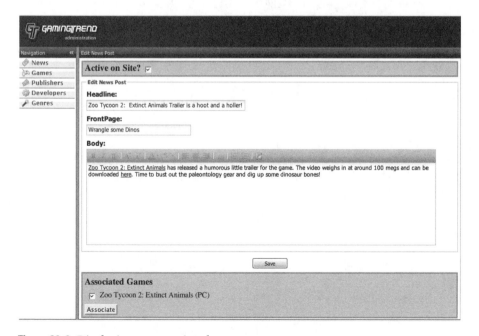

Figure 20-6. *Displaying our associated games*

Of course, you may have noticed that the form we just added pointed to a mythical associate method that doesn't yet exist. We'll need to create this associate method in /app/controllers/posts_controller.rb and we'll want it to set the associated games for this news post to whatever was submitted in our form. In the posts controller, add the following method:

```
def associate
    @post = Post.find(params[:id])
    @post.update_attributes(@params['post'])
    redirect_to post_url(@post)
 end
```

An added bonus of this method is that any previous association entries will be wiped out by our update_attributes call, so this one method can also be used to remove an association from the game when a staff member simply unchecks a value in the form. Of course, what we need now is a way to add new games to the list of associated games. We'll do that by adding a new AJAX-based form to our page. We'll use this new form to allow a staff member to search against the games database and have the results of that search inserted as additional options in the associated games form. In essence, we'll dynamically add options to the associate form, so we'll add the new form to our existing list like this:

```
<div id="add_game_associations">
    <label>Associated Games</label>
    <% form_for :post, :url => { :action => "associate", :id => @post } do |f| %>
        <ul>
        <% @post.games.each do |g| %>
            <li>
                <%= check_box_tag 'post[game_ids][]', g.id, 1 %>
                <%= "#{g.Title} (#{g.Console})" %>
            </li>
        <% end %>
        <div id="results"></div>
        </ul>
        <%= submit_tag 'Associate' %>
    <% end %>

    <label>Add Games to Associate </label>
    <% form_remote_tag :url => '/games/search', :html => {:id => "search"} do -%>
        Search: <input type="text" id="search_form" name="search" />
        <%= submit_tag 'Search' %>
    <% end -%>
</div>
```

This form will submit whatever was entered into its text field to another missing method. This time, the missing method is the search method in the games controller (/app/controllers/games_controller.rb), so let's add that method now:

```
def search
  @results = Game.find(:all,
                       :conditions => ["Title like ?", "%" + params[:search] + "%"],
                       :limit => 20)
end
```

This method will take the submitted parameter and use it in a search against the Title field in the games table. To push those results back into our existing page, we'll create an RJS template—create a new file named search.rjs in /app/views/games, and place the following commands in it:

```
page['search'].reset
page['results'].replace_html(:partial => 'association', :collection => @results)
```

All we're doing in this RJS template is erasing the content from the search form and dumping our results into the result div on the current page (which you should remember was inside our associate games form). To keep things simple, we're using a partial to render the output of our results collection, so we need to create a new partial in /app/views/games named _association.rhtml. That partial should look like this:

```
<li>
  <%= check_box_tag 'post[game_ids][]', association.id, nil %>
  <%= "#{association.Title} (#{association.Console})" %>
</li>
```

It should look familiar, because that's exactly the same format that we're using for the associated games in our first form. The only difference is that we are setting the check boxes on these elements to be unchecked. You can see the display of the page in Figure 20-7.

Figure 20-7. *The new add game associations form*

If we submit that form to search for games named "splinter cell", the results appear in the associated games form that you can see in Figure 20-8.

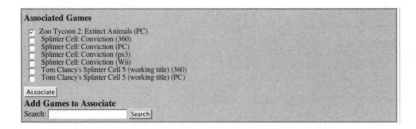

Figure 20-8. *Search results added to our associated games form*

Simply check a few of the games, and click the Associate button to submit the form and associate our additional games to this news post (see Figure 20-9).

Figure 20-9. *Additional games are now associated to our news post.*

It's a nice little solution that makes it easy to associate a large number of records without having to dump the full list of games into the page. Our final show page (/app/views/posts/ show.rhtml) should look like this:

```
<%= ext_layout('Edit News Post') %>

<div id="content">
  <div id="activated">
    <label for="post_Active" style="display: inline; margin-right: 5px;">Active ➥
on Site?</label>
    <%= in_place_checkbox :post, :Active, :checked => true, :unchecked => false %>
  </div>
  <div id="edit_form">
    <script type="text/javascript" charset="utf-8">
      Ext.onReady(function(){
        Ext.form.Field.prototype.msgTarget = 'side';
        var post = new Ext.form.Form({
          labelAlign: 'top',
          url:'<%= post_url(@post) %>'
        });
        post.add(
          post.fieldset(
            {legend:'Edit News Post'},
            new Ext.form.TextField({
            fieldLabel: 'Headline',
```

```
          name: 'post[Headline]',
          growMin:225,
          allowBlank:false,
          grow: true,
          value:"<%= @post.Headline.gsub("\n", "").gsub('"', '\"'). ➥
gsub("'", "\'").gsub("\r", "") %>"
        }),

        new Ext.form.TextField({
          fieldLabel: 'FrontPage',
          name: 'post[FrontPage]',
          width:225,
          allowBlank:false,
          maxLength:26,
          value:"<%= @post.FrontPage.gsub("\n", "").gsub('"', '\"'). ➥
gsub("'", "\'").gsub("\r", "") %>"
        }),

        new Ext.form.HtmlEditor({
          id:'Body',
          fieldLabel:'Body',
          name: 'post[Body]',
          enableFont: false,
          value: "<%= @post.Body.gsub("\n", "").gsub('"', '\"').gsub("'", "\'").➥
gsub("\r", "") %>",
          width:750,
          height:200
        })
      )
    );

    post.addButton('Save', function(){
      if(post.isValid()){
        post.submit({
          params:{
            action: "update",
            _method: "put",
            commit:"Save",
            id: <%= @post.id %>
          }, waitMsg:'Saving News Post Now...'
        });
      } else {
        Ext.MessageBox.alert('Errors', 'Please fix the errors noted.');
      }
    }, post);

    post.render('edit_form');
```

```
      });
      </script>
   </div>

   <div id="add_game_associations">
      <label>Associated Games</label>
      <% form_for :post, :url => { :action => "associate", :id => @post } do |f| %>
         <ul>
            <% @post.games.each do |g| %>
              <li>
                 <%= check_box_tag 'post[game_ids][]', g.id, 1 %>
                 <%= "#{g.Title} (#{g.Console})" %>
              </li>
            <% end %>
            <div id="results"></div>
         </ul>
         <%= submit_tag 'Associate' %>
      <% end %>

   <label>Add Games to Associate </label>
      <% form_remote_tag :url => '/games/search', :html => {:id => "search"} do -%>
         Search: <input type="text" id="search_form" name="search" />
         <%= submit_tag 'Search' %>
      <% end -%>
   </div>
</div>
```

Summary

With that last little touch, we're at a good stopping point, as we've finished up a solid base for the new administration system. We've connected our models to the legacy database, cleaned up a lot of worthless fields, and created a new standard set of interfaces to give the administration site a new sheen. Along the way, you learned about some of the issues that come into play when the database doesn't match Rails conventions and how you can work around them. You also learned about building a more advanced interface using Ext and looked at ways to optimize the workflow to create a new administration interface that not only looks good but should respond faster and make the daily workload a bit easier on the staff as well.

CHAPTER 21

∎∎∎

Enhancing the Gaming Site

This was certainly a large project, wasn't it? It's the kind of project that we could really fill up a whole book with on its own, as we moved into other areas of the application such as supporting reviews, video uploads, and an article review/approval system—and this is just the backend administration system. You can imagine the fun we could have if we roll Rails out to the main site and explore the challenges of deploying a Rails application that handles a pretty fair amount of traffic onto a typical single-server scenario (handling issues such as fine-tuning our database queries and indexes, implementing caching, and of course, monitoring the performance of our application).

In the meantime, however, there are still plenty of fun things to do in the administrative application that we built. This chapter contains a few ideas to get you started.

Build Your Own Generator

As you saw in Chapter 18, generators can be a great tool for automating routine installation tasks. One aspect that we didn't cover in that chapter was the ability to create a generator that we could pass additional parameters into. The way we do this is by making the generator inherit from `Rails::Generator::NamedBase` instead of `Rails::Generator::Base`. Doing so allows us to use parameters passed in from the command line in our generator. You can read more about this at `http://wiki.rubyonrails.org/rails/pages/UnderstandingGenerators`. Experiment with this, and modify your generator to install only a single theme based on a parameter that is passed in when the generator is called.

Add Login Capabilities

One area that we didn't address for our application is the user authentication and administration needs of the application. Of course, by this point we've implemented those so many times you could probably add them blindfolded, so I thought it would be good practice for you to implement the user authentication for this application yourself. If you look at the current database schema for users, you can see that it has a structure like this:

```
create_table "Users", :id => false, :force => true do |t|
    t.column "userID",   :integer, :limit => 8, :null => false
    t.column "username",  :string, :limit => 20,  :default => "", :null => false
    t.column "password",  :string, :limit => 20,  :default => "",  :null => false
    t.column "firstname", :string, :limit => 30,  :default => "",  :null => false
```

```
      t.column "lastname",  :string, :limit => 30,  :default => "",:null => false
      t.column "status",  :string, :limit => 10,  :default => "", :null => false
      t.column "email",  :string, :limit => 100, :default => "news@consolegold.com"
      t.column "last_login_ip", :string,   :limit => 15
      t.column "last_login_host", :string, :limit => 100, :default => "", ➥
   :null => false
      t.column "last_login_dt", :datetime, :null => false
    end
```

Currently those fields are used like this:

- *userID*: This is the primary key used to identify the user.

- *username*: This is the user's login name. This field cannot be renamed, as it's used on the front end as well.

- *password*: This is the user's password stored as an MD5 hash.

- *firstname*: This is the user's first name. This field cannot be renamed, as it's used on the front end as well.

- *lastname*: This is the user's last name. This field cannot be renamed, as it's used on the front end as well.

- *status*: This is used to indicate the status of the user. In the old system, there were three possible statuses: Admin, Staff, and Deactivated. The Admin and Staff levels were used for some basic role-based permission settings.

- *email*: The e-mail address of the user is stored here. This field cannot be renamed, as it's used on the front end as well.

- *last_login_ip*: This was used as a tracking mechanism to capture the IP address that the user last logged in from. You should be able to capture this from request.env['REMOTE_ADDR'].

- *last_login_host*: This was used to capture the remote host name based on the IP address using PHP's gethostbyaddr function. Because this merely slows down the login process while this remote host is looked up and doesn't really provide any additional value, I'd recommend removing this field.

- *last_login_dt*: This captures the datetime that this user last logged into the administration system. Of course, because you're already going to be updating this record with the last_login_ip every time users log in, you could simply change this to an updated_at field and not have to bother with it.

With that information, you should be able to do any necessary conversions of the table and create the user model that will allow it to hook into our legacy database. On the positive side—other than a few fields that need to be present for display on the front end of the web site—you have a fair amount of freedom to reinvent this area. In fact, you could even implement a solution like the restful_authentication plug-in (as long as you added in those required fields).

Of course, you'll also notice that the users model touches most of the other tables that we've built, so be sure to test out your relationships among the models. Also, you'll want to modify your create methods for things such as news posts and game records to capture the user ID of the staff member who created them.

You might also want to think about how you'll handle removing somebody from the staff.

Associate Publishers, Developers, and Consoles to News Posts

In our news post administration, we built a tool to display and modify the association of games to each news post. However, you might recall that earlier we discussed how the site associates multiple items to each news post. Why don't you see if you can finish out this process by adding the ability to associate publishers, developers, and consoles to a news post? Associations among publishers and developers would probably benefit from using the same process that we used for associating games; however, the list of possible consoles is much shorter (possible options within the database include Xbox, 360, PS2, PS3, PSP, Cube, GBA, DS, WII, PC, and Nokia) and therefore probably doesn't need to bother with any AJAX lookups. See if you can come up with an alternative approach for this list.

Create a Consoles Constant

Of course, now that you've built that interface to associate a console to a news post, allow me to point out a potential point of pain for the code. What's going to happen in a few years when Sony announces the PlayStation 4 (PS4)? Currently, that means we'd have to go through every place in the code where we're generating this list of options—such as on the news post editing page, the form to create a new game, or the page to edit an existing game—and add that additional option. That's not exactly efficient, and it opens up the opportunity for mistakes where we might forget to add the PS4 to one of the lists.

A better solution would be to move this list of potential consoles to either the database or into a constant that can be edited in one place. To make things simple for now, why don't you go ahead and create a new constant named CONSOLES that will contain this array of possible consoles and modify all of our code to use that constant instead?

Add Box Art and Screenshot Uploads

In our games show template (/app/views/games/show.rhtml), we added the ability to display the box artwork for a game and any screenshots that have already been uploaded for it. Because we've already covered image uploads in several other projects, we didn't address adding the ability to upload box shots or screenshots in this application. Why don't you see if you can add the attachment_fu plug-in to this project and incorporate it into the design to accommodate this need? For screenshots, you may also want to take another look at adding an option for batch file uploads using SWFupload (we discussed this in Chapter 17). Be sure that, when you create the images, you're associating them correctly to the game record.

Add Support for Games Reviews

The site has developed into a full-fledged gaming news and reviews site, and while we've built the news portion of our gaming site, we're still missing the reviews portion. This is an important feature of the site that helps to drive a lot of traffic through it. On the plus side, the staff has been fairly unhappy with the old review process, so we have the opportunity to re-create the reviews table any way we want—we just need to import the existing reviews into the new format after we're done. The requirements for a game review are fairly simple: we need to capture a large amount of text for the actual review and a set of numeric scores to rate things such as graphics, sound, controls, game play, value, overall score, and of course, an active/inactive flag. The review form itself will need to have rich text editor support in order to allow the staff to format the text.

Think also about how you will handle the associations. A game review will only need to be associated with a single game. For that reason, I would probably recommend that you implement the ability to create the game review as an additional tab on the games' show template—perhaps just a single tab that will display either the current review or a form to create a new review. Another idea would be to include the ability to add revisions of the review using the acts_as_versioned plug-in.

Add Long Content Support

The site will also need the ability to create content that can span multiple pages, such as articles and press releases. Adding these will probably require you to add new navigation links into the application. The forms themselves will probably look fairly similar to the form that we're using to create a new game review, as they'll need to have rich text editor support. Both of these will need to be associated with multiple elements in the same way that we associate news posts. You'll find the tables that you'll need to use for these named PressReleases and Articles. So go ahead and build support for these in your version of the application. Keep in mind that you'll also probably need to do some cleanup on each table's schema first.

Add the Acts as Paranoid Plug-In

One concern that the site owner has about the site is the risk of staff members deleting records inadvertently (or maliciously). The old administration system handled this by limiting access to the delete button to only administrative members of the staff. For the redesign, though, it would be better if anyone could delete a record without needing to notify an administrator. You can do this fairly easily (and safely) through the use of another Rick Olsen plug-in by the name of Acts as Paranoid, which overrides ActiveRecord's delete method to simply set a deleted_at field in the table to the current timestamp. This would require a change to the basic finders used on the front end to look for only records where deleted_at is NULL, but it's a minor SQL change that we can live with considering the additional benefits that it provides us (as a side note, Acts as Paranoid also overrides the default find method for the model as well to only find records that aren't marked as deleted).

Here's the interesting challenge: how will you provide a means for the site owner to go back through and permanently delete a record after it's been marked for deletion by the staff? In this application, where the number of deletes from the database is a fairly small number, I would probably build an observer watching for deletes on the models and kick off an e-mail to the site owner that specifies the records that were deleted. In that e-mail, I would probably build a hidden link to permanently delete the record using the `destroy!` method.

Move Logic to Models

Did you notice that in our news post show template (`/app/views/posts.show.rhtml`) we've got this really big and ugly `gsub` method thats whole purpose is to simply clean up our data?

```
{legend:'Edit News Post'},
  new Ext.form.TextField({
    fieldLabel: 'Headline',
    name: 'post[Headline]',
    growMin:225,
    allowBlank:false,
    grow: true,
    value:"<%= @post.Headline.gsub("\n", "").gsub('"', '\"').gsub("'", "\'").➡
gsub("\r", "") %>"
  }),
```

Even worse, it's repeated three times in this same page. That shouldn't mesh well with our sensibilities to keep things clean or DRY, so try moving this cleanup process into either a method in the Post class or a helper method. Keep in mind that the goal is to avoid duplicating this code—not just simply move it out of the view.

Summary

With those tasks, you're well on your way to having the core administrative needs of the application completed. But don't stop now—there are plenty of other areas that we haven't addressed yet, such as how to support video uploads, staff blogs, and reports on staff productivity (i.e., providing our friend Ron with a report of who's adding content to the site and who's not).

Beyond that, keeping an eye on Ext-JS is a very good idea. The library seems to be in a constant state of development (a point that has not always made writing a book that uses it very much fun), and new features are constantly being added. Even as this book is going to print, there's already a preview of an upcoming 2.0 release that adds some exciting new features, such as grouping rows in grids, multiple document interface (MDI) features, anchored layouts, and scrolling tabs.

Extending Monkey Tasks

The following exercise offers additional enhancements for Monkey Tasks.

Enhance with Ext-JS

Fortunately, we don't have any legacy database issues to deal with in Monkey Tasks. However, I'm sure we could benefit from implementing some of the Ext widgets. For example, you could convert your daily task lists to be displayed in a grid component, you could add support for dialogs to create new tasks and message boxes to notify users when things have changed, or you could go hog wild and completely change the entire application's look and feel into something more like a desktop application using the Ext border layout component.

## PART 8

Integrating with a RESTful Application Using Edge Rails (Rails 2.0)

One of the biggest challenges in writing a book of Rails projects is the fact that Rails has always been something of a moving target. What was once the standard way of accomplishing a task can be dramatically changed in an upcoming version of Rails. While this can make writing a book more difficult, it does make developing applications in Rails fun and exciting as new solutions to common web development pains are added to our arsenal.

With that being said, we're going to close out this book with a project using the latest version of the upcoming Rails 2.0 development code (called edge Rails). To make it interesting, we'll take advantage of one the coolest new features in Rails 2.0—Active Resource, a library for integrating with RESTful APIs—and we'll discuss some of the interesting changes coming to our beloved framework.

■ ■ ■

## CHAPTER 22

Brief Overview of Highrise

In March of 2007, 37signals released their latest product—an online contact relationship manager by the name of Highrise. Highrise is an absolutely fantastic marriage of Rails development and product design that brings a much simpler and relevant paradigm to the idea of relationship management. It brings the focus back on the people—the contacts that we have with them and the things that we need to do to keep those relationships moving forward.

To quote 37signals's own blog when they officially announced the product, Highrise was designed to handle common scenarios, such as:

- See all follow-ups scheduled for this week

- Review Susan's notes before calling her contact at the printer

- Set a reminder to write Steve a thank-you note next Friday

- Review all conversations I've had with Chris from Apple

- Organize interview responses for potential candidates online

- See a list of all the designers your company has hired in the past

- Enter notes from a call with a potential client

- See all the people your company knows at the *New York Times*

- Schedule a follow-up sales call with Jim in three months

- Review all the people tagged "Leads 2006"

However, even better than Highrise's feature list is the fact that the application was written with the same REST-based design principles that we've explored in earlier chapters—so the interface is its own API. This provides us with a solid and easy-to-explore method of integrating our applications with Highrise. Before we can start integrating Highrise, though, let's do a brief overview of what Highrise is and how a normal user would use it.

Creating a Highrise Account

Our first step to using and integrating Highrise is to create a new Highrise account. So go to www.highrisehq.com and follow the steps to pick a plan (Highrise offers several different plans ranging in cost from free to $149 a month).

After you pick a plan, you'll be asked to create the main administrative user for your account as well as to configure a few key settings such as the time zone and web address that will be used to access your account (see Figure 22-1). Once your account is created, you'll receive an e-mail confirmation with the details of your new Highrise account and be prompted to log in.

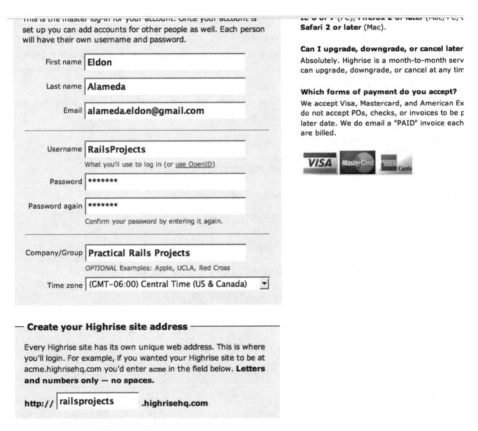

Figure 22-1. *Creating a new account*

Sign in for the first time, and you'll notice that you're immediately presented with one of the key design patterns that 37signals advocates—a highly interactive and informative blank slate. Rather than presenting an utterly empty first page, waiting for the user to add his or her data to the system, 37signals uses this area as an opportunity to provide links to tutorials, helpful tips, and screenshots to hold the hand of someone who's just starting out with the application. With one glance at the page in Figure 22-2, you should immediately be able to see what a difference this can make for a new user.

Figure 22-2. *The starting page*

Within the application, you'll notice that in addition to the Welcome tab, that there are four main tabs:

- *Dashboard*: The Dashboard tab provides you with a high-level overview of the latest activities within your account. This page allows you to quickly preview all of your upcoming tasks and recent contacts.

- *Contacts*: In the Contacts tab, you can view and manage all of your contacts. From here, you can also create tasks, enter notes, or associate people with companies.

- *Tasks*: The Tasks tab enables you to edit and view the tasks that you have created in Highrise.

- *Cases*: The Case section provides a simple way of grouping together related notes, files, and so forth. So if I were planning a birthday party for my daughter, I might create a new case where I could store contact information from party supply vendors, pictures of potential birthday cake designs, and invitation lists.

As much fun as it might be to go over everything that is available within the Highrise application, doing so would be far outside of the scope of this projects book, so let's just hit a few highpoints that you'll need to understand when we start integrating our Rails application to Highrise. The features that we'll need to be concerned with are the abilities to create contacts within Highrise, to maintain a history of our interactions with each contact via notes, and to be proactive in our dealings with each contact by creating tasks that keep the relationships moving forward.

Creating Contacts

As I stated before, the primary focus of Highrise is on people, so it makes sense that one of our first tasks within our new Highrise account will be to add our own contacts. Highrise makes this easy by providing several ways we can add contacts to the application. First, we could enter contacts manually within the application, as you can see in Figure 22-3.

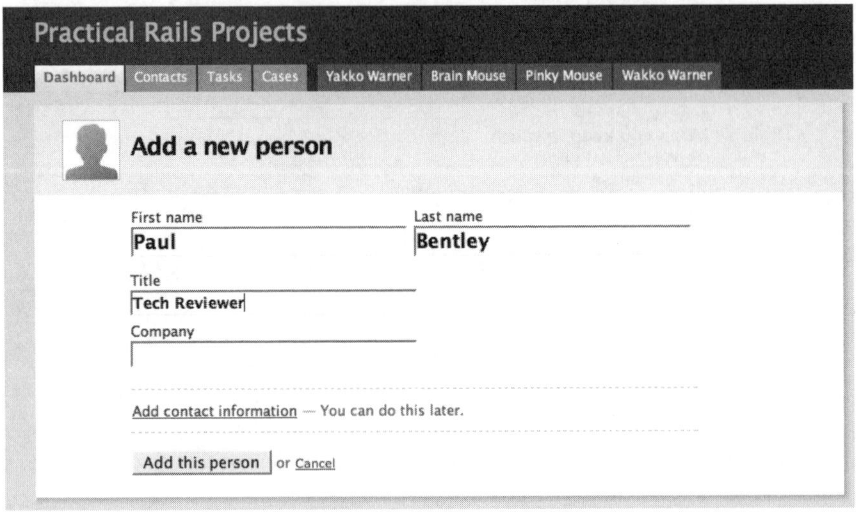

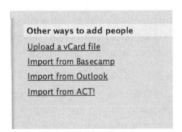

Figure 22-3. *Adding contacts to Highrise*

But, if you have a large pool of contacts, adding each contact manually could become a fairly painful task of copying and pasting each person's information from your existing address books into Highrise. Fortunately, Highrise also supports bulk importing of contacts from a variety of popular systems including Basecamp, Microsoft Outlook, ACT, or even a simple vCard (see Figure 22-4).

Other ways to add people

Upload a vCard file

Import from Basecamp

Import from Outlook

Import from ACT!

Figure 22-4. *Import options*

Once we have some contacts added to your Highrise account, we can begin to manage those relationships from a "what do I need to do next" perspective.

The idea is that, as soon as you complete an interaction with a contact, you should log it as a note within Highrise and immediately schedule the next to-do item for that person. For example, if I were a used car salesman, I would immediately create an account for a recent contact and place information about what the potential ~~sucker~~ customer was looking for, what his price range was, and so on. Then, I would create a task for myself to make a follow up call to that person in a few days and try to talk him into buying a car.

Creating Tasks

Speaking of creating tasks, tasks are amazingly easy to deal with within Highrise. Not only can a simple task be created within the Tasks panel but tasks can be created from all the major areas of the application so that they can be directly associated with a person, a company, or even a case.

Another core feature of creating tasks is the ease with which we can specify a timeline for that task's completion. We can specify general ranges such as Today, Tomorrow, This week, Next week, and Later, or we can choose to set a specific date and time, as shown in Figure 22-5.

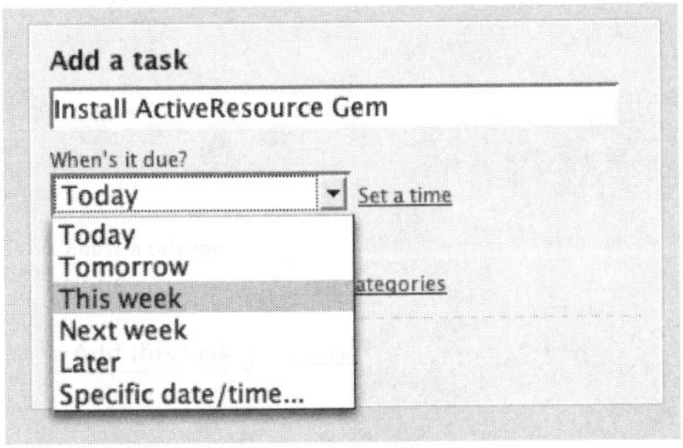

Figure 22-5. *Creating a new task*

Finally, we can also assign each new task a specific category. By default, the application comes with a common set of categories (such as call, demonstration, e-mail, lunch, meeting, and thank-you), but we can also create our own categories to further customize the application to our specific needs. Assigning categories to our tasks makes it easier to visually identify them when looking at our upcoming tasks list, as Figure 22-6 shows.

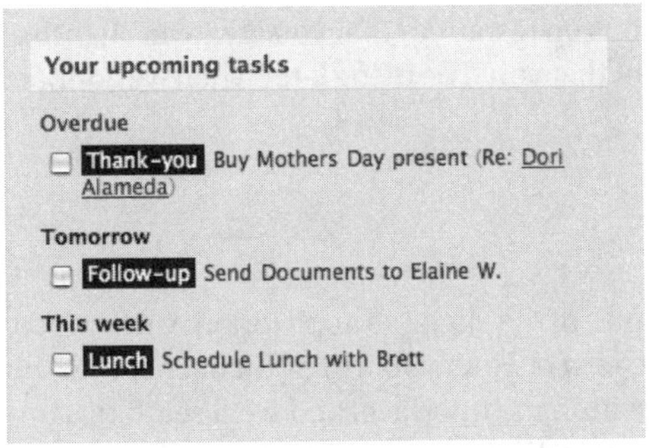

Figure 22-6. *An upcoming task list*

Highrise Has More to Offer

With that basic understanding of contacts and tasks, we've covered enough information for our purposes in this project. Yet we've just barely touched the tip of the iceberg of all the features of Highrise. We didn't even cover some of the cool things such as the e-mail drop boxes, managing permissions with groups, or using tags to keep things organized. For that reason, I highly recommend that you take the time to go through the product tour on the main Highrise web site and explore the application yourself. There are a lot of features that have been done right in Highrise, and that means that there's a lot that we can glean from Highrise for designing our own application.

A Special Note About Permissions

One of the important features to be aware of within Highrise is the permissions system: whenever a new resource is created within Highrise, the creator has the ability to set a variety of permission options for that resource, which restricts the people who can view or edit it. The available options are shown in Figure 22-7.

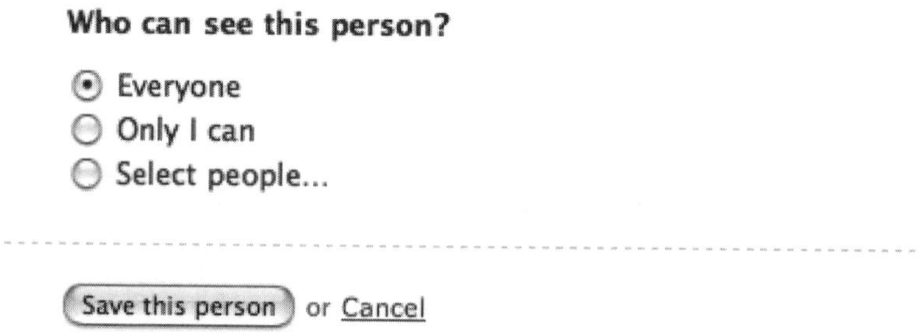

Who can see this person?

⦿ Everyone
◯ Only I can
◯ Select people...

- -

(Save this person) or Cancel

Figure 22-7. *Setting permissions for a person*

Ensuring correct permissions for your user account is important because, when we connect our application to Highrise via the API, you'll be connecting with that user account. So your requests via the API will only be able to view the items that your user account has permission to see. Therefore, if you decide to set permissions on resources that you create in Highrise, make sure that you don't deny access to the account that you'll be using later when we connect via the Highrise API.

Summary

In this chapter, we covered a few of the core principles of the Highrise application, such as people and tasks and how those should be used. In the next chapter, we'll dig a bit deeper into the application as we explore the API that is inherent within the interface, and we'll set things up for building our own application that pulls its data from Highrise.

■ ■ ■

## CHAPTER 23

Integrating to the Highrise REST API

In the last chapter, we took a birds-eye view of Highrise: what it is, what it was designed for, and some of the common actions that we need to understand to use the application. With that simple understanding of how Highrise works, its time for us to begin exploring the fun world of integrating Highrise's data into our own applications. Highrise was created with the goal that the interface would also be the API, so it falls right in line with the RESTful design patterns we've explored in previous projects.

Exploring the API

If you haven't already, open a web browser to your Highrise account, and navigate to the Contacts tab. Once there, go ahead and click one of your contacts, so we can view the information. You should be looking at a screen similar to mine, shown in Figure 23-1.

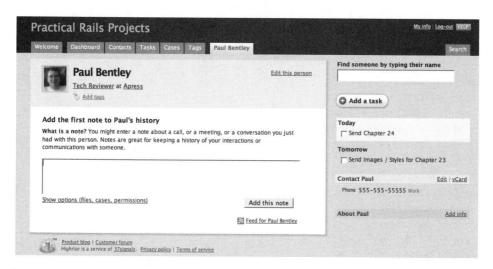

Figure 23-1. *Viewing a contact in Highrise*

If you notice, your URL should look something like http://railsprojects.highrisehq.com/people/1129096. Now, let's modify that by adding a .xml to the very end of the URL string, so it will look like this: http://railsprojects.highrisehq.com/people/1129096.xml. When you load that page, the browser should display an XML format of our contact that looks like this:

```xml
<?xml version="1.0" encoding="UTF-8"?>
<person>
  <author-id type="integer">27034</author-id>
  <background></background>
  <company-id type="integer"></company-id>
  <created-at type="datetime">2007-06-02T17:11:26Z</created-at>
  <first-name>Paul</first-name>
  <group-id type="integer"></group-id>

  <id type="integer">1129096</id>
  <last-name>Bentley</last-name>
  <owner-id type="integer"></owner-id>
  <title>Tech Reviewer</title>
  <updated-at type="datetime">2007-06-04T01:15:10Z</updated-at>
  <visible-to>Everyone</visible-to>

<contact-data>
  <phone-numbers>
    <phone-number>
      <id type="integer">849120</id>
      <location>Work</location>
      <number>555-55-5555</number>
    </phone-number>
  </phone-numbers>

  <web-addresses>
  </web-addresses>
  <email-addresses>
    <email-address>
      <address>paul@apress.com</address>
      <id type="integer">519484</id>
      <location>Work</location>

    </email-address>
  </email-addresses>
  <instant-messengers>
    <instant-messenger>
      <id type="integer">849121</id>
      <location>Work</location>
      <protocol>AIM</protocol>
```

```
      <address>Paul</address>
    </instant-messenger>
  </instant-messengers>
  <addresses>
    <address>
      <city>Kansas City</city>
      <country></country>
      <id type="integer">312057</id>

      <location>Work</location>
      <state>MO</state>
      <street>1005 Walnut St</street>
      <zip></zip>
    </address>
  </addresses>
</contact-data>
</person>
```

■**Note** Some browsers (e.g., Internet Explorer) may try to hide the XML content and show only a blank white page. If yours does this, simply view the source of the page to see the XML content.

Now, change that extension from `.xml` to `.atom` to see the RSS feed available for this contact, or change it to `.vcf` to receive a vCard format. By now, you should have figured out that all this magic is happening because of our good friend from previous RESTful Rails projects—the `respond_to` block.

As cool as it is to be able to discover the API elements ourselves by exploring the interface, it would get old to go through the process of finding all the elements that we would need for our integration. Fortunately, though, we don't have to, as 37signals has released official API documentation that you can read at `http://developer.37signals.com/highrise/`. There, you can find information about accessing all the resources, using HTTP Basic authentication to log in, and even a sample Ruby script that can be used to explore the API from an irb (interactive Ruby) console.

Consuming RESTful APIs

Throughout the course of this book, you've seen how easy it is to create RESTful APIs within modern Rails applications, but the one area that we haven't really covered is how to consume external RESTful data directly into our applications.

If we wanted to be hard core, we could build something ourselves using the `Net::HTTP` Ruby library or even making system calls out to `cURL` and reading back the responses. However, there's no need to reinvent the wheel when we've already got a powerful library by the name of Active Resource.

Active Resource, which was first announced during DHH's keynote address at RailsConf 2006, is an easy library for consuming REST-based resources. In fact, you could almost consider Active Resource to be a simpler cousin of Active Record, except instead of providing an interface to databases, it provides the interface to RESTful applications. With Active Resource, we can simply define a model class for an external REST resource like so:

```
class Post < ActiveResource::Base
  self.site = http://localhost:3000/blog/post
end
```

And that little three-line class method suddenly opens up a world of connectivity, so that interacting with the REST-based API at the other end can be as simple as making calls such as these:

```
posts = Post.find :all    # retrieve back a list of all posts
post = Post.find(5)       # retrieve the post with the id of 5
post = Post.find :first   # retrieve the first post
```

And we're not limited to merely retrieving data either; Active Resource also provides us with familiar methods for creating new data as well:

```
post = Post.new(:title => 'My AR based Post',
                :body => 'This is my first post via ActiveResource')
post.save
```

Obviously, Active Resource is an amazing library for interacting with RESTful applications, and thus it's the perfect library for us to utilize in our integration. The downfall of using Active Resource is that, at the time of this writing, it is still in a prerelease state and is currently planned for inclusion with Rails 2.0 (it will actually replace Action Web Service). Until Rails 2.0 comes out and Active Resource is automatically included with the install, we have to do a bit more work than usual to set up an application to use the latest version of edge rails with Active Resource.

■**Note** Because we're going to be using code from the edge version of Rails, there is a much greater risk of changes to the core that could invalidate our project in this module. The project was tested with the latest version of edge rails as late in the process as possible, so it should be fine. However, it's always a good idea to check both the errata for the book and the RailsProjects.com forums, as I'll be doing my best to periodically retest the application and make any necessary modifications to the code available for download until Rails 2.0 comes out.

Creating a New Edge Rails Project

In the past, the changes between stable and edge Rails releases were less dramatic, and we would normally be able to make our application use edge Rails by simply running the command rake rails:freeze:edge from within an existing Rails application. That freeze:edge task pulls down the latest version of Rails into the /vendor/rails directory, and the next time we start up our Rails application, it utilizes that local copy of the framework.

Unfortunately, though, that process won't work for us in this case. We need to create an edge Rails project using the lates edge Rails. Rails 2.0 will bring a fairly large number of changes to not only the main Rails libraries but also to the structure of our Rails applications themselves. Therefore, we need to instead pull down a local copy of edge Rails and use the `rails` command from that library to create our new application (so that the application's structure is created correctly).

Pulling Down the Edge Version of Rails

We could pull down our initial copy of edge Rails by checking out the latest Rails trunk via a Subversion (SVN) checkout:

```
svn co http://dev.rubyonrails.org/svn/rails/trunk src/railsedge
```

However, I didn't want to assume that everyone is comfortable with Subversion, so instead, we'll use a process that will provide us with the easiest (from a technical understanding) method for creating our edge Rails application, though it may require an extra step or two.

Our first step is to create a new project from scratch; its name will be irrelevant since we'll really only be using this application to store the latest version of Rails:

```
rails edgerails
```

Now that we have a base application, go ahead and open a command prompt in the root of our new application, and run the freeze edge task to pull down the latest version of Rails:

```
rake rails:freeze:edge
```

```
(in /Users/darkel/projects/edgerails)
rm -rf vendor/rails
mkdir -p vendor/rails
REVISION not set. Using HEAD, which is revision 6937.
touch vendor/rails/REVISION_6937
A    vendor/rails/railties
A    vendor/rails/railties/test
(...output ommited for brevity...)
```

■**Note** In working through the examples in this chapter, I noticed an oddity occurring when freezing rails. For some reason, the first attempt to freeze the edge version of Rails would pull down all the latest libraries yet include Action Web Service instead of Active Resource. Immediately running the `rake rails:freeze:edge` command again correctly pulled down Active Resource instead of Action Web Service.

As you freeze your Rails application to the edge version, keep an eye on the libraries that are being copied to ensure that you do get Active Resource (otherwise, this project won't work). You may need to run the command twice.

Creating an Edge Rails Application

Now that we have a local copy of the current edge version Rails, let's use this version to create our new development project. Go back to your main projects folder, and let's create a new project named scheduler:

```
ruby edgerails/vendor/rails/railties/bin/rails scheduler
```

```
create
      create  app/controllers
      create  app/helpers
      create  app/models
      create  app/views/layouts
(...Output ommitted for brevity...)
```

But we're not quite done just yet—even though our scheduler application was built using edge Rails, if we were to start it up now, it simply uses the current version of Rails installed onto our system (and will most likely crash). We need to freeze the edge Rails into our scheduler application as well. While we could simply run the edge:freeze task again from within our scheduler application, that would be a little wasteful, as it would mean that we would now have two or more copies of the Rails edge code on our hard drive (depending on how many edge applications we were developing). If you're running Rails on a Mac or Linux/Unix-based system, you can bypass that wastefulness by simply creating a symbolic link from the /vendor/rails folder of your scheduler application that points to the frozen Rails that's stored in your edgerails folder.

```
ln-s ~/projects/edgerails/vendor/rails vendor/rails
```

If you're running Windows, you'll have to run rake rails:freeze:edge in your application.

■**Caution** There seem to be some compatibility issues when attempting to run an edge Rails project from prepackaged Rails solutions such as Instant Rails on Windows. It's best to avoid these types of solutions for doing edge development, so if you're currently using InstantRails on Windows, I recommend building this project somewhere else, such as on an inexpensive virtual private server available from web sites such as www.rimuhosting.com or www.slicehost.com.

We can test that our application is using the edge version of Rails by starting our web server (mongrel_rails start) and viewing the default index.html page at http://localhost:3000. When you click the "About your application's environment" link, you should see a line that indicates that you're running on Edge Rails like in Figure 23-2.

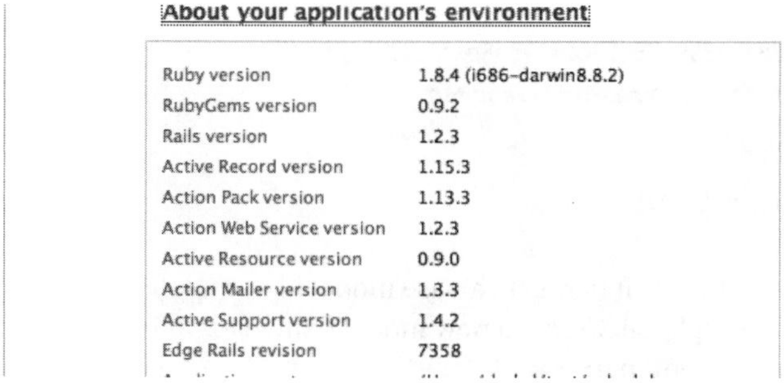

About your application's environment

Ruby version	1.8.4 (i686–darwin8.8.2)
RubyGems version	0.9.2
Rails version	1.2.3
Active Record version	1.15.3
Action Pack version	1.13.3
Action Web Service version	1.2.3
Active Resource version	0.9.0
Action Mailer version	1.3.3
Active Support version	1.4.2
Edge Rails revision	7358

Figure 23-2. *Viewing that our application is running edge Rails*

Alternatively, if you've gotten in the habit of automatically deleting the index.html file from /public, you can still obtain this information from the command line. Open a command line prompt in the root of your application, and run ruby script/about:

```
About your application's environment
Ruby version            1.8.4 (i686-darwin8.8.2)
RubyGems version        0.9.2
Rails version           1.2.3
Active Record version   1.15.3
Action Pack version     1.13.3
Action Web Service version  1.2.3
Active Resource version 0.9.0
Action Mailer version   1.3.3
Active Support version  1.4.2
Edge Rails revision     7358
Application root        /Users/darkel/test/scheduler
Environment             development
Database adapter        sqlite3
```

Testing Our Connectivity

Now that we have a new edge Rails application installed, we can begin setting up a couple of basic models so we can test our connectivity to Highrise and validate that we have Active Resource working before we start building out our new application.

The first step in testing our connectivity is to grab your authentication token from within your Highrise account. Go to the User Account tab in the My Info section, and find the "Reveal authentication token for feeds/api" link. Once you click the link, you'll see something like Figure 23-3.

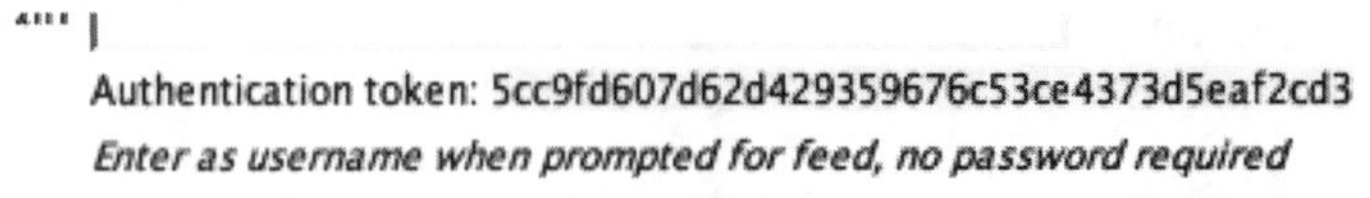

Authentication token: 5cc9fd607d62d429359676c53ce4373d5eaf2cd3

Enter as username when prompted for feed, no password required

Figure 23-3. *An authentication token for the API*

Copy your authentication token, and use it to create a base model in our application that you'll use to make your connection to Highrise. Create a new model named highrise.rb in /app/models/ and place the following content in it:

```
class Highrise < ActiveResource::Base
  self.site = "http://5cc9fd607d62d429359676c53ce4373d5eaf2cd3:X@railsprojects.➥
highrisehq.com"
end
```

There's not a lot to this model—basically, all we're doing is setting the site variable with the address of our external API. We'll then use this model as the primary model that all of our other models will inherit from, so that we only have to set this site value once. Obviously, you'll need to replace the authentication token used in my example with the one from your own account, as well as setting your own subdomain key.

Now that we have our base Highrise model created, let's create a model that will map to a resource in Highrise. Create a new model in app/models named person.rb, and we'll leave it fairly empty for now:

```
class Person < Highrise
end
```

Now, let's open script/console, so we can test that our person model is able to connect to our Highrise account:

```
ruby script/console
```

```
Loading development environment.
```

```
>> Person.find :first
```

```
=> #<Person:0x26f5968 @prefix_options={}, @attributes={"updated_at"=>
Sun Jun 03 21:14:12 UTC 2007, "title"=>nil, "contact_data"=>#➡
<Person::ContactData:0x26f1340 @prefix_options={}, @attributes=➡
{"web_addresses"=>nil, "addresses"=>[#<Person::ContactData::Address:0x26cb8c0➡
@prefix_options={}, @attributes={"city"=>"Kansas City", "zip"=>"66213", ➡
"country"=>"United States", "id"=>312059, "street"=>"123 test lane", ➡
"location"=>"Home", "state"=>"KS"}], "email_addresses"=>[#<Person::ContactData::➡
EmailAddress:0x26e2098 @prefix_options={}, @attributes={"id"=>517659, "address"=>➡
"eldon@email.com", "location"=>"Work"}], "phone_numbers"=>nil, ➡
"instant_messengers"=>nil}, "background"=>nil, "id"=>1128922, "group_id"=>nil, ➡
"company_id"=>1128921, "owner_id"=>nil, "first_name"=>"Eldon", "author_id"=>nil, ➡
"visible_to"=>"Everyone", "last_name"=>"Alameda", "created_at"=>Sat Jun 02 ➡
17:06:26 UTC 2007}
```

```
>> joecool = Person.new(:first_name => 'Joe', :last_name => 'Cool')
```

```
=> #<Person:0x2618220 @prefix_options={}, @attributes={"first_name"=>"Joe",➡
"last_name"=>"Cool"}
```

```
>> joecool.save
```

```
=> true
```

If we go back to our Highrise account now, we can validate that our new user, Joe Cool, was created successfully within Highrise (see Figure 23-4).

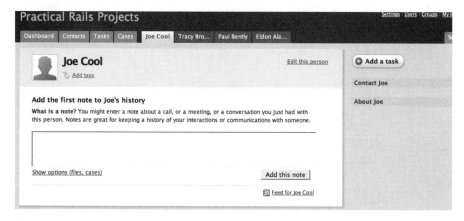

Figure 23-4. *A new user created via ActiveResource*

Summary

In this chapter, we've set up a new Rails project based on edge Rails and set ourselves up to utilize the upcoming Active Resource library within our new project. To test our configuration, we also began setting up the connection to our Highrise account and validated that we could both pull data out and push new data into our Highrise account. In the next chapter, we'll take our new configuration and build a simple application based on the data from that account.

■ ■ ■

## CHAPTER 24

Building the Appointment Scheduler

In the last chapter, we took some giant steps towards our final application by building out some of the models that we can use to connect to Highrise via Active Resource. Now, let's finish things up by putting together a little application that will utilize the data from our Highrise account for all of its data.

What Are We Going to Build?

For this last project, we're going to build a simple application for a friend who is starting up a home-based business selling vitamin and other health-related drinks, pills, and powders. The nature of his business, though, requires one-on-one consultation, so he spends half of his days at his home office calling leads and responding to e-mails and the other half on the road going from customer to customer to review results, take and deliver orders, and give samples of new products.

Highrise provides him pretty much all the functionality he needs for keeping track of his customers and maintaining a proactive approach towards his interactions with them. For each customer, he records all of his interactions into the notes field in Highrise. Then, after he completes each interaction with a customer, he sets up a new task to follow up with that customer using a generic timeframe (e.g., next week). When the specified time arrives, he uses that reminder to contact customers and nail down a specific date and time for follow-up visits. So at any time, his upcoming task list is composed of customers with generic timeframes for contacts and customers with appointments on specific dates and times. This seems to work really well for him, and overall, he's extremely happy with Highrise.

The one thing that he wishes he had in Highrise, though, is a single display showing him all of his upcoming appointments and where they are physically located on a map. He believes that this visual display would be a vital tool for him, as it would help him to more efficiently schedule appointments during the days that he is already in the general area visiting another customer.

Fortunately for us, he doesn't see the need in completely reinventing the wheel though, as he is really happy with the Highrise interface, so we only need to extend a limited amount of functionality into our application for him. First off, our application needs to pull down a list of his upcoming tasks and map each of the customer addresses onto an interactive map that he can use. Ideally, he'd also like to be able to view any notes for each of those specific customers and have the ability to create notes about the person as well.

Putting Together Our Layout

With this basic understanding of what we want to build, I put together the high-level layout for our application shown in Figure 24-1.

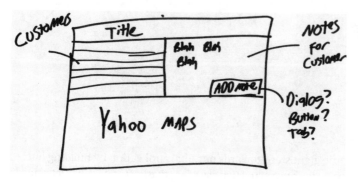

Figure 24-1. *A simple layout for our application*

To accomplish this layout, we'll need to pull in a few extra JavaScript resources.

For one, we'll implement the interactive map functionality through the use of the Yahoo Maps API. Second, once again we'll utilize the Ext-JS framework to help us put together an advanced layout for our friend. We'll take advantage of Ext's border layout support to build the look and feel of our application, while we'll use the grid component to provide a clean way to display our list of upcoming tasks.

Installing Ext

You should remember the overview of the Ext-JS framework back in Chapter 18 (if not, it would be a good idea to review that chapter). If you followed along with that chapter, you should still have a generator that you can use to install Ext into our application with a simple command like this:

```
ruby script/generate extjs
```

If you didn't build that generator, then you'll need to download the Ext framework from http://extjs.com/download (I'm using version 1.1 in this application). Once you unzip the archive, you'll need to copy a few key files out of there and into our application:

- Copy the four adapter JavaScript files (effects.js, prototype.js, scriptaculous.js, and ext-prototype-adapter.js) out of /adapter/prototype, and paste them into the /public/javascripts folder, overwriting the existing versions with the ones from the Ext archive.

- Copy the ext-all.js file from the root of the archive folder into /public/javascripts.

- Copy ext-all.css from /resources/css into /public/stylesheets.

- Copy the default folder and all its contents from /resources/images into /public/images.

These files along with the `application.css` file from the code archive for this project are all we need from Ext to build the look and feel of our application.

Using Yahoo Maps

Sure, Google Maps is the more commonly used option in Rails examples. In fact, there are literally hundreds of tutorials, plug-ins, and so on for using Google Maps, available online and in print. Perhaps that's why so many people overlook the nice features that Yahoo Maps offers. For example, in my experience, I've found that the Yahoo Maps license has traditionally been easier to use for personal or intranet applications. Second, Yahoo Maps also offers the option of a Flash-based map in addition to the standard AJAX-based version. I actually prefer the Flash-based map, as it seems to offer better performance, and I've been able to take advantage of the additional drawing capabilities.

Obtaining an Application ID

The first step in using Yahoo Maps is to obtain an application ID from Yahoo. This application uniquely identifies your application when you make requests to the Yahoo Maps API. To obtain your application ID, you'll need to go to `https://developer.yahoo.com/wsregapp/index.php` and complete the application. Once you have your ID, you'll include it in any calls that we make to Yahoo Maps, such as this call to include Yahoo Maps in a page directly from the Yahoo servers (so there's no need to download it locally):

```
<script type="text/javascript" src="http://maps.yahooapis.com/v3.04/fl/➡
javascript/apiloader.js?appid=[YOUR APP ID HERE]"> </script>
```

Instantiating a Map

After you've included the Yahoo Maps library in your page, you can create a new map within your page with a few simple commands:

```
var map = new Map("mapContainer","[YOUR APP ID]","66213",5);
```

This function creates a new map object within the specified target `mapContainer`, using your application ID, with the map centered on zip code `66213`, and at a zoom level of 5.

Our Layout Script

With our necessary JavaScript libraries installed, our Yahoo application ID, and that quick overview of how we can create a Yahoo map, let's go ahead and put together our layout file, which will pull in our JavaScript libraries and style sheets.

Create a new file named `application.html.erb` in `/app/views/layouts/`. Within this file, place the following content:

```
<html>
<head>
  <meta http-equiv="Content-type" content="text/html; charset=utf-8">
  <title>Welcome to the Party</title>
```

```
  <script type="text/javascript" src="http://maps.yahooapis.com/v3.04/fl/➥
javascript/apiloader.js?appid=[YOUR APP ID]"> </script>
  <%= javascript_include_tag 'prototype' %>
  <%= javascript_include_tag 'scriptaculous' %>
  <%= javascript_include_tag 'ext-prototype-adapter' %>
  <%= javascript_include_tag 'ext-all' %>

  <%= stylesheet_link_tag 'ext-all' %>
  <%= stylesheet_link_tag 'application' %>
</head>
  <body>
    <div id="container">
      <%= yield %>
    </div>
  </body>
</html>
```

■**Tip** You probably noticed that we're using a new file extension for our layout template. That's because Rails 2.0 will begin the deprecation of our beloved `.rhtml` and `.rxml` file extensions. Instead, we'll be using file extensions like `.html.erb` and `.xml.builder` in their place. Why, you may ask? It's designed to do some cleanup of the way that our templates work by baking the MIME convention into the template name and making the purpose of our templates clearer. So rather than using the same `.rhtml` file extension to handle multiple needs such as view files, e-mail templates, and so on, we'll now use these extended file extensions.

It's a good practice to start using this new format. However, there's not a huge rush as our "old" extensions will still work until Rails 3.0.

The Home Controller

With our layout created, the next thing we'll do is add a controller that will serve as the home page for our application (aptly naming it home):

`ruby script/generate controller Home index`

```
    exists  app/controllers/
    exists  app/helpers/
    create  app/views/home
    exists  test/functional/
    create  app/controllers/home_controller.rb
    create  test/functional/home_controller_test.rb
    create  app/helpers/home_helper.rb
    create  app/views/home/index.html.erb
```

We'll also configure the root of our application to point to our new home by adding the following line to our routes.rb in /config:

```
ActionController::Routing::Routes.draw do |map|
  map.root :controller => "home"
  map.connect ':controller/:action/:id'
  map.connect ':controller/:action/:id.:format'
end
```

Next, we'll edit the index.html.erb file that our generator created in /app/views/home to house our initial layout divs:

```
<div id='header' class="ylayout-inactive-content">
  <h1>Welcome to the Party</h1>
</div>
<div id="content">
  <div id="map_pane" class="ylayout-inactive-content">
    <div id="mapContainer"> </div>
  </div>
  <div id="add_note" class="ylayout-inactive-content"> </div>
  <div id="notes" class="ylayout-inactive-content"> </div>
  <div id="customers_grid"class="ylayout-inactive-content"> </div>
</div>
```

Let's quickly break down the divs that we created in this template and what content we plan to place in each:

- map_pane: Used to display the Yahoo map

- add_note: Used to hold the form for creating a note for a customer

- notes: Used to display any notes for a customer

- customers_grid: Used to display a list of customers with upcoming tasks

To meet our initial application design, we'll utilize the border layout component from the Ext-JS framework to pull these divs together into our layout. To do that, we can add a small bit of JavaScript to the top of this template:

```
<script type="text/javascript" charset="utf-8">
    Ext.onReady(function() {
        layout = new Ext.BorderLayout(document.body, {
            north: {
                split:false,
                initialSize:50
            },
            center: {
                titlebar:false,
                autoScroll: true
            }
        });
```

```
                layout.beginUpdate();
                layout.add('north', new Ext.ContentPanel('header'));
                var innerLayout = new Ext.BorderLayout('content', {
                    south: {
                        split:true,
                        initialSize: 300,
                        minSize: 200,
                        maxSize: 500,
                        autoScroll:true,
                        collapsible:true,
                        titlebar:true
                    },
                    center: {
                        autoScroll:true,
                        titlebar:true
                    },
                    east: {
                        split:true,
                        autoScroll:true,
                        titlebar:true,
                        initialSize: 470,
                    }
                });
            innerLayout.add('east', new Ext.ContentPanel('notes', {title: 'Notes'}));
            innerLayout.add('east', new Ext.ContentPanel('add_note',➥
    {title: 'Add Note'}));
            innerLayout.add('center', new Ext.ContentPanel('customers_grid',➥
    {title: 'Customers'}));
            innerLayout.add('south', new Ext.ContentPanel('map_pane', {title:'Map'}));
            layout.add('center', new Ext.NestedLayoutPanel(innerLayout));
            layout.endUpdate();
        });
</script>

<div id='header' class="ylayout-inactive-content">
  <h1>Welcome to the Party</h1>
</div>
<div id="content">
  <div id="map_pane" class="ylayout-inactive-content">
    <div id="mapContainer"> </div>
  </div>
  <div id="add_note" class="ylayout-inactive-content"> </div>
  <div id="notes" class="ylayout-inactive-content"> </div>
  <div id="customers_grid"class="ylayout-inactive-content"> </div>
</div>
```

And with that little bit of JavaScript, our page currently looks like Figure 24-2.

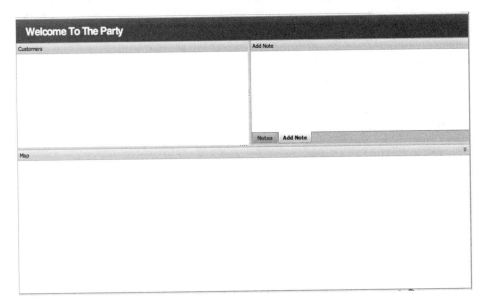

Figure 24-2. *Our page layout after adding the Ext border layout*

Plugging In Our Map

With our layout well on its way, we can now focus on adding some actual content to our page. We'll start by adding our Yahoo Maps component into the map_pane div. Since you already included the Yahoo Maps JavaScript file from our application layout file, it's now just a matter of creating a Map object within our page and having it target the mapContainer div (which is inside the map_pane div).

We can do this simply by adding a bit of JavaScript into the map_page div:

```
<div id="map_pane" class="ylayout-inactive-content">
    <div id="mapContainer"> </div>
    <script type="text/javascript">
        var map = new Map("mapContainer","[YOUR APP ID]","66213", 5);
        map.addEventListener(Map.EVENT_INITIALIZE, onInitialize);

        function onInitialize( eventData ) {
            map.addTool ( new PanTool(), true );
            navWidget = new NavigatorWidget("close");
            map.addWidget(navWidget);
        }
    </script>
</div>
```

All we've done here is create a new `Map` object as we had discussed earlier, but to enhance the usability of the map, we added a few extras as well. First off, we added the ability for the user to click and drag the map to pan the map in different direction by adding the `PanTool` with the `map.addTool ( new PanTool(), true );` line. We also added a Yahoo-provided navigator widget into the map (`navWidget = new NavigatorWidget("close");`), which provides a tool that can be used to control the current zoom of the map.

Because we didn't want to risk those widgets failing to load while we were waiting for the map to finish loading, we used the ability to attach event listeners to wait for the map to fully initialize before adding those widgets to our new map.

With those changes to our page, Figure 24-3 shows the map loaded into our map pane. We also get some extra cool points for the fact that if we resize that container frame, the Yahoo map resizes accordingly as well (no scroll bars for us).

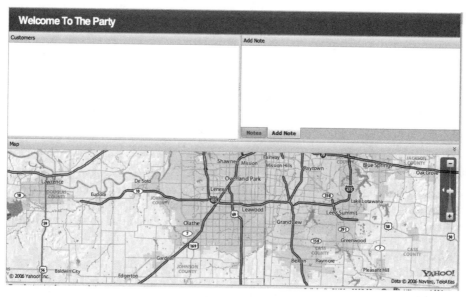

Figure 24-3. *Yahoo maps added to our application*

Adding Our Task List

In the last chapter, we created a Person model that we could use to connect to our Highrise data. Now, we need to create a way to connect our application to the list of tasks within Highrise. According to the Highrise API, a task is represented like this:

```
<task>
    <id type="integer">1</id>
    <recording-id type="integer"></recording-id>
    <subject-id type="integer"></subject-id>
    <subject-type></subject-type>
    <category-id type="integer"></category-id>
    <body>An untimed task for today</body>
```

```
        <frame>today</frame>
        <alert-at type="datetime"></alert-at>
        <created-at type="datetime"></created-at>
        <author-id type="integer">1</author-id>
        <updated-at type="datetime"></updated-at>
</task>
```

We'll only be interested in a few of these fields:

- *id*: This is (obviously) the ID of the task used by Highrise.

- *subject-id*: This stores the ID of the record this task is associated with. If the `subject_type` is `Party`, this is the ID of a person. If the `subject_type` is `Kase`, this ID refers to a case.

- *body*: This is the actual text of the task.

- *frame*: If a task was created with a generic timeframe, it will be returned here. Possible values include `today`, `tomorrow`, `this_week`, `next_week`, or `later`.

- *alert-at*: If a task was given a specific date and time, it will be stored here.

Now that we know what data we want out of Highrise, let's build an Active Resource model for interacting with our tasks. Create a new file named `task.rb` in /app/models, and set it up like this for now:

```
class Task < Highrise
end
```

Once you've saved that Task model, we can fire up a `script/console` to test that our new model is able to talk to Highrise:

```
ruby script/console
```

```
Loading development environment.
```

```
>> t = Task.find :first
```

```
=> #<Task:0x274a1c0 @prefix_options={}, @attributes={"alert_at"=>nil, "updated_at"
=>Tue Jun 05 17:46:53 UTC 2007, "recording_id"=>nil, "body"=>"Evaluate Results",
"id"=>157688, "subject_type"=>"Party", "frame"=>"this_week", "category_id"=>200290,
 "owner_id"=>27034, "subject_id"=>1169836, "author_id"=>27034, "done_at"=>nil,
 "created_at"=>Tue Jun 05 17:46:53 UTC 2007}
```

Getting the Upcoming Tasks

It looks like we're on our way, as we're able to communicate with our Highrise account to pull down the tasks. However, for the purposes of our application, doing a `Task:find :all` would give us too much data, as it would return all tasks including those that are already completed.

What we need is a way to pull back only the tasks that are currently incomplete (regardless of whether they're overdue or not). Fortunately, there's a method available within the API that allows us to retrieve only the upcoming tasks. We just need to change our requests to instead pull from /tasks/upcoming.xml. We'll map to that from our model by creating a new class method named upcoming:

```
class Task < Highrise
  def self.upcoming
    find(:all, :from => :upcoming)
  end
end
```

Armed with that new method, let's modify our controller to retrieve that list of upcoming tasks into the current page. Open home_controller.rb, and edit the index method:

```
class HomeController < ApplicationController
  def index
    @tasks = Task.upcoming
  end
end
```

The only problem with this list is that it will only provide us with the upcoming tasks— what we really need is a way to also retrieve in the associated person for each task; otherwise, we won't be able to display the necessary customer name or display the customer on our map. Unfortunately, Active Resource doesn't have a powerful associations mapping feature like Active Record, so we can't just put in anything like a :has_one :person. Instead, we'll have to build a method to manually pull in the associated person for a given task. We can do this by adding a person method to our Task model:

```
class Task < Highrise
  def self.upcoming
    find(:all, :from => :upcoming)
  end

  def person
    Person.find( subject_id )
  end
end
```

So now if we have a task within an instance variable named @task, we can find the name of the person associated to that task by calling @task.person.first_name and @task.person.last_name. That wasn't too painful, was it?

Now, this method works, but there is a problem with it: each time we make one of those calls to the person method, our application is going to make a new request back to Highrise for the associated person data. That's not exactly a very good use of our network resources, and it will almost certainly add unnecessary delay to our application. We can fix this by making a small modification to that person method to locally cache the person object we retrieve and use that cached version in response to all subsequent requests. So let's modify our `person` method like this:

```
def person
  @person ||= Person.find(subject_id)
end
```

It's a small change, but oftentimes, the littlest things like this add up to huge gains or hits on the performance of an application.

As long we're modifying our models, having to call `@person.first_name` and `@person.last_name` as separate requests is a bit terse, since we know that we're going to want to display customer names in our application. Let's create a new method within the Person model that will join those together for us. Add a `name` method to our Person model that looks like this:

```
class Person < Highrise
  def name
    "#{first_name} #{last_name}".strip
  end
end
```

Displaying Our Upcoming Tasks

Now that we've got an `@tasks` instance variable loaded with our upcoming tasks, it's time for us to add the necessary code to display that list of tasks within our page. To do this, though, will require us to go a bit deeper into some JavaScript configuration, since we want to display our list of upcoming tasks in an Ext grid component as well as map each customer's location on our Yahoo map.

Rather than just dumping the whole JavaScript code here, I'll try to make it a little easier to follow by breaking down some of the critical steps involved with creating this functionality and showing the full template with the new JavaScript added at the end.

Setting Up Our Variables

Our first step is to create a few JavaScript variables to store the data we'll use for our grid:

```
var ds; // holds our data store
var grid; //reference to our grid component
var columnModel; // definition of the columns
```

To make it easier for us to get our task list into the grid's data store, we'll create a JavaScript array to store our upcoming tasks. We'll then populate this array by iterating over our `@tasks` instance variable—pushing each task into the JavaScript array.

```
var gridData = [
  <% for task in @tasks %>
    <% for address in task.person.contact_data.addresses %>
```

```
    [
      '<%= task.subject_id %>',
      '<%= task.person.name %>',
      '<%= task.body %>',
      '<%= task.frame || task.alert_at.localtime.to_s(:appt) %>',
      '<%= address.street %>',
      '<%= address.city %>',
      '<%= address.state %>',
      '<%= address.zip %>'
    ],
  <% end %>
<% end %>
];
```

That should seem pretty straightforward, with the exception of the section where we attempt to populate the array with the due date.

You see, each task will either have a generic timeframe that it's due (e.g., tomorrow, next week), which will be stored as the frame, or it will have a specific datetime variable stored as the alert_at variable. Since we want to display whichever one isn't blank, we'll need to utilize the || (or) method like this:

```
task.frame || task.alert_at
```

However, if we need to display the alert_at variable, we'll want to clean it up a bit for better display. We'll clean it up by first converting it to our application's local time zone by calling task.alert_at.localtime. Once we have the variable in the local time zone, we can reformat it into a form that makes sense for us, which we'll do by creating a new custom time format extension.

■**Tip** Traditionally, we would add a configuration item like a custom time format to the bottom of our environment.rb. However, that's no longer going to be the case in future version of Rails. You'll notice that, in our config folder, we now have a folder named initializers. Rather than cluttering up our environment.rb file with a large amount of miscellaneous bits of code, we can store each of those custom configuration items into separate files stored in this initializers folder, and they'll automatically be included and loaded when Rails::Initializer runs.

This change should keep our configuration files a bit more organized and make it easier for plug-in authors to add custom configuration items into our Rails environment.

You need to create a new file named timeextensions.rb in /config/initializers, and we'll place our custom time conversion extension in that file:

```
ActiveSupport::CoreExtensions::Time::Conversions::DATE_FORMATS.merge!( :appt =>➡
  "%I:%M%p on %a, %B %d" )
```

After that, we'll need to restart our application so that our new Time extension will be loaded. Once we do, we could then call `task.alert_at.localtime.to_s(:appt)` to have a response like 3:00pm on Thu, June 07, which is certainly a lot easier on the eyes than the standard `datetime` format.

Building the Data Store

Going back to our JavaScript configuration, the next major step will be to build a function that we can call to read that new `gridData` array that we just created and use it to build an Ext data store:

```
function setupDataSource() {
  ds = new Ext.data.Store({
    proxy: new Ext.data.MemoryProxy(gridData),
    reader: new Ext.data.ArrayReader(
      {id: 0},
      [
        {name: 'id'},
        {name: 'customer'},
        {name: 'task'},
        {name: 'dueDate'},
        {name: 'street'},
        {name: 'city'},
        {name: 'state'},
        {name: 'zip'}
      ]
    )
  });
  ds.load();
}
```

This function will create a new data store and store it in the `ds` variable. Now that we have a data store created, our next step is to create a `ColumnModel` object to store our configuration of which fields we want to display in our grid. All we need to display in the grid is the customer's name, the task that we need to do for that customer, and the current timeframe or appointment time for that task. We'll configure this data by creating another function that will build our column model object with the fields that we want to display:

```
function getColumnModel() {
  if(!columnModel) {
    columnModel = new Ext.grid.ColumnModel(
      [
        {
          header: 'Customer',
          width: 250,
          sortable: true,
          dataIndex: 'customer'
        },
```

```
      {
        header: 'Task',
        width:250,
        sortable: true,
        dataIndex: 'task'
      },
      {
        header: 'Date Due',
        width:100,
        sortable: true,
        dataIndex: 'dueDate'
      }
    ]
  );
  }
  return columnModel;
}
```

Now that we have functions to build the data store and column models, we'll create a function that will build the grid for us and display it in the customers_grid div:

```
function buildGrid() {
  grid = new Ext.grid.Grid(
    'customers_grid',
    {
      ds: ds,
      cm: getColumnModel(),
      autoSizeColumns: true
    }
  );
  grid.render();
}
```

With all of those functions built, we can create our grid with just two simple function calls:

```
setupDataSource();
buildGrid();
```

So after putting all of this together in our /app/view/home/index.html.erb, it currently looks like this:

```
<script type="text/javascript" charset="utf-8">
  Ext.onReady(function() {
    var ds; //hold our data
    var grid; //component
    var columnModel; // definition of the columns
```

```
var gridData = [
  <% for task in @tasks %>
    <% for address in task.person.contact_data.addresses %>
        '<%= task.subject_id %>',
        '<%= task.person.name %>',
        '<%= task.body %>',
        '<%= task.frame || task.alert_at.localtime.to_s(:appt) %>',
        '<%= address.street %>',
        '<%= address.city %>',
        '<%= address.state %>',
        '<%= address.zip %>'
      ],
    <% end %>
  <% end %>
  ];

  function setupDataSource() {
    ds = new Ext.data.Store({
      proxy: new Ext.data.MemoryProxy(gridData),
      reader: new Ext.data.ArrayReader(
        {id: 0},
        [
          {name: 'id'},
          {name: 'customer'},
          {name: 'task'},
          {name: 'dueDate'},
          {name: 'street'},
          {name: 'city'},
          {name: 'state'},
          {name: 'zip'},
        ]
      )
    });
    ds.load();
  }

  function getColumnModel() {
    if(!columnModel) {
      columnModel = new Ext.grid.ColumnModel(
        [
          {
            header: 'Customer',
            width: 250,
            sortable: true,
            dataIndex: 'customer'
          },
```

```
            {
              header: 'Task',
              width:250,
              sortable: true,
              dataIndex: 'task'
            },
            {
              header: 'Date Due',
              width:100,
              sortable: true,
              dataIndex: 'dueDate'
            }
          ]
      );
    }
    return columnModel;
}

function buildGrid() {
  grid = new Ext.grid.Grid(
    'customers_grid',
    {
      ds: ds,
      cm: getColumnModel(),
      autoSizeColumns: true
    }
  );
  grid.render();
}

setupDataSource();
buildGrid();

layout = new Ext.BorderLayout(document.body, {
  north: {
    split:false,
    initialSize:50
  },
  center: {
    titlebar:false,
    autoScroll: true
  }
});
```

```
    layout.beginUpdate();
      layout.add('north', new Ext.ContentPanel('header'));
      var innerLayout = new Ext.BorderLayout('content', {
        south: {
          split:true,
          initialSize: 300,
          minSize: 200,
          maxSize: 500,
          autoScroll:true,
          collapsible:true,
          titlebar:true
        },
        center: {
          autoScroll:true,
          titlebar:true
        },
        east: {
          split:true,
          autoScroll:true,
          titlebar:true,
          initialSize: 470,
        }
      });
      innerLayout.add('east', new Ext.ContentPanel('notes', {title: 'Notes'}));
      innerLayout.add('east', new Ext.ContentPanel('add_note', ➥
{title: 'Add Note'}));
      innerLayout.add('center', new Ext.GridPanel(grid, {title: 'Customers'}));
      innerLayout.add('south', new Ext.ContentPanel('map_pane', {title:'Map'}));
      layout.add('center', new Ext.NestedLayoutPanel(innerLayout));
    layout.endUpdate();
  });
</script>

<div id='header' class="ylayout-inactive-content">
  <h1>Welcome to the Party</h1>
</div>

<div id="content">
  <div id="map_pane" class="ylayout-inactive-content">
    <div id="mapContainer"> </div>
    <script type="text/javascript">
      var map = new Map("mapContainer","wlsfitters","66213",5);
      map.addEventListener(Map.EVENT_INITIALIZE, onInitialize);
```

```
  function onInitialize( eventData ) {
    map.addTool ( new PanTool(), true );
    navWidget = new NavigatorWidget("close");
    map.addWidget(navWidget);
  }
</script>
</div>

<div id="add_note" class="ylayout-inactive-content"> </div>
<div id="notes" class="ylayout-inactive-content"> </div>
<div id="customers_grid"class="ylayout-inactive-content"> </div>
</div>
```

The preceding code will display our upcoming task in a grid on the page, like you can see in Figure 24-4.

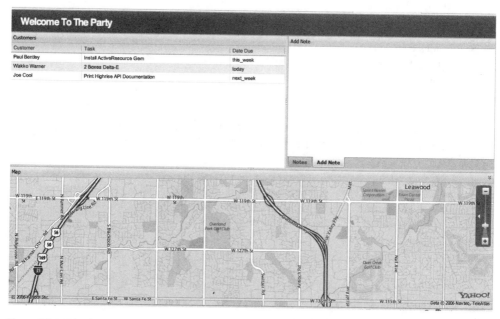

Figure 24-4. *Displaying our upcoming tasks in a grid*

Displaying Customers on the Map

There are a number of different ways to display a location on a Yahoo map, but they all fall into the same basic pattern. We first create a new marker object that contains the information that we want to display. We then place that marker on our map by using methods such as addMarkerByLatLon (if we have the latitude and longitude) or addMarkerByAddress (which will attempt to geocode the address into a latitude and longitude coordinated for us).

Creating the Marker

There are a number of different methods that we can use to create markers within the Yahoo Maps API:

- `CustomImageMarker`: Allows us to specify a custom image to use as a marker

- `CustomPOIMarker`: A prebuilt marker that expands when the user clicks it

- `CustomSWFMarker`: Allows us to specify a custom SWF marker

The easiest of those solutions, and the one that we'll use, is the `CustomPOIMarker` method (POI stands for point of interest, in case you were wondering).

To create a new marker using the `customPOIMarker` method, we'll need to pass the method a few variables:

- `index`: The label the marker will display

- `title`: The text that will display when the marker is moused over

- `description`: The text that will display when the marker is clicked or expanded

- `marker color`: The color of the marker on the map

- `stroke color`: The color of the marker in its expanded state

To add markers to our map, we'll create another function in our JavaScript to cycle through all of the records in the data store, create a marker for each of them, and add them to our map using the `addMarkerByAddress` method. We'll add this method to our configuration directly after the place where we create the `gridData` array and before our `setupDataSource` function:

```
<% end %>
];

function displayOnMap() {
  totalRecords = ds.getCount();
  for (var x=0; x < ds.getCount(); x++) {
    marker = new CustomPOIMarker(  ds.getAt(x).data.customer, ➡
ds.getAt(x).data.task, ds.getAt(x).data.street + '<br />' +ds.getAt(x).data.city➡
 + ' ' + ds.getAt(x).data.state + ' ' + ds.getAt(x).data.zip, 'OxFF0000', ➡
'OxFFFFFF');
    address = ds.getAt(x).data.street + ' ' + ds.getAt(x).data.city + ' ' + ➡
ds.getAt(x).data.state + ' ' +        ds.getAt(x).data.zip;
    map.addMarkerByAddress( marker, address);
  }
}

function setupDataSource() {
  ds = new Ext.data.Store({
```

With that function built, we just need to call it. However, we want to make sure that we don't call it until our data store is fully loaded, so we'll attach it to the on load event of the data store and call it after we build our grid:

```
setupDataSource();
buildGrid();
ds.on('load', displayOnMap());
```

With that last touch, our application now looks like Figure 24-5.

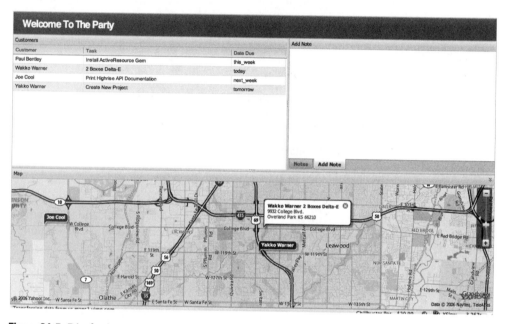

Figure 24-5. *Displaying customer tasks in the grid and on the map*

Managing Notes

All that's left for our little application is to build in the ability to view and add notes for a specific customer. Our first step in doing that is to create a model to interface to our customers' notes residing in the Highrise application. Create a new file named note.rb in /app/models, and place the following code in it:

```
class Note < Highrise
end
```

Next, we'll add a method to our Person model to pull in the associated notes for a customer.

```
class Person < Highrise
  def notes
    Note.find(:all, :from => "/people/#{id}/notes.xml")
  end

  def name
    "#{first_name} #{last_name}".strip
  end
end
```

With the method added, we can now make a call to @person.notes to pull back an array of all notes for a specific customer. Let's go ahead and modify our page to display our list of notes.

Displaying Notes

In our index.html.erb template, we created a div named notes, which is where we'll display the notes for a selected customer. In a few moments, we'll make some modifications to our grid component to allow our friend to simply click a customer to view the notes for that selected customer using an AJAX call, but we'll set up the initial display of the page to show the first record from the data store.

For now, let's modify the notes div to contain an H1 header and a call to render a collection partial to iterate over our notes array. For both of these calls, we'll set the initial display of our notes to use the first record from the data store by calling index 0 of our @tasks array (i.e., the first record):

```
<div id="notes" class="ylayout-inactive-content">
  <h1 id="notes_name">Notes for <%= @tasks[0].person.name if @tasks.any? %></h1>
  <div id="notes_list">
    <%= render :partial => 'notes', :collection => @tasks[0].person.notes if ➥
@tasks.any? %>
  </div>
</div>
```

Now, we simply need to create a partial to display our notes. Create a new file named _notes.html.erb in /app/views/home, and place the following line of code in it:

```
<p><%= notes.body %></p>
```

Adding Notes

Adding a note is equally easy, as once again we'll use a partial. Locate the add_notes div in our index page, and let's add the following line to it:

```
<div id="add_note" class="ylayout-inactive-content">
  <%= render :partial => 'add_note', :locals => {:subject_id => ➥
 @tasks[0].person.id} if @tasks.any? %>
</div>
```

Now, we'll create a new partial named _add_note.html.erb in /app/views/home in which we'll place the following form:

```
<% form_for :note, :url => {:controller => "notes", :action => "create"} do |n| %>
  <fieldset>
    <legend>Add A Note</legend>
    <ol>
      <li><label for="body">Add a Note:</label><%= n.text_field 'body' %></li>
      <%= n.hidden_field :subject_type, :value => 'Party' %>
      <%= n.hidden_field :subject_id, :value => subject_id %>
      <li><%= submit_tag 'Create', :class => 'submit' %></li>
    </ol>
  </fieldset>
<% end %>
```

This form should be pretty standard fare for you at this point, though I'd like to point out that there are two hidden fields that we're passing along with the form submission. First is the subject_type that we'll always set to Party, since we want this note to be associated to a person. Next, we have the subject_id value, which is the ID of the person that we want this note to be associated with—you'll notice that we're passing this value into the partial as a local variable.

Someone very observant might have noticed that we're missing an important part of creating a note—a place to post the note. The form in our partial is pointed to the create method in a notes controller. Unfortunately, that controller doesn't exist yet, so we need to create it:

```
ruby script/generate controller notes
```

```
    exists  app/controllers/
    exists  app/helpers/
    create  app/views/notes
    exists  test/functional/
    create  app/controllers/notes_controller.rb
    create  test/functional/notes_controller_test.rb
    create  app/helpers/notes_helper.rb
```

Now, with our new notes controller built, let's add in our create method so that our form has a destination:

```
class NotesController < ApplicationController
  def create
    @note = Note.new(params[:note])
    @note.save
    redirect_to root_url
  end
end
```

Our method is fairly straightforward: we'll simply create a new note based on the parameters submitted in the form, save it (which will push it up to Highrise), and then redirect the request to the home page.

With those modifications, our page now looks like Figure 24-6, as it displays the notes for a customer.

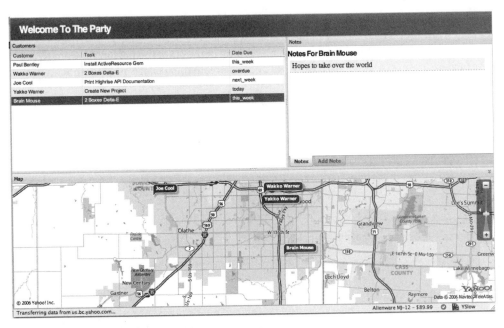

Figure 24-6. *The page displaying a customer's notes*

Using AJAX to Update Displayed Notes

All that's left to finish up our application for our friend is some minor RJS and AJAX calls to allow him to view and add notes for more than just the top record. We'll do that by changing the notes that are displayed and the subject_id in the add note form when our friend selects a customer in the grid component. To do that, we'll attach an on-click event to the grid.

Let's go back into our JavaScript, find our buildGrid function again, and add an event listener for a row click on the grid:

```
function buildGrid() {
  grid = new Ext.grid.Grid(
    'customers_grid',
    {
      ds: ds,
      cm: getColumnModel(),
      autoSizeColumns: true
    }
  );
```

```
grid.on("rowclick", function(grid) {
  new Ajax.Request('/notes/update_page/' + grid.getSelectionModel().➥
getSelected().data.id, {asynchronous:true, evalScripts:true}); return false;
  });

  grid.render();
}
```

When our friend clicks a row in the grid, he will kick off an AJAX call back to the update_page method in the notes controller—passing in the ID of the person we want to use (note/update_page/#{person_id}). Now, we need to create that update_page method in the notes controller:

```
class NotesController < ApplicationController
  def create
    @note = Note.new(params[:note])
    @note.save
    redirect_to root_url
  end

  def update_page
    @person = Person.find(params[:id])
  end
end
```

The update_page method merely pulls back the person object that we're interested in from Highrise and passes control over to an RJS template. So let's create our RJS template—a file named update_page.rjs in /app/views/notes—which should have the following RJS commands:

```
page.replace_html 'notes_name', "Notes for #{@person.name}"
page.replace_html  'notes_list', :partial => 'home/notes', :collection => ➥
 @person.notes
page.replace_html 'add_note', :partial => 'home/add_note', :locals => ➥
{ :subject_id => @person.id }
```

Our RJS template just replaces the contents of three sections: it updates the header area of our notes to display to show the correct customer name, updates the notes list using the same partial, and replaces the add note form with a new one using the correct person's ID.

■**Tip** Actually, in Rails 2.0, the proper file extension for an RJS template like this should be update_page.js.rjs in much the same manner as we're changing our .rthml templates to html.erb. However, templates with these new extensions are not being found by default when the renderer tries to display the associated template currently, so to use our RJS file would require adding an explicit render call at the end of our controller.

Summary

With that final addition, we've completed our Active Resource application. This was a great application to play with, because not only did we get to play with the upcoming Active Resource library but we also go to take a look at some of the upcoming changes to Rails by using edge Rails. To add the cherry on top, we also put together some pretty nice interface elements using the Ext-JS framework and the Yahoo Maps API. All in all, although it wasn't a very complex application, since it only has one page, it was probably the most fun for me to build, and it's one that has plenty of opportunities for you to expand on and build a deeper integration with Highrise.

■ ■ ■

Enhancing Our Rails 2.0 Application

This project was a fun (albeit at times frustrating) one to create. Rails 2.0 is going to have a significant number of changes to some of the common ways that we do things within the framework. While these changes might require a shift in the way that we develop our applications, I have to say that most of these changes are going to be for the best. It is a perfectly acceptable thing to break backward compatibility to keep the framework fresh and relevant and drop that "freshman fifteen."

With that in mind, I've added only a few additional exercises relevant to our specific project, but I also added a list of some of the cool and exciting new features of Rails 2.0 that you can experiment with in our edge Rails application.

Enhancing the Highrise Project

This section contains exercises to enhance our Highrise project.

Cache Customer Data

While our example application allows us to always ensure that we have the most up-to-date data out of Highrise, it's not exactly an efficient use of our resources. A better approach would be to work in some logic to locally store (or cache) information to reduce the number of requests to Highrise and most likely improve the response times of our application.

For example, you could set up a cron job to automatically update a locally stored version of customer data every hour, or you could set up a user-managed "refresh my content" button.

Create Appointments

While we created the necessary models and interface to view and create notes in Highrise, we limited ourselves to only creating a view of upcoming appointments. What if our friend liked the application so much that he also wanted to use it to create the appointments directly?

To do that, you would need to create a view of all customers—not just the ones with appointments already scheduled—and you would need to create an interface within the application that would allow our friend to create a new task and schedule a time. If you do this, I would try to create something comparable to the same manner in which tasks are scheduled within Highrise already. Also, make sure that you create your tasks as associated to the correct customer.

Edit a Customer

Going along with the theme of expanding our integration to Highrise, how about creating the ability to edit a customer's address or phone number details directly from this interface?

New Features in Edge Rails

As an added bonus, here's a list of some of the other new Rails 2.0 features that you can use to enhance the Highrise project or just experiment with.

Sexy Migrations

One feature that I'm particularly excited to begin implementing is Rails support for what are called sexy migrations; see `http://dev.rubyonrails.org/changeset/6667`. Sexy migrations provide enhancements to our migration process, so where traditionally we might create a migration for a post table like this:

```
create_table :posts do |t|
  t.column :blog_id, :integer
  t.column :user_id, :integer
  t.column :title, :string
  t.column :permalink, :string
  t.column :body, :text
  t.column :created_at, :datetime
  t.column :updated_at, :datetime
end
```

sexy migrations allow us to create the exact same table structure like this:

```
create_table :posts do |t|
  t.integer :blog_id, :user_id
  t.string :title, :permalink
  t.text :body
  t.timestamps
end
```

Sexy, indeed.

Automatically Generated Migrations

Another nice new migration feature is the one that adds the ability to automatically generate the add/remove column names from a well-named migration; see http://dev.rubyonrails.org/ changeset/7216. If you created a new migration like this:

```
ruby script/generate migration AddSslFlagToAccount
```

you would find that your newly created migration would already contain this in the up migration:

```
add_column :accounts, :ssl_flag, :type, :null => :no?, :default => :maybe?
```

and this in the down migration:

```
remove_column :accounts, :ssl_flag
```

Pretty sweet, huh? Your migrations can either have camel case names or use underscores as the separators for this functionality.

Database Commands

A new set of rake tasks was added for basic database management (see http:// dev.rubyonrails.org/changeset/6849), so we can now manage our databases without having to run any of those external database utilities (like mysqladmin).

So you can now create the database defined in database.yml with a simple rake db:create call or remove that database from your system with a rake db:drop command.

We can completely remove that database and rebuild it using our migrations with a single rake db:reset command—even cooler still.

View Routes

Another new rake task has been added (see http://dev.rubyonrails.org/changeset/7149) for viewing all of the named routes that your routes files have generated—very useful when you're dealing with RESTful routes and can't remember the exact format for how to link to a new nested resource.

Query Caching

In the current version of Rails, if you were to make a request for a record like this:

```
User.find 123
```

and then later in that same request made the same query again:

```
User.find 123
```

Rails would simply obey your request and make two hits to the database in response to your requests. In Rails 2.0, however, we have a new feature named query caching that, quite simply, will remember that you've already retrieved that data and return a cached version of that result in response to the second query (assuming that no inserts, deletes, or updates have occurred between the two requests).

RESTful Routing Improvements

Rails 2.0 also adds support for declaring :has_many and :has_one relationships within our routes for RESTful resources (see http://dev.rubyonrails.org/changeset/6588). Before, where we might have declared a nested resource like this:

```
map.resources :posts do |posts|
  posts.resources :comments
  posts.resources :images
  posts.resource :user
end
```

with Rails 2.0, we'll be able to declare it like this:

```
map.resources :posts, :has_many => [ :comments, :images ], :has_one => :user
```

Features Removed from the Framework

One of the goals of Rails 2.0 was also to remove some of the bloat from the core framework and make features that should be optional available as plug-ins rather than automatically bundled into every Rails application.

Some of the more interesting features that are being moved into a plug-in or removed entirely are explained in the following sections.

Pagination (http://dev.rubyonrails.org/changeset/6992)

Pagination has been removed from Rails 2.0 and moved into a plug-in named Classic Pagination. Of course, most Rails developers recommend using the Will Paginate plug-in instead.

Scaffold (http://dev.rubyonrails.org/changeset/7429)

The scaffold command has been removed completely from Rails 2.0. The recommendation is to use the scaffolding generator from now on.

JavaScript Helpers

Many of the script.aculo.us JavaScript helpers are also being removed and pushed into plug-ins, including these:

- In-place Editing (http://dev.rubyonrails.org/changeset/7442)

- Auto-completion (http://dev.rubyonrails.org/changeset/7450)

"Acts as" Features

The common "Acts as" features have been removed from the Rails core and moved into separate plug-ins:

- Acts as List (`http://dev.rubyonrails.org/changeset/7443`)

- Acts as Nested Set (`http://dev.rubyonrails.org/changeset/7453`)

- Acts as Tree (`http://dev.rubyonrails.org/changeset/7454`)

Summary

As you can see, Rails 2.0 is going to offer a fairly significant number of changes that should both reduce the size of the framework itself and reduce the amount of code that we need to create to configure our applications. If I had to describe Rails 2.0 in a single word, I would call it "streamlined." As you complete the exercises I suggested for the scheduler application and experiment with the new features I highlighted, I think that you'll agree with me—Rails 2.0 is a good thing.

If you want to keep current with what's going on in edge Rails development, you should keep an eye on any change sets from the official tracking RSS feed at `http://dev.rubyonrails.org/timeline` or on Ryan Daigle's excellent site (`http://ryandaigle.com/`), where he provides periodic summaries of edge Rails changes.

Index

Find it faster at http://superindex.apress.com